LAW AND MEMORY

Legal governance of memory has played a central role in establishing hegemony of monumental history, and has forged national identities and integration processes in Europe and beyond. In this book, a range of contributors explore both the nature and role of legal engagement into historical memory in selected national, European, and international law. They also reflect on potential conflicts between legal governance, political pluralism, and fundamental rights, such as freedom of expression. In recent years, there have been numerous monumental commemoration practices and judicial trials about correlated events all over the world, and this is a prime opportunity to undertake an important global comparative scrutiny of memory laws. Against the background of mass re-writing of history in different parts of the world, this book revisits a fascinating subject of memory laws from the standpoint of comparative law and transitional justice.

ULADZISLAU BELAVUSAU is Senior Researcher in European Law at the T.M.C. Asser Institute (The Hague), University of Amsterdam, the Netherlands.

ALEKSANDRA GLISZCZYŃSKA-GRABIAS is Senior Researcher in Human Rights at the Institute of Law Studies of the Polish Academy of Sciences, Poland.

LAW AND MEMORY

Towards Legal Governance of History

Edited by

ULADZISLAU BELAVUSAU

T.M.C. Asser Institute – University of Amsterdam

ALEKSANDRA GLISZCZYŃSKA-GRABIAS

Polish Academy of Sciences

CAMBRIDGE
UNIVERSITY PRESS

CAMBRIDGE
UNIVERSITY PRESS

University Printing House, Cambridge CB2 8BS, United Kingdom

One Liberty Plaza, 20th Floor, New York, NY 10006, USA

477 Williamstown Road, Port Melbourne, VIC 3207, Australia

314-321, 3rd Floor, Plot 3, Splendor Forum, Jasola District Centre, New Delhi - 110025, India

79 Anson Road, #06-04/06, Singapore 079906

Cambridge University Press is part of the University of Cambridge.

It furthers the University's mission by disseminating knowledge in the pursuit of education, learning and research at the highest international levels of excellence.

www.cambridge.org
Information on this title: www.cambridge.org/9781107188754
DOI: 10.1017/9781316986172

First published 2017

A catalogue record for this publication is available from the British Library

Library of Congress Cataloging in Publication data
Names: Belavusau, Uladzislau, editor. | Gliszczyńska-Grabias, Aleksandra, editor.
Title: Law and memory : towards legal governance of history / edited by Uladzislau Belavusau, T.M.C. Asser Institute, University of Amsterdam [and] Aleksandra Gliszczyńska-Grabias, Polish Academy of Sciences.
Description: Cambridge, United Kingdom; New York, NY, USA: Cambridge University Press, 2017. | Includes bibliographical references and index.
Identifiers: LCCN 2017035931 | ISBN 9781107188754 (hardback)
Subjects: LCSH: Libel and slander—Europe—Criminal provisions. | Political crimes and offenses—Law and legislation—Europe. | International crimes. | History—Research—Law and legislation—Europe. | Collective memory—Government policy—Europe.
Classification: LCC KJC8465 .L39 2017 | DDC 345.4/025—dc23 LC record available at https://lccn.loc.gov/2017035931

ISBN 978-1-107-18875-4 Hardback
ISBN 978-1-316-63859-0 Paperback

CONTENTS

List of Contributors *page* ix
Acknowledgements xi

Introduction: Memory Laws: Mapping a New Subject in Comparative Law and Transitional Justice 1
ULADZISLAU BELAVUSAU AND ALEKSANDRA GLISZCZYŃSKA-GRABIAS

PART I International Law 27

1 The United Nations Human Rights Committee's View of the Past 29
ANTOON DE BAETS

2 The Role of International Criminal Tribunals in Shaping the Historical Accounts of Genocides 48
MARINA AKSENOVA

3 The 'Right to Truth' in International Law: The 'Last Utopia'? 70
PATRICIA NAFTALI

PART II European Law (Council of Europe and the European Union) 89

4 *Kononov* v. *Latvia* as an Ontological Security Struggle over Remembering the Second World War 91
MARIA MÄLKSOO

5 Testing the 'Uniqueness': Denial of the Holocaust vs Denial of Other Crimes before the European Court of Human Rights 109

PAOLO LOBBA

6 Legislating History: The European Union and the Denial of International Crimes 129

LUIGI CAJANI

PART III National Perspectives within the European Union 149

7 Challenging Historical Facts and National Truths: An Analysis of Cases from France and Greece 151

IOANNA TOURKOCHORITI

8 Legal Silences and the Memory of Francoism in Spain 175

ALFONS ARAGONESES

9 Politics of Public Knowledge in Dealing with the Past: Post-communist Experiences and Some Lessons from the Czech Republic 195

JIŘÍ PŘIBÁŇ

10 Adjudication in Latvian Deportation Cases: References to International Law 216

IEVA MILUNA

11 Judging the *Conducător*: Fascism, Communism, and Legal Discontinuity in Post-War Romania 228

COSMIN SEBASTIAN CERCEL

12 Dealing with the Past in and around the Fundamental Law of Hungary 246

MIKLÓS KÖNCZÖL

13 On the Politics of Resentment, Mis-memory, and Constitutional Fidelity: The Demise of the Polish Overlapping Consensus? 263

TOMASZ TADEUSZ KONCEWICZ

PART IV Perspectives beyond the European Union 291

14 Defending Stalinism by Means of Criminal Law: Russia, 1995–2014 293
NIKOLAY KOPOSOV

15 Cutting the Umbilical Cord: The Narrative of the National Past and Future in Ukrainian De-communization Policy 310
LINA KLYMENKO

16 Banning Genocide Denial – Should Geography Matter? 329
ROBERT A. KAHN

17 "From Banning Nakba to Bridging Narratives": The Collective Memory of 1948 and Transitional Justice for Israelis and Palestinians 348
JEREMIE M. BRACKA

18 Historical Revisionism and the Settler State: The Canadian Experience 374
MICHAEL MORDEN

19 Defense of Democracy and the Preservation of Collective Memory through Criminal Legislation: The Challenges of Reconciliation in Peru 395
SALVADOR HERENCIA CARRASCO

Epilogue: Beyond 'Memory Laws': Towards a General Theory of Law and Historical Discourse 413
ERIC HEINZE

Index 435

CONTRIBUTORS

MARINA AKSENOVA is a postdoctoral researcher at iCourts, the Faculty of Law – University of Copenhagen (Denmark).

ALFONS ARAGONESES is a lecturer at Universitat Pompeu Fabra (Barcelona, Spain) and an affiliate researcher at the Max Planck Institute for European Legal History (Frankfurt, Germany).

ANTOON DE BAETS is Professor of History, Ethics and Human Rights at the University of Groningen (the Netherlands).

ULADZISLAU BELAVUSAU is Senior Researcher in European Law at the T.M.C. Asser Institute (the Hague) – University of Amsterdam (the Netherlands).

JEREMIE M. BRACKA is a PhD candidate and a lecturer at the Law Faculty of Monash University (Melbourne, Australia). He is also a visiting scholar at Tel Aviv University (Tel Aviv, Israel).

LUIGI CAJANI is Lecturer in Modern History at the Università La Sapienza di Roma (Italy).

COSMIN SEBASTIAN CERCEL is Assistant Professor of Law at the Faculty of Social Sciences, the University of Nottingham (UK).

ALEKSANDRA GLISZCZYŃSKA-GRABIAS is Senior Researcher in Human Rights Law at the Polish Academy of Sciences (Warsaw, Poland).

ERIC HEINZE is Professor of Law and Humanities at Queen Mary University of London (UK).

SALVADOR HERENCIA CARRASCO is a PhD candidate and Director of the Human Rights Clinic – Human Rights Research and Education Centre of the University of Ottawa (Canada).

ROBERT A. KAHN is a Professor at the School of Law at the University of St. Thomas (USA).

LINA KLYMENKO is a researcher at the Karelian Institute at the University of Eastern Finland (Finland).

TOMASZ TADEUSZ KONCEWICZ is Professor of Law and Director of the Department of European and Comparative Law at the University of Gdańsk (Poland); 2017–18 Fellow at the Program in Law and Public Affairs (LAPA), Princeton University; attorney-at-law.

MIKLÓS KÖNCZÖL is Lecturer in Jurisprudence at Pázmány Péter Catholic University, and Research Fellow at the HAS Centre for Social Sciences, Institute for Legal Studies (Budapest, Hungary).

NIKOLAY KOPOSOV is a visiting professor at Emory University (Atlanta, USA).

PAOLO LOBBA is a postdoctoral researcher at the Department of Legal Studies at Bologna University (Italy).

MARIA MÄLKSOO is Senior Lecturer in International Security at the University of Kent–Brussels School of International Studies (Belgium).

IEVA MILUNA is Lecturer in International Law at the Riga Graduate School of Law (Latvia) and Member of the Advisory Council on International and European Law at the Latvian Ministry of Foreign Affairs.

MICHAEL MORDEN is a research associate at the Mowat Centre, at the University of Toronto School of Public Policy and Governance (Canada).

PATRICIA NAFTALI is FRS–FNRS Postdoctoral Researcher at the Université libre de Bruxelles (Belgium).

JIŘÍ PŘIBÁŇ is Professor of Law at Cardiff School of Law and Politics (UK).

IOANNA TOURKOCHORITI is a lecturer at the National University of Ireland, Galway (Ireland).

ACKNOWLEDGEMENTS

This book is the result of our fruitful cooperation with a number of distinguished institutions and individual scholars. Two of them, Eric Heinze (*Queen Mary University of London*) and Wojciech Sadurski (*University of Sydney*), deserve our special and infinite gratitude for their extraordinary support and invaluable advice throughout the whole process, from the book proposal to the final stage of publication. Much of our fascination with the subject of memory laws and freedom of expression has been, in fact, inspired by the outstanding work of these two leading philosophers of law.

While we were editing the chapters at a later stage, we received the splendid news that our project 'MELA' (*Memory Laws in European and Comparative Perspective*) – created as a research consortium in four EU countries – had been awarded a prestigious *HERA* grant for the next three years. We are indebted to the European Commission for this opportunity to transform our initial research into a wider international project. Apart from HERA, we would like to thank the Amsterdam Center for Contemporary European Studies (*ACCESS-Europe*) for their institutional support. In June 2016 they sponsored our international conference in Amsterdam, which gathered most of our authors and enabled a critical discussion of their draft chapters.

Furthermore, we are much obliged to a number of prominent scholars who have generously shared their precious advice on this book, including Antoon De Baets and Dimitry Kochenov (*Groningen*), Eva-Clarita Pettai (*Tartu*), Gábor Halmai (*EUI, Florence*), Luiza Bialasiewicz, Ester Herlin-Karnell, Magdalena Jozwiak, Matthijs Lok, Christian Noack and Claske Vos (*Amsterdam*), Grażyna Baranowska (*Poznań*), Sévane Garibian (*Geneva*), Armen Mazmanyan (*Yerevan*), Emanuela Fronza (*Bologna*), Amos Goldberg (*Jerusalem*), Yevgeni Klauber (*Tel Aviv*), Pavel Molek and Hubert Smekal (*Brno*), Thérèse O'Donnell (*Strathchlyde*), and Carlos Closa (*Madrid*). In addition, Uladzislau Belavusau would like to extend his gratitude to Eyal Benvenisti (*Cambridge*) and Daniele Gallo (*Rome*) for hosting him as a visiting scholar at, respectively, the *Tel Aviv University* and *LUISS Guido Carli University* in 2015–16, as well as to Janne Nijman (*the Hague*) for her indispensable academic backing. Likewise, Aleksandra Gliszczyńska would like to thank Roman Wieruszewski (*Poznań*) for offering his unremitting academic support and advice, and Wojciech Kozłowski (*Warsaw*) for stimulating exciting professional challenges.

Our special thanks also go to Bartosz Sucharski for donating his enchanting drawing for our book cover, crafted in the best traditions of the Polish placard school. Finally, thanks to everyone at Cambridge University Press and, in particular to Elizabeth Spicer, for their friendly and patient editorship. Last but not least, many thanks to our authors for their thoughtful contributions, advice, and endurance.

Aleksandra and Uład
January 2017

Introduction

Memory Laws: Mapping a New Subject in Comparative Law and Transitional Justice

ULADZISLAU BELAVUSAU AND ALEKSANDRA GLISZCZYŃSKA-GRABIAS

1 Preface

Legislative and judicial practice in recent years abounds with attempts to regulate historical discussion and collective memory through law. Legal regulation of memory is by no means a remnant of the past. In the twenty-first century it remains a vivid reality.

The legal governance of history is often addressed under the tag of *memory laws* (French *lois mémorielles*; German *Erinnerungsgesetze*, etc.). Such laws enshrine state-approved interpretations of crucial historical events. They commemorate the victims of past atrocities as well as heroic individuals or events emblematic of national and social movements. They date back centuries and continue to spread throughout Europe and the world.

Memory laws affect us in various, often controversial ways. They sometimes impose criminal penalties on speech or conduct deemed offensive to the plight of heroes or victims. In that punitive form, memory laws impose limits on democratic freedom of expression, association, the media, or scholarly research. Yet memory laws reach beyond the bounds of criminal law. Children everywhere grow up reading state-approved texts designed to impart not merely a knowledge, but an interpretation of history. Governments everywhere designate national memorial ceremonies or authorize the construction of public monuments.

Curiously, most analyses of memory laws have been written by political scientists, sociologists, and historians rather than *law*-yers.[1] Social

[1] See for example, M. J. Osiel, *Mass Atrocity, Collective Memory, and the Law* (New Brunswick, NJ: Transaction, 1997); P. Vidal-Naquet, *Assassins of Memory. Essays on the Denial of the Holocaust* (New York: Columbia University Press, 1992); S. Moyn, *Human Rights and the Use of History* (New York and London: Verso, 2014).

scientists often scrutinize memory laws as central to the *politics* of memory, that is to the political means by which events are classified, commemorated, or discarded to influence community values and attitudes.[2] Accounts written by lawyers, by contrast, rarely examine memory laws as a global phenomenon. They focus instead on geographically limited laws and judgments.[3] In this regard, the issue of Holocaust denial largely dominates the literature on memory laws by legal scholars, followed by country-specific memory laws and legal practices.[4]

In consolidating accounts by both lawyers and non-lawyers, this volume seeks to fill the "comparative" gap in the literature, revisiting memory laws as a phenomenon of global law and transitional justice. The book offers accounts from various national jurisdictions and from transnational law. The authors ask how law certifies historical narratives, entails claims about historical truth, prescribes commemorative practices, and excludes ineligible accounts.

This introductory chapter aims, in its second section, to systemize the genesis and history of memory laws, and to explain the proliferation of this Western phenomenon within diverse legal systems. It traces the role of the Holocaust in the turn to law within both international and national regimes after World War II. We also examine the mechanics of that spillover in various legal settings. The third section summarizes accounts presented in this book, and explores claims about the benefits and flaws of legal intervention into the marketplace of historical ideas. In conclusion, we ponder the current place and prospects of memory laws as a dynamic

[2] E.g., S. Löytömäki, *Law and the Politics of Memory: Confronting the Past* (Oxford and New York: Routledge, 2014); A. De Brito et al. (eds.), *The Politics of Memory and Democratization* (Oxford: Oxford University Press, 2011); M. Mälksoo, 'The Memory Politics of Becoming European: The East European Subalterns and the Collective Memory of Europe', *European Journal of International Relations* 15:4 (2009), 653–80.

[3] E.g., J. M. Tamarit-Sumalla, *Historical Memory and Criminal Justice in Spain: A Case of Late Transitional Justice* (Cambridge: Intersentia, 2013). A. Sarat and T. R. Kearns, *History, Memory, and the Law* (Ann Arbor, MI: University of Michigan Press, 1999). L. Hennebel and T. Hochman (eds.), *Genocide Denial and the Law* (Oxford University Press, 2011); C. Joerges and N. S. Ghaleigh, *Darker Legacies of Law in Europe: The Shadow of National Socialism and Fascism over Europe and Its Legal Traditions* (Oxford: Hart, 2003).

[4] See R. Kahn, *Holocaust Denial and the Law: A Comparative Study* (Basingstoke and New York: Palgrave, 2004). The exceptions are some Italian and French publications, e.g. G. Resto and V. Zeno-Zenkovich (eds.), *Riparare Risacrcire Ricordere: Un Dialogo tra storici e giuristi* (Naples: Editoriale Scientifica, 2012); D. Losurdo, *Il Revisionismo Storico: Problemi e miti* (Rome-Bari: Laterza, 1996). A. Garapon, *Peut-on réparer l'histoire? Colonisation, esclavage, Shoah* (Paris: Odile Jacob, 2008).

subject of both law and transitional justice. That subject is driven by continuous inter-disciplinary input from lawyers, historians, and scholars from various branches of social sciences.

2 Genealogies and Rise of Memory Laws

> That there shall be on the one side and to others a perpetual Oblivion, Amnesty, or Pardon of all that has been committed since the beginning of these Troubles, in what place, or what manner soever the Hostilitys have been practis'd . . . That they shall not act, or permit to be acted, any wrong or injury to any whatsoever; but that all that has pass'd on the one side, and the other, as well before as during the War, in Words, Writing, and Outrageous Actions, in Violence, Hostilitys, Damages and Expences, without any respect to Persons or Things, shall be entirely abolish'd in such a manner that all that might be demanded of, or pretended to, by each other on that behalf, shall be bury'd in eternal Oblivion.
>
> [Treaty of Westphalia, 1648][5]

The political deployment of memory traces back to the origins of the modern, "post-Westphalian" state, where we discover patterns still at work in today's world. In the aftermath of the Thirty Years' War, even the rigorously fanatic John Calvin preached Christian forgiveness. He demanded that rivals cast off hatred and revenge, and banish all remembrance of injustice.[6] That kind of sermon may well inspire awe, but it is above all military security and social pragmatics that will favour Calvin's approach. What emerges might generously be called a forgiveness model, or more shrewdly an *oblivion* model. In the Treaty of Westphalia (1648), a stepping-stone in the development of modern international law, states are expressly obliged to enforce amnesties and pardons for all wartime wrongdoings. Public rituals surrounding local and national hostilities will, to safeguard the emerging nation states, remain vigilantly prudent. Hence, the possibilities of collective public practices of remembrance and commemoration in the seventeenth century – the age of classical political rationalism of Thomas Hobbes – were essentially limited.[7] That politics

[5] Title II. *Peace Treaty between the Holy Roman Emperor and the King of France and Their Respective Allies [Treaty of Westphalia]*, Avalon Project: Documents in Law, History and Diplomacy, available at: http://avalon.law.yale.edu/17th_century/westphal.asp.

[6] B. Vivian, *Public Forgetting: The Rhetoric and Politics of Beginning Again* (University Park, PA: Penn State University Press, 2010), 43.

[7] C. Volk, 'Struggle, Dissent and Debate: Politics and Memory in Europe', *Eutopia: Ideas for Europe Magazine*, 18 July 2014, available at: www.eutopiamagazine.eu/en/christian-volk/columns/struggle-dissent-and-debate-politics-and-memory-europe.

of sheer silence, aimed at preventing public discord, haunts much of our world today.[8]

A century later, we nevertheless find the French Revolutionaries introducing an approach ostensibly opposite to that model. Austerely rationalist Jacobins orchestrate a nation's march into an enlightened future. That future ends up defined in express opposition to France's past. Earlier institutions – indeed the entirety of the *ancien régime* – came to be presented as ignorant and antiquated. In contrast to medieval Christian oblivion,[9] we now find a model of *zealous remembrance*, which, to this day, will compete with, yet will also interweave with the oblivion model.[10] Among the revolutionaries' mnemonic novelties we discover prescribed rituals of civic remembrance, comprehensive museum reforms (including state appropriation of church property),[11] and the creation of republican state archives.[12] The state modernized the very concepts of "past" and "future" through its new republican calendar (*calendrier républicain français*), and by decreeing a clock divided into one hundred hours of one hundred minutes.[13] Twentieth-century revolutions will replicate those simulacra of modernity, notoriously those of Kim II-Sung's North Korea and Pol Pot's Cambodia. Throughout the eighteenth century, museums evolved from "cabinets of curiosity" towards the sites of glory and podiums of state achievements. Rather than displaying their collections in random order,

[8] See in particular, chapter by Alfons Aragoneses in the present volume, explaining the role of silence in the legal governance of memory in post-Francoist Spain.

[9] On the Medieval forms of commemoration, see E. Brenner, M. Franklin-Brown and M. Cohen (eds.), *Memory and Commemoration in Medieval Culture* (Burlington, VT: Ashgate, 2013).

[10] Even in France itself, this competition between zealous remembrance and oblivion will be present through much of the nineteenth and twentieth centuries. For a most vivid episode of the post-Napoleonic restoration of monarchies and propagated politics of forgetting in France and the Netherlands, see *inter alia*, M. M. Lok, '"Un oubli total du passé"? The Political and Social Construction of Silence in Restoration Europe (1813–1830)', *History & Memory* 26:2 (2014), 40–75.

[11] A. McClellan, *Inventing the Louvre: Art, Politics, and the Origins of the Modern Museum in Eighteenth-Century Paris* (Berkeley, Los Angeles, London: University of California Press, 1994).

[12] About the role of archives in mnemonic policies, see P. Nora, 'Between Memory and History: Les Lieux de mémoire', *Representations* (Special Issue "Memory and Counter-Memory") 26 (1989), 7–24.

[13] The calendar was adopted by the Decree of 24 October 1793 and abolished on 1 January 1806 by Emperor Napoleon I. It was used again briefly during the Paris Commune of 1871. A new clock was also decreed with a day divided into one hundred hours of one hundred minutes. The decimal system eventually became the world standard for all other measures except time.

museums gained a sense of organization and taxonomy. On 10 August 1793, the first anniversary of the monarchy's demise, the Louvre opened its doors, enabling free access to the former French royal collection for all citizens.[14] From that moment forward, French republicanism will dictate not only the nation's future, but also its past. This effectively transformed museums and public collections from elite trifles into instruments of republican citizenship and social management, engineering national unity, or rather cultural homogeneity, along with encouraging active political participation and a strong invitation to commemorate and remember the heroes and victims.[15] That monumental invitation to remember was part and parcel of imagining a new community of national states that highlighted heroism and willingness to sacrifice for the sake of state. Such chief collective virtues were later translated into the duties of the citizen under the republican citizenship paradigm. History has been represented as the struggle of citizens for the glory of imagined civic communities, embraced by states.[16] It has thus played a strong didactic function in setting role models, prescribing mourning for victims and assigning a dichotomist sense of guilt to all the rivals of a nation state. The 1776 Declaration of Independence, promulgated in Philadelphia by peoples' representatives within the North American colonies, fashions the *history of the present King of Great Britain* as *a history of repeated injuries and usurpations, all having in direct object the establishment of an absolute tyranny over these states.*[17] Those words will shape the minds of countless Americans. In reality, however, the colonies were paying lower taxes and enjoyed an average quality of life higher than their old-world counterparts, not to mention that they were inflicting on their own indigenous peoples and African slaves a "tyranny" more devastating than any wrought under George III.[18] Prescription of collective memory via legal instruments has served as a means to legitimize socio-political reality and to homogenize a group.[19]

[14] A. McClellan, *Inventing the Louvre: Art, Politics, and the Origins of the Modern Museum in Eighteenth-Century Paris* (University of California Press, 1999).

[15] For a popular account of museums and citizenship, see T. Bennett, *The Birth of Museum* (London and New York: Routledge, 1995).

[16] B. Anderson, *Imagined Communities: Reflections on the Origin and Spread of Nationalism* (London: Verso, 1991).

[17] The text is available at: www.archives.gov/exhibits/charters/declaration_transcript.html.

[18] See G. G. Norquist, 'Tea, Taxes, and the Revolution', *Foreign Policy* (3 July 2012), available at: http://foreignpolicy.com/2012/07/03/tea-taxes-and-the-revolution/.

[19] See Z. Meral, 'A Duty to Remember? Politics and Morality of Remembering Past Atrocities', *International Political Anthropology* 5:1 (2012), 29–50; For the arguments against duty to remember, see A. De Baets, *Responsible History* (New York and Oxford: Berghahn, 2009), 147–57.

A century later, in Bismarck's Europe, we find the Prussian empire continuing that project of manufacturing myths of continuity from past heroism to present glory.[20] The French model – some might say "myth" – of citizenship had infiltrated the language of law to the degree that the Treaty of Versailles (1919) stipulated a specific "War Guilt Clause", assigning full responsibility for all loss and damage incurred during World War I to Germany.[21] Far from Westphalian oblivion, Versailles constructed transnational law through a discourse of foundational guilt. Through the spread of national secular states and global colonialism, law's mnemonic narratives increasingly pervaded constitutional ideals of citizenship far beyond the Western world, as witnessed, for example, in post-Ottoman Turkey, with the cult of Atürk,[22] or in post-imperial Japan, with censorship of militarist history,[23] or even in nowadays Portugal, with granting of citizenship to the descendants of the Sephardic Jews as acknowledgement of the memory of sufferings and exclusions.[24]

However, the truly universalized "duty to remember" emerged in the aftermath of World War II, with mediatized criminal proceedings, most famously during the international military tribunal in Nuremberg (1945–6),[25] the Israeli trials of Adolf Eichmann (1961)[26] and Ivan Demjanjuk

[20] The process that was eloquently captured by Friedrich Nietzsche in his "Ultimately Meditations", in particular, in *Vom Nutzen und Nachteil der Historie für das Leben* [On the Use and Abuse of History for Life, 1874]. This is one of four essays written by Friedrich Nietzsche between 1873 and 1876 under the title of *Unzeitgemässe Betrachtungen* [Untimely Meditations].

[21] Article 231 of the Treaty of Versailles. This provision sets up later articles in the Reparations part of the Treaty. Germany was required to conduct war crimes proceedings against the Kaiser and other leaders for waging an aggressive war, which largely resulted in acquittals and were widely perceived as a sham, even in Germany. See R. B. Henig, *Versailles and After, 1919–1933* (London and New York: Routledge, 1995).

[22] B. Ince, *Citizenship and Identity in Turkey: From Atatürk's Republic to the Present Day* (London and New York: I. B. Tauris, 2012).

[23] L. Hein and M. Selden (eds.), *Censoring History: Citizenship and Memory in Japan, Germany and the United States* (Armonk, NY: ME Sharpe, 2000).

[24] The Parliament of Portugal has recently decided to grant citizenship to descendants of persecuted Sephardic Jews, whose ancestors were expelled in the fifteenth century. See *The Guardian*, 29 January 2015, available at: www.theguardian.com/world/2015/jan/29/portugal-citizenship-descendants-persecuted-sephardic-jews.

[25] See M. J. Bazyler, 'The Holocaust, Nuremberg and the Birth of Modern International Law', in D. Bankier and D. Michman (eds.), *Holocaust and Justice: Representation and Historiography of the Holocaust in Post-War Trials* (Jerusalem, New York and London: Yad Vashem & Berghahn Books, 2010), 45–58. See also A. De Baets, 'The Impact of the Universal Declaration of Human Rights on the Study of History', *History and Theory* 48 (2009), 20–43.

[26] The trial has been particularly renowned due to the journalism and philosophical account of H. Arendt, *Eichmann in Jerusalem: A Report on the Banality of Evil* (New York: Penguin, 1994; first published in 1963). See also C. Douzinas, 'History Trials: Can Law Decide History?', *Annual Review of Law and Social Science* 8 (2012), 273–89.

(1986–8),[27] or the French trial of Klaus Barbie (1987).[28] These trials gave sense to the new distinctly modern legal concept of "genocide".[29] Such a concept became central to conceptualizing past horrors as criminal The UN General Assembly adopted the Convention on the Prevention and Punishment of the Crime of Genocide on 9 December 1948 as a General Assembly Resolution 260.[30] Not only was it the first crime with a retroactive effect, the subsequent prohibition on Holocaust denial in various countries has set an arch-example of the contemporary legal regulation of memory. Denial, minimization, and gross trivialization of the fact of annihilation of 6 million Jews by Nazis has been criminalized by a number of Western democracies either as a form of hate speech (*Volksverhetzung*, or incitement to hatred) or as a distinct crime of genocide denial.[31] The list of subsequent trials beyond Germany included, for example, Canada's proceedings against James Keegstra (1984)[32] and Ernst Zündel (1985),[33] or the Holocaust denier David Irving's libel action brought in Britain against the American historian Deborah Lipstad.[34] In this regard

27 T. Teicholz, *The Trial of Ivan the Terrible: State of Israel vs. John Demjanjuk* (New York: St. Martins, 1990, 2nd edn).

28 T. Morgan, 'Voices from the Barbie Trial', *The New York Times Magazine*, 2 August 1987, available at: www.nytimes.com/1987/08/02/magazine/voices-from-the-barbie-trial.html.

29 G. Della Morte, 'International Law between the Duty of Memory and the Right to Oblivion', *International Criminal Law Review* 14 (2014), 427–40. Likewise, Louis Joinet's 1997 Set of Principles to Combat Impunity prepared for the UN Sub-Commission on human rights expressly mentions a duty to remember as a State duty to avoid historical revisionism and denialism (E/CN.4/Sub.2/1997/20/Rev.1). See P. Naftali, 'Crafting a "Right to Truth" in International Law: Converging Mobilizations, Diverging Agendas?', *Penal Field* 13 (2016), available at https://champpenal.revues.org/9245.

30 The notion of genocide was first introduced in the essay of Raphael Lemkin, 'The Crime of Barbarity', see J. T. Fussel, *Comprehensive Bibliography: Writings of Raphael Lemkin*, available at www.preventgenocide.org/lemkin/bibliography.htm; See also A. Filipa Vrdoljak, 'Human Rights and Genocide: The Work of Lauterpacht and Lemkin in Modern International Law', *European Journal of International Law* 20:4 (2009), 1163–94.

31 *Volksverhetzung* is a criminal offence under Section 130 of the Criminal Code (*Strafgesetzbuch*) in Germany. Similar provisions about incitement of group hatred have been enshrined in most of continental European criminal codes. In Germany, in can lead to up to five years' imprisonment. For many years that criminal clause was interpreted as covering Holocaust denial, while in the 1990s special provisions on Holocaust denial as well as most recently, on justifying or glorifying the Nazi government were added. Similar self-standing (i.e. separate from "hate speech") provisions on Holocaust denial exist these days in various countries, from Israel to France.

32 S. Mertl and J. Ward, *Keegstra: The Trial, the Issues, the Consequences* (Saskatoon: Western Producer Prairie Books, 1985).

33 R. Lenski, *The Holocaust on Trial: The Case of Ernst Zündel* (Decatur, AL: Reporter Press, 1990).

34 Later on, Irving was convicted in Austria (2006). Dr. Lipstadt chronicled her five-year legal battle in *History on Trial: My Day in Court with David Irving* (New York: Ecco, 2005).

the most eminent precedent in international law is the 1996 decision of the UN Human Rights Committee, which upheld the conviction of the French scholar Robert Faurisson.[35] One of the most featured Holocaust deniers, Faurisson received a special award for "courage" from the Iranian President Mahmoud Ahmadinejad at an "academic" event in Teheran in February 2012, emblematic of the notorious political culture of Holocaust denialism in the Islamist world.[36]

Apart from demonstrating respect by acknowledging the suffering of millions of Jewish victims, criminalization of Holocaust denial after World War II has transformed social reality and led to a global spread of memory laws in three ways:

(1) It advanced the Judaic version of repentance, in contrast to Christian rituals of "oblivion" and ideals of forgiveness, where only direct victims can pardon perpetrators and several generations provide extensive mourning[37];
(2) Together with prohibitions on displays or commerce in Nazi and other extremist memorabilia, symbols and literature,[38] anti-negationist laws have, some would argue, promoted a reductively binary vision of World War II, with absolutized guilt of Nazi Germans and their collaborators, in contrast to the mega-praise of the winning allies. This narrative commonly omitted inconvenient episodes. Thus, the tacit consent to transfer Sudetenland to Germany under the Munich Agreement (1938); the Molotov-Ribbentrop's partition of Poland (1939); the Katyń massacre, which was long attributed to the Germans, while in fact committed by Soviet NKVD; the carpet bombing of Dresden in February 1945 under British and US orders; the massive rapes of German and Hungarian women by Soviet soldiers; the atomic bombings of Hiroshima and Nagasaki by the US forces in August 1945; and other *causes célèbres*

[35] *Faurisson* v. *France* (550/1993) 1996.

[36] J. Weissman, 'Holocaust Denier Receives Award at Iranian Film Festival', *Huffington Post*, 14 February 2012, available at: www.huffingtonpost.co.uk/joseph-weissman/faurisson-iranian-film-festival_b_1274572.html; See also M. Litvak and E. Webman, *From Empathy to Denial: Arab Responses to the Holocaust* (London: Hurst, 2009).

[37] See U. Belavusau, 'Historical Revisionism in Comparative Perspective, Law, Politics, and Surrogate Mourning', *EUI Working Paper* 12 (2013), 5–6. For the account of Judaic "apology", see A. Momigliano, S. Berti and M. Masella-Gayley, *Essays in Ancient and Modern Judaism* (Chicago and London: University of Chicago Press, 1994), 58–66. For a general account of apology, see A. Lazare, *On Apology* (Oxford University Press, 2004).

[38] To give just one, out of many European examples, Section 86a (use of symbols of the unconstitutional organizations) of the German Criminal Code outlaws Nazi symbols and insignia.

before, during, and in the aftermath of World War II stand as tragically anti-heroic episodes. The binarist narrative ends up eagerly exploited by radical groups in such states as Austria, Germany, or Japan – on the right and the left – to advance their credo that European governments manipulate the past to prop up an elitist world;

(3) These memory laws have proved instrumental to the politics of coming to terms with past (*Vergangenheitsbewältigung*) in Germany and other countries.[39] On the one hand, these monumental dichotomist "good-bad" of "victim-perpetrator" versions of history have been extremely successful in bringing up admirable generations of post-war German civil society, who not only acknowledge guilt for the massive annihilation but also always take into account this traumatic past in building a more emancipating and tolerant future.[40] On the other hand, such memory laws have been central to the concept of "militant" (*streitbare* or *wehrhafte*) democracy, which excludes incitement to hatred from constitutionally protected rights of free expression in order to preserve liberal democracy.[41]

Furthermore, the monumental legal prescription of historical truth has fulfilled a remarkable role in the project of Europe's unification. Leading European (EU and Council of Europe) institutions have nonetheless built their normative concepts upon the value of acknowledging past crimes and avoiding future ones, precisely through their policies of political and cultural integration.[42] The Maastricht Treaty (1992) has reinforced this discourse as a foundational myth for EU competences in fundamental rights and the project of EU citizenship, both formalized since then as primary law.[43] Likewise, the soft law of the Union has shaped a strong legal invitation to remember via various resolutions of

[39] See T. Adorno, 'What Does Coming to Terms with the Past Mean?', in G. Hartman (ed.), *Bitburg in Moral and Political Perspective* (Bloomington, IN: Indiana University Press, 1986), 114–29.

[40] D. Michman (ed.), *Remembering the Holocaust in Germany, 1945–2000: German Strategies and Jewish Responses* (New York: Peter Lang, 2002).

[41] For a scrutiny of the concept of militant democracy, see U. Belavusau, 'Hate Speech and Constitutional Democracy in Eastern Europe: Transitional and Militant?', *Israel Law Review* 47:1 (2014), 27–61.

[42] For a detailed analysis, see A. Sierp, *History, Memory and Trans-European Identity: Unifying Divisions* (New York: Routledge, 2014), 125–27.

[43] See Joerges and Ghaleigh (eds.), *Darker Legacies of Law in Europe*. See also S. Smismans, 'The European Union's Fundamental Rights Myth', *Journal of Common Market Studies* 48:1 (2010), 45–66.

the Parliament and Commission.[44] Those legal initiatives capitalize on the rhetoric of the Holocaust as a mega-atrocity. They address the fiction of the common memory of EU citizens as a new specific element of pan-European identity, whose symbolical core is founded on the ethical lessons of the World War II.[45] In fostering a European *demos*, EU institutions have been capitalizing on moral commitment to the past as a promise of a better future. Central to this vision of EU citizenship and its core values has been the *Europe for Citizens Program* launched in December 2006 by Decision 1904/2006/EC of the European Parliament and of the Council.[46] The Program, initially established for the period from 2007 to 2013, was in itself an extensive transnational memory law supporting a series of activities and organizations that promoted "Active European Citizenship". Driving on the activist paradigm of citizenship, seen as the encouragement of civil society to solemnize the Holocaust and other atrocities of totalitarian regimes, the Program has become an important aspect in fostering European integration and in "developing a sense of common identity among European citizens based on recognised common values, history and culture". Furthermore, one of the Program's four action lines is explicitly devoted to "Active European Remembrance".[47] In the renewed *Europe for Citizens Program 2014–2020*, the "European remembrance" of totalitarianism was further reinforced with increased funds going towards action in this area, available for various research institutes, associations of survivors, museums, and organizations active in the promotion of human rights, as well as in the creation of additional channels of communication

[44] E.g., European Parliament Resolution of 23 October 2008 on the Commemoration of the Holodomor, the Ukraine artificial Famine (1932–33), Official Journal of the European Union, 21 January 2010, C 15 E/78; European Parliament Resolution of 2 April 2009 on European Conscience and Totalitarianism; Resolution on the Remembrance of the Holocaust, Anti-Semitism and Racism 2005; Resolution on a Political Solution of the Armenian Question, Doc. A2-33/87. These numerous soft laws illustrate the rise of the alleged right to have one's memory recognized by others, at least, within a peer group, on transnational – in this case European Union – level.

[45] The European politics of memory are well discussed in literature by now, see for example, P. den Boer et al. (eds.), *Europäische Erinnerungsorte* (München: Oldenbourg, 2012); H. Rousso, 'Das Dilemma eines europäischen Gedächtnisses', *Zeithistorische Forschungen* 1 (2004), 363–78; T. Judt, 'The Past is Another Country. Myth and Memory in Postwar Europe', *Theoria: A Journal of Social & Political Theory* 87 (1996), 36–69.

[46] A detailed description of the program is available on the webpage of the EU Commission: http://eacea.ec.europa.eu/citizenship/index_en.php.

[47] Action 4 "Active European Remembrance", available at: http://eacea.ec.europa.eu/citizenship/programme/action4_en.php.

across the EU by networking organizations which were formerly only active at the domestic level.[48]

Yet recent developments of EU law indicate the substantial evolution of the activist citizenship discourse on historic memory, from *invitation to remember* towards *duty to remember*.[49] This paradigm of memory-building straightforwardly outlaws the denial, trivialization, and minimization of certain atrocities. Since the adoption of Framework Decision 2008/913/JHA,[50] this second paradigm has become currently most controversial in EU law and the politics of memory.[51] Previously, a prescription to remember via criminalization of revisionist practices has been emblematic of republican forms of citizenship in nation states. This somewhat outdated vision of citizenship links common goals of community to foundational historical myth(s). Republican citizenship, thus, seeks to reproduce a morally unbiased population and its symbolical duty to commemorate history and community values. As was convincingly argued, the European Union – although proclaiming duties of citizenship in primary law[52] – does not demand any duties of EU citizens in practice.[53] Such a duty-less citizenship is a great achievement too, in line with a progressive shift from community and population towards individual values and dignity. It, therefore, raises many questions voiced in this book as to why EU law has recently opted for criminal restrictions on the free market of historical ideas. This turn mimics the "duty to remember" imposed on citizens in several Member States, in contrast to encouraging a critical dialogue on memory in the EU. In this volume, we leave it up to authors to

48 A. Littoz-Monnet, 'The EU Politics of Remembrance: Can Europeans Remember Together?', *West European Politics* 35:5 (2012), 1182–202.

49 E. Fronza, 'The Punishment of Negationism: The Difficult Dialogue between Law and Memory', *Vermont Law Review* 30 (2006), 609–26.

50 EU Council Framework Decision on Combating Certain Forms and Expressions of Racism and Xenophobia by Means of Criminal Law, 2008/913/JHA. For a detailed account of the controversial history of the Decision's adoption, see M. Bell, *Racism and Equality in the European Union* (Oxford University Press, 2008) 164–8. About the Decision, see chapter by Luigi Cajani in the present volume.

51 L. Pech, 'The Law of Holocaust Denial in Europe. Towards a (Qualified) EU-Wide Criminal Prohibition', *Jean Monnet Working Paper NYU School of Law* 10:9 (2009), 1–51; L. Cajani, 'Criminal Laws on History: The Case of the European Union', *Historien* 11 (2011), 19–48.

52 Under Article 9 TEU and Article 20 TFEU, every person holding the nationality of a Member State is a citizen of the Union. Nationality is defined according to the national laws of that State. Citizenship of the Union is complementary to, but does not replace, national citizenship. EU citizenship comprises a number of rights and duties in addition to those stemming from citizenship of a Member State.

53 D. Kochenov, 'EU Citizenship without Duties', *European Law Journal* 20–4 (2014), 482–98.

decide whether law's purpose should be to invite citizens to remember or rather to impose the duty of memory.

Holocaust denial laws have been followed by at least four – interlinked and not necessarily chronologically distinctive – streams of memory laws after World War II:

(1) The first stream encompasses attempts to retrospectively recognize atrocities and prohibit genocide negationism in an effort to mimic restrictions on Holocaust denials. The most discussed example of such memory laws are the recent attempts of legal recognition (in France, Switzerland, Slovakia, Greece) of the Armenian genocide, that is the Ottoman government's extermination of approximately 1.5 million Armenians from their historic homeland within present-day Turkey.[54] Yet so far, judiciaries in France (2008)[55] and before the European Court of Human Rights (2013)[56] have been reversing the criminalization of Armenian genocide denial, finding it incompatible with freedom of speech, in contrast to the prohibitions on Holocaust denial. Such a stance raises a question of the magnification of a certain hierarchy amongst genocides, with *Shoah* occupying a special place in the monumental legal doctrine of historic memory.[57] Similar questions have been also advanced with regard to specific-country attempts to enact memory laws, covering, *inter alia*, the prescription of positive-negative roles of French colonialism in France,[58] the recognition of *Holodomor* – a policy of mass starvation orchestrated by Bolsheviks during 1932–3 with 2.4 to 7 million victims – in the Ukraine,[59] Asian controversies about laws on the commemoration of Japanese military

[54] For statistics of legal and declarative recognition, see the web-resource: www.armenian-genocide.org/recognition_countries.html.

[55] Décision du Conseil Constitutionnel, n. 2012-647 DC (28 February 2012).

[56] On 28 January 2015, the Grand Chamber of the ECtHR had hearings in case *Perinçek* v. *Switzeland* [No 27510/08]. In its prevision decision [December 2013], the Court held that criminal measures against an Armenian genocide denier in Switzerland violated his freedom of expression.

[57] For a comment on the previous decision of the Court in *Perinçek* [December 2013], see Uladzislau Belavusau, *Armenian Genocide* v. *Holocaust in Strasbourg: Trivialization in Comparison*, available at: www.verfassungsblog.de/en/armenian-genocide-v-holocaust-in-strasbourg-trivialisation-in-comparison/.

[58] E.g., Loi n. 2005-158 du 23 février 2005 portant reconnaissance de la Nation et contribution nationale en faveur des Français rapatriés, Journal officiel, 24 février 2005.

[59] Ukrainian law no. 376-V of 28 November 2006, Vidomosti Verkhovnoi Rady Ukrajiny, 2006. No. 50, 504.

during World War II,[60] etc. The French discussion on the borders of law in prescribing historical memory, subsequent to a series of legislative attempts to regulate colonial historiography, has stimulated academic popularity of the very tag "memory laws" (*les lois mémorielles*).[61]

(2) The second stream addresses falls of twentieth-century dictatorships in the period after World War II and the legal prescriptions of historical commemoration in the subsequent democratic regimes. Such legal means cover both legislative and judicial impositions of truth about victims and condemnations of perpetrators. The most eminent European example in this group is the Law on Historic Memory in Spain (2007).[62] Likewise, this group covers rich legislative practices and jurisprudence by Latin American courts fixing various mechanisms of transitional justice, while instrumentalizing the invitation and duty to remember via legal means.[63]

(3) The third stream was triggered by the de-communization and collapse of the Soviet empire and is, therefore, geographically limited to the countries of Central and Eastern Europe and the ex-Soviet Union. The dilemma of so-called *Historikerstreit* is particularly emblematic for this group as historians long dispute the singularity of the *Shoah* and comparability of Nazi and Stalinist repressions.[64] This diverse group covers judicial sagas on the Katyń massacre (the execution of Polish officers in the 1930s by the Soviets, which was attributed to the Nazi regime for a long time),[65] the constitutional revision of the national history in Hungary,[66] the recognition and prohibition of denial of the

60 Osiel, *Mass Atrocity, Collective Memory, and the Law*; Vidal-Naquet, *Assassins of Memory. Essays on the Denial of the Holocaust*.

61 S. Garibian, 'Pour une lecture juridique des quatre lois "mémorielles"', *Esprit* February (2006), 158–73.

62 *La Ley por la que se reconocen y amplían derechos y se establecen medidas en favor de quienes padecieron persecución o violencia durante la Guerra Civil y la Dictadura [Ley de Memoria Histórica]*, 31 October 2007.

63 See M. C. Campasi, 'From a Duty to Remember to an Obligation to Memory? Memory as Reparation in the Jurisprudence of the Inter-American Court of Human Rights', *International Journal of Conflict & Violence* 8:2 (2014), 61–74; S. Garibian, 'Ghosts Also Die: Resisting Disappearance through the "Right to Truth" and the Juicios por la Verdad in Argentina', *Journal of International Criminal Justice* 1 (2014), 1–24.

64 M. Geyer and S. Fitzpatrick (eds.), *Beyond Totalitarianism: Stalinism and Nazism Compared* (Cambridge University Press, 2009).

65 See ECtHR *Janowiec* v. *Russia* (Appl. No. 55508/07 and 29520/09), Judgment (Grand Chamber) 21 October 2013.

66 See, T. Ország-Land, 'New Hungarian Constitution Shirks Responsibility for the Holocaust', *New English Review*, September 2011, available at: www.newenglishreview.org/custpage.cfm/frm/96102/sec_id/96102.

fact of the Soviet occupation of the Baltic states,[67] and the EU's resolutions recognizing and commemorating Stalinist repressions,[68] etc.

(4) Finally, the fourth stream deals with genocides and other mass atrocities subsequent to the introduction of the crime of genocide in international law. This group is, to a large degree, intertwined with the second stream of "transitional" memory laws and is different from the third stream as it spreads geographically further than ex-Soviet Union and CEE. This group of judicial and legislative engagements with memory covers international criminal proceedings subsequent to crimes against humanity in Rwanda,[69] former Yugoslavia,[70] the spectacular trials of the former heads of the Khmer Rouge in Phnom Pench,[71] and the barriers to the commemoration of the mass displacement of Palestinians ("Naqba" laws) in Israel,[72] etc.

3 Memory Laws: Examples and Comparative Assessment

Memory laws are a contentious normative issue, and while on the one hand it seems that no state, no law, no well-ordered polity can do without them, objections against the very idea of memory laws (let us emphasize: not against some specific laws which may be badly drafted, disproportionate to their aims, unreasonable or unduly oppressive, but against the very idea of the laws *per se*) are powerful. The co-editors of this volume do not pretend to be neutral or agnostic on this issue, we do not want to claim that the principle is non-controversial. Just to the contrary, precisely because these laws can trigger so many concerns, objections, and misgivings, the issue deserves a nuanced, comprehensive, and subtle treatment – which we hope this volume achieves.

[67] L. Mälksoo, *Illegal Annexation and State Continuity: The Case of the Incorporation of the Baltic States by the USSR: A Study of the Tension between Normativity and Power in International Law* (Leiden and Boston: Martinus Nijhoff Publishers, 2003).

[68] Declaration of the European Parliament on the Proclamation of 23 August as European Day of Remembrance of Victims of Stalinism and Nazism.

[69] International Criminal Tribunal for Rwanda, established in 1994. This is not to forget that Rwanda has also introduced a European-styled punitive memory law, outlawing the denial of the genocide.

[70] International Criminal Tribunal for former Yugoslavia, established in 1993.

[71] The Extraordinary Chambers in the Courts of Cambodia (ECCC), commonly known as the Khmer Rouge Tribunal, is a court established to try the most senior responsible members of the Khmer Rouge for crimes perpetrated during the Cambodian genocide.

[72] High Court of Justice Decision 3429/11, *Alumni of the Arab Orthodox High School in Haifa et al. v. The Minister of Finance et al.* (25 January 2012, not yet published) [the "Naqba Law" case].

The misgivings about the very concept of memory laws have to be treated seriously, and the critics of such laws must similarly be treated with the respect they deserve. Perhaps a good point to start is with the very principle of the functions of law: law, we are told, not without reason, is mainly to regulate the community in an imperative, coercive way, rather than to declare "truths" about the presence and the past. This was perhaps best put by a prominent French lawyer, Robert Badinter, in his impassioned critique of a series of proposed French memory laws: "laws are not billboards for campaign advertising. They are created to given the polity" – and then he went on to deplore that the law "has come to be seen as a kind of soothing ointment for emotional suffering". These are deliberately sarcastic and exaggerated claims, but in the spirit of generosity let us give them the most reasonable interpretation, even if only in the temporarily assumed capacity of devil's advocates. The law is peremptory. The law does not describe, announce, declare. The law determines the prescribed behaviour of individuals, authorities, and other public and private entities within its jurisdiction. To use the law for making a statement rather than to regulate behaviour, to interpret the past rather than determine the future actions, and to express a political or moral judgment rather than issue a legal norm of behaviour is to fundamentally misunderstand and distort the central nature and function of law in a society.

Yet obviously much more is at stake than merely a misunderstanding of the function and role of law: the stakes are practical, not theoretical or academic. The dominant concerns of critics of memory laws are that such laws will lead to censorship, "thought police", restrictions of freedom of expression and academic freedoms. These fears are not to be dismissed lightly – and their strong traces are present also in a number of chapters in this volume, for instance in Luigi Cajani's chapter "Legislating History: The European Union and the Denial of International Crimes", who points out that many historians viewed some aspects of the Council Framework Decision of 28 November 2008 on Combating Certain Forms of Racism and Xenophobia by Means of Criminal Law as a possible tool of censorship, because they directly affect the historical interpretation of historical events. A related objection, about school teachers' freedom, was raised by Robert Badinter in the aforementioned speech, when he objected to the proposed French statute of 2005, which would require including a reference to the positive role of the French colonial presence overseas in school curricula. Obviously, one may observe, in the European legal tradition freedom of expression and academic freedom are not absolute – but they are very important nevertheless, and can be restricted only for a limited number of reasons, to which the restrictions must be very narrowly tailored. Article 10 of the European Convention of Human Rights does not explicitly mention a proper ideological orthodoxy as one of the grounds of legitimate restriction of freedom of expression. Can such a prescribed version of the truth be hidden behind the values of "the prevention of disorder", "the reputation or rights of others", "the protection of morals", "public safety" – which are among the catalogue of justifiable grounds for speech restrictions (Art. 10 (2) ECHR)? Probably only in cases of some, narrowly drawn memory laws. Yet, remember, we are dealing here with the very principle of memory laws as such, rather than with strength and weaknesses of *particular* laws . . .

Concerns that memory laws intrude upon freedom of expression come in a left-wing and right-wing (for a lack of better descriptors) versions. Left-wingers deplore the self-aggrandizement of the state, to the detriment of spontaneous, societal interactions, which is the proper space where judgments about the past should be formed, negotiated, challenged, and tested. When the state assumes a role of declaring a truth about the past – especially, about a recent past, with the nexus between the past and the present being relatively clear – it usually does so for self-serving, often imperial reasons. Perhaps the most pathological example of such a law is Vladimir Putin's law of May 2014, described by Nikolay Koposov in his chapter "Defending Stalinism by Means of Criminal Law: Russia, 1995–2014" – a law unashamedly meant to protect the memory of Stalinism against that of millions of its victims. That state-centred memory laws may be self-serving and used to actually stifle a healthy debate about the unwholesome past is shown by Jiří Přibáň in his chapter on the politics of public knowledge and legal justice in the context of dealing with the past in the Czech Republic. The Czech lustration process is shown there as, paradoxically perhaps, inhibiting the public discussion about the totalitarian past, its political impact, and the responsibility of the perpetrators. However, the freedom-of-expression-based objections to memory laws are often dressed in a right-wing rhetoric of warnings against the dreaded political correctness: intellectual fashions, which, allegedly, have a chilling effect upon independent intellectuals and academics.

Freedom of speech (and, in association, freedom of academic pursuit and teaching), while dominant amongst the criticisms of memory laws, is not the only concern raised against the very idea of such laws. To use the instruments of criminal law (of course, not all memory laws belong to that category) may be seen as detrimental to the principles of a fair trial, natural justice, and equitable process. In her chapter on the role of the

International Criminal Tribunal in shaping the historical accounts of genocide, Marina Aksenova perhaps does not raise that objection explicitly but usefully identifies a dichotomy between the individualized purposes of a criminal trial, which is to dispense justice in a fair way (and, let us add, with a proper presumption of the innocence of a defendant) versus the purpose of communicating a certain narrative of a "historical truth" and making value judgments about the history.

Others may be concerned by additional invidious effects of memory laws, including promotion of divisiveness, both within and between societies and nations. Luigi Cajani even writes about "memory wars", referring to the clashes of state-endorsed memories between different states, and in particular between those states, mainly in Western Europe, which are more attentive to the memory of Nazi and fascist totalitarianism and in particular of the Holocaust, and those emerging from the Communist domination, in Eastern and Central Europe, which are more sensitive to the crimes of communist totalitarianism. Can these different sensitivities be reconciled? Maria Mälksoo in her chapter about the European Court of Human Rights case *Kononov* v. *Latvia* shows a specific case of a "memory war": that between Latvia's memory of Soviet crimes in its territory and Russian memory of the Great Patriotic War and the USSR's role in defeating Nazi Germany. However, more worrisome perhaps, memory laws have also a deeply antagonizing potential within the societies where they are in force: a case of Spain described in the chapter by Alfons Aragoneses may serve as evidence both of the unintended negative consequences of the politics of official amnesia, which immediately followed Franco's death, and also of the intended consequences. State-endorsed memory, oddly symbolized by the very title of the 2007 statute: the Historical Memory Act. Controversies around decommunization and lustration in post-communist states provide another example of divisive effects of official memory. After all, in all these societies there is inevitable and inescapable disagreement as to the assessment of the period of state socialism (or of the Franco regime, in the case of Spain): the official endorsement of one viewpoint of the controversy is politically costly (because it alienates a section of the population) and morally objectionable (because it goes against the liberal principle of neutrality of the state). One may maintain, naturally, that no such neutrality is warranted when the assessment of the authoritarian and/or oppressive regime is at issue. And yet the very fact of an actual disagreement in the society about the details of such an assessment suggests that an evaluation endorsed officially by the law creates a danger of leaving those who disagree beyond the pale of the political community; even if only in a symbolic way, they are placed in a position of second-class citizenship. To say that they have brought it upon themselves by siding with the wrong viewpoint is, for liberals, not a satisfactory response because it relies upon an idea of moral uniformity that is anathema to a liberal approach to law. Hence, it is often said, such evaluations are better left outside the sphere of authoritative actions of the state, and relegated to the operations of civil society, education, history, private media, and public opinion.

By this time a reader may have acquired an impression that the authors of this introduction took the "devil's advocate" position so seriously that the role became their second nature. Not so. We believe that while the objections to memory laws have to be taken very seriously, they do not amount to intractable moral, political, or legal obstacles to the very principle of constructing collective memory by, among other things, legal means. In fact, no society can do without it: authoritative decisions about the minimum content of school curricula, about grants and subsidies to museums, broadcasting, or the arts, will inevitably have some content-sensitive dimensions which, among other things, will create a depiction, interpretation, or understanding of the society's past. And while, under our definitions, these actions do not amount to memory laws *sensu stricto*, they are invoked here to show that the law and the state can never be fully agnostic about the collective past. The question therefore is not *whether* but *how*?

Different countries, national and polities, and different *pasts* and circumstances will yield different answers – the issue, as with everything about the "law and society" inquiry, is eminently context-sensitive. It is no coincidence that the main locus of memory laws contemplated in this volume is Europe: the continent of "Bloodlands" and the Holocaust, of fascism and communism, of genocide and war crimes. And while we do not want to undermine the persistence of these mass evils elsewhere (and the discussions of cruel Latin American regimes, of the historical treatment of Canada's Indigenous people, or of the Israeli-Palestinian conflict etc. indicate that we are perfectly aware of the non-European dimensions of the problem), the gravitational pull of European memory laws is beyond any doubt. This not only provides a hint about why memory laws are, in one or another form, inescapable, but also why they are important, indeed often necessary.

A good point at which to begin a defence of the very principle of memory laws is that many of them have aims which are fully convergent with the traditional aims of law, including those of criminal law, and provide for similar guarantees of integrity of legal process. Even such a harsh critic of many memory laws as Robert Badinter, already invoked above, fully accepted the French *loi Gayssot* of 1990 (an anti-Holocaust denial law), stating that the law "primarily targets revisionism, which in this case is simply a camouflage for anti-Semitism, incitement to racial hatred and hatred of a community, all of them offences subject to the force of criminal law". Many memory laws described and discussed in this volume have a similar function and nature: rather than establishing a single, orthodox version of the past, they prosecute for verbal assaults on the dignity of the victims of past mass crimes and their descendants. The wrongs they target, either in the form of dignitary and reputational harms, or of incitement to violence or hatred – belong to a traditional catalogue of social evils that the criminal law may and should address. This is what various legal frameworks on the denial of crimes or glorification of those crimes (in particular, crimes of genocide and war crimes) have in common.

Yet obviously not all memory laws have the form of criminal prohibitions, and address the actions, which are properly deemed criminal in a free and democratic society. Many of them are perfectly legitimate, and non-restrictive of individual freedom, acts of the community to identify the common legacy and symbolically declare the wrongness of past evils, committed in the name of a nation, state, class, with effects which may persist into the present. Remembrance Days, educational and awareness-raising projects, museums and other institutions, the removal of symbols of totalitarianism. Such actions and laws do not only enjoy local significance, confined to the state or region in which they take place. They may also contribute to a broader sense of common legacy, for instance in Europe. As the European Commission put it well in its Report to the European Parliament and to the Council, on the "memory of the crimes committed by totalitarian regimes in Europe" (22 December 2010, COM(2010) 783 final), "it is important to address knowledge gaps concerning the totalitarian past of all [EU] Member States, and especially concerning the period of time in which Eastern and Western Europe have lived two different experiences" (Part 3). Furthermore, the Report added: "The memory and awareness of the tragic past and of the crimes committed by totalitarian regimes should bring together the peoples of Europe. It is important to contribute to the recognition of, and support for, all victims of the totalitarian regimes that have devastated Europe" (id). This is what we may call a cosmopolitan or supranational dimension of the memory laws: they may contribute to a sense of togetherness and commonality, rather than mutual suspicion and distrust.

Nonetheless, perhaps the main rationales for well-drafted, well-designed memory laws concern their role in shaping and promoting collective identity and understanding at the national or even local scale. Rather than contributing to the myths of glorious past, to the self-aggrandizement of the current elites, and to the sense of moral and political superiority, they may help achieve a self-understanding that each nation's complex past consists of the moments of glory and those which are shameful, that no nation is either a collective villain or a hero. They are a sign of the maturity of a collective: proof that a given state has assumed responsibility (if not legal, then moral and political) for crimes and serious violations of human rights in the past, either by the state and its officials, or its citizens. States do not like to remember crimes committed by their compatriots or their nation; like individuals, they have tendencies of amnesia, denial, or trivialization. As a minimum, memory laws help preserve the bare *knowledge* about the past, which is a condition of rational and intelligent self-understanding. Yet by assisting to condemn those aspects of the past which consisted of totalitarianism, oppression, mass crimes, or even genocide, such laws help to protect the democratic order of the state, and its commitment to the rule of law and constitutional liberties.

This, a sceptic will observe, is a very tall order, and an unlikely aim to be achieved when the local elites are notoriously tempted to capture collective memory for their own purposes. We beg to differ: the analyses in this volume do not warrant such a uniform, negative assessment. At least, we ask the readers to hold off their fire until after reading this book. It opens with three chapters on memory in international bodies and tribunals. Antoon De Baets reconstructs the view of history as depicted in the UN Human Rights Committee and finds, surprisingly, that out of the hundreds of decisions, only a fraction may be properly characterized as dealing with historical memories. In De Baets' chapter special attention is given to the cases of Holocaust denial, arising out of France and Canada. The role of the International Criminal Tribunal in shaping historical accounts of genocides is the subject of Maria Aksenova's chapter: she concludes, among other things, that the goal of setting the historical record straight may clash with other goals of trials before the Tribunal, such as deterrence, retribution, restorative justice, and reconciliation. Finally, Patricia Naftali posits the concept of the right to truth, and studies whether this "right" (explicitly recognized by some non-European jurisdictions, for instance by the Inter-American Court of Human Rights) has percolated into the Strasbourg case law. In a refreshing contrast to many, more formalistic studies of the European Court of Human Rights (ECtHR), Naftali describes (also, based on her own interviews) the position of various non-governmental actors involved in the strategic litigation in Strasbourg.

The next part of the volume is devoted to studies on the European law's dealing with the continent's tormented past, both in the EU's and CoE's legal and political settings. In his chapter, Luigi Cajani focuses on the EU Council Framework decision of 28 November 2008 on combating certain forms and expressions of racism and xenophobia by means of criminal law, and carefully traces various steps leading up to the admission of this (controversial, to many) legal instrument, as the key element in European politics of memory. In particular, Cajani reflects on the impact of the EU enlargement upon post-communist states of Central and Eastern Europe, and the resulting clash of collective memories in the Western and Eastern parts of the continent. In the subsequent three chapters of this part of the volume, the ECtHR in Strasbourg plays a special role, as the top, quasi-constitutional court for Europe. Maria Mälksoo discusses in detail the Court case of *Kononov* v. *Latvia*, and shows how the legitimate efforts at transitional justice in post-authoritarian Latvia clashed with the Russian hegemonic, mnemonic narrative about the role of USSR in World War II. After all, it was the first case concerning World War II in which an Allied soldier was convicted for a war crime by another government's court – and such a precedent could not have failed to implicate painful clashes of state-endorsed memories in the two member states of the Council of Europe. Paolo Lobba analyses the ECtHR's case law regarding the uniqueness of the Holocaust, and studies the Strasbourg Court's different phases of distinguishing between Holocaust denial and denial of historical facts other than the Nazi genocide. His descriptive analysis confirms the notorious fact that the memory of the uniqueness of the Holocaust – as a special evil in the recent European history – is perhaps one of the few fixed points in the collective memory of the continent. At the same time, in a normative dimension of his chapter, Lobba proposes the adoption of a strongly civil-libertarian approach by the ECtHR, where restrictions upon the freedom of expression of negationists can be upheld only when tangible symptoms of harm (such as threats to public order) can be shown as properly addressed by the legislation.

Our next section picks up the comparative, national perspectives taken from different EU member states. Ioanna Tourkochoriti examines some recent pieces of legislation, memory laws par excellence on the understanding adopted in this volume, in France, Greece, and Canada, and then compares these national approaches with those adopted by the ECtHR. Tourkochoriti openly draws a distinction between the laws meant to impose a dominant version of historical truth aimed at the formation of national identity on the one hand, and the laws against denial of crimes against humanity, on the other. She further postulates applying the same considerations of respect for freedom of expression to both categories of cases. Spain is the subject-matter of the second chapter in the same section. Alfons Aragoneses traces here an evolution from "the pact of silence" (at the early stages of Spain's transition to democracy) to the "revolt of the grandchildren" aimed at determining the truth and awarding reparations to the victims of the Franco dictatorial rule. Against this background, the author discusses the Historical Memory Act of 2007 – perhaps the most paradigmatic case of memory laws studied in this volume – and concludes, perhaps surprisingly to external observers, that it has not produced any tangible effects (other than regarding reparations) as far as the collective memory of Francoism is concerned. In his chapter on dealing with the past through "politics of public knowledge and legal justice" in the Czech Republic, Jiří Přibáň observes various pathologies of the Czech legal approach to the past, as depicted by a recent, disconcerting "Kundera case" where the famous novelist was found allegedly guilty of some politically discrediting behaviour back in the 1950s. Using this case study, Přibáň argues that the official system of purging those guilty of political collaboration with the system of oppression may, unexpectedly, inhibit public discussion about the totalitarian past. Ieva Miluna discusses in turn the issue of adjudication in deportation cases that took places in Latvia in the light of international law. The whole Baltic region was the theatre of particularly painful mass evils: not only of state terror inflicted by the Stalinist regime but also of mass-scale killings and population displacement. The main argument of this chapter is that national courts, in their war crimes trials, found themselves manoeuvring between the nationally stipulated definitions of international crimes and the international law in force concerning international crimes. In this regard, the role played by the references to international law in Latvia's criminal code was one of the decisive aspects. Cosmin Sebastain Cercel describes a rarely studied case of post-World War II Romania trials dealing with the Romanian participation in the war, and in particular in the Holocaust. This is an intriguing case, in which two murderous totalitarianisms intersected in a complex way: one as a "judge", another as a target of judgment. Not surprisingly, Cercel looks into theoretical shallowness of Stalinism as an ideological frame of dealing with the past, and its inability to properly address the history of the Holocaust. A much more recent attempt to cope with the criminal past of a post-Communist nation is discussed in the chapter by Miklós Könczöl, who examines, against a background of memory laws concerning Hungarian history since the end of the nineteenth century, the Fundamental Law (the Constitution) of 2011 which construes itself as marking a radical caesura between the past and the present. As is known, constitutional changes in Hungary post-2010 have caused a lot of concern about the rule of law in Europe and worldwide, and Könczöl's analysis is particularly useful in helping understand these changes, in the light of constitution-makers; and legislators' attempts to construct their own, consistent, narrative about the recent past. Similarly, Tomasz Tadeusz Koncewicz, in a concluding chapter for this part of the volume, considers a new historical narrative, which became *de rigeur* after the recent presidential and parliamentary elections in Poland, in 2015. In the chapter "On the Politics of Resentment, Mis-memory, and Constitutional Fidelity. The Demise of the Polish Overlapping Consensus?" he shows clearly how harmful it may be to adopt a rhetoric, supported by criminal law and operated through violations of the Constitution, which falsely interprets the past in which Poles were always the victims and never co-perpetrators of historical crimes.

In the last section, the volume looks beyond the European Union. Nikolay Koposov, in his chapter, subjects the Russian historical memory law of 2014 to a harsh criticism showing that, in reversal of the proper pattern of memory laws, the Russian criminal provision, rather than protecting memories of the victims of state policy, in fact protects the memory of the Stalinist state from that of its victims. Koposov's subtle account provides an insight into the divergences among Russian law makers, as evident in the conflict between the two houses of the Russian Parliament: the project of the Council of Federation was more in line with the European standards, but the project of the State Duma, developed along the traditional Soviet approaches, prevailed. Similar controversies, though introduced from the Ukrainian perspective, are analysed in Lina Klymenko's chapter on the narrative of the national past and future in the de-communization policy of Ukraine. Presenting the subject within the context of the ongoing geo-political conflict between Ukraine and Russia, Klymenko focuses on, as she puts it, "interpretive approaches to policy-making that emphasize the role of narratives constructed by political actors in policy-relevant situations". Klymenko also shows how dealing with the Soviet past, through the means of different laws and policies, resonates with Ukrainian aspirations to join the European community. Next, Robert A. Kahn, in his chapter on the geography of banning genocide denial, raises a fascinating intellectually and politically urgent issue of the nexus between a legitimate prohibition and the place where the crimes to which the prohibition applies were committed. Under the "nexus argument", for instance, punishment for Holocaust denial is perfectly legitimate in Germany but not necessarily in India, while Rwandan genocide denial should be prosecuted in Rwanda but not necessarily in France, etc. While the "nexus argument" may, superficially at least, benefit from the support of the context-sensitivity principle, Kahn provides a thought-provoking debunking of the argument, and shows that it is vulnerable to at least three criticisms: from the revolution in communications around the globe, from demographical dispersal of the survivors and descendants of the victims, and from geopolitics which indicates that there may be global risk arising out of the glorification of mass crimes, even if committed in a relatively discrete part of the globe. Jeremie Bracka discusses the collective memories of the Israelis and Palestinians focused upon the events of 1948, and their role in shaping Israeli and Palestinian national identities. Bracka believes in the need to forge a bridging narrative, based on an honest and full account of the past, in order to transcend a conflict-based culture rooted in polarized, clashing narratives. The Canadian experience of dealing with the treatment of its Indigenous peoples is the topic of the chapter by Michael Mordon. Looking at the work and impact of three commissions charged with attainment of truth and reconciliation, Mordon explores in detail the impact of these bodies upon Indigenous narratives, but also concludes that their impact upon the non-Indigenous narratives was negligible. Finally, Salvador Herencia Carrasco scrutinizes the impact of the decisions of the Inter-American Court of Human Rights on the prosecution of grave human rights violations perpetrated by military regimes in Latin America, the topic that still remains less well known to the European readers. Looking in particular at the experience of Peru, the author considers many of the challenges for the restitution of memory, going beyond traditional measures of transitional justice, such as the construction of sanctuaries in the places of mass graves or the opening of the National Museum of Memory.

The book ends with an Epilogue by Eric Heinze: "Beyond 'Memory Laws': Towards a General Theory of Law and Historical Discourse". While in this introduction we have mapped the genesis, evolution, and major examples of memory laws, in the closing essay Heinze offers a proposal for a seminal normative theory of memory laws. For this purpose, Heinze develops a taxonomy of memory laws, distinguishing between non-regulatory and regulatory laws, and suggests that the latter need not be necessarily punitive. Indeed, non-punitive yet regulatory laws seem to be of special significance in Heinze's scheme. Further, he indicates a distinction between substantive and expressive weight of law, and uses this distinction to emphasize the expressive significance of memory laws.

For all the healthy diversity among contributions to this volume, a number of common themes emerge. They identify some dangers of allowing politicians and law makers to authoritatively manage the collective memory of a given community. A holistic and interdisciplinary insight helps to define some constant trends which emerge at the intersection of law and memory.

For one thing, it is clear that many states lead various battles for memory. They often use law as the weapon in these battles, in order to "protect", no matter what, some particular memories of the past and the suffering of the nation. This may be clearly seen in the memory-oriented conflicts between Ukraine or the Baltic States, on the one hand, and Russia, on the other. Perhaps we could offer a hypothesis that if it were not for an aggressive Russian propaganda and military threats of Putin's epoch, the mnemopolitics in the region might have been much more peaceful, more in line with forgetting than with current zealous traumatized remembrance. The more Russian politics distances itself from consensus-seeking and the more aggressively it imposes its own version of the past, the more radically the states which had been victims of Soviet domination insist on their own versions of history. Also various Institutes of Memory or Remembrance, established as administrative promoters of memory laws and which have been mushrooming in particular in Central and Eastern European states (Poland, Czech Republic, Ukraine, etc.), became instruments for shaping the contours of collective memory. Their role as depositors of sources about history is invaluable but, on the other hand, they are often used and misused by politicians who access documents in the "lustration" processes.

Yet another regularity which may be noted about instrumentalizing memory-oriented conflicts are various phenomena of emulating some paradigm cases of negationism prohibition (Holocaust or Armenian denial ban) in order to justify nationalist memory constructivism. Poland with its current legislative project on defamation of the Nation, Russia with the Federal Law "On Entrenchment of the Victory of the Soviet People in the Great Patriotic War of 1941–1945", or Hungary with legal and political white-washing its wartime collaborationism with Nazis are some of the recent examples. In such a narrative, supported by criminal law sanctions, Poles, Russians, or Hungarians are solely victims or saviours of others. Their own faults in the past must be erased from memory of future generations while the memory of their victimhood is to be continuously amplified.

Equally significant as classical memory laws is also "legal silence" in constructing historical memory, parallel and often in contrast to zealous remembrance. The silence in forgetting about some dates, events, or persons effectuated by permitting only one version of the past may be deafening. It occasionally results from some "pacts of memory" between ancient regimes and new elites, in the process of transition. Vivid examples of such "pacted memories" are Israel's Nakba law or Spain in which a long-lived silence about Franco regime's atrocities have been, at a certain point, replaced by the law mandating a restoration of the memory by a restrictive law.

4 Conclusions

In Greek mythology, the personification of memory, *Mnemosyne*, spawned nine Muses, including *Calliope* (Poetry), *Clio* (History), *Melpomene* (Tragedy), and *Polyhymnia* (Hymns). In a similar way, a heterodox mass of state-orchestrated memory laws, policies, and practices – impressively spread after the French revolution – mothered contemporary requisites of republican citizenship: academic history, museums, architecture and naming in urban space, national heroic epos, and commemoration of victims-citizens. Legal governance of memory, thus, has played a central role in establishing the hegemony of monumental history, and has forged national identities and integration processes in Europe and beyond. Yet memory laws also contribute to complacency among citizens who seem at times too readily relegating debates about history and culture to the cloistered confines of legislatures and courtrooms. In this book, we invite our authors to unpack both the nature and the role of legal engagement into historical memory in specific jurisdictions and cases, as well as to reflect on potential conflict of legal governance of memory with values of democratic citizenship, political pluralism, and fundamental rights, such as freedom of expression.

Recent years have been full of monumental commemoration practices and memory laws about correlated events all over the world. Thus, today seems to be the perfect moment to undertake such a global comparative scrutiny of memory laws. Against the background of mass re-writing of history and denialism of historical facts in different parts of the world, it is time to revisit the fascinating subject of memory laws from the standpoint of comparative law and transitional justice.

PART I

International Law

1

The United Nations Human Rights Committee's View of the Past

ANTOON DE BAETS

1 Introduction

The year 2016 marked the fiftieth anniversary of one of world's most important human rights treaties, the International Covenant on Civil and Political Rights.[1] The Covenant was unanimously adopted in 1966 and entered into force in 1976. At the latter occasion, an Optional Protocol regulating a complaints procedure was established: individuals were given the opportunity to submit complaints to the United Nations, on the condition that they were related to one of the human rights stipulated in the Covenant.[2] As of 2016, this complaint procedure had yielded around 2,500 complaints – an average of fifty a year. Complaints are admissible only if they come from individuals, if all domestic remedies have been exhausted, and if the state against which the complaint is directed has ratified both the Covenant and the Protocol.[3]

The complaints are brought before the United Nations Human Rights Committee, an international body of eighteen independent human rights experts. Although its views on individual cases are not legally binding, the Committee is the most authoritative interpreter of the Covenant, which itself is legally binding. In addition, it publishes guidelines to interpret the Covenant in the form of *General Comments*, as well as reports on the follow-up that states give to its views. Over the years, the complaints procedure has become one of the most important instruments for human

[1] This chapter was presented as a paper at conferences on truth commissions in Hanover, Germany (2015) and law and memory in Amsterdam, the Netherlands (2016). All websites mentioned in this chapter were last visited on 20 June 2017.

[2] The *substantial* human rights are Articles 6–27 of the International Covenant on Civil and Political Rights (ICCPR).

[3] Technically, complaints are 'communications'; complainants are 'authors'; and the decisions of the Human Rights Committee (HRC) are 'views'. The case citation structure in the notes is: *Author versus country* (number/year of communication) year of adoption of views.

rights protection in the world, and many of the Committee's views have resonated widely.

The complaints archive of the United Nations is publicly accessible in its entirety.[4] For historians, one subset of the archive is particularly intriguing; namely the grievances that citizens have filed concerning past wrongs. They prompt several questions: What historical issues has the Committee dealt with? How has it handled questions of time, memory, and history? Finally, in handling them, are there any discernable patterns? A specific factor points in the direction of patterns: the Covenant rights and the Protocol rules themselves impose a rather strict logic and unity. But other factors point in the opposite direction. First, it is not part of the Committee's mission to develop a consistent philosophy of time, memory, and history.[5] When complaints regarding the fate of imprisoned or tortured historians were submitted to the Committee, for example, the fact that the victims were historians was irrelevant; it simply viewed them as citizens who were victims.[6] Second, the Committee is not expressly bound by any doctrine of precedent. Finally, individual Committee members serve for two years and are allowed to express separate opinions.

One might ask: Does this dispel the hope to discover any such patterns? This is what I attempt to unravel here. I selected the 108 most relevant cases via a keyword search in the complaints archive and studied them, together with the Covenant and the *General Comments*.[7] I then analysed the various memory and history issues they raised in order to identify the Committee's view of the past. The table on next page provides a compass with which to follow this analysis.

2 View of Time

Before we can analyse the Committee's views of memory and history, we need to investigate the substratum for these views, that is, the way in which

[4] See tbinternet.ohchr.org/_layouts/treatybodyexternal/TBSearch.aspx?Lang=en&TreatyID=8&DocTypeID=17.

[5] Compare A. De Baets, 'The Impact of the Universal Declaration of Human Rights on the Study of History', *History and Theory* 48:1 (2009), 21–3 (discussing the Declaration's general view of history).

[6] Remarkably, all relevant cases came from Uruguay when it was still a dictatorship; the HRC invariably tried to protect these historians: *Landinelli Silva* v. *Uruguay* (34/1978) 1981; *Martínez Machado* v. *Uruguay* (83/1981) 1984; *Conteris* v. *Uruguay* (139/1983) 1990; *Cariboni* v. *Uruguay* (159/1983) 1990.

[7] I also consulted numerous HRC *Concluding Observations* based on its consideration of periodic country reports.

The United Nations Human Rights Committee's view of the past (1976–2015)

	View of time (as a substratum)		***View of memory (as a right)***
T1	*Time-collapsing factors:* Rules of *ratione temporis* and non-retroactivity; rule of personal, not broad historical, claims; rule not to reassess historical evidence	M1	Right to mourn
		M2	Right to commemorate
		M3	Right, no duty, to remember
		M4	No memory laws banning historical views
		M5	Tradition not a limit to free expression
T2	*Time-expanding factors:* Principle of heirs; principle of state succession; principle of continuing violations; principle of imprescriptibility; principle of legality; view of past generations and ancestors; view of past eras		***View of history (as a right)***
		H1	Right to the truth about the past
		H2	Right to information about the past
		H3	State's duty to investigate past crimes
			View of history (as a craft)
		H4	Protection of historical opinions
		H5	Right to err
		H6	Principles of objectivity, neutrality, non-discrimination in history education
		H7	Principle of honesty in historical research

the Committee's work is influenced by its view of time. This is in itself a complex matter as it involves several factors that shrink the time scope of the Committee, and countervailing factors that expand it.

(T1) Although there is no time limit to submit complaints, the Committee's grasp of time is structurally limited by several Protocol rules. The most important is the rule of *ratione temporis* (by reason of time): the complaint must relate to an event that occurred after the relevant state ratified the Protocol. This rule is an application of the fundamental principle of non-retroactivity, which stipulates that laws and treaties cannot be imposed retroactively. It implies, above all, that an act cannot be a crime if no pre-existing law prohibited it (*nullum crimen sine lege*, no crime without

a prior law; Article 15 of the Covenant).[8] Another rule stipulates that the complaints procedure is designed for individuals claiming themselves to be victims of a violation. This means that an *actio popularis* (a complaint in the public interest) or a challenge of legal provisions deemed to be contrary to the Covenant *in the abstract* is not admissible. It is not allowed, for example, to submit broad historical claims involving Article 1 of the Covenant (the right to self-determination, which is a collective right). The purpose of the complaints procedure is to adjudicate concrete individual violations, not to redress all the injustices of history.[9] This rule is partly the reason why the Committee's use of historical concepts is rather rare. In one case about indigenous peoples, it adopted a notion of 'historical inequity', but this was exceptional.[10] Bound by the strict Protocol rules, it could not and did not go much further in developing a historical vocabulary. A third rule prescribes that the Committee cannot mount fact-finding operations itself. It depends on the parties (the authors and the state) for its information. As it is not a court of last instance, it does not generally re-assess findings of fact by domestic courts, even when the latter are based on contested historical records.[11] These rules have severely restricted the temporal scope of the Committee.

(T2) In other inventive ways, however, the Committee has been capable of enlarging its horizon. To begin with, two readings of the *ratione temporis* rule can push the time limit forward into the future. The first provides that if authors die during a proceeding, their heirs can continue the case.[12] The second applies the principle of state succession, which stipulates that successor governments are held to the obligations of their predecessors. This is justified because human rights belong to the people and compliance with them is not affected by regime change, including dismemberment into more than one state. The Committee applied this principle after the break-up of the USSR and Yugoslavia, for example.[13] A third principle – crucial for our

[8] For examples, see *Julian and Drake* v. *New Zealand* (601/1994) 1997; *Sankara* v. *Burkina Faso* (1159/2003) 2006.

[9] For examples, see *AD* v. *Canada* (78/1980) 1984; *Marshall* v. *Canada* (205/1986); *EP* v. *Colombia* (318/1988) 1990; *Gorji-Dinka* v. *Cameroon* (1134/2002) 2005; *Azouz* v. *Algeria* (1798/2008) 2013.

[10] *Lubicon Lake Band* [Ominayak] v. *Canada* (167/1984) 1990.

[11] For examples, see *Jonassen* v. *Norway* (942/2000) 2002; *Howard* v. *Canada* (879/1999) 2005.

[12] For examples, see *Des Fours Walderode* v. *Czech Republic* (747/1997) 2001; *Sanlés* v. *Spain* (1024/2001) 2004; *Anton* v. *Algeria* (1424/2005) 2006.

[13] S. Joseph and M. Castan, *The International Covenant on Civil and Political Rights: Cases, Materials, and Commentary* (Oxford University Press, 2013), 908–9.

purposes – prescribes that a complaint is admissible when the violation it refers to started before ratification of the Protocol but continued, or had effects which themselves constituted violations, after that date. This is called the 'principle of continuing violations'. The Committee defines 'continuing' as an affirmation, after the entry into force of the Protocol, by act or by clear implication, of previous violations by the state party. This principle has been of paramount importance in several domains, but perhaps most important in cases of enforced disappearances.[14]

Notably, two fundamental time principles with a strong potential to expand the Committee's temporal perspective have not played a significant role. The first is the imprescriptibility principle, stipulating that international crimes such as genocide, crimes against humanity, war crimes, slavery, torture, and enforced disappearance are exempted from time bars. These crimes are imprescriptible for as long as their perpetrators live, as long as they can be prosecuted, as long as their victims or their immediate descendants survive, and as long as they can be judicially investigated. The scale on which these crimes occur, however, generally exceeds the individual level (except for cases of torture and disappearance), which probably explains why the principle has only played a minor role in a system exclusively focusing on individual complaints. When the Committee has noted it, it has done so implicitly and indirectly. The second principle that is not frequently invoked is the legality principle, according to which (among others), the term 'pre-existing law' refers not only to domestic and statutory criminal law, but also to criminal law, which is international and customary. Article 15.2 of the Covenant stipulates that an act or omission is criminal when 'at the time when it was committed, it was criminal according to the general principles of law recognized by the community of nations'. This formula reflects the natural law basis of human rights.[15] It highlights the awareness that some acts have long been generally considered criminal and that any national written criminal law to the contrary

[14] For applications of the principle in cases of indigenous peoples, confiscation, and enforced disappearance, see *Lovelace* v. *Canada* (24/1977) 1981; *SE* v. *Argentina* (275/1988) 1990; *RAVN* v. *Argentina* (343/1988, 344/1988, 345/1988) 1990; *Aduayom* v. *Togo* (422/1990, 423/1990, 424/1990) 1996; *Simunek* v. *Czech Republic* (516/1992) 1995; *Könye* v. *Hungary* (520/1992) 1994; *EK and AK* v. *Hungary* (520/1992) 1994; *Bousroual* v. *Algeria* (992/2001) 2006; *Yurich* v. *Chile* (1078/2002) 2005; *Cifuentes* v. *Chile* (1536/2006) 2009; *Yusupova* v. *Russia* (2036/2011) 2015.

[15] The natural law conception of the legality principle can be traced back to at least 1789 (the Alien Tort Statute). See A. De Baets, 'Historical Imprescriptibility', *Storia della Storiografia* 59–60 (2011), 128–49.

cannot change this. The invocation of Article 15.2, however, has not played an important role before the Committee.[16]

Up until this point, I have referred to rules and principles which determine the time framework within which the Committee operates. Yet some complaints have elicited views from the Committee which also laid bare something about its time conception. Once, for example, the Committee paid explicit attention to the concepts of ancestors and past generations in its views.[17] In *Hopu and Bessert* v. *France* [1997], the term 'family' was given an extraordinarily broad interpretation by taking into account tradition when defining it.[18] The authors, two ethnic Polynesian inhabitants of Tahiti (an overseas possession of France), complained in 1993 that a hotel complex had been constructed on the burial grounds of their ancestors. They failed, however, to establish a family or kinship link between the remains found in these burial grounds and themselves. Forensic tests showed only that the remains predated the arrival of Europeans in Polynesia. Nevertheless the Committee demonstrated surprising sensitivity to the intergenerational link, finding as follows:

> The Committee considers that the authors' failure to establish a direct kinship link cannot be held against them . . . where the burial grounds in question pre-date the arrival of European settlers and are recognized as including the forebears of the present Polynesian inhabitants of Tahiti. The Committee therefore concludes that the construction of a hotel complex on the authors' ancestral burial grounds did interfere with their right to family and privacy.

It should be noted, however, that four Committee members dissented from the above finding. They argued that the term 'family' did not include all members of an ethnic group or 'all one's ancestors, going back to time immemorial'.[19] *Hopu and Bessert* has not become a part of acknowledged customary law.[20] Nevertheless we can conclude that, in this particular case, the Committee displayed a certain sensitivity to the role of past generations, if not in its conclusions, then at least in its considerations.[21]

16 For an example, see *Baumgarten* v. *Germany* (960/2000) 2003.

17 For an example in which the HRC dealt with the concept of future generations, see *EHP* v. *Canada* (67/1980) 1982.

18 *Hopu and Bessert* v. *France* (549/1993) 1997.

19 *Ibid.*, para 10.3, dissenting opinion, para 4. Compare *Vakoumé* v. *France* (822/1998) 2000. See also Salvioli's discussion of 'family' in his opinion in *Benaziza* v. *Algeria* (1588/2007) 2010.

20 See *Diergaardt* v. *Namibia* (760/1997) 2000.

21 Another type of enduring link between family members – the right to inherit nobility titles over generations – was not embraced by the HRC. See *Hoyos Martínez de Irujo* v. *Spain* (1008/2001) 2004; *Carrión Barcáiztegui* v. *Spain* (1019/2001) 2004.

The last feature of the Committee's time conception has revealed itself in the many cases where it had to decide whether the confiscation of property by past regimes and the failure of successor regimes to provide compensation for it were reprehensible under the Covenant's non-discrimination guarantee (Article 26 of the Covenant). In several of these 'discrimination cases', the Committee held that it was reasonable to distinguish between victims of injustice in different historical periods. It held that while a government dealing with the injustices of a previous regime should do so in a non-discriminatory way, it was not discriminatory if it failed to also clean up the remnants of injustices of regimes further back in time.[22]

An understanding of the rules under which the Committee is accountable, the principles it holds and has (or has not) applied, and the views of short- and long-term time conceptions it was inspired to give in particular cases are of paramount importance, as they trickle down in its views of memory and history and form the bedrock for assessing them.

3 View of Memory (as a Right)

(M1) Starting from a peculiar time conception in dealing with the past, the Committee has developed a memory regime with special features. The first of these features seems surprising: the Committee has never explicitly defended in its majority views a right to mourn in private for the deceased victims of human rights violations, although this would have been logical in all those cases where the right to life was violated. The reason for this is probably, if not certainly, that the right to mourn is so self-evident that it barely deserves mention. The dignity-based human rights doctrine strongly implies such a right to mourn as an integral part of the rights to privacy and thought (Articles 17–18 of the Covenant). Several statements of individual

[22] For examples, see *Drobek* v. *Slovakia* (643/1995) 1997; *Malik* v. *Czechoslovakia* (669/1995) 1998; *Schlosser* v. *Czech Republic* (670/1995) 1998; *X* v. *Czech Republic* (1961/2010) 2015; *B and C* v. *Czech Republic* (1967/2010) 2015. See also *Simunek* v. *Czech Republic* (516/1992) 1995; *Somers* v. *Hungary* (566/1993) 1996; *Adam* v. *Czech Republic* (586/1994) 1996; *Des Fours Walderode* v. *Czech Republic* (747/1997) 2001; *Pezoldova* v. *Czech Republic* (757/1997) 2002; *Fábryová* v. *Czech Republic* (765/1997) 2002; *Brokova* v. *Czech Republic* (774/1997) 2002; *Blazek* v. *Czech Republic* (857/1999) 2001; *Marik* v. *Czech Republic* (945/2000) 2005; *Neremberg* v. *Germany* (991/2001) 2001; *Kríž* v. *Czech Republic* (1054/2002) 2005; *Blücher von Wahlstatt* v. *Czech Republic* (1491/2006) 2010; *Sechremelis* v. *Greece* (1507/2006) 2011; *Ondracka* v. *Czech Republic* (1533/2006) 2007; *Lange* v. *Czech Republic* (1586/2007) 2011; *Bergauer* v. *Czech Republic* (1748/2008) 2010; *BK* v. *Czech Republic* (1844/2008) 2012; *TW and GM* v. *Slovakia* (1963/2010) 2014.

Committee members confirm this assumption. In 2009, while considering the disappearance case *Cifuentes* v. *Chile* [2009], two Committee members observed that:

> When the State has been responsible [for a disappearance, *adb*], it is not only ethically but also legally unacceptable for it to fail to provide family members with the answers they need to be able to mourn, as is their right, disappeared persons who have been extrajudicially executed . . . If the person has died, family members must be allowed to exercise their right to mourn the person so that they may try to continue on as best as they can under such tragic circumstances, and the State should guarantee them that right.[23]

Sometimes the Committee has implicitly asserted a right to mourn. In *Schedko* v. *Belarus* [2003], the author of a complaint was not informed of the date, hour, or place of the execution of her son (who was convicted of murder and sentenced to death).[24] In addition, the body was not returned for burial and the location of the grave was unknown to her. The Committee commented as follows:

> The Committee considers that the authorities' initial failure to notify the author of the scheduled date for the execution of her son, and their subsequent persistent failure to notify her of the location of her son's grave amounts to inhuman treatment of the author, in violation of Article 7 of the Covenant [the right not to be subjected to inhuman treatment, *adb*].[25]

The Committee has regularly insisted that burial places of victims need to be officially recognized and human remains returned to the family.[26] It is also noteworthy that while the right to mourn derives from Articles 17–18

[23] *Cifuentes* v. *Chile* (1536/2006) 2009, dissenting opinion of Keller and Salvioli, paras 12–31, especially 29, 31. For cases about the right to mourn before the ECtHR see: ECtHR *Płoski* v. *Poland* (Appl. No. 26761/95), Judgment 12 November 2002, paras 35–9; ECtHR *Éditions Plon* v. *France* (Appl. No. 58148/00), Judgment 18 May 2004, para 47; ECtHR *Hachette Filipacchi Associés* v. *France* (Appl. No. 71111/01), Judgment 14 June 2007, para 46. See also the Inter-American Commission on Human Rights *Report no. 21/00; Case 12.059: Carmen Aguiar de Lapacó* v. *Argentina* (1999), paras 2, 15 (a case initiated in the context of the so-called 'truth trials').

[24] *Schedko* v. *Belarus* (886/1999) 2003.

[25] *Ibid.*, para 10.2. See also *Staselovich* v. *Belarus* (887/1999) 2003; *Sultanova* v. *Uzbekistan* (915/2000) 2006; *Saimijon* v. *Uzbekistan* (959/2000) 2006; *Khalilova* v. *Tajikistan* (973/2001) 2005; *Aliboeva* v. *Tajikistan* (985/2001) 2005; *Shukurova* v. *Tajikistan* (1044/2002) 2006; *El-Alwani* v. *Libya* (1295/2004) 2007; *El-Hassy* v. *Libya* (1422/2005) 2007; *Kovaleva* v. *Belarus* (2120/2011) 2012.

[26] With respect to the official recognition of burial places, see: *Sankara* v. *Burkina Faso* (1159/2003) 2006, paras 12.2, 14; and for the return of remains, see: *Azouz* v. *Algeria* (1798/2008) 2013, para 10(d); *Saadoun* v. *Algeria* (1806/2008) 2013, para 10(d).

of the Covenant, the Committee has called some aspects of its violation a breach of Article 7.

(M2) The right to mourn in private has a natural extension to the right to mourn and commemorate in public, drawing on the rights to free expression and peaceful assembly (Articles 19 and 21 of the Covenant). In *General Comment 31*, the Committee observed that states were obliged to give reparations to individuals whose rights were violated, and that this could include 'measures of satisfaction, such as public apologies [and] public memorials'.[27] In addition, it has frequently pronounced itself on the issue of suppression or obstruction of public commemorations organized to honour victims of human rights violations. In a series of Belarusian cases, the Committee systematically upheld the right to organize peaceful commemorative activities. In *Kovalenko* v. *Belarus* [2013], for example, a peaceful assembly aimed at commemorating the victims of Stalinist repression in the Soviet Union was broken up by the authorities.[28] According to the Committee, this was a violation of the rights to free expression and peaceful assembly.[29]

The right to commemoration further extends to anniversaries of historical events, either with or without victims to remember. In *Laptsevich* v. *Belarus* [2000], for example, the author distributed leaflets without authorization.[30] These leaflets mentioned the anniversary of the proclamation of independence of the People's Republic of Belarus, a short-lived attempt to create an independent Belarusian state between March 1918 and January 1919. According to the authorities, the leaflets contained a distorted version of history and disturbed the public order. The Committee was not convinced: it ruled that Belarus had failed to justify the need for prior authorization of public meetings during which material was disseminated or speeches made, and found a violation of the right to free expression.[31]

27 *General Comment 31* (on general legal obligations) (2004), para 16. See also United Nations (UN), *Basic Principles and Guidelines on the Right to a Remedy and Reparation for Victims of Gross Violations of International Human Rights Law and Serious Violations of International Humanitarian Law* (2005), principles 22(e)–(g).

28 *Kovalenko* v. *Belarus* (1808/2008) 2013.

29 *Ibid.*, para 8.8. See also *Belyazeka* v. *Belarus* (1772/2008) 2012.

30 *Laptsevich* v. *Belarus* (780/1997) 2000.

31 *Ibid.*, paras 8.1, 8.4–8.5. See also *Velichkin* v. *Belarus* (1022/2001) 2005; *Gryb* v. *Belarus* (1316/2004) 2011; *Komarovsky* v. *Belarus* (1839/2008) 2014; *Protsko* v. *Belarus* (1919/2009) 2013; *Evrezov.* v. *Belarus* (1099/2010) 2014; *Aleksandrov.* v. *Belarus* (1933/2010) 2014; *Bazarov.* v. *Belarus* (1934/2010) 2014; *Symonik* v. *Belarus* (1952/2010) 2014; and *Surgan* v. *Belarus* (1969/2010) 2015.

(M3) Whereas the Committee has robustly endorsed a *right* to memory, as in the above, it has turned its back on any imposition of a *duty* to remember. This can be unambiguously inferred from three of its principles (M3–M5). First, the Committee has attached a high value to Article 18.2 of the Covenant:

> No one shall be subject to coercion which would impair his freedom to have or to adopt a religion or belief of his choice.

This non-coercion principle was reaffirmed in *General Comment 22*, which stipulated that:

> [P]olicies or practices that have the same intention or effect as direct coercion . . . are inconsistent with Article 18, paragraph 2.[32]

It was once more recalled in *General Comment 34*:

> Any form of effort to coerce the holding or not holding of any opinion is prohibited. Freedom to express one's opinion necessarily includes freedom not to express one's opinion.[33]

In other words, citizens have a *right* to remember (including a right to mourn and commemorate) as part of their rights to privacy and thought and freedoms of expression and assembly, but they are *not* obliged to comply with a *duty* to remember imposed on them by others or by the state. They cannot be forced to mourn or commemorate against their will.

(M4) A similar reasoning applies to memory laws, i.e. laws that prescribe or proscribe certain views of historical figures, symbols, dates, or events. Scores of countries have adopted such laws. In *Faurisson* v. *France* [1996], the Committee was very critical of one such memory law – the Gayssot law under which Holocaust denier Robert Faurisson was convicted in France – and similar Holocaust denial laws.[34] But at the time it said that it was not its task to evaluate such laws in the abstract, and therefore it did not ask France to repeal it.[35] Individual Committee members, however, feared that the Gayssot law suggested:

> that the State party had attempted to turn historical truths and experiences into legislative dogma that may not be challenged.[36]

[32] *General Comment 22* (on freedom of thought) (1993), para 5, 8.

[33] *General Comment 34* (on the freedoms of opinion and expression) (2011), para 10. For a full discussion, see: A. De Baets, *Responsible History* (New York and Oxford: Berghahn, 2009), 144–54.

[34] *Faurisson* v. *France* (550/1993) 1996.

[35] *Ibid.*, para 9.3.

[36] *Ibid.*, concurring opinion of Evatt, Kretzmer, and Klein, para 9.

Fifteen years later, the Committee's opinion had markedly evolved. In its *General Comment 34*, it explicitly rejected memory laws *if* they proscribed certain historical views:

> Laws that penalize the expression of opinions about historical facts are incompatible with the obligations that the Covenant imposes on States parties in relation to the respect for freedom of opinion and expression.

A footnote clarified that these laws were known as 'memory laws', even adding an explicit reference to *Faurisson*.[37] Recalling this view in 2012, the United Nations Special Rapporteur on Free Expression, Frank La Rue, called upon states to repeal laws that prohibited discussion of historical events because 'history should always be open to discussion and debate'. He added:

> By demanding that writers, journalists and citizens give only a version of events that is approved by the Government, States are enabled to subjugate freedom of expression to official versions of events.[38]

In 2013, the United Nations Independent Expert on the Promotion of a Democratic and Equitable International Order declared that:

> Such laws [defamation, blasphemy and memory laws, *adb*] have totalitarian implications and consequences, violate human dignity, the right to open debate, academic freedom, and ultimately lead to intellectual stagnation and self-censorship, which have adverse consequences on the ability of people to participate in decision-making. . . . States should . . . repeal legislation that is incompatible with Articles 18 and 19; in particular . . . memory laws and any laws that hinder open discussion of political and historical events.[39]

All this means that, in addition to memory laws *proscribing* historical views, those *prescribing* historical views should be rejected *if* they are coercive and make the expression of alternative views impossible.

(M5) Some states also invoke domestic traditions as grounds for restricting free expression about the past. This is not in conformity with

[37] *General Comment 34*, para 49: 'Laws that penalize the expression of opinions about historical facts are incompatible with the obligations that the Covenant imposes on States parties in relation to the respect for freedom of opinion and expression. [footnote 116]'. Footnote 116 stipulates: 'So called "memory-laws"; see communication No. 550/93, *Faurisson* v. *France*. See also the concluding observations on Hungary (CCPR/C/HUN/CO/5) para 19.'

[38] UN, *Report of the Special Rapporteur on the Promotion and Protection of the Right to Freedom of Opinion and Expression* (A/67/357; 2012), para 55.

[39] *Report of the Independent Expert on the Promotion of a Democratic and Equitable International Order, Alfred-Maurice de Zayas* (A/HRC/24/38) (2013), para 38, 56(e).

the Covenant. Article 19.3 exhaustively lists the legitimate grounds for restricting free expression: the rights or reputations of others, or the protection of national security, public order, public health or morals. Tradition is not on this list. In *General Comment 34*, the Committee emphasized that:

> [I]t is not compatible with the Covenant for a restriction [on free expression] to be enshrined in traditional, religious or other such customary law.[40]

In 2014, La Rue and other rapporteurs jointly declared that:

> Certain types of legal restrictions on freedom of expression can never be justified by reference to local traditions, culture and values.[41]

One of the legitimate grounds, however, is public morals. The notion of tradition is often surreptitiously introduced under this guise and equated to the notion of morals. In *General Comment 22*, however, the Committee emphatically distinguished the two, observing that:

> [T]he concept of morals derives from many social, philosophical and religious traditions; consequently, limitations on the freedom to manifest a religion or belief for the purpose of protecting morals must be based on principles not deriving exclusively from a single tradition.[42]

In sum, the Committee has categorically rejected duties to remember imposed by others (coercion in the realm of thought, memory laws, suppression in the name of particular traditions). At the same time, however, persons imposing duties to remember on themselves are merely exercising their right to memory.

4 View of History (as a Right)

(H1) While in memory issues an affective bond with the past prevails, in history issues what is at stake is a cognitive link with the past. The needs of victims and their relatives to be informed about the human rights violations to which they were subjected in the past – most often in an atmosphere of

40 *General Comment 34*, para 24, also para 32. See also G. Reid, 'The Trouble with Tradition: When "Values" Trample over Rights', in Human Rights Watch, *World Report 2013* (Washington, DC: Human Rights Watch, 2013), 20–8. The restrictive HRC view of tradition is in line with its restrictive view of a 'margin of appreciation' for states parties: see *General Comment 34*, para 36 and *Länsman* v. *Finland* (511/1992) 1994, para 9.4. But see *Hertzberg* v. *Finland* (61/1979) 1985, para 10.3, opinion of Opsahl.

41 *Joint Declaration on Universality and the Right to Freedom of Expression* (2014), para 1f.

42 *General Comment 22*, para 8. See also UN Economic and Social Council, *Siracusa Principles on the Limitation and Derogation Provisions in the International Covenant on Civil and Political Rights* (1985), paras 27–8.

widespread silence, secrecy, and lies – have been underscored by a new right that has gradually emerged since the 1990s. Called the 'right to the truth',[43] it holds that everybody has a right to know the truth about past human rights violations: surviving victims and relatives of deceased victims in the first instance, but also the society at large.[44] This new right is based on a combination of the rights to information, to an effective remedy, and to be free from inhuman treatment (Articles 19, 2.3 and 7 of the Covenant respectively). It is so strong that neither a change of government, nor an amnesty law, nor the passage of time (particularly the deaths of perpetrators and victims) can affect it. In *Quinteros* v. *Uruguay* [1990], the mother of a woman who had disappeared in 1976 submitted a complaint in 1983.[45] In the Committee's view (in 1990), it said it understood:

> [t]he anguish and stress caused to the mother by the disappearance of her daughter and by the continuing uncertainty concerning her fate and whereabouts. The author has the right to know what has happened to her daughter. In these respects, she too is a victim of the violations of the Covenant suffered by her daughter, in particular of Article 7 [the right not to be subjected to inhuman treatment, *adb*].[46]

In other words, the absence of truth and the lingering uncertainty were seen as forms of inhuman treatment and mental suffering.[47] And for the first time, the relatives of a direct victim of human rights violations were recognized as victims of a human rights violation themselves. After *Quinteros*, the Committee emphasized time and again that the lack of knowledge of existential facts (i.e. facts about life and death) was

[43] For more on the right to truth, see chapter by Patricia Naftali in the present volume.

[44] Foundational texts (available at www.concernedhistorians.org/content/to.html) are: UN Commission on Human Rights, *Updated Set of Principles for the Protection and Promotion of Human Rights through Action to Combat Impunity* (2005), principles 1–18, 23, 34; UN, *Basic Principles and Guidelines on the Right to a Remedy and Reparation*, principles 22(b), 24; UN, *International Convention for the Protection of All Persons from Enforced Disappearance* (2006), preamble, articles 8, 24(2); UN Working Group on Enforced and Involuntary Disappearances, *General Comment on the Right to the Truth in Relation to Enforced Disappearance* (2010), in *Report*, 12–17; Resolutions of the UN Human Rights Council (formerly Commission on Human Rights) about the right to the truth in 2005–6, 2008–9 and 2012; and studies on the right to the truth from the Office of the UN High Commissioner for Human Rights (OHCHR) in 2006–7 and 2009–11. For a history of the right to the truth (previously the right to know), see De Baets, *Responsible History*, 154–65.

[45] *Quinteros* v. *Uruguay* (107/1981) 1990.

[46] *Ibid.*, para 14.

[47] See *Bousroual* v. *Algeria* (992/2001) 2006; *Cifuentes* v. *Chile* (1536/2006) 2009; *Benaziza* v. *Algeria* (1588/2007) 2010; *Saadoun* v. *Algeria* (1806/2008) 2013; *Mechani* v. *Algeria* (1807/2008) 2013; *Rizvanović* v. *Bosnia and Herzegovina* (1997/2010) 2014, etc.

a form of inhuman treatment. In *Rizvanović* v. *Bosnia and Herzegovina* [2014], to cite a particularly tragic example, it condemned as inhuman the obligation imposed on the family of a disappeared person to have that person declared dead in order to be eligible for compensation.[48] The right to the truth is also of pivotal importance to historians because, in a certain sense, what is called the 'right to the truth' in international law today is nothing less than a crucial (though not the only) component of a 'right to *historical* truth' or a 'right to history'.

(H2) The right to the truth is supported by two other guarantees. The first is a right to information about the past, which enables individuals to access knowledge in the possession of public bodies, especially information about themselves and their relatives. In *Pezoldova* v. *Czech Republic* [2002] – a telling case even though not explicitly connected to the right to the truth – the author complained that while seeking restitution for property confiscated by the state, she had been denied access, between 1991 and 2001, to the archival file which could have proved her restitution claim.[49] In the absence of any satisfactory explanation by the state in this regard, the Committee ruled that the author's right to an effective remedy was violated.[50] In its *General Comment 34*, the Committee indicated that:

> Article 19, paragraph 2 embraces a right of access to information held by public bodies. Such information includes records held by a public body, regardless of the form in which the information is stored, its source and the date of production.[51]

The formula 'regardless of . . . the date of production' is notable because it also refers to laws regulating public archives. The Committee has regularly encouraged states to make public all documents relevant to human rights violations, including military archives, in order to enable individuals to file complaints based on evidence from these archives and to exercise their right to the truth.[52]

[48] *Rizvanović* v. *Bosnia and Herzegovina* (1997/2010) 2014, paras 9.6, 11. See also *Durić* v. *Bosnia and Herzegovina* (1956/2010) 2014; *Hero* v. *Bosnia and Herzegovina* (1966/2010) 2014; *Selimović* v. *Bosnia and Herzegovina* (2003/2010) 2014.

[49] *Pezoldova* v. *Czech Republic* (757/1997) 2002.

[50] *Ibid.* paras 7.1, 11.3, 11.4, 11.6, partly concurring opinions.

[51] *General Comment 34*, para 18.

[52] See, for example, HRC, *Concluding Observations* for Paraguay, UNDoc. A/50/40, paras 192–223 (1995), paras 201, 216; Brazil CCPR/C/BRA/CO/2 (2005), para 18. See also UN, *Report of the Special Rapporteur on the Promotion and Protection of the Right to Freedom of Opinion and Expression, Frank LaRue* (A/HRC/20/17; 4 June 2012), para 91.

(H3) In order to have teeth, the right to the truth should entail a corresponding duty on the part of states to investigate human rights violations themselves. As early as 1982, the Committee emphasized such a state duty to investigate.[53] Time and again it has referred to this duty, particularly in cases of international crimes and especially in countries where amnesty laws impeded the investigation of past violations, such as Argentina, Chile, Uruguay, or Algeria.[54]

5 View of History (as a Craft)

(H4) In its *General Comment 34*, the Committee formulated two fundamental principles for those who held and expressed historical opinions. It observed that:

> Paragraph 1 of Article 19 requires protection of the right to hold opinions without interference. This is a right to which the Covenant permits no exception or restriction . . . All forms of opinion are protected, including opinions of a political, scientific, historic, moral or religious nature.[55]

The above commentary emphasizes the absolute and non-derogable right *to hold* opinions of a historical nature. Such historical opinions clearly encompass memories, interpretations of past events and explicit moral judgments about the conduct of historical figures.

This principle is reinforced by the non-coercion principle, as formulated in Article 18.2 of the Covenant (and already explained above). Applied to the context of historical research, writing, and teaching, this principle means that

[53] *Optional Protocol*, Article 4(2); *General Comment 6* (on the right to life) (1982), para 4; *General Comment 20* (on the prohibition of torture) (1992), paras 14–15, *General Comment 26* (on the continuity of obligations) (1997), para 4, *General Comment 31*, paras 15, 18. The first disappearance case brought before the HRC, *Bleier* v. *Uruguay* (A/37/40) (1982), paras 13–15, emphasized the duty to investigate.

[54] For a case, see *Rodríguez* v. *Uruguay* (322/1988) 1994, paras 12–14. See also *SE* v. *Argentina* (275/1988) 1990; *RAVN* v. *Argentina* (343/1988, 344/1988, 345/1988) 1990; *Vargas* v. *Chile* (718/1996) 1999; *Acuña* v. *Chile* (717/1996) 1999; *Benaziza* v. *Algeria* (1588/2007) 2010; *Zarzi* v. *Algeria* (1780/2008) 2011; *Berzig* v. *Algeria* (1781/2008) 2012; *Azouz* v. *Algeria* (1798/2008) 2013; *Saadoun* v. *Algeria* (1806/2008) 2013; *Djebbar* v. *Algeria* (1811/2008) 2012; *Sedhai* v. *Nepal* (1865/2009) 2013; *Khirani* v. *Algeria* (1905/2009) 2012; *Fedsi* v. *Algeria* (1964/2010) 2014; *Bousseloub* v. *Algeria* (1974/2010) 2014; *Bhandari* v. *Nepal* (2031/2011) 2014; *Basnet* v. *Nepal* (2051/2011) 2014. See also many of the HRC *Concluding Observations*. In 1988, the Inter-American Court of Human Rights delivered a pioneering judgment in a disappearance case, *Velásquez Rodríguez* v. *Honduras* (*Judgment of 29 July 1988* [1988], paras 166–81, 184, 194), emphasizing that changes of government did not affect state duties to prevent, investigate, punish, and compensate human rights violations.

[55] *General Comment 34*, para 9.

historians and others are not obliged to *express* historical opinions or adopt those of others. If they do, however, such opinions merit strong protection.[56]

(H5) The other principle is the right to be wrong. In the words of the Committee:

> The Covenant does not permit general prohibition of expressions of an erroneous opinion or an incorrect interpretation of past events.[57]

This right to err echoes the views of John Stuart Mill, who in 1859 famously argued that erroneous and false opinions are valuable because they challenge disbelievers to refute them in order to come closer to the truth. In the process, some of the supposedly erroneous or false information could turn out to be true after all.[58]

(H6) As the Committee has a vast and worldwide mandate, it should come as no surprise that it offers only a few further general guidelines in the areas of history education and research beyond the aforementioned principles. In the domain of education, the Committee condemned discriminatory views in the school system in *Ross* v. *Canada* [2000].[59] Another important case is *Hartikainen* v. *Finland* [1981], which laid down the principles of objectivity and neutrality.[60] Hartikainen was a teacher and free thinker, who complained about the fact that Finnish children who did not attend religious instruction courses were obliged to take courses about the history of religions and ethics instead. He argued that this undermined the liberty of parents to ensure the education of their children in conformity with their own convictions (Article 18.4 of the Covenant). The Committee, however, stipulated that this was not the case, on the condition that:

> such alternative course of instruction [was] given in a neutral and objective way and respect[ed] the convictions of parents and guardians who do not believe in any religion.[61]

[56] Statements of fact are distinguished from statements of opinion; while facts are susceptible to a truth/falsity proof, opinions are less so. This distinction is an important foundation of legal epistemology. Expressing statements of opinion enjoys stronger protection than expressing statements of fact. See, e.g., *General Comment 34*, para 47: 'Defamation laws . . . should not be applied with regard to those forms of expression that are not, of their nature, subject to verification [by which are meant opinions, *adb*].' Or para 49: 'Laws that penalize the expression of opinions about historical facts'.

[57] *General Comment 34*, para 49.

[58] J. S. Mill, *On Liberty* (London: Parker and Sons, 1859), chapter 2.

[59] *Ross* v. *Canada* (736/1997) 2000, para 11.5–11.6.

[60] *Hartikainen* v. *Finland* (40/1978) 1981.

[61] *Ibid.*, para 10.4; *General Comment 22*, para 6. See also *Waldman* v. *Canada* (694/1996) 1999, concurring opinion, para 2.

Taken together, *Ross* and *Hartikainen* laid down the principles of non-discrimination, objectivity, and neutrality in history education.

(H7) Finally, the Committee's handling of the *Faurisson* case about Holocaust denial – already mentioned – indirectly sheds light on its view of historical research.[62] In *Faurisson*, the Committee did not discuss Holocaust denial as a form of hate speech that merited prohibition (Article 20.2 of the Covenant), but as a form of free expression that could be restricted (Article 19.3 of the Covenant). In doing so, it did not concentrate, however, on Holocaust denial as a form of pseudo-history (as historians would do), but rather on Holocaust denial as a vehicle for anti-Semitism. Nonetheless, we learn something about the Committee's perception of responsible history in the process, especially in the individual opinions accompanying the majority view. Three Committee members denounced Faurisson's views because they:

> [implied,] under the guise of impartial academic research, that the victims of Nazism were guilty of dishonest fabrication, that the story of their victimization is a myth and that the gas chambers in which so many people were murdered are 'magic'.

And they added:

> While there is every reason to maintain protection of *bona fide* historical research against restriction, even when it challenges accepted historical truths and by so doing offends people, anti-Semitic allegations of the sort made by the author, which violate the rights of others in the way described, do not have the same claim to protection against restriction.[63]

This means that Holocaust denial, and by extension other forms of genocide denial, violate the rights of others, because by suggesting that the victims of genocide lie about what happened and thus falsify history, they maliciously defame the reputation of genocide survivors and harm the memory of those who did not survive it. Such defamation and privacy invasion, in violating the dignity of the victims, do not merit the

[62] In its *Concluding Observations* for Japan, CCPR/C/JPN/CO/5 (2008), para 22, the HRC also condemned denial of the 'comfort women' system during World War II, lamenting that 'few history textbooks contain[ed] references to the [. . .] issue'.

[63] *Faurisson* v. *France* (550/1993) 1996, concurring opinion of Evatt, Kretzmer, and Klein, paras 6, 10. For a discussion (in Dutch), see A. De Baets, 'De zaak-Faurisson: De klacht van een holocaustontkenner bij het VN-Mensenrechtencomité' ['The Faurisson Case: The Complaint of a Holocaust Denier before the HRC'], *Ex Tempore* 34:2 (2015), 96–105. For other Holocaust-related cases, see *Ross* v. *Canada* (736/1997) 2000, *Zündel* v. *Canada* (953/2000) 2003, and *Zündel* v. *Canada* (1341/2005) 2006.

protection of free expression. From this judgment, we can clearly infer that the Committee considers intellectual honesty in historical research to be of fundamental importance, echoing the views of Max Weber.[64]

6 Conclusions

This chapter has unpacked the United Nations Human Rights Committee's views of the past by analysing the dimensions of time, memory, and history as they appear in its *General Comments* and in 108 relevant individual complaints brought before it. The analysis first reviewed the rules restricting the Committee's temporal scope and the principles expanding it. Next the Committee's views on the rights to memory and history were discussed, as well as the principles according to which historical teaching and research are required to develop.

The particular set-up of the United Nations complaints procedure imposed a time regime of immediacy on the Human Rights Committee. The rules of *ratione temporis* and non-retroactivity, of personal victimhood (thus excluding broad or abstract historical claims), and of not reassessing historical evidence used by domestic courts all restricted the Committee's temporal scope. Accordingly, the Committee did not develop a historical vocabulary of any significance. Nevertheless, it extended its horizon in several ingenuous ways, allowing it sometimes to penetrate deeper into the traumatic pasts of victims: by admitting standing to heirs in cases where complainants die; by requiring successor regimes to fulfil the obligations of their predecessors, and above all through the principle of continuing violations. In selected cases, the Committee has also displayed a certain sensitivity towards the role of past generations and towards differentiation between past regimes. The fundamental time principles of imprescriptibility and legality have been of lesser importance: even though these principles considerably facilitate the widening of the time scope, they normally play a role in large-scale crimes, and except for cases of torture and disappearance, are usually absent at the level of individual violations.

Within this time framework, the Committee has defended a strong memory regime. Paradoxically, this is best reflected in an omission: the Committee has said little about a right to mourn in private, in all probability because this right is universally accepted. The Committee has ruled systematically in favour of peaceful public commemorations, which can often

[64] M. Weber, *Wissenschaft als Beruf* (originally 1918; Munich: Duncker & Humblodt, 1919), spoke about 'intellektuelle Rechtschaffenheit'.

be seen as a natural extension of mourning. In other words, the Committee has appealed implicitly to states to respect the right to mourn, and explicitly to allow peaceful commemorations. The Committee's strong memory regime is also discernible in its firm rejection of all forms of coercion, be it under the guise of duties to remember imposed on individuals by others, memory laws imposed on individuals by the state, or traditions invoked as grounds for restricting free expression. Likewise, the Committee has helped develop a strong right to history in the shape of an individual and collective right to the truth about the human rights violations of the past, which cannot be affected by regime changes, amnesty laws, or the deaths of victims or perpetrators. This right is supported by the right of citizens to access information held by public bodies, and a corresponding state duty to investigate past crimes.

The Committee has also identified strong basic principles for the exercise of the historian's craft, but understandably it has not set forth detailed principles in this domain. From a human rights perspective, opinions about history – such as memories, interpretations of the past or explicit moral judgments about the conduct of historical figures – are not obligatory, but once uttered, they merit strong protection even if they prove to be wrong in the end. Other principles have been understandably rather general and self-evident: history education should obey the principles of objectivity, neutrality, and non-discrimination, and historical research should observe the principle of honesty.

The mission of the Human Rights Committee has never been to develop a consistent philosophy of time, memory, and history, nor to judge the injustices of the past in the abstract. All in all, the Committee, although tied to many rules, has built an infrastructure of iron principles for the rights to memory and history. Some – such as objectivity or honesty – are mere repetitions of age-old and still cherished maxims. But in applying the continuing violations principle, in helping develop the right to the truth, in stressing the duty of a state to investigate past crimes even after a change of regime, and in devoting explicit attention to memory issues and historical opinions in its recent *General Comment 34*, it has made innovative contributions. As a legal body, the Committee has developed consistent basic principles about the past and how to cope with it. These principles protect our bond with the past and shape our understanding of history to a far larger degree than we may be aware of.

2

The Role of International Criminal Tribunals in Shaping the Historical Accounts of Genocide

MARINA AKSENOVA

1 Introduction: Two Identities of International Criminal Trials

An international consensus on the need to prosecute and punish mass atrocities is arguably the strongest evidence of the existence of a global collective consciousness. The Nuremberg Tribunal challenged the traditional world order centring on states and their intentions and overlooking abuses sanctioned by the state or flowing from state policy. This tribunal was the first international court tasked with trying individuals responsible for crimes committed on a large scale by an oppressive regime. Despite some dissenting voices, the Nuremberg trials were neither show trials, nor a purely domestic criminal law process. They were rather a way of expressing international outrage with Germany's aggression through judicial means. Ever since this historic shift occurred, the field of international criminal law has been increasingly vested with a mounting number of objectives – deterrence, retribution, transitional justice, reconciliation and, finally, setting the historical record. Some of these goals are conflicting. This chapter critically assesses the latter objective and situates it among other considerations. The crime of genocide, first prosecuted internationally by ad hoc tribunals in the 1990s, exemplifies the main argument in this chapter: providing a historical account of events is an essential and inalienable part of international criminal law, but it is limited in scope and subject to strict legal requirements.

Aksenova's contribution was funded by the Danish National Research Foundation Grant no. DNRF105 and conducted under the auspices of iCourts, the Danish National Research Foundation's Centre of Excellence for International Courts.

Introduction to this volume provides a comprehensive typology of memory laws that emerged following World War II.[1] Increasing attempts to regulate and/or legally recognise past atrocities point in the direction of the growing traction – in academic and policy circles alike – of the very concept of 'memory laws', or, borrowing from Eric Heinze, 'laws affecting historical memory'.[2] This chapter is concerned with the fourth category of memory laws identified in Introduction, namely legislative and judicial practices following the integration of the crime of genocide in international law.[3] In particular, the focus is on the role of the two modern international criminal tribunals – the International Criminal Tribunal for Rwanda (ICTR) and the International Criminal Tribunal for the Former Yugoslavia (ICTY) – in shaping the historical narrative of genocides in Rwanda and Srebrenica, respectively.

History is frequently written through judgments evaluating and giving weight to conflicting accounts of events. Heinze's distinction between the expressive weight of a certain historical version endorsed by the law, irrespective of that version's substantive weight, is only emphasised when one talks about the judgments of international criminal tribunals. Expressive weight refers to the opportunity of a claim to be heard and discussed, while substantive weight is rather factual and normative claims, as discussed in epistemic communities.[4] International tribunals are bodies tasked with singling out the facts relevant to the case at hand, while simultaneously shaping collective memory pertaining to the world's biggest evils. Legal documents emanating from these courts involve in-depth historical analysis and propose a certain narrative contextualising legal findings. The tribunals are therefore uniquely placed to attribute expressive weight to a certain version of events.

The process of judicial history-writing is particularly evident in the work of international courts for two main reasons. First, international cases strongly affect both the nation in question *and* the collective consciousness of the global community. Domestic proceedings may also resonate internationally, but do not, usually, have the same clout of impartiality

1 Introduction by Uladzislau Belavusau and Aleksandra Gliszczyńska-Grabias in the present volume.

2 Heinze argues that this term is more suitable for it allows us to understand 'broader processes through which law guides the public's understanding of the past'. See Epilogue by Eric Heinze in the present volume.

3 Introduction by Uladzislau Belavusau and Aleksandra Gliszczyńska-Grabias in the present volume.

4 Heinze, *supra* note 2.

as their international counterparts. Secondly, the issues brought to the attention of international courts are complex and involve many actors at different levels of state hierarchy, making the attribution of responsibility contingent on the broader cultural, historical, and political background. Historical narratives are particularly prominent in international prosecutions of mass atrocities. The magnitude of events leading to the commission of international crimes has the potential to build national collective identities. At the same time, responsibility must be apportioned on an individual basis. This 'scaling down' from communal to individual requires detailed contextualisation. This is why the narrative-setting function finds its strong expression in international criminal law.

The crime of genocide sits at the apex of the group of offences with highly traumatic connotations for future generations. It criminalises the destruction of individuals as a collective entity, on the basis of their belonging to a group defined by certain characteristics. This act is particularly heinous for it attacks persons and denies them right to exist *as a group*. Hanna Arendt referred to genocide as 'an attack upon human diversity as such, that is, upon a characteristic of the 'human status' without which the very words "mankind" or "humanity" would be devoid of meaning.'[5] The convoluted logic underlying acts of genocide threatens the whole humankind due to its capacity to indoctrinate and turn humans against each other. The dangerous potential of genocide, historically tested, elevates it to the status of the most odious international crime.

Unlike war crimes or crimes against humanity, genocide was not prosecuted at Nuremberg. Thus this crime only came within the purview of international criminal law in the 1990s with the creation of the ICTY and ICTR. It is understandable that both tribunals grappled with the enormity of the crimes in question and with the immense responsibility of trying genocide for the first time in history. The *Akayesu* judgment delivered by the ICTR in 1998 is one of the most significant documents produced by the international tribunals as it contains the world's first conviction for the crime of genocide.[6] The first ICTY sentence for genocide followed shortly after – in 2001 – in the *Krstić* case.[7]

[5] H. Arendt, *Eichmann in Jerusalem: A Report on the Banality of Evil* (1965), 268, 269.

[6] *Prosecutor* v. *Akayesu*, ICTR Case No. 96-4-T, Trial Chamber Judgment, 2 September 1998 ('*Akayesu* Trial Judgment').

[7] *Prosecutor* v. *Krstić*, ICTY Case No. IT-98-33-T, Trial Judgment, 2 August 2001 ('*Krstić* Trial Judgment').

This chapter argues that any international criminal trial assumes two identities – *social* and *legal*. These identities are interconnected, but yet distinct. As a legal event, an international criminal trial pronounces on the individual guilt or innocence of the alleged perpetrator of mass atrocities. In their legal sense, international trials pursue traditional criminal law objectives of retribution and deterrence, and, at least in theory, adhere to the liberal principles of legality and due process. Simultaneously these trials are social events. They fulfil an important communicative function in modern societies by actively reflecting consensus about the values agreed upon internationally. The Preamble of the Rome Statute of the International Criminal Court (ICC) points out that 'all peoples are united by common bonds, their cultures pieced together in a shared heritage'.[8] International criminal law is thus at the core of the emerging global collective consciousness and international prosecutions of offences such as genocide 'activate' this consciousness.

The paradox is in the nature of interaction between the legal and the social identities of an international criminal trial. Legal identity provides the basis for establishing the credibility of its social counterpart. An international judgment must follow the rules accepted within its own discipline to be perceived as legitimate and gain wider traction as a communicative symbol. The narrative-setting function of international criminal law is thus both limited and reinforced by the traditional criminal law values.[9]

The following section analyses the purposes of international criminal trials as compared to their domestic counterparts. It draws specific attention to the aim of setting the historical record and its boundaries. Section three dwells on these boundaries and explores the idea of a criminal trial as a reflection of the global collective consciousness. Section four discusses the creation of the accounts of genocide by the ad hoc tribunals in the light of the constraints imposed by the legal identity of international trials. It is argued that at least three legal principles shaped historical accounts pertaining to the crime of genocide. These principles are *legality*, *individual criminal responsibility*, and *disciplinarity*.

[8] Preamble, Rome Statute of the International Criminal Court, adopted 17 July 1998.

[9] Groome argues 'the Security Council [while establishing the ICTY] placed the truth-finding process within the walls of a courtroom in which individual criminal responsibility would be determined'. D. Groome, 'The Right to Truth in the Fight against Impunity' *Berkley Journal of International Law* 29:1 (2001), 186.

2 Narrative-Setting Function of (International) Criminal Law

The objectives of international criminal courts and tribunals are not well defined in their constitutive instruments. Such a deficiency might well have a historical explanation. The Nuremberg and Tokyo Charters – the predecessors of the statutes of modern international criminal courts and tribunals – did not elucidate this issue primarily because the purpose of their existence was clearly understood by the drafters. The destiny of those responsible for the worst acts of aggression in the twentieth century was hotly debated prior to the adoption of the Charters and criminal trial was chosen as the most adequate response. Thus the International Military Tribunal (IMT) and International Military Tribunal for the Far East (IMTFE) arose out of necessity and their main objective was set at bringing former Nazi perpetrators to justice by virtue of a criminal trial. There was no need to further elucidate the mandate of these two tribunals thereby putting at risk fragile legal and political compromise reached by the victorious powers during the negotiations.[10]

The ICTY and ICTR Statutes, drafted in a succinct manner, continue the tradition of obscurity when it comes to the goals of international criminal justice by avoiding clear statements on the matter. The Rome Statute of the ICC provides some hints in the Preamble where it talks about the objective of ending impunity and preventing crimes, without any further elaboration.[11]

In contrast with the vague or non-existent formulations in the statutes of international courts and tribunals, domestic penal law often provides more direct evidence as to the purposes it intends to achieve by prohibiting certain conduct and imposing punishment on the perpetrators for violating these prohibitions.[12] It is rare that domestic criminal justice systems pursue

[10] R. Overy, 'The Nuremberg Trials: International Law in the Making', in P. Sands (ed.), *From Nuremberg to the Hague: The Future of International Criminal Justice* (Cambridge University Press, 2003), 1–29.

[11] W. Schabas, *The International Criminal Court: A Commentary on the Rome Statute* (Oxford University Press, 2010), 898.

[12] For example, the German Penal Code expressly acknowledges proportionality to the seriousness of offence – central to the retributive philosophy of punishment – and dangerousness of the offender as indicators for the administration of penalties. The Russian Penal Code places strong emphasis on restoring social order through punishment of those who violated it. This objective can be traced back to the general idea of retribution but has stronger moral appeal. Prevention of crime and rehabilitation of the offender are also expressly recognised aims of the system of criminal justice. See Article 62 Strafgesetzbuch

the purpose of creating a certain narrative of events as their general goal.[13] The central premise of national penal law is that criminal responsibility is individual in nature. Criminal law is therefore a tool for establishing the truth only about the specific controversy. The inquiry is limited in scope in that it is focused on the attribution of responsibility in each case.[14] With few notable exceptions discussed below, there is no expectation, as a rule, that national judges will embark on the journey of history writing. The legal identity of a regular domestic criminal trial thus prevails over the social one.

National proceedings become the source of history making only in *exceptional* circumstances. According to Ruti Teitel, the process whereby criminal trials become the instruments of history production usually occurs in the time of transition.[15] The moment of rupture in the society denotes the collapse of a shared collective identity rooted in political, cultural, and historical reality. It is, then, the law that is vested with the task of recreating this lost identity by sacrificing individual rights to the societal interest in establishing a historical record.[16] The traditional punishment rationales aimed at individuals, such as proportionality, are qualified or modified by the collective interest at stake.

The most famous and widely cited example of such national identity building through criminal prosecution is the trial of the Nazi bureaucrat Adolf Eichmann by the court in Jerusalem in 1961 for crimes perpetrated against the Jewish people. Hanna Arendt observed, 'it was history that, as far as the prosecution was concerned, stood in the center of the trial'.[17] Another telling example is the Frankfurt Auschwitz Trial of 1963–5, which is frequently seen as 'breaking the wall of silence' around the Holocaust in West Germany.[18] These series of trials, concerning twenty-two officials charged under German penal law for their involvement in the Auschwitz-Birkenau death and concentration camp complex, followed a period of

(German Criminal Code), 13 November 1998 [StGB], as amended; Article 43 Ugolovnii Kodeks RF (Russian Criminal Code), 24 May 1996, as amended.

13 This statement refers to the general aims of domestic criminal justice systems and does not touch upon specific instances of criminalisation aimed at historical revisionism discussed elsewhere in this volume.

14 R. Teitel, *Transitional Justice* (Oxford University Press, 2000), 72.

15 *Ibid.*

16 *Ibid.*, 76.

17 Arendt, *supra* note 5 at 19 as cited by R. Wilson, 'Judging History: The Historical Record of the International Criminal Tribunal for the Former Yugoslavia', *Human Rights Quarterly* 27 (2005), 910.

18 D. Pendas, 'Seeking Justice, Finding Law: Nazi Trials in Postwar Europe', *The Journal of Modern History* 81 (2009), 347–68, at 367.

clemency and amnesty that prevailed in Germany and all over Europe in the 1950s. According to Devin Pendas, the long-term effects of the Auschwitz Trial on public opinion in Germany have been significant and contributed to the culture of openness and remorse with respect to the Nazi past.[19]

In contrast with domestic courts, international tribunals pursue the objective of history writing as *a rule* rather than *an exception*. The UN Secretary General, in his 2004 report to the UN Security Council, generously summarised multiple objectives of international criminal justice and named setting the historical record of events as one of the purposes of international trials.[20] Academic literature also does not shun away from this goal: there is an opinion shared by some scholars that international criminal law serves as a medium for communication of a certain narrative of historical truth.[21]

In its first sentencing judgment in *Erdemović*, the ICTY Trial Chamber underscored its truth-seeking mandate as complementary to its primary duty to prosecute and punish. As Dermot Groome points out, the ICTY tended – in the early case law – to emphasise its role in establishing the truth based on reliable and credible evidence.[22] The argument in *Erdemović* was that discovering the truth about the evil perpetrated in the former Yugoslavia was fundamental for reconciliation and rebuilding the rule of law.[23] This reasoning is consonant with the judgment of the European Court of Human Rights (ECtHR) in *Al Nashiri v. Poland* whereby the Court found that Poland's involvement in the CIA rendition programme rendered it responsible for violating Article 3 of the European Convention on Human Rights, prohibiting torture.[24] In particular, the ECtHR reproached the high level of confidentiality that Polish authorities attached to national investigations. The Court acknowledged

[19] *Ibid.*, 368.

[20] The Secretary-General, *Report of the Secretary-General on the Rule of Law and Transitional Justice in Conflict and Post-Conflict Societies*, U.N. Doc. S/2004/616 (2004), at 38.

[21] J. Galbraith, 'The Pace of International Criminal Justice', *Michigan Journal of International Law* 31:79 (2009–10), 89; R. Steinke, *The Politics of International Criminal Justice. German Perspectives from Nuremberg to the Hague* (Oxford: Hart Publishing, 2012), 9; Wilson, *supra* note 17, 917 citing L. Douglas, *The Memory of Judgment: Making Law and History in the Trials of the Holocaust* (New Haven, CT: Yale University Press, 2001), 6; Groome, *supra* note 9, 175.

[22] See Groome, *supra* note 9, 185.

[23] *Prosecutor* v. *Erdemović*, Sentencing Judgment, Case No. IT-96-22T, 29 November 1996, at 21.

[24] ECtHR, *Al Nashiri* v. *Poland* (Appl. No. 28761/11), Judgment, 24 July 2014.

the challenges of prosecuting terrorism cases, but recognised the overriding public interest to know the truth about what happened. What is particularly striking is the Court's acceptance of the fact that the right to truth does not belong solely to the victim or their family, but also to the general public.[25]

Richard Wilson helpfully outlines the trends in socio-legal scholarship criticising history making as a purpose of criminal trials – international and domestic.[26] He distinguishes among what he calls the 'Partiality Thesis', which contends that law is too limited in scope to reveal the whole story; the 'Incompatibility Theory' holding that law and history have different instruments of inquiry – legal thinking requires embracing only one account, while history is essentially pluralistic;[27] finally, the 'Law is an Ass Thesis', presupposing that law has its internal logic distorting the accuracy of historical representation.[28]

These reflections precede Wilson's main claim consisting of two parts.[29] First, domestic or international courts pronouncing on the issues of massive human rights violations simply cannot avoid the process of interpreting history. The nature of collective violence, such as genocide, requires establishing the context, therefore inevitably inviting determinations of historical significance. Secondly, international courts, such as the ICTY, are better suited to fulfil this objective than their domestic counterparts. Wilson, accordingly, differentiates the narrative-setting function of criminal trials in national proceedings and internationally. National proceedings frequently serve the interests of state identity building and are thus subjugated to political controversies. This results in theatrical trials based on a distorted or oversimplified historical narrative. In contrast, international courts are in a position to deliver a more balanced and accurate historical account because they are free from the political interests of individual states.[30]

[25] *Ibid.*, para. 495.

[26] These challenges do not only arise out of criminal trials; other UN bodies tasked with interpreting the past encounter similar tensions. For example, Antoon De Baets' contribution to this volume focuses on the UN Human Rights Committee's views of the past. While the Committee's mission is not, strictly speaking, to develop time, history and memory, De Baets argues that it has openly engaged with these themes and broadened the scope of the right to truth. See chapter by Antoon De Baets in the present volume.

[27] See also Heinze, *supra* note 2, 7.

[28] Wilson, *supra* note 17, 912–4.

[29] The thesis referred to here is found in Wilson, *supra* note 17. He later elaborated his ideas in an excellent book R. A. Wilson, *Writing History in International Criminal Trials* (Cambridge University Press, 2011).

[30] Wilson, *supra* note 17, 918 *et sq.*

The first part of Wilson's argument – namely that certain historical narrative is an inalienable part of any criminal trial dealing with mass atrocities – presents little controversy. Indeed, history writing in the context of international criminal law is the rule rather than the exception. Wilson's second claim is more contestable, however, because international judicial bodies are not free from external political pressure originating from states and regional organisations alike. The legitimacy of the ICC, and to a lesser extent of the ICTY and ICTR (in the past), depends on their recognition by external actors, which often serve as pressure groups influencing prosecutorial strategies or funding decisions.[31]

It is particularly challenging to accommodate the purpose of setting the historical record when it is linked to the other goals of international criminal law, such as reconciliation.[32] The idea of 'ultimate truth' as a path to reconciliation surfaced as early as the first ICTY judgment, but these two goals are not as interconnected as it is argued in *Erdemović*. Reconciliation may require holding different parties to account, rather than prosecuting perpetrators from one side of the conflict, as it happened at the ICTR, when the Hutu perpetrators were tried for genocide, but crimes committed by the Tutsis were overlooked. It does not follow that the accounts produced on the basis of international trials are not truthful, but rather their scope is limited. Consequently, there is little empirical evidence reconciliation actually took place in Rwanda, let alone that the ICTR contributed to it.[33] Recent ethnic tensions between the Hutu-led government and Tutsis in Burundi only confirm the latter point.

3 International Trials as Social Performances

Accepting that international criminal law is symbolic, in that it allows for prosecuting only a handful of perpetrators, releases some pressure from

[31] The ICTY/R were set up pursuant to the resolutions of the UN Security Council (UNSC Resolutions 827 (1993) and 955 (1994) respectively). Because of their geographically limited mandate and UN backing, their dependence on the will of individual states was limited. The situation is different for the ICC as this is a treaty-based court largely relying on the contributions and support by its individual members.

[32] Fredrick de Vlaming is arguing for more transparency and impartiality of the prosecutorial strategies. F. de Vlaming in L. Reydams *et al.* (eds.), *International Prosecutors* (Oxford University Press, 2012), 570–1; *Cf.* Galbraith, *supra* note 22, 89.

[33] S. Kendall and S. Nouwen, '"Legacy Talk" at the International Criminal Tribunal for Rwanda', EJIL Talk, 2 May 2016, available at www.ejiltalk.org/legacy-talk-at-the-international-criminal-tribunal-for-rwanda/#more-14276.

the courts to unveil all of the truth about the conflict. The symbolic function of international criminal law is encrypted in its social identity and follows from the formation of the global collective consciousness. The idea first emerged in the seminal work of Emile Durkheim entitled *The Division of Labour in the Society*. Durkheim identified two distinct consciousness that exist within each individual: one is personal and characterises each one of us separately, whereas the other one is collective in that it comprises states common to the whole of society. The two coexist in every person and give rise to a solidarity, which binds the individual to society.[34] Since the time when this claim had been made in the beginning of the twentieth century, a new additional type of consciousness emerged – that is a global one, which exists in every individual, along with personal and collective consciousness, and embraces a set of characteristics not unique to a particular society, but common to all in the interconnected world order.

In *the Division of Labour in the Society*, Durkheim argued that modern societies subsist on interdependence stemming from the allocation of functions to different actors. He later modified his view to account for a more complex picture rooted in value systems that are expressed by religious or quasi-religious practices.[35] The deep unsettling query of Durkheim's analysis is his search for the moral foundations of the new legal order. He comes to realise that the division of labour and the distribution of tasks is insufficient to facilitate the processes of integration, thus he turns to religion. The special emphasis is on the process of expressing beliefs – religious ritual is a method for the society to renew itself and tie together its members. Religion consists of acts, which have the object of perpetually making and remaking the soul of the collectivity and of individuals, thus its function is to strengthen the bonds attaching the individual to the society.[36] For Durkheim, religion has a social function, both as a system of communication of ideas and sentiments and as a means of specifying and regulating social relationships.[37]

Applying Durkheim's ideas to modern international criminal trials, it is possible to conceptualise them as religious rituals. Jeffrey Alexander

[34] E. Durkheim, *The Division of Labour in Society* (orig. pub.1893, ed. Basingstoke: Macmillan, 1984), 61.

[35] R. Cotterrell, *Emile Durkheim: Law in a Moral Domain* (Stanford, CA: Stanford University Press, 1999), 49–51

[36] E. Durkheim, *The Elementary Forms of the Religious Life* (London: George Allen & Unwin Ltd 1912), 471.

[37] S. Lukes, *Emile Durkheim: His Life and Work: A Historical and Critical Study* (Stanford, CA: Stanford University Press, 1973), 471, citing Durkheim, *supra* note 34, 98.

offers a contemporary take on the issue of symbolic integration of different groups in modern societies by drawing on the field of performative studies.[38] He acknowledges that societies are still permeated by symbolic, ritual-like activities. The key word is 'ritual-like' because for Alexander rituals proper are mostly present in societies with simpler organisation, characterised by a shared belief system. Thus, the participants in the ritual nearly automatically identify with the symbolic objects of interaction.[39] When it comes to modern highly fragmented societies, cultural practices are better viewed as a social performance rather than a ritual.

Alexander's argument proceeds as follows: social performance consists of a number of elements including actors, scripts, background representations, and audience. In simpler societies these elements are *fused*, or tightly linked to each other. Religious rituals are examples of social performances when the audience does not need to be convinced because it already shares the beliefs that the actors are transmitting. With increasing social complexity, the elements of any social performance become *de-fused*. The successful social performance *re-fuses* the elements by bringing them together in a coherent fashion.[40] Failure to do so may render the social performance unconvincing, thus obstructing the delivery of the symbolic integrative message indented by the cultural practice in question.

The first international prosecutions of genocide at the ICTY and ICTR were undoubtedly social performances carrying a strong message of condemnation and giving effect to the values agreed upon internationally. The judges were 'actors' tasked with ensuring the delivery of this message to a highly diverse and fragmented audience.

4 Shaping the Account of Genocide in an International Courtroom

If one perceives international criminal trials as social performances *per* Alexander, then it is important to define instruments that make 'pieces of the puzzle' fit together in a way convincing to the general public. As argued in the Introduction, trials are constrained by legal principles because these notions make trials credible. Thus, the success of the whole endeavour

[38] J. Alexander, 'Cultural Pragmatics: Social Performance between Ritual and Strategy', in J. Alexander, B. Giesen and J. Mast (eds.), *Social Performance: Symbolic Action, Cultural Pragmatics and Ritual* (Cambridge University Press, 2006), 29.

[39] *Ibid.*

[40] *Ibid.*, 32.

depends on whether international judges stay within the limits of the discipline and adhere to the core principles of criminal law – individual criminal responsibility and legality. This process can also be seen as securing social, or perceived, legitimacy of international criminal justice. The following section elaborates on these pillars in the context of genocide prosecutions.

4.1 *Legality*

The principle of legality requires prohibited conduct to be thoroughly reflected in the law. The underlying idea is that an individual must be fairly warned about the prohibited conduct prior to any demands on his or her liberty. Paradoxically, international criminal law emerged as a discipline without a vast body of law to rely upon. It started with the creation by the Allied powers of the IMT in Nuremberg – a judicial organ designed to rule on questions of individual criminal responsibility of those accountable for mass atrocities.[41] The decision to set up a court was a matter of compromise among the winning powers – the British delegation initially insisted on summary executions for the perpetrators of war crimes while the Soviets and the Americans were in favour of trials in front of the military tribunal, granted that the former group preferred show trials to regular criminal processes.[42] This compromise extended to a variety of matters, including the nature of the tribunal and the style of the proceedings. Framing the charges against the accused presented one of the toughest challenges, both in legal and political terms.[43] The general sentiment was to punish aggression and unabridged militarism, which explains why war crimes and crimes against peace were central during the prosecutions in Nuremberg.

The absence of any legal precedent regarding the crimes prosecuted internationally inspired the work of the United Nations War Crimes Commission set up in 1943 to assist with finding the substantive definitions. The primary task of this body was to investigate the facts and formulate legal opinions relating to war crimes and penal liability of the

[41] United Nations, *Agreement for the prosecution and punishment of the major war criminals of the European Axis* ('London Agreement'), 8 August 1945, 82 U.N.T.C. 280.

[42] Overy, *supra* note 10.

[43] R. Jackson, 'Nuremberg in Retrospect: Legal Answer to International Lawlessness,' *XXXC American Bar Association Journal* 813–6 and 881–7 (October 1949). Reproduced in G. Mettraux (eds.), *Perspectives on the Nuremberg Trial* (Oxford University Press, 2008), 358–9.

perpetrators.[44] Consequently, war crimes as a category made an early entrance onto the scene of international criminal law and largely dominated it. Article 6 of the Nuremberg Charter extended the jurisdiction of the IMT over war crimes, together with crimes against peace and crimes against humanity.[45]

The notion of crimes against humanity was originally introduced as an extension of war crimes and served the practical purpose of addressing atrocities committed by the Nazi regime against its own Jewish citizens. The records of the United Nations War Crimes Commission indicate that crimes against humanity were included in the Charter, primarily due to the fact that war crimes were traditionally directed only against foreign citizens. The Commission held that 'offences committed by the enemy could not technically be regarded as war crimes *stricto sensu* on account of one or several elements, which are of different nature'.[46] The reference was made to the nationality of victims. Bassiouni highlights the evolutionary nature of crimes against humanity as a legal phenomenon that grew out of necessity imposed by the circumstances into a distinct category.[47] Despite inclusion in the Nuremberg Charter, crimes against humanity did not get an independent standing immediately. The IMT discussed war crimes and crimes against humanity together under the same subheading, pointing out the required nexus between the two categories of crimes.[48] Genocide crystallised as a legal category only following the Nuremberg trial.[49] Cognisant of the horrendous nature of crimes committed during the Holocaust, Raphael Lemkin coined the term as early as 1943. Factually

[44] History of the United Nations War Crimes Commission and the Development of the Laws of War compiled by the United Nations Commission (London: His Majesty's Stationary Office, 1948) ('UN War Crimes Commission'), available at www.cisd.soas.ac.uk/Files/docs/97813052-history-of-the-unwcc-chapter-8.pdf ('UN War Crimes Commission Reports'), 169.

[45] Article 6, United Nations, *Charter of the International Military Tribunal – Annex to the Agreement for the prosecution and punishment of the major war criminals of the European Axis ('London Agreement')*, 8 August 1945.

[46] UN War Crimes Commission Reports, at 174.

[47] M.C. Bassiouni, 'Revisiting the Architecture of Crimes Against Humanity: Almost a Century in the Making, with Gaps and Ambiguities Remaining – the Need for a Specialized Convention', in L. N. Sadat (ed.) *Forging a Convention for Crimes Against Humanity* (Cambridge University Press, 2011), 44.

[48] *The Trial of German Major War Criminals by the International Military Tribunal Sitting at Nuremberg*, Germany, 21 November 1945 (1946), 224–5, 248 *et sq*.

[49] It must be noted that the brief overview in this chapter does not do justice to the vast amount of literature pertaining to the crime of genocide. *E.g.* W. Schabas, *Genocide in International Law: The Crime of Crimes* (Cambridge University Press, 2009).

speaking, *genocide* referred to the same set of events that were covered by crimes against humanity.

Notwithstanding the existence of the concept, the crime of genocide was not included in the Nuremberg Charter. Early during the negotiations for the Charter, the American delegation suggested extending the jurisdiction of the tribunal to the crime of 'genocide', or destruction of racial minorities and subjugated population, but this offence was never included in the final text agreed by the Allied powers and was not discussed in the final stages of the drafting of the document. The indictment presented by the Prosecution to the IMT nonetheless referred to *deliberate and systematic genocide* – this description was not an independent charge, however, but referred to an attack upon the physical and biological existence of a given protected group in the context of the extermination as a crime against humanity. The Nuremberg judgment does not mention genocide at all.[50]

This historical particularity demonstrates one of the key arguments in this chapter: international criminal law evolved and keeps evolving according to a certain script or a narrative, which is neither directly linked to the actual events in history nor entirely detached from them; rather the transformation happens as a matter of progressive interpretation. While the substantive weight of the crimes committed during World War II remained unchallenged, their expressive weight fluctuated and became more nuanced with time.[51] In this regard, Jeffrey Alexander notes that the IMT was only the *first* step towards universalising Jewish suffering. He underlines that the focal point of the Nuremberg trial was the unacceptability of the aggression, which was at that time perceived as the ultimate evil; the suffering of Jews was a corollary or a consequence of the Nazi aggression.[52] Only later, the mass killings of Jews acquired an independent standing as a tragedy in public opinion and transformed itself from an event to an archetype of suffering.[53]

The fact that genocide was not one of the crimes prosecuted at Nuremberg might have prompted states to establish the prohibition via an international treaty just two years after the Nuremberg trial.[54] This historical omission

[50] G. Mettraux, *International Criminal and Ad Hoc Tribunals* (Oxford University Press, 2005), 194–5.

[51] See Heinze, *supra* note 2.

[52] J. C. Alexander, *Trauma a Social Theory* (Polity Press, 2012), 46.

[53] *Ibid.*, at 60. Paolo Lobba in his chapter in the present volume points to the unique place the Holocaust occupies in the history of the European identity building. He describes the nature of Holocaust as an event that shaped the collective memory of the continent.

[54] UN General Assembly, *Convention on the Prevention and Punishment of the Crime of Genocide*, 9 December 1948, United Nations ('Genocide Convention 1948').

served as a compensatory mechanism in the legal arena allowing for codification to take place at a rapid pace. In 1946, the UN General Assembly (GA) first defined genocide as a:[55]

> Denial of the right of existence of entire human groups, as homicide is the denial of the right to live of individual human beings; such denial of the right of existence shocks the conscience of mankind, results in great losses to humanity in the form of cultural and other contributions represented by these human groups, and is contrary to moral law and to the spirit and aims of the United Nations.

Just two years later, in 1948, the GA adopted the Convention on the Prevention and Punishment of the Crime of Genocide (Genocide Convention).[56] Article II of the Convention contains a definition of genocide reproduced nearly verbatim in the Statutes of the ad hoc tribunals, hybrid courts and the ICC.[57] This rigidity of legal construction distinguishes genocide from other international crimes that altered their content with the passage of time.

Genocide is any of the following acts (the list is exhaustive) committed with intent to destroy, in whole or in part, a national, ethnical, racial, or religious group: killing members of the group; causing serious bodily or mental harm to members of the group; deliberately inflicting on the group conditions of life calculated to bring about its physical destruction in whole or in part; imposing measures intended to prevent births within the group; forcibly transferring children of the group to another group.[58] Destruction is understood as a physical destruction, thus discrimination or causing suffering won't suffice for the purposes of this crime.[59] The attack is on a group as a collective entity, in whole or in part, meaning that either the perpetrator intended to destroy a considerable number of individuals belonging to a group or targeted individuals who constitute a 'significant' or 'emblematic' section of that group.[60]

The characteristics bringing groups under the protection of the Genocide Convention are limited to cultural, religious, ethnical, or national only. There is strong opposition to expanding the definition of

[55] UN GA Resolution 1946 96(I).

[56] Genocide Convention 1948.

[57] Article 4 of the ICTY Statute, Article 2 of the ICTR Statute, Article 6 of the Rome Statute of the ICC.

[58] Article II of the Genocide Convention 1948.

[59] *Krstić* Appeal Judgment, para. 25.

[60] Mettraux, *supra* note 50, at 221; *Prosecutor* v. *Krstić*, ICTY Case No. IT-98-33-A, Appeal Judgment, 19 April 2004 ('*Krstić* Appeal Judgment'), paras. 12, 16, 21 and 37.

genocide for a fear of diluting it.[61] Because the law is not flexible in this regard, the context of atrocity must be thoroughly studied in order to establish whether the group indeed belongs to the protected category.[62] The *Krstić* Trial Chamber expressly admitted that the boundaries of these entities may be difficult to establish and the analysis of the socio-historical context is thus important.[63]

The first ever conviction for genocide in the *Akayesu* case demonstrated this complexity: the Rwandan Tutsi were not a religious group, nor could they be distinguished from Hutus on the basis of nationality.[64] The Tutsi had been officially classified in Rwanda as an 'ethnic group', but they shared with Hutus the main features of ethnic identification – language and culture.[65] Wilson traces the evolution of the ICTR reasoning in this regard. In *Akayesu*, the Trial Chamber first concluded that the Tutsis do not meet the criteria as an ethnic or racial group for the purposes of the Genocide Convention. It then conferred protection to the group by reference to the *travaux preparatoire* and the intention of the drafters to protect any 'stable and permanent group'.[66] Rwanda's law and society conferred such status upon Tutsis. Arguably, the rigidity of law led to a questionable interpretation of the notion of a 'protected group' in *Akayesu*.[67]

In the 1999, the *Kayishema* Trial Chamber reversed this interpretation and declared that the Tutsis were killed on the basis of their ethnicity.[68] This ruling did not resolve one of the main criticisms of the *Akayesu*

61 On 20 October 2015, the ECtHR rendered a judgment examining in detail the definition of the crime of genocide. The Court's Grand Chamber remained highly divided as to what comprises a 'protected group' and whether additional categories may be added to the definition contained in the Genocide Convention. The Majority ruled against expanding the definition. See ECtHR, *Vasiliauskas* v. *Lithuania* (Appl. No. 35343/05), Judgment (Grand Chamber), 20 October 2015

62 The discussion about what constitutes a protected group and other elements of genocide continues nowadays with many scholars and members of the civil society holding conflicting views about the legal qualification of the Holodomor in Ukraine and the massacre at Katyn in Poland. In Ukraine, a large section of the population starved following orders issued by Joseph Stalin, while in Katyn the Soviet army exterminated the intelligentsia as part of the invasion of Poland in 1940.

63 *Krstić* Trial Judgment, para. 557.

64 W. Schabas, 'Judicial Activism and the Crime of Genocide', in S. Darcy and J. Powerdly (eds.), *Judicial Creativity at the International Criminal Tribunals* (Oxford University Press, 2010), 71.

65 *Ibid.*

66 *Akayesu* Trial Judgment, paras. 511–6.

67 Wilson, *supra* note 29, 178.

68 *Prosecutor* v. *Clelment Kayishema and Obed Ruzindana*, Case No. ICTR-95-1-T, Trial Chamber Judgment, 21 May 1999, para. 312.

approach, namely its failure to account for the subjective perception of the division by the Hutu perpetrators who exploited extremist racial ideology based on popular mythology. In the following *Rutuganda* case, the view was altered again: the judges recognised the subjective view of ethnic group membership and concluded that it is impossible to adopt a formal policy on the matter, thus determination must be made on a case-by-case basis.[69] Wilson points to the fact that the ICTR eventually never solved the enigma of the Tutsi identity.[70]

4.2 *Individual Criminal Responsibility*

The judges usually choose one interpretation of evidence over all others and ensure the observance of the rules of legal inquiry, limiting the scope and depth of their historical assessment. One of the major factors constraining historical assessment in the course of international trials is the need to attribute individual criminal responsibility for collective wrongs. It is precisely the collective aspect of international criminality that begs for extended analysis of the causes, context, and networks that facilitated the commission of offences. At the same time, individuals accused always remains at the centre of the 'story' constructed during trial. This limits the extent to which alternative interpretations can be furnished within one judgment.

The ad hoc tribunals faced an uneasy task of establishing individual criminal responsibility of the accused, while simultaneously disentangling highly complex sets of circumstances leading to the crimes of genocide in Bosnia and Rwanda. For example, in *Krstić*, the Trial Chamber drew on a variety of evidence to paint a picture of what happened in and around Srebrenica during those few days in July 1995.[71] At the same time, the judges emphasised the limited nature of legal inquiry:

> The Trial Chamber leaves it to historians and social psychologist to plumb the depths of this episode of the Balkan conflict and to probe for deep-seated causes. The task at hand is a more modest one: to find, from the evidence presented during the trial, what happened during that period of about nine days and, ultimately, whether the defendant in this case, General Krstić was criminally responsible, under the tenets of international law, for his participation in them.[72]

[69] *Prosecutor* v. *Georges Anderson Rutuganda*, Case No. ICTR-96-3-T, Trial Chamber Judgment, 6 December 1999, paras. 56–8.
[70] Wilson, *supra* note 29, 184.
[71] *Krstić*, Trial Judgment, para. 4.
[72] *Ibid.*, para. 2.

The first ICTY conviction for genocide in *Krstić* case ended with the Presiding Judge Almiro Rodrigues drawing a distinction between collective and individual responsibility. He admitted that the Serbian forces committed some of the heinous acts in the former Yugoslavia, but 'to associate this evil with Serbian identity would be an insult to the Serbian people'. Equally monstrous, in the view of the Presiding Judge, was not to attach individual responsibility for these acts. Thus, the delivery of the judgment ended with the emotional statement directed at the convicted person and broader community alike '[i]n July 1995, General Krstić, you agreed to evil'.[73]

It must be noted that the Trial Chamber convicted General Krstić for participating in the joint criminal enterprise to commit genocide; hence the above statement refers to him in this capacity – as someone who shared the intent of the perpetrators. He was sentenced to forty-seven years of imprisonment accordingly.

General Krstić was deputy commander of the Drina Corps, one of the corps which constituted the army of Republika Srpska, often known as the VRS. The Trial Chamber established that on 11 July 1995, just a few days before the atrocities happened, Krstić entered Srebrenica together with General Ratko Mladić and arranged for buses to transfer the civilian population. The Appeals Chamber agreed with the Trial Chamber that the crimes occurred in the VRS zone of responsibility and that by 15 July 1995 Krstić knew of the genocidal intent of some of the VRS staff members.[74] Krstić also knew that by allowing Drina Corps resources to be used he contributed to the executions of Bosnian Muslims. At the same time, evidence suggested that he was not a *supporter* of this plan. The appellate judges therefore concluded that Krstić's responsibility is best described as that of 'aider and abettor'. His sentence was reduced to thirty-five years of imprisonment due to the fact that the convicted person did not share a specific intent destroy protected groups, which is a crucial element of genocide.

Judge Shahabuddeen in his partial dissenting opinion in *Krstić* highlighted the difference between the intent of the perpetrator and the intent of the aider and abettor in relation to the crime of genocide – the former

[73] ICTY Press Release, Radislav Krstić becomes the First Person to be Convicted of Genocide at the ICTY and is Sentenced to 46 Years Imprisonment, 2 August 2001, available at www.icty.org/en/press/radislav-krstic-becomes-first-person-be-convicted-genocide-icty-and-sentenced-46-years, last accessed 2 February 2016.

[74] *Krstić*, Appeal Judgment, paras. 135–7.

intends to commit genocide, while the latter intends to provide means by which the perpetrator, if he wishes, can realise his intent to commit genocide.[75]

The *Krstić* Appeal judgment recognised to some extent the symbolic function of international criminal law by singling out one particular offence, genocide, as deserving 'special condemnation and opprobrium'.[76] The reasoning is that genocide 'is a crime against all of humankind, its harm being felt not only by the group targeted for destruction, but by all of humanity'.[77] At the same time, the judges felt obliged to specify Krstić's contribution to the crime and re-adjusted his sentence based on his lower level of culpability.

4.3 *Disciplinarity*

Mass atrocities involve responsibility of the variety of actors at different levels of state hierarchy. An interaction of multiple factors, including group pressure and group identity building, results in the situation producing crimes. A network of individuals, organisations and sometimes states thus contribute to the escalation of hostilities. This phenomenon is often called 'system' or 'systemic' criminality.[78] How to address system criminality and apportion responsibility for the wrongs? If one views trials as 'social performances', it is essential for their credibility to deal with responsibility of an individual, a state, or an entity within the constraints of the specific discipline. This is so because the rules are defined for each particular branch law and merging them in an attempt to reach justice in one holistic process appears too far-fetched.

An example of a failed attempt to treat responsibility holistically is the following instruments, which were introduced at Nuremberg, but which have not received recognition in modern international criminal law: conspiracy, membership in a criminal organisation and lowering the standard of fault. Conspiracy charge failed in Nuremberg (but not in Tokyo); the Rome Statute of the ICC famously rejects criminal responsibility of legal entities, and modern international courts and tribunals have developed a

[75] *Krstić*, Appeal Judgment, Partial Dissenting Opinion of Judge Shahabuddeen, para. 66.
[76] *Krstić*, Appeal Judgement, para. 36.
[77] *Ibid.*
[78] A. Nollkaemper and H. van der Wilt (eds.), *System Criminality in International Law* (Cambridge University Press, 2009).

sophisticated body of precedents aimed at scrupulously assessing personal culpability.

Leora Bilsky brilliantly argues how restitution litigation of the 1990s pursued the Nuremberg objective of addressing the liability of a legal entity, but did so while avoiding the limitations of criminal law. The legacy of Nuremberg has indeed been challenged by the Holocaust restitution actions brought before the American courts in the 1990s. They were settled for large amounts, provoking criticism by legal scholars and historians alike.[79] The Nuremberg legacy withstood the challenge precisely because the restitution litigation took place within the constraints of civil law, hence the expectations vested on what these civil proceedings could achieve were different from those vested in an (international) criminal trial.

Another telling example of the 'division of labour' among different branches of law is the refusal of the International Court of Justice (ICJ) to apply the test of 'overall control' introduced by the ICTY Appeals Chamber in *Tadić*. In 2007, the ICJ had to rule on Bosnia's claim that Serbia had committed genocide during the war in Bosnia. When resolving the issue, the Court, *inter alia*, discussed whether the acts of genocide were committed by persons or organs whose conduct is attributable to Serbia. The Court answered this question in the negative, rejecting Bosnia's claim that the conduct of the VRS is attributable to Serbia as a conduct directed or controlled by the state.[80] The ICJ was invited to apply the *Tadić* test of 'overall control' in resolving this issue. The ICJ refused to do so and, instead, applied a stricter test of 'effective control' developed by the ICJ in the *Nicaragua* case.[81] The ICJ explained that while it attached great weight to the ICTY's finding relating to the events that happened during the conflict, it could not use the ICTY's legal test of 'overall control' because it was developed for a purpose *not related* to the attribution of state responsibility for acts committed by paramilitary units.[82] The issue of aims and purposes of each discipline is thus intrinsically related with the legal standards it upholds.

79 Leora Bilsky, 'Transnational Holocaust Litigation', *European Journal of International Law* 23:2 (2012), 349.

80 *Case Concerning the Application of the Convention on the Prevention and Punishment of the Crime of Genocide (Bosnia and Herzegovina* v. *Serbia and Montenegro)*, I.C. J. Reports 2007 ('*Genocide* Judgment'), para. 412.

81 *Military and Paramilitary Activities in and against Nicaragua (Nicaragua* v. *United States of America)*, ICJ Reports 1986, para. 65.

82 *Genocide* Judgment, paras. 402–4.

Finally, the *Gacaca*, or grassroots lay court system, that emerged in Rwanda as an alternative to the prosecutions by the ICTR and domestic national courts is another example of a self-contained regime operating in accordance with its own rules and reinforcing the idea of trials as social performances. *Gacaca* may be described not only in legal terms as a community justice mechanism dealing with low-level perpetrators of genocide, but also as a social process or a cultural practice aimed at overcoming the trauma of genocide and defining the relationship between different political opponents.[83]

5 Conclusion

The challenge in implementing the goal of narrative setting in international context is thus not to lose sight of the main function of a criminal trial. The court of law is not designed to make value judgments about the history *in abstracto*, but rather to adjudicate on a set of facts, using the legal tools available to it. Legal inquiry is neither a sufficient nor a satisfying exercise for the purposes of establishing a comprehensive account of events, yet it is usually authoritative enough to provide a meaningful insight into the situation and to attribute additional expressive weight to a certain version of happenings. The important caveat is to treat legal inquiry as *limited in scope*.

The purpose of this chapter was to make sense of these limitations by viewing trials as having two distinct identities – social and legal – that are interconnected. This conceptualisation promotes adherence to legal rules for they ensure the credibility of the performance, or, in other words, perceived legitimacy of the trial. The ad hoc tribunals prosecuting genocide for the first time in the history of international criminal law were constrained by the rigidity of the definition of genocide, and thus bound by the principle of legality. The judges faced the task of reflecting individual culpability of the accused even at the expense of painting a wider picture of events. Finally, the ad hoc tribunals were cognisant of the impossibility of extending the reach of the discipline beyond jurisdictional constraints. Therefore, it is inevitable and natural that in pursuing the objective of setting the historical record, their inquiry was limited in scope.

[83] R. Haveman, 'Doing Justice to Gacaca', in A. Smeulers and R. Haveman (eds.) *Supranational Criminology: Towards a Criminology of International Crimes* (Antwerp, Oxford, and Portland: Intersentia, 2008), 359.

What do these observations mean for the future prosecutions of genocide by international courts and tribunals? First and foremost, any labelling of certain atrocities as 'genocide' will involve thorough consideration of the legal definition of this crime. In this regard, the rigidity of the 1948 formula, currently accepted in international criminal law, may come under criticism. As *Akayesu* demonstrated, this characterisation may prove too rigid to capture the nature of crimes committed in the specific case, thereby prompting judges to engage in creative interpretation of law at the expense of the credibility of the whole trial. Secondly, jurisdictional matters (also stemming from the notion of legality) will play an essential role in prosecuting genocide. For example, many observers describe offences committed by Daesh against members of the Yazidi community as genocide, but without an appropriate forum to adjudicate on the matter, these acts may never receive legal recognition as such.[84] Finally, individual focus of prosecutions will persist due to a strong criminal law component embedded in international criminal justice. Even if one accepts history writing as one of the goals of this discipline, the idea of individual criminal responsibility will remain an element *fusing* together history and law by making trials sound performances in their legal sense.

[84] Neither Iraq nor Syria is a State Party to the Rome Statute. Consequently, prosecution of crimes committed on their territory by non-State Party nationals at the ICC is only possible upon the referral by the UN Security Council, which, at the time of writing, remains highly unlikely. The creation of an international or a hybrid tribunal with the specific mandate is another option yet to be explored.

3

The 'Right to Truth' in International Law: The 'Last Utopia'?

PATRICIA NAFTALI

> It is now essential that science should not be asked to judge and that law should not be asked to pronounce truth.
>
> Bruno Latour[1]

1 Introduction

The rise of a 'right to truth' presumably owed to victims of gross human rights violations in the discourse of international law seems to epitomise the way law attempts to regulate individual and collective memory, revisionism, and denialism of historical events and mass atrocities. The first decade of 2000 has witnessed a linguistic turn from the 'duty to remember' to the assertion of the existence of a 'right to truth' as a general human right – and even to a *people's* right. Its historical origins lie within the second stream of memory laws mentioned by the co-editors of this book in their genealogy of memory laws, particularly with the Latin American transitional justice initiatives.[2] Unlike most chapters in this volume, which deal with criminal legislation or specific memory laws, this chapter focuses on the use of human rights language to reclaim the memory of the past as an individual and collective entitlement.

Originally developed in the context of enforced disappearances, as the right of victims' relatives to know the fate and whereabouts of the

1 From 'Scientific Objects and Legal Objectivity', in A. Pottage and M. Mundy (eds.), *Law, Anthropology and the Constitution of the Social: Making Persons and Things* (Cambridge University Press, 2004), 73–114, at 113.

2 See Introduction by Belavusau and Gliszczynska-Grabias in the present volume.

disappeared,[3] the 'right to truth' has expanded to encompass victims' right to obtain information on the circumstances of serious human rights violations. While the existence of the 'right to truth' as a free-standing right remains controversial,[4] inter national courts have played a crucial role in bringing this concept to reality, inferring it from other existing rights, such as the right to access justice[5] or the right not to be subjected to torture or to inhuman or degrading treatment or punishment.[6]

It now features high on the agenda of the international community to implement politics of truth and memory related to State-sponsored abuse. In his book *The Last Utopia: Human Rights in History*,[7] Samuel Moyn wonders whether human rights have supplanted earlier political utopias, which now belong to fallen universalist ideologies. The same question can be raised about the 'right to truth' in the context of post-conflict rebuilding and transition to democracies. For instance, in the name of the 'right to truth', truth and reconciliation commissions, trials, public apologies, memorials, museums, and other memory-related practices are now commonly promoted in post-war societies as a 'vital safeguard against the recurrence of violations'.[8] This right is presented as interconnected with the State's 'duty to preserve memory' of atrocities, which is 'aimed at preserving the collective memory from extinction and, in particular, at guarding against

[3] See T. Scovazzi and G. Citroni, *The Struggle against Enforced Disappearance and the 2007 United Nations Convention* (Leiden: Martinus Nijhoff Publishers, 2007). See also Article 24(2) of the 2006 *International Convention for the Protection of All Persons from Enforced Disappearances*, entered into force in December 2010, which provides that '[e]ach victim has the right to know the truth regarding the circumstances of the enforced disappearance, the progress and results of the investigation and the fate of the disappeared person'. United Nations [UN] General Assembly Res 61/177 (20 December 2006), UN. Doc. A/RES/61/177.

[4] See, *inter alia*, United Nations Office of the High Commissioner for Human Rights [hereafter OHCHR], report *The Right to Truth* (7 June 2007), UN. Doc A/HRC/5/5/7, para. 17.

[5] Inter-American Court of Human Rights [hereafter IACtHR], *Bámaca-Velásquez* v. *Guatemala*, Judgment on merits, 25 November 2000, para. 201.

[6] Human Rights Chamber of Bosnia-Herzegovina, *Selimovic* v. *Republika Srpska* (the *Srebrenica* Cases), 7 March 2003, para. 191.

[7] S. Moyn, *The Last Utopia. Human Rights in History* (Cambridge: Harvard University Press, 2010).

[8] UN Commission on Human Rights [UNCHR], *Updated Set of Principles for the Protection and Promotion of Human Rights through Action to Combat Impunity. Addendum*, prepared by Diane Orentlicher (8 February 2005), UN. Doc. E/CN.4/2005/102/Add.1, p. 7; UNCHR, *Final Report on the Question of the Impunity of Perpetrators of Human Rights Violations (Civil and Political) prepared by Louis Joinet*, UN Doc. E/CN.4/Sub.2/1997/20/Rev1 (2 October 1997).

the development of revisionist and negationist arguments'.[9] This puzzling evolution seems to point to an ever-increasing faith in human rights. For instance, knowing the truth regarding the causes and circumstances of atrocities would facilitate the 'healing' of victims and their 'catharsis'; bring 'closure' to victims' relatives; 'restore their dignity'; foster 'reconciliation' between divided societies in the aftermath of violent conflicts; and, finally, strengthen accountability for violations and the rule of law.[10]

Against this backdrop, it would be difficult not to see the advent of the 'right to truth' as a progress of international law and victims' rights in particular, as most scholars and human rights practitioners do.[11] However, are we dealing with yet another example of rights inflation and the 'rhetoric of rights'?[12] Is the recent legalisation of 'truth' a legal revolution or a rhetorical façade, the crystallisation of an innovative right or the mere recycling of existing rights? To answer this question, I examine legal mobilisations of the 'right to truth' to gain insights into the potential value of this concept. The first section argues that 'the right to truth', as advocated by its global promoters, is and has been historically used as a revolutionary tool to reform various areas of international law. The second section discusses the effects of mobilisations of the 'right to truth' on the Inter-American Court of Human Rights (IACtHR) and European Court of Human Rights (ECtHR) case-law to assess to what extent they have accommodated the subversive potential of the 'right to truth'.[13] Finally, the conclusion highlights the utopian and dystopian aspects of globalised politics of truth in order to point to some effects of the institutionalisation of the 'right to truth' in the domestic and international spheres.

[9] *Ibid.*

[10] See e.g., *Ban Ki-moon's Secretary General's Message for 2011 on the International Day for the Right to the Truth*: www.un.org/en/events/righttotruthday/2011/sgmessage.shtml and UNHRC [UN Human Rights Council], *Report of the Special Rapporteur on the Promotion of Truth, Justice, Reparation and Guarantees of Non-Recurrence, Pablo de Greiff*, A/HRC/24/42 (28 August 2013), paras. 20 and 90. All URLs were last accessed on 31 May 2016.

[11] R. Aldana-Pindell, 'An Emerging Universality of Justiciable Victims' Rights in the Criminal Process to Curtail Impunity for State-Sponsored Crimes', *Human Rights Quarterly* 26:3 (2004), 605–86; G. Park, 'Truth as Justice: Legal and Extralegal Development of the Right to Truth', *Harvard International Review* 31:4 (2010), 24–7.

[12] S. Scheingold, *The Politics of Rights: Lawyers, Public Policy, and Political Change*, 2nd ed. (University of Michigan Press, 2004), 41.

[13] For an account of the 'right to truth' in the context of the UN Human Rights Committee, see chapter by Antoon De Baets in the present volume. See also chapter by Salvador Herencia Carrasco in the present volume for an overview of the IACtHR jurisprudence related to the issue of memory and its relevance for Peru's transition.

2 A Potentially Revolutionary Category: Reforming International Law through the 'Right to Truth'

Within the last two decades, the 'right to truth' has been mobilised in Courts by various actors as a catalyst to challenge political constraints in the domestic sphere. In order to fully grasp the importance of the recognition of the 'right to truth' in the perspective of their architects, this section draws on their strategic litigation through their press releases, reports, and third-party interventions or *amicus curiae* briefs. In particular, it shows how this narrative device has been litigated to extend international human rights law to new terrains beyond enforced disappearances to include: States' prerogative to grant amnesties, State secrecy and national security, and finally, victim-centred reparations aimed at accompanying the grieving of family members of victims and preserving the memory of victims or historical events.

2.1 *From Limiting to Prohibiting Amnesties*

Political transitions in Latin America around the mid-1980s witnessed a generalisation of amnesties to the benefit of perpetrators of political violence. Here, the 'right to truth' provided a resource in the middle of the 1990s to challenge the idea of amnesties as State prerogatives, with a view to inflect the political and legal context overly favourable to politics of pardon and oblivion. First, amnesties were not prohibited under international law; on the contrary, they were encouraged in internal armed conflicts,[14] and mostly upheld by Supreme Courts in most Latin American countries.[15] In addition, they were justified by the international community as tools of peace making and by successor regimes as politics of national reconciliation.[16]

Against this backdrop, the 'right to truth' has been mobilised in Argentina in 1995,[17] and later on in the Inter-American system, to limit

[14] Article 6(5) of Protocol Additional to the Geneva Conventions of 12 August 1949, and Relating to the Protection of Victims of Non-International Armed Conflicts (Protocol II), 1125 U.N.T.S. 609 (8 June 1977).

[15] N. Roht-Arriaza and L. Gibson, 'The Developing Jurisprudence on Amnesty', *Human Rights Quarterly* 20 (1998), 843–85.

[16] See more generally S. Lefranc, *Politiques du pardon* (Paris: Presses Universitaires de France, 2002).

[17] Cámara Federal en lo Criminal y Correccional de la Capital Federal, *Emilio Mignone s/Presentación en la Causa 761 'Hechos Denunciados Como Ocurridos en el Ambito de la Escuela Superior de Mecánica de la Armada'*, reg. n°3/95 (20 April 1995), II, para. 2.

the effects of amnesty laws on criminal investigations into the fate of the disappeared,[18] under the motive that although amnesty laws prevented perpetrators to be prosecuted, the 'right to truth' of families and society remained a sufficient *rationale* to reopen *criminal* investigations into the fate of all the disappeared and to document State terrorism, including the identity of perpetrators.[19] The 'right to truth' envisioned was, however, more ambivalent towards punishment than the protagonists were later willing to admit, as their insistence on an individualised judicial truth, obtained through criminal investigations, suggests a broader punitive agenda to collect criminal evidence against State agents for later use.[20]

At the same time, the proliferation of truth and reconciliation commissions (TRC) in the Americas – in Chile, El Salvador, Haïti, and Guatemala – was also seen as alternative contributions to an emerging 'right to truth' of victims and societies on the broad historical circumstances of past abuse.[21] The 1994 post-apartheid South African TRC, which was mandated to grant individualised and conditional amnesties, represented a turning point in that following its 'truth in exchange of amnesty' model, blanket and 'amnesic amnesties' started to be delegitimated and opposed to 'accountable amnesties'.[22] More recently, advocates of prosecutions have more radically challenged amnesties for impeding on victims' 'right to truth', a vision that the IACtHR has come to endorse.[23] Nonetheless, the absolute prohibition of amnesties for serious crimes still remains highly controversial in international law.[24]

[18] M. Abregú, 'La Tutela Judicial del Derecho a la Verdad en la Argentina', *Revista IIDH* 24 (1996), 11–48.

[19] Human Rights Watch/Americas and Centre for Justice and International Law, *Memorial en Derecho* Amicus Curiae *Presentado a la Excma. Cámara Federal en lo Criminal y Correccional de la Capital Federal en el Asunto 'Mignone Emilio F., s/ Presentación en Causa n° 761 (E.S.M.A.)'*, *Revista IIDH* 21 (1995), 149–71, para. 2.

[20] P. Naftali, 'Toute la vérité, rien que la vérité? Les mobilisations du 'droit à la vérité' sur les disparitions forcées dans les affaires Mignone et Lapacó en Argentine', in J. Allard et al. (eds.), *La vérité en procès. Les juges et la vérité politique* (Paris: LGDJ, 2014), 73–93.

[21] P. Hayner, 'Fifteen Truth Commissions – 1974 to 1994: A Comparative Study', *Human Rights Quarterly* 16:4 (1994), 597–655, at 611; J. Pasqualucci, 'The Whole Truth and Nothing but the Truth: Truth Commissions, Impunity and the Inter-American Human Rights System', *Boston University International Law Journal* 12 (1994), 321–70, at 329–31.

[22] R. Slye, 'The Legitimacy of Amnesties Under International Law and General Principles of Anglo-American Law: Is a Legitimate Amnesty Possible?', *Virginia Journal of International Law* 43 (2002), 173–247, at 245.

[23] See Section 3.1.

[24] M. Freeman and M. Pensky, 'The Amnesty Controversy in International Law', in F. Lessa and L. Payne (eds.), *Amnesty in the Age of Human Rights Accountability: Comparative and International Perspectives* (Cambridge University Press, 2012), 42–65.

2.2 *Limiting State Secrecy Abuse and Promoting Politics of Transparency*

Lately, the 'right to truth' has also been mobilised beyond contexts of State crimes to curtail State secrecy policies and promote good governance, including in 'ordinary' democracies. Here, truth activists attempt to spark a paradigm shift from States' 'secrets privilege' in domestic legislations to a human rights-based principle of openness of public administrations. For instance, as part of the 'right to truth', *Open Society Justice Initiative* (OSJI) advocates a general right of access to State-held information, irrespective of the existence of any specific freedom of information act or legislation.[25] The NGO generally promotes national laws on access to public documents, including military, police and intelligence records, mainly in Latin America and Eastern Europe.[26] It thus litigates for a 'right to truth' arising, among other sources, from the right to freedom of expression before the IACtHR (Article 13 of the American Convention on Human Rights, hereafter ACHR)[27] and ECtHR (Article 10 of the European Convention on Human Rights, hereafter ECHR).[28]

For these advocates, the potential of the 'right to truth' in connection with the right to freedom of expression is manifold. First, the recognition of a 'right to information' would entail an unprecedented right to access classified archives. For instance, in *Gomes Lund* v. *Brazil* before the IACtHR,[29] which concerns the failure of Brazil to declassify military records on the repression of a communist guerrilla movement in 1972 during the

[25] *Amicus brief* submitted by OSJI, ARTICLE 19 *et al.* before the IACtHR in the case *Claude Reyes* v. *Chile*, 28 March 2006, paras. 20, 34, and 46, available at www.opensocietyfoundations.org/sites/default/files/court-amicus-brief-3282006.pdf; OSJI, application to the ECtHR *al-Nashiri* v. *Poland*, 6 May 2011, at 72, available at www.opensocietyfoundations.org/sites/default/files/echr-al-nashiri-application-20110506.pdf.

[26] See OSJI work on freedom of information available at www.opensocietyfoundations.org/topics/freedom-information.

[27] OSJI *et al.*, *Amicus Curiae Submission in the Case Gudiel Álvarez et al. ('Diario Militar')* v. *Guatemala*, 10 May 2012, para. 15, available at www.opensocietyfoundations.org/sites/default/files/inter-american-court-diario-militar-amicus-20120827.pdf.

[28] OSJI, written comments in ECtHR *El-Masri* v. *Ex-Yugoslav Republic of Macedonia* (Appl. No. 39630/09), Judgment (Grand Chamber) 21 March 2012 [El-Masri case], para. 133 [OSJI *El-Masri* Brief] and in ECtHR *Janowiec* v. *Russia* (Appl. Nos. 55508/07 and 29520/09), Judgment (Grand Chamber) 21 October 2013, 16 January 2013 [OSJI *Janowiec* Brief], available at www.opensocietyfoundations.org/sites/default/files/echr-janowiec-written-comments-20130116.pdf.

[29] IACtHR, *Gomes Lund and others* v. *Brazil* (*Guerrilha do Araguaia*), Judgment, 24 November 2010.

dictatorship, OSJI argued that 'grounding the right to truth on Article 13 would grant both victims and the general public an unambiguous basis for claiming a judicially enforceable right of access to relevant information held by the State, including classified records'.[30] This may also influence the ECtHR, which has traditionally been reluctant to apply Article 10 of the ECHR to cases related to access to State-held information.[31]

Second, the 'right to truth' would be instrumental to counter State denial for human rights violations. For instance, *El-Masri* v. *Macedonia* before the ECtHR was the first case before an international Court in which accountability was sought for the CIA extraordinary renditions programme led by George W. Bush after 9/11 with the complicity of a few European States. While the petitioner alleged that he was secretly arrested and detained by Macedonian authorities as an Al-Qaida terrorist suspect and handed over to CIA agents who transferred him to a CIA-run secret prison in Afghanistan where he was tortured, Macedonia repeatedly denied its role in the global rendition programme. In addition, previous efforts to seek justice in US Courts were dismissed at the pre-trial phase on the grounds of the validity of the 'state secrets privilege' argument, declaring that 'the very subject of litigation is itself a state secret'.[32] However, truth entrepreneurs argue that denials of access to information relevant to historical truth and based on national security arguments would have to be justified by the State under the strict necessity test of Article 10, 2° ECHR, which would shift the burden of proof of the necessity of secrecy on to the authorities. In addition, society's 'right to truth' would be another compelling public interest to balance – and possibly outweigh – State secrecy interests invoked to refuse disclosure.[33] OSJI also raised this argument before the ECtHR in *Janowiec and others* v. *Russia*, which relates to

[30] OSJI *et al.*, *Amicus Curiae Submission in the Case of Gomes Lund and Others* v. *Brazil to the Inter-American Court of Human Rights* [OSJI *Gomes Lund Amicus*], 1 June 2010, para. 104, available at www.opensocietyfoundations.org/sites/default/files/araguaia-amicus-english-20100601.pdf; OSJI, *Litigation: Gomes Lund* v. *Brazil*, 13 January 2015, available at www.opensocietyfoundations.org/litigation/gomes-lund-v-brazil.

[31] Article 10 has been mainly interpreted as a right of governmental *non-interference*, i.e. as a negative duty to abstain from interfering with information circulating freely. For instance, in *Leander* v. *Sweden*, the ECtHR stated that Article 10 did not entail *per se* a positive duty of States to give information to citizens. However, since 2006, a few decisions seem to invert this trend. See generally W. Hins and D. Voorhoof, 'Access to State-Held Information as a Fundamental Right under the European Convention on Human Rights', *European Constitutional Law Review* 3 (2007), 114–26.

[32] *El-Masri* v. *United States*, Fourth Circuit, 479 F.3d 296, at 310.

[33] See e.g., OSJI *Gomes Lund Amicus*, para. 101.

the Katyn massacres of 20,000 Polish prisoners of war by Stalin's secret police in 1940 when the USSR invaded Poland.[34] In this case, the Russian government refused to disclose classified documents to the prisoners' relatives who had filed a criminal investigation, as well as all the investigative files and the decision to terminate proceedings. Finally, the link between the 'right to truth' and Article 10 is particularly important for truth activists to extend the beneficiaries of the former from the individual victim to the public and the media in general.[35]

2.3 *Promoting a Broader Approach to Reparations at the ECtHR*

The 'right to truth' has further been used to suggest reforms of the ECtHR case-law in the area of reparations. In the ECtHR system, the primary remedy is a simple declaration of a violation. However, Article 41 ECHR provides that the Court 'shall, if necessary, afford just satisfaction to the injured party'. Most frequently, the Court grants financial compensation in cases of disappearances.[36] Before the Strasbourg Court, both OSJI and REDRESS, a human rights NGO that defends torture survivors to obtain access to justice and reparations, have recently challenged this limited approach to reparations.

First, they invited the Court to embrace a psychologically sensitive approach to reparations in cases of State denial by stressing the therapeutic benefits of officially acknowledging truth for victims of gross violations.[37] In *Varnava and others* v. *Turkey*, which concerns the disappearance of Greek-Cypriots who went missing in the course of the Turkish military operation in Northern Cyprus in 1974, REDRESS asked the judges to generally move beyond financial compensation and to 'award additional forms of satisfaction'[38] in line with a restorative, victim-centred approach to reparations. REDRESS mentioned the 'right to truth' as a

[34] OSJI *Janowiec* Brief, para. 124.

[35] ECtHR, *Al Nashiri* v. *Poland* (Appl. No. 28761/11), Judgment, 24 July 2014, para. 483.

[36] See e.g., ECtHR, *Musayeva* v. *Russia* (Appl. No. 12703/02), Judgment, 3 July 2008.

[37] REDRESS Submission to the Grand Chamber in the *El-Masri* v. *Macedonia* case [REDRESS *El-Masri* Brief], 12 April 2012, para. 30, available at www.redress.org/downloads/El%20Masri%20-%20Grand%20Chamber%20brief.pdf and OSJI *El-Masri* Brief, para. 142.

[38] REDRESS intervention submission in *EctHR Varnava and Others* v. *Turkey* (Appl. Nos. 16064/90, 16065/90, 16066/90, 16068/90, 16069/90, 16070/90, 16071/90, 16072/90, and 16073/90), Judgment (Grand Chamber) 2 October 2008, para. 45, available at www.redress.org/Varnava%20Brief%20Final%202%20Oct%2008.pdf.

form of reparation owed to victims of disappearances and their next-of-kin, claiming that the Court had already implicitly inferred such a right as part of the right to be free from torture or ill-treatment (Article 3 ECHR), the right to an effective remedy (Article 13), and the right to an effective investigation and to be informed of the results (a procedural obligation under Articles 2, 3, 5, and 13).[39]

Second, REDRESS and OSJI challenged the ECtHR reluctance to reorder an investigation in the operative part of the judgment when the State has repeatedly failed to undertake one. According to the NGOs, as long as the truth is not elucidated, the ECtHR should consider that a persisting duty to investigate exists as a means of reparation when a State has violated both its duty to carry a thorough investigation into allegations of abuse and the right to an effective remedy.[40]

3 The 'Right to Truth' in Comparative Perspective

How successful have these attempts been in devising the contours of the 'right to truth'? As strategic litigation efforts have mainly focused on the IACtHR and ECtHR, the following sections assess to what extent the latter have recognised the 'right to truth' and whether this has any concrete implications.

3.1 The Inter-American Court of Human Rights: Between a Retributive and Restorative Approach

The IACtHR has evolved from the refusal to recognise this right in 1997, under the motive that it is 'inexistent in the American Convention',[41] to the declaration in 2000 that it is embedded in the right to access justice, as expressed in the following *dictum*:

> in the circumstances of the instant case, the right to the truth is subsumed in the right of the victim or his next of kin to obtain clarification of the facts relating to the violations and the corresponding responsibilities from the competent State organs, through the investigation and prosecution established in Articles 8 and 25 of the Convention.[42]

[39] *Ibid.*, paras. 14–15.

[40] REDRESS *El-Masri* Brief, paras. 25–8; OSJI *El-Masri* Brief, paras. 160–4.

[41] IACtHR, *Castillo-Páez* v. *Peru*, Judgment on merits, 3 November 1997, para. 86.

[42] IACtHR, *Bámaca-Velásquez* v. *Guatemala*, Judgment on merits, para. 201.

As the excerpt shows, the vision of truth developed by the judges from San José seems to mainly stem from a judicial and retributive approach. Firstly, in terms of legal foundations, the Court implicitly rejects that the 'right to truth' is autonomous,[43] preferring to derive it from the general duty to guarantee the rights contained in the ACHR (Article 1,1), together with the right to a fair trial (Article 8) and the right to judicial protection (Article 25). So far, it generally refuses to derive it from Article 13 governing freedom of expression,[44] contrary to the consistent demands of the Inter-American Commission and human rights groups such as OSJI. However, in *Gomes Lund* v. *Brazil*, the Court exceptionally accepted to derive the 'right to truth' from Article 13, further stating that:

> in cases of violations of human rights, the State authorities cannot resort to mechanisms such as official secret or confidentiality of the information, or reasons of public interest or national security, to refuse to supply the information required by the judicial or administrative authorities in charge of the ongoing investigation or pending procedures.[45]

Secondly, the Court further construes the 'right to truth' as a right to punitive justice, as illustrated by its unprecedented case-law on amnesties. Since 2001 onwards, it has evolved from a mitigating position, whereby the 'right to truth' was seen as a palliative to amnesties,[46] to a radical position outlawing amnesty laws, under the motive, *inter alia*, that they impede on victims' 'right to truth'.[47] In addition, it has strengthened victims' procedural access to all stages of the investigation and prosecution, thereby improving the status of victims in the proceedings.[48] Thirdly, it prioritises a criminal investigation of the 'right to truth' over non-judicial inquiries in case of potential conflict between TRCs and prosecutions, stating that 'the "historical truth" documented in the reports of special commissions does not complete or replace the State's obligation to establish the legal

[43] IACtHR, *Blanco Romero* v. *Venezuela*, Judgment, 28 November 2005, para. 62.

[44] IACtHR, *Case of the Rochela Massacre* v. *Colombia*, Judgment, 11 May 2007, para. 147; *Las Dos Erres Massacre* v. *Guatemala*, Judgment, 24 November 2009, para. 151.

[45] IACtHR, *Gomes-Lund* v. *Brazil*, para. 202. In two subsequent judgments, the Court clarified that it did not overturn its case-law, but that this decision was based on the particular circumstances of the case, as a specific request for information had been filed by the victims. See *Family Barrios* v. *Venezuela*, Judgment, 24 November 2011, para. 290 sq., footnote 378 and *Gudiel Álvarez et al.* (*'Diario Militar'*) v. *Guatemala*, Judgment, 20 November 2012, para. 269.

[46] IACtHR, *Castillo-Páez* v. *Peru*, paras. 89–90.

[47] IACtHR, *Barrios Altos* v. *Peru*, Judgment on merits, 14 March 2001, para. 43.

[48] IACtHR, *Case of the Rochela Massacre* v. *Colombia*, Judgment, 11 May 2007, para 195.

truth through judicial proceedings'.[49] Even though it acknowledges that TRCs and archive centres can contribute to 'historic truth'[50] and 'to build and safeguard historical memory',[51] it favours the ascertainment of truth through criminal investigations of all perpetrators. In disappearance cases, the Court recognises that victims' families have a substantial right to know the fate of the disappeared, and, in the event of death, the State has a duty to locate and identify mortal remains according to 'all possible technical and scientific means'[52] and to return the bodies to their family in order to allow proper burial according to their customs and religious beliefs.[53]

However, the Court also endorses a restorative vision of the 'right to truth' and recognises its collective dimension, especially when it comes to reparations. In addition to ordering further investigations into the violations, it has conceptualised a range of moral and symbolic reparation measures aimed at 'recovering the memory of the victims, re-establishing their reputation, consoling their next of kin or transmitting a message of official condemnation of the human rights violations in question and commitment to the efforts to ensure that they do not happen again'.[54] For instance, it has compelled States to erect memorials for the remembrance of specific historical events,[55] hold ceremonies of commemoration and issue public apologies to victims,[56] or publish excerpts of its judgment in the media.[57]

In sum, far from being redundant, the 'right to truth' has refined and 'enriched'[58] the content of existing rights in the IACtHR case-law, granting victims a status to participate in all proceedings related to the elucidation of the crimes and to formulate symbolic reparations aimed at preserving the memory of events or victims of State abuse. However, its most radical

[49] See, *inter alia*, IACtHR, *Almonacid Arellano et al.* v. *Chile*, 26 September 2006, para. 150; *Zambrano Vélez* v. *Ecuador*, Judgment, 4 July 2007, para. 128.

[50] IACtHR, *Goiburú et al.* v. *Paraguay*, Judgment, 22 September 2006, para. 81 at 93.

[51] IACtHR, *Zambrano Vélez* v. *Ecuador*, Judgment, 4 July 2007, para. 128.

[52] IACtHR, *Case of the 'Mapiripán massacre'* v. *Colombia*, Judgment, 15 September 2005, para. 305.

[53] IACtHR, *Villagrán-Morales et al.* v. Guatemala, Judgment on reparations, 26 May 2001, para. 102.

[54] *Ibid.*, para. 84.

[55] IACtHR, *Case of the 'Mapiripán massacre'* v. *Colombia*, Judgment, 15 September 2005, para. 315.

[56] *Ibid.*, para. 314; *Moiwana Community* v. *Surinam*, Judgment, 15 June 2005, para. 216.

[57] *Bámaca-Velásquez case* (reparations), para. 84.

[58] L. Burgorgue-Larsen and A. Ubeda de Torres, *Les grandes décisions de la Cour interaméricaine des droits de l'homme* (Brussels: Bruylant, 2008), 749.

contribution to a fragmented international law consists in granting victims an unprecedented enforceable right to have perpetrators prosecuted and punished, which remains a minority position in international law.[59]

3.2 *The European Court of Human Rights: To Recognise or Not to Recognise?*

Although the 'right to truth' has been expressly recognised more than a decade ago by the IACtHR, it has only recently permeated the ECtHR under the influence of global truth activists. Even though the ECtHR first avoided answering REDRESS claims about the 'right to truth' in *Varnava and Others* v. *Turkey*, it eventually addressed them in later judgments, although in an ambivalent way.

In the 2011 case of *Association '21 December 1989'* v. *Romania*, concerning the failure of Romania to investigate the circumstances of the massacres of anti-government protesters during the Romanian revolution in 1989, the ECtHR found a procedural violation of Article 2 (right to life) and pointed out:

> the importance of the right of victims and their families and dependants to know the truth about the circumstances of events involving massive violations of fundamental rights such as the right to life, which implies the right to effective judicial investigation and the possible right to compensation.[60]

Here, the ECtHR exceptionally reordered the State to conduct an effective investigation as a measure of reparation, seemingly announcing a more flexible stance to reparations.

However, in *El-Masri* v. *Macedonia*, it did not take this approach. In that judgment, the Court mentioned the impediment on victims' 'right to truth' as part of the inadequate character of the investigation under the procedural duties of Article 3 (right to be free from torture or inhuman treatment). It further regretted that '[t]he concept of "State secrets" has often been invoked to obstruct the search for the truth' in rendition cases.[61] The recognition of the 'right to truth' is nevertheless controversial, as illustrated by the individual opinions of judges. A few judges oppose a separate and specific analysis of the 'right to truth' and consider it 'redundant'

[59] On this issue, see more generally A. Seibert-Fohr, *Prosecuting Serious Human Rights Violations* (Oxford University Press, 2009).

[60] ECtHR, *Association '21 December 1989'* v. *Romania* (Appl. No. 33810/07), Judgment, 24 May 2011, para. 144.

[61] *El-Masri* case, para. 191.

with the procedural right to a thorough investigation into gross violations under Articles 2 and 3 ECHR.[62] The Court has indeed consistently held that an effective investigation implies clarification of all facts, victims' access to the procedure and inquiry results, and public scrutiny.[63] Others consider the Court 'too timid' in recognising the 'right to truth' under the motive that it is '[neither] a novel concept in [the ECtHR] case-law, and nor is it a new right'.[64] The latter judges also argued that '[a] more explicit acknowledgment of the right to the truth in the context of Article 13 of the Convention [right to an effective remedy], far from being either innovative or superfluous, would in a sense cast renewed light on a well-established reality'.[65] Thus, they endorse a right to factual truth, construed as a 'right of access to relevant information about alleged violations, both for the persons concerned and for the general public'.[66] In this context, the allusion to the 'right to truth' in the judgment appears mostly symbolic, as it did not trigger any substantial change in the Court case-law. For example, the Court has not reordered any investigation as a measure of reparation, which is in line with its general principle of the discretion of States to choose how to conform with ECtHR decision (Article 46). The Court has also not embraced a more diversified spectrum of restorative measures of reparations and equally refuses to grant other remedies.

A few months earlier, in *Janowiec* v. *Russia*, before the Grand Chamber referral, the fifth Chamber referred to the manipulation of history by the Soviet and Polish communist authorities (who imposed an official version of the Katyn massacres as killings orchestrated by the Nazis) as an additional element of suffering of the relatives in the context of Article 3, stating that:

> The Court appreciates that the applicants suffered a double trauma: not only had their relatives perished in the war but they were not allowed, for political reasons, to learn the truth about what had happened and were forced to accept the distortion of historical fact by the Soviet and Polish Communist authorities for more than fifty years.[67]

[62] *Ibid.*, Joint concurring opinion of Judges Casadevall and López Guerra.

[63] See *inter alia*, ECtHR *Aksoy* v. *Turkey* (Appl. No. 21987/93), Judgment, 18 December 1996; ECtHR *McKerr* v. *The United Kingdom* (Appl. No. 28883/95), Judgment, 4 May 2001, paras. 157–60.

[64] *El-Masri* case, Joint Concurring Opinion of Judges Tulkens, Spielmann, Sicilianos, and Keller, para. 5.

[65] *Ibid.*, para. 7.

[66] *Ibid.*, para. 4.

[67] ECtHR, *Janowiec* v. *Russia* (Appl. Nos. 55508/07 and 29520/09), Judgment, 16 April 2012, para. 156.

This excerpt shows a willingness on the part of Strasbourg judges to also consider obstacles to the 'right to truth' as a *substantial* violation of the right to be free from torture and inhuman or degrading treatment or punishment under Article 3. However, the Grand Chamber later reversed the decision. Not only did it remain silent on the 'right to truth',[68] but it also treated the failure of Russia to disclose the investigative files and to submit to the Court copies of the classified decision terminating the criminal case as a violation of the State procedural duty to cooperate with the Court (Article 38). This was thus a finding of a procedural violation *vis-à-vis* the *Court* itself, not a substantive violation vis-à-vis the *applicants' right to truth*.[69]

In addition, like the majority of the IACtHR decisions under the ACHR, the ECtHR refuses to consider the 'right to truth' under Article 10 of the ECHR. In the *El-Masri* case, it rejected as 'manifestly ill-founded' the applicants' claim that the authorities' refusal to acknowledge and disclose the victim's rendition violated his and the public's 'right to truth' under Article 10.[70] However, the Court symbolically recognised that the 'right to truth' regarding the relevant circumstances of the case does not belong solely to the victim and his or her family, but also belongs to the general public.[71] In addition, although the Court does not recognise a 'right to truth' arising from Article 10, it increasingly condemns States under Article 10 when they invoke unjustified restrictions to classified documentation.[72] Even if the ECtHR refuses to connect the 'right to truth' with the right to freedom of expression, its case-law under Article 10 has thus started shifting regarding access to information.

So far, the specificity of the 'right to truth' compared to existing rights remains unclear in the Strasbourg case-law. The ECtHR's hesitance to give a distinct meaning to the 'right to truth' is likely to frustrate truth activists, who want to derive more than mere symbolic recognition from the Court's case-law. As it stands now, the ECtHR falls below the aspirations of its promoters, while the IACtHR has generally endorsed the latter's claims. However, even if the full potential of the 'right to truth' imagined by truth

[68] See, however, partially dissident opinion of Judges Ziemele, Gaetano, Laffranque and Keller, paras. 9 and 24.

[69] ECtHR *Janowiec* v. *Russia* (Appl. Nos. 55508/07 and 29520/09), Judgment (Grand Chamber) 21 October 2013, para. 216.

[70] *El-Masri*, paras. 264–5. See also *Al-Nashiri* v. *Poland*, paras. 581–2.

[71] *Al-Nashiri* v. *Poland*, para. 495.

[72] ECtHR, *Youth Initiative for Human Rights* v. *Serbia*, Judgment, 25 June 2013, para. 20.

activists is not yet realised at the ECtHR, this may open up avenues for further litigation.

4 Conclusion: Between Utopia and Dystopia

Notwithstanding the ongoing challenges of the recognition of the 'right to truth' before the ECtHR, the concept has gained momentum in UN human rights bodies, which accommodate a maximalist vision of the 'right to truth'. In addition to promoting trials and truth commissions as privileged institutions to implement the 'right to truth',[73] the UN Office of the High Commissioner for Human Rights recommends best practices regarding programmes of witness protection in trials of gross violations of human rights, the preservation of archives related to State abuse, and the use of forensic techniques to exhume mass graves and identify human remains.[74] The 'right to truth' increasingly becomes a UN institutional symbol for memory practices, as illustrated by the creation of both a special rapporteur position[75] and an 'International Day for the Right to the Truth'.[76]

This institutionalisation of truth-seeking practices reconfigures the discourse of international law in the direction of new utopias. The idea that, through law, it becomes possible to shed light on 'the truth' about State-sponsored abuse and counter State denialism, is one of them. In this sense, the idea of a 'right to truth' might be mystifying in the light of the difficulties to enforce State cooperation in the context of highly politically motivated crimes. Whether the 'right to truth' is exercised through TRCs or Courts, the dependency of investigators or prosecutors on State cooperation and their over-reliance on perpetrators' or witnesses' accounts reflects the inherent limitations of truth-seeking mechanisms.[77] It also raises false expectations that an objective conception of truth can be reached through

[73] OHCHR, *Study on the Right to Truth*, UN Doc. E/CN.4/2006/91 (2006); *Rule-of-Law Tools for Post-Conflict States: Truth Commissions* (2006).

[74] OHCHR, annual reports *Right to the Truth*, A/HRC/12/19 (21 August 2009) and A/HRC/15/33 (28 July 2010); *Report on the Right to the Truth and on Forensic Genetics and Human Rights*, A/HRC/15/26 (24 August 2010); *Report on the Seminar on Experiences of Archives as a Means to Guarantee the Right to the Truth*, A/HRC/17/21 (14 April 2011).

[75] UNHRC, Resolution 18/7 *Special Rapporteur on the Promotion of Truth, Justice, Reparation and Guarantees of Non-recurrence*, A/HRC/18/7 (29 September 2011).

[76] UNGA Resolution, *Proclamation of 24 March as the International Day for the Right to the Truth concerning Gross Human Rights Violations and for the Dignity of Victims*, A/RES/65/196 (21 December 2010).

[77] N. Combs, *Fact-Finding without Facts: The Uncertain Evidentiary Foundations of International Criminal Convictions* (Cambridge University Press, 2010); R. Wilson,

particular epistemologies recently sanctified by international law in the context of mass atrocities, which espouse the language of scientific truth, such as 'forensic science'.[78]

Furthermore, the normalisation of the 'right to truth' as a multifaceted, polysemic category undermines its enforceability, given the evasiveness of its definition and contours.[79] The flexibility of the norm, praised by scholars and practitioners as a way to better adapt a situation to local realities,[80] also encourages States to favour the least politically costly option available to them. This is clearly exemplified by States' interventions at the UN Panel on the 'right to truth' organised by the Human Rights Council in Geneva in 2010 to clarify its content and legal status.[81] States' accounts reveal relativist, *à la carte* interpretations of the concept, which point to the political uses of the 'right to truth'. For instance, delegates from Morocco, Colombia, Brazil, and Uruguay omitted the judicial and punitive facet of the 'right to truth' from their statements, precisely at a time when prosecutions for past human rights abuse were hindered by amnesty laws or lack of political will. Another utopia concerns truth activists' faith in the progressive defeat of impunity towards which international law would lead us,[82] contrary to empirical evidence[83] and the constant surge of amnesties.[84] For instance, the contribution of truth commissions to the fight against impunity remains largely rhetorical because they predominantly operate within contexts of

The Politics of Truth and Reconciliation in South Africa: Legitimizing the Post-Apartheid State (Cambridge University Press, 2001).

78 On the limits of forensic expertise as an applied science and the epistemological controversies on its objectivity, see M. Klinkner, 'Forensic Science Expertise for International Criminal Proceedings: An Old Problem, a New Context and a Pragmatic Resolution', *The International Journal of Evidence and proof* 13:2 (2009), 102–29 and from the same author, 'Proving Genocide? Forensic Expertise and the ICTY', *Journal of International Criminal Justice* 6:3 (2008), 447–66.

79 See more generally, Y. Naqvi, 'The Right to the Truth in International Law: Fact or Fiction?', *International Review of the Red Cross* 88:862 (2006), 245–73.

80 J. Méndez, 'Accountability for Past Abuses', *Human Rights Quarterly* 19:2 (1997), 255–82.

81 UNHRC, *Panel Discussion on the Right to Truth* following Resolution 9/11 (13th session, 9 March 2010).

82 N. Roht-Arriaza and J. Mariezcurrena (eds.), *Transitional Justice in the Twenty-First Century: Beyond Truth versus Justice*, 1st ed. (Cambridge University Press, 2006); Amnesty International, 'Commissioning Justice', April 2010, London, ed. *Amnesty International*, index POL 30/004/2010.

83 UNHRC, *Report of UN Special Rapporteur on the Promotion of Truth, Justice, Reparation and Guarantees of Non-recurrence*, UN Doc A/HRC/24/42 (2013), para. 24 ('In practice, only a fraction of those who bear responsibility for violations are ever even investigated.').

84 L. Mallinder, *Amnesty, Human Rights and Political Transitions: Bridging the Peace and Justice Divide* (Oxford: Hart Publishing, 2008), 19.

legal or *de facto* amnesties. The anti-impunity turn has also given way to an era of confessions and apology over human rights violations,[85] which further reflects the moralisation of international law. Finally, the utopia of the therapeutic function of the 'right to truth', both for victims and societies, attests to the increasing psychologisation of international law.[86] However, these assumptions on the transformative impact of truth-telling technologies on individuals and societies largely function as articles of faith[87] and tend to replicate problematic representations of victims in terms of intimacy and agency.[88] For instance, on behalf of the 'healing power of truth', State-sponsored ceremonies to (re)bury the dead for family members often equate with politics of forced closure, allowing little or no room for the possibility of irreversible loss and indefinite bereavement.

These newly assigned roles of international law should also not obscure some of the more insidious risks or effects of these utopias. On the dystopian side, the proliferation and bureaucratisation of truth-seeking practices have led to a managerialisation of memory practices, which transforms political problems into technical ones. However, as Martti Koskeniemmi argues, 'managerialism has its concealed normativity that privileges values and actors occupying dominant positions in international institutions'.[89] Unsurprisingly, the politics of truth and memory promoted by the UN human rights bodies are contingent on their own structural bias. For instance, the United Nations have avoided civil society memorial initiatives aimed at commemorating their own responsibility in the Srebrenica massacres of July 1995 in Bosnia-Herzegovina.[90]

[85] M. Gibney *et al.* (eds.), *The Age of Apology. Facing Up to the Past* (Pennsylvania University Press, 2008).

[86] On the therapeutic ethos of truth commissions, see C. Moon, 'Healing Past Violence: Traumatic Assumptions and Therapeutic Interventions in War and Reconciliation', *Journal of Human Rights* 8:1 (2009), 71–91.

[87] D. Mendeloff, 'Truth-Seeking, Truth-Telling, and Postconflict Peacebuilding: Curb the Enthusiasm?', *International Studies Review* 6:3 (2004), 355–80; E. Daly, 'Truth Skepticism: An Inquiry into the Value of Truth in Times of Transition', *International Journal of Transitional Justice* 2:1 (2008), 23-41; J. Clark, 'Transitional Justice, Truth and Reconciliation: An Under-Explored Relationship', *International Criminal Law Review* 11:2 (2011), 241–61.

[88] T. Madlingozi, 'On Transitional Justice Entrepreneurs and the Production of Victims', *Journal of Human Rights Practice* 2:2 (2010), 208–28.

[89] M. Koskenniemi, 'The Politics of International Law – 20 Years Later', *European Journal of International Law* 20:1 (2009), 16.

[90] O. Simic, '"Pillar of Shame": Civil Society, UN Accountability and Genocide in Srebrenica', in O. Simic and Z. Volcic (eds.), *Transitional Justice and Civil Society in the Balkans* (New York: Springer, 2013), 181–99.

The lack of accountability of the United Nations for the Srebrenica massacres has thus been paired with an Alzheimer's-like official politics, which points to the asymmetry of politics of remembrance and mourning. In addition, the *régimes* of truth and reconciliation fuel an entire memory industry composed of 'truth experts' that has become global and highly lucrative.[91] The advent of the 'right to truth' arguably plays into a memory lobby dominated by a few western international human rights NGOs who tend to replicate 'toolkits' and standardised models of truth-seeking,[92] from Kosovo[93] to Colombia,[94] with the support of the United Nations human rights bodies[95] and domestic NGOs which have internalised the global transitional justice agenda.[96] Despite formal emphasis on the importance of local context,[97] the quasi-systematic intervention of these new global experts in the aftermath of atrocities tends to depoliticise the issue of how sovereign people wish to address a violent past by resorting to hegemonic models of truth inquiry most often ill-adapted to local realities.[98] Finally, victims' testimonies in TRCs or trials for human rights violations are often silenced or edited for

[91] K. Bilbija and L. Payne (eds.), *Accounting for Violence: Marketing Memory in Latin America* (Durham and London: Duke University Press, 2011); K. Theidon, 'Editorial Note', *International Journal of Transitional Justice* 3:3 (2009), 295–300.

[92] J. Subotic, 'The Transformation of International Transitional Justice Advocacy', *International Journal of Transitional Justice* 6:1 (2012), 106–25; R. Nagy, 'Transitional Justice as Global Project: Critical Reflections', *Third World Quaterly* 29:2 (2008), 275–89; N. Fritz, 'Made to Order? Transitional Justice Initiatives in the Developing World, or the Truths We Should Be Telling' in C. Eisgruber and A. Sajo (eds.), *Global Justice and the Bulwarks of Localism in Human Rights Context* (Leiden: Martinus Nijhoff Publishers, 2005), 317–31.

[93] A. Di Lellio and C. McCurn, 'Engineering Grassroots Transitional Justice in the Balkans: The Case of Kosovo', *East European Politics and Societies* 27:1 (2013), 129–48.

[94] D. Lecombe, *'Nous sommes tous en faveur des victimes'. La diffusion de la justice transitionnelle en Colombie* (Paris: LGDJ, 2014).

[95] See e.g., L. Kent, *The Dynamics of Transitional Justice: International Models and Local Realities in East Timor* (Oxford: Routledge, 2012); P. Naftali, 'The Politics of Truth: on Legal Fetishism and the Rhetoric of Complementarity', *Revue Québecoise de Droit International* (special issue December 2015), 101–28.

[96] See note 93.

[97] See e.g., UN Secretary General 'Report on The Rule of Law and Transitional Justice in Conflict and Post-Conflict Societies' (2004), UN Doc S/2004/616 at paras. 15–20.

[98] Of course, this does not mean that domestic actors do not ultimately resist, appropriate, or transform these international models. See e.g., D. Lecombe, 'Nous sommes tous en faveur des victimes'. *La diffusion de la justice transitionnelle en Colombie* (Paris: LGDJ, 2014); J. Rowen, '"We Don't Believe in Transitional Justice": Peace and the Politics of Legal Ideas in Colombia', *Law and Social Inquiry* 41 (2016, doi:10.1111/lsi.12262).

diverse agendas,[99] including the vested interests of the promoters of the global transitional justice project.

As Jean Carbonnier once wrote, '[i]t is so rare for the law to proclaim its own limits'.[100] If the 'right to truth' thus embodies several utopian projects to further expand the functions and boundaries of international law, it oscillates between promise and pathos, legal innovation and legal fetishism, idealism, and imperialism. Given its elusiveness, the 'right to truth' will undoubtedly continue to inspire more actors to try to erode other highly sensitive State prerogatives or other areas governed by secrecy. Whether it can serve as an antidote to the denialism of atrocities, whether it will become a tool for consensual, mainstream, or subversive truths, or whether it triggers new paradigms or more illusions for victims of State crimes remains to be seen and assessed on a case-by-case basis.

[99] See *inter alia* R. Wilson, note 77 and B. M. French, 'Technologies of Telling: Discourse, Transparency, and Erasure in Guatemalan Truth Commission Testimony', *Journal of Human Rights* 8:1 (2009), 92–109.

[100] J. Carbonnier, *Flexible droit. Pour une sociologie du droit sans rigueur*, 10th ed. (Paris: LGDJ, 2001), 74. Personal translation from French ('Il est si rare que le droit proclame ses propres limites').

PART II

European Law
(Council of Europe and the European Union)

4

Kononov v. *Latvia* as an Ontological Security Struggle over Remembering the Second World War

MARIA MÄLKSOO

1 Introduction

More than seventy years apart from today, the Second World War is still the past that refuses to pass. This chapter examines a case that illuminates broader mnemonical and legal reverberations of the events of the war as it unfolded in the European periphery in 1944. If law is a medium of collective remembrance, what role is allocated to international legal rulings by states fighting for the wider recognition of their central mnemonic narratives? This chapter delves into the uncharted relations between international adjudication and the ontological security-seeking behaviour of states. Ontological security refers to a sense of a continuous and stable 'self', having that sense confirmed by the others and being thus reassured about one's own continuity in, and confidence vis-à-vis the world.[1] As the

This contribution was supported by the institutional research funding (IUT20-39) of the Estonian Ministry of Education and Research and the Mobilitas post-doctoral programme of the European Social Fund (GSHRG060MJ).

1 For the various applications of ontological security from psychoanalysis and social theory to International Relations (IR), see R. D. Laing, *The Divided Self: An Existential Study in Sanity and Madness* (London: Tavistock, 1960); A. Giddens, *The Constitution of Society: Outline of the Theory of Structuration* (Berkeley and Los Angeles, CA: University of California Press, 1984), and A. Giddens, *Modernity and Self-Identity: Self and Society in the Late Modern Age* (Stanford, CA: Stanford University Press, 1991); J. Huysmans, 'Security! What Do You Mean? From Concept to Thick Signifier', *European Journal of International Relations* 4:2 (1998), 226–55; C. Kinnvall, 'Globalization and Religious Nationalism: Self, Identity, and the Search for Ontological Security', *Political Psychology* 25:5 (2004), 741–67; J. Mitzen, 'Ontological Security in World Politics: State Identity and the Security Dilemma', *European Journal of International Relations* 12:3 (2006), 341–70; B. Steele, *Ontological Security in International Relations: Self-Identity and the IR State* (New York: Routledge, 2008); A. Krolikowski, 'State Personhood in Ontological Security Theories of International Relations and Chinese Nationalism: A Sceptical View', *Chinese Journal of International Politics* 2:1 (2008), 109–33; A. Zarakol, 'Ontological (In)Security and State Denial of Historical Crimes: Turkey and Japan', *International Relations* 24:1 (2010), 3–23, and A. Zarakol, 'States and Ontological

pursuit of ontological security is allegedly central to the human condition,[2] driving by extension also state behaviour, states seek to perform actions in order to underwrite their notions of 'who they are'.[3] Besides physical survival as a legal person,[4] continuity as a certain kind of actor is thus essential for states. Retaining a sense of continuous state identity becomes particularly acute in periods of political transformation, such as in transitions from non-democratic to democratic regimes or from the suppression by a foreign power to self-government.[5] Transitional legal rulings therefore entail considerable potential as political tools in the identity-building contestations of states dealing with a repressive period in their overlapping histories in various ways. The invoking of international judicial authorities such as the European Court of Human Rights (ECtHR) in the course of these ontological security-seeking struggles of states allows us to interrogate the function and the weighting role of international court rulings on the contested historical memory in question.[6]

My central argument is that as international court rulings enable the legal crystallisation of particular mnemonic narratives, they can reinforce

---

Security: A Historical Rethinking', *Cooperation and Conflict* 52:1 (2017), 48–68; A. Lupovici, 'Ontological Dissonance, Clashing Identities, and Israel's Unilateral Steps towards the Palestinians', *Review of International Studies* 38:4 (2012), 809–33; S. Croft, 'Constructing Ontological Insecurity: The Insecuritization of Britain's Muslims', *Contemporary Security Policy* 33:2 (2012), 219–35; T. Solomon, 'Attachment, Tautology, and Ontological Security', *Critical Studies on Security* 1:1 (2013), 130–2; K. Gustafsson, 'Memory Politics and Ontological Security in Sino-Japanese Relations', *Asian Studies Review* 38:1 (2014), 71–86; B. Rumelili, 'Identity and Desecuritisation: The Pitfalls of Conflating Ontological and Physical Security', *Journal of International Relations and Development* 18:1 (2015), 52–74, and B. Rumelili (ed.), *Conflict Resolution and Ontological Security: Peace Anxieties* (New York: Routledge, 2015); J. Subotić, 'Narrative, Ontological Security, and Foreign Policy Change', *Foreign Policy Analysis* 12:4 (2016), 610–27; C. Rossdale, 'Enclosing Critique: The Limits of Ontological Security', *International Political Sociology* 9:4 (2015), 369–86; M. Mälksoo, 'Memory Must be Defended': Beyond the Politics of Mnemonical Security, *Security Dialogue* 46:3 (2015), 221–37.

2 C. Browning, 'Ethics and Ontological Security', in J. Nyman and A. Burke (eds.), *Ethical Security Studies: A New Research Agenda* (London and New York: Routledge, 2016), 160–73. See also the special issue 'Ontological Securities in World Politics', *Cooperation and Conflict* 52:1 (2017), especially the introduction by C. Kinnvall and J. Mitzen, 3–11.

3 Zarakol, 'Ontological (In)Security and State Denial of Historical Crimes', 3.

4 See Art. 1 of the Montevideo Convention on the Rights and Duties of States, 1933.

5 Note, however, that unlike in IR, state identity and continuity have an identical meaning in international legal sense. See K. Marek, *Identity and Continuity of States in Public International Law* (Geneva: Librairie Droz, 1954); J. R. Crawford, *The Creation of States in International Law*, 2nd edn (Oxford University Press, 2007).

6 See Preface and Introduction in the present volume.

or undermine the international status of competing biographical narratives of states contesting for the affirmation of their respective 'life-stories', and the consistency of their 'selves' thereof.[7] This proposition is illustrated with an analysis of the *Kononov* v. *Latvia* case in the ECtHR, offering a microcosm of Russia's and the Baltic states' competing claims on ontological security in pursuing a particular pan-European remembrance of the Second World War.

The *Kononov* case enables a close-up study of the complex relationship between law and memory against the backdrop of Russia's 'memory wars' with its former Soviet subjugate states, whereby Russia's hegemonic mnemonic narrative of the 'Great Patriotic War' and the USSR's role in defeating Nazi Germany clashes with the critical accounts of the Soviet crimes in the occupied territories.[8] The debates and proceedings on the *Kononov* v. *Latvia* case in the ECtHR in 2008[9] and 2010[10] have been examined from the perspectives of international criminal and humanitarian law, human rights law, and transitional justice.[11] This chapter explores the case through the lens of ontological security, taking the *Kononov* case to be an emblematic illustration of competing Russian and Baltic claims on the narrative consistency of their state 'selves' and their conflicting bids on the legitimate remembrance of the Second World War and the Soviet legacy in general.[12] This case and the surrounding discussions offer an

[7] This resonates closely with Eric Heinze's discussion in the present volume about law's tendency to add *expressive*, rather than *substantive weight* to a preferred version of history, promoting it at the expense of alternative versions which are equally competing for the authoritative shaping of public understandings of the past.

[8] M. Mälksoo, 'Nesting Orientalisms at War: World War II and the "Memory War" in Eastern Europe', in T. Barkawi and K. Stanski (eds.), *Orientalism and War* (New York: Columbia University Press, 2013), 177–95.

[9] ECtHR, *Kononov* v. *Latvia* (Appl. No. 36376/04), Judgment, 24 July 2008.

[10] ECtHR, *Kononov* v. *Latvia* (Appl. No. 36376/04), Judgment (Grand Chamber), 17 May 2010.

[11] G. Pinzauti, 'The European Court of Human Rights' Incidental Application of International Criminal Law and Humanitarian Law: A Critical Discussion of Kononov v. Latvia', *Journal of International Criminal Justice*, 6 (2008), 1043–60; L. Mälksoo, 'Casenote on *Kononov* v. *Latvia*', *The American Journal of International Law*, 105:1 (2011), 101–8; A. Buyse, 'The Truth, the Past and the Present: Article 10 ECHR and the Situations of Transitions', in A. Buyse and M. Hamilton (eds.), *Transitional Jurisprudence and the ECHR: Justice, Politics and Rights* (Cambridge University Press, 2011), 131–50; J. A. Sweeney, 'Transitional Criminal Justice at the ECtHR: Implications for the Universality of Human Rights', *Baltic Yearbook of International Law* 12:1 (2012), 183–210.

[12] See also N. Muižnieks, 'Latvian-Russian Memory Battles at the European Court of Human Rights', in N. Muižnieks (ed.), *The Geopolitics of History in Latvian-Russian Relations* (Riga: Academic Press of the University of Latvia, 2011), 219–38.

evocative window into the contested readings of the conduct and consequences of the war in the East European 'bloodlands'.[13] The political repercussions of the ECtHR's verdict on the case demonstrate how international legal rulings can be invoked as validating or discrediting states' biographical self-narratives (of which mnemonical narratives occupy a central place). By extension, while ontological security as applied in the study of international relations refers to the close nexus between state identity and its sense of security, it can be embedded in, or confirmed by, international legal rulings. Besides underscoring the diverging directions of Latvia's and Russia's politics of transitional justice, the case of *Kononov* v. *Latvia* also illustrates their respective appeals on the ECtHR as a political resource in their distinct struggles of coming to terms with the Soviet past.[14]

Kononov v. *Latvia* has furthermore a strong transnational resonance for the broader European community. The case highlights how justice established in trials addressing past international wrongdoings and human rights abuses can itself become a new form of remembrance, and the respective legal decision, consequently, a vehicle of collective memory at a pan-European scale.[15] Legal processes help to establish and buttress a particular historical account, while records of the trial and judgment remain enduring representations of the newly established 'regime of truth'.[16] The historical accounting of the criminal trial has therefore noteworthy 'truth effects' besides the production of justice.[17] As transitional historical accountings draw a line that redefines a past and reconstructs actors' political identities,[18] 'the jurisprudence serves a fixative role', as the finality of legal judgment could settle contested understandings of history.[19] Trials of transitional historical justice seek not just to adjudicate individual responsibility, but to draw a normative line between a condemnable past and a legitimate present, to publicly instantiate the past wrongdoings in order to establish the truth about the event in controversy vis-à-vis the predecessor regime. As such, they enable

[13] T. Snyder, *Bloodlands: Europe between Hitler and Stalin* (New York: Basic Books, 2010).

[14] Cf. the chapters by Koposov, Klymenko, Přibáň, Miluna, Cercel, and Könczöl in the present volume.

[15] See D. Levy and N. Sznaider, *Human Rights and Memory: Essays on Human Rights* (University Park, PA: The Pennsylvania State University Press, 2010), 18–19.

[16] R. G. Teitel, *Transitional Justice* (Oxford University Press, 2000), 72.

[17] *Ibid.*, 72–3.

[18] *Ibid.*, 8.

[19] M. Hamilton and A. Buyse, Introduction in A. Buyse and M. Hamilton (eds.), *Transitional Jurisprudence and the ECHR: Justice, Politics and Rights* (Cambridge University Press, 2011), 6.

the establishment of a historical record at the highest legal standard of certainty, as well as a public airing of the country's past through a particular representation of the past regime.[20] It is in that sense legal rulings amount to the 'hardware' of memory,[21] a highly regarded resource for supporting an actor's sense of a continuous 'self' (or its ontological security). Magnifying a particular historical account, international legal proceedings and court decisions likewise entail the potential of becoming sources of interpreting history *in spe*, for history is 'memory seen through [...] documents'.[22]

This chapter outlines first the Latvian-Russian mnemonical disagreement over the assessment of the events of the Second World War in the region, as displayed in the *Kononov* case. It then moves on to argue how a particular interpretation and remembrance of the war and the Soviet legacy more generally sustains the biographical accounts of the states under investigation, bolstering their respective claims on ontological security. The conceptual point of departure for such a take is a narrative understanding of state identity.[23] Accordingly, the biographical narrative is of central importance for state identity 'because it is the locus through which agents "work out" their understanding of social settings and the placement of their Selves in those settings'.[24] The stories states tell about themselves have behavioural consequences: identities are not only *told*, they are also *enacted*. Since states allegedly seek consistency between their self-identity narratives and their behaviour in international politics, to increase their credibility and to defend them from threats to that identity, their international behaviour is expressive of state identity.[25] A state's biographical narrative constitutes and maintains its 'self', giving life to routinised foreign policy actions.[26] The ability to maintain a consistent and socially recognised story about oneself therefore determines the coherent 'actorness' of

[20] Teitel, *Transitional Justice*, 72–3.

[21] Cf. A. Etkind, 'Hard and Soft in Cultural Memory: Political Mourning in Russia and Germany', *Grey Room* 16 (2004), 36–59; A. Etkind, 'Post-Soviet Hauntology: Cultural Memory of the Soviet Terror', *Constellations* 16:1 (2009), 182–200.

[22] J. Winter, 'The Performance of the Past: Memory, History, Identity', in K. Tilmans, F. van Vree and J. Winter (eds.), *Performing the Past: Memory, History, and Identity in Modern Europe* (Amsterdam: Amsterdam University Press, 2010), 12.

[23] E.g., C. Epstein, 'Who Speaks? Discourse, the Subject, and the Study of Identity in International Relations', *European Journal of International Relations* 17:2 (2011), 327–50. See also Steele, *Ontological Security*, 20; F. Berenskoetter, 'Parameters of a National Biography', *European Journal of International Relations* 20:1 (2014), 262–88.

[24] Steele, *Ontological Security*, 7.

[25] *Ibid.*, 11.

[26] *Ibid.*, 3.

states in world politics. Narratives and practices send signals about state's intentions to its international counterparts. It is thus necessary to analyse both discourse and practice; both what is being said and actually done. The conclusion recapitulates the broader implications of the ECtHR's final judgment on the case of *Kononov* v. *Latvia* for the remembrance of the Second World War and the Soviet legacy in Europe at large.

2 *Kononov* v. *Latvia* as a Legal Act in the Baltic-Russian 'Memory War' on the Second World War

The Russian and Baltic readings of the course, consequences, and ramifications of the Second World War, as well as their general assessment of the Soviet legacy, diverge considerably both at the 'collected' (or aggregated individual) and 'collective' levels of social remembrance.[27] Their respective state-led politics of memory have evocatively embodied the antagonistic understandings of the course and results of the war in the region across all five policy domains listed by Thomas U. Berger as the constituents of a country's 'official historical narrative' (i.e. rhetoric, commemoration, education, compensation, and punishment).[28] For the Republic of Latvia, as for the other Baltic states of Estonia and Lithuania, the Soviet Union was one of the aggressors in the Second World War, responsible for their loss of independence for the better part of the second half of the twentieth century. Accordingly, the three Baltic states were subjected to military occupation and subsequent annexation by the Soviet Union following the Molotov-Ribbentrop Pact of 23 August 1939 between the USSR and Germany. Since the incorporation of Estonia, Latvia, and Lithuania into the Soviet Union in 1940 ensued from the illegal threat of force, military aggression, and occupation, these countries continued to exist as states under international law even though they were *de facto* annexed by the Soviet Union (following the legal principle of *ex injuria non oritur jus*, or illegal acts cannot create law).[29] Along with the other Baltic states and Poland, Latvia has consequently emerged as one of the most vocal advocates of criminal and historical justice[30] vis-à-vis former communist regimes,

[27] J. K. Olick, 'Collective Memory: The Two Cultures', *Sociological Theory* 17:3 (1999), 333–48.

[28] T. U. Berger, *War, Guilt, and World Politics after World War II* (Cambridge University Press, 2012), 12.

[29] For the outline of the legal argument, see L. Mälksoo, *Illegal Annexation and State Continuity: The Case of the Incorporation of the Baltic States by the USSR* (Leiden and Boston: Martinus Nijhoff, 2003).

[30] See Teitel, *Transitional Justice* for this taxonomy.

hailing for a pan-European moral, political, and legal condemnation of the totalitarian communist legacy in Europe.[31] In 2010, Latvia was among six East European states calling for the European Commission to criminalise the denial of crimes perpetrated by communist regimes in the same way a number of European Union countries have banned the public condoning, denial and gross trivialisation of the Holocaust.[32]

For the Russian Federation as the legal continuator of the USSR, the 'Great Patriotic War' and the victory thereof marked the emergence of the Soviet Union as a great power internationally, as well as standing for the Soviet people's selfless defence of Europe from Nazism. According to the official Russian line, the incorporation of the Baltic states to the USSR was voluntary, and in any way legitimate, considering the security situation created by Nazi Germany in the build-up to the war. Many Baltic politicians have been vocally critical of the narrative of the Soviet 'Great Patriotic War' as a solely defensive enterprise against Nazi aggression for this narrative invariably ignores or discounts the significance of Nazi-Soviet collaboration under the auspices of the non-aggression treaty of 1939.

The case of *Kononov* v. *Latvia* involves a number of vehemently contested issues in the Russian-Baltic memory debates. These include the legal status of Latvia in the Second World War; the problem of how to reckon with the crimes committed in the name of the Soviet regime by Soviet military personnel; the status of persons linked to the military organs of Soviet power in the former Soviet territories that restored their independent statehood in 1991; the question of whether Russia as the 'state-continuator' of the Soviet Union in international legal terms has inherited any responsibility for the internationally wrongful acts of the Soviet regime; and last not least, could an individual who fought on the side of the Allies in the Second World War be tried for war crimes.[33] *Kononov* v. *Latvia* furthermore exemplifies the Baltic-Russian disagreement on the alleged universality of the Nuremberg principles.[34] While the Baltic states have pushed for holding the standard formulated at Nuremberg to be universal in the context of the Second World War, Russia has essentially spoken for the discriminatory concept of war crimes, arguing that in terms of *jus in bello*, more was permitted

[31] For a comprehensive account, see E.-C. Pettai and V. Pettai, *Transitional and Retrospective Justice in the Baltic States* (Cambridge University Press, 2014).

[32] The other five signatories of the request were Bulgaria, the Czech Republic, Hungary, Lithuania, and Romania. See further M. Mälksoo, 'Criminalizing Communism: Transnational Mnemopolitics in Europe', *International Political Sociology* 8:1 (2014), 82–99.

[33] Muižnieks, 'Latvian-Russian Memory Battles . . .', 219–21.

[34] The customary international law principles recognised in the Statute of the Nuremberg International Military Tribunal and the jurisprudence of this Tribunal.

to the warring party whose war could have been considered just in terms of *jus ad bellum* (i.e. legitimate self-defence against the aggression by Nazi Germany). Consequently, Russia has claimed the Nuremberg precedent not to be practically applicable to the nationals of the victorious Allies.[35]

The case of *Kononov* was brought before the ECtHR on the issue of the retroactive application of criminal sanctions by a former 'Red partisan' commander Vasily Makarovich Kononov, who after having been decorated as a war hero during the Soviet times, was charged with war crimes after Latvia's independence had been restored.[36] According to the case against Kononov that passed through all three stages of the Latvian court system, Kononov had led a group of Soviet partisans who killed nine inhabitants of the eastern Latvian village of Mazie Bati on 27 May 1944 for their alleged collaboration with the German forces occupying the country at the time. According to Kononov's account, this was planned as an act of retaliation since previously villagers had given away the location of the Soviet Major Chugunov's nearby platoon to the Germans, which was consequently destroyed. Allegedly, the villagers had been hiding weapons provided by the Germans and were collaborating with them. Kononov affirmed that he had not been personally involved in killing any villagers, claiming furthermore that his unit's orders had actually been to capture the 'traitors' and put them on a trial in a Soviet military court.[37]

The 2008 judgment by the ECtHR's former Third Section found Latvia to be in violation of Art. 7 of the European Convention on Human Rights (ECHR) when convicting Kononov for a war crime by a narrow margin of four votes against three.[38] Art. 7 para 1 sentence 1 of the ECHR reads as follows:

> No one shall be held guilty of any criminal offence on account of any act or omission which did not constitute a criminal offence under national or international law at the time when it was committed.[39]

The crux of the matter, however, was more revealingly stated by Judge Egbert Myjer of the Netherlands in his concurring opinion to the chamber's judgment, which had reached a conclusion that Kononov's actions

[35] Mälksoo, 'Casenote on *Kononov* v. *Latvia*'.

[36] Kononov was born in Latvia in 1923. He was a citizen of Latvia until April 2000 when he took up Russian citizenship instead.

[37] *Kononov* v. *Latvia*, 2008, para 22.

[38] *Ibid.*, paras 7 and 41.

[39] ECHR, as amended by Protocols Nos. 11 and 14, supplemented by Protocols Nos. 1, 4, 6, 7, 12, and 13.

in 1944 did not amount to a war crime. As Judge Myjer substantiated his siding with the Court's ruling:

> I must explain that my perception is somehow tainted by my own national background. I was born in the Netherlands just after the Second World War and grew up with the perception that the Nazis and their collaborators were entirely in the wrong and those who fought against the Nazis (including members of resistance groups) were completely in the right. Whatever acts the resistance groups had committed against the occupying German forces or against Netherlands nationals who had collaborated with them, it had always been for the right cause.[40]

Accordingly, Judge Myer's conclusion was to put aside what he called 'the double *occupation* viewpoint of the Latvian Government' (emphasis in the original), maintaining that just like in Netherlands, 'there was no justification for a pro-Nazi attitude or active collaboration with the Nazis in Latvia either'.[41] The discriminatory understanding of war crimes as evocatively aired by Judge Myjer's concurring opinion was later echoed by Pavel Laptev, Russian representative at the Court at the time, who argued in an interview with *Kommersant* that 'within the limits of reason' any means to fight Nazism were essentially justified.[42] This perspective determined the applicability of the rules protecting civilians in war according to their personal political sympathies, thus refuting a foundational principle of international humanitarian law.

Only two years later, however, the Grand Chamber of the ECtHR reversed the previous judgment of the Court's former Third Section. In this final judgment of 17 May 2010 in the case of *Kononov* v. *Latvia*, the Grand Chamber found, by fourteen votes to three, that Latvia had not violated Art. 7 of the ECHR, which enshrines the prohibition of retroactive application of criminal law when convicting the former Soviet partisan Vasily Kononov for a war crime committed in Latvia during the Second World War.[43] Symptomatically to the dividing lines of the debate, the Russian Federation continued to intervene in the process before the Grand Chamber as a third-party state in support of Kononov,[44] while Lithuania stepped in for Latvia.

[40] *Kononov* v. *Latvia*, 2008, Judge Myjer's concurring opinion, para 9.

[41] *Ibid.*, para 10.

[42] S. Bartul', Pavel Laptev: 'Srok Zhizhni Evropeiskogo Suda Mozhet Byt' Sokrashen' [Pavel Laptev: The Length of Life of the European Court may be Shortened], *Kommersant*, 31 May 2010.

[43] *Kononov* v. *Latvia*, 2010.

[44] The Russian authorities and media kept a keen eye on the *Kononov* case ever since it was being tried in the Latvian courts, with the lower house of the Russian Duma and the

Hence, contra the discriminatory understanding of war crimes that had informed the original ECtHR ruling in the *Kononov case*, the Grand Chamber upheld the war crimes conviction of Kononov by the previous rulings of the Latvian courts. The Court thereby established an important precedent in applying the Nuremberg standards also to the winners of the Second World War, recognising these as the universal normative benchmark regardless of the perpetrators' allegiance to the supposedly more rightful *jus ad bellum*.[45] The successful Latvian appeal at the ECtHR on the *Kononov* case constituted a significant triumph for the broader Baltic politics of seeking recognition to their distinct experiences with twentieth-century totalitarian regimes and the legal treatment of the internationally wrongful acts committed by the Soviet communist regime on a par with the crimes of the Nazis.[46] Latvian Member of the European Parliament Sandra Kalniete who chairs the informal group Reconciliation of European Histories in the European Parliament welcomed the Grand Chamber's judgment as a step towards historical justice.[47]

The Russian Ministry of Foreign Affairs, in its turn, called the Court's final judgment 'a very dangerous precedent' that represented:

> an attempt to cast doubt on several key legal and political principles that emerged following the Second World War and the postwar settlement in Europe, particularly with regard to the prosecution of the Nazi war criminals . . . [T]he Grand Chamber has actually agreed today with those who seek to revise the outcome of World War II and whitewash the Nazis and their accomplices . . . [T]he decision seriously damages the credibility of the Council of Europe in general and may be viewed as an attempt to draw new dividing lines in Europe and to destroy the continent's emerging consensus on pan-European standards and values.[48]

Federation Council passing declarations in support of Kononov in 1998, 2000, and 2001; President Putin sent a personal greeting to Kononov on the latter's eightieth birthday in 2003, and President Medvedev sent his condolences to Kononov's family following Kononov's death in 2011. See Muižnieks, 'Latvian-Russian Memory Battles . . .', 222. It has been estimated that Russia spent 5 Million Russian roubles on Kononov's defence. S. Bartul', 'Partizan Vasili Kononov Proigral Svoyu Pobedu', *Kommersant*, 18 May 2010.

45 Mälksoo, 'Casenote on *Kononov* v. *Latvia*'.

46 Mälksoo, 'Criminalizing Communism: Transnational Mnemopolitics in Europe'.

47 See eureconciliation.wordpress.com/2010/05/18/a-pivotal-judgment-of-the-echr-no-impunity-for-perpetrators-of-war-crimes-sandra-kalniete-mep/ (last accessed: 3 October 2016).

48 Statement by the Russian Foreign Ministry Following the Pronouncement on 17 May 2010, of the Ruling of the Grand Chamber of the European Court of Human Rights in the Case of Vasily Kononov.

The ECtHR's acceptance of the position of Latvia in the case of *Kononov* was consequently seen as marking 'a legally baseless and politically detrimental shift in the Court's legal approaches to the assessment of events and outcomes of the Second World War'. Speaking on behalf of the Russian Federation, the statement of the Russian Ministry of Foreign Affairs promised to draw 'appropriate conclusions' on the ruling, including with regard to the construction of Russia's relations with the Court and the Council of Europe as a whole.[49] The Russian State Duma, in its turn, expressed its 'deep concern' over delivery of this judgment, which was regarded as:

> not only . . . a dangerous court precedent and a change of legal approaches to the assessment of the events of the Second World War, but also as an attempt to initiate revision of judgments rendered by the International Military Tribunal for Nuremberg.

Accordingly, the Grand Chamber judgment was perceived as 'justif[ying] the actions of the Latvian authorities pursuing the policy of revanchism and chauvinism' as well as 'encourag[ing] those State leaders who call for revision of the results of the International Military Tribunal for Nuremberg'. The Duma maintained that:

> One has to be sorry about the fact that a number of politicians in the world increasingly side with those political forces that seek to justify Nazi ideology, demolish established post-war world order and that seek to encourage aggressive nationalism. Such a tendency is dangerous since it leads to revival of fascism, and justifies war crimes committed during the Second World War.[50]

The Russian State Duma thus dubbed the final ruling on *Kononov* v. *Latvia* as 'of purely political nature', as it was allegedly 'not based on universally accepted principles and norms of the international law'. Moreover, 'serious negative consequences' were foreseen 'for the participants in the Second World War, who fought on the side of the Allies, which might be manifested in their criminal prosecution for commission of war crimes'.[51] Likewise, President Medvedev suggested that the 'open reassessment of a verdict previously reached definitely has political motives behind it', and

[49] *Ibid.*

[50] The Fifth State Duma of the Federal Assembly of the Russian Federation, *Statement as regards Delivery of the Judgment by the Grand Chamber of the European Court in the Case of Kononov* v. *Latvia*, 21 May 2010.

[51] For a more balanced legal assessment of the judgment on *Kononov* by the Grand Chamber, see A. I. Kovler, 'Follow-up to Kononov, Human Rights', *Case-Law of the European Court of Human Rights* 9 (2010), 74–9.

could 'undermine the basis of international law',[52] while Andrei Klimov, the deputy chairman of the Duma's International Affairs Committee, claimed that a 'continuation of this logic will ultimately lead to whitewashing of Hitler and his accomplices'.[53]

In response, the Latvian Ministry of Foreign Affairs denounced attempts to exercise pressure on the ECtHR, maintaining that:

> ECtHR judgment in the Kononov case confirms the generally recognized principle of international law that responsibility for the committed war crimes shall be individual and effective, and that such crimes may not be justified by the perpetrator's belonging to a certain state, political, ideological or other group.[54]

Yet, the Grand Chamber had, in fact, stood clear of taking an explicit stand on the lawfulness of Latvia's incorporation into the USSR in 1940,[55] effectively refusing to add substantive weight on this major bone of contention between the parties of the debate.[56] However, if Latvia was first illegally occupied by the USSR and only then by Germany, and in case the first Soviet occupation was violent and repressive enough, the villagers of Mazie Bati could have hardly had any legal or moral duty to prefer one occupier to another – quite contrary to the implication made by Judge Myjer[57] and the even more evocative official Russian position on the case.

3 *Kononov* v. *Latvia* as a Clash of Competing Claims on Ontological Security

I suggest that the *Kononov* case challenged fundamentally both Latvia's and Russia's self-narratives as particular kinds of states, although in different ways, drawing on their specific interpretations of the events and consequences of the Second World War and their ensuing self-defined

52 President Dmitry Medvedev Sees Politics behind Kononov Case, *The Voice of Russia*, 29 May 2010.

53 L. Korotun, 'Verdict of Kononov's Guilty Justifies Fascism', *The Voice of Russia*, 21 May 2010. For further discussion of the case in the Russian media, see Muižnieks, 'Latvian-Russian Memory Battles . . .'.

54 Available at: www.mfa.gov.lv/en/news/latest-news/10548-european-court-of-human-rights-recognizes-acts-committed-by-vasiliy-kononov-as-a-war-crime (last accessed: 3 October 2016).

55 *Kononov* v. *Latvia*, 2010, para 210.

56 But cf. ECtHR *Kolk and Kislyiy* v. *Estonia* (Appl. No. 23052/04 and 24018/04), Judgment, 17 January 2006, and ECtHR *Penart* v. *Estonia* (Appl. No. 14685/04), Judgment, 24 January 2006.

57 *Kononov* v. *Latvia*, 2008, Judge Myjer's concurring opinion. See further Mälksoo, 'Casenote on *Kononov* v. *Latvia*'.

ontological security requirements. Not prosecuting Kononov for crimes committed during the time of the war would have discredited Latvia's efforts at post-communist transitional justice, undermining the country's central biographical narrative which is based on the legal principle of state continuity with the pre-war republic and the remembrance of the Second World War as a sequence of foreign occupations (i.e. first, Soviet; then Nazi; then again Soviet).

For Russia, a Soviet veteran's prosecution of war crimes by its former Soviet subjugate state was clearly disruptive for its central state-endorsed mnemonic narrative as the critical and heroic contributor in defeating Nazi Germany. Latvia's pursuance of historical justice threatened to dilute the moral supremacy of the Soviet human sacrifice among the anti-Hitler Allied coalition. Russia's support of Kononov thus appeared almost imperative for its defence of the country's memory and sense of honour in relation to the 'Great Patriotic War'. Latvia's charges against Kononov were thus interpreted as if constituting a normative threat[58] to Russia's identity as a great and victorious European power. It appears that for the current Russian leadership, a sense of ontological anxiety was generated by the ECtHR's final proceedings on the case rather than by Kononov's actual deeds in the Latvian village of Mazie Bati in 1944. It was not Kononov's responsibility for the killing of Latvian villagers *per se*, including burning alive a woman in the final stages of pregnancy, that produced a radical disconnection with the hegemonic mnemonic narrative of the 'Great Patriotic War' and the role of the Soviet Union in fighting Nazism, but rather the European Court's eventual siding with Latvia in its charge against the Soviet veteran. ECtHR's ruling on the *Kononov* case threatened Russia with an imperative to fundamentally reassess its official account of the war as a selflessly defensive and indeed self-sacrificing enterprise. This was regarded as highly problematic in Russia for the victorious 'Great Patriotic War' has emerged as a major resource for the positive sense of the Russian post-Soviet 'self' during the Putin era, forming the backbone of the country's contemporary state-sanctioned biographical narrative. The ontological significance of the war for the modern Russian construction of its state identity is evocatively reflected in the recent amendment to the country's Criminal Code, whereby the 'dissemination of false information on the activities of the Soviet Union during World War II' and the 'rehabilitation of Nazism' are explicitly criminalised.[59]

[58] I. Creppell, 'The Concept of Normative Threat', *International Theory* 3:3 (2011), 450–87.

[59] Art. 354.1., *The Criminal Code of the Russian Federation*. See further Koposov in the present volume.

While accepting the role of the continuator state of the Soviet Union in international legal terms, the Russian Federation has persistently refused to assume legal responsibility for the internationally wrongful acts of the Soviet regime, both within its current borders and beyond. Russia's lack of political penitence towards the other Eastern European nations and states affected by the Soviet repressive policies has made it an antipode of a 'sorry state', unwilling to publicly express contrition for past human rights abuses in order to promote reconciliation between the former repressor state and the repressed.[60] Meanwhile, the Putin regime has cunningly appropriated the discourses of human rights and genocide prevention for its own identity-political projects. Russia's own record in criminal-judicial measures adopted vis-à-vis the perpetrators of the human rights violations of its antecedent regime remains notoriously absent.[61] Russia's chosen transitional justice model has been aimed at impunity rather than accountability. In the meantime, the Kremlin's rhetorical stance on various kinds of 'Nazis', past and present, is strongly punitive, in a curious contradiction to the Putin regime's support to far-right parties in Europe.

To be sure, fundamental transitions (be they political, economic, ideological, or all at once, as has been the case with Russia's emergence from the USSR) present fundamental challenges for maintaining the consistency of the self-concept of a state. 'Coming to terms with the past' calls for the revision of the state's mnemonic vision of itself, thus destabilising its identity and potentially endangering its continuous agency in international politics.[62] The status-related costs entailed with a critical revision of a past 'self' are not just emotionally charged, but have concrete political consequences. In Russia's case, the unqualified renouncing of the communist regime after the collapse of the USSR would have made it difficult to concurrently 'inherit' the desirable legacy of the Soviet Union in the international system as its 'state continuator' (i.e. Russia's privileged position in the international system through the permanent membership of the UN Security Council, or its great power status in general). Against that backdrop, Russia's notorious strategic silence[63] about certain problematic

[60] Cf. J. Lind, *Sorry States: Apologies in International Politics* (Ithaca, NY: Cornell University Press, 2008).

[61] N. Adler, 'Country Study: Russia', in L. Stan and N. Nedelsky (eds.), *The Encyclopedia of Transitional Justice* (Cambridge University Press, 2012), 406.

[62] Mälksoo, 'Memory Must Be Defended', 224.

[63] R. Fivush, 'Speaking Silence: The Social Construction of Silence in Autobiographical and Cultural Narratives', *Memory* 18:2 (2010), 88–98; K. Knutsen, 'Strategic Silence: Political Persuasion between the Remembered and the Forgotten', in A. Dessingué and

chapters in the life of this antecedent 'self' is not actually inconsistent with the basic premises of the ontological security theory. The political handling of its communist past has been further complicated for Russia by the additional challenges the collapse of the antecedent regime has presented for its spatial continuity. Losing a considerable chunk of the formerly inhabited space, as well as millions of Russian compatriots to the newly independent states at Russia's borders has forced the country to fundamentally reconsider (and thus far not particularly successfully) its historical self-definition as an empire rather than a nation-state.

In sum, both Latvia's and Russia's discourses and actions regarding the *Kononov* case stemmed from and sought to guard their central state-endorsed ontological security narratives, highlighting the countries' mutual importance for the constitution of their identities as certain kinds of states. Taking Kononov to court on charges of war crimes in the Second World War was logically consistent with the grand narrative of the Latvian state identity based on legal continuity with the pre-Second World War republic.[64] This case was part of the country's endeavour to come to terms with its Soviet legacy while constructing a continuous state identity after restoring sovereign statehood in the throes of the collapsing Soviet Union. Latvia's appeal on the original ruling on *Kononov* by the ECtHR moreover highlights the significance allocated to the European affirmation of Latvia's central mnemonic narrative ordering its contemporary sense of 'self'. Likewise, the *Kononov* case evidently challenged Russia's state identity for it threatened to disrupt its state-endorsed biographical narrative as a selfless liberator of Europe from Nazism, inducing thus a sense of disconnection with the exclusively heroic self-image in the context of the war. For Russia, the *Kononov* case thus emerged as an event that 'refuse[s] to be readily incorporated in the national myth of glory and sacrifice'.[65] The final ruling of the ECtHR on the case thus created a radical disjuncture for the hegemonic state-sponsored Russian mnemonic narrative of the 'Great Patriotic War'. It is noteworthy that 'Europe' has been a significant point of reference for both Russia and Latvia in the search for wider recognition of their respective biographical narratives and remembrances of the

J. Winter (eds.), *Beyond Memory: Silence and the Aesthetics of Remembrance* (Abingdon and New York: Routledge, 2016), 125–39.

64 N. Muižnieks, 'History, Memory and Latvian Foreign Policy', in N. Muižnieks, *The Geopolitics of History in Latvian–Russian Relations* (Riga: Academic Press of the University of Latvia, 2011), 7–18.

65 J. Edkins, *Trauma and the Memory of Politics* (Cambridge University Press, 2003), 108. Cf. Zarakol, 'Ontological (In)Security and State Denial of Historical Crimes'.

Second World War. As the Baltic states continue to call for broadening the spectrum of an official pan-European remembrance of this war as the clash of two totalitarian 'evils', Russia's emphasis remains on the USSR's contribution to the Allied victory as part of the already well-established Western narrative of the Second World War as the 'good war' of fighting against a single tyranny.[66]

4 Implications for European Remembrance of the Second World War

The proceedings in the case of *Kononov* show evocatively how transitional historical justice, as pursued by Latvia and Russia in their distinct ways, is connected to the preservation of the respective state identities over time. *Kononov* v. *Latvia* is an emblematic example of the legal process that Latvia resorted to during its post-Soviet transition in order to preserve its ontological consistency as a continuous state with the pre-war republic. For Russia, this case encapsulates multiple, and yet to be successfully surmounted tensions in its hegemonic mnemonic narrative of the 'Great Patriotic War' and the Soviet legacy more generally. While for Latvia this case has enabled a public airing of the Baltic states' difficult predicament between Nazi Germany and the Soviet Union in the context of the Second World War, *Kononov* induced fundamental ontological insecurity in Russia, undermining its state-sanctioned mnemonic account of the war as a noble and selfless struggle for the freedom of the whole of Europe. Paraphrasing Lawrence R. Douglas, while the ECtHR's ruling enabled to 'clarify or elucidate the historical record' for Latvia, it failed 'to police a history that ha[d] already been adequately clarified' for Russia.[67]

The case of *Kononov* v. *Latvia* has thus wider repercussions for the so-called 'Western front' of the East European 'memory wars' over the Second World War.[68] ECtHR's 2008 ruling on *Kononov* demonstrated how the mental line drawn under the war in Nuremberg had essentially been a necessary compromise for Western Europe in order to move on with life in the immediate aftermath of war horrors. It is hardly surprising

[66] See further M. Mälksoo, 'The Memory Politics of Becoming European: The East European Subalterns and the Collective Memory of Europe', *European Journal of International Relations* 15:4 (2009), 653–80.

[67] L. R. Douglas, *The Memory of Judgment: Making Law and History in the Trials of the Holocaust* (New Haven, CT: Yale University Press, 2001), 256.

[68] Mälksoo, 'Nesting Orientalisms'.

that the compromise which had turned a blind eye towards assessing the role of the Soviet Union in the war and measuring the Soviet conduct by the same normative yardstick that had been applied to the crimes of the Nazis, began to unravel as the former 'captive nations' of the Soviet bloc had a chance to start sorting out their own records of the war and the ensuing Soviet suppression. 'We have to understand the Western Europeans', Estonian historian Toomas Hiio wrote after the first ECtHR's ruling on the *Kononov* case.[69] 'But this understanding is not a one-way street, nor an obligation of Eastern Europeans', he added, for 'there can be no justification for the selective application of international law'.[70] In the resonating words of Valters Nollendorfs, Chairman of the Board at the *Occupation Museum* Association of Latvia, 'crimes have to be prosecuted and justice has to be brought' for 'justice not carried out is just as bad as the injustice that has taken place'.[71]

The European Court's final ruling on the *Kononov* case sits in the broader backdrop of the emerging pan-European re-assessment of the legacies of the two totalitarian regimes of twentieth-century Europe, with various mnemonic/historiographical and legal-political implications.[72] International judgments, such as the ECtHR Grand Chamber's ruling in the *Kononov* v. *Latvia* case are transformative opportunities for shaping the historical accounts of the (Allied) war crimes in the Second World War in general. As the *Kononov* v. *Latvia* turned out to be the first case concerning the Second World War in which an Allied soldier was convicted for a war crime by another government's court, the final ruling of the ECtHR in this case established an important precedent in applying the pertinent standards of international law also to the winners of the war.[73] The *Kononov* judgment points at the gradual transformation of the wider European assessment of the complex legacies of the Second World War in Eastern Europe. The verdict which came out in favour of Latvia and against

[69] Hiio was in charge of historical research in the Estonian International Commission for Investigation of Crimes against Humanity, the predecessor of the current Estonian Institute of Historical Memory wherein he serves as a member of the board.

[70] T. Hiio, 'Lahtikistud Ajalugu' [A History Torn Open], *Eesti Päevaleht*, 6 August 2008. For further Estonian reactions to the *Kononov* case, see M. Arpo, 'Professor Martens, tule tagasi!' [Come Back, Professor Martens!], *Eesti Päevaleht*, 2 August 2008; R. Maruste, 'Sõjakurjategijaid oli mõlemal poolel' [There Were War Criminals on Both Sides], *Pärnu Postimees*, 29 May 2010.

[71] C. Bigg, 'Amid V-Day Festivities, Soviet Partisan Braces for War Crimes Verdict', *Radio Free Europe/Radio Liberty*, 7 May 2010.

[72] Pettai and Pettai, *Transitional and Retrospective Justice*, Chapter 7.

[73] Mälksoo, 'Casenote on *Kononov* v. *Latvia*'.

the plaintiff Vasily Kononov could accordingly be read as promoting a particular kind of memory at the European level.[74]

Nonetheless, the contestation over the legitimate and proper remembrance of the Second World War goes on. Vindicated by the European Court's decision on the *Kononov* case, Latvian Minister of Justice has announced its preparation to claim occupation damages from Russia along with its two Baltic counterparts.[75] Meanwhile, Russia has taken concrete steps to detach itself from the jurisdiction of the Court. Resonating with the warning to draw 'appropriate conclusions' on the ECtHR's *Kononov* ruling, the State Duma recently adopted a law enabling Russia not to implement judgments of the European Court if 'in conflict with constitution'.[76] While the final ruling of the Court is drawn upon and evoked as a resource of national identity and memory-building in the former Soviet space, the *Kononov* case highlights the significance allocated to international legal rulings by states seeking to reinforce their mutually contested biographical narratives.

The final ECtHR ruling in the *Kononov* case has not eliminated the mnemonical dividing lines between Russia and the Baltic states in regard to the Second World War and the Soviet legacy in general. The case has only underscored various normative lines of contestation still prevalent among distinct European communities of memory. The decisiveness of the *Kononov* ruling for shaping public discourse about the Soviet criminal legacy across Europe needs to be further contextualised in the ECtHR's rulings on a variety of post-communist justice measures and their complex interactions with other forces seeking to make their imprint on historical remembrance of the Second World War and the role of the USSR in it.

[74] But cf. ECtHR *Vasialiauskas* v. *Lithuania* (Appl. No. 35343/05), Judgment (Grand Chamber), 20 October 2015. For a broader discussion on the persisting lack of equivalence between the ECtHR's treatment of 'post-Communist' and 'post-Nazi' cases, see A. Gliszczyńska-Grabias, 'Communism Equals or Versus Nazism? Europe's Unwholesome Legacy in Strasbourg', *East European Politics and Societies and Cultures* 30:1 (2016), 74–96.

[75] See www.just.ee/sites/www.just.ee/files/news-related-files/declaration_05_11_15_.pdf (last accessed: 3 October 2016).

[76] See kommersant.ru/doc/2870960 (last accessed: 3 October 2016).

5

Testing the "Uniqueness": Denial of the Holocaust vs Denial of Other Crimes before the European Court of Human Rights

PAOLO LOBBA

1 Introduction

The European Court and the European Commission of Human Rights (ECtHR or Court; and ECommHR or Commission, respectively) have long dealt with expressions denying the existence of the Holocaust. Invariably, the "Strasbourg jurisprudence" has found that such statements do not merit protection under the free speech principle encapsulated in Article 10 of the European Convention on Human Rights (ECHR). In so doing, the Strasbourg organs have progressively developed an *exceptional legal regime* which, relying upon the so-called "abuse clause" under Article 17 ECHR, departs from the ordinary "necessity test" envisaged under Article 10.

This exceptional regime was initially applied very sparingly and thus remained largely unchallenged and poorly theorised, until recently when other forms of deplorable expressions regarding tragic events of the past raised the issue of its actual scope of applicability. Essentially, it has become necessary to determine whether the strict approach adopted by the Court and Commission in relation to Holocaust denial extends to expressions disputing the reality of other historical facts. Thus the question has become whether, under the Strasbourg jurisprudence, Holocaust denial remains *unique*, i.e. whether it may justify restrictions on free speech while the denial of other grave crimes remains protected speech.

The first opportunity to test the Court's jurisprudence against other forms of denialism emerged in the recent case of *Perinçek* v. *Switzerland*,[1]

The views expressed herein are those of the author and do not necessarily reflect those of the United Nations.

[1] ECtHR, *Perinçek* v. *Switzerland* (Appl. No. 27510/08), Judgment (Grand Chamber), 15 October 2015 (hereinafter *Perinçek* (2015)); ECtHR, *Perinçek* v. *Switzerland*, Judgment (Second Section), 17 December 2013 (hereinafter *Perinçek* (2013)).

which stemmed from a conviction for having disputed the characterisation of the extermination and mass deportations suffered by the Armenians in 1915 and following years as genocide. Ten years after the statements on which the conviction took place were made, the case culminated in a Grand Chamber judgment, which crystallises some important principles about the criminalisation of negationism.

At the same time the *Perinçek* judgment has also provoked much controversy among politicians, victims, and academics, reflecting the highly divisive and utterly political nature of the salient issue, namely the recognition of the Armenian genocide. Although the Grand Chamber prudently avoided pronouncing thereupon, its dictum cannot but exert an influence on the underlying debate, and risks being invoked instrumentally to further political aims. This wider significance of the Court's *Perinçek* ruling should not be regarded as surprising, as the Court is frequently confronted with the issues raised by public representations of history and memory, and their role in the construction of the identity of a given social group, as well as the possible use, misuse, and abuse of historical information under the guise of free speech.[2] Insofar as the Court is thus called upon to evaluate restrictions on the possibility to debate aspects relating to collective memory, it clearly finds itself entangled in the awkward position of being the arbiter of a people's history.

The focus of this chapter, however, is primarily on the *Perinçek* judgment's legal, rather than historical and political, significance. In this regard it may be said that the Court's ruling adopts a liberal approach to free speech, suggesting that generally the denial of historical events may only be punished when it amounts to incitement to hatred or violence, while at the same time it confirms that special treatment applies to Holocaust denial, the insidious tenor of which does not require specific evidence, but

[2] As illustrations of the interplay between historical and legal assessments, see e.g., ECtHR, *Fatullayev* v. *Azerbaijan* (Appl. No. 40984/07), Judgment, 22 April 2010; ECtHR, *Monnat* v. *Switzerland* (Appl. No. 73604/01), Judgment, 21 September 2006; ECtHR, *Ždanoka* v. *Latvia* (Appl. No. 58278/00), Judgment (Grand Chamber), 16 March 2006; ECtHR, *Chauvy and Others* v. *France* (Appl. No. 64915/01), Judgment, 29 June 2004, including the *Concurring Opinion of Judge Thomassen*. On the associated issue of memory laws, see e.g. E. Fronza, 'Negazionismo (diritto penale)', in *Enciclopedia del Diritto. Annali 8* (Milan: Giuffrè, 2015), 633–58; T. Hochmann, *Le négationnisme face aux limites de la liberté d'expression* (Paris: Pedone, 2013); L. Cajani, 'Criminal Laws on History', *Historein* 11 (2011), 19–48; P. Nora, 'Gedächtniskonjunktur', *Transit – Europäische Revue* 22 (2001–2), 18–31; A. Gliszczyńska-Grabias, 'Memory Laws or Memory Loss?', *Polish YB of Int'l L.* (2014), 155–80.

automatically derives from the historical context of the states that were involved in the perpetration of the Nazi atrocities.

Accordingly, the principal aim of this chapter is to examine whether the different treatment afforded to the denial of the Holocaust and to the denial of other historical facts has been convincingly justified by the Court. The goal is not to analyse whether the Holocaust is a unique historical event, but rather whether it calls for a *unique legal regime with respect to negationism*. In order to meaningfully examine this issue, it is necessary at the outset to explore the particulars of the exceptional principles that the Commission and the Court have applied to Holocaust denial, which evolved through three stages of jurisprudence, marked by the interaction between Articles 10 and 17 of the ECHR. The overview provided of the precedents which marked these stages exposes the functioning of the abuse clause and its scope of applicability, as well as how this clause has been adapted to deal with denialism.

Following the above analysis, the chapter turns to an in-depth examination of *Perinçek* by describing and critically analysing the judgments handed down, in turn, by the Chamber and the Grand Chamber of the ECtHR. Two critical questions raised by this case are then addressed. The first is whether, and to what extent, the *Perinçek* judgment on the Court's position on the scope of applicability and *modus operandi* of the abuse clause, with particular attention paid to the issue of whether denialism *as such* will still fall under Article 17, and if so to the attendant consequences of such a finding. The second question is whether the denial of the Holocaust remains subject to unique judicial treatment, and if so whether this differentiation can be justified in relation to the denial of other past tragedies, in particular the one inflicted upon Armenians by the Ottoman Empire, which was at the heart of the *Perinçek* judgment.

2 Setting the Scene: The Interplay between Articles 10 and 17

The judgments of the Court in *Perinçek* must be assessed against the tortuous path followed by the ECtHR jurisprudence on the denial of the Holocaust. Although the Court has regularly rejected any application seeking protection for expressions of Holocaust denial, there have been variations in the legal basis and reasoning that supported such decisions. The analysis that follows purports to shed light on whether the denial of the Holocaust has been subjected by the Court to a *special* or *unique* legal regime.

Denialism-related precedents are marked by the interaction between Articles 10 and 17 of the ECHR. A restriction on free speech is ordinarily addressed pursuant to Article 10, which enshrines the right to freedom of expression.[3] According to well-established Strasbourg case law, state interference was found to be in compliance with Article 10 where the restrictive measure in question: (i) was prescribed by law; (ii) pursued a legitimate aim; and (iii) was necessary in a democratic society and proportionate to the legitimate aim pursued. The key element of the test is the last step, in which the judges seek to strike a balance between the various interests at stake, deciding the case in the light of all its factual circumstances.

Article 17, in turn, removes from the protection of the Convention any activity aimed at destroying any of the rights set forth in the ECHR.[4] However, the application of Article 17 has not been consistent. In some cases expressions considered to constitute activities aimed at destroying a right set forth in the ECHR have been categorically excluded from the subject-matter scope of the ECHR in accordance with what has been termed the "guillotine effect" of the abuse clause,[5] while in other cases Article 17 has been employed as a principle of interpretation within the framework of Article 10.

3 The Evolution of the Exceptional Regime Applied to Holocaust Denial

In the jurisprudence concerning Holocaust denial, despite some internal ambiguity and inconsistency three stages may be identified, which depend on the role assumed by the abuse clause in the judges' reasoning.

[3] See generally D. Voorhoof, 'The [ECHR]: The Right to Freedom of Expression [...]', *Human Rights* 7:2 (2015), available at http://hdl.handle.net/1854/LU-6900860, 1–40; J.-F. Flauss, 'The [ECtHR] and the Freedom of Expression', *Indiana Law Journal* 84:3 (2009), 809–49.

[4] See generally H. Cannie and D. Voorhoof, 'The Abuse Clause and Freedom of Expression in the [ECHR]', *Netherlands Quarterly of Human Rights* 29:1 (2011), 54–83; D. Keane, 'Attacking Hate Speech Under Article 17 of the [ECHR]', *Netherlands Quarterly of Human Rights* 25:4 (2007), 641–63; Y. Arai, 'Prohibition of Abuse of the Rights [. . .]', in P. Van Dijk et al. (eds.), *Theory and Practice of the [ECHR]* (Antwerpen: Intersentia, 4th ed., 2006), 1083–92; S. van Drooghenbroeck, 'L'article 17 de la Convention européenne des droits de l'homme est-il indispensable?', *RTDH* 46 (2001) 541–66.

[5] G. Cohen-Jonathan, 'Le droit de l'homme à la non-discrimination raciale', 46 *RTDH* (2001) 665–88, at 665.

3.1 First Stage: Application of General Principles on Freedom of Expression

The first phase of case law on Holocaust denial involves a small number of cases heard by the (now abolished) Commission during the 1980s.[6] The distinguishing feature of this stage was that Article 17 did not come into play. During this phase the application of Article 17 was confined to two early cases in which the Court excluded, by virtue of Article 17's guillotine effect, antidemocratic activities[7] and racist expressions[8] from the protection of the Convention.

In contrast, the judicial analysis of Holocaust denial applications was at that time conducted pursuant to the *ius commune* of Article 10, meaning that the cases were assessed in the light of all their circumstances, and that the respondent state was required to demonstrate that the interference with the right to free speech was necessary and proportionate in a democratic society.

The restricted scope of application of Article 17 in this initial stage also clearly emerges in *Lowes* v. *United Kingdom*.[9] Despite the fact that the case concerned anti-Semitic activities, including conduct akin to denialism, the application was dismissed pursuant to Article 10, suggesting that only blatantly racist conduct – not even anti-Semitism – justifies the application of the abuse clause.

3.2 Second Stage: Application of Article 17 as a Principle of Interpretation

The case of *Kühnen* v. *Germany*,[10] which concerned neo-Nazi propaganda, marks the beginning of the middle phase, setting a precedent that would later be followed in Holocaust denial cases.[11] The abuse clause contained

[6] EcommHR, *X.* v. *Germany* (Appl. No. 9235/81), 16 July 1982; EcommHR, *T.* v. *Belgium* (Appl. No. 9777/82), 14 July 1983.

[7] EcommHR, *Parti Communiste d'Allemagne c. Allemagne* (Appl. No. 250/57), 20 July 1957.

[8] EcommHR, *Glimmerveen and Hagenbeek* v. *the Netherlands* (Appl. No. 8348/78 & 8406/78), 11 October 1979.

[9] EcommHR, *Lowes* v. *United Kingdom* (Appl. No. 13214/87), 9 December 1988.

[10] EcommHR, *Kühnen* v. *Germany* (Appl. No. 12194/86), 12 May 1988. In the same vein, see EcommHR, *B.H., M.W., H.P. and G.K.* v. *Austria* (Appl. No. 12774/87), 12 October 1989; EcommHR, *Ochensberger* v. *Austria* (Appl. No. 21318/93), 2 September 1994.

[11] EcommHR, *F. P.* v. *Germany* (Appl. No. 19459/92), 29 March 1993; EcommHR, *Walendy* v. *Germany* (Appl. No. 21128/92), 11 January 1995; EcommHR, *Remer* v. *Germany* (Appl. No. 25096/94), 6 September 1995; EcommHR, *Honsik* v. *Austria* (Appl. No. 25062/94), 18

in Article 17 was applied here by the Commission not as a case-killer provision – i.e. as one generating the guillotine effect – but rather as an *interpretative aid*, affording guidance within the necessity test under Article 10.[12] In all cases falling under this second stage, the Commission showed an unusual deference to the assessments undertaken at the domestic level, which were affirmed quite uncritically.[13] Moreover, the specific circumstances of each case were neither examined in any detail nor on a case-by-case basis, with Holocaust denial being automatically presumed to be a typical Nazi-inspired activity.

In the case of *Kühnen*, the Commission made a second, significant change to its previous interpretation of the abuse clause, broadening its *scope of application*. Whereas the text of Article 17 targets conduct "aimed at the destruction of the rights and freedoms set forth" in the ECHR, the Commission extended its reach to activities vaguely defined as those running counter to the "basic values underlying the Convention".[14]

3.3 *Third Stage: Article 17 as Categorically Excluding Holocaust Denial from the Protection of Article 10*

In the third phase, the Court relied upon the guillotine effect of the abuse clause to exclude Holocaust denial from the protective umbrella of Article 10 altogether. This shift in approach dates back to the landmark *Lehideux* case, in which the Grand Chamber ruled that the negation of "clearly established historical facts – such as the Holocaust – [. . .] would be removed from the protection of Article 10 by Article 17".[15]

While in *Lehideux* the new role assigned to the abuse clause was only announced, but not applied, two subsequent cases demonstrate its

October 1995; EcommHR, *Nationaldemokratische Partei Deutschlands* v. *Germany* (Appl. No. 25992/94), 29 November 1995; EcommHR, *Rebhandl* v. *Austria* (Appl. No. 24398/94), 16 January 1996; EcommHR, *Pierre Marais* v. *France* (Appl. No. 31159/96), 24 June 1996; EcommHR, *D. I.* v. *Germany* (Appl. No. 26551/95), 26 June 1996; EcommHR, *Hennicke* v. *Germany* (Appl. No. 34889/97), 21 May 1997; EcommHR, *Nachtmann* v. *Austria* (Appl. No. 36773/97), 9 September 1998; ECtHR, *Witzsch* v. *Germany (1)* (Appl. No. 41448/98), 20 April 1999. See, for an account of many of these decisions, G. Cohen-Jonathan, 'Négationnisme et droits de l'homme', 32 *RTDH* (1997), 571–97, at 573–85.

[12] Cohen-Jonathan, 'Le droit de l'homme', at 667–68. Cf. van Drooghenbroeck, 'L'article 17', at 553–5 (considering Article 17 an *arrière-fond interprétatif superflu*).

[13] See e.g. EcommHR, *Walendy* v. *Germany* (the law), p. 6; EcommHR, *Nachtmann* v. *Austria* (the law), para 2, pp. 5–6.

[14] EcommHR, *Kühnen* v. *Germany* (the law), para 1, p. 6.

[15] ECtHR, *Lehideux and Isorni* v. *France* (Appl. No. 24662/94), 23 September 1998, para 47.

potential. In *Garaudy*, the Court recalled with approval the precedent of *Lehideux*, and explained that Holocaust denial falls under Article 17 because it "undermines the values on which the fight against racism and anti-Semitism are based" and, as such, is "incompatible with democracy and human rights".[16]

Arguably, the judgment in *Garaudy* implicitly restricts the scope of Article 17, requiring the showing of an *antidemocratic or anti-Semitic intent* underlying acts of denialism. The validity of this (moderately reassuring) thesis, however, appears to be challenged by subsequent decisions.

In *Witzsch* v. *Germany (2)*, the applicant did not contest the existence of the Holocaust *per se*, but rather the responsibility of Hitler and his party for the extermination of Jews.[17] The case does not present any indicia of racism, nor do the judges uncover a pro-Nazi purpose underlying the expressions. The abuse clause is nonetheless applied, apparently on account of "the applicant's disdain towards the victims of the Holocaust".[18]

This latter finding is not grounded on a strong factual basis, but rather *presumed* by the Court. This aspect weakens the above-envisioned hypothesis that Article 17 is in effect invoked upon a showing of racist or antidemocratic intent. Further doubts are raised by the fact that, conversely, some cases concerning patently racist or anti-Semitic expressions were dismissed pursuant to Article 10 alone.[19] The conclusion is that Article 17 attaches to Holocaust denial *as such* and its application is divorced from a finding of racist or antidemocratic intent, which the Court apparently *presumed* to permeate any statement of the kind. In contrast, the treatment of other racist or totalitarian conduct is not comparably uniform.

4 The *Perinçek* Case as the Litmus Test for the Court's Case Law on Denialism

4.1 *Background to the Case and Criminal Proceedings in Switzerland*

Doğu Perinçek ("the applicant") is a Turkish politician, holding the position of incumbent president of the Patriotic Party (formerly the Workers Party).

16 ECtHR, *Garaudy* v. *France* (Appl. No. 65831/01), 24 June 2003 (the law), para 1(i), p. 29.

17 ECtHR, *Witzsch* v. *Germany (2)* (Appl. No. 7485/03), 13 December 2005.

18 *Ibid.*, (the law), para 2, p. 8.

19 See e.g. ECtHR, *Seurot c. France* (Appl. No. 57383/00), 18 May 2004; ECtHR, *Balsytė-Lideikienė* v. *Lithuania* (Appl. No. 72596/01), 4 November 2008; ECtHR, *Gollnisch c. France* (Appl. No. 48135/08), 7 June 2011.

Convicted in the so-called "Ergenekon trials" for directing a terrorist organisation seeking to overthrow the Turkish government, he was released from prison in March 2014. In the past the ECtHR had already ruled in his favour in two cases brought against Turkey.[20]

At the root of Perinçek's instant application was his conviction by Swiss courts of racial discrimination pursuant to Article 261 bis(4) of the Penal Code,[21] due to his public statements that the characterisation of the crimes perpetrated against Armenians as genocide was an "international lie". Importantly, he did not deny the *existence* of the massacre as such, but rather its *legal classification* as genocide.

The Swiss Federal Tribunal reasoned that Article 261 bis(4) applies to any genocide and crime against humanity – not only to the Holocaust – as long as there exists a comparable "general agreement" about the underlying facts and legal characterisations.[22] This requirement was deemed to have been met with respect to the Armenian genocide, owing to the attendant "broad consensus of the community", notably among historians.[23] Consequently, the Tribunal found that the applicant had disputed the generally accepted legal characterisation of the Ottoman crimes, and that he did so for racist and nationalistic motives.[24]

In Europe, the Swiss verdict against Perinçek represents the first (but not the only) criminal conviction for denial of the Armenian genocide.[25]

4.2 The Judgment of the Grand Chamber

In his application before the Court, Perinçek submitted that his conviction in Switzerland violated the right to freedom of expression enshrined in Article 10 ECHR. The Grand Chamber, by ten votes to seven, upheld the

[20] ECtHR, *Perinçek c. Turquie* (Appl. No. 46669/99), 21 June 2005 (violation of Article 10); ECtHR, *Socialist Party and Others* v. *Turkey* (Appl. No. 21237/93), Judgment 25 May 1998 (violation of Article 11).

[21] "[A]ny person who on any of these grounds [i.e. race, ethnic origin or religion] denies, trivialises or seeks justification for genocide or other crimes against humanity."

[22] Tribunal fédéral (Switzerland), ATF 6B_398/2007, 12 December 2007 (hereinafter Tribunal fédéral (2007)), paras 3.4 and sub-paragraphs.

[23] Tribunal fédéral (2007), para 4 and sub-paragraphs.

[24] *Ibid.*, paras 5.2 and 7.

[25] See Tribunal fédéral (Switzerland), ATF 6B_297/2010, 16 September 2010 (so-called *Ali Mercan* case). Moreover, civil proceedings against Bernard Lewis were brought in France, resulting in an order to make (symbolic) reparation (see Tribunal de grande instance de Paris (France), judgment of 21 June 1995).

judgment of the Chamber (rendered, in turn, by a five-to-two majority), finding that the applicant's right had been violated and that such finding constitutes in itself just satisfaction. Below is a concise summary of the Grand Chamber's argument.

4.2.1 Preliminary Issue: The Applicability of Article 17

A preliminary issue was whether the application was admissible under Article 17 ECHR. Of note is that Article 17 was first deemed to apply to activities that "run counter to the basic values underlying the Convention", including expressions denying clearly established historical facts and crimes against humanity.[26] In subsequent cases the Court added that Article 17 also covers statements aimed at "justifying war crimes such as torture or summary executions"[27] or at the "glorification of war crimes, crimes against humanity or genocide".[28] In practice, however, the abuse clause has thus far been applied only to one specific type of denialism, namely the denial of the Holocaust.

Although the earlier precedents might have allowed for a summary dismissal of the application in *Perinçek*, the Court declined to do so, resolving instead to refine its jurisprudence on Article 17. The Grand Chamber thus found that the "decisive point" under the abuse clause is whether the conduct sought to "stir up hatred or violence" and the applicant sought to rely on the Convention to engage in activities aimed at the destruction of the rights encapsulated therein.[29] In the circumstances of the *Perinçek* case, such conditions of applicability were not "immediately clear" to the Court. Therefore the evaluation of Perinçek's conduct was joined to the analysis of the merits under Article 10.[30] It is noteworthy that the Grand Chamber departed from the approach taken by the Chamber, which discounted the relevance of Article 17 altogether.[31]

4.2.2 The Merits of the Application

The thrust of the decision focuses on whether the interference with Perinçek's rights under Article 10 was necessary in a democratic society. The Grand Chamber had to balance the right to freedom of expression

[26] See § 3, *supra*.
[27] ECtHR, *Orban and others* v. *France* (Appl. No. 20985/05), Judgment, 15 January 2005, para 35.
[28] ECtHR, *Fáber* v. *Hungary* (Appl. No. 40721/08), Judgment, 24 July 2012, para 58.
[29] *Perinçek* (2015), para 115.
[30] *Ibid.*
[31] *Perinçek* (2013), para 54.

against the right to respect for private life, which is affected by statements undermining the identity, and thus the dignity, of Armenians.[32] In order to strike such a balance, the judgment confronts two critical areas: the first revolving around the applicant's expressions, and the second relating to the international, European, and Swiss normative frameworks.

4.2.2.1 The Applicant's Statements The Grand Chamber's first point is that the applicant's statements fall within a class of expression entitled, in the Court's jurisprudence, to *heightened protection* under Article 10, since they (i) qualify as political speech and hinge on a matter of public interest[33] and (ii) do not amount to a call for hatred or intolerance.[34]

In particular, the Grand Chamber takes issue with the Swiss courts' finding that the applicant acted with a racist motive. In the Grand Chamber's view, the "overall thrust" of the statements shows that they were directed against "imperialists", with no allegations hinting at a falsification of history concocted by Armenians.[35] Nor can any incitement to hatred or intolerance be inferred from the applicant's position and the "wider context" of the utterances. In this regard, the Grand Chamber distinguished the *Perinçek* case from those regarding the denial of the Holocaust, in which, for "historical and contextual reasons", it had "invariably" presumed their inciting character.[36] The same "automatic presumption" is declared to be inapplicable to the present case, apparently on the grounds of a *geographical and temporal hiatus* between the applicant's expressions in Switzerland and the Armenian events, which occurred in the Ottoman Empire approximately ninety years prior thereto. That being the case, the Grand Chamber goes on to examine whether there are any concrete elements indicating a potentially racist or antidemocratic agenda, and finds none.

The judges then move on to scrutinise the existence of a pressing social need, going through geographical and historical factors, among others. The relevant section begins with yet another comparison between denial of the Armenian and the Jewish massacres.[37] The Grand Chamber points out that the inherent connection found between Holocaust denial and anti-democratic and anti-Semitic ideologies is owed to the *historical context* of

[32] *Perinçek* (2015), paras 156, 198–203, 227.
[33] *Ibid.*, para 231.
[34] *Ibid.*, paras 232–41.
[35] *Ibid.*, paras 232–3.
[36] *Ibid.*, para 234.
[37] *Ibid.*, paras 242–8.

the states from which the relevant litigation arose, all of which were states involved in the commission of the Nazi horrors.

In contrast, Switzerland lacked any such "direct link" with the events of 1915–16.[38] Nor did its national context expose any indicia of a tense atmosphere that could lead to "serious frictions" between the Turks and Armenians residing within its territory. Turning to the situation in Turkey, the Grand Chamber finds that the measures taken against the applicant had no "rational connection" with the aim of protecting the rights of the Armenians living in Turkey.[39] There was no indication either that the statements were a cause of hostility against them, or that a criminal conviction in Switzerland would make them feel any safer.

Lastly, the Court's analysis gauges the extent to which Perinçek's speeches affected the rights of the Armenians.[40] Here the Grand Chamber reiterates that the statements can neither be regarded as "particularly upsetting" or "virulent" nor as having had a widespread dissemination.[41] In sum, there is no specific evidence to support a finding that they caused serious prejudice to the dignity of the Armenians.

4.2.2.2 The Normative Framework The Grand Chamber next examines the legal landscape in Europe regarding criminal law restrictions on denialism. The conclusion is that such legislation varies significantly and no discernible trend emerges; but that the Swiss provision, however, represents the most restrictive option.[42]

The judges continue their analysis of the normative framework by observing that, under international law, Switzerland was not required to take the restrictive measure against the applicant,[43] because his utterances did not amount to incitement to hatred and international norms fall short of creating an obligation for genocide denial *as such* to be criminally punished.

The next aspect under consideration concerns the effect that the domestic courts' qualification of the events of 1915–16 as genocide had on the

[38] *Ibid.*, para 244.

[39] *Ibid.*, para 246. Cf. *Perinçek* (2015), 'Joint Dissenting Opinion of Judges Spielmann, Casadevall, Berro, De Gaetano, Sicilianos, Silvis and Kūris' (hereinafter *Perinçek* (2015), 'Joint Dissenting Opinion'), paras 6–7 (harshly criticising the majority for watering down the principle of universal protection of human rights).

[40] *Perinçek* (2015), paras 251–4.

[41] *Ibid.*, para 253.

[42] *Ibid.*, para 257.

[43] *Ibid.*, paras 258–68.

applicant's rights.[44] The Grand Chamber emphasises that the Swiss judiciary relied on conflicting yardsticks to sanction the genocidal nature ascribed to the Ottoman conduct. In light of such discrepancies, it remains unclear, in its view, whether or not the criminal conviction resulted from a mere divergence between Perinçek's opinion and "the prevailing views in Swiss society".[45]

4.2.3. Conclusions of the Grand Chamber

The reasoning culminates in a balancing exercise between the applicant's right to freedom of expression and the Armenians' right to protection of their dignity.[46] The Grand Chamber, after recapitulating all the factors it went through in its analysis, concludes that: (i) the statements concern a matter of public interest and do not qualify as a call for hatred or intolerance, and thus merit a heightened protection; (ii) the context in which they were made is not characterised by special tension or historical overtones; (iii) the statements do not affect the dignity of the Armenians to the extent that they require a criminal law response in Switzerland; (iv) Switzerland was under no international obligation to criminalise such statements; (v) Swiss courts appear to have censured the applicant for having expressed an opinion that diverges from the established opinions in Switzerland; and (vi) the government's interference materialises in a serious measure, a criminal conviction.

Hence, the Grand Chamber finds that, in the light of the context, the restriction on the applicant's right to freedom of expression was not necessary in a democratic society and that, accordingly, Article 10 was violated.[47] As a further consequence of this finding, the Grand Chamber declines to apply Article 17.

5 Another Episode in the Ongoing Saga on the Role of Article 17

The *Perinçek* case represented a timely opportunity for the ECtHR to review its case law on the exact function of Article 17. Two aspects remained to be settled: its scope of applicability, especially when it came to denialism, and its *modus operandi*, i.e. the way in which it was applied.

44 *Ibid.*, paras 269–71.
45 *Ibid.*, para 271.
46 *Ibid.*, paras 274–81.
47 *Ibid.*, paras 280–2.

As to the former, the Chamber and Grand Chamber judgments clarified that the abuse clause, despite previous open-ended dicta on the point, is not unconditionally applicable to the *unqualified denial* of any "clearly established historical facts". As regards the latter, the judges in Strasbourg opted to retain a certain margin of manoeuvre, thus confirming that they regard Article 17 as the Court's "wild card".

5.1 The Scope of Applicability of the Abuse Clause

We shall first examine the import of the Court's findings in *Perinçek* on the scope of applicability of the abuse clause (Article 17). It is worth recalling that Article 17 was conceived, in the wake of World War II, as an additional safeguard against the threats posed by groups or individuals pursuing *totalitarian aims*.[48] In this early stage, its application proved to be infrequent, being confined to two cases in which the Court applied it to antidemocratic or manifestly racist activities.[49]

Starting in the 1980s and continuing through the 1990s, the abuse clause came into play principally in litigation concerning Holocaust denials. As shown above,[50] the incorporation of Holocaust denial into the category of totalitarian activities was invariably *presumed*, including in cases wherein this element had not been established by domestic courts.

In its more recent decisions, the Court *expanded the scope* of Article 17. It firstly declared the provision to be applicable to denialism as such, without explicitly requiring any further showing.[51] Secondly, it effectively applied Article 17 to a wide range of expressions whose connection to the Article's original anti-totalitarian purpose was not specifically probed.[52]

In *Perinçek* the Court had perforce to engage with the far-reaching principles laid down in the precedents dealing with Holocaust denial because,

[48] P. Le Mire, 'Article 17', L.-E. Pettiti et al. (dir.), *La Convention européenne des droits de l'homme* (Paris: Economica, 2nd ed., 1999), 509–22, at 510–12.

[49] See footnotes 5–6, *supra*.

[50] See § 3.3, *supra*.

[51] See § 3.3, *supra*.

[52] See e.g. ECtHR, *W.P. and Others* v. *Poland* (Appl. No. 42264/98), Inadmissibility Decision 2 September 2004 (anti-Semitism); ECtHR, *Norwood* v. *United Kingdom* (Appl. No. 23131/03), Inadmissibility Decision 16 November 2004 (Islamophobia); ECtHR, *Pavel Ivanov* v. *Russia* (Appl. No. 35222/04), Inadmissibility Decision 20 February 2007 (anti-Semitism); ECtHR, *Hizb Ut-Tahrir and Others* v. *Germany* (Appl. No. 31098/08), Inadmissibility Decision 12 June 2012 (calls for violent destruction of Israel and killing of its inhabitants, and justification of suicide attacks); ECtHR, *Molnar* v. *Romania* (Appl. No. 16637/06), Inadmissibility Decision 23 October 2012 (hate speech devoid of calls to violent or unlawful action).

on their face, they would have allowed a summary dismissal of the application pursuant to Article 17. Thus the Court decided to refine its case law, holding that the abuse clause may only apply to expressions that are directed to stir up hatred or violence.[53] This provision, therefore, may not be applied to denialism *as such*, absent a case-specific assessment as to whether such statements are intended to provoke hatred or violent action. The two benches, however, although concurring in the formulation of the principle in the abstract, took a different approach to its application to the facts of the case. While the Chamber decidedly excluded a finding that the statements amounted to hate speech, and hence unambiguously declined to invoke the abuse clause, the Grand Chamber's holding was much more nuanced. It did not rule that the statements did not constitute incitement, but only that this point was not "immediately clear". As a consequence, it examined the application in light of Articles 10 and 17 jointly.

In this way, the Grand Chamber did not entirely sanction the idea that disputing the legal classification – but not the existence – of a historical event could not, as such, be contemptuous to the victims. Indeed, in the Author's view, drawing a distinction between the denial of the existence of an event and the denial of its legal qualification is, to an extent, artificial. For example, claiming that the Armenian massacres and mass deportations did not constitute genocide is paramount to denying *the reality of a factual element* of the Ottomans' criminal enterprise, that is, their intention to destroy, in whole or in part, the Armenian group as such – an element which is inferred, in turn, by a series of other equally significant factual circumstances.

At the same time, it is noteworthy that the Court confirmed the limited scope of Article 17, thus standing by its pronouncement that this avenue may only be pursued in "extreme cases".[54] This clarification was much needed in order to establish the limits to what could be regarded as an expansive trend in the Court's reading and application of the abuse clause – a trend which, if continued, could undermine the right to free speech, in the sense of legitimising restrictions on expressions that, although disquieting, do not expose any tangible symptoms of harm.

Nevertheless, the Court's present (commendable) dictum notwithstanding, Article 17 remains susceptible to a *broad and discretionary application*. First, the "novel" requirement of incitement to hatred or violence must be seen in relation to the Court's settled position on hate speech,

[53] *Perinçek* (2015), para 115; *Perinçek* (2013), para 52.
[54] ECtHR, *Paksas* v. *Lithuania* (Appl. No. 34932/04), Judgment 6 January 2011, para 87.

which brings within the scope of the abuse clause even expressions devoid of any calls for unlawful conduct or violent action.[55] Nor does the abuse clause target only "explicit and straightforward" statements; it also extends to more subtle and allusive forms of expression.[56]

Most importantly however, the notion of "incitement to hatred" is vague, and thus prone to oscillating interpretations. When it comes to denialism, it can hardly be questioned that most attempts to challenge the reality or magnitude of a traumatic event, no matter if well- or ill-intentioned, will almost certainly be seen by the victims as disquieting and insulting speech.[57] It follows that the gist of the Court's assessment is likely to focus on whether the conduct had a contemptuous aim and caused serious prejudice to the victims, which is bound to be a very subjective assessment, open to a wide spectrum of diverging understandings, as attested to by the Grand Chamber's bitter split in *Perinçek*.[58]

This blurred frontier between licit and illicit speech may have a chilling effect on the voicing of opinions that "offend, shock or disturb the State or any sector of the population", which the Court has long proclaimed should be permitted.[59]

5.2 *The Unsettled Functioning of the Abuse Clause*

The precedents on antidemocratic activities reveal two fundamental ways in which Article 17 operated, i.e. as either interpretative aid, or as a "case-killer" provision (through its guillotine effect). A notable study has uncovered a wealth of "undesirable consequences" flowing from the guillotine effect.[60] Among others, the rejection of an application on such a basis occurs with no, or at best only a superficial, examination of the context, nor is the proportionality of the state interference strictly scrutinised.

[55] See e.g. ECtHR, *Molnar* v. *Romania*, para 23; ECtHR, *Vejdeland and Others* v. *Sweden* (Appl. No. 1813/07), Judgment 9 February 2012, para 55; ECtHR, *Féret* v. *Belgium* (Appl. No. 15615/07), Judgment 16 July 2009, para 73.

[56] ECtHR, *M'Bala M'Bala* v. *France* (Appl. No. 25239/13), 20 October 2015, para 40.

[57] See *Perinçek* (2015), para 238.

[58] See *Perinçek* (2015), 'Joint Dissenting Opinion', para 4; *Perinçek* (2015), 'Additional Dissenting Opinion of Judge Silvis, Joined by Judges Casadevall, Berro and Kūris' (hereinafter *Perinçek* (2015), 'Additional Dissenting Opinion'), para 9.

[59] ECtHR, *Handyside* v. *United Kingdom* (Appl. No. 5493/72), Judgment 7 December 1976, para 49.

[60] Cannie and Voorhoof, 'The Abuse Clause', 68–72.

More problematically, states are relieved from the onus of convincingly justifying the restrictive measure, and thus their repressive practices risk being legitimised.

The Court has responded to this criticism in a number of its recent decisions, including the Grand Chamber's judgment in *Perinçek*, in which the application of Article 17 did not fully exclude or obliterate a proper legal analysis.[61] The proportionality of the interference, however, continued to be disregarded. Moreover, Article 17 still allows for applications to be summarily declared inadmissible, i.e. via decisions where exhaustive reasoning is not required and to which judges are not entitled to annex separate opinions.[62]

These pitfalls in Article 17's role as a case-killer add to some ambiguities surrounding its procedural function, which has fluctuated between being an "admissibility filter" to exclude patently ill-founded applications, and an "interpretative aid" at the stage of the merits. In *Perinçek*, the Grand Chamber confirmed this dual role, specifying that Article 17 may be resorted to at the stage of admissibility only where it is "immediately clear" that its requirements are met.[63]

To borrow from the language of a dissenting opinion in *Perinçek*, the Court has "kept its options open" regarding the functioning of the abuse clause.[64] One may query though: What has been, thus far, the provision's *added value* in the necessity test? Indeed, there is no indication that it has somehow had an impact on the usual structure or outcome of the ordinary analysis under Article 10.

On the other hand, there is a risk that Article 17 can end up alleviating the pressure, both *on states* to thoroughly justify the interference and *on Strasbourg judges* to deliver compellingly reasoned decisions. Therefore, it is argued that the Court should either articulate a set of narrow and measurable criteria that effectively ensure the application of Article 17 to only the most extreme cases,[65] or exclusively rely on the ordinary regime under

[61] ECtHR, *Kasymakhunov and Saybatalov* v. *Russia* (Appl. No. 26261/05 & 26377/06), Judgment 14 March 2013; ECtHR, *M'Bala M'Bala c. France*.

[62] See e.g. ECtHR, *Hizb Ut-Tahrir and Others* v. *Germany*; ECtHR, *Molnar c. Roumanie*.

[63] *Perinçek* (2015), paras 114–15.

[64] *Perinçek* (2015), 'Additional Dissenting Opinion', para 8.

[65] See, for an interpretative proposal which relies on the selective criteria of gravity, univocal aim, and existence of countervailing interests, P. Lobba, 'Holocaust Denial before the [ECtHR]: Evolution of an Exceptional Regime', *European Journal of International Law* 26:1 (2015), 237–53, at 250–1.

Article 10, which has proved perfectly capable of addressing insidious speech.[66]

6 Denial of the Holocaust: Special or Unique?

In *Perinçek*, the Court takes great pains to justify why the exceptional regime elaborated with respect to Holocaust denial is inapplicable to the denial of other historical facts, trying to avoid giving the impression that it is sanctioning a hierarchy between different, equally painful, events.[67] This aspect, however, proves to be the most controversial issue determined by the Court, with the Grand Chamber's majority thinning to nine judges and partially distancing itself from the Chamber's judgment.

The Chamber, back in 2013, had relied on two arguments to distinguish *Perinçek* from the cases involving Holocaust denial. In the first place, it seemed to infer a different *degree of consensus* as to the legal qualification of the events of 1915–16 compared to that ascribed to the Nazi crimes.[68] In so ruling, the Chamber, in effect, raised doubts as to the correctness of the genocidal nature ascribed to the Armenian events. Secondly, it noted a *different impact* of the two types of expression, which justified different responses.[69] The Chamber seemed to suggest that whereas Holocaust denial is a main vehicle of anti-Semitism and thus requires constant vigilance internationally, denials targeting the Armenian massacre cannot be said to have the same repercussions.

The Grand Chamber carefully avoided engaging in the debate about the proper qualification of the Armenian massacre. In this regard, it made

[66] See e.g. ECtHR, *Zana* v. *Turkey* (Appl. No. 18954/91), Judgment 25 November 1997; ECtHR, *Sürek* v. *Turkey (1)* (Appl. No. 26682/95), Judgment 8 July 1999; ECtHR, *Sürek* v. *Turkey (3)* (Appl. No. 24735/94), Judgment 8 July 1999; ECtHR, *Osmani and Others* v. *the Former Yugoslav Republic of Macedonia* (Appl. No. 50841/99), Inadmissibility Decision 11 October 2001; ECtHR, *Seurot* v. *France* (Appl. No. 57383/00), Inadmissibility Decision 18 May 2004; ECtHR, *Balsytė-Lideikienė* v. *Lithuania* (Appl. No. 72596/01), Judgment 4 November 2008; ECtHR, *Le Pen* v. *France* (Appl. No. 18788/09), Inadmissibility Decision 20 April 2010; ECtHR, *Gollnisch* v. *France* (Appl. No. 48135/08), Inadmissibility Decision 7 June 2011.

[67] For a criticism of the distinction endorsed in *Perinçek* (2013) between the treatment of the denial of the Holocaust and that of other crimes, see U. Belavusau, 'Memory Laws and Freedom of Speech', in A. Koltay (ed.), *Comparative Perspectives on the Fundamental Freedom of Expression* (Budapest: Wolters Kluwer, 2015), 537–58, at 548–50; see also P. Lobba, 'A European Halt to Laws Against Genocide Denial?', *European Criminal Law Review* 4:1 (2014), 59–77, at 68–9, 72–3.

[68] *Perinçek* (2013), para 117.

[69] *Ibid.*, para 119.

clear that legislation against Holocaust denial is justified not so much because the Holocaust is a clearly established historical fact, but because its negation "must invariably be seen as connoting an antidemocratic ideology and anti-Semitism".[70]

Interestingly, while the majority trod lightly in its approach to the legal characterisation of the Ottoman crimes, seven dissenting judges straightforwardly proclaimed their genocidal nature to be "self-evident".[71] Quite aside from the judges' dubious expertise in the field of contemporary history, such sweeping and conclusory assertions will hopefully remain an isolated exception in the consistent tendency of the Strasbourg jurisprudence not to get involved with ongoing historical and political debates.

Shifting away, then, from matters concerning the factual assessment and legal qualification of past events, the Grand Chamber justified the automatic presumption of harm applied to Holocaust denial with its inherent association with racist and totalitarian ideologies, which derives from historical and contextual reasons.[72] Despite a *prima facie* resemblance to the first Chamber's logic, the Grand Chamber made two novel points in this regard.

Firstly, it reaffirmed that the principles applied to the negation of the Holocaust stand out as unique; all other types of denialism require specific evidence to attest to their qualification as hate speech. In the latter area, the Court will likely subject the domestic courts' justifications to critical review, as it did in *Perinçek*.[73] This is consistent with an effective "European supervision" over national repression of disturbing speech, which may often be driven by political expediency rather than genuine public order concerns.

This is not to say that the Court has barred states from making denialism a crime.[74] Restrictions of the kind, however, have to be grounded on some *tangible symptoms of harm*, such as incidents wherein perpetrators maliciously falsified history, justified crimes, or issued particularly virulent statements disseminated in a form that is impossible to ignore. In sum, states cannot impose a blanket ban on denialism, but are required to strike a reasonable balance between the protection of the victims' dignity and the public's right to free speech. In this way, the Court intended to guard against unwarranted restrictions on

[70] *Perinçek* (2015), para 243. See also *Ibid.*, para 253.

[71] *Perinçek* (2015), 'Joint Dissenting Opinion', para 2.

[72] *Perinçek* (2015), para 234. See, for a similar approach, Conseil constitutionnel (France), 2015-512 QPC, 8 January 2016, para 10.

[73] See e.g. *Perinçek* (2015), paras 232–3.

[74] But see *Perinçek* (2015), 'Joint Dissenting Opinion', para 2.

freedom of expression, aimed at preventing the irrebuttable presumption that has been applied to Holocaust denial from spilling over into other forms of denialism, irrespective of whether the disputed events and legal classifications can be considered as clearly established.[75]

The second key point made by the Grand Chamber might be regarded as planting the seeds for the erosion, or at least a cautious delimitation, of the unique principles governing Holocaust denial. In upholding the presumption of harm applied to such expressions, the Grand Chamber appeared to justify it only on account of the *historical experience of the states from which the denialism cases before the Court arose*, which had all perpetrated or aided and abetted the commission of the Nazi crimes and could thus be seen as being under a special moral obligation to distance themselves from any attempt to downplay or call into question those atrocities.[76] Although this passage does not lend itself to a clear-cut interpretation, it might be read as a retrospective limitation upon the far-reaching principles regulating Holocaust denial. If scrupulously applied, this dictum could call for a context-sensitive analysis (in lieu of summary rejection) of complaints originating in countries that were not involved in the commission of the Nazi crimes. The automatic presumption triggering the guillotine effect would in this way be restricted to a narrowly defined group of states. With the exception of these particular contexts, restrictions on free speech would require the usual wealth of justifications on part of domestic authorities, in keeping with the principles laid down with respect to other forms of denialism.

7 Conclusions

It must be cautioned that the Grand Chamber fell short of unequivocally adopting the interpretation outlined above. Yet its judgment in *Perinçek* has paved the way for a future development of the Court's jurisprudence towards a position whereby the principles applied to Holocaust denial do not substantially deviate from those applied to pernicious or inflammatory speech in general, including the negation of other traumatic historical events. Whether the uniform treatment we are hereby advocating for will be grounded by the Court on Article 10 alone, Article 10 interpreted in the light of Article 17, or Article 17 alone, is at this point of diminished importance. What matters the most is that the Court's analysis be not relegated

[75] Cf. *Perinçek* (2013), para 117.
[76] *Perinçek* (2015), para 243.

to a superficial content-based, context-unrelated assessment, but came with the typical in-depth evaluation of all relevant circumstances that, over the past decades, has earned the Court the authority it presently enjoys worldwide.

Should the Court indeed follow the interpretation posited in this chapter, the issue of a patent disparity in the treatment between denial of the Holocaust and the denial of other crimes would be minimised, albeit not entirely resolved. It seems highly unlikely, and hardly acceptable, that the Court, in processing applications of Holocaust denial, would decline to rely on the rules and approaches that have produced adequate results in other hate speech cases. It should be noted, further, that the *Perinçek* Grand Chamber put forward a *dual presumption*: not only is the close association between Holocaust denial and anti-Semitism presumed, but so too is it presumed that the "special moral responsibility" of states that were involved in the Nazi crimes translates into a pressing social need on the part of these states to enforce a blanket criminal prohibition against Holocaust denial, independent of its tendency to incite hatred or violence. This being the current case law, the Court should at a minimum allow such presumption(s) to be rebutted by applicants.

As we have sought to demonstrate, the unique legal treatment accorded to Holocaust denial – upheld in *Perinçek* – is hard to justify and it seems likely to be increasingly challenged by other groups of victims who feel that their dignity deserves equal protection. Future cases will tell whether the Court will continue to stand by this dichotomy, or opt for the progressive harmonisation of its principles on denialism.

6

Legislating History: The European Union and Denial of International Crimes

LUIGI CAJANI

1 Introduction

On 28 November 2008, the Council of the European Union approved the Framework Decision on Combating Certain Forms and Expressions of Racism and Xenophobia by Means of Criminal Law,[1] which in addition to mandating the Member States to take measures to punish, as declared in the title, racist and xenophobic crimes,[2] adds a set of various forms of denial related to historical events which constitute crimes, more precisely acts:

> publicly condoning, denying or grossly trivializing crimes of genocide, crimes against humanity and war crimes as defined in Articles 6, 7 and 8 of the Statute of the International Criminal Court, ... [and] the crimes defined in Article 6 of the Charter of the International Military Tribunal appended to the London Agreement of 8 August 1945, directed against a group of persons or a member of such a group defined by reference to race, colour, religion, descent or national or ethnic origin when the conduct is carried out in a manner likely to incite to violence or hatred against such a group or a member of such a group.[3]

[1] Council Framework Decision 2008/913/JHA of 28 November 2008 on Combating Certain Forms and Expressions of Racism and Xenophobia by Means of Criminal Law, *Official Journal of the European Union*, 6.12.2008, L 328/55–L 328/58 (hereinafter Council Framework Decision 2008/913/JHA). For a deeper analysis, see B. Renauld, 'La décision-cadre 2008/913/JAI du Conseil de l'Union européenne: du nouveau en matière de lutte contre le racisme?', *Revue trimestrielle des droits de l'homme* 81 (2010) 119–40; L. Pech, 'The Law of Holocaust Denial in Europe. Toward a (qualified) EU-wide Criminal Prohibition', in L. Hennebel and T. Hochmann (eds), *Genocide Denials and the Law* (Oxford University Press, 2011) (hereinafter Hennebel and Hochmann (eds), *Genocide Denials*), 185–234; P. Lobba, 'La lotta al razzismo nel diritto penale europeo dopo Lisbona. Osservazioni sulla decisione quadro 2008/913/GAI e sul reato di negazionismo', *Ius17@unibo.it* 3 (2011), 109–58.

[2] "Publicly inciting to violence or hatred directed against a group of persons or a member of such a group defined by reference to race, colour, religion, descent or national or ethnic origin" (Council Framework Decision 2008/913/JHA, art. 1, § 1 a).

[3] Council Framework Decision 2008/913/JHA, art. 1, § 1 c and d).

The fundamental assumption of this Framework Decision is the nexus between racism and xenophobia on the one hand, and the denial of international crimes on the other. At the core of this connection lies the Holocaust, the denial of which is punished because it is considered tantamount to anti-Semitism, i.e. racism. At the same time, since the Holocaust is a historical event the punishment for denying, condoning, or grossly trivializing it makes it possible to extend the idea to punish the "denial, condoning, or grossly trivializing" to other historical events, which however may be more difficult to define as a form a racism. Likewise, this nexus is flawed with a conceptual short circuit: in fact the denial of the Holocaust entails the denial of the *reality* of the event, whilst in other cases, like the "genocide" committed against the Armenians in the Ottoman Empire during the First World War, the denial concerns only the *legal qualification* of the event, i.e. its characterization as "genocide" as opposed to being placed in another category of international crimes.

In addition, the two main elements of the Framework Decision, the counteraction of racism and xenophobia, have been present in State legislation since many years, and have been the cornerstone of the *International Convention on the Elimination of All Forms of Racial Discrimination*, adopted by the General Assembly of the United Nations on 21 December 1956. In contrast, the legislation criminalizing the denial of the Holocaust and other historical events has a more recent and controversial history. In this chapter, I first highlight the main elements of this legislation, and then analyse the long path which had led to the adoption of the Framework Decision, the various ways it has been implemented in the legislation of the EU Member States, and finally the serious concern it has raised among historians with respect to its possible impact on freedom of research and expression.

2 The Legislation on the Denial of the Holocaust and Other Historical Events

The first law punishing the denial of the Holocaust was introduced in Israel in 1986.[4] In Europe, similar provisions appeared in 1990 in France when the *Loi Gayssot*[5] was approved, during a moment when the fight against anti-Semitism seemed particularly urgent in the light of the activity of

[4] Denial of Holocaust (Prohibition) Law, 5746-1986, Article 2.

[5] Loi n 90-615 du 13 juillet 1990 tendant à réprimer tout acte raciste, antisémite ou xénophobe. With respect to the enforcement of this law, see *La lutte contre le négationnisme. Bilan et perspectives de la loi du 13 juillet 1990 tendant à réprimer tout acte raciste, antisémite ou*

Holocaust deniers like Robert Faurisson, and in the aftermath of a particularly outrageous episode of anti-Semitism – the desecration of the Jewish cemetery of Carpentras.[6] This law, while proclaiming the general intent of suppressing "every act of racism, anti-Semitism or xenophobia", imposed one year's imprisonment and a heavy fine to those who would "dispute (*ceux qui contestent*) the existence of one or more crimes against humanity defined by Article 6 of the Charter of the International Military Tribunal appended to the London Agreement of 8 August 1945". This latter instrument constituted the legal basis of the Nuremberg Trial.[7] The *Loi Gayssot* recognized the competences of both international and French courts to identify and try such crimes against humanity.[8]

This law is emblematic of the explicit connection between the crimes of denialism, on the one hand, and racism, anti-Semitism, and xenophobia on the other. It should be noted that the reference to Article 6 of the Charter is limited to the crimes against humanity cited therein, thus excluding crimes against peace and war crimes.

Other European states soon followed the French example, albeit with substantive differences. Sometimes "Nazi crimes" were explicitly mentioned; in other cases there was a general reference to "crimes against humanity" or "genocides"; and in some cases other forms of criminal conduct were

---

xénophobe. Actes du colloque du 5 juillet 2002 à la cour d'appel de Paris Commission nationale consultative des Droits de l'homme (CNCDH) (Paris: La documentation française, 2003).

[6] J. B. Wolf, *Harnessing the Holocaust. The Politics of Memory in France* (Stanford, CA: Stanford University Press, 2004), 137–42.

[7] The crimes are as follows:

> (a) Crimes against peace: namely, planning, preparation, initiation or waging of a war of aggression, or a war in violation of international treaties, agreements or assurances, or participation in a common plan or conspiracy for the accomplishment of any of the foregoing; (b) War crimes: namely, violations of the laws or customs of war. Such violations shall include, but not be limited to, murder, ill-treatment or deportation to slave labor or for any other purpose of the civilian population in occupied territory; murder or ill-treatment of prisoners of war or persons on the seas, killing of hostages, plunder of public or private property, wanton destruction of cities, towns or villages, or devastation not justified by military necessity; (c) Crimes against humanity: namely, murder, extermination, enslavement, deportation, and other inhumane acts committed against any civilian population, before or during the war; or persecutions on political, racial or religious grounds in execution of or in connection with any crime within the jurisdiction of the Tribunal, whether or not in violation of the domestic law of the country where perpetrated.

[8] For more details on the French context and intricacies of memory legislation and jurisprudence in France, see chapter by Ioanna Tourkochoriti in the present volume.

added to denial, e.g. "minimization". Furthermore, specific conditions were sometimes required in order to commence a prosecution, e.g. the existence of a danger to public peace.[9] In 1992, Austria made it an offence punishable by imprisonment of one to ten years (twenty in case of particularly serious offences) to "deny, grossly minimize, approve or try to justify" genocide and other Nazi crimes.[10] Switzerland followed suit in 1993 with a law punishing those who "deny, grossly minimize or try to justify a genocide or other crimes against humanity" with a fine or imprisonment up to three years.[11] In 1994, Germany, after ten years of parliamentary debates,[12] added a paragraph to Section 130 of the *Strafgesetzbuch*, under the heading of *Volksverhetzung*, which punished – with a fine or a prison sentence of up to five years – "whosoever publicly or in a meeting approves, denies or downplays an act committed under the rule of National Socialism . . . in a manner capable of disturbing the public peace".[13] A Belgian law of 1995 punished the "denial, minimization, justification or approval" of the Nazi genocide with a fine or imprisonment ranging from eight days to one year.[14] In 1995, Spain introduced a new Article 607.2 to its Penal Code, which punished both the denial and the justification of genocide – without specifying the Holocaust or any other particular genocide, and without mentioning crimes against humanity.[15] In 1997, Luxembourg introduced new penal regulation of racist behaviours, including Article 457.3 of the Penal Code, which punished those who had "disputed, minimized, justified or denied the existence of one or more crimes against humanity and war crimes defined by Article 6 of the Charter of the International Military Tribunal appended to the London Agreement of 8 August 1945". It recognized the jurisdiction of Luxembourgian, foreign, and international courts for the trial of these crimes. The law envisaged a prison term of eight days

[9] E. Fronza, 'The Criminal Protection of Memory: Some Observations about the Offence of Holocaust Denial', in Hennebel and Hochmann (eds), *Genocide Denials*, 155–81.

[10] Bundesverfassungsgesetz, mit dem das Verbotsgesetz geändert wird (Verbotsgesetz-Novelle 1992).

[11] Loi fédérale 18 June 1993.

[12] T. Wandres, *Die Strafbarkeit des Auschwitz-Leugnens* (Berlin: Duncker & Humblot, 2000), 110–2.

[13] Bundesrepublik Deutschland, *Strafgesetzbuch*, section 130, § 3.

[14] Loi tendant à réprimer la négation, la minimisation, la justification ou l'approbation du génocide commis par le régime national-socialiste allemand pendant la seconde guerre mondiale, 23 mars 1995.

[15] Ley Orgánica 10/1995, de 23 de noviembre, del Código Penal. For more on the legal engagements into historical memory in Spain, see chapter by Alfons Aragoneses in the present volume.

to six months and/or a fine from 10,001 to 1,000,000 francs. These provisions were extended to genocides committed not only by the Nazis, and for such cases only Luxembourgian and international courts were recognized.[16]. In 2002, Romania decided to punish "organizations and symbols with a fascist, racist or xenophobic character" and propagation of a cult of personality of persons responsible for crimes against peace and humanity and war crimes and found guilty by a national or international court.[17] In addition, the denial of the Holocaust was explicitly mentioned and punished by imprisonment ranging from six months to five years.[18]

3 The Making of the Framework Decision on Racism and Xenophobia

In the meantime, this legislative trend went up from the national to the supranational level when, in 1996, the European Union launched a Joint Action to Combat Racism and Xenophobia,[19] which established the judicial cooperation of the Member States in order to fight, amongst others, the following forms of criminal conduct: "public incitement to discrimination, violence or racial hatred"; "public condoning, for a racist or xenophobic purpose, of crimes against humanity and human rights violations"; and "public denial of the crimes defined in Article 6 of the Charter of the International Military Tribunal appended to the London Agreement of 8 April 1945 insofar as it includes behaviour which is contemptuous of, or degrading to, a group of persons defined by reference to colour, race, religion or national or ethnic origin". This initiative was not effective, but was picked up again by the Commission on 29 November 2001 with its first version of the Framework Decision.[20]

Article 4 of this first proposal followed in the footprints of the Joint Action of 1996, albeit with some important differences. In particular, for

[16] Loi du 19 juillet 1997 complétant le code pénal en modifiant l'incrimination du racisme et en portant incrimination du révisionnisme et d'autres agissements fondés sur des discriminations illégales.

[17] Ordonanța de urgență a Guvernului no. 31/2002, Articles 1 and 2.

[18] *Ibid.*, art. 6.

[19] Joint Action of 15 July 1996 adopted by the Council on the basis of Article K.3 of the Treaty on European Union, concerning action to combat racism and xenophobia (96/443/JHA), *Official Journal of the European Union*, 24.7.1996, L 185/5–L 185/7.

[20] Proposal for a Council Framework Decision on combating racism and xenophobia (COM(2001) 664 final – 2001/0270(CNS), *Official Journal of the European Union*, 26.3.2002, C 75 E, 269–73.

the punishment of the denial or trivialization of the crimes prosecuted by the Nuremberg Tribunal and the requirement of contemptuous or degrading circumstances were dropped, with the likelihood of disturbing the public order introduced to replace them.

This proposed Framework Decision met with strong resistance at the diplomatic level. In fact the Member States, according to its Article 16 § 1, had to take the necessary measures to comply with it by 30 June 2004. Yet this did not happen.[21] In fact, a meeting of the Council for Justice and Home Affairs on 2–3 June 2005 confirmed that an agreement was still far from being achieved. The president in office of the Council, Luxemburger Luc Frieden, said during a press conference:

> We had a very political discussion about that Framework decision today. I think this is less a legal document but rather more a political document . . . The draft Framework decision, as amended many times by me and the working group over the past months, has found large support, though not unanimous.[22]

He further stated that the main obstacle had been the different points of view among the Member States on the sensitive issue of freedom of expression:

> That means that in some countries freedom of expression knows almost no boundaries, certainly no boundaries imposed through criminal law sanctions. For others, freedom of expression does have limits. Those are limits that freely elected parliaments put into the criminal code, where the interests of others are in conflict with some fundamental human rights. This is a debate that one can have for ages.[23]

Thus the progress of the draft Framework Decision was halted for some time, until January 2007, when at the beginning of the German term of presidency of the Council of the European Union the German Minister of Justice, Brigitte Zypries, announced her intention to bring about its adoption in order to extend the legislation criminalizing the denial of

[21] For further information on this phase of the negotiations about the Framework decision, see M. Bell, 'European Union Strategies to Combat Racism and Xenophobia as a Crime', in R. Nickel, A. Coomber, M. Bell, T. Hutchinson, and K. Zahi (eds), *European Strategies to Combat Racism and Xenophobia as a Crime* (Brussels: European Network Against Racism: 2003), 31–8.

[22] Justice and Home Affairs, Press Release 2 June 2005: "No agreement on the framework decision on combating racism and xenophobia at the Justice and Home Affairs Council" (available at www.eu2005.lu/en/actualites/communiques/2005/06/02jai-rx/index.html) (retrieved 31 July 2016).

[23] *Ibid.*

genocides, notably the Holocaust, to all the Member States.[24] This marked the beginning of the last phase of the approval process, which was eventually successful, albeit thanks to many compromises which visibly influenced the final text.

Thus the prosecution of the various forms of denial listed in Article 1 §1 of the Framework Decision ("publicly condoning, denying or grossly trivializing") depends on many circumstances: it must be public, and "carried out in a manner likely to incite to violence or hatred". In the same article, § 2 gives Member States the freedom to "choose to punish only conduct which is either carried out in a manner likely to disturb public order or which is threatening, abusive or insulting". The following § 4 similarly enumerates a set of options concerning the tribunals entitled to define an historical event as an international crime, which cannot be denied:

> Any Member State may, on adoption of this Framework Decision or later, make a statement that it will make punishable the act of denying or grossly trivialising the crimes referred to in paragraph 1(c) and/or (d) only if the crimes referred to in these paragraphs have been established by a final decision of a national court of this Member State and/or an international court, or by a final decision of an international court only.

Other articles also prescribe prosecution of the "instigation, aiding and abetting" of the aforementioned forms of criminal conduct (Article 2); make these offences punishable with maximum criminal penalties of no less than between one and three years of imprisonment (Article 3); establish racist and xenophobic motivation as an aggravating circumstance for any other crime (Article 4); define liability and penalties for legal persons (Articles 5 and 6); and provide that the prosecution of the forms of criminal conduct defined in Articles 1 and 2 "shall not be dependent on a report or an accusation made by a victim of the conduct, at least in the most serious cases" (Article 8).

Article 9 § 1 establishes the boundaries of the jurisdiction for these forms of criminal conduct, as follows:

> Each Member State shall take the necessary measures to establish its jurisdiction with regard to the conduct referred to in Articles 1 and 2 where the conduct has been committed:
>
> (a) in whole or in part within its territory;
> (b) by one of its nationals; or
> (c) for the benefit of a legal person that has its head office in the territory of that Member State.

[24] I. Traynor, 'Germany Bids to Outlaw Denial of Holocaust across Continent', *The Guardian*, 16 January 2007.

4 The Implementation of the Framework Decision by the EU Member States

Article 10 (§ 1) of the *Framework Decision* set 28 November 2010 as the deadline for Member States to comply with its provisions. In terms of its implementation, Article 1 §§ 2 and 4 had already offered a wide range of options, but these were not sufficient for some Member States, who found the Framework Decision to be in conflict with their traditions of free speech. These member states accepted the Decision only after the inclusion of a "safeguard clause" in Article 7 § 2, as follows:

> This Framework Decision shall not have the effect of requiring Member States to take measures in contradiction to fundamental principles relating to freedom of association and freedom of expression, in particular freedom of the press and the freedom of expression in other media as they result from constitutional traditions or rules governing the rights and responsibilities of, and the procedural guarantees for, the press or other media where these rules relate to the determination or limitation of liability.

In practical terms, this clause impedes the programmatic attempt to homogenize the legislation of the Member States, as is reflected in the subsequent implementation process.

In fact, Ireland, Denmark, Sweden, the Netherlands, and the United Kingdom have not made any changes to their legislation to bring it in line with the Framework Decision, considering that the norms of their penal laws punishing racism and xenophobia sufficiently cover its requirements. Of particular interest is the debate which took place at the House of Lords in 2007, where great concern was expressed about the definition of the forms of criminal conduct in Article 1 of the Framework Decision, especially with regard to "grossly trivializing" as being too vague.[25] Furthermore, the punishment for Holocaust denial was considered problematic. On this last point the Government reassured the Lords that it did not intend to make Holocaust denial a criminal offence, because that would represent an "unnecessary infringement on freedom of expression", and because in a case where a denial would be "expressed in a way that is threatening, abusive, or insulting and incites racial hatred, or is likely to do so", then it would be punishable under the Public Order Act 1986.[26] In 2011, Finland increased

[25] House of the Lords, Committee Office: The Lord Grenfell, Chairman of the Select Committee on the European Union, to the Rt Hon Vernon Coaker MP, Parliamentary Under Secretary of State, Home Office, 19 April 2007, 24 May 2007.

[26] House of Lords Debates, vol. 691, 20.4.2007, col. WA 97.

the punishment for racist and discriminatory behaviours, yet without introducing crimes of denial.[27] Germany only slightly modified its previous legislation, in 2011, by adding to article 130 § 1 of the *Strafgesetzbuch* a reference to "individuals" as a potential target, whilst before only "groups" were mentioned.[28] This article, as has been alluded to, dealt only with the Holocaust. Nothing has been changed in the German Penal Code concerning the other crimes against humanity or war crimes because – as stipulated in the preparatory report for this law – they are considered already covered by Article 140 of the *Strafgesetzbuch*, which imposes imprisonment up to three years or a fine for the public approval of a wide array of crimes, ranging from sexual offences to high treason to counterfeiting of money, and including crimes against humanity and war crimes in general.[29]

Amongst the States which have in one way or another adopted the Framework Decision (some of them after the deadline) are Malta,[30] Slovakia,[31] and Latvia[32] (2009), Lithuania[33] and Hungary[34] (2010), Bulgaria (2011),[35] and Greece (2014).[36] However, there are some substantive

[27] Laki 511/2011 rikoslain muuttamisesta Annettu Helsingissa 13 paivana toukokuuta 2011, Suomen Saadoskokoelma, 20 May 2011.

[28] Gesetz zur Umsetzung des Rahmenbeschlusses 2008/913/JI des Rates vom 28. November 2008 zur strafrechtlichen Bekämpfung bestimmter Formen und Ausdrucksweisen von Rassismus und Fremdenfeindlichkeit und zur Umsetzung des Zusatzprotokolls vom 28. Januar 2003 zum Übereinkommen des Europarats vom 23. November 2001 über Computerkriminalität betreffend die Kriminalisierung mittels Computersystemen begangener Handlungen rassistischer und fremdenfeindlicher Art, 16 March 2011.

[29] Deutscher Bundestag – 17. Wahlperiode, Drucksache 17/3124: Entwurf eines Gesetzes zur Umsetzung des Rahmenbeschlusses 2008/913/JI des Rates vom 28. November 2008 zur strafrechtlichen Bekämpfung bestimmter Formen und Ausdrucksweisen von Rassismus und Fremdenfeindlichkeit und zur Umsetzung des Zusatzprotokolls vom 28. Januar 2003 zum Übereinkommen des Europarats vom 23. November 2001 über Computerkriminalität betreffend die Kriminalisierung mittels Computersystemen begangener Handlungen rassistischer und fremdenfeindlicher Art, Begründung A, III.

[30] Act No. XI of 2009: An Act further to amend the Criminal Code, Cap. 9.

[31] Zákon č. 300/2005 Z. Z. z 20. mája 2005 Trestný Zákon v znení zákona č. 650/2005 Z. z., v znení zákona č. 692/2006 Z. z., v znení zákona č. 218/2007 Z. z., v znení zákona č. 491/2008 Z. z., v znení zákona č. 497/2008 Z. z., v znení zákona č. 498/2008 Z. z., v znení zákona č. 257/2009 Z. z.

[32] Grozījumi Krimināllikumā, 74–1, adopted by the Parliament on 1 July 2009.

[33] Baudžiamojo kodekso 95 straipsnio pakeitimo bei papildymo, kodekso papildymo 170[2] straipsniu ir kodekso priedo papildymo įstatymas, 2010 m. birželio 15 d. Nr. XI-901, Vilnius.

[34] 2010. evi LVI. torveny a Buntető Torvenykonyvről szolo 1978. evi IV. torveny modositasarol.

[35] Darzhaven vestnik, No. 33/26 April 2011.

[36] Βουλή των Ελλήνων, Τροποποίηση του ν. 927/1979 (Α' 139) και προσαρμογή του στην απόφαση - πλαίσιο 2008/913/ΔΕΥ της 28ης Νοεμβρίου 2008, για την καταπολέμηση

differences in these legislative texts. First of all, the provision of Article 1 § 1 (c, d) specifying that the various forms of denial can be prosecuted when "carried out in a manner likely to incite to violence or hatred" is generally absent (exceptions are Bulgaria and Malta). Lithuania made use of the clause envisaged in the previous Article 1 § 2 and declared that the denial would be prosecuted when carried out in a threatening, abusive, or insulting manner or when it disturbed public order. Significant differences also concern the designation of the official bodies entitled to define historical events as international crimes. In some countries, such as Malta, Latvia, and Hungary, there is no indication at all. In other states (Slovakia), only international courts are mentioned. In other cases, both international and national courts as well as the national parliament (Greece) and the European Union (Lithuania) are included, thus going beyond the provisions of the Framework Decision. Italy was the latecomer with its law of 2016,[37] which does not introduce denial as a separate crime. Rather, it included it as an aggravating circumstance in a 1993 law, which prosecutes general crimes of a racist nature. Likewise, the Italian law gives no indication about which official bodies which are competent to interpret historical events as international crimes.

5 The Case of Crimes by Communist Regimes

In 2007, during the last phase of the debate on the Framework Decision, another controversy arose concerning an issue that was particularly sensitive for the "new" EU States which were previously behind the Iron Curtain. The three Baltic countries, Poland, and Slovenia demanded that the crimes perpetrated by the Soviet regime be included in the Framework decision.[38] This initiative was not extemporaneous: already in 2006 the Parliamentary Assembly of the Council of Europe had passed a resolution which called for the international condemnation of the crimes committed

ορισμένων μορφών και εκδηλώσεων ρατσισμού και ξενοφοβίας μέσω του ποινικού δικαίου (L 328) και άλλες διατάξεις. For an analysis of the Greek law, see chapter by Ioanna Tourkochoriti in the present volume.

[37] Legge 16 giugno 2016, n. 115: Modifiche all'articolo 3 della legge 13 ottobre 1975, n. 654, in materia di contrasto e repressione dei crimini di genocidio, crimini contro l'umanità e crimini di guerra, come definiti dagli articoli 6, 7 e 8 dello statuto della Corte penale internazionale.

[38] C. Barbier, D. Ghailani, and P. Pochet, 'European Briefing: Digest', *Journal of European Social Policy* 17 (2007), 271–84, at 277.

by totalitarian communist regimes, and not only those of the past but also those still in power.[39]

This demand met with opposition from, *inter alia*, the United Kingdom,[40] and eventually the proponents gave it up in exchange for a declaration of the Council, which promised a future reconsideration of the issue, as follows:

> The Framework Decision is limited to crimes committed on the grounds of race, colour, religion, descent or national or ethnic origin. It does not cover crimes committed on other grounds, for example by totalitarian regimes. However, the Council deplores all of these crimes [. . .] The Berlin declaration adopted on 25 March 2007 stated that "European integration shows that we have learnt the painful lessons of a history marked by bloody conflict". In that light the Commission will organize a public European hearing on crimes of genocide, crimes against humanity and war crimes committed by totalitarian regimes as well as those who publicly condone, deny, grossly distort or trivialize them, and emphasizes the need for appropriate redress of injustice and – if appropriate – [will] submit a proposal for a framework decision on these crimes.[41]

One year later, on 8 April 2008, a public hearing on the crimes of totalitarian regimes was actually organized by the Slovenian presidency of the Council of the European Union. Many speakers harshly condemned the double-standard employed with respect to Nazi and communist crimes, which was widespread in Western Europe for cultural and political reasons and was reflected in the then-current draft of the Framework Decision.[42] The lenient attitude towards today's Russia and its President Vladimir Putin, who extolled the role of the Soviet army as liberator of Europe, was also criticized. For these reasons the previous "Soviet satellite" States felt that the Framework Decision did not duly acknowledge their suffering under the Soviet Union and the installed domestic

[39] Parliamentary Assembly of the Council of Europe, Resolution 1481 (2006): Need for international condemnation of crimes of totalitarian communist regimes (adopted on 25 February 2006).

[40] House of the Lords, Committee Office: The Lord Grenfell, Chairman of the Select Committee on the European Union, to the Rt Hon Vernon Coaker MP, Parliamentary Under Secretary of State, Home Office, 19 April 2007.

[41] Council of the European Union, Interinstitutional File: 2001/0270(CNS) DROIPEN 94, Brussels, 26 November 2008.

[42] S. Kalniete, 'Divergences within European politics with Regard to Communist Totalitarianism', in P. Jambrek (ed.), *Crimes Committed by Totalitarian Regimes* (Ljubljana: Slovenian Presidency of the Council of the European Union, 2008) (hereinafter Jambrek (ed.), *Crimes*), 245–50; G. Valdis Kristovskis, 'The Need for a Reappraisal of the European History', in Jambrek (ed.), *Crimes*, 223–5.

communist regimes. Likewise, the proposed concept of genocide was criticized for excluding political and social groups, a decision which was taken by the United Nations in 1948, when the Convention on the Prevention and Punishment of the Crime of Genocide was approved, owing to the pressure of the Soviet Union, and which has also been reflected in the Statute of the International Criminal Court.[43] At the end of the hearing the Lithuanian delegation proposed a set of initiatives to investigate the crimes of communist and other totalitarian regimes in Europe and to promote awareness about them, including, *inter alia*, the establishment of a commemoration of their victims on 23 August, the day when the Molotov-Ribbentrop pact was signed in 1939.[44] Thus, an equal responsibility for the outbreak of the Second World War was placed on both Germany and Soviet Union. This demand was fulfilled only a few months later, on 23 September 2008, by the European Parliament, which declared 23 August as the *European Day of Remembrance for Victims of Stalinism and Nazism*.[45]

The particular concern of post-communist States for their own history is also reflected in some of their laws implementing the Framework Decision. The Czech Republic had already introduced Article 261a into its Penal Code of 2000, which conflated the Nazi and the communist crimes, as follows:

> Whoever publicly denies, questions, approves or tries to justify Nazi or communist genocide or other crimes against humanity committed by Nazis or communists shall be punished by a term of imprisonment from six months to three years.[46]

Likewise, Hungary[47] and Lithuania[48] have explicitly mentioned communist crimes in their approval of the Framework Decision.

[43] R. Racinskas, 'Historical Justice for Europe: Why, When and How?', in Jambrek (ed.), *Crimes* 13–19; D. Žalimas, 'The Need for Equal Treatment of Nazi and Soviet crimes', in Jambrek (ed.), *Crimes*, 81–4.

[44] E. Zingeris, 'Transition from the "Gulag Empire" to the Western civilisation - issues of remembrance and education', in Jambrek (ed.), *Crimes*, 255–8.

[45] Declaration of the European Parliament on the proclamation of 23 August as European Day of Remembrance for Victims of Stalinism and Nazism, *Official Journal of the European Union* 14 January 2010, C 8/ E 57–59.

[46] Zákon ze dne 25. října 2000, kterým se mění zákon č. 140/1961 Sb., trestní zákon, ve znění pozdějších předpisů.

[47] See *supra* note 34.

[48] See *supra* note 33.

6 Historians Criticize the Framework Decision

The aforementioned Zypries' declaration of 2007 awakened the attention of the broader public towards the Framework Decision and unleashed a wave of negative reactions among historians. British historian and political scientist Timothy Garton Ash wrote that this initiative, however well-intentioned, was "very unwise . . . [and] it would further curtail free expression – at a time when it is under threat from many quarters".[49] Similarly, German historian Eberhard Jäckel asserted in an interview that the denial of the Holocaust was "a stupid thing to do", which, however, did not require punishment unless it incited hatred, and which could be combated more effectively by "information".[50] Likewise, Italian historians reacted against the Italian Minister of Justice, Clemente Mastella, who, inspired by Zypries, wanted to immediately introduce a law criminalizing the denial of the Holocaust:[51] in one single day more than 200 scholars signed a petition asserting that such a law was dangerous, useless, and counterproductive, because: (1) it would provide deniers with "the opportunity to present themselves as defenders of freedom of expression"; (2) in its efforts to impose historical truth, the State would expose this truth to the risk of losing all legitimacy and would undermine "confidence in the free confrontation of stances and in free historiographical and intellectual research"; and (3) laws criminalizing incitement to violence, incitement to racial hatred, and the praising of crimes against humanity already existed in Italy. The petition concluded with the assertion that civil society alone was empowered to struggle against Holocaust denial by means of "a cultural fight, by ethics, and by steadfast policy".[52] Furthermore, the French association *Liberté pour l'histoire* protested against the Framework decision, pointing out, *inter alia*, the "perverse effects" of *Loi Gayssot*,[53] which had already been denounced at the time of its approval by historians Pierre Vidal-Naquet[54] and Madeleine Rebérioux.[55]

[49] T. Garton Ash, 'A Blanket Ban on Holocaust Denial Would be a Serious Mistake', *The Guardian*, 18 January 2007.

[50] 'Historiker Jäckel: Holocaust-Leugner mit Ignoranz strafen (Moderation: Gabi Wuttke)', *Deutschlandradio*, 1 February 2007 (retrieved 31 July 2016).

[51] A. Tarquini, 'Mastella: negare la Shoah sarà reato', *l'Unità*, 20 January 2007.

[52] 'Noi storici contro la legge che punisce chi nega la Shoah', *l'Unità* 23 January 2007. The petition was launched by Marcello Flores, Simon Levis Sullam, and Enzo Traverso.

[53] P. Nora, 'Liberté pour l'histoire!', *Le Monde*, 10 October 2008.

[54] P. Vidal-Naquet, 'Qui sont les assassins de la mémoire?', *Idem, Les assassin de la mémoire. «Un Eichmann de papier» et autres essais sur le révisionnisme*, édition revue et augmentée, postface de Gisèle Sapiro (Paris: La Découverte, 2005), 206.

[55] M. Rebérioux, 'Le Génocide, le juge et l'historien', *L'Histoire* 138 (novembre 1990), 92–4.

The concern of historians spread also beyond the borders of the European Union. In particular, the General Assembly of the International Committee of Historical Sciences (ICHS), held in Beijing on 17–18 September 2007, approved a motion expressing great alarm at this possible intrusion of the law into the field of historical research.[56] A few days before the Beijing meeting, the American Historical Association had issued a communication concerning the Framework decision, stating that any scientific research may only be assessed by experts belonging to the same research field. Therefore, should a historian distort his evidence, the only measures to be taken against him, by colleagues specialized in the same field, must be the exclusion from academic posts and, in extreme cases, from publications. It concluded that: "if any other body, especially a body with the right to initiate legal proceedings and impose penalties, seeks to influence the course of historical research, the result will inevitably be intimidation of scholars and distortion of their findings".[57]

7 Conceptual Pitfalls of the Framework Decision

In the introduction I identified the equalization of denial of the *reality* of an historical event with the contestation of its *legal definition* as one of the main pitfalls of the Framework Decision (and of similar laws). While the former can be considered insulting to the victims because it entails the accusation of lying, the latter is only a matter of interpretation, characteristic for the work not only of historians but also of lawyers. Obviously it is difficult and even impossible to obtain general agreement on the legal definition of historical events involving international crimes. Scholars' opinions differ about the definition of genocide in terms of the requisite intent and methods of perpetrators and of the characteristics of the victims.[58] In particular, this is the case of the Armenians massacred in the Ottoman Empire during the First World War,[59] of the famine victims in Ukraine in

[56] General Assembly of the ICHS, Beijing, 17–18 September 2007 (available at: www.cish .org/: retrieved 31 July 2016).

[57] AHA Statement on the Framework Decision of the Council of the European Union on the Fight against Racism and Xenophobia, *Perspectives* 45:8 (2007).

[58] S. Straus, 'Contested Meanings and Conflicting Imperatives: A Conceptual Analysis of Genocide', *Journal of Genocide Research* 3:3 (2001), 349–75.

[59] Most scholars maintain that it must be considered as genocide, but this definition has been contested for instance by Bernard Lewis (Y. Auron, *The Banality of Denial. Israel and the Armenian Genocide* (New Brunswick, London: Transaction Publishers, 2003) 226–30) and by G. Lewy in his book *The Armenian Massacres in Ottoman Turkey: A Disputed Genocide* (Salt Lake City, UT: The University of Utah Press, 2005).

1932–3,[60] and more recently of the massacres in Srebrenica[61] and Darfur.[62] Some scholars limit the definition of genocide only to the Holocaust,[63] in the context of the debate about its uniqueness.[64] Others extend it to a great number of historical events, including the "colonial genocides", like the fates of the Hereros, of the Australian Aborigines, and of the Native Americans, even going back in history to antiquity.[65] Henry Huttenbach, editor of the *Journal of Genocide Research*, in 2002 depicted the state of the question as follows:

> To date, genocide . . . lacks both a satisfactory conceptual definition and a consensus as to the inner make-up of genocide. Without a conceptual

[60] For a review of the relevant literature, see Y. Bilinsky, 'Was the Ukrainian Famine of 1932–1933 Genocide?', *Journal of Genocide Research* 1:2 (1999), 147–56.

[61] W. A. Schabas, *Genocide in International Law. The Crime of Crimes* (Cambridge, New York, Melbourne, Madrid: Cambridge University Press, 2000), 189–201; *Application of the Convention on the Prevention and Punishment of the Crime of Genocide (Bosnia and Herzegovina v. Serbia and Montenegro), Judgment, I.C.J. Reports 2007 - Application de la convention pour la prévention et la repression du crime de génocide (Bosnie-Herzégovine c. Serbie-et-Monténégro), arrêt, C.I.J. Recueil 2007;* I. Delpla, Xavier Bougarel, and Jean-Louis Fournel (eds), *Investigating Srebrenica. Institutions, Facts, Responsibilities* (New York, Oxford: Berghahn Books, 2012); and the interview given by Yehuda Bauer to Radio Televizija Republike Srpske: *Bauer: U Srebrenici je bilo masovno ubistvo, a ne genocide* (RTRS, 29.6.2015: retrieved 31 July 2016).

[62] *Report of the International Commission of Inquiry on Darfur to the United Nations Secretary-General, Pursuant to Security Council Resolution 1564 of 18 September 2004*, Geneva, 25 January 2005; J. Hagan and W. Rymond-Richmond, *Darfur and the Crime of Genocide* (Cambridge, New York, Melbourne, Madrid, Cape Town, Singapore, São Paulo: Cambridge University Press, 2009).

[63] G. I. Langmuir, 'Continuities, Discontinuities and Contingencies of the Holocaust', in J. Frankel (ed.), *The Fate of the European Jews, 1939–1945, Continuity or Contingency? (Studies in Contemporary Jewry XIII)*, New York - Oxford, Oxford University Press, 9–29.

[64] S. T. Katz, *The Holocaust in Historical Context, Vol. 1: The Holocaust and Mass Death before the Modern Age* (New York, Oxford: Oxford University Press, 1994); M. Levene, 'Is the Holocaust Simply Another Example of Genocide?', *Patterns of Prejudice* 28:2 (1994), 3–26; A. Margalit and G. Motzkin, 'The Uniqueness of the Holocaust', *Philosophy & Public Affairs* 25:1 (Winter, 1996), 65–83; G. D. Rosenfeld, 'The Politics of Uniqueness: Reflections on the Recent Polemical Turn in Holocaust and Genocide Scholarship', *Holocaust and Genocide Studies* 13:1 (1999), 21–63; A. S. Rosenbaum (ed.), *Is the Holocaust Unique? Perspectives on Comparative Genocide* (Boulder, CO: Westview Press, 2009, third edition, 1995 first edition).

[65] B. Kiernan, *Blood and Soil: A World History of Genocide and Extermination from Sparta to Darfur* (New Haven, CT: Yale University Press, 2007); N. Finzsch, 'If It Looks Like a Duck, If It Walks Like a Duck, If It Quacks Like a Duck: Comment on "Can there be Genocide without the Intent to Commit Genocide?" by Guenter Lewy', *Journal of Genocide Research* 10:1 (2008), 119–26; J. Sarkin, *Colonial Genocide and Reparations Claims in the 21st Century: The Socio-Legal Context of Claims under International Law by the Herero against Germany for Genocide in Namibia, 1904–1908* (Westport, CT: Praeger Security International, 2009).

> definition one is impeded in separating genocidal events from the non-genocidal; and, lacking a basic blueprint, it is unclear how and what to compare and, thereby, determine distinctive singularities and commonalities separating and linking genocides.[66]

Things are no less debated in the cases of crimes against humanity and war crimes. British philosopher Anthony Grayling, for instance, asserts that the air raids carried out by the Allied forces against German and Japanese cities during the Second World War were crimes against humanity.[67]

To dictate and enforce, via a punitive provision, the interpretation of a historical event is therefore an infringement of freedom of research. Not only is juridical inquiry carried out according to a specific logic, its procedures and goals differ substantially from historical methodology. By definition, moreover, historical research is constantly evolving, a characteristic which conflicts with the nature of a final sentence of a court which, even if passed by a majority of the judges of a court, has the definitive force of *res judicata*. Furthermore, some Member States also give the right to define historical events to national Parliaments, and these kinds of definitions do not follow a legal logic, but rather solely serve the political agendas of the moment. The contrasting definitions of national courts, international courts, and national Parliaments create a dangerous chaos, whereby a statement which is perfectly legitimate in one State may be a criminal offence in another.

Another problem is of a technical juridical nature and is connected with the meaning of the three forms of criminal conduct foreseen in the Framework Decision: whilst *denial* can be clearly enough defined (insofar as it refers both to the *reality* and to the interpretation of a historical event), the meaning of *condoning*, and especially of *grossly trivializing* is rather uncertain and vague, and can therefore lead to greatly divergent interpretations in separate individual trials. According to some legal scholars, in fact, forms of criminal conduct such as "condoning" or "trivializing" (in various national legislations one can also find other more or less synonymous terms, like "justification" or "minimization") can apply even when a historical event defined as an international crime is explained, or its gravity is diminished according to the context where it happened, for instance

[66] H. R. Huttenbach, 'From the Editor: Towards a Conceptual Definition of Genocide', *Journal of Genocide Research* 4:2 (2002), 167–75, here 167.

[67] A. C. Grayling, *Among the Dead Cities* (London: Bloomsbury, 2006).

if it is considered as a reaction to a perceived danger or to a previous act of violence by the victims.[68]

8 Conclusions

Laws that dictate a certain definition of a historical event and enforce it by use of the penal code mark a turning point in the story of the social and political use of history. These laws are not the sole domain of the European Union. In 2006 the Ukrainian Parliament passed a law declaring the Holodomor, the famine which hit the country during the 1930s, as a genocide against the Ukrainian people and deemed its denial as unlawful.[69] In 2014, the Russian Parliament approved an amendment to the Penal Code, which punishes – by jail terms up to three years or a fine – the denial or approval of crimes recognized by the International Military Tribunal established in 1945 and the spreading of false information about the Soviet Union's activities during the Second World War.[70] These laws are the result of two, sometimes concurrent, inputs: on the one hand, the pressure of social interest groups, which are particularly strong in the wider context of the "memory wars", which in turn are part of the "memory boom" which has become diffused worldwide during the last three decades;[71] and on the other hand the propaganda strategies of political powers on both the domestic and on the international level, as for instance in the cases of Ukraine or of Armenia, which strive to have the specific tragedies suffered by their nations recognized internationally as genocide. By adopting the

[68] E. Fronza, 'Profili Penalistici del Negazionismo', *Rivista Italiana di Diritto e Procedura Penale* n.s. XLII (1999), 1034–74, here 1050, 1061–2.

[69] G. Kasianov, 'The Great Famine of 1932–1933 (Holodomor) and the Politics of History in Contemporary Ukraine', in S. Troebst (ed.), *Postdiktatorische Geschichtskulturen im Süden und Osten Europas. Bestandsaufnahme und Forschungsperspektiven* (Göttingen: Wallstein Verlag, 2010), 619–41. See also chapter by Lina Klymenko in the present volume.

[70] N. Koposov, 'Une loi pour faire la guerre: La Russie et sa mémoire', *Le Débat* 181 (2014) 103–15. See also the chapter by Koposov in the present volume.

[71] Among the vast literature on this theme, see: P. Nora, 'Gedächtniskonjunktur', *Transit - Europäische Revue* 22 (2001–2002), 18–31; J. Winter, 'The Generation of Memory. Reflections on the "Memory Boom" in Contemporary Historical Studies', *Canadian Military History* 10:3 (2001), 57–66; M. Cherif Bassiouni, 'International Recognition of Victims' Rights', *Human Rights Law Review* 6:2 (2006), 203–79; R. N. Lebow, 'The Future of Memory', *Annals of the American Academy of Political and Social Science* 617 (May 2008), 25–41; P. Lagrou, 'Europe as a Place for Common Memories? Some Thoughts on Victimhood, Identity and Emancipation from the Past', in M. Blaive, C. Gerbel and T. Lindenberger (eds), *Clashes in European Memory: The Case of Communist Repression and the Holocaust* (Innsbruck, Wien, Bozen: StudienVerlag, 2011), 281–8.

Framework Decision, the European Union has given a very strong impetus to this legislative trend, and not only among its Member States.

One can formally distinguish between laws which are simply a "declarative statute"[72] and those which punish the denial of a historical event. The former aim at a kind of moral reparation to the victims, often with an admission of culpability and an explicit educational intent, like the French *loi Taubira*.[73] In this sense they could be considered as just another form of the politics of memory, like the building of monuments or the establishment of commemorative events, with no tangible harm. However, experience shows that these laws tend to be the first step towards the introduction of penal laws making denial a crime. This is evident in the French case, where the first, purely declarative, law of 2001 on the Armenian genocide was followed, under pressure from the French-Armenian lobbies, by a set of parliamentary initiatives aimed at punishing the denial of the Armenian genocide, mimicking the pattern of the *loi Gayssot*.[74] All these attempts have so far failed, either at the parliamentary level or, when successful there, at the level of the *Conseil Constitutionnel*.[75] Yet their lobbyists have not given up, and again an initiative has been introduced at the *Assemblée nationale*, which on 1 July 2016 adopted an amendment to the law on press freedom (the same to which the *loi Gayssot* referred) punishing the denial of every genocide, crime against humanity, war crimes, and enslavement.[76] This stance concerns not only all the crimes foreseen by the Article 6 of the Charter of the International Military Tribunal but also, in particular, the crimes foreseen by the French laws on the slave trade and the Armenian genocide. This bill, as of this writing, awaits approval by the *Sénat*.

These laws seriously endanger freedom of research and expression, not only for historians but for everyone who is involved in communicating history, such as teachers and journalists. Such dangers are well illustrated by the recent case of German historian Heinz Richter, who in

[72] D. Fraser, 'Law's Holocaust Denial: State, Memory, Legality', in Hennebel and Hochmann (eds), *Genocide Denials*, 3–48.

[73] Loi n. 2001-434 du 21 mai 2001 tendant à la reconnaissance, par la France, de la traite et de l'esclavage en tant que crime contre l'humanité, art. 2: "Les programmes scolaires et les programmes de recherche en histoire et en sciences humaines accorderont à la traite négrière et à l'esclavage la place conséquente qu'ils méritent".

[74] For more on the French case, see chapter by Ioanna Tourkochoriti in the present volume.

[75] Conseil Constitutionnel, *Décision n° 2012-647 DC du 28 février 2012*.

[76] Assemblée nationale, XIVe législature Session extraordinaire de 2015–16, Compte rendu intégral Deuxième séance du vendredi 01 juillet 2016.

2011 published a book about the Battle of Crete in 1941.[77] In the book, he explained the German retaliations against civilians as having been provoked by the war crimes perpetrated by Greek partisans against the German military, and was therefore charged, on the basis of the law of 2014, at the court of Rethymno (Crete) with denial of the crimes of Nazism against the Cretan people with defamatory intent. Richter was eventually acquitted in February 2016.[78] The Academy of Athens, despite expressing disagreement with Richter's point of view, defended his right to freedom of research and criticized the prosecutor,[79] while Greek historians acted as witnesses on behalf of Richter in the court proceeding. This example aptly captures the necessity for, and the possible effectiveness of, mobilization by historians in the face of punitive memory laws.

[77] H. A. Richter, *Operation Merkur. Die Eroberung der Insel Kreta im Mai 1941* (Mainz – Ruhpolding: Verlag Franz Philipp Rutzen, 2011) (Greek translation: Η μάχη της Κρήτης, Αθήνα: Εκδόσεις Γκοβόστη, 2011).

[78] Λινα Γιανναρου, Αθωώθηκε ο Γερμανός ιστορικός Χάιντς Ρίχτερ, Η Καθημερινή, 11 February 2016.

[79] Η υπόθεση ποινικής δίωξης Χάιντς Ρίχτερ, *Η Καθημερινή*, 20 December 2015.

PART III

National Perspectives within the European Union

7

Challenging Historical Facts and National Truths: An Analysis of Cases from France and Greece

IOANNA TOURKOCHORITI*

> A history entirely rewritten and judged from the perspective of the victims and the conquered is a denial of history.[1]

1 Introduction

The need to express our collective disapproval of atrocities against humanity through memory laws is certainly justifiable.[2] But how far should such laws extend? Should they limit the expression of statements that contest those facts' existence? Memory laws can serve to prescribe or proscribe[3] an official version of historical truth. Using the mechanisms of state constraint against opinions that are contrary to this official version of the truth can be very dangerous for individual and collective liberties. The denial of crimes against humanity is a criminal offense in various European legal orders, e.g. France.[4] The European Union has endorsed this approach through a Council Framework Decision[5] that crystallizes legislation already existing in a number of Member States and asks others to consider enacting measures criminalizing this category of speech. This chapter examines a

* I would like to thank Eric Heinze for detailed comments on a previous draft. Thanks go also to Thomas Hochmann, Antoon De Baets, Luigi Cajani, Uladzislau Belavusau, Aleksandra Gliszczynska-Grabias, Cosmin Cercel, Robert Kahn, and to an anonymous reviewer for interesting suggestions.

1 P. Nora, 'Historical Identity in Trouble' in *Liberté pour l'Histoire*, available at www.lph-asso.fr/index.php?option=com_content&view=article&id=152&Itemid=182&lang=en.

2 See chapter by Eric Heinze in the present volume.

3 See chapter by Antoon De Baets in the present volume.

4 By the famous "Loi Gayssot," Law No. 90-615 of 13 July 1990, Tendant à réprimer tout acte raciste, antisémite ou xénophobe, *Journal Officiel de la République française*, of 4 July 1990, at 8333.

5 Council Framework Decision No. 208/913/JAI of 28 November 2008, *O.J.* No. L 328/55, 12 July 2008. See chapter by Luigi Cajani in the present volume.

number of cases where courts have imposed legal sanctions on those who made claims either denying the Holocaust,[6] or challenging elements of national identity that seemed inacceptable to national authorities, as well as legislative proposals attempting to impose an official version of historical facts.

In 2011, the French government proposed legislation that would criminalize the denial of the Armenian genocide.[7] The French Constitutional Council invalidated the proposal.[8] In Turkey, cases have emerged where authors who discuss that genocide face charges for "denigration of the Turkish nation."[9] The Greek authorities refused to register an association formed to promote the cultural interests of the "Macedonian Nation." The European Court of Human Rights (ECtHR) held that Greece was in violation of the group's freedom of association in this case.[10]

France maintains a number of legislative texts that recognize genocides having taken place at different moments in history, both French and global. Recently, there was a legislative attempt to include in a legal text a clause according to which the French school programs should "recognize the 'positive role' of the French presence overseas."[11] The proposal sought to consecrate through law an official truth on the French colonial past. The proposal was suppressed, however, following the intervention of President Jacques Chirac after the request of five eminent French historians.[12]

[6] HRC, *Faurisson* v. *France* (Appl. No. 550/1993), Decision 8 November 1996 (The author was a professor of literature at the Sorbonne until 1973 and at the University of Lyon until 1991. He was removed from his chair, after expressing doubts on the existence of gas chambers), ECommHR *Garaudy* v. *France* (Appl. No. 65831/01), Inadmissibility Decision 7 July 2003.

[7] 'Les Députés Pénalisent la Négation des Genocides', *Le Monde*, 22 December 2011.

[8] Decision No. 2012-647 DC, of 28 February 2012, available at www.conseil-constitutionnel.fr/conseil-constitutionnel/francais/les-decisions/acces-par-date/decisions-depuis-1959/2012/2012-647-dc/decision-n-2012-647-dc-du-28-fevrier-2012.104949.html.

[9] In reference to article 301 of the Turkish Penal Code. In the case of novelist Orhan Pamuk charges were eventually dropped, see BBC News, *Court Drops Turkish Writer's Case*, 23 January 2006, available at www.news.bbc.co.uk/2/hi/europe/4637886.stm.

[10] ECtHR *Sidiropoulos and Others* v. *Greece* (Appl. No. 57/197/841/1047), Judgment 10 July 1998, ECtHR *Affaire Maison de la Civilisation Macédonnienne et Autres c. Grèce* (Appl. No. 1295/10), Judgment 9 July 2015.

[11] Article 4 of proposition of law of 23 February 2005, critique by F. Laroussi, 'Le nouveau revisionnisme', *Le Monde*, 12 May 2005, P. Nora, 'Liberté pour l'Histoire', *Le Monde*, 11 October 2008.

[12] L. Van Eeckhout, 'Une disposition adoptée avec l'aval du gouvernement français; Des députés UMP et UDF trouvent légitime d'intervenir pour que l'orientation des manuels soit conforme aux valeurs de la République', *Le Monde*, 11 June 2005; R. Branche, C. Liauzu, G. Meynier, and S. Thénault, 'La Résponsabilité des historiens face à l'histoire coloniale', *Le Monde*, 20 September 2005.

The ECtHR has issued conflicting decisions on the topic. It held Greece in violation of the Convention for refusing to protect the freedom of association of a group with aims contrary an official version of history constitutive of the modern Greek national identity. However, the same court declined to protect free expression for persons who have denied crimes against humanity. It declared inadmissible the application of Roger Garaudy for violation of article 10 of the European Convention on Human Rights[13].

This chapter analyzes various legal attempts to impose an official version of the truth. A nation's collective consciousness can be manifest either as a national identity, which dictates the acceptance of an "official" version of history, or as a specific way of handling our collective *malaise* towards atrocities committed by humanity. Using state constraint, especially through criminal law, is not justified in view of the "imaginary institution" of the nation state. This chapter argues that there is no difference between the cases of imposing of a dominant version of the truth, necessary to the formation of national identity, and the denial of crimes against humanity. Thus the difference in the case law of the ECtHR is not justified.

2 Imposing an Official Version of History through the Law: Some French and Greek Cases

According to the framework decision 2008/913/JHA[14] of the Council of European Union, the Member States of European Union "should consider" criminalizing "publicly condoning, denying or grossly trivializing crimes of genocide, crimes against humanity and war crimes,"[15] as well as "publicly condoning, denying or grossly trivializing the crimes defined in article 6 of the Charter of the International Military Tribunal appended to the London Agreement of 8 August 1945, . . . when the conduct is carried out in a manner likely to incite to violence or hatred against such a group or a member of such a group."[16] This requirement that the speech be carried out in a way that is likely to incite to violence or hatred raises the standards of protection of speech and allows for the distinction between academic speech that does not have this tendency and other categories

[13] *Garaudy* v. *France*.
[14] See note 6.
[15] Article One, 1, c. See chapter by Luigi Cajani in the present volume.
[16] Article One, 1, d.

of speech that may have it. Nevertheless, the mere existence of a clause imposing criminal sanctions upon the denial or trivialization of historical facts can lead academics to adventures before courts, as the cases analyzed below show. Their very existence can have unintended consequences and in particular a "chilling effect" upon academic discourse, which can deprive societies of important information and analysis that is crucial to their self-understanding.

France currently maintains five memory laws.[17] The first one is the "Gayssot" law,[18] which criminalizes the denial of the existence of one or more crimes against humanity, as defined by article 6 of the Charter of the International Military Tribunal appended to the London Agreement of 8 August 1945 and recognized by the Nuremberg judgments and subsequent judgments handed down in France. The "Arménie" law[19] recognizes the Armenian genocide of 1915 and was enacted after the request of French citizens of Armenian origin. The "Taubira" law[20] recognizes the Atlantic slave trade as a crime against humanity. It aims to denounce colonialism, including the clause "the curriculum and the research programs in history and the humanities will give the slave trade and slavery the consequent place they deserve." The "Mekachera" law "rehabilitated colonialism."[21] The "Mekachera" law "concerning the gratitude of the nation towards its repatriated French Citizens" was a legislative attempt to include in a legal text a clause according to which the French school programs should "recognize the 'positive role' of the French presence overseas."[22] This proposal to consecrate an official truth on colonial

[17] For a list of those laws see *Liberté pour l'Histoire*, available at: www.lph-asso.fr/index.php?option=com_content&view=article&id=54&Itemid=19&lang=en.

[18] Of 13 July 1990 modifying the law of 1881 on "Freedom of the Press." Currently the Art. 24 bis of the same law criminalizes l'existence d'un ou plusieurs crimes contre l'humanité tels qu'ils sont définis par l'article 6 du statut du tribunal militaire international annexé à l'accord de Londres du 8 août 1945 et qui ont été commis soit par les membres d'une organisation déclarée criminelle en application de l'article 9 dudit statut, soit par une personne reconnue coupable de tels crimes par une juridiction française ou international."

[19] Law No. 2001-70 of 29 January 2001 "Relative à la reconnaissance du génocide arménien de 1915," available at www.legifrance.gouv.fr/affichTexte.do?cidTexte=JORFTEXT000000403928&dateTexte=&categorieLien=id.

[20] Law No. 2001-434 of 21 May 2001 "Tendant à la reconnaissance de la traite et de l'esclavage en tant que crime contre l'humanité": available at www.legifrance.gouv.fr/affichTexte.do?cidTexte=JORFTEXT000000405369&categorieLien=id.

[21] R. Remond, 'History and the Law', in *Liberté pour l'Histoire*, available at www.lph-asso.fr/index.php?option=com_content&view=article&id=154&Itemid=184&lang=en.

[22] Article 4 of proposition of Law of 23 February 2005, critique by Laroussi, 'Le nouveau revisionnisme', Nora, 'Liberté pour l'Histoire'.

French past in a law which aimed to compensate inequalities and injustices among repatriated officers of the French army and *harkis* – that is local collaborators of the colonial regime – was suppressed following the intervention of President Jacques Chirac after the request of five eminent French historians.[23] A dozen other bills were submitted to the Assemblies defining as crimes against humanity a number of historical events in France and elsewhere in the world, such as the "Gypsy Genocide" (1939–45), the Ukrainian genocide of 1932–3" and the "Genocide in the Vendée of 1793–4."[24] As commentators have noted, most of these legislative texts pose problems from within legal practice and may unduly reflect the concerns of pressure groups.[25] Legal advisory bodies and in particular the Conseil d'État have not had the opportunity to warn of potential technical difficulties in the application of these laws.

In 2011, the French government proposed legislation that would criminalize the denial of the Genocides.[26] The law punished the denial or minimization of the existence of one or more crimes of genocide "recognised as such under French law." It punished, as the principal offense, those who "have contested or minimised in an excessive manner . . . the existence of one or more crimes of genocide as defined under article 211-1 of the Criminal Code which are recognised as such under French law," irrespective of the means of expression or public communication used.[27] The same law extended the right granted to certain associations to join proceedings as a civil claimant, in particular in order to draw the inferences from the establishment of this new offense.[28]

[23] Van Eeckhout, 'Une disposition adoptée avec l'aval du gouvernement français; Des députés UMP et UDF trouvent légitime d'intervenir pour que l'orientation des manuels soit conforme aux valeurs de la République', Branche, Liauzu, Meynier, and Thénault, 'La Résponsabilité des historiens face à l'histoire coloniale'.

[24] See F. Chandermangor, 'The Historian at the Mercy of the Law' in *Liberté pour l'Histoire*, available at www.lph-asso.fr/index.php?option=com_content&view=article&id=150&Itemid=179&lang=en.

[25] *Ibid.*

[26] 'Les Députés Pénalisent la Négation des Genocides', *Le Monde*, 22 December 2011. Although the legislation draft was considered contrary to the Constitution by the French Constitutional Council, the newly elected French President committed to bringing a new text before the Parliament which would pass the control of Constitutionality, see infra part II.C.

[27] The proposed legislation introduced article 24–ter into the Law of 29 July 1881 on the freedom of the press. The sanctions foreseen were a term of imprisonment of one year and a fine of EUR 45,000.

[28] Article 2 of the same law amending article 48–2 of the Law of 29 July 1881.

The French Constitutional Council invalidated the proposal on rule of law grounds.[29] It noted that a legislative provision having the objective of "recognising" a crime of genocide would not itself have the normative scope, which is characteristic of the law.[30] The French Assembly of representatives enacted a law recently that criminalizes the denial of crimes against humanity when they take place in circumstances "inciting to hatred or violence."[31] The French Senate very recently adopted the same law.[32] The French government estimates that the Council will find the law in conformity with the Constitution, since it associates the negation of crimes against humanity with incitement to hatred. Nevertheless, the risk always exists that incitement will be interpreted very broadly. Very recently the same Council held that the Gayssot Law is in conformity with the Constitution as it aims to limit an abuse of the exercise of freedom of expression.[33] According to the Council, the law is proportionate to the aims of the legislator, as it targets some particularly grave manifestations of anti-Semitism and racial hatred.[34] It prohibits only the "implicit or explicit" negation or the exaggerated minimization of crimes. The law does not aim to prohibit historical debates. It remains to see whether French courts will apply the law in a way that does not prohibit historical debates in the future. So far they have interpreted the notion of "denial" very broadly.[35] The French *Cour de Cassation* has held that expressing doubts on the number of victims or grossly minimizing the number of victims in bad faith are acts constitutive of the offense.[36]

[29] Decision No. 2012-647 DC of 28 February 2012, available at www.conseil-constitutionnel.fr/conseil-constitutionnel/francais/les-decisions/acces-par-date/decisions-depuis-1959/2012/2012-647-dc/decision-n-2012-647-dc-du-28-fevrier-2012.104949.html.

[30] Decision No. 2012-647 DC, Considérant 6.

[31] 'L'Assemblée adopte un amendement pénalisant la contestation des crimes contre l'humanité', *Le Monde*, 2 July 2016, available at www.lemonde.fr/politique/article/2016/07/02/l-assemblee-adopte-un-amendement-penalisant-la-contestation-des-crimes-contre-l-humanite_4962343_823448.html#kLTqM4M3fUhbYFoB.99.

[32] 'Feu vert au Sénat à la pénalisation du négationnisme du Génocide Arménien et l'Apologie de l'Esclavage', *France Soir*, 14 October 2016, available at www.francesoir.fr/politique-france/feu-vert-au-senat-la-penalisation-du-negationnisme-du-genocide-armenien-et.

[33] Décision No. 2015-512 QPC of 8 January 2016, available at www.conseil-constitutionnel.fr/conseil-constitutionnel/francais/les-decisions/acces-par-date/decisions-depuis-1959/2016/2015-512-qpc/decision-n-2015-512-qpc-du-8-janvier-2016.146840.html.

[34] *Ibid.*, Considérant 8.

[35] L. Pech, 'The Law of Holocaust Denial in Europe', in L. Hennebel and T. Hochmann (eds.), *Genocide Denials and the Law* (Oxford University Press, 2011), 186–234, at 201.

[36] Cour de Cassation, Chambre Criminelle, 17 June 1997, No. de pourvoi: 94-85126, available at www.legifrance.gouv.fr/affichJuriJudi.do?idTexte=JURITEXT000007068633.

The attempt to criminalize the denial of genocides through law sparked an enormous controversy as to whether it is appropriate for the Parliament to "make history" instead of the historians.[37] The existence of memory laws in France has already led historians to legal adventures. The historian Bernard Lewis was prosecuted for some comments he made during an interview with two journalists of the newspaper *Le Monde* in 1993[38] on the occasion of the publication of French translations of two of his books, *The Arabs in History*[39] and *Race and Slavery in the Middle East.*[40] In that interview, although he recognized that hundreds of thousands of Armenians had died, he expressed some doubts as to whether there was a deliberate political decision to systematically annihilate the Armenian nation. Shortly after this interview he published another article in *Le Monde* where he was tracing some differences between the Armenian case and the Holocaust.[41] The criminal prosecution was dismissed, as French law at the time incriminated the denial of the Holocaust only. Nevertheless, the first instance court of Paris (civil jurisdiction) found civil responsibility on the basis of article 1382 of the French Civil Code.[42] According to the court the historian, by stating that there was no "serious proof" for the Armenian genocide, "did not meet his duties of objectivity and prudence on such a delicate topic."[43]

The Taubira law, which recognized the Atlantic slave trade as a crime against humanity without foreseeing a criminal sanction for its denial, was the reason that led the historian Olivier Pétré-Grenouilleau to an adventure for his book *Les Traites Négrières*,[44] published in 2004. This book had been awarded the prestigious Senate history book award established "to recognize a historical work that meets scholarly standards and also contributes to the citizens' education."[45] In a newspaper interview related to the award, the historian declared that he viewed the Atlantic slave trade as a crime against humanity. He rejected the term "genocide," however, as it

[37] See for instance Robert Badinter, 'Le Parlement n'est pas un Tribunal', *Le Monde*, 14 January 2012, Bernard Acoyer, 'L'histoire n'a pas à être définie parla loi', *Le Monde*, 27 February 2010.

[38] 'Pourquoi les Turcs refusent-ils toujours de reconnaître le génocide arménien?', *Le Monde*, 16 November 1993.

[39] London/New York: Hutchinson's University Library, 1954.

[40] Oxford University Press, 1990.

[41] 'Les Explications de Bernard Lewis', *Le Monde*, 1 January 1993.

[42] According to which: "Any act of a person which causes damage to another makes him by whose fault the damage occurred liable to make reparation for the damage."

[43] TGI de Paris, 21 June 1995, available at www.voltairenet.org/article14133.html.

[44] Published by Gallimard in the prestigious collection "Bibliothèque des Histoires" in 2004.

[45] See Remond, 'History and the Law'.

implied systematic extermination. The slave traders did not, on his view, aim for the disappearance of their slaves as they saw their labor power as having a commodity value.[46] Following these declarations, a group from the Caribbean, Guyana, and Réunion attempted to file a legal action against Pétré-Grenouilleau considering that the Taubira law gave them that possibility.[47] The group tried to use the possibility to join proceedings as a civil claimant under clauses of the Taubira law that gives this option to associations "which aim at defending the memory of the slaves and the honor of their descendants" in cases of "provocation to hatred," "defamation," and "insult."[48] The lawsuit was clearly not founded and the group later withdrew it claiming that their initiative had been misunderstood by the general public.[49] The case led nineteen historians to file a petition in favor of repealing the Gayssot and Taubira laws.[50]

A number of French historians have noted public uneasiness about contradictory elements in French history. The ideology of the French Revolution and the culture of the rights of man, a paradigm commonly seen by the French as emblematic throughout Europe, coexists with darker elements. These include the political instability to which the French Revolution led, the Collaboration in the 1940s, and the decolonization and the War in Algeria.[51] Pierre Vidal Naquet has analyzed the great discontent that the democracy of the "rights of Man" feels toward the torture practiced "in the margins of legality" on the colonies, especially Algeria.[52] This feeling of guilt, an irrational feeling, is not the proper guide for legislative policy. As I argue in section 2, guilt is part of the French collective consciousness and it contains rational and irrational elements. The French are expressing a position against moral relativism through these laws. Nevertheless, the danger always exists that societies

[46] *Ibid.*

[47] See L. Daireau, 'L'affaire Olivier Pétré-Grenouilleau: Eléments de chronologie', available at www.clionautes.org/spip.php?article925.

[48] Art. 48-1 of the Law of 29 July 1881 as modified by law of 21 May 2001.

[49] A. de Baecque, 'Il s'est Fait Traiter', *Libération*, 15 March 2006, available at www.liberation.fr/portrait/2006/03/15/il-s-est-fait-traiter_33167.

[50] The petition was signed by the most notorious French historians: Jean-Pierre Azéma, Élisabeth Badinter, Jean-Jacques Becker, Françoise Chandernagor, Alain Decaux, Marc Ferro, Jacques Julliard, Jean Leclant, Pierre Milza, Pierre Nora, Mona Ozouf, Jean-Claude Perrot, Antoine Prost, René Rémond, Maurice Vaïsse, Jean-Pierre Vernant, Paul Veyne, Pierre Vidal-Naquet et Michel Winock see Daireau, *supra* n. 47.

[51] Nora, 'Historical Identity in Trouble'.

[52] P. Vidal Naquet, *Le Torture dans la République, Essai d'Histoire et de Politique Contemporaines (1954–1962)* (Paris: La Découverte/Maspero, 1983), at 15.

lose control of the irrational elements at play within their collective consciousness and that they limit excessively individual liberties, such as freedom of expression.

The need to protect the official version of history and of the national identity in Greece has led to a series of cases handled before courts. Greece has twice been held in violation of article 11 of the European Convention of Human Rights (ECHR),[53] for its courts' failures[54] to register an association called the "Home of Macedonian Civilisation."[55] The Greek court of first instance refused registration finding that the goals of the association ran contrary to national interests.[56] The appellate court engaged in a long historical analysis to support the argument that the Macedonian nation forms part of the Greek nation. It cited "facts" from antiquity to recent years. It referred to the dialect of the local populations, and their religion, myths, and traditions to trace similarities between the Macedonians and those elsewhere in the Greek world.[57] The court claimed that the Macedonian kings acted "not just as Greeks but as pan-Hellenists, in the

[53] According to article 11:

> Freedom of assembly and association. 1. Everyone has the right to freedom of peaceful assembly and to freedom of association with others, including the right to form and to join trade unions for the protection of his interests. 2. No restrictions shall be placed on the exercise of these rights other than such as are prescribed by law and are necessary in a democratic society in the interests of national security or public safety, for the prevention of disorder or crime, for the protection of health or morals or for the protection of the rights and freedoms of others. This Article shall not prevent the imposition of lawful restrictions on the exercise of these rights by members of the armed forces, of the police or of the administration of the State.

[54] According to article 78 of the Greek Civil Code an association acquires legal personality "as soon as it has been entered in a special public register (of associations) held at the court of first instance for the place where it has its headquarters."

[55] The first case was in ECtHR *Sidiropoulos and Others* v. *Greece* (Appl. No. 57/197/841/1047), Judgment 10 July 1998, and the second in ECtHR *Affaire Maison de la Civilisation Macédonnienne et Autres c. Grèce* (Appl. No. 1295/10), Judgment 9 July 2015.

[56] The aims of the association were

> (a) the cultural, intellectual and artistic development of its members and of the inhabitants of Florina in general and the fostering of a spirit of cooperation, solidarity and love between them; (b) cultural decentralisation and the preservation of intellectual and artistic endeavours and traditions and of the civilisation's monuments and, more generally, the promotion and development of [their] folk culture; and (c) the protection of the region's natural and cultural environmentsee Id, para 8.

[57] For an English translation see ECtHR *Sidiropoulos and Others* v. *Greece* (Appl. No. 57/197/841/1047), Judgment 10 July 1998 para 11.

sense that they incarnated the old idea of the creation of a unified Greek State by bringing together the smaller Greek territories."[58]

One wonders whether it is appropriate for justices to put forward a version of the historical truth that is convenient for the political purposes that the law envisages. The court situates the emergence of "Macedonia" as a Slavic State and "the Macedonian nation" as a specific nation in early twentieth century. It sees the establishment of the "Home of Macedonian Civilization" as part of a wider effort to create a Macedonian Question with international ramifications. This would mean in reality "to dispute the Greek identity of Macedonia and its inhabitants by indirect [. . .] means and [. . .] to undermine Greece's territorial integrity."[59]

For the ECtHR in *Sidiropoulos and others* v. *Greece* the Greek ruling violates the group's freedom of association as protected by article 11 of the ECHR.[60] Maintaining national security and preventing disorder are certainly legitimate aims. However, upholding cultural traditions and historical and cultural symbols in this way is no such aim.[61] The restrictions to freedom of association were not necessary as the ECtHR found no relevant threat to Greece's territorial integrity, national security, or public order. "Mention of the consciousness of belonging to a minority and the preservation and development of a minority's culture could not be said to constitute a threat to democratic society."[62] A mere suspicion of the intention of the association's founders could not be held as representing a danger to Greece's territorial integrity.[63]

The absence of willingness among Greek courts to abide by this ruling led to a second case before the ECtHR on the same issue.[64] When the applicants tried to have the "Home of the Macedonian Civilization" registered anew by the Greek first instance court,[65] the court rejected the application for a second time. Its justification was that the aim of the Constitution of the association presupposes the existence of a Macedonian civilization ethnically autonomous from Greek civilization.[66] Since no such nation exists, the association would have no purpose.

58 *Ibid.*

59 *Ibid.*

60 *Ibid.*, at para 47.

61 *Ibid.*, paras 37–9.

62 *Ibid.*, para 19.

63 *Ibid.*, para 45.

64 ECtHR *Affaire Maison de la Civilisation Macédonnienne et Autres c. Grèce* (Appl. No. 1295/10), Judgment 9 July 2015.

65 On the basis of article 78 of the Greek Civil Code, see *supra* n. 36.

66 *Ibid.*, para 8.

The Court of Appeals affirmed the ruling.[67] It undertook a historical and geographical analysis of the term "Macedonia" concluding that, before the Second World War, the concept "Macedonian nation" never existed. The refusal to register the association could be justified with reference to the protection of "public order," a criterion limiting the freedom of association under ECHR 11(2). For the court the use of the term "Macedonian" would endanger the peaceful coexistence of the inhabitants of Florina. The Supreme Court of Ordinary Jurisdiction rejected unanimously the association's appeal. It affirmed the reasoning of the Court of Appeals.[68] The ECtHR again found a violation of ECHR article 11 repeating its reasoning in *Sidiropoulos*. The ECtHR noted that the applicants did not aim to promote the idea of a Macedonian minority in Greece. There was nothing to indicate any danger to public order.[69] It stressed that under its case law, danger to public order is a criterion that is to be evaluated *a posteriori* and not *a priori*.[70] For the ECtHR the local authorities in Greece could always *a posteriori* control whether the association's activity could be limited in reference to the need to protect the public order.

The Greek Law implementing the European Council Framework Decision 2008/913/JHA on criminalizing the denial of crimes against humanity[71] has also led to litigation in cases where the protection of national identity is at stake. Although this legislation reaffirms legitimate values and the condemnation of atrocities, it also creates dangers to the freedom of expression of historians. The legal adventures of Heinz Richter a German historian and academic, Professor at the University of Manheim, illustrate this point. Fortunately, the first instance criminal courts held in this case that the law is unconstitutional.[72] Professor Richter was prosecuted on the

[67] *Ibid.*, paras 10–11.

[68] *Ibid.*, para 13.

[69] *Ibid.*, para 40.

[70] *Ibid.*, para 42.

[71] Law 4285/2015 of 9 September 2014, O. J. 191 A' of 10 March 2014. The relevant offense is defined as

> publicly condoning, denying or grossly trivializing crimes of genocide, crimes against humanity and war crimes, the Holocaust and the Nazi crimes that have been recognized by decisions of international courts or the Greek parliament when the behavior turns against a group of persons or a person which can be defined in reference to race, color, religion, genealogical origins, ethnic or national origins, sexual orientation, gender identity or handicap when this behavior manifests itself in a way that can incite violence or hatred or has a threatening aim or aims to slander a group or a member of such a group

Id article 2, amending Law 927/1979 article 1 para 1.

[72] Text (in Greek) available at anamorfosis.net/blog/?attachment_id=11879.

basis of this law, shortly after the Greek translation of his book the *Battle of Crete*.[73] The book recounts events during the German occupation of the Greek island in the Second World War. It describes acts of violence committed by the local resistance movement composed by civilian population against wounded German soldiers and against the dead bodies of German soldiers. Richter describes these acts as part of an "ancient Cretan tradition of contempt of death, which meant that those acts did not intend to degrade the bodies of the dead soldiers."[74] Richter describes the battle of Crete as the "last 'clean' military enterprise of the WWII and the beginning of a 'dirty war' began, which included attacks by an autonomous resistance movement [not part of the Greek army] and retaliation by the German occupant army."[75] The book stirred enormous controversy as it was considered to be justifying the German atrocities as a response to the violent acts committed by the locals against the German soldiers. Richter stresses facts little known to the general public, describing violent acts committed by both sides, in a way considered inappropriate by local citizens. Richter's defense argued that the historian is emphasizing the absurdity of war and the fact that both sides, invaders and local population, were victims of the situation.[76] The book explains how the battle of Crete led to the movement of Greek resistance and to retaliatory acts by the invading army. Richter discusses the 'idealism' of the German soldiers with the aim to explain how they were the victims of a totalitarian regime that exploited their patriotism, made them instruments of its propaganda, and sent large numbers of them to their deaths .[77] Richter's defense claimed that the law was contrary to the Greek Constitution's clauses protecting freedom of expression and to article 10 ECHR.

The first instance criminal court in Crete held the law to be unconstitutional, violating the clauses that protect freedom of expression and academic freedom.[78] The law could be held constitutional only to the extent that it concerns speech that is threatening, defamatory or can provoke hatred. Speech that just denies or trivializes or even approves of these

[73] H. A. Richter, *Operation Merkur: Die Eroberung der Insel Kreta im Mai 1941* (Rutzen: Ruhpolding, 2011).

[74] According to the comments of the defense counsel Dr. Athanasios Anagnostopoulos, available at anamorfosis.net/blog/?p=11819.

[75] H. A. Richter, *Operation Merkur: Die Eroberung der Insel Kreta im Mai 1941*, Greek Transl. (Athens: Govostis, 2011), at 440.

[76] *Ibid.*

[77] *Ibid.*

[78] See *supra* n. 65.

crimes should be protected. The court held that the laws that "recognize" historical facts cannot in a democratic and pluralist society constitute the basis of binding rules which lead to legal prohibitions and sanctions. This is so even if they express a majority opinion. Nevertheless, the court struggled with a clause in the Greek law on the negation of crimes against humanity that have been recognized by decisions of the Greek Parliament. The EU Council Framework Decision refers only to outlawing the negation of crimes described in article 6 of the Charter of the International Military Tribunal appended to the London Agreement of 8 August 1945. The Greek law refers to the crimes that have been recognized by the Greek Parliament. The court considered it unconstitutional, holding that the Parliament exceeded the constitutional limits of the legislative function, violated the constitutional principle of the legality of crimes, and attempted to intervene in the function of the judiciary. The decision in Richter's case regarding the role of the Parliament referred generally to the role of the judiciary/legislature but was also based on article 1(4) of the Framework Decision which provides that Member States may punish crimes referred to in paragraph 1(c) and/or (d) insofar as they have been established by a final decision of a national court of the Member State and/or an international court. The Framework Decision does not give any capacity to local parliaments. This distinction between the cases recognized as crimes against humanity by local parliaments in Europe and the reference to the crimes against humanity recognized by European institutions is not justifiable. The need to consolidate collective memory through legislation, either at the national or at the European level, can lead to the same dangers for the academic freedom of historians. It can also lead to the same difficulties concerning the appropriate use of the law, as I argue below.

Before the implementation in Greek law of the Council Framework decision, the Greek Supreme Court of Ordinary Jurisdiction was reluctant to accept limitations of speech for denial and trivialization of crimes against humanity under preexisting legislation prohibiting incitement to racial or ethnic hatred.[79] The Supreme Court has protected the freedom of expression of the author of a book denying the Holocaust.[80] In this decision, the Supreme Court notes the importance of freedom of expression, which includes the possibility to evaluate, judge, and interpret historical

[79] Law 927/1979 of 22/28 June 1979, Official Journal, A' 139.

[80] Greek Supreme Court of Ordinary Jurisdiction, Case number 3/2010. The case concerned the book "Jews, the Whole Truth" by Konstantinos Plevris.

facts and the persons associated with those according to their ideological opinions. This case, though does not raise any issues that would be crucial to the understanding of national identity in Greece.

3 Social Imaginaries and Freedom of Expression

Should the laws enforce an official version of historical truth upon those who negate some atrocities committed by humanity in the past? These atrocities are considered to be so profoundly offensive to humanity that we feel the need to proclaim our condemnation of them with an act of a parliament or an international treaty. The expressive force of this consecration symbolizes profound disapproval of atrocities committed by some groups over others in the past. Having parliaments pass such laws expresses some values of our collective consciousness today, both at the European level and the national level. Our need to use the expressive function of the law in order to affirm these values seems to create problems of methodology and of compatibility with freedoms that we also consider fundamental and in need of protection, such as academic freedom or freedom of association. European collective consciousness is expressed in the form of guilt for the atrocities that happened during the Second World War and in the need to reaffirm our condemnation. National collective consciousness in Greece dictates limiting freedom of expression of historians and associations that are offering an alternative narrative of facts constitutive of national identity.

The examples of France and Greece show more clearly how the relevant discourses relate to the self-conception of the nation. The idea of national identity is an element of the "collective consciousness" that Durkheim discusses.[81] An element, which holds a community together by assuring allegiance around some deeply held values. As Benedict Anderson notes, European national identity is a social construct, an imaginary identity.[82] Cornelius Castoriades emphasizes that history is poièsis – "creation and ontological genesis in and through the acting and the representing/discourse of men."[83] History is a constructive representation. It forms the nation's self-understanding. The self-conception of a nation assigns meaning to elements of life that are neither rational nor irrational, but

[81] E. Durkheim, *The Elementary Forms of Religious Life* (New York: The Free Press, 1995), 426.
[82] B. Anderson, *Imagined Communities* (London, New York: Verso 1983), 6.
[83] C. Castoriadis, *L'Institution Imaginaire de la Société* (Paris: Seuil, 1995), at 8.

imaginary.[84] The nation's self-image is formed through imaginary meanings, which valorize, structure, and give hierarchy to the whole of objects and ideas. The imaginary is a frame of interpretation, which supports the personal and social self-conception and which concerns what is called the "real."[85] The imaginary provides a structure for understanding reality inside a social frame. Castoriadis proposes the conception of the imaginary as escaping determination and as something that is recreated constantly. These thoughts are particularly relevant in reference to national self-identity, which is formed and reformed throughout time. Interpretations which seem to deviate from this self-conception are seen as threatening this vision. This is particularly relevant concerning the *Richter* case in Greece and the Mekachera law in France.

For Castoriadis, who is following on this point Hans-Georg Gadamer[86] and Martin Heidegger[87] social space and everything it "contains" is constituted by its temporality, by the social construction of time. The life of a society takes place in the explicit and implicit reference to the past, to the tradition, and to what has been acquired. It is also present in the "future," in anticipation, uncertainty, and enterprise.[88] The social-historical, the time space in which we "situate" all "reality," and the social-historical reality itself, is the product of the social-historical institution.[89] Society is instituted on the imaginary level thanks to the preferred narratives in a process, which implies distinction, choice, position, and gathering of specific ideas. These narrations are reflected themselves among others in the legislative texts and in judicial discourse. The logic of identity presupposes an ontological decision in the world of thought. It unifies and categorizes the various elements through official court discourse. In this respect, the Greek cases reaffirm national identity by excluding those who supposedly threaten it.

For Durkheim, collective consciousness arises somewhere in between the sphere of the rational and the irrational.[90] He links the excesses of the manifestations of collective consciousness to collective representations and to the idea of collective "effervescence" where the use of the rational

[84] *Ibid.*, at 225.
[85] *Ibid.*, at 242.
[86] H. Georg-Gadamer, *Truth and Method* (New York: Continuum, 2004).
[87] M. Heidegger, *Being and Time* (New York: Harper Perennial, 1962).
[88] Castoriadis, *L'Institution Imaginaire*, at 325.
[89] *Ibid.*
[90] Durkheim, *The Elementary Forms of Religious Life*, 15.

faculties fades.[91] Concerning the denial and trivialization of crimes against humanity, the collective consciousness in Europe after the Second World War has crystallized around a sense of guilt for the terrible atrocities committed in its midst. The use of legal constraints by the state in these cases manifest the excesses in the irrationality of collective consciousness. The limitation of free expression is not appropriate for the management of European collective consciousness. For Durkheim, societies punish in order to defend themselves when they think that the values that they consider fundamental for their existence are violated.[92] Not harming others is one fundamental value, and societies should punish when this principle is violated. They should not punish though to enforce the values that on the imaginary level hold them together as a society when no harm to others exists. Nietzsche noted that the more insecure a society is, the harsher it tends to punish in case of violation of its laws.[93] As the community's power and self-confidence grow, criminal law becomes milder.[94] Michel Foucault also noted that societies punish in order to defend themselves, to assure their existence.[95] In *Discipline and Punish* he describes the transition from harsh punishment to the more "humane" system of punishment dominant in contemporary democratic nation states as going together with a legitimizing myth, the social contract.[96] Under the *Ancien Régime*, whenever someone violated the law, an offense to the *dignitas* of the Sovereign was at stake, which necessitated vengeance in his name. Contemporary democratic regimes, by contrast, punish in order to defend themselves.[97] National identity forms part of this mythological element that binds us with others in the context of the state. For Marx national identity belongs to the false consciousness of the ideological superstructure: a fictive bond that conceals social stratification and class interest.[98] Whether we accept any of those interpretations on the role of national identity or not, its protection is too vague a criterion to dictate the enactment of legislation that limits expression that challenges it. This is certainly relevant for the case of

[91] *Ibid.*
[92] É. Durkheim, *The Division of Labor in Society* (New York: The Free Press), 42.
[93] F. Nietzsche, *On the Genealogy of Morality* (Indianapolis/Cambridge: Hackett, 1998), 47.
[94] *Ibid.*
[95] M. Foucault, *Discipline and Punish, The Birth of the Prison*, Engl. transl. by Alan Sheridan (New York: Vintage, 1995).
[96] *Ibid.*, 89.
[97] *Ibid.*, 90.
[98] See for instance in his *German Ideology*, in R.C. Tucker (ed.) *The Marx-Engels Reader* (New York: Norton, 1978), 195.

the fragile Greek identity, the feeling of guilt for colonialism in France, and the feeling of guilt for the Holocaust in Europe. States cannot legitimately limit freedom of expression or association in the name of a fictive identity that they have constructed for themselves as constitutive of the "nation." Limiting expression that challenges a vision of national identity is a sign of insecurity.

Despite the expressive functions of legislative proclamations as to the existence of certain crimes against humanity, there is something perplexing in very act of the legislative branch in proclaiming these crimes and in imposing penalties for their denial. Legislating in the area of the *is* means transcending the *is*/*ought* distinction. The task of the law is to regulate about the *ought* not about the *is*. The law should impose standards of behavior that are necessary for the interaction among citizens. The task of historians is to provide interpretations about the *is*, about facts. Courts and the judiciary are deciding about issues that belong to the level of the *ought*. Claims about historical facts should not be part of the legal discourse but part of the academic debates among historians. If parliaments consider it appropriate to express collective disapproval for atrocities committed in the past and to undertake a symbolic action by recognizing them through a memory law, this text should not create liability for persons expressing interpretations of historical facts that are different from the dominant interpretation. This was correctly noted by the Greek criminal court in the *Richter* case.[99]

The dangers for free expression in these laws lie in the difficulty that exists in any attempt to distinguish between fact and opinion within historical discourse. Interpreting the past is the quintessence of historical research. It involves reference to and interpretation of facts and giving them meaning within the interpretative scheme of each historian. In historical discourse it is difficult to distinguish between narration of fact and expression of opinion on the facts. As Paul Ricoeur notes, we expect that the historian must express his or her subjectivity of a certain quality, which will inspire in the reader instructed by it to achieve a "subjectivity of reflection."[100] Historians reconstruct events or series of events. They establish hypothesis and ask questions about facts.[101] Their task is not to restore things "such as they happened," but rather to recompose and elaborate a historical understanding.[102] Historians seek relations between the phenomena that

99 Text (in Greek) available at anamorfosis.net/blog/?attachment_id=11879.

100 P. Ricoeur, *History and Truth* (Evanston: Northwestern University Press, 1965), 22.

101 *Ibid.*, 23.

102 *Ibid.*, 24.

they consider important to discuss; they analyze and recompose historical facts.[103] History is a science of the human societies, as such it is based upon a judgment of importance that is made by the historian himself or herself.[104] Often history uses many schemes of interpretation which are often "pre-critical, wavering between determinism and probability."[105] The language of the historian is necessarily equivocal. It attempts to make sense of events that have happened in the past, separated from the historian by a temporal distance. The historian is struggling to find concepts that will allow him or her to describe what is other in terms that are common to his time.[106] Unlike the mathematician who denominates and determines the structure of a notion, the historian needs to re-present and thus to imagine and re-place in the background of historical distance some events.[107] Furthermore, the historian is trying to reconstruct what others have experienced. That task is inevitably "inexhaustible." It has its own limits, the limits of "intellectual approximation."[108]

Altering the process of how history is written means denying the subtlety and the nuance that is the work of historical research. It means denying "temporal differences and transitions" removing "the factors of transformation and the conditions of change" from the liberty of the historian.[109] The *Richter* trial is indicative of this fact. The historian was trying to show how dehumanizing war is for both sides. The attacking side, the German invaders as paratroopers, and the local populations of Greece felt equally the objectification that war leads to. Richter was prosecuted for bringing into the understanding of historical fact the nuance and the critical attitude that is expected from the work of historians. For Ricoeur history finds its completion in the reader, the student and the public.[110] History is part of self-knowledge. We "have need of history" to get out of our subjectivity and experience in and beyond ourselves.[111] The critique of elements that we consider constitutive of our national identity must be allowed as it promotes our collective self-understanding. The *Richter* case shows that

[103] *Ibid.*
[104] *Ibid.*, 26.
[105] *Ibid.*, 27.
[106] *Ibid.*
[107] *Ibid.*, 27–8.
[108] *Ibid.*, 28.
[109] Nora, 'Historical Identity in Trouble'.
[110] Ricoeur, *History and Truth*, 32.
[111] *Ibid.*, 33.

fundamentally challenging the self-understanding of the modern Greek identity can be a factor that promotes this self-understanding.

The collective consciousness in France is aware of the difficulties in imposing penalties upon historians as the decision of the *Conseil Constitutionnel* on the law on the denial of genocides shows. The French, by proclaiming some crimes against humanity through the law, are taking a position against moral relativism. In this case collective consciousness manifests itself as guilt for the crimes against humanity that were committed in the midst of Europe. Even in this case some caution is required. The feeling of guilt is an emotion that belongs to the irrational sphere of our collective consciousness. We are running the risk of losing control of this irrational element and of limiting excessively freedom of expression. The unintended consequences of this limitation can be legal adventures for valuable participants in our public dialogue as the *Pétré-Grenouilleau* case shows.

Protecting the sensibilities of the victims is a cause whose value weakens if someone considers the numerous crimes against humanity that have taken place and which have not been recognized in a legal text. As Pierre Nora notes,[112] the broadening of the concept of crime against humanity leads to a systematic "victimization" that could be expanded to include a series of crimes against humanity that history is full of. This is a case of slippery slope par excellence, which would lead to the legal commemoration of significant events that took place and which would limit significantly the possibility of historians to write and comment about them.

4 Judging History before International Courts: Is the Inconsistency in Protecting Freedom of Expression Justified?

International and national courts have issued split decisions on memory laws. The ECtHR has not found violations in cases where penalties were imposed for denial or trivialization of the Holocaust. As to the denial of the Armenian genocide it has been more protective of freedom of expression. This contradictory attitude does not seem justified in light of the former analysis of collective consciousness.

In *Faurisson* v. *France*[113] the United Nations Human Rights Committee, the International Covenant on Civil and Political Rights (ICCPR) supervisory

112 Nora, 'Historical Identity in Trouble'.

113 The author, who was a professor of literature at the Sorbonne until 1973 and at the University of Lyon until 1991 when he was removed from his chair, expressed doubts on the existence of gas chambers for extermination purposes.

body, held that the conviction of Faurisson and his publisher for denying crimes against humanity established by the Nuremberg Tribunal[114] met the legal requirements of the treaty and was "necessary" in the struggle against racism and anti-semitism. The Committee referred to article 19(3)(a) ICCPR to stress that the "respect of the rights or reputations of others" "may relate to the interests of other persons or to those of the community as a whole."[115] "The statements made by the author read in their full context were of a nature to as to raise or strengthen anti-semitic feelings, the restriction served the respect of the Jewish community to live free from fear of an atmosphere of anti-semitism."[116]

The European Commission on Human Rights[117] in the past has declined to protect freedom of expression in cases of Holocaust denial.[118] The European Court of Human Rights declared inadmissible the application of Roger Garaudy for violation of article 10 of the European Convention on Human Rights.[119] Garaudy had been convicted in France for publicly defaming a group of persons, the Jewish community. He had suggested that the dominant conception of the Holocaust was based on deliberate distortions of history by "the Israeli-Zionist lobbies in France and the

[114] In application of the French Law of 13 July 1990. The French state put forward that the law is not punishing the expression of an opinion, "but the denial of a historical reality universally recognized," *Ibid.*, para 7.10.

[115] *Ibid.*, para 9.6.

[116] *Ibid.*, para 9.7.

[117] The European Commission of Human Rights was from 1954 until 1998 the institution, which examined and determined the admissibility of complaints for violation of the rights protected by the European Convention on Human Rights. Protocol 11 replaced the part-time Commission and Court by a single full-time Court and gave direct access to individuals to the Court.

[118] The Commission found a series of application inadmissible: ECommHR *X.* v. *Germany* (Appl. No. 9235/81), Inadmissibility Decision 16 July 1982, DR 29, p. 194, ECommHR *T.* v. *Belgium* (Appl. No. 9777/82), Inadmissibility Decision 14 July 1983; ECommHR *H., W., P. and K.* v. *Austria* (Appl. No. 12774/87) Inadmissibility Decision 12 October 1989, DR 62, p. 216, ECommHR *Honsik* v. *Austria* (Appl. No. 25062/94) Inadmissibility Decision, 18 October 1995, DR 83-A, p. 77, ECommHR *Nationaldemokratische Partei Deutschlands* v. *Germany* (Appl. No. 25992/94) Inadmissibility Decision 29 November 1995, DR 84, p. 149, ECommHR *Irving* v. *Germany* (Appl. No. 26551/95) Inadmissibility Decision 29 June 1996, ECommHR *Marais* v. *France* (Appl. No. 31159/96), Inadmissibility Decision 24 June 1996, DR 86, p. 184. Although the relevant national judgments were found to constitute an interference with the applicants' freedom of expression, the interference was always held to be "necessary in a democratic society" within the meaning of article 10, see Pech, 'The Law of Holocaust Denial in Europe', at 214.

[119] *Garaudy* v. *France*.

United States."[120] The ECtHR expressed doubts as to the methodological approach of the applicant holding that "denying the reality of clearly established historical facts, such as the Holocaust, . . . does not constitute historical research akin to a quest for the truth,"[121] substituting its judgment for that of the community of experts as to what constitutes the proper methodology of history. The ECtHR further associates the denial of crimes against humanity to racial defamation of Jews and to incitement to hatred of them.[122] Thus "the main content and tenor of the applicant's book are markedly revisionist and run counter to the fundamental values of the Convention, as expressed in its Preamble, namely justice and peace."[123] The conviction was thus an interference with liberty "necessary in a democratic society" within the meaning of article 10 § 2 of the ECHR.[124] The question that emerges is what are the limits of the truth of the historian and the truth of the judge. To what extent is the judge competent to evaluate whether any book written is based upon a clear historical methodology or not? Expert testimony is not a safe solution in this case as there is disagreement even among historians about the meaning of specific historical events. Leading French jurist Simone Weil, an Auschwitz survivor, noted in reference to this case that the law "lets the negationnists appear as martyrs, victims of an official truth. Thanks to it, the negationnists will be able to drive the debate on freedom of expression off course."[125]

In Turkey, cases have emerged where authors who discussed the same genocide faced charges for "denigration of the Turkish nation" in reference to article 301 of the Turkish Penal Code.[126] In a number of cases that have come up against Turkey before the ECtHR concerning the denial

[120] *Garaudy* v. *France*, para 10. The applicant was sentenced to a suspended term of three months' imprisonment and a fine of FRF 20,200, *Ibid.* at 12. He put forward that his book was part of a study he had intended to make of the three major monotheist religions, after examining Roman Catholic and Islamic fundamentalism he had intended to extend his study to political Zionism, which he considered to be a form of fundamentalism, *Ibid.*, para 17.

[121] *Ibid.*, para 23.

[122] *Ibid.*

[123] *Ibid.*

[124] *Ibid.*, para 24.

[125] Interview with Simone Weil in L'Événement du Jeudi, 27 June–3 July 1996, cited in S. Epstein 'Abbé Pierre and the French Negationists', in Robert S. Wistrich ed. *Holocaust Denial, The Politics of Perfidy* (Berlin/Boston: Walter de Gruyter & Co KG and Jerusalem: Hebrew University Magnes Press, 2012), 85–108.

[126] In the case of novelist Orhan Pamuk, charges were eventually dropped, see BBC News, *Court drops Turkish Writer's Case*, 23 January 2006, available at http://news.bbc.co.uk/2/hi/europe/4637886.stm.

of the Armenian Genocide the Court has found violation of freedom of expression.[127] In these cases where limitations of speech in order to protect the Turkish national identity were at stake, the ECtHR protected freedom of expression.

In *Perinçek* v. *Switzerland* the applicant had been convicted in Austria for denying the Armenian genocide.[128] According to the Turkish government, the applicant's discourse "qualified as political speech" which was not confined to statements touching exclusively upon domestic issues or to mainstream speech.[129] The applicant aimed only at having an impact upon the controversy dominant at the time in Switzerland on the recognition of the relevant events of 1915 and the following years as genocide and the criminalization of its denial.[130] The Armenian government submitted that the comments were a "racially motivated insult to Armenians and an invitation to Turks to believe them to be liars."[131] The Swiss courts thus, "had the usual margin of appreciation to decide whether the statements could harm social harmony by infringing the dignity of the Armenians."[132] The ECtHR ruled anew in in favor of freedom of expression. This is political speech, which did not amount to incitement to hatred or intolerance.[133]

[127] ECtHR *Güçlü* v. *Turkey* (Appl. No. 27690/03) Judgment 10 February 2009. The provision was later repealed (lawyer and politician arguing that Turkey had to "come to terms" with the Armenian genocide and engage in an open debate on the issue was convicted under a legal provision proscribing propaganda against Turkey's territorial integrity). ECtHR *Dink* v. *Turkey* (Appl. Nos. 2668/07, 6102/08, 30079/08, 7072/09 and 7124/09) Judgment 14 September 2010 (prominent Turkish-Armenian writer and journalist had been convicted of denigrating "Turkishness," a criminal offence under article 159 of the Turkish Criminal code as then in force, which was later superseded by article 301 of the Turkish Criminal Code of 2005). ECtHR *Cox* v. *Turkey* (Appl. No. 2933/03), Judgment 20 May 2010, paras 27–45 (US citizen who had taught in Turkish universities was deported from Turkey in 1986 and banned from re-entering the country for alleging in front of students and colleagues that the Turks "had massacred Armenians." ECtHR *Altuğ Taner Akçam* v. *Turkey* (Appl. No. 27520/07) Judgment 25 October 2011 (professor of history who published extensively on the events of 1915 and had been the subject of several criminal investigations. He complained before the ECtHR of the inclusion of article 301 within the Turkish Criminal Code, which, he argued, allowed him to be prosecuted for his scholarly work on the Armenian topic).

[128] ECtHR *Perinçek* v. *Switzerland* (Appl. No. 27510/08), Judgment of 15 October 2015, para 96.

[129] *Ibid.*, para 173.

[130] *Ibid.*

[131] *Ibid.*, para 177.

[132] *Ibid.*

[133] *Ibid.*, paras 231–3.

The divergence between previous older decisions of the ECtHR not finding violation to freedom of expression for limits imposed upon Holocaust denial and the decisions finding violation in the denial of other genocides is not justified. As a matter of principle, freedom of expression should be protected in both cases. These reasons concern what writing history is and whom history is done for. In this frame offense about something concerning our self-conception does not justify limitations, as analyzed above. Similarly, the dangers that the existence of prohibitions on writing about historical work can lead to are the same as well. No matter how compelling the need is in contemporary Europe to condemn an event as appalling as some crimes against humanity, the dangers of abuse of the law and of judicial adventures for academics who are informing the public persist.

As I argued earlier, our emotions manifest themselves in our collective consciousness. In France those emotions and especially the feeling of guilt dictate a firm position against value relativism. This conception is also expressed in the EU Council Framework decision. However we are running the risk of losing control of our emotions, which belong to the irrational part of our collective consciousness, and of limiting individual freedoms too much. Our legal systems contain contradictions.[134] On the one hand the need to commemorate and condemn atrocities. On the other, the need to protect individual freedoms, which makes more sense in the case of minority opinions. In these conflicts the advantage should be given to the protection of minority opinions. There does not seem to be a principled reason for a difference between Holocaust denial and the denial of the Armenian genocide. The ECtHR should adopt a consistent approach defending freedom of expression in all these cases.

5 Conclusion

Maintaining laws that criminalize the denial or trivialization of crimes against humanity, can have pernicious unintended consequences upon important constitutional freedoms such as academic freedom and the freedom of association. These laws are usually the result of collective disapproval of some of the worse atrocities committed throughout history. As a matter of principle though, giving legal form to the collective consciousness in this way can lead to dangerous slippery slopes where it is difficult to halt the irrational elements within collective consciousness

[134] I thank Cosmin Cercel for a reminder of this point.

in a way that is compatible with intellectual freedom. Even if the relevant clauses in the Council Framework decision associate the expression of the denial or trivialization to incitement to violence and hatred, not all European Union states have introduced this requirement into their legislation. And even if they have, the very existence of a clause of the kind can lead historians and other valuable contributors to our collective search of meaning to long-lasting adventures before courts. Our public dialogue in our collective sense of meaning for humanity should be wide open and allow the expression of interpretation of historical facts that might seem idiosyncratic or even offensive and disturbing for the collective narratives of a society in its search of self-understanding throughout history.

8

Legal Silences and the Memory of Francoism in Spain

ALFONS ARAGONESES

1 Introduction: War of Memories in Spain

From the very beginning of the construction of the European Union, European laws, solemn declarations, and political statements have made reference to history. References to armed conflicts such as the two world wars, or to the various dictatorships of the twentieth century, are easy to find in European 'soft' law, from declarations recognizing the facts of mass atrocities to an EU Council Decision criminalizing genocide denials.[1] At other times they take the form of preambles or 'songs of the law', interpreting or supporting the legitimacy of the rules.[2]

In 2008, the European Parliament decided to highlight this memory of the European project by establishing 23 September as a day of remembrance of the victims of Nazism and Stalinism.[3] One year later the same Parliament approved a resolution on European conscience and totalitarianism.[4] Similar resolutions were approved by the Parliament about other historical events, such as the Holodomor.[5]

This research was funded by the Spanish ministry of Economy and Competitivity (DER2014-56291-C3-1-P).

[1] I.e. Council Framework Decision 2008/913/JHA of 28 November 2008 on combating certain forms and expressions of racism and xenophobia by means of criminal law, *Official Journal of the European Union* (*OJ*), 6 December 2008, L 328/55–L 328/58. See also chapter by Luigi Cajani in the present volume.

[2] M.-T. Fögen, *Das Lied vom Gesetz* (München: Carl-Friedrich-von-Siemens-Stiftung, 2007).

[3] European Parliament: Declaration of 23 September 2008 on the proclamation of 23rd August as European Day of Remembrance for Victims of Stalinism and Nazism. *OJC 8 E*, 14 January 2010, 57–9.

[4] European Parliament: Resolution of 2 April 2009 on European Conscience and Totalitarianism. *OJ* C 137 E, 25–7.

[5] European Parliament: Resolution of 23 October 2008 on the commemoration of the Holodomor, and the Ukraine artificial famine (1932–33). *OJ C* 15 E, 78–80.

Interestingly, a proposal for a similar resolution regarding Franco's regime was presented before the European Parliament one year later. However, the members of the Parliament were unable to agree on a declaration condemning Franco's 1936 coup d'état. The Christian Democrats, following the conservative Spanish *Partido Popular* (People's Party), refused to join in. In the end, the Parliament decided to issue a statement from its President, at the time a Spaniard himself, José Borrell,[6] followed by other statements by various MEPs. Mr. Borrell condemned the coup d'état and Francoism. The Spanish conservative MEP Jaime Mayor Oreja refused to do the same and warned of the danger of meddling with historical memory. In the words of Mayor Oreja:

> We must not change our attitude, and many Spaniards believe it to be an historical mistake to try to promote a second transition today. It is an historical mistake to unilaterally destroy the essence of our Constitution of harmony; it is historically foolish to introduce the debate on the right to self-determination in Spain, the creation within Spain of new nations that have never existed; it is an historical mistake because it moves us away from the harmony we have created.[7]

This contrast between the European Parliament's declaration concerning Nazism and Stalinism and the proposed resolution concerning Francoism perfectly captures the conflict that persists in Spain between the different collective memories of the Civil War and Francoism.

This conflict has also had legal repercussions in Spain, with one set of laws making references to the country's democratic past, and other laws and judicial decisions pointing to its dictatorial past. This makes memory laws in Spain a controversial subject. At the national level we find only one legal provision clearly in line with memory laws – the provision in the Criminal Code proscribing the denial of the Holocaust.[8] There are no laws imposing a particular version of the Francoist past, nor punishing the denial of the crimes of the dictatorship. Even the Historical Memory Act of 2007 does not proscribe Francoist ideology.[9] Therefore it would be an

[6] European Parliament: 70 years after General Franco's coup d'état in Spain (Statements by the President and the political groups), *OJ*, Minutes, C 303E, 15 and following.

[7] Statement of MEP Jaime Mayor Oreja. See previous footnote.

[8] Ley Orgánica 1/2015, of 30 March modifying the Ley Orgánica 10/1995 of 23 November of the Criminal Code, *BOE* 77, 31 March 2015, 27061–176.

[9] Ley 52/2007, of 26 December recognizing rights and establishing measures for those who suffered persecution or violence during the civil war and the dictatorship, *BOE* 310, 27 December 2007, 53410–6.

exaggeration to consider that Spanish law has adopted a severe regulation of historical memory.

The current situation dates back to the lack of a formal process of transitional justice and memory legislation during the transition. Yet the political transition, which took place between the years 1975 and 1982 and which allowed for the continuity of Francoist institutions and legal behaviours beyond the transition to democracy, also partially explains the Spanish anomaly in the Western European context. The legislator and the drafters of the Constitution decided not to erase the precedent of Francoist law. They also opted for silence: no condemnations of the dictatorship and no references to the anti-Francoist opposition or the victims of Francoism are to be found. The consequence was what Boaventura de Sousa Santos calls a 'palimpsest of legal cultures'. This lack of regulation led to the creation of a legal culture combining elements of the old Francoist system and the new democratic one.[10]

This silence also has legal and political consequences in the legal system. As stated by Eric Heinze in this volume, 'Not to legislate is also to legislate. Legal power acts through law's proceedings, but also though law's abstentions'.[11] Legal vacuums can be occupied by pre-existent discourses or by new ones. In Spain, the narratives about the dictatorship that had already existed occupied the silent space left by the legislator, that is, the Francoist nationalist discourses, together with their references to the Civil War and the years of 'peace' that followed. This has led to the acceptance of Francoism as something natural, as being a part of the Spanish national identity.

The legal system is not only a normative order – it also contains a narrative, values, and culture that have an influence on collective identity and the political system. According to Christian Giordano, this narrative often refers to history in search of consensus, common values, and ideas, with the aim of legitimizing the law.[12]Re-conceiving the past as a way of legitimizing a legal institution or national identity has been also studied by António Hespanha.[13]

[10] B. Sousa Santos, 'The Heterogeneous State and Legal Pluralism in Mozambique', *Law & Society Review* 40 (2006), 39–75, at 47.

[11] See chapter by Eric Heinze in the present volume.

[12] C. Giordano, 'The Past in the Present: Actualized History in the Social Construction of Reality', *Focaal* 26:28 (1996), 97–107.

[13] A. M. Hespanha, 'Legal History and Legal Education', *Rg-Rechtsgeschichte* 4 (2004), 41–56, at 41.

In this way, the lack of a clear legal and political discourse has allowed Francoism to become naturalized. That is, it has led to the general acceptance of the dictatorship as a natural part of Spanish history and culture, and the acceptance of the symbols of this dictatorship as part of the Spanish landscape. Law has played a role in this process.

This explains the indifference of Spanish institutions towards the demands of the victims. Likewise, it explains the remaining Francoist monuments and street names,[14] along with the lack of commemoration of the victims of the dictatorship, or any commemoration of the liberation of the Nazi camps to which approximately 9,500 Spanish Republicans were deported.

In this chapter I discuss the laws that contributed to this culture of oblivion and acceptance of Francoism during both the dictatorship (1936–75) and the transition (1975–82). I explain the origins of the memorialist movements, which began around the year 2000, and how the state institutions reacted to them by initially attempting to satisfy the victims with new memory laws. Finally, I describe the current panorama of these conflicting memories today.

2 The Memory of Francoist Law: 1939–1975

On 18 July 1936, a part of the military, some of the conservatives, and the pro-fascist Falange party executed a coup d'état. This military coup failed in the industrialized areas, mostly in Andalusia and in the Mediterranean coast. With financial and military support from Nazi Germany and Fascist Italy, Franco's African troops successfully returned to the Peninsula, turning the failed coup into a Civil War that lasted three years.

In April 1939 Franco's victory put an end to the war, but the repression continued. The regime was founded on a narrative of the war that presented Francisco Franco as the *caudillo* (charismatic chieftain, or leader) of Spain, delivered by the Grace of God and the coup, and the Civil War as a National Uprising and a Holy Crusade. From 1939 until 1975, the remembrance of this 'crusade' played an important role in legitimizing the regime created by a coup d'état, an act that defied both the Criminal Code and the Constitution of the epoch. Street names and monuments throughout

[14] That is, the Francoist Mausoleum in San Lorenzo de el Escorial, or the Monument to the Francoist fighters of the Ebre battle in Tortosa. The local Government of Madrid decided recently to remove all Francoist street names. See 'El Ayuntamiento de Madrid cambiará el nombre de 30 calles franquistas', *El Mundo*, 23 December 2015.

the country memorialized references to the war. Both 18 July (the date of the coup, which was dubbed 'the National Uprising') and 1 April ('Victory Day') were highlighted as national holidays in Spain's official calendar. From 1942 onwards, all cinemas were obliged to show a NO-DO (documentary or newsreel) before every screening, which very often depicted episodes from the war or reconstruction efforts.

The law also contained references to the war. Starting from early repressive legislation, such as the 'Law against free-Masonry and Communism' or the 'Political Responsibility Act', to decrees regulating minor issues,[15] Spanish law directly or indirectly assumed the legitimacy of the Civil War.

The defeat of the Axis powers in 1945 and the social and economic changes of the 1960s forced the regime to undergo deep transformations. The institutionalization of the dictatorship made its survival possible during a time of growing complexity and state intervention in the economy. The main pillars of the regime – the authority of Francisco Franco and National Catholicism – remained, while new rational elements were also introduced, contributing to the aforementioned 'palimpsest of legal cultures'.[16]

Legitimacy by origin (the Civil War) was combined with arguments of legitimacy by exercise (particularly economic growth). References to the war did not disappear, but underwent a mutation. Instead of 'war' or 'victory', the word 'peace' was introduced into the political discourse. A massive campaign was organized to commemorate the twenty-fifth anniversary of the victory in the Civil War, yet the phrase used referred not to 'victory' but to 'peace': '25 Years of Peace'.[17] The word 'peace' started to appear in the names of institutions, streets, schools, and even the hospital where Franco himself died in 1975. However, the legitimacy of origin and the references to religion and the eternal nation did not entirely disappear. An example of this mixture can be found in the decree that declared amnesty for certain political criminals. Published on 1 April 1964, hitherto

[15] For example, the 'Orden of 6 May 1970 concerning validation of studies in universities not located in the national area during the Crusade of Liberation', *BOE*, 132, 3 June 1970, 8569.

[16] Sousa Santos, 'The Heterogeneous State and Legal Pluralism in Mozambique'.

[17] For more on the campaign '25 Years of Peace', see F. Fernández-Crehuet, 'Recht und Fiktion im Franco Regime', in F. Fernández-Crehuet López and A. M. Hespanha (eds.), *Franquismus und Salazarismus: Legitimation durch Diktatur* (Frankfurt am Main: Vittorio Klostermann, 2008), 3–12. See also A. Aragoneses 'El derecho bajo el franquismo. Transformaciones del sistema jurídico español (1936–1978)', in M. Capellà and D. Ginard (eds.), *Represión política, justicia y reparación: La memoria histórica en perspectiva jurídica (1936–2008)* (Palma: Plural, 2009), 123–39.

the 'Day of Victory' and henceforth the 'Day of Peace', it included references to peace but also to the victory, the Crusade, and the head of state.[18]

In 1959 Franco's gigantic mausoleum, the *Valle de los Caídos*, or the Valley of the Fallen, was inaugurated. This monument, located in San Lorenzo de El Escorial some fifty kilometres northeast of Madrid, was designed to honour the National Crusade and Franco. However, the monument was also meant to play an important role in the creation of a new narrative in the 1960s: the discourse of reconciliation. The bodies of thousands of Republican soldiers were transported to the monument, without their relatives' permission.[19] The goal of this operation was to combine the old discourse of victory with a newly created discourse of reconciliation, imposed on the defeated by the victors.

The context of this propaganda operation generated a perception of the dictatorship as something 'natural', as the only possible response to the instability during the Second Republic, as the only path to the transition to modernity.[20] Francoism was presented as the source of stability, economic growth, social well-being, and modernization. This is important because that narrative survived Franco and became one of the pillars of the 'acceptance of impunity' by the victims during the transition.

3 Amnesty, Oblivion, and Democratic Normality: 1977–1999

On 20 November 1975, Francisco Franco Bahamonde died. The Spanish head of state did not pass away in prison, nor was he executed by partisans. Franco was never tried for his crimes before any court. Instead, he died in agony in the *La Paz* (Peace) hospital, which he had personally inaugurated in 1964. He was buried on 23 November in the *Valle de los Caídos.*

20 November 1975 marks the beginning of the Spanish transition to democracy. Yet it was not until 1978 that the democratic Constitution was promulgated. We can conclude that the transition finished in 1982 with the victory of the social democratic PSOE party in the general elections. The transition was marked by political violence from anti-democratic forces, from terror groups like ETA in the Basque Country and the extreme leftist

[18] Decreto 786/1964, of 1 April, granting a general pardon on the occasion of the 25 years of Spanish Peace. *BOE* 84, 7 April 1964, 4313.

[19] See the documentary 'Avi et trauré d'aquí', produced by Catalan Public Television TV3 and directed by Montse Armengou and Ricard Belis (2013).

[20] M. Fraga, *Horizonte Español* (Madrid: Editora Nacional, 1965).

GRAPO, from police and paramilitary forces, and from extreme-right organizations.[21]

After Franco's death, King Juan Carlos I was appointed Head of the State. The *Ley de reforma política*[22] was passed by the Francoists in 1976 by the *Cortes*, the corporatist Francoist parliament. The law initiated the dismantling of the Francoist institutional framework and opened a path towards democratization. It provided a framework for the general elections of 1977, won by the UCD, a centre-right party founded by former Francoists and conservative opponents. Thus the transition started with a deal between Francoist politicians and opponents under pressure from the military. This explains why no references to the victims were made either in the law or in the political discourse of the time.

In 1976 the Government enacted a first Amnesty, via a 'Decreto Ley',[23] for opponents of Francoism and civil servants of the Spanish Republic.[24] The Parliament elected in June 1977 began discussion of another very important law, the *Ley de Amnistía*, or Amnesty Act.[25] This legislation represents both a cornerstone in democracy-building as well as an important element in the construction of a culture of impunity and oblivion. The law is still in force today, and its legal effects continue to block attempts to ascertain and assign legal responsibility for serious human rights violations.

In its first article, the Amnesty Act declares that general amnesty will be granted to 'all acts with a political motive (*de intencionalidad política*), irrespective of their effects, which were classified as crimes but were committed before 15 December 1976', as well as all the acts of the same nature made between 15 December 1976 and 15 July 1977, provided that the political motives behind these acts had been aimed at 'the re-establishment of public liberties or autonomy for the territories of Spain'.

Article 2 of the Act is even more important and has had a more lasting effect in Spanish law and society. According to this article, the following cases are included in the amnesty 'in any case': 'Crimes that may have been committed by authorities, civil servants, and public order agents with the aim of investigating and prosecuting acts included in this law'; i.e. with the

[21] S. Baby, *Le Mythe de la Transition Pacifique: Violence et Politique en Espagne (1975-1982)* (Paris: Casa de Velázquez, 2013).

[22] Ley 1/1977, of 4 January of Political Reform. *BOE* 4, 5 January 1977, 170–1.

[23] A "Decreto-Ley" is a "Ley" enacted first by the Government and later ratified by the Parliament.

[24] Real Decreto-Ley 10/1976, of 30 July concerning Amnesty. *BOE* 186, 4 August 1976, 15097–8.

[25] Ley 46/1977, of 15 October, concerning Amnesty. *BOE* 248, 17 October 1977, 22765–6.

aim of repressing opponents of Francoism. This provision has blocked any initiative to bring individuals responsible for serious human rights violations before a court, blazing what Rafael Escudero[26] has called 'the path to impunity'.

The Amnesty Act also sealed what has been called the 'pact of silence' of the transition to democracy. According to Escudero, the victims accepted silence in exchange for democracy: the tension and violence of the transition did not allow any other options.[27] At the same time, however, the urge for democracy and the modern legitimacy discourses of the 1960s also put the demands of the victims in second place.

In the words of Alejandro Baer, the victims and legislators 'opted for a tacit agreement to leave the legacy of the war and the dictatorship out of the political debate', a strategy he termed the 'pact of silence'.[28] We can conclude that there was no transitional justice. What occurred was, in the words of Bartolomé Clavero, a 'constituent amnesty' and an oblivion: the Constitution of the new democratic regime was based on the oblivion of the crimes of Francoism.[29]

Nevertheless, both before and after the ratification of the Constitution, some laws and decrees were enacted that acknowledged certain rights for the victims of the Civil War. In April 1976, a royal decree[30] declared that the soldiers of the Republican Army had the same rights as those of the Francoist forces under the Spanish War Mutilated Soldiers Act, enacted in March of that year.[31] Similarly, a 1979 law granted pension rights and medical assistance to relatives of victims on both sides of the Civil War,[32] although it excluded those whose death was 'caused by execution of a death sentence' or 'derived from violent action on the part of the victim'.

[26] R. Escudero, 'Road to Impunity: The Absence of Transitional Justice Programs in Spain', *Human Rights Quarterly* 36 (2014), 123–46.

[27] *Ibid.*, 132.

[28] A. Baer, 'The Voids of Sefarad: The Memory of the Holocaust in Spain', *Journal of Spanish Cultural Studies* 12 (2011), 95–120, at 98.

[29] Expression of B. Clavero, *España 1978: La amnesia Constituyente* (Madrid: Marcial Pons, 2014).

[30] Decreto 3025/1976 of 23 December regulating pensions for those Spaniards who suffered mutilation due to the war and could not enter in the Cuerpo de Caballeros Mutilados de Guerra por la Patria. *BOE* 9, 11 January 1977, 522.

[31] Ley 5/1976, of 11 March, of 'Mutilados de Guerra por la Patria'. *BOE* 63, 13 March 1976, 5209–15.

[32] Ley 5/1979, of 18 September concerning pensions, medical, pharmaceutical, and social assistance for the benefit of widows and relatives of Spaniards who died in the past civil war. *BOE* 233, 28 September 1979, 22605–6.

In a law enacted in 1984, the rights of both the members of the Republican Army and the police forces were explicitly recognized.[33]

The transitional government policy combined amnesty and impunity in its granting of certain social rights for a few victims of the Civil War. Francoism was not condemned by either the Government or the Spanish Tribunals. There is no reference in the Constitution to the dictatorship, the democratic opposition, or the crimes of the dictatorship. The transition conceived the democratic system as a natural continuation of the dictatorship. Antonio Baylos has noted that 'the drafters of the constitution chose not to define the dictatorial regime as a permanent state of exception. This would have allowed for the elimination of all Francoist laws and judicial decisions'.[34]

A new actor in the Spanish legal and political system, the Constitutional Tribunal, could have changed this legal approach to the past, but in 1982 it decided to consider Francoist law as fully valid and to deem the democratic law as the continuation of Francoist law. The Court decided a case lodged by Juan Bautista Santaella, a former member of the Spanish Republic Army who, in 1979, demanded the recognition of all the rights he had according to a Decree of 1936. The Constitutional Court decided that the law of the Francoist territory in the Civil War was the one which was imposed over the whole Spanish territory, and, therefore that Republican law could not be considered as law by the present legal system.[35]

This result was, according to the Constitutional Court, based on 'the hard reality of history', which could not be avoided. The Court indirectly endorsed full legality to Francoist legislation, even though it was illegitimate by origin, while outlawing the legal system put in place during the democratic Spanish Republic (1931–9). According to the court, the Francoist regime was not a permanent state of exception, but a valid, legitimate legal system.

In another case, in 1983, an association of Aviators of the Second Republic claimed they had the right to enjoy the same rights as the Francoist aviators. The Constitutional Court declared that it lacked the competence to correct the lack of action on the part of the legislator in the sphere of

[33] Ley 37/1984, of 22 October, recognizing the rights and services to those who were members of the Armed Forces, Public Order Forces of the Republic. *BOE* 262, 1 November 1984, 24433.

[34] A. Baylos, 'Derechos económicos e indemnizaciones derivados de la memoria histórica', in J. A. Martín Pallín and R. Escudero (eds.), *Derecho y memoria histórica* (Madrid: Trotta, 2008), 185–208, at 188.

[35] Decision of the Constitutional Tribunal 28/1982 of 26 May, *BOE* 137, 9 June 1983, 19–21.

the rights of civil servants of the Spanish Republic.[36] According to Baylos, these decisions helped the 'democratic normalization of the past'.[37]

The pact of silence was not discussed after 1981. Some organizations considered the Constitution to be a starting point for the recognition of rights of the victims and the elaboration of an official, democratic policy of remembrance. However, a failed coup attempt in 1981 brought certain democratization processes to a close. The social democratic *Partido Socialista Obrero Español*, PSOE, won the general elections in 1982 and put an end to the reparation measures that had been timidly initiated under the previous governments. Only in 1990 did the government acknowledge the right to financial compensation for a small subset of former political prisoners, namely those who had spent more than three years in prison and were older than sixty-five.[38]

Spanish society did not protest against this culture of silence. Spain's entry into the European Community (1986), together with economic growth and new cultural freedom, obscured the unresolved problems of justice and memory. In his novel *La Buena letra*, Rafael Chirbes illustrates these developments with the story of a family of defeated Republicans who abandon their ideals and past in the name of economic growth and well-being.[39] This reality of the 1980s and 1990s is also depicted in cultural creations such as the films of Pedro Almodóvar, in which a modern cosmopolitan Spanish society enjoys its freedom without concern for its past history. Luisa Elena Delgado's analysis of Almodóvar's films from this perspective is both insightful and telling.[40]

I recall here only one judicial case during this period: the Ruano case. Enrique Ruano was a student who died in 1969 at the hands of the police. The regime press presented his death as a suicide, but in 1995 his relatives sued the police officers. The defendants claimed innocence and demanded application of the Amnesty Act. The judge was willing to accept this only on the condition that they admitted to having committed a crime for political reasons. The defendants would not accept this condition, and they were acquitted for lack of evidence. This decision of the *Audiencia Provincial de*

[36] Decision of the Constitutional Tribunal 63/1983 of 20 July, *BOE* 189, 9 August 1983, 21657–9.

[37] Baylos, 'Derechos económicos e indemnizaciones', 188.

[38] Ley 4/1990, of 29 June, of General State Budget for 1990. *BOE* 156, 30 June 1990, 18669–710.

[39] R. Chirbes, *La Buena letra* (Barcelona: Anagrama, 2007).

[40] L. E. Delgado, *La nación Singular: Fantasías de la Normalidad Democrática Española (1996–2011)* (Madrid: Siglo XXI, 2014), at 33.

Madrid can be seen as having opened a gate for using the Amnesty Act as a mechanism to access the truth, but this gate was never used.[41]

Despite being passive towards the Francoist past between 1977 and 2008, the Spanish legal system at the same time reacted to past violations of human rights in other parts of the world. Judges of the Audiencia Nacional initiated procedures against former repressors in Chile and Argentina, invoking universal jurisdiction. Obviously these were cases against Argentinean and Chilean individuals who had committed crimes in their respective countries. However, this changed many Spaniards' perception of justice and universal jurisdiction, fuelling the demands of associations in 2008 and the years that followed.

4 The Rebellion of the Grandchildren and the *Historical Memory Act*: 1999–2011

The novel *Blutorangen* by Verena Boos magnificently portrays the shift in the Spanish culture of memory in the final years of the twentieth century.[42] A Spanish student goes to Munich on an Erasmus Programme exchange in the 1990s. There she meets Germans of her age whose grandparents were Spanish antifascists. Her political conscience is awakened, and she starts questioning many aspects of her Spanish identity and its relationship with the past. She then becomes involved with the movement for the defence of historic memory in Spain. Maite, the novel's main character, is the paradigmatic figure of what Margalida Capellà has called 'the rebellion of the grandchildren', which occurred when a generation of young Spaniards, being the grandchildren of those who fought in the Civil War, suddenly realized the abnormality of Spain's culture of memory and, as young adults, created and propelled the movement for historic memory.[43]

The year when the first mass graves were exhumed, 1999, can be said to mark the beginning of this 'rebellion of the grandchildren'. After almost twenty years of silence and transition, a new generation started joining efforts with people of older generations to demand justice and reparation. However, in addition to generational factors this phenomenon is also explainable by cultural and economic factors. This young generation had greater access to a university education and to alternative channels of communication.

[41] Audiencia Provincial de Madrid, Auto, 19 December 1995.

[42] V. Boos, *Blutorangen* (Berlin: Aufbau Verlag, 2015).

[43] M. Capellà, 'La rebelión de los nietos', *La Vanguardia*, 26 October 2008.

These young Spaniards, together with their older counterparts, formed organizations like the *Asociación para la Recuperación de la Memoria Histórica*, as well as local and regional associations. They provided support for, and even participated in, exhumations; they endorsed the review of Francoist judicial decisions; and they sought recognition for the democratic struggle against Francoism.

Such was the general atmosphere when the PSOE won the national elections in March 2004. The new government took several steps to attempt to respond to the demands of this 'memorialist movement'. Parliament declared 2006 the Year of Historical Remembrance,[44] and it started funding public remembrance policies. In that year, 2006, the government presented a bill for historical remembrance that generated strong opposition from the main conservative party (*Partido Popular* or *PP*), founded by former Francoists, as well as the conservative media. The climate of political tension and the attack from the right-wing media influenced the debate around the *Ley de Memoria Histórica* (Historical Memory Act), which was passed into law in December 2007.[45]

Following the 'grandchildren's rebellion', democratic remembrance and human rights organizations demanded the annulment of court sentences against Republicans who had fought against Franco's insurrection. They also asked that the state take responsibility for the exhumation of mass graves and demanded reparations for all victims. The Act itself did not provide the associations for the victims of Francoism with a satisfactory answer to their demands.[46]

Intense debates were held concerning the *Ley de Memoria*. The right wing PP accused the PSOE of 'breaking the spirit of the Transition'.[47] It repeatedly referred to 'the wounds of the Civil War', which it accused the left-wing parties of reopening.[48]

Actually this law is not, strictly speaking, a memory law. The popular name, the Historical Memory Act, does not reflect its content. The official title is 'Law recognizing rights and establishing measures for those who

[44] Ley 24/2006, of 7 July, declaring 2006 the Year of Historical Memory. *BOE* 162, 8 July 2006, 12309.

[45] Ley 52/2007, of 26 December, recognizing rights and establishing measures for those who suffered persecution or violence during the civil war and the dictatorship. See footnote 10.

[46] See E. Nizkor, 'The question of impunity in Spain and crimes under Franco', 2014. Available at: www.derechos.org/nizkor/espana/doc/impuspa.html (last accessed 4 January 2017).

[47] 'El PP rechaza la ley de memoria y dice que rompe el pacto de concordia sobre el pasado', *El País*, 6 December 2007.

[48] 'Rajoy: Abrir heridas del pasado no conduce a nada', *El País*, 6 September 2008.

suffered persecution or violence during the civil war and the dictatorship'. It does not impose or even support a particular reconstruction of history. It only declares annullable the judicial decisions of the Francoist Courts, regulates the financial support to relatives and pensions for certain groups and victims, and forbids political acts in the Valley of the Fallen. Likewise, it only regulates the documentation centre of the Civil War, without imposing a particular vision of it.

In the law's preamble, Francoism is indirectly condemned by expressing adherence to the 'content of the Report of the Parliamentary Assembly of the Council of Europe signed in Paris the 17th March 2006',[49] which 'strongly condemns the extensive and wide-ranging human rights abuses committed by the Franco regime in Spain from 1939 to 1975'.[50] The preamble acknowledges the suffering of the victims of the dictatorship. At the same time however, there are references to the 'spirit of the transition' in which the law would find its legitimacy.

The Law does not annul the judicial decisions handed down by exceptional tribunals: the military *Consejos de Guerra* or War Courts, the special jurisdiction against communism and freemasons, the tribunals for political responsibilities, or the Public Order Court (special tribunals created to repress political opponents). Article 2.1 only declares that these decisions were 'unjust and illegitimate'. Article 3 states that the tribunals or courts who made these decisions were illegitimate as well. Yet the Law does not go so far as to declare these decisions void and illegal. Escudero has explained the difference between nullity and 'annullability'.[51] The illegitimacy of these decisions is clear from a democratic point of view. However, if they are not declared void, they remain part of the legal system.

According to the Historical Memory Act, the victims of those court decisions, in many cases taken by exceptional military courts, may petition the Spanish Ministry of Justice for a 'declaration of reparation and personal acknowledgement', which is important from a political and symbolic point of view. Yet it does not change anything in terms of their legal validity and nor does it create a right to compensation for damages.

[49] Ley 52/2007, of 26 December recognizing rights and establishing measures for those who suffered persecution or violence during the civil war and the dictatorship. *BOE* 310, 27 December 2007, 53410.

[50] Parliamentary Assembly. Council of Europe. Report of the Committee on Political Affairs and Democracy. Report. Document 10737. Rapporteur: Mr. Brincat.

[51] R. Escudero, 'Nulidad/ilegitimidad de las Sentencias Franquistas', in R. Escudero (ed.), *Diccionario de memoria histórica: Conceptos contra el olvido* (Madrid: Catarata, 2011), 84–9.

Articles 11 to 14 of the Act regulate the administrative duty to assist relatives and associations in the exhumation of bodies in mass graves. According to legal scholars, this violates international law, which considers the state to be the party responsible for mass violations of human rights and therefore responsible for the exhumation of the bodies from mass graves.[52]

Articles 15 to 17 of this Act order the removal of Francoist symbols and forbid political acts in the Valley of the Fallen, Francisco Franco's mausoleum, which is of great symbolic importance for Franco supporters. In accordance with these articles, the remaining statues of Franco were removed from public spaces, although other monuments and street names still exist in many Spanish cities.

The law left the interested associations unsatisfied. While it gave them, and citizens in general, some means to obtain financial assistance from the state for the exhumation of bodies or the removal of symbols, recent episodes have shown how difficult it is for the Spanish state and society to confront its past. The first such episode was the reaction of the conservative *Partido Popular* to the 2015 decision of Madrid's city council to change Francoist street names, proving that this legislative directive is still far from effective.[53] Another example is the elimination of funding for exhumations by the ruling national *Partido Popular* government.

Nevertheless, the Spanish Historical Memory Act has fostered the intervention of local authorities in removing Francoist monuments and has also been used as a basis for regional laws and public policies of remembrance.

Following the 2003 elections, the Catalan government created a special 'General Agency of Democratic Remembrance' and funded several local associations and government projects. In 2006, before the Historical Memory Act was enacted, the new regional Constitution of Catalonia (*Estatut d'Autonomia*) declared in Article 54 that the Catalan government 'and the other public authorities shall work for the knowledge and the

[52] M. Capellà, 'Represión política y derecho internacional: Una perspectiva comparada (1936–2006)', in M. Capellà and D. Ginard (eds.), *Represión política, justicia y reparación: La memoria histórica en perspectiva comparada (1936–2008)* (Palma: Plural, 2009), 161–254, at 240; J. Chinchón, *El tratamiento judicial de los crímenes de la Guerra civil y el franquismo en España. Una visión de conjunto desde el derecho internacional* (Bilbao: Universidad de Deusto, 2012), at 23 and following; J. Bonet Pérez/R. A. Alija Fernández, *Impunidad, derechos humanos y justicia transicional* (Bilbao: Universidad de Deusto, 2009), 45.

[53] 'El Ayuntamiento de Madrid cambiará el nombre de 30 calles franquistas', *El Mundo*, 23 December 2015.

maintenance of the historical memory of Catalonia as a collective heritage'. In accordance with this article's mandate, in 2007 the Catalan Parliament created the Democratic Memorial with the task of developing 'public policies of remembrance directed by the civic action of retrieving, commemorating, and fostering democratic memory'.[54] In 2009 the same Parliament approved the Mass Graves Act, building on the Historical Memory Act to assist the relatives and associations in the identification and exhumation of mass graves.[55]

Just recently the Balearic Parliament also adopted a Mass Graves Act.[56] It protects the mass graves and regulates their identification and opening, as well as the exhumation of the remaining bodies.[57] It considers the enforced disappearances of the Civil War and Francoism as 'crimes against humanity'.[58] This legal categorization could make it possible to include this act in the category of laws that 'prescribe or proscribe certain views of historical figures, historical dates, historical symbols, or historical events'.[59]

This wave of regional laws related to historical memory may be seen as creating a dichotomy between the legal silence of Spanish national law on the one hand, and the legal activism of some autonomous regions on the other. It demonstrates the existence of different political and memorialist cultures, which use the law to pursue their own ends.

The trajectory of the Historical Memory Act has not been very successful since 2011. A controversial lawsuit that went before the *Tribunal Supremo* – the *Garzón* case[60] – and the victory in the Parliamentary elections of the conservative *Partido Popular*, which was opposed to this law and to memory laws in general, has rendered many aspects of this law non-applicable and/or deprived them of real legal effect, for example by simply eliminating funding for the exhumations.

[54] Llei 52/2007 of the Democratic Memorial, *DOGC* 5006, 12 November 2007, 45172–9.

[55] Llei 10/2009 on localization and identification of persons who disappeared during the Civil War and the under Franco, *DOGC* 5417, 9 July 2009, 55065–71.

[56] Llei 10/2016, concerning the recovery of disappeared persons during the Civil War and Francoism, *BOIB* 76, 16 June 2016, 18241–7.

[57] Article 1, of the Llei 10/2016.

[58] Articles 2 and 10 of the Llei 10/2016.

[59] See Antoon De Baets' chapter in this book.

[60] 'Garzón abre la primera causa de la historia contra el franquismo', *El País*, 17 October 2008. See Audiencia Nacional, For the Resolution of Justice Baltasar Garzón. Juzgado Central de Instrucción no 5: Auto of 16 October 2008 (Diligencias Previas PA 399/2006 V).

In 2006, in the light of the strength at that time of the memorialist movement, a group of associations filed a lawsuit in the National Court seeking an investigation of Francoist crimes. The controversial judge Baltasar Garzón was put in charge of this investigation. Garzón was a renowned judge, responsible for the indictment of Argentinean and Chilean authorities for crimes committed during the dictatorships in those countries. Garzón sought to open a general investigation for crimes against humanity committed during the Francoist dictatorship, arguing that such crimes against humanity did not fall under the general 1977 amnesty.[61] The problem was that, according to Spanish law, the *Audiencia Nacional* had the right to claim universal jurisdiction for crimes committed abroad, but not for crimes committed in Spain. So technically Judge Garzón was not competent to start an investigation. In the end Judge Garzón recused himself amid a strong and controversial political and social debate. Responsibility for the investigation went to the territorial courts.

Two far-right organizations nevertheless proceeded to sue Garzón for perversion of Justice (*prevaricación*) in 2009. The lawsuit created a major scandal, and on 27 February 2012 the Spanish Supreme Court issued its decision 101/2012.[62] The Court declared Garzón not guilty, but imposed an interpretation of the Spanish legal system that ran contrary to the demands of the associations. According to this decision, the 1977 Amnesty Act precludes investigation of the crimes of Francoism. In the Court's opinion, transition is considered to be a 'perfect model'. The Court also established the doctrine according to which the 'search for truth is a legitimate and necessary aspiration and must avail itself of all the disciplines and professions, especially of historians. But it is not a matter for judges'. The crimes of Francoism, according to this view, entail no legal consequences, but rather only scholarly ones.

As Escudero reminds us, with this decision the 'Supreme Court further rejected the international legal doctrine that establishes a duty to investigate the destiny of disappeared persons, even if it is not possible to punish those who are guilty'.[63]

This legal approach to the crimes of Francoism runs parallel to the dismantling of the Historical Memory Act following the victory of the *Partido Popular* in the 2011 general elections. Over the course of three

[61] Vid Juzgado Central de Instrucción no 5: Auto of 16 October 2008.

[62] Tribunal Supremo. Sentencia 101/2012, 27 February 2012, Caso Manos Limpias y Asociación Libertad e Identidad vs. Baltasar Garzón.

[63] Escudero, 'Road to impunity', op. cit., at 124.

consecutive General Annual Budgets, starting in 2012, the new government has eliminated appropriations for the exhumation of mass graves.[64] On 4 November 2015, a journalist asked President Rajoy for clarification of the non-allocation for the Historical Memory Act. The president's response was that 'the budgetary allocation [for Historical Memory] has been zero',[65] clearly presenting his government's lack of support for this law as an achievement, leaving the Act in many aspects without force due to the lack of financial support.

Something similar happened in Catalonia after the 2010 elections. The new government, formed by the liberals and Christian Democrats of *Convergència i Unió*, reduced the budget for Historical Memory and cut back staffing at the Democratic Memorial. It also changed its approach to democratic remembrance by promoting a discourse that treats the victims of the two sides of the Civil War and the victims of the Francoist dictatorship on equal terms.[66]

5 Francoism Forgotten; World War II Remembered: 2011–2015

As already explained, political and legal systems make reference to the past to legitimize themselves.[67] In this sense, the current Government is also using history to legitimize itself. Similar as in the case of Hungary, also analysed in this book,[68] the efforts to reinterpret medieval history and the time of the Catholic Monarchs are quite remarkable.[69]

In spite of the anti-Semitism growing in social and political discourses,[70] Spanish institutions have been making a great effort to involve Spain in

64 'Rajoy completa una legislatura de olvido económico a las víctimas del franquismo'. Eldiario.es, 4 August 2015; 'La promesa que Rajoy sí cumplió'. *El País*, 5 October 2013; 'El Gobierno elimina el presupuesto de la Memoria Histórica'. *El Mundo*, 29 September 2012.

65 The full answer can be found on the Spanish government website: www.lamoncloa.gob.es (last accessed: 4 January 2017).

66 'El Memorial dóna veu als monistrolencs que van patir la guerra civil'. *Regió7*, 7 May 2015.

67 Giordano, 'The past in the present'.

68 See chapter by Miklós Könczöl in the present volume.

69 See the Public television serial 'Isabel' about the Catholic Monarchs, produced by Televisión Española directed by Javier Olivares and broadcasted between 2012 and 2014.

70 Observatorio de Antisemitismo. Casa Sefarad-Israel, Estudio sobre antisemitismo en España. Informe de resultados (Madrid: Casa Sefarad-Israel, 2012). See also A. L. Menny, 'Antisemitism in Spain: A Religion-Based Anti-Judaism?' *Proceedings/International conference "Antisemitism in Europe Today: The Phenomena, the Conflicts"* (Berlin: Jüdisches Museum, 2013), 1–13.

a cosmopolitan culture of remembrance. As Daniel Levy and Natan Sznaider have described, the Holocaust has become the cornerstone in the construction of a global culture of remembrance.[71] Spanish institutions have organized acts of Holocaust remembrance since 2005 and are seeking legislative changes to increase Spanish participation in this global remembrance culture.[72]

In 2014, a new education act introduced the Jewish Holocaust into the primary and secondary school curricula.[73] Royal decrees implemented this act and established the pedagogical content to be included in the secondary[74] and primary schools.[75] These include provisions to make the teaching of World War II and the Holocaust compulsory for all schools. At the same time, no reference to the Republicans deported to Nazi camps or the victims of Francoism was included. In other words, the government is trying to describe fascism as a part of the history of *other* states instead of an important part of its own past, similar to what is happening in countries like Hungary.[76]

In 2015, an act was adopted that granted Spanish citizenship to Sephardic Jews.[77] To some extent this could be considered 'as acknowledgement of the memory of sufferings and exclusions', in the sense explained by Uladzislau Belavusau and Aleksandra Gliszczyńska-Grabias, of Sephardic Jews who were expelled in 1492.[78] Furthermore, this law also tries to promote the inclusion of Spain in the European memory of the Holocaust. In the law's preamble, the Holocaust is described as an 'everlasting link' between Sephardic Jews and the memory of the Holocaust, as the Holocaust caused 'the brutal sacrifice of thousands of Sephardic Jews'.

In 2015 the Spanish Parliament implemented the Framework Decision of the European Council of 28 November 2010 on reform of criminal

[71] N. Sznaider and D. Levy, 'Memory Unbound: The Holocaust and the Formation of Cosmopolitan Memory', *European Journal of Social Theory* 5 (2002), 87–106.

[72] See Baer, 'The Voids of Sefarad'.

[73] Ley Orgánica 8/2013, of 9 December, to Improve Quality of Education (LOMCE). *BOE* 295, 10 December 2013, 97858–921.

[74] Real Decreto 1105/2014, of 26 December establishing the basic content of Secondary Education. *BOE* 3, 3 January 2015, 169–546.

[75] Real Decreto 126/2014, establishing the basic content of Primary Education. *BOE* 52, 1 March 2014, 19349–420.

[76] See chapter by Miklós Könczöl in the present volume.

[77] Ley 12/2015 of 24 June granting Spanish citizenship to Sephardim originally from Spain. *BOE* 151, 25 June 2015, 52557–74

[78] See Introduction by Uladzislau Belavusau and Aleksandra Gliszczyńska-Grabias in the present volume.

legislation with regard to Holocaust denial.[79] The new article 510.1.c of the Criminal Code, amended in 2015, punishes anyone found guilty of 'publicly denying, trivializing in a grave manner, or exalting the crimes of genocide or crimes against humanity'.[80]

These legislative reforms follow the general trend of remembering the Holocaust. The coming generations in Spain will be educated within the culture of human rights. Not surprisingly however, in the educational guidelines as well as in the Spanish Citizenship law, Spanish institutions avoid mentioning both the complicity between Adolf Hitler and Francisco Franco and the ambivalent role played by Franco during the Holocaust. Franco saved only a few thousand Jews at the very end of the war, while at the same time he allowed the deportation of both Jews and Spanish Republicans to Nazi camps. This silence over the fate of Franco's victims stands out in contrast to the historical-cultural references to World War II and the Holocaust.

6 Conclusion: Legal Silence and the Naturalization of Francoism

The Spanish state refuses to commemorate the victims of Francoism or to fulfil the mandates of the Historical Memory Act, which is once again present in political debates. These decades of oblivion and normalization of the dictatorship, which started in the 1960s, constitute serious obstacles to the development in Spain of public policies of remembrance similar to those being implemented in the heart of Europe.

The normalization of the Valley of the Fallen as a monument deprived of political symbolism is symptomatic of this situation. In 2016, an online travel agency included a special hotel offer that could strike many as peculiar: rooms were made available in the Hospedería de la Santa Cruz del Valle de los Caídos, the Francoist monument where Francisco Franco,

79 Ley Orgánica 1/2015, of 30 March modifying the Ley Orgánica 10/1995 of 23 November of the Criminal Code, *BOE* 77, 31 March 2015, 27061–176. See chapter by Luigi Cajani in the present volume.

80 While a 1995 reform of the criminal code had previously specified Holocaust denial as a crime, a 2007 decision of the Constitutional Court declared this article void for violating fundamental rights: A. Rubí Puig and P. Salvador Coderch, 'Genocide Denial and Freedom of Speech Comments on the Spanish Constitutional Court's Judgment 235/2007, November 7th', INDRET 4 (2008). Available at: www.indret.com/pdf/591_en.pdf (last accessed: 4 January 2017).

José Antonio Primo de Rivera, and 30,000 soldiers are buried.[81] And the gigantic monument to the battle of the Ebre River still stands in Tortosa, Catalonia and enjoys legal protection.[82]

The above phenomena reveal the degree to which Francoism has been naturalized in Spanish contemporary history, without criticism or questioning by Spanish institutions. The silence of the law in the seventies and eighties was only apparently neutral. In fact, the gap created by the lack of an official narrative about the dictatorial past has been occupied by the old narrative created between 1939 and 1978, which survived the death of Francisco Franco.

[81] Seen at www.booking.com (last accessed: 4 January 2017).

[82] This monument was inaugurated by Francisco Franco himself to glorify the Francoist soldiers who fought in the Ebre battle. It still stands today and is protected by municipal regulations.

9

Politics of Public Knowledge in Dealing with the Past: Post-communist Experiences and Some Lessons from the Czech Republic

JIŘÍ PŘIBÁŇ

1 Introduction

History is a battlefield of present politics. Dealing with the past reveals power struggles and strategies of the present. Past events are both denounced and glorified by political agents of the present hoping to weaken their enemies.

However, the past also contains injustices and political crimes and any decision not to deal with them in the present only reaffirms them and confirms the unjust status of their victims. Not to deal with past injustices thus compromises the legitimacy of the present system of positive law.

To deal, or not to deal with the past, indeed, is an important question. This question, however, is inseparable from questions of which past is to be dealt with and how it is to be dealt with.

After the fall of communism, new democratic regimes engaged in the process commonly labelled as 'dealing with the past' to address the former regimes' injustices and illegitimacy. However, in some countries, such as Poland and Hungary, this post-communist liberal democratic politics has been challenged by new politics of conservative populism drawing on the idea of discontinuity between post-1989 liberal democracy and illiberal regimes emerging after the constitutional regime change orchestrated by Prime Minister Viktor Orbán in Hungary in 2011 and the parliamentary victory of Jaroslaw Kaczynski in Poland in 2015.[1] Even the post-communist past is thus being dealt with as illegitimate and the undemocratic and illiberal past that was to be dealt with after the 1989 revolutions reappears in new political practices of the present.

[1] For a detailed analysis, see chapter by Miklós Könczöl (on Hungary) and chapter by Tomasz Tadeusz Koncewicz (on Poland) in the present volume.

In October 2013, a political movement ANO 2011 (YES 2011 movement), formed by a billionaire entrepreneur and former career communist accused of collaborating with the secret police Andrej Babiš, surprisingly won nearly 19 per cent of the vote in the parliamentary election in the Czech Republic by campaigning against corruption in particular and party politics in general. The ANO movement became a junior partner in the coalition government formed by the Czech Social Democratic Party and Mr. Babiš became its deputy prime minister.

One was almost tempted to say that this result was a final stage of dealing with the country's communist past when the electorate preferred to challenge the country's present political élites with their corrupt practices and remained indifferent to the ANO movement leader's murky past. Nevertheless, while successfully leading the ANO movement in the electoral campaign of 2013, Mr. Babiš, who was a Slovak national in communist Czechoslovakia, launched a legal action against the Nation's Memory Institute of Slovakia to clear his name against accusations of collaboration with the communist secret police. In June 2014, the district court of Bratislava ruled that, due to the lack of evidence, Mr. Babiš cannot be considered a former StB (the communist secret police of Czechoslovakia) agent and the appeal court confirmed this original judgment a year later. The communist past, including the possible StB collaboration of Andrej Babiš, proved relatively unimportant during the 2013 parliamentary elections, yet it was considered important enough by him to sue the Nation's Memory Institute of Slovakia and legally prove his innocence before Slovak courts.

Despite these recent twists in Central European politics, it is important to critically assess general patterns of the post-1989 democratization and social transformation politics in different countries of the former Soviet bloc. The emerging public domain and democratic institutions of post-communist Central European countries were confronted with political crimes and injustices of the past and therefore had to respond to the demand of constitutional and legal remedies 'dealing with the past'. Legality became one of the most important discursive and integrative techniques of dealing with the past in post-communist democratic societies. Administration and juridification of collective memory became a hallmark of post-communist historical justice.

Furthermore, the general concept of historical justice is impossible to separate from specific politics of public knowledge and its ideological contestations in the emerging pluralistic and democratic condition. The process of searching for historical justice thus shows that collective memory is not accumulative but always selective and this selection significantly affects party politics and ideologies in post-communist countries.

This chapter opens by summarizing and critically reflecting on the Kundera case which significantly affected the public debate about the communist past in the Czech Republic. Different forms of historical justice – restitutions, rehabilitations, retributions, and preventive lustrations are then briefly discussed to highlight underlying differences between the symbolic and pragmatic need to deal with the past. I argue that the lustration process handled by state bureaucrats paradoxically inhibited the public discussion of the totalitarian past, its political impact and responsibility. Political uses of the lustration law and other legal acts, such as *The Act of Public Access to Files Connected to Activities of Former Secret Police* No. 140/1996, contributed to the post-communist political neurosis and continue to operate as significant objects of party politics and ideological conflicts in the Czech political and public sphere.

The establishment of *The Institute for the Study of Totalitarian Regimes* in the Czech Republic in 2007 – almost two decades after the Velvet Revolution – is another example of this political neurosis and party politics selecting and administering particular public interpretations of modern political history. No other case illustrates its disciplining and policing functions better than the Kundera affair when the novelist was scandalised not so much for what he allegedly did or did not do in 1950 but because he refused to communicate with the Institute's researchers in 2008.

The production of public knowledge by the Institute and its disciplinization effects were illustrated by the question asked by the Institute's researchers and journalists: 'If Kundera is not guilty, why does he not speak to us?' Instead of searching for historical facts and details, the Institute thus operated as a public institution producing specific knowledge, interpretations, and discourses on recent national history and thus only contributes to *the neurotic collective memory* – an example of Halbwachs's classic notion of collective memory which has been typical of post-communist political, legal, and moral experiences. Subsequent changes in the Institute's focus and personnel between 2012 and 2014, caused by previous political changes in the Senate, the upper chamber of Parliament of the Czech Republic electing and recalling members of the Institute's Council as its supreme body, only confirm the Institute's function in general politics of public knowledge and collective memory. However, unlike relatively banal political and ideological conflicts regarding the Institute's mission, its politics of public knowledge and collective memory is stretching far beyond partisan politics and remains best illustrated by its early actions and controversies, such as the Kundera case.

2 The Kundera Case

On Monday, 13 December 2008, a Czech weekly magazine *Respekt* published information that Milan Kundera, the most distinguished Czech novelist, apparently reported a young man and agent Miroslav Dvořáček to the state police on 14 March 1950.[2] The denunciation nearly resulted in a death sentence for Dvořáček who eventually spent fourteen years in communist prisons.

At that time, Kundera was a student of the Academy of Film Arts who had just been expelled from the communist party. These circumstances led to speculations regarding his possible fear of further persecution, including the possibility of criminal charges for not reporting a suspect stranger who stayed overnight at the student dormitory of which Kundera was a senior student supervisor.

Kundera, a former enthusiastic young communist who nevertheless distanced himself from the official ideology in early days of the Czechoslovak communist regime in the 1950s and subsequently dedicated a number of his novels to the unmasking of the 'communist kitsch', thus became suspected of hiding his own skeleton in the closet like so many other intellectuals and artists of the last century. The mass media were locked in heated debates whether Kundera's work, therefore, could be interpreted as a kind of apology for morally repulsive deeds from times of 'the artist as a young man' – something similar, for instance, to the story of a Hungarian film director István Szabó who collaborated with the secret police between 1957 and 1963 and wrote some forty-seven reports about his friends and teachers.[3] Some commentators even concluded that this revelation was yet another evidence of artistic and moral weakness of Kundera's novels[4] while others were shocked by the aggressiveness of attacks on the novelist,[5] especially among younger journalists.[6]

[2] P. Třešňák and A. Hradilek, 'Udání Milana Kundery' (Milan Kundera's Denunciation), *Respekt* weekly magazine, 13 October 2008. The English version of the article is available at: http://respekt.ihned.cz/c1-36380440-milan-kundera-s-denunciation.

[3] News was published by R. Ungvary in the Hungarian magazine *Élet és Irodalom* on 27 January 2006.

[4] A. Tomský, 'Stín udání v pozadí Kunderova díla' (A Shadow of Denunciation in Kundera's Work), *Lidové noviny* daily newspaper, 15 October 2008.

[5] K. Hvížďala, 'V říši hluku je ticho urážkou' (Silence is an Insult in the Empire of Noise), *Euro* weekly magazine, 29 October 2008.

[6] One of the most illustrative examples of this radicalism reflecting on the whole scandal and public responses to it is Adam Drda's article 'Milan je můj kamarád a dal bych za něj pravou ruku!' (Milan Is My Buddy and I Would Give My Right Hand For Him!), *Babylon* magazine 3:XVIII, 25 November 2008.

As if six decades old actions were to be judged and condemned by the public to distinguish and reiterate what is to be treated as morally right and wrong today.

3 Scandalizing, or Dealing with the Past? Reflections on the Kundera Case

Is the Kundera case yet another example of history catching up with its subjects, or is it rather an example of Kundera's sceptical view of humankind always preferring judging to thinking, in this case judging the writer's actions irrespective of whether they actually had happened?

This extraordinary case is a good example of the state of historical research dealing with the Czech communist past, its media presentation, and perceptions by the public. The most striking fact is that the information was forwarded to the weekly *Respekt* by a young researcher of *The Institute for the Study of Totalitarian Regimes* Adam Hradilek. Hradilek abandoned historical science methodology of verification of police documents and co-wrote a journalistic article with one of the magazine's editors Petr Třešňák. Together, they used a heroic narrative contrasting Dvořáček's courage and Kundera's possible denunciation assumingly long buried in the famous man's past.

When asked whether they actually spoke to Kundera, the historian Hradilek and the journalist Třešňák both said that they had faxed a list of questions to what they believed was the novelist's private fax number and decided to publish all documents after they had not received any response. Furthermore, it was revealed that one of the central figures of the whole case, Iva Militká, was Hradilek's relative. Militká actually was the person who let Dvořáček stay in her student room in 1950. She informed Hradilek that her then boyfriend and later husband Miroslav Dlask told her on his deathbed that, at that time, he had told his friend Kundera about Dvořáček's presence in the dormitory and that Kundera logically had to be the one who reported it to the police.

Instead of historical research, we thus have a possible love triangle almost worthy of a Kundera novel – Dvořáček staying in Militká's room while her boyfriend Dlask shared the information with his friend Kundera who, according to Dlask's version revealed to the historian by Dlask's wife Militká, informed the police. Instead of investigative journalism supported by historical science and further evidence, we have a complex of personal interests fabricated into a scandalous and scandalizing story. Neither the journalist nor the historian bothered to interview other possible participants of the tragic event. For instance, Zdeněk Pešat, a historian and Dlask and Kundera's former fellow student, subsequently made a statement according to which it actually was not Kundera but Dlask who reported on his love rival Dvořáček and used Kundera's name and date of birth when giving details to the police officials.[7] This version could be supported by the fact that Dlask refused to talk about the event with his wife Militká all his life.

On top of it, *Respekt* magazine did not bother to contact ordinary policemen serving at the police station at that time. Had they done so, Hradilek and Třešňák would have discovered that the report allegedly made by Kundera at 4 PM was in fact written after the police arrest of Dvořáček late in the evening and therefore at the time when the criminal investigation police (not the secret police or intelligence service) was interrogating Dlask, Militká, and many other students from the dormitory. This information was revealed by the former police officer Alois Pašek in November 2008[8] but never commented on by *Respekt* magazine.

To conclude on this extremely souring scandal, Kundera was forced to make a public statement in which he compared the magazine's treatment to 'the assassination of an author'[9] and said that he had nothing to do with the whole event. He thus refused to give in to the media and the young historian Hradilek's pressure to 'cooperate in the interest of historical truth'. As if the irony of history was catching up with the novelist yet again – this time the irony of post-communist history of 'dealing with the communist past' which wanted to bring him to another public trial – Kundera's silence and refusal to respond to the magazine's set of questions was bizarrely taken as another indication of possible guilt – exactly according to the obscene logic of the world governed by noise in which silence is a crime.[10]

7 'Czech Literary Historian Zdeněk Pešat's Statement on Kundera Case', *České noviny* (The Czech Press Agency Website), 15 October 2008. See 'Was Milan Kundera a Communist Snitch?', *Time*, 18 October 2008. Available at http://content.time.com/time/arts/article/0,8599,1851772,00.html.

8 'Former Czechoslovak Investigator Questions Kundera's Guilt-Press', *České noviny* (The Czech Press Agency Website), 13 November 2008. The investigator Alois Pašek was interviewed by the daily newspaper *Právo*, which published the report on 13 November 2008.

9 See, for instance, K. Connoly, 'Kundera hits out at "communist collaborator" claims', *The Guardian*, 13 October 2008. Available at: www.guardian.co.uk/books/2008/oct/13/milan-kundera-collaborator-dvoracek.

10 Yasmina Reza responded to the scandal with a brief comment in *The Guardian* in which she actually used the sentence 'In the empire of noise, silence is a crime'. See Y. Reza, 'Two weeks in books: in defense of Milan Kundera', *The Guardian*, 18 October 2008. Available at: www.guardian.co.uk/books/2008/oct/18/2.

The most striking fact is that research of this particular history was done under the auspices of *The Institute for the Study of Totalitarian Regimes* – a special body set up by the Czech Parliament in 2007 to deal with the past beyond the common framework of legal justice and in the context of both historical science and public morality. The historian Hradilek thus utterly discredited the Institute's role when he: (a) 'sold' the story to the weekly magazine without using appropriate historical methodology; (b) under the veil of impartial historical research was covering his family history; (c) did not respond to information and further evidence fundamentally challenging his conclusions; (d) eventually published a report for the Institute which focused on Dvořáček's personal history while hardly mentioning the role of Milan Kundera.

Publishing two different versions of the same event – one scandalizing Kundera, for *Respekt* magazine, and the other summarizing plain facts, for the Institute – the historian Hradilek ended up in the same camp like the regime he was supposed 'to study'. In the weekly *Respekt*, he and the journalist Třešňák twisted details and circumstances of a particular historical event by making it part of a pretentious moralistic narrative in which a highly respected 'hero' was to turn out to be a 'villain'! Contrary to the magazine's story, the name of Milan Kundera is mentioned only in one sentence in a report co-written for the Institute with another researcher Martin Tichý and published in spring 2009.[11]

4 Acts of Rehabilitative and Restitutive Justice

I consider this lengthy case study introduction necessary to outline what actually is at stake in any process of 'dealing with the past', especially its institutional and public morality framework. The ultimate failure of one of the Institute's employees actually is a symptom of a much larger problem of all post-communist societies and their forms of 'dealing with the past', especially politicization of the public memory and moral panic driven by the fear of common guilt of all those living through the communist past. However, before analysing specific forms of dealing with the past, I want to focus on traditional forms of legal justice and how they dealt with the past and responded to the post-communist political and social search for historical justice.

[11] A. Hradilek and P. Tichý, 'Osudová mise Moravcova kurýra. Příběh plukovníka letectva ve výslužbě Miroslava Dvořáčka' (The Fatal Mission of Moravec's Courier), *Paměť a dějiny (Memory and History)* 1 (2009), 72–86.

Returning to or dealing with the past is a common measure of addressing any forms of injustice and looking for their remedy, from restitutive and rehabilitative to retributive criminal justice. Nevertheless, the slogan of 'dealing with the past' is mainly studied in the context of transitional justice, post-authoritarian/post-totalitarian transformations and democratic constitution-making and state-building.[12] In this context, a particular period of national history is labelled as 'unjust' or 'lawless' and a common triad of rehabilitative, restitutive, and retributive justice is further supplemented by specific legal, moral, and political measures to facilitate symbolic condemnation of the past unjust regime and its replacement by a new legitimate social and political order.

Historical justice is selective rather than comprehensive. This operation of cutting a symbolic difference between the unjust past and the present struggling to bring justice to both victims and the general public may be fully contained by common legal acts, such as rehabilitation laws restoring the moral and civic credits of victims of the past regime and compensating them for their persecution. Before addressing the specific role of the Czech *Institute for the Study of Totalitarian Regimes* and other forms of non-legal or quasi-legal dealing with the past, let us therefore briefly summarize common post-revolutionary measures of rehabilitative and restitutive justice.

The Czechoslovak *Act of Judicial Rehabilitation*, No. 119/1990 of the Collection of the Laws legislated full rehabilitation of individuals unjustly prosecuted and imprisoned. The Act re-established full integrity and criminal law rehabilitation of those people and granted them financial compensation for the period of their imprisonment, the loss of jobs, trial costs, and health harms.[13] This entitlement was granted even to prisoners' relatives. The law also included a clause stating that compensation for other losses such as property, employment, and educational discrimination would be drafted in specific laws under the new government's programme of political rehabilitation. The act came into effect on 1 July 1990 and rehabilitated all

[12] For comparisons of post-communist and post-World War II political and legal choices, see especially L. Huyse, 'Justice after Transition: On the Choices Successor Elites Make in Dealing with the Past', *Law & Social Inquiry* 20:1 (1995), 51–78; on South Africa, see especially A. Boraine, J. Levy and R. Scheffer, *Dealing with the Past: Truth and Reconciliation in South Africa* (Cape Town: IDASA, 1997); for another complex volume of essays covering different countries in transition, see N. Biggar (ed.), *Burying the Past: Making Peace and Doing Justice after Civil Conflict* (Washington, DC: Georgetown University Press, 2003).

[13] See Section 23 of the Act No. 119/1990 Collection of Laws.

individuals sentenced for political offences between 25 February 1948 and 31 December 1989.

Furthermore, restitution laws providing for either natural restitution (*restitutio in integrum*) or financial compensation of property unjustly expropriated by the past regime were enacted immediately after the regime change in 1989. The Czechoslovak restitution laws were one of the most important priorities of the new democratic legislature elected in the first free parliamentary election in 1990. The Czechoslovak Federal Assembly (Parliament of the Czech and Slovak Federal Republic) legislated a number of laws to enact the process of restitution, especially *The Act of Mitigation of the Consequences of Certain Property Losses* No. 403/1990 of the Collection of Laws, *The Act of the Regulation of Church Property* No. 298/1990 of the Collection of the Laws, and *The Act of Extrajudicial Rehabilitation* No. 87/1991 of the Collection of Laws.

Restitution was perceived as the return of unjustly expropriated property and therefore as a part of the broader process of rehabilitation understood as the law mitigating injustices and harms done by the communist regime. This process of dealing with the unjust past was enacted by a series of specific laws during the first years of the legal and political transformation, formulated in the opening section of the Act No. 480/1991 of the Collection of Laws,[14] which established the legal assumption that the communist regime breached both the principle of human rights and its own laws.[15]

5 Symbolism and Pragmatism of Dealing with the Past: The Lustration Law and Post-communist *Political Neurosis*

Any legislation dealing with the past has both *pragmatic* and *symbolic* meaning.[16] While the pragmatic meaning of laws dealing with the past consists of their providing practical remedies, compensations, and punishments for past crimes and injustices, the symbolic meaning is given by value-based political arguments and moral judgments incorporated in those laws and expressed through the medium of legality.

[14] See Act No. 480/1991 Collection of Laws, para 1.

[15] For further details regarding the Czechoslovak restitution laws and comparisons with other post-communist Central European countries, especially Hungary's prospective interpretation of government's restitution policies, see J. Přibáň, *Legal Symbolism: On Law, Time and European Identity* (Aldershot: Ashgate, 2007), 168–75.

[16] For the distinction of symbolic and pragmatic elements in law, see Přibáň, *supra* n. 15, 166–7.

Post-communist 'transitional' laws obviously are a mixture of pragmatic and symbolic elements but it is still possible to classify them according to the level and importance of either pragmatic or symbolic purposes concepts, and consequences. Purely technical provisions of restitution laws compensating for communist expropriations thus have hugely symbolic meaning for victims of expropriations or their relatives, but also can symbolically operate within the public sphere and often with different evaluations from those directly involved in the process of legal restitutions.[17]

Similarly, the most technical provisions such as lustrations in state-owned industrial companies and public institutions had a symbolic value. Czechoslovak and, later, Czech lustration laws prohibited former communist officials and some high-profile repressive job holders, such as secret police officers and communist militia members, from taking specific jobs in the new democratic administration. Drawing on the principle of 'democracy defending itself' and originally designed as a temporary measure to protect the emerging democratic system from persons formerly committed to the suppression of any pro-democratic movements and activists, the law respected the supremacy of democratic legitimacy and therefore did not cover democratically elected offices. Former communist officials, secret police officers, and their agents active before the Velvet Revolution thus still could enter the new democratic political domain through the process of parliamentary and local elections, almost exclusively on the now slightly renamed but ideologically unreconstructed Communist Party of Bohemia and Moravia ballot list.[18]

Despite all limitations and controversies surrounding the enactment of lustrations, the law effectively protected the system of administration and justice from those directly involved in the communist regime's persistence, policies, and repressions. Its pragmatic goals were determined by the need to provide personal safeguards for the emerging rule of law and the constitutional state.[19]

[17] For further details, see J. Přibáň, *Dissidents of Law: On the 1989 Velvet Revolutions, Legitimations, Fictions of Legality and Contemporary Version of the Social Contract* (Aldershot: Ashgate, 2002), 107–9.

[18] D. Kosař, 'Lustrations and Lapse of Time: Dealing with the Past in the Czech Republic', *European Constitutional Law Review* 4:3 (2008), 460–87.

[19] For further details, see J. Přibáň, 'Oppressors and Their Victims: The Czech Lustration Law and the Rule of Law', A. Mayer Rieckh and P. De Greiff (eds.), *Justice as Prevention: Vetting Public Employees in Transitional Societies* (New York: Social Science Research Council, 2007), 308–47.

At the same time, the law's symbolic role was enormous in the first half of the 1990s. It was perceived as one of few successful policies of decommunization, which involved elements of moral retribution beyond the system of criminal justice. Lustrations were considered both a technique of enhancing the stability of new democracy and an administrative measure for dealing with the communist past by effectively discriminating against those responsible for the past crimes and injustices. It was part of the Czech decommunization policy based on the idea of practical measures necessary to protect the new democratic regime and temporarily eliminate potentially disloyal individuals from public administration.

Indeed, the law functioned as an efficient filter separating former communist officials and their agents from institutions of new democratic administration. Contrary to the criticisms that the lustration act created an atmosphere of fear and suspicion, it contributed to the stabilization of the Czech post-communist society in its early stages of social and political transformation.[20] For instance, it reduced anxiety and uncertainty regarding new political élites.

However, the law's moral symbolic impact on dealing with the communist past turned out problematic when it became clear that a number of those listed under the category of secret police agents actually were actively involved in the struggle against the communist regime. They could appear on the list of secret police agents for many different dubious reasons and, though commonly not causing any harm to anyone, now were subject of the same lustration law sanctions as those who used to interrogate, blackmail, and even torture them.[21]

The lustration law's symbolic role of dealing with the past, therefore, was criticized for exactly its administrative and bureaucratic nature, which ruled out more profoundly moral processes of dealing with the past, such as truth and reconciliation commissions or various public institutes of national memory. The lustration process handled by state bureaucrats paradoxically inhibited the public discussion of the totalitarian past, its political impact and responsibility. The instrumental dealing with the past by legislation contributed to the growing public indifference and marginalization of moral issues of the political past and their subsequent political uses in the form of what can be described as post-communist *political neurosis*.

[20] M. Gillis, 'Lustration and Decommunisation', in J. Přibáň and J. Young (eds.), *The Rule of Law in Central Europe* (Aldershot: Ashgate, 1999), 56–81.

[21] Přibáň, *supra* n. 15.

6 History of Documentation and Publication of Communist Secret Police Information

To understand the state of post-communist political neurosis, of which the Kundera case was the most prominent example, it is important to analyse internal dynamics and different aspects of disclosing and archiving facts and information related to the communist regime and its legal regulation and changes in the Czech Republic in the last two decades.

The process of dealing with the past hardly could be limited to the expertise and privileged power positions of the highest constitutional authorities. The public demanded more information about and evaluations of the communist past and this politics of disclosure gradually became a central point of politics of dealing with the past, especially after controversial and even disenchanting effects of the lustration law which was a central pillar of decommunization politics of the 1990s.[22]

The idea of publishing secret police registers and of giving public access to secret police files was mainly inspired by the German legislation and coincided with the first prolongation of the lustration law in 1996. In the same year, Parliament enacted *The Act of Public Access to Files Connected to Activities of Former Secret Police*, No. 140/1996 of the Collection of Laws of the Czech Republic. The law originally granted access only to persons potentially affected by secret police activities. Nevertheless, the statute was amended in 2002[23] so that the main registers of secret police collaborators could be made available to the general public.

According to the current regulation, any adult person who is a citizen of the Czech Republic can file a request to access the secret police files and documents collected between 25 February 1948 and 15 February 1990. The access, which is provided by the Ministry of Interior, therefore is not limited to the person's data and files. Nevertheless, the Ministry protects the constitutional rights of personal integrity and privacy of other individuals who might be mentioned in the files demanded by the applicant. The Ministry therefore must make all information possibly affecting those constitutional rights inaccessible to the applicant unless it is related to the activities of the secret police and its collaborators. The applicant thus can access any details regarding the identity of secret police agents but would

[22] *Ibid.*; see also A. Kaniowski, 'Lustration and Decommunisation: Ethical and Theoretical Debates', in M. Krygier and A. Czarnota (eds.), *The Rule of Law after Communism: Problems and Prospects in East-Central Europe* (Aldershot: Ashgate, 1999), 212–47.

[23] See Act No. 107/2002 of the Collection of Laws of the Czech Republic amending Act No. 140/1996.

not be able to see information related for instance to their marital life or health problems. This shift of the state policy naturally resulted in a number of legal cases in which individuals demanded their names be removed from the registers and moral reputation re-established.

However, the idea of publishing communist secret police information was inseparable from calls for investigation and prosecution of communist political crimes. Responding to these calls, Parliament set up *The Office for Documentation and Investigation of the Crimes of Communism*. The office originally operated as part of the Ministry of Interior and, from 1 January 2002, as part of the Service of the Criminal Investigation Police.[24] It was to continue the job of collecting and archiving information regarding the communist regime which had been previously done by two other governmental offices – *The Office for Documentation and Investigation of the Secret Police (StB) Activities* of the Ministry of Interior and *The Centre for Documentation of Lawlessness of the Communist Regime* of the Ministry of Justice (originally set up as part of the Prosecution Office). The office's task was to map all injustices, atrocities and crimes related to the communist regime and its officials. It was to archive past political injustices and crimes and thus create a memento for future generations. Apart from this moral job, the office also had a specific criminal justice task: filing cases and prosecuting individuals who still were subject to criminal liability.[25]

7 Politics of National Memory and *The Institute for the Study of Totalitarian Regimes*

The policy of public access to the communist secret police files responded to the demand to disclose all available information regarding the past regime's repressive nature and keep it in the public domain as a warning sign, learning experience, and moral legitimation of the present democratic regime. It also contained and effectively neutralized risks of 'wild' publications of these files by unauthorized agents, though discussions regarding which information should be made available on the Internet still go on. However, these problems are not considered central political issues by Czech society anymore.

At the same time, this *imperative of public knowledge* and knowing more about the communist past did not substitute for the absence of criminal justice like, for instance, in South Africa. All information still relevant in

[24] The Office was set up from two different administrative offices under the Ministry of Interior on 1 January 1995.

[25] For further details, see Přibáň, *supra* n. 15.

terms of criminal justice was to be forwarded and used by the criminal prosecution office. Drawing on these policies, *The Institute for the Study of Totalitarian Regimes* was eventually set up in the Czech Republic in 2007 to synthesize earlier attempts at archiving and, where still possible, prosecuting political crimes of the communist regime.

Another important reason behind the establishment of the Institute was the fact that other post-communist countries, most notably Poland and Slovakia, set up their institutes of national memory. *The Institute of National Remembrance* was established in Poland in 1998[26] and *The Nation's Memory Institute* was established in Slovakia in 2002.[27] Both institutions were designed as independent bodies searching for facts about the totalitarian (not only communist but also fascist/Nazi occupation) past and presenting them to both legal authorities and the general public.

The Act of *The Institute for the Study of Totalitarian Regimes and the Archive of Security Forces*[28] opens with the statement: 'Those who do not know their past are doomed to repeat it'. In the same preamble, the Parliament of the Czech Republic recognizes its duty to deal with the consequences of totalitarian regimes and expresses its will 'to investigate and recall the consequences of the activity of criminal organizations based on the Communist and Nazi ideologies advocating suppression of human rights and rejecting the principles of a democratic state in the years 1938–1945 and 1948–1989'.[29]

[26] The Polish Institute of National Remembrance was set up by a bill enacted by Parliament on 18 December 1998 and started its work on 1 July 2000.

[27] Act of the National Council (Parliament) of the Slovak Republic No. 553/2002 Collection of Laws both founded the Nation's Memory Institute and implemented the policy of disclosure of documents regarding the activity of state security authorities in the period 1939–89.

[28] Act No. 181/2007 Collection of Laws of 8 June 2007 on *The Institute for the Study of Totalitarian Regimes and the Archive of Security Forces.*

[29] The following subsection of the preamble emphasizes the importance of historical knowledge for condemnation of totalitarian ideologies and politics. It reads:

> The knowledge of historical sources and other evidence relating to the above regimes and events leading to their establishment makes it easier to understand the consequences of systematic destruction of the traditional values of European civilization, deliberate violation of human rights and freedoms, moral and economic decline accompanied with judicial crimes and terror against proponents of different opinions, replacement of a functioning market economy with directive control, destruction of the traditional principles of proprietary rights, abuse of education, science and culture for political and ideological purposes, and reckless destruction of nature. Citizens' education in these subjects contributes to the strengthening of democratic traditions and enhancement of civil society and at the same time helps to accomplish the ideals of justice, describe the committed crimes and identify their organizers and executors.

In the same Act, the legislator summarizes essential characteristics of the process of dealing with the past, especially when it acknowledges 'the need to preserve the memory of the huge number of victims and of the losses and damage suffered by the Czech people and other peoples in the territory of the Czech Republic at the time of totalitarian dictatorships' and 'patriotic traditions of social resistance against occupation and expressions of totalitarianism, which reflected the citizens' struggle for freedom and democracy in defending human rights and human dignity'. However, Parliament also reiterates the democratic state's 'obligation to prosecute crimes against peace and humanity and war crimes', 'obligation to indemnify all those who suffered damage caused by the state that violated human rights, the international law as well as its own laws', and 'obligation to allow the public maximum possible access to the secret activity of the totalitarian and authoritative regimes security services, as an expression of its conviction that unlawful acts of any totalitarian or authoritative regime against citizens must not be protected by secrecy or forgotten'.[30]

[30] Similarly, The National Council of the Slovak Republic (Slovak Parliament) defined the role of The Nation's Memory Institute in Slovakia in the Act of the National Council of the Slovak Republic No. 553/2002 Collection of Laws.

The Act's Preamble reads:

> The National Council of the Slovak Republic, keeping in mind:
>
> - the large number of victims, losses and damages, incurred by the Slovak Nation and the members of minorities living in Slovakia in the years of the Second World War and after its ending,
> - patriotic traditions of the Slovak Nation in fighting occupants, fascism, and communism, the deeds of citizens acting in the interest of a free and democratic Slovakia and acting to protect freedom and human dignity,
> - the duty to persecute crimes against peace, humanity and crimes of war, as well as
> - the duty of our State to rectify the wrongdoings to all those who suffered damage on behalf of a State, which violated human rights and its own laws,
> - the duty of our State to disclose the activity of repressive authorities, which was kept in secrecy in the period of oppression 1939–89 and to establish responsibility for subduing our Mother Country, murdering, enslaving, committing robberies and degrading others, the moral and economic decline accompanied by judicial crimes and terror against those of different opinions, the destruction of traditional principles of property rights, misuse of upbringing, education, science and culture for political and ideological purposes to express our persuasion that those who do not know their past, are condemned to repeat it, and that no unlawful act on behalf of the State against its citizens may be protected by secrecy or forgotten, agreed on the present Act.

The Act's opening parts thus synthesize major principles and policies of the post-communist Czech democratic state's dealing with the past, most notably its retrospectively constructed constitutional obligations to provide for measures of retributive, restitutive, and rehabilitative justice, supplemented by effective policies of publication of information related to repressive forces of totalitarian regimes.

The Institute's job description, therefore, consists of: (a) the collection of all information that still may be pragmatically used within the system of legal justice; (b) the construction of a morally normative collective memory of the nation. It is to conduct independent historical research, yet symbolic and normative expectations of research outcomes are already outlined by the legislator in the Act establishing the Institute.

The Institute is expected to act as an independent research institution but its organizational structure is typical of an administrative governmental body, with the Director as a chief administrator in the civil servant position. Furthermore, the seven member strong Council of the Institute is elected by the Senate of the Czech Republic (Parliament's upper chamber).[31] Parliament's possible interests are thus exercised through its upper chamber's election, which makes the Institute part of political and ideological conflicts.

8 Scientific Legitimation of Collective Memory?

Regarding the establishment of the Institute, it is important to note that the law has always been criticized by both the democratic and communist left, which perceived it as a tool of ideological propaganda used by conservative political parties which were in the coalition government between 2006 and 2009. Apart from communists, the Social Democratic Party politicians commonly doubt the Institute's role and some social democratic leaders openly speak of their plans to close it down in the future.

The very existence of the Institute, therefore, is politically controversial and criticisms of the Institute's political and ideological role did not

[31] Similarly, the Slovak Nation's Memory Institute is defined as 'a public institution' by the Act of the National Council of the Slovak Republic No. 553/2002 Collection. It is headed by the Board of Directors, which has nine members. The Chair and four other members are elected by the National Council of the Slovak Republic, two members are appointed by the President of Slovak Republic, and two by the Government of Slovak Republic. The tenure of the members is six years. After the first election, as prescribed by law, two members elected by the parliament, one appointed by the President, and one by the Government were chosen by lot for a shortened tenure of three years.

disappear after the Academic Council of the Institute was established in July 2008 as an expert advisory body, the power of which is to issue research recommendations to the Institute's research activities.

Forming the Academic Council, the Institute hoped to increase its disputed prestige of an independent and academically legitimized research institution. Criticized by politicians for its propaganda role and equally attacked by fellow historians for its dubious outcomes, the Institute aimed at increasing its prestige by accommodating more scientific legitimacy. However, the Institute's existence is troubled by the very paradox of dealing with the past based on the idea that collective memories can be shaped, contained, and organized by a public institution rather than open debates stimulated by the public itself and drawing on multiple discourses including political, academic, moral, and legal ones.

The Institute resembles other quasi-legal and quasi-judicial institutions, such as the South African Truth and Reconciliation Commission and the Polish or Slovak institutes of national memory or remembrance, which seek to file as much information as possible in the hope of producing public knowledge and constituting collective memories.[32] These institutions act as machines designed to use collective memories to shape and codify new collective identities.[33]

Dealing with the past always facilitates the constitution of new collective identities for political societies by synthesizing 'new' collective memories. The Institute's role fits exactly into this production of collective memories, which is to shape the national identity. Its historical research and production of information manipulates collective memory as a mode of self-reflection of a social group, its history and identity.

However, collective memory is a mode of internal perspective, which constitutes the group's *living* memory and remembers only those elements of the past which are still meaningful for the group, its unity, its identity, and its continued existence. Collective memory constitutes the history of the group but this history hardly can be produced, codified, controlled, and guaranteed by a public body such as institutes of national memories in post-communist Europe.

Indeed, collective memories require a referential framework limiting possibilities of the interpretation of the community's history and public institutions function in this way. However, the collective memory reconstructs the *meaningful* past, which is eventually always determined by the

[32] M. Halbwachs, *The Collective Memory* (New York: Harper-Colophon Books, 1980).

[33] For the notion of machine memories, see Přibáň, *supra* n. 15, 65.

present social life.[34] Although laws and public institutions may be a very effective form of codifying the collective memory of a political society and the symbolic universe of its identity,[35] the living generations engage in integrative manipulation of the past in profoundly more complex modes of social communication. Political institutions and laws are only part of this complexity, susceptible to manipulations and partisan uses, and therefore cannot be in control of the constitution of politically correct and morally desirable collective memories.

9 Dealing with the Past as Its Forgetting

The constitution of collective memory and identity is always determined by the present state of a political society but hardly by its institutional and legally or politically normative framework. Politics can play an important role in the institutionalization and the limits of legal and moral dealing with the past. Specific strategies of political agents of the present determine society's *access to the past* but, typically, none of these ways of dealing with the past can satisfy the public and there is always a 'past to be dealt with'.

In the context of the Czech Institute for the Study of Totalitarian Regimes, this manipulation of collective memories and dealings with the past by the present political condition and moral constellations is illustrated, for instance, by the exclusion of the period between 1945 and 1948 which, though politically and internationally different from the periods 1938–45 and 1948–89, had been politically, legally, and morally problematic. During this time, millions of ethnic Germans had been expelled from Czechoslovakia and other East European countries because of the widespread collaboration of this population with the Nazi occupation regime and active involvement in ethnic cleansing and other repressions against the rest of populations during the Second World War. Despite having international legal justification in the Postdam Treaty, these expulsions, nevertheless, had been accompanied by various forms of collective violence and atrocities of the post-war revenge, which can

[34] M. Halbwachs, *On Collective Memory* (Chicago, IL: The University of Chicago Press, 1992), 40.

[35] See, for instance, S. Veitch, 'The Legal Politics of Amnesty', in E. Christodoulidis and S. Veitch (eds.), *Lethe's Law: Justice, Law and Ethics in Reconciliation* (Oxford: Hart Publishing, 2001), 33–45.

hardly be defended in terms of current political standards, legal norms, and moral convictions.

The example of limiting the Institute's historical investigations to the years 1938–45 and 1948–89, now officially labelled 'totalitarian' despite huge differences, for instance, between the Stalinist early 1950s period and the relatively liberal second half of the 1960s peaking in the Prague Spring of 1968, only proves common sociological knowledge that every collective memory and historical justice is selective rather than comprehensive. Every dealing with the past subsequently also involves 'undealing with the past'. Every politics of memory involves politics of active forgetting.

Although morally disturbing and always controversial, this internal dynamics runs through political history and its best ancient illustration is probably Cicero's speech in the Senate two days after the assassination of Caesar when he called for *oblivione sempiterna delendam* – eternal oblivion of the act. Winston Churchill's speech in Zurich in 1946 is another fine example of this politics of active forgetting because, though explicitly mentioning the need to punish those guilty of war crimes and to deprive Germany of the power to rearm and launch another aggressive war, Churchill reiterates Gladstone's call for 'a blessed act of oblivion' and the need to 'turn our backs upon the horrors of the past'.[36]

10 Concluding Remarks: On Public Knowledge and Neurotic Collective Memory

More important than the exclusion of the post-war revengeful atrocities from the study of and dealing with the past is the Czech legislator and government's delay in establishing *The Institute for the Study of Totalitarian Regimes*. The fact that these constitutional bodies considered it necessary to institutionally frame the nation's collective memory and produce the body of authoritative public knowledge nearly two decades after the collapse of the communist regime shows how prominent the past has become in the present political and ideological struggles and how moral arguments are designed to be won through the authority of public bodies.

The state in which a political institution pretends to act as a mental institution disciplining and morally ordering the collective body of a polity

[36] W. Churchill, 'Zurich Speech, 19 September 1946' available at The Churchill Society, London, www.churchill-society-london.org.uk/astonish.html. About historical dynamics of oblivious versus active memorization, see Introduction by editors in the present volume.

is impossible to explain by merely using some kind of the Durkheimian methodology and concepts of collective memory and identity. The constitution of public bodies such as the Institute, especially their claim of scientific research-based legitimacy, indicates that this institutional setting is designed to produce a specific and morally definite body of *public knowledge*.

What is important is knowledge rather than memory and morality rather than law. If we accept Michel Foucault's claim that sovereignty was typical of the rule of absolutist monarchy while modernity created new forms of governmentality based on policing and social discipline,[37] we have to conclude that the Institute's organization and functions, rather than legal justice typical of courts, are closer to the policing and disciplinization of public morality.

This policing function of the Institute came to its full force exactly during the Kundera affair when the novelist was scandalized not so much for what he allegedly did or did not do in 1950 but because he refused to communicate with the Institute's researchers in 2008. The production of public knowledge does not grant any *right to silence*. Those in charge of producing the public knowledge can use any method of extracting missing facts of the past including the orchestrated provocation of a suspect by speculating about his possible guilt in the mass media.

The guilt of keeping silence about one's personal history is unforgivable for those searching for the Truth and feeling entitled to reveal it to the rest of society. 'If Kundera is not guilty, why does not he speak to us?' asked those behind the scandal. In the world governed by the media noise, silence is always suspicious if not criminal. Unsurprisingly, the Institute came under heavy fire from academic historians, politicians including those from the conservative right-wing parties, and the general public.

The Kundera case is not important because it would be a 'celebrity author caught naked' kind of the tabloid scandalization story managed by state-paid historians searching for and authorizing the official truth about the communist past. It is important because it shows that the post-communist regime's production of public knowledge about the communist past cannot eliminate a fundamental discursive conflict between personal stories and official history. The case mainly proved that even post-communist societies consider suspicious and untrustworthy those individuals who

[37] See, for instance, M. Foucault, 'The Birth of Biopolitics', in M. Foucault (ed.), *Ethics. Essential Works of Foucault 1954–1984*, Vol 1 (London: Penguin Books, 2000), 73–9.

carefully protect their private life and personal history and remain unwilling to collaborate with political institutions set up to 'clarify and understand the communist past'. The typically modern struggle of a man against the public intrusion into his private life, so extreme during communist times, thus carries on in the form of *the post-communist neurotic collective memory*. The recent rise of varieties of political populism in Hungary, Poland, and other countries of the former Soviet bloc is just one of its many examples, now complicated by the common and potentially fatal crisis of the European Union and its inability to deal with its both past and present.

10

Adjudication in Latvian Deportation Cases: References to International Law

IEVA MILUNA

1 Introduction

Following the collapse of the USSR and Latvia's renewal of its independence, its accession to international law instruments adopted during its fifty years of occupation induced Latvians to think about the adjudication of international crimes committed on Latvian soil during the occupation regime.[1] As a result, Latvia's criminal laws were amended so that victimized States would be able to adjudicate international crimes that were long known to the international community. The main argument of this chapter is that national courts, in their 'war crimes trials', found themselves manoeuvring between the nationally stipulated definitions of international crimes and the international law in force concerning international crimes. In this regard, the role played by the references to international law in Latvia's criminal code was one of the decisive aspects.

While the practice of all three Baltic States is of a similar nature, in this chapter I confine myself mainly to discussion of the major cases in Latvia, in some instances touching also upon similar cases in Estonia and Lithuania as well. It has frequently happened that cases from the Baltic States have reached the European Court of Human Rights (ECtHR) with regard to definitions of and adjudication of international crimes at the national level. However, the ECtHR has not been a fourth instance court, but only the guardian of whether the effect of interpretation of relevant national and international laws is compatible with the European Convention on Human Rights (ECHR). Nonetheless the ECtHR has been involved in the Latvian examination of international crimes in cases from Latvia in light of their definitions in international law.

[1] E.C. Pettai and V. Pettai, *Transitional and Retrospective Justice in the Baltic States* (Cambridge University Press, 2015), 3.

Section 2 of this chapter discusses the adjudication by national and international courts in the so-called 'deportation cases', as these form the core practice of 'war crimes trials' in Latvia. Section 3 is devoted to examination of the role of international law in amending the national laws of Latvia and in bringing perpetrators to justice.

2 Adjudication in Deportation Cases

The Baltic States experienced two large deportations of its people by the USSR to remote places in Russia; in 1941 and 1949. In 1941, 10,000 Estonians, 15,081 Latvians, and 13,600 Lithuanians, comprising the respective countries' economic, cultural, and intellectual elites, were deported to Siberia.[2] In 1949, 40,500 Latvians, 33,500 Lithuanians, and 20,500 Estonians, including entire families, were deported, being labelled as bandits and nationalists, bandits' accomplices, and Kulaks.[3] Later the deportations were acknowledged to be without foundation and all deportees were rehabilitated.[4] Following the collapse of the USSR, the parliaments of the Baltic States became engaged in the task of prosecuting international crimes committed on their soil. It has often been noted that Baltic States' Criminal Codes in Soviet times contained definitions of international crimes worded in such a way as to prevent the trial of USSR perpetrators for the crimes committed during the Soviet regime.[5] Thus the parliaments of the respective Baltic States were endowed with the task of formulating international crimes in accordance with internationally agreed definitions.

The discussion of the Latvian deportation cases entails an examination of the rules of the Latvian Criminal Code which were in force at the time of adjudication of the crimes. Section 68.1 of the Latvian Criminal Code,

[2] ECtHR *Larionovs and Tess* v. *Latvia* (Appl. Nos. 45520/04 and 19363/05) Inadmissibility Decision 25 November 2014 (para 12); K. Inkuša, 'Mass Deportations of 1949 in Latvia as a Crime Against Humanity – A Fair Legal Reality for Social and Political Groups in the Context of the Genocide Convention?', *Baltic Yearbook of International Law* 9 (2009), 73; L. Mälksoo, 'Soviet Genocide? Communist Mass Deportations in the Baltic States and International Law', *Leiden Journal of International Law* 14 (2001), 764; Pettai and Pettai, *Transitional and Retrospective Justice*, 46.

[3] Mälksoo, 'Soviet Genocide?', 765; Pettai and Pettai, *Transitional and Retrospective Justice*, 52.

[4] *Larionovs and Tess* v. *Latvia* (para 25); Pettai and Pettai, *Transitional and Retrospective Justice*, 53.

[5] L. Mälksoo, 'The Definition of Genocide and the Role of Soviet International Lawyers: Reflections on the Socialist Legacy in International Law', *Baltic Yearbook of International Law* 6 (2006), 114.

entitled 'Crimes against humanity, genocide' in fact prescribed criminal responsibility for genocide as a type of crime against humanity:

> for the commission of crimes against humanity, also for genocide, irrespective of whether they have been committed in time of war or in time of peace, as these offences are defined in international law . . . , that is, the intentional commission of acts with the aim of full or partial extermination of a national, ethnic, racial, or social group, or groups of common belief or religion as such, by killing, or inflicting serious bodily injuries or mental harm, deliberately inflicting upon the group conditions of life aimed at bringing about its physical destruction in whole or in part, and by deprivation or restriction of economic, political or social human rights of a native population with the same intent.[6]

However, crimes against humanity as a separate international crime were not criminalized.[7] As can be seen from the above-quoted section, genocide was defined by the Latvian Criminal Code as an attack upon, among other groups, a social group and group of common belief or religion by depriving or restricting economic, political, and/or social human rights of the basic population.[8] As will be further seen, owing to its very imprecise character this definition has caused a lot of discussion in both the national and international courts.

In the early adjudications the Latvian national courts were not very elaborate in terms of analysing the national criminal law rules and their compliance with international law. In the case of *Noviks*, which concerned organizing Latvian deportations to Siberia, the Latvian Supreme Court was guided by the definition of genocide stipulated in Section 68.1 of the Latvian Criminal Code.[9] The Latvian Supreme Court acknowledged that Noviks committed genocide against the citizens of Latvia, whom he considered as socially dangerous and detrimental to the regime, a finding which was in compliance with the requirements established by Section 68.1 of the Latvian Criminal Code. The court also stipulated that this qualification complied with the Genocide Convention. These conclusions of the national court did not discuss the issue of whether social groups can be targeted in cases of genocide.

[6] Inkuša, 'Mass Deportations of 1949', 73–4.

[7] Pettai and Pettai, *Transitional and Retrospective Justice*, 98.

[8] M. Paparinskis, 'Deportāciju prāvas: Starptautisko tiesību skatupunkts', *Jurista Vārds* 16:371 (2005) gada 3.maijs.

[9] Pettai and Pettai, *Transitional and Retrospective Justice*, 65–6.

Further, in the case of *Farbtuhs*, which also concerned deportations of Latvian citizens to Siberia,[10] the Latvian Supreme Court ruled that Farbtuhs was responsible for the crime proscribed by Section 68.1 of the Latvian Criminal Code, as his action was targeted against a group of individuals on the basis of their social status and political conviction.[11] Moreover, the Latvian Supreme Court stated that this acknowledgment complies with the conventional norms. The judgment also refers to the 8 August 1945 Charter of the International Military Tribunal for Nuremberg (Nuremberg Charter) trial and its Section 6.(c), which stipulates that genocide also includes acts which are committed against civilian populations on the basis of their political convictions with the purpose of their total or partial destruction.[12] It needs to be mentioned that this does not comply with the wording of Section 6.(c) of the Nuremberg Charter. It is also rather unclear how the reference to the Nuremberg Charter encompasses the fact that social and political groups were targeted groups of genocide. At the same time, it is obvious that the Latvian courts considered genocide as a form of crime against humanity.

In another deportation case, the case of *Savenko*, the Latvian Regional Court referred to the Genocide Convention and erroneously stated that, according to the Convention, social groups and groups of common belief or religion are protected.[13] The Latvian Regional Court correctly referred to Section 6.(c) of the Nuremberg Charter, which defines crimes against humanity. Furthermore, the Latvian Supreme Court established that the acts of Savenko were targeted against civilian groups, on the basis of their social status and political convictions, and that this fully complies with the definition of genocide under conventional law.[14] Thus, the Latvian Supreme Court continued to maintain that genocide encompasses cases of targeting social groups and groups of common belief or religion, and that genocide is a form of crime against humanity.

In the case of *Tess*, who also participated in organizing the deportations of Latvians, the Regional Court of Latvia ruled that he committed the crime of genocide with the purpose of destroying a social group as such, making reference to the Genocide Convention and the Nuremberg

[10] *Ibid.*, 97.
[11] Judgment of the Supreme Court of the Republic of Latvia, Nr. PAK-17, 12 January 2000.
[12] *Ibid.*
[13] Judgment of Kurzeme Regional Court of the Republic of Latvia, Nr. K-23/13, 7 July 2000.
[14] Judgment of the Supreme Court of the Republic of Latvia, Nr. PAK-15, 7 February 2001.

Charter.[15] The Regional Court elaborated on the fact that the 26 November 1968 Convention on the Non-Applicability of Statutory Limitations to War Crimes and Crimes Against Humanity (1968 Convention) declared that no statutory limitations existed with respect to genocide, even if these crimes do not qualify as crimes in accordance with the State law where they have been committed.[16] Furthermore, the Regional Court rightly stated that the Genocide Convention did not proscribe the targeting of a social group or group of certain common belief or religion, as provided for in Section 68.1 of the Latvian Criminal Code and mentions States which have extended the list of targeted groups.[17] The Regional Court also analysed Section 6. (c) of the Nuremberg Charter, which provides that acts of genocide include those which are targeted against groups of individuals on the basis of their political conviction.[18] Tess was convicted of genocide with the purpose of destroying a social group, although this does not exclude the possibility that a national group was targeted.[19] The Regional Court of Latvia referred to the practice of different international courts and tribunals in its finding that Tess was guilty of genocide with the purpose of destroying a social group, thus extending the definition of genocide. Also, the Latvian Regional Court, having analysed several judgments of the special courts (International Criminal Tribunal for the Former Yugoslavia [ICTY], International Criminal Tribunal for Rwanda [ICTR]) and certain domestic provisions (including the new criminal law of Estonia), found that State practice and general principles of international law permitted the retroactive application of domestic criminal law in exceptional cases, such as the present one, for punishment of the international crime of genocide. [20]

In another deportation case, the *Larionovs* case,[21] the Regional Court of Latvia makes an even stronger argument on the basis of international law, recalling that the State legal system also comprises principles of international law, which were made binding upon Latvia by the 4 May 1990 Declaration on the Renewal of Independence of the Republic of Latvia.[22] Thus, Article 7 of the ECHR does not prohibit the jurisdiction of a court and the imposition of punishment upon a person for any act or omission

15 Paparinskis, 'Deportāciju prāvas'.
16 *Ibid.*
17 *Ibid.*
18 *Ibid.*
19 *Ibid.*
20 *Larionovs and Tess* v. *Latvia*, para 93.
21 Pettai and Pettai, *Transitional and Retrospective Justice*, 101.
22 Judgment of Zemgale Regional Court of the Republic of Latvia, Nr. K06-3/03-1, 25 September 2003.

in accordance to the general principles of law recognized by civilized nations.[23] The Regional Court of Latvia also referred to Section 45.1 of the Latvian Criminal Code, which states that there is no statutory limitation for crimes against humanity, crimes against peace, war crimes, or genocide.[24] The Latvian court did not analyse whether the prohibition of genocide existed as a customary rule of international law at the time of commission of the crime.[25] With regard to the extension of the definition of genocide to cover the targeting of social groups, the Regional Court of Latvia referred to the fact that since the adoption of the 1948 Genocide Convention new experiences should be taken into account, and that the 1948 Universal Declaration of Human Rights prohibits discrimination on the basis of social origin.[26] Thus the Regional Court did not consider the finding that the Latvian Criminal Code proscribes genocide against a social group as mistaken.[27] Moreover, the national court defined genocide as a type of crime against humanity and stated that the most important characteristic of genocide is the fact that it is perpetrated against a specific group of persons on the basis of certain criteria.[28] The ECtHR, in its review and ruling, referred to the national court's finding that, with respect to *mens rea*, Larionovs was aware of the historical, political, and social processes that were taking place and was aware of the repression and deportations that had taken place in 1940 and 1941.[29] The ECtHR found that national courts considered that the Latvian legislator defined the crime of genocide as a special category of the crimes against humanity.[30]

The individuals found guilty in the *Larionovs* and *Tess* cases both referred their cases to the ECtHR, which joined their applications. They claimed that the national proceedings were unreasonably long, and their right to fair trial had been violated as they were punished in accordance with laws that did not exist at the time of the commission of crimes (violations of Articles 6 and 7 of the ECHR). The ECtHR on its part found that Larionovs and Tess had not exhausted their effective local remedies, namely that they had not referred their cases to the Latvian Constitutional Court, thus potentially reopening the criminal cases.

23 *Ibid.*
24 *Ibid.*
25 Paparinskis, 'Deportāciju prāvas'.
26 Judgment of Zemgale Regional Court of the Republic of Latvia, Nr. K06-3/03-1, 25 September 2003.
27 *Ibid.*
28 *Larionovs and Tess* v. *Latvia*, para 54.
29 *Ibid.*, para 55.
30 *Ibid.*

At the same time, the ECtHR declared that Article 7 of the ECHR does not prohibit the retroactive application of criminal law, but embodies more generally the principle that only the law can define a crime and prescribe a penalty, as well as the principle that the criminal law must not be extensively construed to the accused's detriment, for instance by analogy.[31] The ECtHR has pronounced that a constitutional complaint can only be lodged against a legal provision and not against a judicial or an administrative decision as such.[32] In this case that meant establishing whether the applicants' conviction of the crime proscribed by Section 68.1 of the 1961 Criminal Code for acts committed in March 1949 was directly related to any legal provisions which could reasonably be questioned as being contrary to the Constitution of Latvia.[33] While the crime was proscribed by Section 68.1 of the 1961 Criminal Code, its retrospective application was provided for by Section 6.1 and Section 45.1 of the 1961 Code.[34] The ECtHR declared that the definition of the crime could be subject to constitutional review.[35] The Latvian government provided relevant examples of the Constitutional Court's case-law, which demonstrates, *inter alia*, that Article 92 of the Constitution of Latvia includes the guarantees enshrined in Article 7 of the ECHR.[36] The ECtHR elaborated on the fact that the cases relied on by the Latvian government demonstrate that it is the practice of the Constitutional Court to examine the compatibility of legal provisions not only with the Constitution itself, but also with the ECHR.[37] The Court thus found that the relevant domestic law provisions concerning the retroactive application of criminal law and the scope of the crime itself could be challenged before the Constitutional Court as being contrary to the human rights enshrined in the Constitution of Latvia.[38] The ECtHR finally declared that in the renewed examination of the case the authorities will be bound by the judgment of the Constitutional Court and its interpretation of the impugned provision, and that the two-step remedy envisaged by Latvian law can be considered as capable of providing redress in the circumstances of the case.[39]

[31] *Ibid.*, para 146.
[32] *Ibid.*, para 148.
[33] *Ibid.*, para 149.
[34] *Ibid.*, para 150.
[35] *Ibid.*, para 151.
[36] *Ibid.*, para 154.
[37] *Ibid.*, para 158.
[38] *Ibid.*, para 159.
[39] *Ibid.*, para 162.

3 The Role of International Law

Taking into account the discussion over whether a social group and/or group of common belief or religion can be targeted in cases of genocide, it should be borne in mind that Section 68.1 of the Latvian Criminal Code refers to definitions of crimes against humanity and genocide *as they have been established by 'the respective conventional norms'* (emphasis added). This practice with regard to international crimes has remained until today in the Baltic States' criminal laws. It thereby fully satisfies the principle of *nullum crimen sine lege*, as the definition of international crimes can be based on applicable international laws, whether customary or treaty provisions.

In the cases of *Noviks*, *Farbtuhs*, and *Savenko*, the Latvian courts referred to international law rules, however, these references do not contribute to the main discussion of whether social and political groups can be targeted under international law in the cases of genocide. The Latvian courts used this argumentation because they considered genocide as a form of crimes against humanity. Thus, it can be concluded that the reference in Section 68.1 of the Latvian Criminal Code to international law has been misleading with respect to the national courts' reasoning.

In the case of *Tess* the Latvian court determined, with an implicit reference to binding international law applicable to the definition of genocide, that it was still genocide committed against a social group, and that part of international practice refers to the fact that genocide can be carried out against a social group. In the cases of both *Larionovs* and *Tess*, the Latvian courts made an even stronger reference to binding international law, stating that Latvia acceded to the international law instruments in its 4 May 1990 Declaration on the Renewal of Independence of the Republic of Latvia, thus crimes could be adjudicated on the basis of international law.

At the same time, the joint case of *Larionovs and Tess v. Latvia* induced a discussion by the ECtHR concerning the relevance of international laws. The ECtHR made an approving reference to the national court of appeals, which evaluated the international rules on genocide both in customary international law and treaty provisions, and found that the court of appeals concluded that in the international community the concept of genocide is not limited to an act directed against a national, ethnic, racial, or religious group, and that the list of criteria mentioned in the 1948 Genocide Convention cannot be considered as exhaustive.[40] Thus the national court of appeals concluded that genocide is an international crime and that in

40 *Ibid.*, para 63.

domestic legislation it may be defined in a different manner from the 1948 Genocide Convention, if in substance it corresponds to all of the characteristics of a crime against humanity.[41] As a result the national court of appeals found that Section 68.1 of the Latvian Criminal Code is not contrary to the 1948 Genocide Convention.[42]

The role of international law was also discussed by the ECtHR in the *Larionovs and Tess* v. *Latvia* case, in which the ECtHR referred to the domestic courts, which reasoned that the lack of any statutory limitations with respect to 'crimes against humanity including genocide', irrespective of the date of their commission and whether they had been committed during times of war or in a time of peace, was not only provided for in national law but also spelled out in the 1968 Convention.[43] Section 68.1 of the Criminal Code referred to the definition of the crime 'by the respective normative treaty legislation' and contained a reference to international law.[44] Thus, the court rejected the applicants' argument that their convictions were related merely to an interpretation and application of the relevant provisions of national law.[45] Rather, the court found that their convictions were based on provisions of the national criminal law, which transposed the relevant provisions of international law.[46]

Moreover, the role of international law appears in some other Soviet regime-related national adjudications of cases that have reached the ECtHR – *Penart* v. *Estonia*,[47] *Kolk and Kislyiy* v. *Estonia*,[48] *Kononov* v. *Latvia*,[49] and *Vasiliauskas* v. *Lithuania*.[50] The case of *Penart* v. *Estonia* concerns historical events, which took place in 1953. Penart directed the killing of O.R.R. – a person hiding in woods from the Soviet oppressions by occupation authorities. Penart was also in charge of other operations against other persons hiding in woods, including V.S. and P.M., both of whom were killed. Penart was found guilty of crimes against humanity because he had organized

41 *Ibid.*
42 *Ibid.*
43 *Ibid.*, para 151.
44 *Ibid.*
45 *Ibid.*
46 *Ibid.*
47 ECtHR *Penart* v. *Estonia* (Appl. No. 14685/04), Inadmissibility Decision 24 January 2006.
48 ECtHR *Kolk and Kislyiy* v. *Estonia* (Appl. Nos. 23052/04 and 24018/04) Inadmissibility Decision of 17 January 2006.
49 ECtHR *Kononov* v. *Latvia* (Appl. No. 36376/04) Judgment 24 July 2008; ECtHR *Kononov* v. *Latvia* (Appl. No. 36376/04), Judgment (Grand Chamber) 17 May 2010.
50 ECtHR *Vasiliauskas* v. *Lithuania* (Appl. No. 35343/05) Judgment (Grand Chamber) 20 October 2015

the killing of a person hiding from the authorities because of his (in the case of O.R.R.) political convictions. Penart argued that they were not civilians and also argued that the *nullum crimen sine lege* principle had been violated because these were not crimes against humanity at the time of their commission. He also alleged that Article 7 of the ECHR had been violated.[51]

At that time Criminal Code of 1946 of the Russian Soviet Federal Socialist Republic (SFSR) had been applicable in the Estonian territory and it did not include crimes against humanity. Only in 1994 was the Estonian Criminal Code amended to include crimes against humanity. The court noted however that the killing of civilians was considered as a crime against humanity in accordance with the Nuremberg Charter. The court also referred to the 1968 Convention, which states that no statutory limitations apply to crimes against humanity. It is my view that the reference to international law in the Estonian Criminal Code also played a role. The court stipulated that these were crimes against humanity in accordance with international law at the time of their commission. The court also provided the argumentation that the Soviet Union was a party to the London Agreement of 1945, by which the Nuremberg Charter was enacted. The Soviet Union was also a Member of the United Nations, thus it could not claim that it did not know of these international law principles. As a result, Penart's claim was considered as manifestly ill-founded.

In a deportation case, *Kolk and Kislyiy* v. *Estonia*, Kolk and Kislyiy were convicted in 2003 of crimes against humanity, as they participated in civilian deportations in 1949. Kolk and Kislyiy complained that at that time the 1946 Criminal Code of the SFSR was applicable in Estonia, while amendments concerning crimes against humanity were established in the Criminal Code of Estonia only in 1994. Here too international law played a role, as the Estonian appeals court referred to the fact that Article 3 of the Constitution of Estonia stipulates that generally recognized principles and rules of international law were an inseparable part of the Estonian legal system.[52] The national courts of Estonia thus found that these were crimes against humanity that were committed in 1949, as such acts had been defined by the Nuremberg Charter and the Nuremberg Judgment and had been affirmed as principles of international law by the UN General Assembly in 1946.[53] Kolk and Kislyiy also alleged a violation of Article 7 of the ECHR in that they had been punished on the basis

[51] Pettai and Pettai, *Transitional and Retrospective Justice*, 109.

[52] *Ibid.*, 276.

[53] *Ibid.*, 109.

of the retroactive application of criminal law. However, the ECtHR made reference to historical facts and the 'Molotov-Ribbentrop Pact'. Furthermore, the court explicitly stated that deportations were expressly criminalized under the Nuremberg Charter and were not linked with the specific context of World War II, as the 1968 Convention refers to the crimes against humanity committed in both wartime and in peace time. The court noted that Estonian domestic law refers to rules of both general international law and international agreements, and that the ECtHR's role is only to see whether the effects of interpretation of law by the domestic courts is compatible with the ECHR. The court concluded that the acts committed by the claimants were crimes against humanity, and that the Soviet Union was a Party to London Agreement and Member of the United Nations, hence all the principles were known to it. The court also concluded that there was no reason to question Estonia's application of domestic law in the light of international law.

In the case of *Kononov* v. *Latvia*, which led to both Chamber and Grand Chamber judgments, the court in fact affirmed that the national conviction of Kononov's war crime was well-founded.[54] The case concerned the killing and burning alive of nine people in a village of Latvia in 1944, when Latvia was under double occupation during World War II.[55] Like Kolk and Kislyiy, Kononov also alleged a violation of Article 7 of the ECHR, whereby the Latvian courts had convicted him for war crimes under Section 68.3 of the Criminal Code, which also refers to relevant legal conventions.[56] The courts of Latvia declared that Kononov was accused of war crimes in light of the 1968 Convention, and that it complied with what had been stipulated in international agreements to which Latvia was a party.[57] The Grand Chamber concluded that Kononov's conviction of war crimes did not constitute a violation of Article 7, paragraph 1 or paragraph 2,[58] as at the time of commission of the crimes by Kononov, his offences were sufficiently accessible and foreseeable.[59]

[54] Cf. chapter by Maria Mälksoo in the present volume.

[55] Pettai and Pettai, *Transitional and Retrospective Justice*, 103; N. Muiznieks 'Latvian-Russian Memory Battles at the European Court of Human Rights', in N. Muiznieks (ed.), *The Geopolitics of History in Latvian-Russian Relations* (Riga: Academic Press of the University of Latvia, 2011), 221.

[56] ECtHR *Kononov* v. *Latvia*, para 3.

[57] *Ibid.*, paras 45–6.

[58] *Kononov* v. *Latvia*, Grand Chamber, paras 245–6; Pettai and Pettai, *Transitional and Retrospective Justice*, 280.

[59] *Ibid.*, para 244.

In the case of *Vasiliauskas* v. *Lithuania*, Vasiliauskas complained that his conviction for genocide was in breach of Article 7 of the ECHR because the national courts' broad interpretation of the crime had no basis in international law. In that case, the Grand Chamber of the ECtHR found that there was not a sufficient basis for a finding that customary international law, as it stood in 1953, included political groups.[60] The court declared that it was not obvious that the ordinary meaning of the terms 'national' or 'ethnic' could be extended to cover partisans, and that such a finding would be an interpretation by analogy to the applicant's detriment, which rendered his conviction unforeseeable.[61]

4 Conclusions

In Latvia, the adjudication of crimes committed during the Soviet regime has raised issues concerning the implementation and application of international law in the national legal order. In the so-called 'deportation trials' the national courts had to deal with the application of relics from the past, i.e. the laws of the Soviet regime, which contained definitions of a different scope than in current international law. Thus the national courts had to manoeuvre between the nationally stipulated definitions of international crimes and international law.

These national cases, which reached the ECtHR, involved a situation whereby the core of the national courts' finding on the relevant questions lay in the national laws (which often referred to international laws) and the national court system. The Baltic States' laws have adopted the practice, when defining international crimes in the national criminal codes, of referring to internationally agreed rules of law and definitions. This practice provides an answer to many questions, as references to international law means reference to human rights, international criminal law, international humanitarian law, and other fields. It is to be hoped for that the national courts in the Baltic States will use this reference effectively, so that indeed their adjudication of international crimes will be in compliance with internationally agreed rules and standards.

60 *Vasiliauskas* v. *Lithuania*, para 175.
61 *Ibid.*, para 183.

11

Judging the *Conducător*: Fascism, Communism, and Legal Discontinuity in Post-War Romania

COSMIN SEBASTIAN CERCEL

1 Introduction

Romania's troubled legal past remains to stay an enigma for both legal historians and legal theorists alike. Coming to terms with the intricate legacy of the unjust law[1] brought by what we term today as the totalitarian experience, calls for a thorough engagement with the dialectical relation of continuity and discontinuity linking our arguably democratic present to the crises of the past. This hermeneutical and historical enterprise requires in itself not only a necessary interdisciplinary gaze but also a specific focus on 'the fraying edges of the law',[2] on its pathology,[3] and on its shifts from one regime of legality to another. In following this line, my aim is to

This text developed out of my interventions at the Ninth Roundtable for the Semiotics of Law (19 September 2009), Poznań, Poland, the Genealogies of Memory Project Conference 2013 (27 November 2013), Warsaw, Poland, and the Legislating and Justice History workshop in Amsterdam (1–2 June 2016) occasioned by the advancement of this book. The argument I defend here has also benefitted from my visiting lectureship at the Sorbonne School of Law (March and December 2015). I thus wish to thank the organisers, discussants and participants at these conferences, especially Ulad Belavusau, Eric Heinze, Saygun Gokariksel, Artemy Kalinovsky, Ronnie Lippens, and Stephen Skinner for their helpful comments. I am also indebted to Pierre Legrand for his kind invitation allowing me to refine my reflection within the framework of the seminar I delivered in Paris. I am further grateful to Andru Chiorean, David Fraser, and Simon Lavis for their generous interest in my work. I am, of course, thankful to the editors for their invaluable work in setting up this volume. Unless otherwise indicated, all translations are mine. Needless to say, the usual disclaimer applies: I am responsible for any remaining errors or omissions. This chapter is for J. and N.

1 See G. Radbruch, 'Gesetzliches Unrecht und übergesetzliches Recht', *Süddeutsche Juristen-Zeitung* 1 (1946), 105–8, at 105 [*unrichtiges Recht*].

2 W. Maley, 'Beyond the Law: The Justice of Deconstruction', *Law and Critique* 10 (1999), 49–69, at 50.

3 See H. Hart, *The Concept of Law* (Oxford University Press, 1994), 117–23.

put under scrutiny the obscure passage from conservative authoritarian and fascist[4] regimes towards the Stalinist dictatorship of the late 1940s in Romania. Consequently my purpose is to analyse the role played by the process of criminalisation of the authoritarian past both in the attempt at ideological legitimation carried out by the Romanian Communist faction as well as in the broader legal and political framework of the time. I thus intend to explore how the criminal law-based discursive construction addressing the military dictatorship of 1941–4 as a criminal enterprise affected the Romanian state's later legal morphology and its ideological tenets. Equally, my intention is to inquire on the memorial consequences of this mapping of the Antonescu regime and to underline the semiotic and political weight of this legacy. I propose to do so by drawing on the paradoxes entailed by the state of exception, understood here as a philosophical category aiming to investigate the ontological tenets of law and able to offer an insight into the structural legal, historical, and symbolic limits of reconstructing the *nomos* in modernity.[5] From this point of view I shall argue that the post-war trials and the legal framework of the time seeking to address past injustices related to World War II failed to mark a return to a stable polity grounded in a coherent normative construct. The central failure of this project of judging the past relates to the particular way in which it came short of addressing the material history of the Holocaust and articulated the experience of the war. According to the reading I advance in this chapter, this specific failure of the post-war trials took the form of an ideological sublimation of the central positions of the legal and memorial drama at stake, that is, the perpetrators and the victims. By eliding this pivotal ethical distinction in reading the past in order to articulate a constitutional narrative of national and constitutional continuity, the Antonescu trial failed to address the politico-legal mechanism at the core of the Holocaust – the legalised production of *homines sacri*.[6] This chapter asserts that the post-war trials limitations were the result of a nexus of socio-legal factors, such as the presence of a politically charged situation, the theoretical scarcity of Stalinism as an intellectual frame

[4] I borrow this distinction from Roger Griffin. See, R. Griffin, *The Nature of Fascism* (New York: Palgrave Macmillan, 1991), 32–6.

[5] G. Agamben, *State of Exception* (Chicago: University of Chicago Press, 2005 [2003]), 87.

[6] One could thus speak of 'Auschwitz as a site not of extermination, but as the site for the production of material to be destroyed, the ultimate logic of modernity, capitalism and bio-power in the service of the racial vision of the Nazi State': D. Fraser, 'Dead Man Walking: Law and Ethics after Giorgio Agamben's Auschwitz', *International Journal for the Semiotics of Law* 12 (1999), 397–417, at 404.

influencing legal representation, as well as the discursive power of nationalist ideology already embedded in the legal framework.

In order to approach the legal and constitutional confusion reigning in the interregnum emerging at the end of World War II, I shall first address the conceptual framework of the state of exception as developed in the work of Italian philosopher Giorgio Agamben. This step seems necessary first as a matter of historiographical inquiry inasmuch as Agamben's paradigm is able to underline the ambiguous status of legal discourse in the interwar and World War II Romanian context, that of both being caught in the totalitarian maelstrom and of positively taking part in the reign of state sanctioned violence. Second, as a matter of jurisprudential inquiry, the concept of exception enables us to circumvent, even if only provisionally, the entrenched theoretical positions of reading the law in totalitarian contexts as a 'legislative monstrosity',[7] 'statutory lawlessness',[8] or 'laws [that] may be law but [are] too evil to be obeyed',[9] which, each in their own way, tend to eschew law's manifold embeddedness in a modernity gone awry. It might also compel us to reflect on the legal and political nature of such regimes and avoid semantic and legal confusions that all too often insinuate themselves in the analysis of totalitarianism.[10] Last, and this time as a matter of critical inquiry, the paradigm of the exception could be at least serviceable in offering a map of the areas in which law, understood as a structured symbolic discourse, fails in articulating and thus limiting historical violence.

2 Beyond the Law: The State of Exception

To begin with, the state of exception is a limit-concept for legal theory inasmuch as it questions the basic assumptions of continental legal thought and disturbs the cardinal distinction between the normative and the descriptive. As Agamben argues, 'exceptional measures [. . .] find themselves in the paradoxical position of being juridical measures which

[7] L. L. Fuller, 'Positivism and Fidelity to Law: A Reply to Professor Hart', *Harvard Law Review* 71 (1958), 630–72, at 654.

[8] Radbruch, 'Gesetzliches Unrecht', 107.

[9] H. Hart, 'Positivism and the Separation of Law and Morals', *Harvard Law Review* 71 (1958), 523–629, at 620.

[10] With specific reference to Antonescu's dictatorship, Romanian constitutional historians limit themselves to stating that it is 'difficult to define'. For such an example, see E. Focşeneanu, *Istoria Constituţională a României: 1859–2003*, 3rd edn (Bucharest: Humanitas, 2007), 124.

cannot be understood in legal terms'.[11] His analysis, finds its departing point in the somewhat peculiar juridico-political structure present in constitutional practice and constitutional framework of the Western tradition since the eighteenth century,[12] consisting in either the suspension of constitutional guarantees or of the whole constitutional process for a series of actions taken by state authorities with the aim of protecting the constitutional order.

By focusing at this ambiguous practice of going beyond the law in order to uphold its mere existence, Agamben defines the state of exception as a zone of indistinction in the structure of the law,[13] thus isolating a conceptual area where it is logically impossible to make any relevant distinction between law and fact. It is through this 'suspension' of the legal that a zone of indistinction between fact and norm, between force and form, is opened within the fabric of the symbolic framework that would have otherwise been arguably able to sustain the distinction between law and violence and ultimately between politics and life.[14] As Agamben writes, following Carl Schmitt, '[s]ince "there is no rule that is applicable to chaos", chaos must first be included in the juridical order through the creation of a zone of indistinction between outside and inside, chaos and the normal situation– the state of exception'.[15]

The paradox of the exception should be now apparent. Do such legal measures fall under the category of legally or constitutionally justified measures? Or are they purely and simply facts that are indistinguishable from law inasmuch as the law has been debased to the 'force of law',[16] always already underlining its existence yet never actualised outside the realm of exception?[17] And if this is the case, what is the legal meaning, if there is one, of the acts undertaken under the seal of the exception? It is precisely in this sense that the suspension of the law blurs the borders between the stability traditionally attributed to legal normativity and its exterior: '[T]he situation created in the exception has the peculiar characteristic that it cannot be defined either as a situation of fact or as a situation

11 Agamben, *State of Exception*, 1.
12 *Ibid.*, 11–24.
13 *Ibid.*, 41.
14 *Ibid.*, 88.
15 G. Agamben, *Homo Sacer: Sovereign Power and Bare Life* (Stanford: Stanford University Press, 1998 [1995]), 19.
16 Agamben, *State of Exception*, 32–44.
17 A. Schütz, 'Thinking the Law With and Against Luhmann, Legendre, Agamben', *Law and Critique* 11 (2000), 107–36, at 117.

of right'.[18] However, it should be noted that the paradox entailed by the state of exception is not a merely a case arising out of law's incompleteness, one for which the law does not provide any provision or guidance thus compelling the judge to exercise discretion,[19] but purely and simply the status of the legal order within modernity. As Agamben observes, '[l]aw is made of nothing but what manages to capture inside itself through the inclusive exclusion of the *exceptio*: it nourishes itself on this exception and is a dead letter without it'.[20]

While the concept of exception is a central one for both philosophical and jurisprudential inquiry by bringing to the fore the possibility of law's disappearance as a normative category, for the purposes of this chapter I shall try to explore its historiographical and memorial value. This is because the initial theoretical thrust of the concept of exception captures the conceptual grey-zone within the law as primarily a consequence of the accumulation of historical tension and acceleration of time specific to the modern able to paradoxically unravel its ancient origins. Moreover, Agamben's construction of the concept gives a central place to the history of the interwar and World War II if only by examining at some length the paradigmatic case of article 48 of the Weimar Constitution.[21] Indeed, echoes of this troubled history seem to be the frontispiece from which the Agambenian archaeological inquiry excavating the problematic tension between law and lawlessness starts. Perhaps not least, the intellectual and material history of the concept is intimately linked to the dissolution of experience specific to the interwar not only through its theorisation within legal and theoretical circles on the continent during the interwar and wartime, but also through the proliferation of 'states of exception' which have opened the path to the creation of camps and the extermination undertaken during the war. For inasmuch as the exception was a part of the legal discourse of the interwar and wartime authoritarianism, it was also embodied through a manifold set of material practices which found themselves at the core of the production of extermination, racial and ethnic cleansing and the ascent of total war.[22] From this vantage point, reading the post-war trials through the lenses of the exception would enable us to shed

[18] *Ibid.*

[19] Hart, *Concept of Law*, 252.

[20] Agamben, *Homo Sacer*, 19.

[21] *Ibid.*, 14–16.

[22] Evocative of this relation between the intellectual history of the concept of exception and Romanian legal history is Carl Schmitt's presence in Bucharest in 1943 on the occasion of a conference on the 'Historical Condition of European Jurisprudence', let alone his

a new light on the hidden structural limits of the politico-legal pitfalls of the Eastern European post-war period. Equally, such a conceptual framework could also enable us to look beyond the all too often assumed cynical political goals aimed by Stalinism in its project of Communist takeover and to critically engage with the legal and ideological choices the actors of post-war faced within their own intellectual and discursive constraints.

3 Law, Dictatorship, Fascism

Four constitutional moments have marked political life in Romania prior to and during its participation in World War II. Firstly, one can note the instauration of the Royal Dictatorship of King Carol II through the proclamation of the new constitution in 1938[23] replacing the Constitution of 1923,[24] as well as the subsequent suppression of political parties.[25] Another significant moment is King Carol II's abdication in 1940[26] as a result of the territorial losses towards the USSR, Bulgaria, and Hungary during the summer of 1940 and of the pressures orchestrated by Marshal Antonescu, prime minister at that time, backed by other political forces inimical to the royalist faction.[27] The abdication was ensued by the instauration of Marshal Antonescu's military dictatorship and the proclamation of the National Legionary State.[28] In the first stage, the new regime was supported by the Romanian main fascist movement, the Iron Guard. As a consequence, Romania soon signed the Tripartite Pact and entered into the Axis' sphere of influence.[29] As early as January 1941, the Iron Guard, put an end to their collaboration with the military dictator and fully contested the Marshal's authority as head of state. The conflict resolved itself in an intervention of the Army, backed by German assent, quelling

acquaintance with Romanian intellectual figures of the far-right: G. Balakrishnan, *The Enemy: An Intellectual Portrait of Carl Schmitt* (London: Verso, 2000), 246–7.

23 The Constitution of Romania 1938, *Monitorul Oficial* (*M.Of.* hereafter) No. 48, 27 February 1938, 1109–29.

24 The Constitution of Romania 1923, *M. Of.* No. 282, 29 March 1923, 13315–34.

25 Decree Law No. 1422 of 30 March 1938 concerning the dissolution of associations, factions and political parties, *M.Of.* No. 75, 31 March 1938, 1640–1.

26 See, 'King's Carol II Manifesto to Romanians of the 6th of September 1940', in I. Scurtu, *România și marile puteri (1933–1940): Documente* (Bucharest: Editura Fundației România de Mâine, 2000), 232.

27 V. Georgescu, *Romanians: A History* (Columbus: Ohio State University Press, 1991), 210.

28 Royal Decree No. 3151 of 14 September 1940 declaring Romania a National Legionary State, *M.Of.* No. 214 bis, 14 September 1940, 5414.

29 Georgescu, *Romanians*, 212–13.

the fascist rebellion. After three years of war against the USSR, following the fall of the front in Ukraine, King Michael – who has only nominally ruled the country – conducted a *coup d'état* deposing the Marshal and signed an armistice with the Allies. This opened the way to a partial restoration of the Constitution of 1923.

These constitutional moments are not only symptomatic for a broad range of political, legal, and symbolic ambiguities specific to the fascist takeover in Romania or to Romania's participation in the war and, but are also at the origins of the later legal and memorial intricacies of the post-war context. Thus it may prove serviceable to take a closer look at their intrinsic tensions as well as at the ways in which they affected the overall framing of the legal system.

For many a historiographer of the Romanian interwar, the royal dictatorship of 1938 stands as a first assertion of full authoritarian powers, and it thus marks the beginning of Romania's *fall* in the realm of totalitarianism.[30] Consequently, the Constitution of 1938 is retrospectively read as being endowed with a great deal of symbolic signification. As such, it is the very legal mechanism that separates democracy from totalitarianism. At a closer look, one may observe that the process of dissolution of legality and the 'breakdown of democracy'[31] was anything but linear and it was rather build upon an accumulation of gradual increase of executive unregulated power during the interwar. The dissolution of the law during the interwar took various forms such as the use of the state of siege, the recourse to government by decree,[32] the direct nomination of governments, or the practice of passing of legislation criminalising political activities.[33]

The constitutional system of the interwar could be safely termed as 'semi-authoritarian',[34] and was one that decidedly relied on a constant recourse to unregulated state power.[35] However, it was still a regime that at

[30] *Ibid.*, 198–9; K. Hitchins, *Rumania 1866–1947* (Oxford University Press, 1994), 421.

[31] J. J. Linz, *Totalitarian and Authoritarian Regimes* (Boulder: Lynne Rienner, 2000), 137.

[32] Constantin Dissesco, 'L'évolution du droit public roumain', in *Les transformations du droit dans les principaux pays depuis cinquante ans: livre du cinquantenaire de la Société de législation comparée* (Paris: L.G.D.J, 1922), 301.

[33] I have discussed the historical and jurisprudential consequences of this thread of legal measures elsewhere: C. S. Cercel, 'The Enemy Within: Criminal Law and Ideology in Interwar Romania', in S. Skinner (ed.), *Fascism and Criminal Law: History, Theory, Continuity* (Oxford: Hart, 2014), 101–26.

[34] M. Mann, *Fascists* (Cambridge University Press, 2004), 44.

[35] Between 1918 and 1928 no fewer than 12 decrees were issued, instituting or upholding the partial or general state of siege: V. Pantelimonescu, *Starea de asediu: Doctrină, jurisprudentă și legislație* (Bucharest: Cartea Românească, 1939), 32–45.

least formally was committed to the tenets of modern constitutionalism[36] insofar as it guaranteed the classical liberal freedoms and still tried to legitimise their limitation or suspension through exceptional circumstances. For its part, the royal dictatorship stands for a new constitutional regime that cuts itself with the tenets of traditional forms of legality and the creeds of the liberal state. It also marks the entry into a new regime of power and the emergence of a fragile albeit violent resolution of the conflict opposing the King on the one hand, the democratic political forces on the other and the rising power of Romanian fascist movement, the Iron Guard. In this conflict, which is laden with ideological ambiguities and political intricacies inasmuch as during one decade each side collaborated to some extent with the other,[37] one can easily grasp the symptoms of a society caught by an ethos of crisis.[38] The dictatorship of 1938 is thus an ambiguous attempt at countering fascism through its own means, including unbridled state violence, anti-Semitic legislation and administrative practices as well as the staging of ultranationalist ideology.[39]

The emergence of the National Legionary State came as a result of the New Order of Europe entailed by the opening hostilities of World War II and the sudden defeat of France, one of the main guarantors of Romania's sovereignty after the Great War. The territorial losses, the growing local dissent at the wake of the war, as well as the growth of popularity of the far-right, prompted the King to set a new government with Marshal Antonescu as a prime minister. Although a second-rank figure in the political spectrum of the interwar, Antonescu was revered as an uncontested moral and military authority to such an extent that his growing popularity, pro-German activities, and defiance of the King determined the latter to assign him on home arrest prior to nominating him as prime minister.[40] One of the first measures taken by Antonescu in this capacity was to force the King to delegate him the reserved powers. Later on, he pressured for his abdication. As Carol's son, Prince Michael, was approaching majority,

[36] Georgescu, *Romanians*, 198–9.

[37] R. A. Haynes, 'Reluctant Allies? Iuliu Maniu and Corneliu Zelea Codreanu against King Carol II of Romania,' *The Slavonic and East European Review* 85 (2007), 105–34.

[38] For an insightful analysis of the relation between fascism and the crisis of liberal democracies during the interwar see R. Griffin, 'Modernity under the New Order: The Fascist Project for Managing the Future', in M. Feldman (ed.), *A Fascist Century* (Basingstoke: Palgrave Macmillan, 2008), 24–45, at 44.

[39] Georgescu, *Romanians*, 208.

[40] D. Deletant, *Hitler's Forgotten Ally* (Basingstoke: Palgrave Macmillan, 2006), 47–8.

he was crowned king, while the Marshal effectively held executive powers as the Head of the State – *Conducător*.

While the new regime symbolically termed itself as overtly fascist, it also uneasily mitigated the tension between the conservative-leaning militarism of the Marshal and the 'revolutionary'[41] tendencies of the Iron Guard.[42] The latter was constantly pressuring for direct action against the Jewish minority, as well as for retaliation against former central figures of the Royal Dictatorship. The dualism between military authoritarianism and fascism purely and simply could be mainly observed at the organisational level of the administration. As such, unsurprisingly, the Army, the Gendarmerie, as well as the Secret Services were under the control of Antonescu and his loyal followers. For their part, the Ministry of Interior, the police, and the government's representations in the territory (*Prefecturi*) were controlled by the Iron Guard.[43] The latter was further backed by the Legionary Police, a para-military force organised after the model set-up by the SA and the SS.[44] The tension reached a peak as a result of the series of executions perpetrated by the Legionary Police and the assassination of former prime minister and noted Romanian nationalist historian Nicolae Iorga. Moreover, the Guard exacted taxes upon the Jewish population without any legal ground and started an entire campaign of expropriation and deportation of Jewish communities.[45] These policies culminated in the Bucharest Pogrom perpetrated as the first stage of the Legionary Rebellion. Taking control over the Police Headquarters, police stations, and several ministries, the Guardists launched their attack on the Army. The Guardist Ministry of Interior ordered the Jewish districts in Bucharest to be set on fire, the action being followed by a series of deportations, executions, and random shootings exacted mainly by the Corps of Legionary Workers,[46] the trade-union based branch of the Iron Guard. Started on the 21st of January, the uprising was quelled by the 24th by the Army. The main outcome was the proclamation of the National and

41 M. Platon, 'The Iron Guard and the Modern State. Iron Guard Leaders Vasile Marin and Ion I. Moţa and the "European New Order"', *Fascism* 1 (2012), 65–90, at 69.

42 A. Kallis, *Genocide and Fascism: The Eliminationist Drive in Fascist Europe* (London: Routledge, 2009), 221.

43 International Commission on The Holocaust in Romania, in *Final Report*, eds. T. Friling, R. Ioanid and M. E. Ionescu (Iaşi: Polirom, 2004), 109.

44 *Ibid.*, 110.

45 *Ibid.*, 110–15. See also Kallis, *Genocide and Fascism*, 221.

46 International Commission on The Holocaust in Romania, *Final Report*, 110.

Social State under the rule of Marshal Antonescu supported by a technocratic government.

The deposition of the fascist movement was not, however, a return to any form of classical constitutionalism or to any democratic stand. As the country soon ventured in the 'crusade against Bolshevism',[47] by joining the German Barbarossa Plan, the situation would evolve further in changing Romania into an overt ultranationalist polity. As such, the military dictatorship soon implemented further anti-Semitic legal and administrative measures on Romanian territories as well as in the occupied territories under Romanian administration. The racial policies devised against Jewish and Roma population, this time with legal and administrative scrupulousness backed by military warring ethos, are at the origins of the darkest moment in Romanian history.[48] The intermingling between dictatorship understood as the suspension of the legal system, the wartime conditions marked by the dissolution of the categories of limited war, and the discursive hegemony of state-racism in national ideology, all point towards a limit-state of political, legal, and ethical categories founding the state. The National Social State under Antonescu is thus a *nekropolitical*[49] enterprise in which the state and law were reduced to a mere formless existence, but were nonetheless necessary constituents and accomplices of the 'eliminationist drive'.[50] It thus actualised the ultimate hidden structure of the modern state under the guise of 'state racism',[51] enabling both the legal and political apparatus to recreate the old sovereign right of killing within the resolutely modern framework of biopolitical power.

The Antonescu regime is now held liable for Romania's participation in the Holocaust which has been accounted as a death toll ranging from 280,000 to 380,000 Jews,[52] executed, killed, or disappeared as a result of the government's policies in Romania and Romanian-occupied territories. As it has been stated, 'of all the allies of Nazi Germany, Romania bears responsibility for the deaths of more Jews than any country other than

[47] Deletant, *Hitler's Forgotten Ally*, at 81.

[48] V. Solonari, *Purifying the Nation: Population Exchange and Ethnic Cleansing in Nazi-Allied Romania* (Baltimore: Johns Hopkins University Press, 2010), 168–99. With regard to the policies of 'Romanianisation', see also Ş. C. Ionescu, *Jewish Resistance to 'Romanianization'* (Basingstoke: Palgrave Macmillan, 2015).

[49] A. Mbembe, 'Nécropolitique', *Raisons politiques* 21 (2006), 29–60, at 34.

[50] Kallis, *Genocide and Fascism*, 251–5.

[51] M. Foucault, *Il faut défendre la société* (Paris: Gallimard, 1996), 213–35.

[52] International Commission on The Holocaust in Romania, *Final Report*, 179.

Germany itself'.[53] Moreover, as Dan Stone convincingly argues, 'the murder of the Jews of Romania (excluding northern Transylvania, ceded to Hungary in 1940) and Transnistria was essentially an independent undertaking'.[54] However not only did it take sixty years for Romanian authorities to fully recognise the scale of the persecutions exacted against Jewish and Roma population, but many of the political, legal and symbolical intricacies of the Holocaust still continue to haunt both the state's self-representation as well as Romanian legal discourse. Approaching the first legal encounters with the memory of the Holocaust inside the legal framework itself is not only a crucial task in understanding the path from one regime to another, but also the ways in which national and state ideology have been constructed through the ethico-legal rendering of this dark period.

4 Judging the Disaster: Law and Historical Violence

This line of inquiry draws us to a closer analysis of the fourth constitutional moment closing the series of war-time dictatorships. Indeed, the short, partial, and fragile return to democratic and constitutional 'normality' between 1944 and 1947 marks both a politically charged and cultural significant interregnum laden with far-reaching consequences for the fate of Romanian *nomos*, as well as for later Romanian Communist ideology and praxis. As such, the return of democracy is also paradoxically linked to the entry into stage of history of institutionalised, if not already state-steered, Communism. In short, the *coup d'état* staged by King Michael of Romania backed by different factions of the Romanian army and Romanian politics – such as the National Democratic Bloc (that would comprise National Liberals, the Peasants' Party, Social Democrats, and Communists) on the 23rd of August 1944 ousted the military dictator and was soon ensued by an Armistice agreement with the Allies.[55] The Constitution in 1923 was partially put again into force by a decree dating from August 1944,[56] which thus formally ended Antonescu's rule.

53 *Ibid.*, 385.

54 D. Stone, *Histories of the Holocaust* (Oxford University Press, 2010), 36.

55 R. J. Crampton (ed.), *Eastern Europe in the XXth Century and After*, 2nd (London: Routledge, 1997), 228–31. See also J. Rothschild and N. M. Wingfield (eds.), *Return to Diversity[:] A Political History of East Central Europe Since World War II*, 3rd (Oxford University Press, 2000), 105–6; Georgescu, *Romanians*, 220.

56 Royal Decree No. 1626 of 31 August 1944 concerning the establishment of the Rights of Romanians within the frame of the Constitution of 1866 such as modified by the Constitution of 1923, *M. Of.* No. 202, 2 September 1944, 6232.

However, under the Armistice agreement, parts of the traditional sovereignty of the state were questioned inasmuch as the Soviet Union had 'monopoly of interpretation of the Agreement' which it exercised through an intentionally unclear formulation of the legal status of the concluding parties.[57] Moreover, the Agreement already imposed rather unusual obligations which, considering Romania's participation in the war until the 23rd of August seem just and reasonable, but nonetheless question the traditional forms of sovereignty. As such, according to Articles 14 and 15 of the Agreement, the Romanian state was bound to 'undertake to collaborate with the Allied (Soviet) High Command in the apprehension and trial of persons accused of war crimes' and to 'dissolve all pro-Hitler organizations (of a Fascist type) situated in Rumanian territory, whether political, military or para-military, as well as other organizations conducting propaganda hostile to the United Nations, in particular the Soviet Union, and will not in future permit the existence of organizations of that nature'.[58] In retrospect, the provisions of the Agreement are regarded by historians and constitutionalists as being nothing short of a Soviet 'mechanism of takeover'[59] in Romania.[60]

From a legal perspective the constitutional framework of the time remained highly problematic as long as Articles III and IV of the August Decree restating the Constitution of 1923 leave out of its scope the functioning of the legislative and the judiciary.[61] It would be thus safe to affirm that the regime of exceptional measures outside the scope of the constitutional control continued to be in power before the new constitution of 1948 introducing the dictatorship of the proletariat would be affirmed. This legal uncertainty determined partly some of the political developments in Communist takeover, as well as the process of dealing with the Fascist and authoritarian past. In this sense, the passing of the Statute no. 312 of 1945 seeking to prosecute and punish those responsible for bringing

[57] See e.g. the wording of the Armistice Agreement determining the Allied powers in an ambiguous manner alternating the reference between Allied and Soviet powers: The Armistice Agreement with Rumania of 12 September 1944, *Department of State Bulletin*, Vol. XI, No. 273, 17 September 1944, 289–306.

[58] Articles 14 and 15 of the Armistice Agreement with Rumania.

[59] D. Deletant, *Hitler's Forgotten Ally* (Basingstoke: Palgrave McMillan, 2005), 245.

[60] 'The Allied Control Commission formed to oversee the armistice was entirely Soviet-dominated. Its American and British members did not even have the right to travel freely in Romania without the permission of the Soviet authorities': Georgescu, *Romanians*, 223.

[61] Articles III–IV, Royal Decree No. 1626 of 31 August 1944.

the disaster of the country and war crimes[62] takes place in an ambiguous constitutional context.

At this stage, one may legitimately ask who or which is the institutional body asserting the sovereignty by framing the legal definition of a crime and by creating categories necessary to the process of criminalisation? The positive legal answer lies within the emitent of the Statute, which was the Ministry of Justice. Interestingly for the purposes of this chapter, the office of the Ministry of Justice was held by one of the few local prominent leaders of the Communist Party, Lucreţiu Pătrăşcanu.[63] A lawyer by training, who acted during the interwar as council of the defence for illegal Communists and gained a seat in the Parliament as a representative of the legal façade of the Communist Party, the National Peasant Bloc, Pătrăşcanu was also one of the few Romanian Marxists of his time who also made a somewhat important contribution to Marxist theory.[64] Indeed, his book, *Under Three Dictatorships*,[65] written while under house arrest during the early 1940s, offers a compelling reading of the authoritarian turn in Romanian politics during the interwar as a violent answer to the internal tension of local capitalism.[66] However important these insights might appear, a more complex answer would seek to take into account the inherently 'constitutional' dimension of such a statute. Indeed, what symbolically it is created through the process of criminalisation of the former dictatorship is also a form of discursive production of alterity. The new regime therefore marks its difference in respect to the criminal other and draws its own legitimacy from positing this difference. Through this process of criminalisation of the past, a foundational myth of the state is reconstructed and narrated once again.

The fact that the Communist movement was in charge of the prosecution and conviction of the crimes is of course not surprising inasmuch as Soviet troops were present in Romania and the movement was slowly

[62] Statute No. 312 of 24 April 1945 for the prosecution and punishment of those responsible for the disaster of the country or war crimes, *M.Of.* No. 94, 24 April 1945, 4–6.

[63] Crampton, *Eastern Europe in the XXth Century and After*, 225.

[64] For an informed analysis of Pătrăşcanu's contribution to Marxist theory, see C. Rogozanu, 'Lucreţiu Pătrăşcanu', in A. Cistelecan and A. State (eds.), *Plante exotice: teoria şi practica marxiştilor români* (Bucharest: Tact, 2016), 125–84.

[65] L. Pătrăşcanu, *Sous trois dictatures* (Paris: Vitiano, 1946).

[66] This reading, despite its economistic overtones, has served as a basis for an important historiographical contribution to the understanding of Romanian fascism. See, R. Ioanid, *The Sword of the Archangel: Fascist Ideology in Romania* (Boulder: East European Monographs, 1990), 10–11.

trying to rebuild its presence in public life. The situation also provided the Communists with the opportunity not only to tackle the issue of the authoritarian and fascist state violence to which most of them would have been victims, but also to create their basis for a new legitimising framework. To put it simply, in contradistinction to the authoritarian dictatorships of the late interwar the Communist movement had the chance to present itself as a guardian of democracy and a bearer of an authentic democratic ethos – after all the Communist party was part of the National Democratic Bloc. This is not to say that the trial of war criminals was mainly a matter of Communist politics. Rather my claim is that the way in which the actions of the authoritarian regimes were legally framed as crimes in the early years of post-war through an intricate process symbolisation in which national ideology and state responsibility played a key role. A notable part of the politico-legal context of the time was held by the shifting role of the Communist movement, which was the main proxy between the established power in Bucharest and the 'Allied (Soviet) High Command'.

Whilst the framing of the Statute seeking to address Romania's participation in the war and the atrocities committed is rather ambiguous in terms of criminal law wording, as, for instance, the responsibility is defined in relation to persons rather than with acts, while the crime of 'bringing the disaster upon the country' is not defined anywhere else,[67] it also hints at a series of other constitutional and ideological underpinnings. Indeed, the choice of words is symptomatic, inasmuch as 'country' (*ţara*) was by no means a criminal law category and hardly a modern constitutional one. Whereas in common language the country and the state might be interchangeable, under the already modern Romanian legal system of the time, 'the country' did not have a proper juridical meaning. It had, however, one specific meaning as a constitutional archaism traceable back to the Middle Ages – that is

[67] Article 1 defined those 'guilty of the disaster brought on the country' as (a) persons who had backed Hitler or espoused fascism and who bore the political responsibility for allowing German troops to enter Romania; and (b) persons who had given their support to the above deeds, either in speech, writing or by any other means. Article 2 proclaimed those 'guilty of the disaster brought on the country through the commission of war crimes' as persons who had taken the decision to declare war on the Soviet Union and the United Nations, who had treated prisoners in an inhuman manner, who had ordered or carried out acts of terror or cruelty against the population in the war zones, who had taken repressive measures against civilians out of racial or political motives, and who had ordered forced labour or the deportation of people. Conviction under article 1 carried imprisonment for a term of between five years and life, while that under article 2 attracted forced labour for life or the death penalty: Statute No. 312 of 24 April 1945.

the constitutional body which ultimately legitimised the Prince in the elective monarchies of the fourteenth to the eighteenth century.[68] Given that Antonescu used the term *Conducător* (Leader) in defining his office – which was already a constitutional archaism as it evoked one of the offices of the Voyvod title of the Middle Ages – it can be inferred that it was the country, that is the constitutionally organised 'people', which had suffered the tort of dictatorship. In other words, the passive subject of the crime is already the legally constructed 'people', understood here as an abstract legal body. In this sense, not only the state reframes itself through the process of criminalisation, but also restates and redefines the people as a constitutive part of the polity.

The post-war trials developed in this legal framework have been regarded by commentators as a rather problematic attempt in dealing with the trauma of the war and in assigning responsibilities.[69] It has thus been noted the limited extent of the scope of the war trials, the courts leniency towards some of the convicts as well as the random application of the law over territory especially in those areas in Northern Transylvania which during the war had been part of Hungary. As Maria Bucur points out, a tendency can be noted of avoiding dealing with Romanian responsibility for the atrocities which was backed by an ideological conviction that responsibility lied within the foreign former allies – Nazi Germans and fascist Hungarians.[70] Topical in embodying the ethical confusion of the attempt of approaching Romanian Holocaust, the trial of Antonescu offers a series of extremely poignant examples as regards the legal and ideological construction of fascism and Romanian collaborationism.

Due to its importance, and especially to its high coverage in media, the Communist faction in charge now with the machinery of justice organised the trial with care. As noted, the members of the Court and the accusers were carefully chosen through members of the party, access to the trial was limited to a selected audience, and special measures for keeping order were taken. The Court judging the trial was an extraordinary People's

[68] See for instance, G. I. Bratianu, *Sfatul domnesc si adunarea starilor in principatele Romane* (Bucharest: Editura Enciclopedica, 1995 [1947]), 22: the author stresses the meaning of *ţara* as a legal community. See also D. Barbu, *Bizanţ contra Bizanţ* (Bucharest: Nemira, 2001), 88, where the author emphasises the discontinuity between the 'country' and the 'state', the first one being a distinct entity which played a key role in the dialectics of power between the prince and the nobles.

[69] M. Bucur, *Heroes and Victims: Remembering War in Twentieth Century Romania* (Bloomington: Indiana University Press, 2009), 156.

[70] *Ibid.*, 156–8.

Tribunal presided by Alexandru Voitinovici, assisted by Constantin Balcu and seven people's judges, all members of the Communist movement. The public prosecutors were two lawyers Vasile Stoican, seconded by Constantin Dobrian, a procurator at the Court of Appeal in Timişoara and a public accuser, Dumitru Săracu, without legal training, from the ranks of the Communist Party.[71] There were a series of accusations, organised around the lines of the actions of the former Marshal and of the legal framework that was into force. They concerned namely the unlawful war against the Soviet Union, the terror unleashed against workers and peasants, the 'German colonisation of Romania', the economic disaster, the massacres, the deportations and the campaign of 'Romanianisation'.[72] As we can notice, only a part of the accusation dealt explicitly with atrocities of the regime directed against its citizens and against inhabitants of the occupied territories, while the others were referring clearly to the abstract legal entity of the 'country'.

Indeed, in their struggle of redeeming the 'country' the accusers would stress out its sufferings. Two recurrent images will follow closely the accusation act and the interrogatory: that of the oppressed Romanian peasant forced to become a soldier, and that of colonised Romania. By overemphasising the national disaster, the accusers come to a point where there would not be any distinction between the victims and the oppressors, a point where the very oppressors would appear before the world as victims. As stated by one of the public accusers: 'there can be no difference between the massacre of those [Romanian soldiers] young people and that of the massacre in Majdanek'.[73] And as he continues 'I can't make any distinction in sending to death the youth of the Nation and the shooting in forest outskirts of deported people'.[74] The *Conducător* is, thus, guilty first and most of all in bringing a disaster on the country. The tort made wasn't one perpetrated against millions of expressionless victims, but to an abstract legal community, which is through the very act of uttering of this words founded on a fundamental ethical confusion.

However, the central legal, political and semiotic problem here is not the responsibility of the *Conducător*, but the dynamics through which 'the country' receives its innocence by losing the *Conducător*. What the Trial is telling to the state and to the anonymous collaborators of the dictatorship

[71] Deletant, *Hitler's Forgotten Ally*, 249–50.

[72] *Procesul marii trădări naţionale* (Bucharest: Eminescu, 1946), 19–34.

[73] *Ibid.*, 284.

[74] *Ibid.*

is that most of them were victims themselves. Through accepting this complicity in the field of social reality, the legal order creates its 'people', its 'country' as it imagines them to be: 'We are a modest people who never had expansionist tendencies. We had a sole mission: that of preserving our national being of a modest and working people, who never went out of its borders, who never did barbaric acts and always defended its land and its national being'.[75] This is one of the legal embodiments of Romanian Stalinist ideology, which embellishes a reality filled with diffuse anti-Semitism and oppression. One could note the peculiar resemblance between the 'modest people' fighting for their land and the 'sacred war against bolshevism' the same people would engage in years before as well as the radical disjunction between the historical real of giving way to the 'eliminationist drive' and the political symbolic negation of this real.

To put it in Benjaminian terms, the very point of approaching the issue of historical injustice, the lawyers and the public accusers turn away from articulating a discourse from the perspective of the 'tradition of the oppressed'.[76] Rather their attempt is to redeem what was impossible historically to be redeemed. They turn their face from history in order to offer expiation to the state and its mechanism and along with them to the nation. From this point of view the Law before which the *Conducător* is brought and before which the victims could seek release, refrains from re-structuring the power relations. The law doesn't judge historical violence, because ontologically it is inscribed in a history of violence. As Walter Benjamin noted, 'all [law] was the prerogative of the kings or of the nobles – in short of the mighty; and that, *mutatis mutandis*, will remain as long as it exists'.[77] As law is consubstantial with historical violence, addressing it legally is deemed to fail, except under a possibility to judge history itself, and thus to cut off with a tradition that instils that history should be that of the victors. The law, surpassed by mythical violence, fails to bring justice. What we are given in fact is the reproduction of the same mechanism of a culture tainted by barbarism, and linked inescapably to it, a mechanism of mythical violence[78] reproducing itself under the masks of the revolution from above.

[75] *Ibid.*, 302.

[76] W. Benjamin, 'Theses on the Concept of History', in H. Arends (ed.), *lluminations* (New York: Shocken Books, 1969 [1940]), 256 (T VIII).

[77] W. Benjamin, 'Critique of Violence', in M. Bullock and M. W. Jennings (eds.), *Selected Writings*, vol. I (Cambridge: Harvard University Press, 1999 [1921]), 296.

[78] 'There is no document of civilization that is not tainted by barbarism': Benjamin, 'Theses on the Concept of History', 257 (T VII).

5 Conclusion

The trial of Antonescu, taken as a paradigmatic example of judging the past and constructing the new regime of legality, fails to address the material history of the Holocaust and the manifold forms through which the state as such participated in the criminal enterprise. By devising legally the crime as a tort against an abstract legal community that is already founded by the state, it came short in questioning the basic tenets of law's and state part in the dissolution of the polity. This decision had dire ethical consequences – some of which I have tried to point out here. It also had further political consequences as long as by seeking to legitimise itself through an ethical confusion, the Communist movement itself moved away from the tenets of international Communism. It has symbolically embraced the national route, inasmuch as it renounced its revolutionary stand and joined the sphere of state-driven politics. This turn was perhaps hardly a surprise, given the prominent role given to the state in both Stalinist ideology and jurisprudence since the time of the Great Terror, which had forged the dogma of 'a mighty and invincible state'.[79] Furthermore its legal consequences are even more compelling, for the focus on personal dimension of the perpetrators – even if accurate – prevented a discussion of the systemic dimension of the crimes. Law has thus failed to recognise its own suspension and continued its formless and confused existence from one dictatorship to the other.

[79] A. Vyshinsky, *The Law of the Soviet State* (New York: Macmillan, 1961), 49. On the role played by Soviet lawyers in the post-war trials see, F. Hirsch, 'The Soviets at Nuremberg: International Law, Propaganda, and the Making of the Postwar Order', *American Historical Review* 113 (2008), 701–30.

12

Dealing with the Past in and around the Fundamental Law of Hungary

MIKLÓS KÖNCZÖL

1 Introduction

This chapter discusses the role of historical narratives in recent Hungarian legislation, with a special focus on the new constitution, the Fundamental Law of Hungary. It does so by constructing its own narrative about the Fundamental Law, with challenges faced by the Hungarian political elite during the last two decades, and responses given by the constitution-makers. The first section looks at three major challenges legislation tried to deal with after the democratic transition. The first one of these is the question of responsibility (legal, political, and moral) for crimes committed during the Communist regime. The second one is continuity (historical, political, and legal) with the so-called 'historical' (i.e. pre-WWII) constitution. The third problem is the relationship between historical memory and freedom of expression. The second section then looks at two segments of the Fundamental Law of 2011: the preamble (entitled *National Avowal*), and Article U, which was added to the original text just a few days before its entering into force. By adopting a rather detailed constitution with a preamble, rather than just a charter of rights, the constitution-makers made it possible for themselves to take position on a number of questions related to the past.[1] Here, a close reading of the text is intended to reveal the moves by which the preamble outlines Hungarian constitutional history, thereby constructing itself as a milestone in that history, but also as a privileged point of reference, a gateway

[1] See e.g. L. Trócsányi, 'Magyarország Alaptörvényének legfontosabb üzenetei egy igazságügyi miniszter szemszögéből' ('The Most Important Messages of the Fundamental Law of Hungary, from the Perspective of a Minister of Justice'), in E. Balogh (ed.), *Számadás az Alaptörvényről (Giving Account of the Fundamental Law)* (Budapest: Magyar Közlöny Lap-és Könyvkiadó, 2016), 11–18, at 11–12.

between past and present. Concurrent readings of the text are illustrated by examples taken from the political controversy surrounding the drafting process and following the enactment of the Fundamental Law. The third and final section seeks to summarise the lessons that can be learnt from this case study, examining legislation dealing with the past from a normative perspective, looking at the Fundamental Law as part of a historical narrative itself.[2]

2 Responsibility, Continuity, and Freedom of Expression: From 1990 to 2010

After the democratic transition in 1989–90, memories of the Communist era could be expected to appear in legislation. That, however, happened only to a limited extent. The new text of the amended Constitution, to begin with, contained no direct reference to the past, speaking only about 'a peaceful political transition to a constitutional state' (cf. *Act 31 of 1989*). Rather than offering an overarching narrative, new laws focused on the anti-Soviet revolution of 1956.[3] While that was an important and by no means undisputed move, a number of questions remained unanswered. Perhaps the most urgent one was that of responsibility, both for individual criminal acts committed under the Communist regime, and more generally for being part of that regime. The second question concerned continuity. Democratic transition in Hungary took place by way of amending, rather than violating, the rules of the existing legal system, thus maintaining the legal identity of the state. In terms of historical and

[2] This approach is inspired by Bernard Jackson's distinction between stories *in* the trial and the story *of* the trial, cf. B. Jackson, *Law, Fact and Narrative Coherence* (Liverpool: Deborah Charles Publications, 1988). Here, however, there will be three (kinds of) stories at play: the ones told by the constitution-makers; then the process and context of constitution-making as perceived by politicians, lawyers, and the general public; and finally the one told by this chapter, which builds upon the two others. For a brief discussion about the role of the Fundamental Law in shaping a 'national constitutional narrative', see B. Fekete, 'The National Avowal: More than a Conventional Preamble to a Constitution', in Z. Szente, F. Mandák and Zs. Fejes (eds.), *Challenges and Pitfalls in the Recent Hungarian Constitutional Development: Discussing the New Fundamental Law of Hungary* (Paris: L'Harmattan, 2015), 11–24, at 18–20.

[3] See esp. *Act 28 of 1990 on the importance of the Revolution and War of Independence of October 1956*. The first piece of legislation dealing with 1956 was *Act 36 of 1989 on the remedy of convictions related to the 1956 uprising* (the first annulment act). The latter, passed before the first free elections, notoriously avoided using the word 'revolution', and spoke of 'those acting for the social transformation and independence of our country during the national tragedy of 1956' in the preamble.

political identity, however, the situation was much less clear, with much more disagreement within the political elite. Thirdly, the legal means for protecting certain historical narratives had to be elaborated, which necessarily entailed setting limits to the freedom of expression. We shall now look at these three problems in turn, as they appeared in the legislation of the two decades between 1990 and 2010.

2.1 *Responsibility*

The lack of a generally accepted historical narrative notwithstanding, the apparent need to do justice has led to legislation in three areas. First, a series of restitution and annulment acts dealt with the compensation, legal and (partially) material, of those whose rights were violated between 1939 and 1990. A much more sensitive issue was the investigation into the functioning of the Communist secret service and their informers, and particularly the identification of the persons involved. The idea that the complete list of agents should be published was first formulated in 1990. However, it was only in 1994 that the Parliament enacted a law 'on the review of persons in certain important positions' (*Act 23 of 1994*). That latter provided for a partial review only, i.e. only senior public officers were subject to it. In case the review committees (consisting of three judges each) found that someone was either a member of the Nazi Arrowcross Party, or was involved in the work of certain of the Communist secret services, the person could choose either to resign or to have the committee's decision published. The law has been amended several times, with its scope broadened or narrowed, yet a complete publication of the 'agents' lists' was never accomplished.[4]

Likewise, the first bill dealing with the Communist past from the perspective of criminal law opted for a technical solution. Without making any reference to the nature of the regime, it simply provided that for certain crimes committed between 21 December 1944 and 2 May 1990, 'the

[4] See B. Révész, *Források a titkosszolgálatok politológiai tanulmányozásához (Sources for the Political Study of the Secret Services)* (Szeged: JATEPress, 2010), esp. chapter 4. In connection with the access to the files, see the ECtHR *Kenedi* v. *Hungary* (Appl. No. 31475/05), Judgment 26 May 2009. More recently, the Committee of National Remembrance (*Nemzeti Emlékezet Bizottsága*), a research body established by *Act 241 of 2013* (pursuant to Article U, para 3 of the Fundamental Law), has started to publish selective lists of 'holders of Communist power', available at: www.neb.hu/hu/kommunista-hatalombirtokosok-1956, last accessed 23 February 2016.

statute of limitations shall restart on 2 May 1990', if 'the State failed to make a penal claim due to political reasons'. The bill was enacted by Parliament on 4 November 1991, yet the Constitutional Court ruled that the statute was unconstitutional, partly because of its retroactive effects, and partly because of the vagueness of the term 'political reasons' (cf. Decision 11/1992 (III. 5.) AB). After a series of further bills and Constitutional Court decisions, Parliament enacted *Act 90 of 1993*, narrowing the scope of responsibility to crimes recognised by international law and committed during and after the revolution of 1956, and making an explicit reference to the Court's relevant decision.

2.2 *Continuity*

The next law dealing with history, in chronological order, was *Act 1 of 2000*, commemorating the beginning of Hungarian statehood, marked by the coronation of King Stephen I (later canonised as Saint Stephen). The preamble briefly summarises the millennial history of Hungary, focusing on the moment of accession to Europe and Christendom. It emphasises the fact that the Hungarian state and nation have survived, but also the role they have played in protecting the Christian Occident. In the second, much shorter, part of the preamble, the 'Holy Crown', i.e. the alleged crown of Stephen I,[5] is characterised as 'a relic embodying the continuity and independence of the Hungarian state according to the consciousness of the nation and the Hungarian public law tradition'.[6] The normative part of the statute then provides for the transfer of the crown and the coronation insignia from the Hungarian National Museum to the Parliament, and the establishment of the Holy Crown Council (*Szent Korona Testület*), chaired by the President of the Republic and comprising chief state officers.

[5] See the summary of E. Dányi, 'Democracy in Ruins: The Case of the Hungarian Parliament', in D. Grafijczuk and D. Sayer (eds.), *The Inhabited Ruins of Central Europe: Re-imagining Space, History, and Memory* (Basingstoke: Palgrave Macmillan, 2013) (hereinafter Dányi, 'Democracy in Ruins'), 55–78, at 57–63, covering the history of the crown and related political ideas (on which see below), with further references. See also L. Péter, 'The Holy Crown of Hungary, Visible and Invisible', *Slavonic and East European Review* 81:3 (2003), 421–510.

[6] Translation adapted from K.L. Scheppele, 'The Constitutional Basis of Hungarian Conservatism', *East European Constitutional Review* 9:4 (2000) (hereinafter Scheppele, 'The Constitutional Basis of Hungarian Conservatism'), 51–7, at 51.

While transforming the central hall of the Parliament into a *lieu de mémoire* in its own right,[7] the transfer also provoked a fiery debate on the political-symbolic meaning of the crown.[8] Critics of the new legislation interpreted it as the symbol of royal power and the lack of equality, which is, by definition, irreconcilable with republican ideals. Moreover, bringing it into the Parliament was regarded by some as an attempt at its re-sacralisation, violating the separation of church and state, a principle entrenched in the constitution.[9] Supporters of the statute, in turn, pointed out that the text only referred to the crown as a symbol of historical continuity and national independence. The key issue, it seems, is what one understands by 'historical continuity'.

2.3 *Freedom of Expression*

The third piece of legislation from the very end of this period is a memory law *par excellence*: one penalising the public denial of the Holocaust (*Act 36 of 2010*, amending *Act 4 of 1978*, the Penal Code). The newly introduced Section 269/C of the Penal Code contained no explanation concerning the Holocaust itself, and focused on the protection of individual victims' dignity:[10] 'Whoever violates the dignity of a victim of the Holocaust before a wide public by denying the fact of the Holocaust, expressing doubt about it, or trivialising it, commits a felony and shall be punishable with imprisonment of up to three years'. At the same time, Parliament turned down another bill initiating the penalisation of the denial of both Nazi and Communist crimes.

This law marked the end of a lengthy debate, in which the victims' interest was set against freedom of speech.[11] Earlier attempts at penalising

[7] Cf. Dányi, 'Democracy in Ruins', at 57, citing P. Nora, 'Between Memory and History: Les lieux de mémoire', *Representations* 26 (1989), 7–24, and G. C. Bowker, *Memory Practices in the Sciences* (Cambridge: MIT Press, 2005).

[8] On the diversity of views among the parliamentary parties, see the brief overview of P. Nemes, 'Crown Fever', *Central Europe Review* 2:1 (10 January 2000) (available at: www.ce-review.org/00/1/nemes1.html, last accessed 23 February 2016).

[9] See e.g. Scheppele, 'The Constitutional Basis of Hungarian Conservatism', S. Radnóti, 'The Glass Cabinet. An Essay about the Place of the Hungarian Crown', *Acta Historiae Artium* 43:1 (2002), 83–111.

[10] The formulation thus circumvented a possible objection, i.e. that groups of people (such as Holocaust victims) cannot have dignity.

[11] On the same phenomenon in European law, see most recently U. Belavusau, 'Memory Laws and Freedom of Speech: Governance of History in European Law', in A. Koltay (ed.),

Holocaust denial all failed.[12] In the law penalising Holocaust denial in itself, then, the concept of human dignity was used to justify a limitation of the freedom of speech, which actually protected a certain memory. A few months later, after the general elections, Parliament passed *Act 56 of 2010*, amending, among others, Section 269/C of the Penal Code, which now penalised 'public denial of the crimes of National Socialist and Communist regimes'.[13]

A related issue was the criminal prohibition of the public use of Nazi and Communist symbols (the five-pointed red star, the hammer and sickle, the swastika, the SS-logo, and the so-called 'arrowcross'), dating back to 1993. *Act 45 of 1993*, which amended the Penal Code by introducing Section 269/B, stated in its preamble that:

> Extremist political ideologies of the 20th century have, by violently taking power and using it in an exclusive manner, established dictatorships in Europe and Hungary, which neglected human rights and led to the mass extermination of Hungarian citizens . . . [T]he use of symbols of states, organisations, and political movements endorsing the extremist ideologies mentioned above tears painful wounds and is irreconcilable with our constitutional values.

While the Constitutional Court did not find penalising the use of these symbols unconstitutional (cf. Decision 14/2000 (V. 12.) AB), the provision was heavily criticised in Hungary, and in a 2008 decision, the European Court of Human Rights ruled that the ban violated Article 10 of the European Convention of Human Rights.[14]

Comparative Perspectives on the Fundamental Freedom of Expression (Budapest: Wolters Kluwer, 2015), 535–56.

[12] The relevant constitutional principles were developed by the Constitutional Court in another case (Decision 30/1992 [V.26.] AB), by making a distinction between 'inciting hatred' and 'using an offensive or denigrating expression'. It is only in the former case, the Court argued, that the freedom of speech has to yield to other values, most notably to the protection of human dignity. The Court also explained that the truth content of the respective utterances does not matter: the only thing that counts is whether it is capable of arousing hatred, i.e. emotionally preparing for the use of violence. The subsequent case law of the Constitutional Court has been extremely rich. For its discussion, see U. Belavusau, 'Hate Speech and Constitutional Democracy in Central and Eastern Europe: Transitional and Militant?', *Israel Law Review* 47:1 (2014), 27–61 (in particular, 42–27 about relevant decisions of the Constitutional Court of Hungary).

[13] The same provision is now Section 333 of the new Penal Code (*Act 100 of 2012*).

[14] ECtHR *Vajnai* v. *Hungary* (Appl. No. 33629/06), 8 July 2008. Following further ECtHR judgments, another decision of the Constitutional Court (4/2013 (II. 21.) AB) held Sect. 269/B of the Penal Code unconstitutional and annulled it. Section 335 of the new Penal Code penalises the use of totalitarian symbols only if it takes place 'in a manner capable of

3 Attempts of a Coherent Narrative: The Fundamental Law in Context

In 2010, soon after the general elections, the new governing coalition, which now had a majority of two thirds in Parliament, announced that they were going to adopt a new constitution. The document, entitled *The Fundamental Law of Hungary* (*Magyarország Alaptörvénye*), was accepted on 18 April 2011 and signed by the President of the Republic on Easter Monday, 25 April. It entered into force on 1 January 2012. The content of the constitution, as well as the way it was made, provoked much criticism from within Hungary and abroad. In what follows, I shall focus on the memory aspects of its text and context. Consequently, debates will be mentioned to the extent they are relevant for the working of narratives in and around the text.

The making of the Fundamental Law has been part of a broader effort made by the new government to come to terms with the past and to establish some kind of a national consensus through a powerful memory policy. This means that the context of constitution-making comprises a number of other measures, legislative and otherwise, as well as the public perception of, and disagreement about these. I shall confine myself to briefly mentioning some of the latter, to show at least certain ways in which the Fundamental Law has been contextualised before, during, and after its making.

As for the text of the Fundamental Law, it consists of several clearly distinguishable parts. Such a distinction was explicitly intended by its drafters, as it is indicated by both the numbering and the stylistic features of the different parts.

The very first part of the document is further separated from the rest by its title, 'National Avowal' (*Nemzeti hitvallás*). It is in here that most of the efforts to create a coherent historical narrative take place, and it is also the most widely discussed and criticised part of the Fundamental Law.[15] Apart from references to Hungarian history, the National Avowal also contains

disturbing public peace, especially by violating the human dignity or posthumous personal rights of the victims of totalitarian systems'.

15 See e.g. the essays in B. Majtényi and M.D. Szabó (eds.), *Az elveszejtett alkotmány (The Constitution Lost)* (Budapest: L'Harmattan and Eötvös Károly Intézet, 2011) and G.A. Tóth (ed.), *Constitution for a Disunited Nation: On Hungary's 2011 Fundamental Law* (Budapest, New York: Central European University Press, 2012), in particular B. Majtényi, 'Vissza a jövőbe – 1989-től a történeti alkotmányig' ('Back to the Future: From 1989 to the Historical Constitution'), in Majtényi and Szabó (eds.), *Az elveszejtett alkotmány*, 209–12, S. Radnóti, 'A Sacred Symbol in a Secular Country: The Holy Crown', in Tóth (ed.), *Constitution for a Disunited Nation*, 85–109, and Zs. Körtvélyesi, 'From *We the People* to *We the Nation*', in Tóth (ed.), *Constitution for a Disunited Nation*, 111–40.

a series of solemn declarations concerning the concept of the nation, the relationship between the individual and the political community, rights and duties, and so on. Indeed, historical references are formulated as declarative sentences themselves. The (most strictly) relevant parts run as follows:[16]

> We are proud that our king Saint Stephen built the Hungarian State on solid ground and made our country a part of Christian Europe one thousand years ago.
>
> We are proud of our forebears who fought for the survival, freedom and independence of our country.
>
> We are proud of the outstanding intellectual achievements of the Hungarian people.
>
> We are proud that our people has over the centuries defended Europe in a series of struggles and enriched Europe's common values with its talent and diligence.
>
> We recognise the role of Christianity in preserving nationhood. We value the various religious traditions of our country.
>
> We promise to preserve the intellectual and spiritual unity of our nation torn apart in the storms of the last century.
>
> We honour the achievements of our historical constitution and we honour the Holy Crown, which embodies the constitutional continuity of Hungary's statehood and the unity of the nation.
>
> We do not recognise the suspension of our historical constitution due to foreign occupations. We deny any statute of limitations for the inhuman crimes committed against the Hungarian nation and its citizens under the national socialist and the communist dictatorship.
>
> We do not recognise the communist constitution of 1949, since it was the basis for tyrannical rule; therefore we proclaim it to be invalid.
>
> We agree with the Members of the first free National Assembly, which proclaimed as its first decision that our current liberty was born of our 1956 Revolution.
>
> We date the restoration of our country's self-determination, lost on the nineteenth day of March 1944, from the second day of May 1990, when the first freely elected organ of popular representation was formed. We shall consider this date to be the beginning of our country's new democracy and constitutional order.

[16] The text follows the official English version of the consolidated text of 2013 (not yet including the Sixth Amendment enacted on 14 June 2016), published at the website of the Hungarian government, available at: www.kormany.hu/download/e/02/00000/The%20New%20Fundamental%20Law%20of%20Hungary.pdf, last accessed 23 February 2016.

> We hold that after the decades of the twentieth century which led to a state of moral decay, we have an abiding need for spiritual and intellectual renewal.
>
> We trust in a jointly-shaped future and the commitment of younger generations. We believe that our children and grandchildren will make Hungary great again with their talent, persistence and moral strength.

In the previous section, I distinguished between stories related to pre-WWII Hungarian history and those concerning the two dictatorial regimes that followed. I shall now look at these stories as they appear in the National Avowal[17] (and elsewhere in the Fundamental Law) in turn, then reflect on a third one, the story of post-1989 developments.

(1) While stories related to earlier periods may seem to be less relevant for the current constitutional situation than twentieth-century developments, it is also known that several of the world's constitutions go back to the more ancient part of the nation's history.[18] This has been explained by the need to show continuity in a situation where radical changes are just taking place, as in the case of European post-Communist countries.[19] This is partly true for the Fundamental Law, too. The question that arises is, however, with what exactly one wants to establish continuity.[20]

The constitution-makers opted for the beginning of the Kingdom of Hungary as the starting point of their narrative, much in the vein of *Act 1 of 2000*. The following statements then mention survival and fight on the one hand and intellectual virtues on the other, yet without any further reference to identifiable events. Thus, continuity seems to appear in the vaguest possible sense here, as the continuous presence of a Hungarian

[17] See also the discussion of G. Schweitzer, 'Fundamental Law – Cardinal Law – Historical Constitution: The Case of Hungary Since 2011', *Journal on European History of Law* 4:1 (2013), 124–8.

[18] See J.O. Frosini, *Constitutional Preambles at a Crossroads between Politics and Law* (Santarcangelo di Romagna: Maggioli, 2012), 37–9.

[19] See I. Kukorelli and G. Máthé, 'Közjogi értékeink a preambulumban' ('Our Public Legal Values in the Preamble'), in V. Lamm, B. Majtényi and A.L. Pap (eds.), *Preambulum az alkotmányokban (Preambles in Constitutions)* (Budapest: Complex, 2012), 9–22, and B. Fekete, 'Történeti elemek az EU-tagállamok alkotmány-preambulumaiban' ('Historical Elements in Constitutional Preambles of EU Member States'), in V. Lamm, B. Majtényi and A.L. Pap (eds.), *Preambulum az alkotmányokban (Preambles in Constitutions)* (Budapest: Complex, 2012), 33–45.

[20] On the problem of continuity in the Fundamental Law see, most recently, Zs. Körtvélyesi, '*Continuity, Discontinuity and Constitution-Making: A Comparative Account*' (30 January 2016), available at SSRN: http://ssrn.com/abstract=2826131, last accessed 23 February 2016 (hereinafter Körtvélyesi, 'Continuity, Discontinuity and Constitution-Making'), 17–21.

state and a Hungarian nation. It is also from the (historical) perspective of country and nation that Christianity and religious traditions are mentioned. The vagueness on the one hand and the national focus on the other makes it possible for the constitution-makers to make reference to several elements of a possible positive national image without appearing divisive. Religious allusions, for instance, could be open to objections as violating the freedom of conscience or the separation of religious communities and the state. Here, however, Christianity is firmly linked to the history of the nation, its value being attributed to its role 'in preserving nationhood'.[21]

A further parallel with *Act 1 of 2000* is the mention made of the Holy Crown as embodying 'the historical continuity of Hungary's statehood and the unity of the nation'. Here, however, it appears just after a reference to the 'historical constitution', which has provoked much criticism, mainly on the part of Hungarian politicians and legal scholars.

The crown in itself is the symbol of royal power. Calling it 'holy' may evoke religious connotations. In Hungary, however, the Holy Crown has also been used to refer to a public-law concept and a related political doctrine as well. Thus, mentioning the Holy Crown as a symbol of continuity together with the historical constitution, then stating that '[w]e do not recognise the suspension of our historical constitution due to foreign occupations' leads to the conclusion that the constitution-makers intend to return to the constitutional situation preceding the occupation of Hungary first by German, then by Russian troops.[22] Given that until 31 January 1946, Hungary was a monarchy, the so-called 'Doctrine of the Holy Crown' is certainly part of the 'historical constitution'.[23]

[21] This also applies to the motto at the beginning of the text, 'God bless the Hungarians', the first line of the national anthem. See B. Schanda, 'A New Constitution for Hungary: Some Sensitive Issues', *Iustum Aequum Salutare* 7:2 (2011), 153–8, at 157–8. Elsewhere Schanda argues that the quotation may have a special meaning for those believing in God, yet without excluding non-believers from the national community, cf. B. Schanda, 'Az alkotmányjog oktatásáról' ('On Teaching Constitutional Law'), *Fundamentum* 17:1 (2013) 44–6, at 44. In the very last clause of the text, the constitution-makers refer to themselves as 'being aware of [their] responsibility before God and man'. That, however, refers exclusively to 'the Members of the National Assembly elected on 25 April 2010'.

[22] This is reinforced by the later statement that 'our country's self-determination [was] lost on the nineteenth day of March 1944', on which see below.

[23] Cf. Z. Szente, 'The Doctrine of the Holy Crown in the Hungarian Historical Constitution', *Journal on European History of Law* 4:1 (2013) (hereinafter Szente, 'The Doctrine of the Holy Crown') 109–15, at 110; P. Sonnevend, A. Jakab and L. Csink, 'The Constitution as an Instrument of Everyday Party Politics: The Basic Law of Hungary', in A. von Bogdandy and P. Sonnevend (eds.), *Constitutional Crisis in the European Constitutional Area: Theory,*

As for the content of the doctrine, it was first formulated as such in Werbőczy's *Tripartitum*, a law-book from the sixteenth century,[24] where the author combined crown symbolism with an organic conception of the state and a theory of mutual empowerment. In this sense, the Holy Crown is regarded as the source of all political power, with the King and the nobility being members of the Crown. It is the King who creates nobles, while it is the noblemen who elect the King. In different periods, different weight was attributed to the doctrine, and there were shifts in its content as well, but it proved flexible enough to persist even in the twentieth century.[25] After 1920, it was of particular importance for the legitimacy of the 'Kingdom without a King', and also for Hungarian claims to the 'Lands of the Holy Crown'.

It has been pointed out that symbols of Hungarian constitutional history, and the Holy Crown in particular, are open to various interpretations.[26] While the crown is by nature linked to monarchy, and the original version of the Holy Crown Doctrine narrowed the concept of nation to noblemen, during the reforms introduced after the 1848 revolution a different reading emerged. While keeping the doctrine as the constitutional framework, the equality of political rights now meant that all citizens became members of the Holy Crown.[27] While the only explicit reference to 1848 in the Fundamental Law is the listing of 15 March among the national holidays (in Art. J), the opening and closing mottoes also allude to the same historical moment.[28]

Law and Politics in Hungary and Romania (Oxford, Portland: Hart, 2015) (hereinafter Sonnevend, Jakab and Csink, 'The Constitution as an Instrument of Everyday Party Politics') 33–109, at 36.

[24] For an English translation see J. M. Bak, P. Banyó and M. Rady (eds.), *The Customary Law of the Renowned Kingdom of Hungary: A Work in Three Parts* (Budapest: Central European University Press, 2005).

[25] Cf. Sonnevend, Jakab and Csink, 'The Constitution as an Instrument of Everyday Party Politics', 36.

[26] Cf. I. Császár and B. Majtényi, 'Hungary: The Historic Constitution as the Place of Memory', in M. Suksi, K. Agapiou-Josephides, J-P. Lehners and M. Nowak (eds.), *First Fundamental Rights Documents in Europe: Commemorating 800 Years of the Magna Carta* (Mortsel, Cambridge: Intersentia, 2015) (hereinafter Császár and Majtényi, 'Hungary: The Historic Constitution as the Place of Memory') 57–67, at 62–7. See also Szente, 'The Doctrine of the Holy Crown', 112.

[27] See e.g. Császár and Majtényi, 'Hungary: The Historic Constitution as the Place of Memory', at 62–3, quoting M. Tomcsányi, *Magyarország közjoga (The Public Law of Hungary)* (Budapest: Királyi Magyar Egyetemi Nyomda, 1932).

[28] The national anthem, entitled 'Himnusz' ('Hymn') is a poem by Ferenc Kölcsey (1823), combined with the melody of Ferenc Erkel (1844). It was also played on 15 March 1848.

The Fundamental Law further mentions the achievements of the historical constitution in its second part ('Foundation') as an interpretive guideline.[29] It is difficult to imagine what this conception could add to the explicit rules of the constitution, which makes the impression that the reference there only serves to give emphasis to the idea of historical continuity.

(2) This continuity, however, is not unbroken. While the text says that the constitution-makers 'do not recognise the suspension of our historical constitution due to foreign occupations', it also states that the autonomy of the state was lost with the German occupation in 1944, and was regained only with the first free elections in 1990. In terms of law, the text explicitly denies the validity of the 1949 constitution (*Act 20 of 1949*) as 'the basis of a tyrannical rule'. These statements are rather puzzling as they raise the question as to what, then, remains of continuity.

The period between 1944 and 1990 includes at least three moments that may be – and are generally – considered important for twentieth-century Hungarian constitutionalism. The first one is 1945–6. Apart from the fact that Hungary became a republic, it was also a period when a democratic multi-party system started to work – to be soon oppressed through the Communist takeover. The second one is the revolution of 1956. While an even much shorter period, its symbolic power is arguably one of the greatest, as it is reflected by the fact that 23 October, the day the revolution began, is one of the three national holidays according to the Fundamental Law. Thirdly, the period immediately before the free elections in 1990 was of high importance for the shaping of the democratic constitution: the constitutional amendment passed on 18 October 1989 (Act 31 of 1989) and the proclamation of the republic on 23 October in the same year were the key moments marking the end of long negotiations.

Of the three, the post-war changes appear only through an indirect reference, inserted into the text by the Fourth Amendment, as 'the democratic attempt built on a multi-party system in the years after World War II', which was then uprooted by the Communist Party with the help of the Soviet armed forces (Art. U). In the same Article, the revolution of 1956 is

The closing motto, 'Let there be peace, freedom and concord' stems from the manifesto of the revolution, entitled *What Does the Hungarian Nation Wish?*, and printed on the same day.

[29] Art. R, para 3: 'The provisions of the Fundamental Law shall be interpreted in accordance with their purposes, the National Avowal contained therein and the achievements of our historical constitution'. See Sonnevend, Jakab and Csink, 'The Constitution as an Instrument of Everyday Party Politics', esp. at 74.

mentioned, too, but only in terms of its bloody suppression. In that case, however, the National Avowal contains another, again indirect, reference, by expressing agreement 'with the Members of the first free National Assembly, which proclaimed as its first decision that our current liberty was born of our 1956 Revolution'. The democratic transition, apart from the references to the freely elected National Assembly of 1990, does not appear anywhere in the text. It seems that any event from that period of 'lacking sovereignty' can enter the text only if 'legitimate' moments open a window for them.

Another aspect of the missing period is the crimes against humanity committed under the Nazi and Communist regimes.[30] Here again, the reference is occasioned by the rejection of 'any statute of limitations for the inhuman crimes committed against the Hungarian nation and its citizens' under the two dictatorships. This gap is partly filled by the newly introduced Section U, which gives a list of events grounding the responsibility of Communist leaders. Yet also here, the connection to the present is established, on the one hand, by the statement that '[p]olitical organisations having gained legal recognition during the democratic transition as legal successors of the Hungarian Socialist Workers' Party continue to share the responsibility of their predecessors as beneficiaries of their unlawfully accumulated assets', and, on the other hand, by the provisions regulating how 'the operation of the communist dictatorship shall be realistically revealed and society's sense of justice shall be ensured'.

(3) The third period is the one beginning with the democratic transition. The absence of the transition as a process from the historical overview of the National Avowal has been mentioned above. More importantly, anything that happened since the first free elections is almost completely

[30] The statement in the National Avowal that the 'country's self-determination' was 'lost on the nineteenth day of March 1944', i.e. the beginning of the German occupation of Hungary, is often criticised as an attempt to deny the involvement of the Hungarian State in the deportation of Jews to Nazi concentration camps. Recent historical research has shown that the military occupation still allowed some scope for the Hungarian government and the Regent, Miklós Horthy, to manoeuvre, even against the will of Edmund Veesenmayer, the Reich plenipotentiary (*Reichsbevollmächtigter*) for Hungary, in a number of issues. Cf. K. Ungváry, 'Mesterterv? A deportálások döntési mechanizmusa' ('Masterplan? The Decision Mechanism of Deportations'), *Századok* 149:1 (2015), 1–32, esp. at 18–25, with further references.

missing.[31] This may be interpreted in two different ways at least, either as meaning that the constitutional 'present' started on 2 May 1990, and the Fundamental Law is part of that story, or as an indication of the fact that the Fundamental Law marks a new beginning, and the years between 1990 and 2012 are nothing else than an uneventful part of the past. The repeated reference to 1990, and the one to the previous constitution[32] would suggest that the first reading is to prevail, while repealing the 'decisions of the Constitutional Court taken prior to the entry into force of the Fundamental Law' (Closing and Miscellaneous Provisions, para 5) speaks for the second one.

The tension between the two possibilities is due to the distance in time between the substantial constitutional changes in 1989 and the making of the new constitution. This makes it necessary for the constitution-makers to define the relationship of the Fundamental Law to the developments of the last twenty-two years.[33] While the Fundamental Law itself is silent on the issue, exponents of the government sometimes formulate some reasons why making a new constitution became inevitable. According to the first argument, the 1989 preamble of the constitution explicitly stated that a new constitution was forthcoming. Second, the title of the constitution, i.e. Act 20 of 1949, still referred to the original Stalinist document, even though its contents were completely different. Third, the several amendments made since 1989 made it difficult to determine the exact content of the constitution. Fourth, the political and economic crisis that started in 2006 called for new legal solutions, even at the constitutional level.[34] The first reason

[31] The only exceptions being the reference to the successor parties of the Hungarian Socialist Workers' Party in Section U (quoted above), and the statement in the Closing and Miscellaneous Provisions, para 2, that 'This Fundamental Law shall be adopted by the National Assembly pursuant to Sections 19(3)a) and 24(3) of Act XX of 1949 [i.e., the old Constitution]'.

[32] See the previous note, and the discussion of Körtvélyesi, 'Continuity, Discontinuity and Constitution-Making', 17–20.

[33] A document entitled 'Declaration of National Cooperation', passed soon after the 2010 elections as Political Declaration 1 of 2010 (16 June) of the Hungarian National Assembly on National Cooperation anticipates that by stating, in its opening sentence, that '[a]t the end of the first decade of the 21st century, after forty-six years of occupation and dictatorship and *two turbulent decades of transition* Hungary has regained the right and ability of self-determination' (emphasis added). An English translation of the text is available at www.nefmi.gov.hu/english/political-declaration, last accessed 23 February 2016.

[34] See e.g. L. Trócsányi and M. Sulyok, 'The Birth and Early Life of the Basic Law of Hungary', in A.Zs. Varga, A. Patyi and B. Schanda (eds.), *The Basic (Fundamental) Law of Hungary: A Commentary of the New Hungarian Constitution* (Dublin: Clarus, 2015), 1–34, esp. at 7–8.

serves as the basis of a third possible interpretation of the post-1989 period, according to which the democratic transition did not end in 1990 but only in 2012. This narrative regards the making of the Fundamental Law as the last step of a process, by which the basic values of the political community, missing from the 1989 constitution, were finally formulated.[35]

Which of these interpretations is going to be dominant in political discourse is not for the constitution-maker to decide. Nevertheless, political actions related to the Fundamental Law influence the narratives about it. Part of this influence is intentional. Moves such as setting up the 'Table of the Fundamental Law' in government buildings to promote and distribute the text, commissioning artwork for an illustrated edition, or introducing the 'Fundamental Law Day' (25 April, cf. Closing and Miscellaneous Provisions, para 5) are clearly meant to facilitate the perception of the Fundamental Law as an unequivocal *lieu de mémoire*. Yet other measures, such as the (so far) frequent amendments, the enactment of the 'Transitional Provisions' (*Átmeneti rendelkezések*) and their subsequent inclusion into the text of the Fundamental Law itself,[36] work into the opposite direction, partly by undermining the image of stability, and partly by making the impression that constitution-making is used as a means to achieve party-political goals of the moment.

[35] See esp. F. Hörcher, 'Az értékhiányos rendszerváltás. Jogelméleti és politikafilozófiai megfontolások' ('Value-Deficient Transition: Legal Theoretical and Political Philopsohical Considerations'), *Fundamentum* 7:1 (2003), 62–72; F. Hörcher, 'Communal Values in the New Hungarian Fundamental Law: The Habermas-Ratzinger Debate and the Use of the Humanities in Constitutional Interpretation', in E. Bos and K. Pócza (eds.), *Verfassunggebung in konsolidierten Demokratien: Neubeginn oder Verfall eines Systems?* (Baden-Baden: Nomos, 2014), 346–64; F. Hörcher, 'The National Avowal: An Interpretation of the Preamble, from the Perspective of the History of Political Thought', in A.Zs. Varga, A. Patyi and B. Schanda (eds.), *The Basic (Fundamental) Law of Hungary: A Commentary of the New Hungarian Constitution* (Dublin: Clarus, 2015), 35–56; A.Zs. Varga, 'A magalkotmány védelmében' ('In Defence of a Core Constitution'), *Pázmány Law Working Papers* 2011/2 (available at www.plwp.jak.ppke.hu last accessed 23 February 2016), 12–13.

[36] The Transitional Provisions of the Fundamental Law of Hungary were enacted on 30 December 2011, two days before the Fundamental Law entered into force. Section 31, para 2 provided that 'The Transitional Provisions are part of the Fundamental Law'. In its Decision 45/2012. (XII. 29.) AB, passed a year later, the Constitutional Court declared several of the provisions unconstitutional. On 11 March 2013, the Parliament passed the Fourth Amendment of the Fundamental Law, amending it along the lines of the Transitional Provisions. Changes brought in by the Fourth Amendment include Section U (concerning the responsibility of Communist leaders and successor parties, although not mentioning the Hungarian Socialist Party by name, as the Transitional Provisions did) and the Fundamental Law Day.

4 Conclusion

In his 'Theses on Law, History and Time', Costas Douzinas quotes Xenophon's account of the Athenians' decree prohibiting the recollection of crimes committed during the Thirty Tyrants' regime, and the citizens' oath in which they promised 'not to remember the evils' (*me mnesikakein*).[37] 'The two prohibitions on memory', he concludes, 're-founded democratic politics against the ruins of the civil war'.[38] There is, however, another classical quote, this time from Thucydides, describing civic strife from the perspective of language: 'Words had to change their ordinary meaning and to take that which was now given them. Reckless audacity came to be considered the courage of a loyal ally; prudent hesitation, specious cowardice; moderation was held to be a cloak for unmanliness; ability to see all sides of a question, inaptness to act on any'.[39] The former passage is usually read as an argument in favour of keeping silent about the question of responsibility, while the latter suggests that for any workable political community, there needs to be at least a basic moral vocabulary shared by all the citizens. Re-creating a political community makes it necessary to balance the two in a most careful manner.

The drafters of the new Hungarian constitution apparently tried to do both: to keep silent on a number of sensitive issues in order to avoid being divisive, but also to be explicit about matters they considered to be essential for the shaping of citizens' identity. Both efforts take place, partly at least, in the historical narratives present in (and behind) the preamble. The primary aim of this chapter was to show what these narratives are and how they function within the text and its broader political context. It was pointed out that in addition to the narratives in the preamble, also the narratives about the Fundamental Law itself are of relevance for its success as a constitution. I argued that the former mainly respond to issues that have arisen in the course of the democratic transition, such as the questions of

[37] C. Douzinas, 'Theses on Law, History and Time', *Melbourne Journal of International Law* 7:1 (2006) (hereinafter Douzinas, 'Theses on Law, History and Time') 13–27, cf. Xenophon, *Hellenica* 2.4.43. For recent discussions of the Athenian case see A. Wolpert, *Remembering Defeat: Civil War and Civic Memory in Ancient Athens* (Baltimore, London: The Johns Hopkins University Press, 2003) esp. Chapter 4; A. Lanni, 'Transitional Justice in Ancient Athens: A Case Study', *University of Pennsylvania Journal of International Law* 32:2 (2010) 551–94; E. Carawan, *The Athenian Amnesty and Reconstructing the Law* (Oxford University Press, 2013).

[38] Douzinas, 'Theses on Law, History and Time', 27.

[39] Thucydides 3.3.82, quoted from R. Crawley (tr.), *Thucydides, History of the Peloponnesian War* (London: Dent, 1910), 224.

responsibility for Communist (and Nazi) crimes, the commemoration of and compensation for the victims, and the 'historical continuity' of the Hungarian constitution. While trying to embed all these elements into a coherent narrative, the preamble leaves many questions unanswered. Finally, it was observed that by incorporating the so-called Transitional Provisions into the Fundamental Law, the constitution-maker not only changed part of the narratives already present, but also reinforced a narrative about the constitution-making process that is less than positive for the creation of a constitutional identity for the citizens.[40]

[40] The author would like to thank Péter Cserne and Gábor Halmai for their comments and suggestions, as well as István H. Szilágyi and István Tóth-Barbalics for their help with the bibliography, and Antoon De Baets for calling my attention to relevant ECtHR case law.

13

On the Politics of Resentment, Mis-memory, and Constitutional Fidelity: The Demise of the Polish Overlapping Consensus?

TOMASZ TADEUSZ KONCEWICZ

> Genocide, of which the Polish people were not guilty, happened after all on our soil and stigmatized this soil forever . . . Our memory and public consciousness must never forget about this bloody and heinous sign. We cannot pretend that this never happened . . . Our homeland is built first and foremost of memory; in other words only memory of the past gives us a chance to be ourselves. This past is not to be disposed of freely, even though we cannot be held directly responsible for the past in our individual capacity. We are obliged to carry this past inside us, irrespective of how painful it might be. And we should strive to cleanse it . . . all the profanity that happened here on this soil obliges us to perform such an act of cleansing. On this graveyard this obligation really boils down to a respect for one thing: to see our past in truth.[1]
>
> Jan Błoński, *Biedni Polacy patrzą na getto* *(The poor Poles look at the ghetto)*

1 Setting the Scene

1.1 Politics of Resentment

The "politics of resentment" is sweeping across Europe. Yet the concept itself, and its consequences and *modus operandi*, remains far from clear. We continue to lack a conceptual framework to deal with it. We tend to adopt an intuitive understanding of the term and equate it with the politics of protest, i.e. contestation of and revolt against mainstream politics. In this traditional sense the politics of resentment is often analysed together with populism, and the two are even sometimes used interchangeably. Like

To the memory of my late Grandmother, Czesława Strąg, Righteous Among the Nations of the World, who tirelessly taught me that in order to move forward, we must never forget where we came from.

[1] *Tygodnik Powszechny* 2, 11 January 1987. Unless otherwise stated, all translations are mine.

populism, the politics of resentment is not only anti-elitist, but also anti-pluralist.[2] Populism appeals to resentment to exclude "others" from "the people", claiming that only "We" represent the real "We the People" However, the politics of resentment is conceptually different. Being concrete and yet fluid and intuitive at the same time, it penetrates social and political life more deeply and broadly than populism. The politics of resentment translates, and structures, populism. At its deepest level, the "politics of resentment" calls into doubt the very commitments entered into voluntarily. It strikes at the very core of the societal fabric. The politics of resentment is felt differently in the main axes of divergence of the European continent. i.e. in *the West* and *the East*. In the former case, EU law and Europeanization provoke well-known criticisms of the remoteness of Brussels, with resultant civic indifference, thus turning against the mainstream politics and offering a nostalgic return to the nation state. In the homogenous societies of the *East*, the politics of resentment currently does not have an "Other" to turn against,[3] and, as a result it has fed off the phenomenon that I call "alienating constitutionalism". This provides fertile ground for a sweeping politics of resentment. The incessant pressure of Europeanization and the drive to "catch-up" with what was not long ago accepted as a superior Western standard has provoked a backlash against the elite-driven and technocratic politics, wherein public discourse was dominated by strict legalism and a top-down approach, and people were relegated to the symbolic "casting the vote moment". There was almost an aura of inevitability to mainstream politics: the choice at the polls could be against a person (party) but never against those policies which were seen as a non-negotiable itinerary to be carried out. The politics of resentment took advantage of the exclusion that defined this "alienating constitutionalism" and transformed itself into a "vindictive constitutionalism", marked by gut-politics, emotions, and revolt against the corrupt political elites and institutions. A phase of "constitutional capture" followed. The predictable and stabilizing liberal narrative of *in the rule of law we trust* has been debunked by an emotional and unpredictable brand of politics.[4] This politics of resentment has never worked on its own.

[2] This is the understanding of populism adopted by J. W. Müller in his insightful analysis *What Is Populism?* (University of Pennsylvania Press, 2016).

[3] This homogeneity and the fear of "the Other" (as evidenced in, e.g., the resistance of Central and Eastern Europe countries to accept immigration quotas) stands in stark contrast to Eastern Europe's past, marked by a diversity that was once unparalleled in the rest of Europe.

[4] See the special Volume no 18/2007 of the *Journal of Democracy: Is East-Central Europe Backsliding?*; and in particular the analysis by I. Krastev, 'The Strange Death of the Liberal Consensus', *Journal of Democracy* 18:4 (2007), 56.

It is always a function and mixture of culture, history, and domestic politics. As a result of this, "bifurcation resentment" works differently in different environments and manifests itself in different guises: Brexit in the UK and more generally anti-European sentiments across the continent; the rise of right-wing parties in Germany, Austria, and France; the spread of hate speech and exclusion of the "Other", including the expulsion of the Roma from France; or more recently the disabling of constitutional checks and balances and exclusion of the political opposition from politics in Poland and Hungary. The rationale behind this resentment – exclusion and distrust – plays out in each and every case mentioned, yet it operates differently, with varying intensity and consequences. However, what interests me here is one particular sphere in which the politics of resentment operates – the public discourse on history and the past. How does the politics of resentment drive new narratives of the past, and how does it reshape them and impose them on the public consciousness?

1.2 "Memory Capture" and "Mis-memory" – Concepts and Manifestations

The "politics of resentment" touches upon history and impacts the way we remember the past. The resentment involved resorts to what I call here *memory capture*, understood as a generic and novel concept that calls into question "We, the Polish people". "Memory capture" is based on a systemic weakening of the inclusive approach to the past, which allows all voices to be heard. It offers a more flattened and one-dimensional explanation of where "We, Poles" came from and what makes up our national identity. "Memory capture" is vindictive: Poland and the Poles have suffered so much in the past that they are now entitled to a greater respect and recognition for their sufferings. Poland has rightful expectations to be a taker, not a giver, because we have already given too much and should now be compensated for all our sacrifices and sufferings.[5]

Crucially for my analysis, memory capture consists of enslaving the past within one dominant narrative and, as a result, entails an imbalance in our

[5] Arguing in 2007 for increased voting rights in the EU for Poland, then-Prime Minister and leader of PiS, Jarosław Kaczyński stated: *We are only demanding one thing, that we get back what was taken from us*, and added that *[i]f Poland had not had to live through the years of 1939–45, Poland would today be looking at the demographics of a country of 66 million*. See, 'Poles in a war of words over voting', BBC News, 21 June 2007, available at http://news.bbc.co.uk/1/hi/world/europe/6227834.stm.

collective remembering and way of looking at the past. Certain elements are exposed and celebrated, while others that do not fit the overarching rationale and narrative are relegated to the margins of public discourse, castigated, and even, as will be shown below, penalized. In the end, the historical debate is tainted by an imbalance and asymmetry. This is where the concept of *mis-memory* enters the picture, distorting our reading of our national history and the past. The high rhetoric adopted is always the same: to protect the good name of Poland. Beneath the surface, though, lurk the true motives of Polish political masters: negation of historical truth by silencing those who dare to speak honestly, without sugar coating, about past events. "Memory capture" and "mis-memory" dictate a vision of the past that is one-dimensional: we suffered and others always plotted against us. Today the day of reckoning has come and Poland must be put back on the pedestal of sufferer and victimized.[6] Anyone who counters our understanding of our past is characterized almost instantaneously as a liar and a traitor.[7] With the passage of a new law (described below), this crusade will progress even faster and in a more disciplined way.

Andrzej Wajda, the renowned Polish movie maker who recently passed away, was a person who, more than anyone else, shaped and expressed the Polish post-1945 spirit and consciousness through his artistic vision and imagination. He had this to say on the state of the Polish soul and national temperament:

> Those who go around shouting "Poland, Poland!" don't always have the deepest and wisest reflections of Poland in their hearts and minds. Slowacki knew this . . . The symbols of tradition and history are alive in our nation, and it has never allowed them to be torn from its memory. But the question is whether these symbols incline us to communal action and true patriotic sentiments, or whether they engender sterile and inert emotions and cheap feelings, serving as a smokescreen for self-satisfaction, arrogance and apathy, indeed chauvinism and even hatred.[8]

[6] This victimhood is a salient feature of the politics of mis-memory in Poland or, as Gross puts it, the "perspective of victimhood is a comfortable vision of one's own history"; J. Tomasz Gross, 'Ten jest z ojczyzny mojej . . . ale go nie lubie' (He Comes from My Homeland . . . and Yet I Don't Like Him), Aneks. *Kwartalnik Polityczny*, 41–2 (1986).

[7] J. Connelly and T. T. Koncewicz, 'Who Are Today's Polish Traitors? Of Politics of Paranoia and Resentment and Missed Lessons from the Past', available at www.verfassungsblog.de/who-are-todays-polish-traitors-of-politics-of-paranoia-and-resentment-and-missed-lessons-from-the-past.html.

[8] Polish quotation comes from www.newsweek.pl/kultura/andrzej-wajda-nie-zyje-rezyser-andrzej-wajda-zmarl-w-niedziele-wieczorem,artykuly,398462,1.html.

This mis-memory manifests itself in many places and under many guises. We now read insinuations that Lech Wałęsa worked for the secret police of Communist Poland. Earlier this year, officials of the Polish Institute of National Remembrance (IPN) seized documents from a vacation house of the deceased former secret police chief, Czesław Kiszczak. One file supposedly contains Wałęsa's signature, showing his assent to act as a "secret collaborator" as well as alleged receipts for payments. This is not the first time that Walesa has faced questions in this regard. In the 1990s rumours surfaced that he was an informer code-named "Bolek", yet no document has emerged showing that such an agent spied on anyone. The IPN is not even sure if Wałęsa's alleged signature is genuine. What is unquestionable is that there is an ongoing stubborn and persistent campaign to show that a man who destroyed a political system was also in its pay. Wałęsa is not the only dissident icon being targeted. Writers Adam Michnik and Jacek Kuroń, former foreign minister Bronisław Geremek, and first post-Communist Prime Minister, Tadeusz Mazowiecki (the latter three now deceased) have likewise attracted accusations of complicity. In Germany or Czechoslovakia the allegations, if true, would imply a moral failing. In Poland they signal treason.

All this raises the question: Are these examples unrelated incidents or do they, rather, hint at an emerging trend in the way of understanding, and looking at, Polish history?[9] It is no coincidence that my analysis has commenced with these random examples. Taken in isolation they could be considered as no more than a disturbing aberration; analysed together, however, they point towards a dangerous and growing trend of rewriting history and the imposition of a new historical narrative.[10] Should we be surprised by this zealous historical turn in Poland? My answer is "no", and that the past – both the most recent and more ancient – holds all the keys to making sense of the sweeping "politics of mis-memory". One cannot fully grasp the rationale behind the *memory capture* and obsession with history without looking behind the lurking ideology and founding myths of the Polish powers. In the eyes of the right-wing and ultra-conservative ruling Law and Justice party (hereinafter PiS, as it is known in Poland based on its Polish acronym), the birth of the Third Republic in 1989 has been deficient since its very beginnings. PiS has been built on and thrived on the premise

[9] See also 'Charlemagne. The Politics of Memory', *The Economist* 9 April 2016.

[10] www.ft.com/content/67532c78-e62d-11e5-a09b-1f8b0d268c39; www.ft.com/content/e05e0500-6f8b-11e2-b906-00144feab49a?ftcamp=published_links%2Frss%2Farts_books%2Ffeed%2F%2Fprodu.

of denouncing the so-called "Round Table Talks" in 1989 as a rotten compromise struck by Lech Walesa (a traitor and secret collaborator with the communists) and Solidarność (Solidarity) with the outgoing communist regime as a means of keeping the old elites alive. According to this narrative, Polish politics and democratic institutions (e.g. judicial constitutional review)[11] are all a sham, and the Third Republic (brought into existence in 1989) has never been a real state, but rather a phantom state based on the intellectual corruption of the political elites, bribery, dysfunctional government, caving in to Brussels, selling off Poland to strangers for peanuts, and waiting at the beck and call of Germany. "Real Poles" were shackled and relegated to the sidelines. Now, "We the PiS" – speaking on behalf of "true Poles" – will reclaim the state from the corrupt elites and purge it of all irregularities, using the tools of censorship, the antagonising rhetoric of "we vs. them", nationalistic undertones, the presentation of Poland as the political lapdog of Germany and the EU, and manipulation of the law. In such "Paranoia-driven" politics, any pocket of independence and potential resistance is seen as dangerous and fuels conspiracy theories. The enemy is omnipresent: both everywhere and nowhere. It is invisible and does not respect rules. As a result, tracking the enemy and/or traitor is crucial and provides the self-renewing justification for the paranoid regime. This is crucial because it shows how headline-grabbing statements on the past and the focus on the current injustices that Poland and Poles are allegedly being subjected to make up the new Polish historical orthodoxy.

2 "My Way or the Highway": Protecting the Good Name of Poland and the "Polish Death Camps" Controversy

2.1 *Criminalizing the Historical Debate*

A powerful example of the resentments driven by politics is provided by the recent draft amendment to the Law on the IPN.[12] While it is not intention here to dissect the new amendments in detail, some of its premises

[11] For more on the constitutional crisis in Poland and its European ramifications, see T. T. Koncewicz, 'Of Institutions, Democracy, Constitutional Self-Defence and the Rule of Law: The Judgments of the Polish Constitutional Tribunal in Cases K 34/15, K 35/15 and Beyond', *Common Market Law Review* 53 (2016), 1753–92.

[12] Act of 18 December 1998 on the Institute of National Remembrance – Commission for the Prosecution of Crimes against the Polish Nation, Official Journal of Laws No. 155, item 1016. At the time of writing the draft was submitted to the Parliament. For an update see www.premier.gov.pl/wydarzenia/decyzje-rzadu/projekt-ustawy-o-zmianie-ustawy-o-instytucie-pamieci-narodowej-komisji.html

need to be examined in order to understand the nature of the threat they represent. It is yet another (and the most serious so far) exemplification of the *politics of mis-memory*. The Law on IPN has been amended by first, adding a new Chapter 6 to the civil law protection of the good name of the Republic of Poland and of the Polish Nation; and second by criminalizing publicly and erroneously assigning to the Polish nation any blame for participation in, organizing, responsibility for, or complicity in the Nazi crimes committed by the III Reich (Art. 55a and Art. 55b). This crime can be committed either intentionally[13] (in which case the penalty is up to five years' imprisonment) or unintentionally[14] (here the penalty would be a fine or restriction of liberty). The crime is subject to the application of the so-called "unconditional protective principle", which means that foreigners as well can be held liable for their statements made abroad, irrespective of whether the same crime is envisaged in the law of their home country. The official press release from the Minister of Justice, (who drafted the new law), presented the law as follows: "*Today the Polish government took an important step in the direction of creating stronger legal instruments allowing us to defend our rights, defend the historical truth, and defend Poland's good name everywhere in the world.*"[15] He alluded to the notorious "Polish death camps" designation appearing every now and then in the foreign media, which can be viewed as suggesting co-responsibility on the part of Poland and the Poles for the crimes committed by Nazi Germany. He vowed to prosecute all those who defame Poland or the Polish Nation.

Nobody in their right mind questions the right of Polish government to set the record straight on the impropriety of the expression "Polish death camps" or to demand necessary actions against those who use this or equivalent expressions. It is the method of enforcement, and the severity of penalty, that are unheard of. The new Law has already sparked a furore

[13] In accordance with Art. 9 §1 of the Polish Criminal Code, *a prohibited act is committed with intent when the offender wants to commit it, namely where there is a desire to commit it or an acceptance of the foreseeable possibility of committing the act.* All translations of the Polish Criminal Code come from N. Faulkner, *The Criminal Code. Kodeks Karny* (Warsaw: BECK, 2012).

[14] Art. 9 §2 of the Polish Criminal Code provides that: *A prohibited act is committed without intent where the offender does not intend to commit it, but does so out of a failure to exercise due care under the circumstances, even though the possibility of committing the prohibited act was foreseen, or could have been foreseen.*

[15] Later in a radio interview he added: "*This will be a project that meets the expectations of Poles, who are blasphemed in the world, in Europe, even in Germany, by allegations that they are the Holocaust perpetrators, and that in Poland there were Polish concentration camps, Polish gas chambers. Enough with this lie. There has to be responsibility.*"

over its scope and range and the severity of its sanctions, and has been criticized as a "blunt instrument"[16] and as yet another example of nationalist revival in Poland and the return of revisionist history,[17] as well as a threat to any open discussion of crimes for which Poles were responsible.[18] Critics have pointed out the possible dangers of limiting free speech and research,[19] and of building the martyrological narrative wherein the world does not understand how much Poland suffered.[20]

The Polish legal system already contains provisions that could be resorted to in cases of alleged falsification of history or of wrongly imputing blame for certain acts and/or behaviours to a person or group of persons. These provisions include: Art. 55 of the Law on IPN (denying Nazi crimes); Art. 133 of the Polish Criminal Code (publicly insulting the Polish nation or Poland)[21]; Art. 212 of the Polish Criminal Code (slander)[22]; and Art. 216 of the Polish Criminal Code[23] (insult). The introduction by way of amendment of Art. 55a and the accompanying penalization provisions means that the Polish legislator deemed Art. 133 of the Polish Criminal Code insufficient to deal with the problem of alleged attacks on the good name of the Polish nation. Art. 55a becomes a self-standing basis for criminal responsibility, independent of whether the action was also slanderous. Under Art. 55a, the latter is a possibility, a side effect, but does not in itself constitute a crime or the imputation of a crime. It is possible, however, for the two provisions (Art. 55a IPN and 133 PCC) to work in conjunction, when a public imputation takes the form of a slander, which cannot be ruled out.

[16] 'Charlemagne. The Politics of Memory', *The Economist* 9 April 2016.

[17] T. Zieve, 'Historians say Polish bill on death camps reference extreme', available at www.jpost.com/Diaspora/Historians-say-Polish-bill-on-death-camps-reference-extreme-464495.

[18] C. Kroet, 'Poland to prosecute for the phrase "Polish death camps"' available at www.politico.eu/article/poland.

[19] M. Lebovic, 'Do the words "Polish death camps" defame Poland? And if so, who's to blame?' available at www.timesofisrael.com/do-the-words-polish-death-camps-defame-poland-and-if-so-whos-to-blame/.

[20] E. Roberts, 'Poland wants to outlaw phrases like "Polish death camps"' available at http://edition.cnn.com/2016/08/17/europe/poland-ban-death-camp-phrase/.

[21] The code uses the full name of the Polish State – "Rzeczpospolita" (Republic).

[22] "*Slandering* another person, a group of people, a business entity or an organizational unit, about conduct or characteristics that may discredit them in the face of the public opinion, or result in a loss of confidence in their ability to perform in a given position, occupation or type of activity" (emphasis mine).

[23] "*Insulting* another person in his or her presence, or publicly in his or her absence with the intention that the insult will reach that person" (emphasis mine).

The introduction of Art. 55a was already foreshadowed in 2006 by the incorporation into the Polish Criminal Code of Art. 132a, which penalized "the public defamation of the Polish Nation" by accusing it of involvement in Nazi or communist crimes. The revisionist rationale in 2006 was a direct response to books published by the Princeton-based academic Jan Tomasz Gross about the events in Jedwabne in July 1941, where Poles burned their Jewish neighbours in a barn.[24] The constitutionality of this so-called "Gross-law" (as one of the academics dubbed it)[25] was challenged before the Polish Constitutional Tribunal by the Ombudsman. One of the central arguments of the Ombudsman was that Art. 132(a) was redundant in light of the existing Art. 133 of the Criminal Code, which penalized publicly "insulting" the Polish Nation. The latter provision focused on the impossibility of distinguishing between the actual truth or falsity of the statements, and instead targeted evaluations only, whereas "slander" levelled at Polish nation would deal with an imputation of facts which could be analysed in terms of their truth or falsity. As such, Art. 132(a) would contravene the constitutionally protected freedom of expression (Art. 54 of the Constitution) and freedom of academic research (Art. 73 of the Constitution). There was a clear danger of a "chilling effect", in that people would abstain from speaking up about the past in public, knowing that their statements could then be subjected to an evaluation of their truth or falsity. In the end, one vision of history would emerge and the public discourse would be centralized around this one-sided narrative of the past.[26]

24 J. T. Gross, *Neighbors: The Destruction of the Jewish Community in Jedwabne*, Poland (Princeton: Princeton University Press, 2001); and J. T. Gross, *FEAR: Anti-Semitism in Poland after Auschwitz, an Essay in Historical Interpretation* (Princeton: Princeton University Press, 2007). These two books have been received with mixed emotions. On the one hand they spawned a collective soul-searching and critical introspection of large segments of Polish society, often unaware of this less glorious part of our past. On the other hand they provoked virulent and intransigent responses from those who have been advocating the "victimhood vision" of Polish history. See the excellent collection of essays and documents compiled in A. Michnik (ed.), *Przeciw antysemityzmowi. 1936–2009*, Vol. III (Universitas, Cracow, 2010) and in particular the part '2001–2004. Wokół zbrodni w Jedwabnem, (On the crime in Jedwabne)', 570–677. For a more revisionist interpretation of Gross's work, see R. Jankowski (ed.), *Cena Strachu. Gross w oczach historyków. Wybór publikacji (The Price of Fear. Gross in the Eyes of Historians. Selected papers)* (Warsaw: Fronda, 2008).

25 A term taken from I. C. Kamiński, 'Kontrowersje prawne wokół przestępstwa polegającego na pomawianiu narodu o popełnienie zbrodni', *Problemy Współczesnego prawa międzynarodowego, Europejskiego i Porównawczego* 8 (2010), 7.

26 Case 5/07, judgment of 19 September 2008. The arguments of the Ombudsman have been reconstructed here on the basis of the judgment's historical part (point 1 of the Court's reasoning).

Even though the Tribunal never dealt with the substance of the application (as it declared the law unconstitutional due to the faulty legislative process used in its passage), the application of Ombudsman provides some pertinent arguments to be taken into account now, in the assessment of the most recent revival of the defamation laws.

2.2 "Polish Death Camps" and (the Missing) Historical Debate. Anticipating the Litigation

"Historical debate" resembles democracy, where all voices are supposed to be heard. As the majority must not oppress the minority, dominant historic narratives cannot exclude minority or less popular views of historical events. Yet the new Polish Law is the most recent proof that in Poland the past continues to be seen as a collection of indisputable truths, not open to divergent interpretations and historical debate. The law under consideration will thus enforce the former while suppressing the latter. The "death camp" blunders and other statements about the past/history of Poland as a nation should be analysed in the context of the more general and well-established principles on the freedom of expression.[27] This is where the

[27] For the sake of completeness, one must bear in mind that even before the new legislation entered into force, Polish courts had already decided three "Polish death camps" cases. With these cases the contours of civil liability began to emerge. In the first case of *Osewski* v. *Die Welt/Axel Springer*, the plaintiff was the grandson of a former prisoner of the Nazi labour camp in Sztum, and himself a former prisoner of the Nazi concentration camp in Deutsch Eylau. The Regional Court in Warsaw dismissed the plaintiff's claims in case in II C 10/11 (judgment of 5 March 2015). On 31 March 2016 the Court of Appeal in Warsaw upheld the first instance judgment (in I ACa 971/15). The second case – *Zapaśnik* v. *Focus Online – Tomorrow/Focus Media GMBH* (I C 726/13) – was decided by the Regional Court in Olsztyn. In this case the plaintiff was a former prisoner of the camp in Lebrechsdorff. In its judgment of 25 February 2015 the plaintiff's claims were rejected. On appeal this judgment was upheld by the Court of Appeal in Białystok in its ruling of 30 September 2015 (case ACa 403/15). Finally, the third case, *Tendera* v. *ZDF*, was heard by the Regional Court in Cracow (IC 151/14) and dismissed on 25 April 2016. On the basis of this case law, we can detect two competing strands in the reasoning of the courts. In the first strand, in order for civil liability to arise there must be a slander directed at an individual addressee. One cannot base an individual claim on the alleged slander of the nation as a whole. While national identity, dignity and pride, and being part of a community are important parts of the consciousness of each human being, nonetheless the expression "Polish death camps" was not aimed at either the plaintiffs or their families. A second strand of reasoning was elaborated on by the Court of Appeal in Warsaw in the *Osewski* case. The Court of Appeal found that it was not necessary that an alleged slander be directed at an individual addressee. The denigration of a community that impacted on the personality of a person strikes at the same time at the dignity of such person. The Court's dismissal of this case was not prompted by the lack of an individual slander, but by the fact that the defendant did everything necessary

new Polish law is at its weakest, as the Polish legislator brushed aside all counter arguments and failed to balance the alleged protection of the good name of Poland against other interests worthy of protection. In particular, freedom of expression is conspicuous by its absence, as the Polish legislator glossed over the necessity to ensure freedom of expression within the context of a historical debate.[28]

Historical debates are no stranger to the docket of the European Court of Human Rights (hereinafter referred to as "the Court"). The Court is well aware of the thin ground it treads upon and the sensitivities involved in its adjudication on historical issues. When faced with interferences with the freedom of expression of authors who make statements dealing with historical occurrences, the Court's method of proceeding can be described as highly contextual and issue specific.[29] What matters is the specificity of

---

to rectify the damage caused by the incriminating statements e.g. by publishing, both online and in paper, an apology and an unequivocal statement that the death camps were constructed and run by Nazi Germany. It is submitted here that the more restrictive first interpretation, which focuses on the individualization of slanderous statements, is more in keeping with other competing interests and the weighing exercise carried out by the Courts (see also the analysis below).

[28] See General Comment no 34 of the Human Rights Committee of the United Nations in Statement no 49 on Art. 19 of the Covenant of Political Rights (adopted during the 102nd Session in Geneva, 11–29 July 2011). Point 49 of the comment reads:

> Laws that penalise the expression of opinions about historical facts are incompatible with the obligations the Covenant imposes on States parties in relation to the respect for freedom of opinion and expression. The Covenant does not permit general prohibition of expression of an erroneous opinion or an incorrect interpretation of past events. Restriction on the right of freedom of opinion should never be imposed and, with regard to freedom of expression, they should not go beyond what is permitted in paragraph 3 or required under art. 20.

Full text available at www2.ohchr.org/english/bodies/hrc/docs/CCPR-C-GC-34.doc.

[29] Over the years the Court's jurisprudence has built up a list of what might be called "background circumstances" – factual elements that play a role in determining whether an interference with given historical statements was "necessary in a democratic society". Such assessments have been extremely contextual and depended on the interplay between the nature and potential effects of such statements and the context in which they were made. Among these circumstances are the manner in which the impugned statements were phrased and the way in which they could be construed. For various constellations and applications, see ECtHR, *Lehideux and Isorni* v. *France* (Appl. No. 24662/94) Judgment (Grand Chamber), 23 September 1998 (para 53); ECtHR *Stankov and the United Macedonian Organisation Ilinden* (Appl. Nos. 29221/95 and 29225/95), Judgment, 2 October 2001 (paras 102, 106); ECtHR, *Radio France and Others* (Appl. No. 53984), Judgment, 30 March 2004 (para 38); ECtHR *Orban and Others* v. *France* (Appl. No. 20985/05), Judgment 15 January 2009 (paras 46, 49, and 51). Also relevant are specific interests or rights affected by the statements. *Stankov and the United Macedonian Organisation Ilinden* involved the national

the past events, with established facts justifying more a robust control over the statements, whereas facts that are still debated may be subjected to an in-depth and critical analysis, which can stir up controversy, in order to move the discussion on the still-debated issues forward. It is essential in democratic societies to ensure that debates surrounding historical events of a particularly serious nature should be able to take place freely. Crucially, seeking historical truth is an integral part of freedom of expression, and the Court's role is not to arbitrate the underlying historical issues, which are part of a continuing debate between historians, a debate which shapes opinion concerning the events which took place and their interpretation. When the issue does not belong to the category of "clearly established historical facts", it must be open to consideration from all possible angles and perspectives. However, the Court must balance the public interest in being informed of historical events that continue to stir up controversy against the need to protect the reputation of those who might be impugned by the statements.

In exercising its supervisory jurisdiction, the Court must look at the alleged interference in light of the case as a whole, including the content of the remarks directed against the applicants and the context in which they were made. In particular, it must determine whether the interference in issue was "proportionate to the legitimate aims pursued", and whether the reasons adduced by the national authorities to justify its sanctions are "relevant and sufficient". In so doing, the Court has to satisfy itself that the national authorities applied standards which were in conformity with the principles embodied in Art. 10 and, moreover, that they based their decisions on an acceptable assessment of the relevant facts. In addition, in the exercise of its European supervisory jurisdiction, the Court must verify whether the authorities struck a fair balance when protecting two values guaranteed by the Convention, which may come into conflict with

symbols of Bulgarians. What was at stake in *Radio France and Others* (paras 31, 34–9) and ECtHR *Chauvy and Others* (Appl. No. 64915) Judgment, 29 June 2004 (paras 52, 69) were the reputations of living persons affected by serious accusations of wrongdoing contained in the contested statements. In *Monnat* (see *infra* note 31, para 60), the statements had been directed against the leaders of the country during the Second World War. In ECtHR *Association of Citizens Radko and Paunkovski* v. *the former Yugoslav Republic of Macedonia* (Appl. No. 74651/01) Judgment, 15 January 2009 (paras 69, 74) the statements had affected the national and ethnic identity of all Macedonians. The Court's case law takes also into account statements' impact by taking into account the manner in which they were disseminated and the possible influence they might have on their addresses, and finally the lapse of time between the statements and the historical events to which they refer.

each other in this type of case; namely the freedom of expression protected by Art. 10 on the one hand, and the right of those persons attacked by a book or statements to protect their reputation, a right which is protected by Art. 8 of the Convention as part of the "right to respect for private life".[30]

In *Monnat* v. *Switzerland*[31] the Court was faced with the issue of the role played by Switzerland in the Second World War. The Court shied away from settling the issues of historical significance. Rather it set the parameters for its weighing exercise and defined its task as considering whether the measures taken were proportionate to the aim pursued. In doing so, the Court formulated three interrelated principles that run through its case law. *First*, the search for historical truth forms an integral part of freedom of expression. *Second*, each case is to be seen in its own context. *Third*, statements that form part of an ongoing debate among historians and/or public debate are often far from settled. When such debate raises or touches upon a matter of extremely serious public concern, it falls within the duty of the media to broadcast information about it. Public debate about a country's history is a matter of extremely serious public concern, and in a democratic state the media has a special role to play in this regard. Such a qualification automatically, under Art. 10(2) of the Convention, limits the scope of restrictions and sanctions member states may impose. In such circumstances the authorities have only a limited margin of appreciation to make a determination that there exists a "pressing social need" to take the measures in question against an applicant. The Court's scrutiny must be most thorough when the measure or sanctions imposed by the national authorities are capable of discouraging the participation of the media in debates over matters of legitimate public concern (e.g. a country's history).

In terms of contextualizing the Polish amendments, the above leads to the conclusion that any public debate over a country's history must be as open and accessible as possible. The interest of the public in the matters

[30] In *Orban*, *supra* note 29, the Court also observed that although the author's statements had not lost their capacity to bring back memories of past suffering, owing to the lapse of time it was not appropriate to judge them with the same degree of severity that might have been justified ten or twenty years earlier. In that connection the Court reiterated that freedom of expression within the meaning of Art. 10 protected not only "information" or "ideas" regarded as inoffensive or as a matter of indifference, but also that which offended, shocked, or disturbed. Accordingly, penalizing a publisher for having assisted in the dissemination of a witness account written by a third party concerning events which formed part of a country's history would seriously hamper contributions to the discussion of matters of public interest, and should not be envisaged without particularly good reason.

[31] ECtHR *Monnat* v. *Switzerland* (Appl. No. 73604/01), Judgment, 21 September 2006.

discussed, and the polarization of public opinion stemming from a lack of agreement over past events, are important factors to be taken into account when assessing whether there is a "pressing social need" for the legislator to take measures interfering with the freedom of expression. As a rule, these factors will strongly favour the uninhibited exchange of ideas and expression of points of view, even those most controversial and sometimes offensive. Historical debate, in a sphere in which it is unlikely that any certainty exists and which is still debated and explored, demands that the exercise of the freedom of expression will cover not only information or ideas that are favourably received or regarded as inoffensive, but also those that offend, shock, or disturb.[32] These statements go hand in hand with the established *dicta* that freedom of expression in matters of public interest is in principle entitled to strong protection, whereas expression that promotes or justifies violence, hatred, xenophobia, or another forms of intolerance cannot normally claim such protection. Statements on historical issues, whether made at public rallies or in media such as books, newspapers, or radio and television programmes, are as a rule seen as touching upon matters of public interest.[33] The right to take part in what the Court calls "a long-standing controversy" relating to an issue of public concern, or a "heated debate", must shield those participating from any too easy interference on the part of the state authorities, so long as the debate does not cross the line and turn into a call for violence, hatred, or intolerance. In addition, while controversial remarks about traumatic historical events are always likely to reopen the controversy and bring back memories of past sufferings, a lapse of time of some forty years or more makes it inappropriate to deal with them with the same severity as events which took place ten or twenty years earlier.[34]

[32] In ECtHR *Cox* v. *Turkey* (Appl. No. 2933/03), Judgment, 20 May 2010 the Court emphasized that the alleged incriminating statements concerned the Kurdish and Armenian questions, which were still the subject of *heated debate, not only within Turkey but also in the international arena, with all those involved voicing their views and counter-views*. It acknowledged that *opinions expressed on these issues by one side could sometime offend the other side*, but stressed that *a democratic society require[d] tolerance and broadmindedness in the face of controversial expressions* (para 42).

[33] For example in *Stankov, supra* note 29 (paras 79, 85, and 97), it was held that freedom of assembly and the right to express one's views through it are among the paramount values of a democratic society. The essence of democracy is its capacity to resolve problems through open debate.

[34] *Lehideux and Isorni* v. *France, supra* note 29 para 55. In the leading case of ECtHR *Perinçek* v. *Switzerland* (Appl. No. 27510/08, Judgment (Grand Chamber), 15 October 2015, the Court qualified this by adding: "Whereas events of relatively recent vintage may be so traumatic as to warrant, for a period of time, an enhanced degree of regulation of statements relating to them, the need for such regulation is bound to recede with the passage

Importantly the case law proceeds from the special importance attached to freedom of expression. Statements that contest, even in virulent terms, the significance of historical events that carry a special sensitivity for a country and touch on its national identity cannot, in and of themselves, be regarded as seriously affecting their addressees. At the same time, in *Perincek* the Court was not ready to exclude that there might exist circumstances in which, in view of the particular context, statements relating to traumatic historical events could result in significant damage to the dignity of groups affected by such events; for instance if they are particularly virulent and disseminated in a form that is impossible to ignore. In order to justify the interference with such speech on the grounds of public security and public order, the state would have to prove that an element of incitement to violence goes along with the speech. In order to justify an interference with free speech on the grounds of protection of others, the state would have to show that the speech interferes with the right of an individual group within a large community, or with the cohesion of an entire ethnic group. In the former case, special sensitivities of an identified group of people would have to be come into play, and in the latter scenario this extra sensitivity and need for extra protection would have to be extended to the entire nation (ethnic group). The latter requirement will be extremely difficult to prove as it would encompass an assumption that all people in the group share the same understanding of their history or its selected aspects. Importantly, in anticipating the possible future challenges to the Polish law before the Court, it is safe to assume that the Court would not look at the nation and the State as a "third person" to be protected. At most, the Court would be willing to look at the interference as aimed at protecting rights (dignity etc.) of individuals (citizens) as members of the nation. The term "another person" was understood as covering individuals claiming to be victims. These individuals make up the "sensitive group" that merits protection against the statements as their specific right.[35] The necessity for

---

of time" (para 250). For more on *Perinçek*, see U. Belavusau, *Perinçek* v. *Switzerland: Between Freedom of Speech and Collective Dignity*, available at http://verfassungsblog.de/switzerland-between-freedom-of-speech-and-collective-dignity/.

[35] In *Perincek* case, *supra* note 34, the Court accepted the possibility of protecting the rights of others as a justification for interference and spoke of "the ethnic group's sense of identity and its members' feelings of self-worth and self-confidence" (para 200) as worthy of the protection, as follows: "With regard to this legitimate aim, a distinction needs to be drawn between, on the one hand, the dignity of the deceased and surviving victims of the events of 1915 and the following years and, on the other, the dignity, including the identity, of present-day Armenians as their descendants" (para 155); further identifying "the rights of

interference in a democratic society would thus be balanced against the sensibilities of a group or a specific right. Poland, or the "Polish nation in its entirety" would not be treated as a third person whose rights merit protection.[36] Rather, the rights of individuals (living, or their ancestors) in their individual capacities would need to be claimed to be the victim of the violation of the Convention. In the Polish case the situation is different though, as some Polish courts tend to accept the protection of the good name of the "People" in the abstract, which strengthens the narrative that our whole identity should be built around a one-dimensional axis of victimhood and suffering.

Armenians to respect for their and their ancestors' dignity, including their right to respect for their identity constructed around the understanding that their community has suffered genocide" (para 227). In light of the case-law, the Court accepted that both ethnic identity and the reputation of ancestors may engage Art. 8 of the Convention under its "private life" heading (para 227). A similar approach was adopted in *Monnat* v. *Switzerland* (*supra* note 31, 21 September 2006). In ECtHR *Putistin* v. *Ukraine* (Appl. No. 16882/03) Judgment, 21 November 2013 (paras 33, 36–41), it was accepted that the reputation of an ancestor could in some circumstances affect a person's "private life" and identity, and thus come within the scope of Art. 8 § 1 of the Convention. In ECtHR *Jelevar and Others* v. *Slovenia* (Appl. No. 47318/07), Inadmissibility Decision 11 March 2014 (para 37), the Court likewise accepted that an attack on the reputation of an ancestor, in the form of a work of literary fiction, could affect a person's rights under Art. 8 § 1 of the Convention.

[36] Case law intimates that those rights that might be used as a counterbalance to freedom of speech would be, first, rights to privacy and dignity (individual); and, second, the right to impart true and objective information. In the former case applicants could claim that the unfettered speech violates their (or their ancestors') rights, whereas in the latter the applicants would rather claim that Poles have a right to be informed, as freely and as broadly as possible, of their collective past, and any restrictions on such information violate this right. It seems that the latter case is the only one in which the Court would be ready to look at the population as a whole and accept that the "communal" right to impart objective information is to be protected (in this vein, see also *Association of Citizens Radko and Paunkovski* v. *the former Yugoslav Republic of Macedonia*). This aspect will likely feature prominently in any future litigation and the argument would be that Polish people have a right to know about their history, good and bad, and that the penalization of reporting on crimes committed by individuals and suggestion that they amount to crimes committed by the Polish Nation, thus defaming its good name, would not survive the Court's scrutiny under the Convention. This is where the breathtaking scope of the new legislation comes into play and becomes problematic. For a comprehensive critical analysis, see I. C. Kamiński, *Projekt nowelizacji ustawy o Instytucie Pamięci Narodowej – Komisji Ścigania Zbrodni przeciwko Narodowi Polskiemu. Ocena w świetle Europejskiej Konwencji o Ochronie Praw Człowieka oraz Konstytucji Rzeczyspopolitej Polskiej* (*Draft Law on the Polish Institute of National Remembrance – Commission for the Prosecution of Crimes against the Polish Nation. Appraisal in the Light of the European Convention of Human Rights and the Constitution of the Republic of Poland)* (unpublished legal opinion commissioned by the Polish Ombudsman, on file with the Author).

One must not forget that the Polish legislator used the term "good name of Poland and the Polish people" in the abstract. There is thus the inherent danger that our entire identity is to be built around victimhood and underpinned by an imposed historical narrative.[37] The new legislation is a two-edged sword. On the one hand, it puts forward a dominant narrative and picks from the past only those pieces that fit within the overarching orthodoxy. On the other hand, it closes off a wider historical debate and penalizes those who are not willing to fall in line. The case law of the Court demonstrates that in historical debates what is truly important is not *who* speaks but *about* what and *how*. The subject matter takes centre stage, and only in the second step of the analysis do we locate the words within a person. It is not a question of protection, but rather the standards expected of a person (politician, historian, layman). Only an intent to deny uncontested past events might justify such interference and the imposition of a deprivation of one's liberty. Lacking this subjective element, all interference (*a fortiori* pecuniary sanctions) would be held to be disproportionate, as was the case in *Perincek*. As the term "Polish death camps" belong to a category of speech that has general significance, any restrictions would have to pass the most severe tests of justification. Nobody in their right mind would deny that "Polish death camps" is indeed misleading and has thus far met with strong and decisive condemnation by Polish authorities, as well as contrite rectification by those behind the faulty statements. The question here is whether the criminal law framework the most adequate for addressing this kind of statement? Within the criminal law framework, the speaker's state of the mind and intentions would have to be the most important factor taken into account. The boundary between negative and ill-thought-out statements on the one hand and incurring criminal responsibility on the other must be demarcated clearly and the latter requires a high standard of proof. Otherwise the balancing between what

[37] The new law aims to make sure that this "belonging to the community" is not tainted by any wrongdoing. However, it is not a plaintiff who is to decide this, but historians. The plaintiff can only make sure that his/her good name is protected and should be freed from any doubts and accusations. His/her subjective claim of being hurt by the statements must be proven based on the facts of each case. There must be no presumption that his/her feelings extend to the nation as such. Plaintiffs cannot, guided by their own feelings of anger and indignation, sue on behalf of all Poles. National history is not only about moments of glory and success, but also includes dark moments, which should be studied, researched, and commented upon with the same scientific rigour. Making a link between the good name of the plaintiff and the nation as such, and translating the "goodness" of particular plaintiffs into the lack of faultiness of a nation, is crossing one bridge too many.

is permissible and free of penal sanction, and what is impermissible and subject to criminal sanction, will be blurred. The question of culpability is thus of central importance.[38] How to show and prove the intention to commit a crime, and distinguish that from those acting negligently? In most cases, the authors of the statements "Polish death camps" did not mean (intend) to falsify Polish history by imputing Polish participation in Nazi-committed atrocities. Yet, under the new law they would be all criminally responsible for their negligent actions.[39] In such a case, freedom of expression would figure prominently and be an overriding consideration. Even in cases of intentional fault, Poland still cannot *automatically* impose punishment. In order to justify prosecution for a knowingly false usage of the term "Polish death camps", Poland would have to still have to show that the statement, as an act, contained some extra subjective element, such as incitement to violence and/or hate speech. It would appear that a criminal conviction for a knowingly false usage of the term "Polish death camps" could be justified only in extreme cases of abusive speech clearly aimed at denigrating the Polish nation or Poles. The threshold to prove that this is indeed the case would be very high.

The expression "Polish death camps" is, however, but one example of the types of cases that might fall within the provisions of the new law. Its scope is much more encompassing, as the "good name of the Republic (Rzeczpospolita)" and "Polish nation" will cover an infinite number of statements that the majority, at any given time, may disapprove of as not "Polish enough". We are in for a historical roller coaster ride and top-down projection of the past and history. The way we understand our past will be left to the whimsical visions of history professed by those in power at any given time, and to the discretion and common sense of public prosecutors. To deploy criminal law, though, to enforce one's vision of the past marks the point at which things get dangerous.

Applying all the above in the context of the "Polish death camps" controversy, these inaccurate statements were made within the context of a debate on the Second World War and as such dealt with issues of public concern and interest. As a result any interference with that kind of speech would

[38] Let us also not forget about the stratification of penalties, which seems to be haphazard. Art. 55a of the Law on IPN (imputing blame) entails a higher sanction than that provided for in Art. 55 IPN (for denial and slandering) or in Art. 133 of the Criminal Code.

[39] The new Law would also capture the words of President B. Obama (!), who in a 2012 used the phrase "Polish death camps" in a speech honouring a Polish war hero; 'White House: Obama misspoke by referring to "Polish death camp" while honoring Polish war hero', *The Washington Post*, 29 May 2012.

be rigorously scrutinized, with the Council of Europe member states enjoying only a limited margin of appreciation. The intent of the person who made such a statement would take centre stage. With respect to the use of the term "Polish death camps", statements were often made out of ignorance or with reference to the territory ("Polish" meaning the camps were built on the territory of Poland). The objective was not to falsify history by imputing responsibility for building and managing concentration camps (i.e. committing atrocities) to the Poles. In other words there was no intent to impugn Poland. Even in the rare instances where such an intent could be found to have existed, the proportionality test would still have a role to play. Given the importance of speech of this kind, criminal liability would be acceptable only in the most extreme cases of a speech inciting to crime, or hate speech. Statements on the "Polish death camps" would have to be accompanied by such "circumstances surrounding the background", and as the *Perinçek* case shows, go beyond statements that are virulent and intransigent.

The Polish law is most controversial – and at its weakest – on the necessity requirements, which would overlap with the rights/interests protected. The Polish case is special because it provides not only for civil liability for infringing the good name of the Republic and of the Polish Nation, but also for criminal responsibility. Protecting the good name of the State and/or Nation is deemed more important than a robust, comprehensive, and inclusive discussion about the nation's past – a discussion that tolerates statements, often shocking and controversial, as long as they add to the ongoing debate of public importance and attract general attention. Historical discourse belongs *ex definitione* to this category. Abusing the legislative process to promote one's vision of the past by silencing all voices of critique, dissent, or even simply doubt, thus becomes a real danger and opens up a space for manipulating facts and past events. In the end, we end up with a flattened and one-sided account of what happened, why, how, and even when.

3 "Seeing the Past in Truth" – A Polish Dream, Myth, or Forlorn Hope?

Controversial aspects of a nation's history must be brought to the fore and discussed openly and dispassionately.[40] The creation of controversy and reopening of the historical debate to probe less-known aspects of our

[40] ECtHR, *Éditions Plon v. France* (Appl. No. 58148/00), Judgment, 18 May 2004 (para 53).

history should form an important part of our common efforts to unearth what lies behind us and what is in front of us. *Seeking* historical truth does not equate to *finding* it. Sometimes the process itself is gratifying, even if a final result is unattainable. This is the price for maintaining an "overlapping consensus" and living in a divided society with competing visions and understanding of our history (some more or less plausible). Every voice is important as long as it adds to the ongoing debate. Nobody should be excluded, much less penalized, for taking part in the exchange and professing his or her own visions of history, which may go against the mainstream (and often momentary) narrative, which has more to do with politics than seeking out historical truth. Imposing sanctions for statements that go against the grain of the mainstream understanding of "what happened" would clearly inhibit the free flow of views and lead to a "one and only" vision of the past. The debate will be flattened and ultimately stifled, as prospective participants who hold different views will be discouraged – and even excluded – from joining the debate. The media will think twice before stirring up a new controversy that would justify interest on the part of the public. Public discussion will suffer as a result. It will become predictable and one-sided, always sitting well within the expectations of the regime and its historical policy.

In trying to understand the current Polish way of historical remembering – or rather our national "mis-memory" – the analysis of T. Judt can be very helpful and instructive.[41] He argues that two kinds of memories emerged from what he calls the "official version of the wartime experience" which became dominant in Europe by 1948. One was that of the things done to "us" by Germans during the war, and the other that of things (however similar) done by "us" to "others" after the war. This created

> Two moral vocabularies, two sorts of reasoning, two different pasts. In this circumstance, the uncomfortably confusing recollection of things dome by us to others *during* the war . . . got conveniently lost. If Germans were guilty, then "we" were innocent. If guilt consisted of being German or working for the Germans and their interests – and it could hardly be denied that in every occupied country such persons had been present and prominent – then innocence had to mean taking an anti-German stance, not only after 1945 but also before. Thus to be innocent a nation had to have resisted, and to have done so in its overwhelming majority, a claim that was perforce

[41] See his brilliant analysis in 'The past is another country: myth and memory in post-war Europe', in J. Werner Müller (ed.), *Memory and Power in Post-War Europe: Studies in the Presence of the Past* (Cambridge University Press, 2002), 157–83. This book is a state-of-the-art statement on what it takes to remember honestly.

> made and pedagogically enforced all over Europe, from Italy to Poland, from the Netherlands to Romania (italics in the original).[42]

This one-sided reading of the past pervaded public consciousness for years to come and created a voluntary and comforting collective amnesia driven by fundamental myths. Crucially, it has built post-war national mythology around "examples and stories which were repeated and magnified, *ad nausea*, in novels, popular histories, radio, newspapers, and especially cinema". Importantly for my analysis, this mythology took on special importance and rationale in the eastern part of Europe. T. Judt rightly points out the communists' interest in

> flattering the recalcitrant local population by inviting it to believe the fabrication now deployed on its behalf by the USSR – to wit, that central and eastern Europe was an innocent victim of German assault, had played no part in its own downfall or in the crimes perpetrated on its territory, and was a full partner in the work of liberation led by Soviet soldiers abroad and communist partisans at home.

The above argument shows that when it comes to Eastern Europe, and Poland in particular, the past is indeed, and continues to be, a "foreign country".[43] Again, as Judt argues

> If the problem in Western Europe has been a shortage of memory, in the other half of the continent the problem is reversed. Here there is too much memory, too many pasts on which people can draw, usually as a weapon against the past of someone else. Whereas the Western European dilemma was confined to a single set of unhappy memories located in the occupation years 1940–44/45, the East Europeans have multiple analogous reference points: 1918–21, 1938, 1939, 1941, 1944, 1945–48, 1956, 1968 and now 1989. For Eastern Europeans the past is not just "another country" but a positive archipelago of vulnerable historical territories, to be preserved from attacks and distortions perpetrated by the occupants of a neighbouring island of memory. It is a dilemma made more cruel by the fact that the enemy is almost always within: most of these dates refer to a moment at which one part of the community (defined by class, religion, or nationality) took advantage of the misfortunes of another to help itself to land, property or power.[44]

At this moment Poland and the Poles find themselves at a critical juncture; stuck between old myths and the narratives of "what happened" on the one hand, and the rejection of any attempts to finally discover the

[42] T. Judt, *supra* note 41, 163.
[43] D. Lowenthal, *The Past is a Foreign Country* (Cambridge University Press, 1985).
[44] T. Judt, *supra*, note 41, 172.

multi-dimensional pasts that Poles are heirs to, and must own up to on the other. With the new legislation, the signal has been sent that the history lessons[45] are far from being internalized. Quite on the contrary, history and the past is instrumentalized to serve the new political masters' vision of the past. Although made with regard to the files of the secret police in Eastern and Central Europe, T. G. Ash's argument in favour of the usefulness of these files in writing reliable history comes to mind here. He argues that *[T]he evidence has to be weighed with very special care. The text must put in the historical context. Interpretation needs both intellectual distance and the essential imaginative sympathy with all the men and women involved, even the oppressors. But with these familiar disciplines, there is a truth that can be found. Not a single, absolute Truth with a capital T, but still a real and important one.*[46] The same admonition applies to confronting one's past and building a memory that would capture the entirety of the historical baggage. Only then will Poles be able to remember honestly and move forward. By revealing the past, we discover the present, and most importantly, build for the future in keeping with the constitutional fidelity that binds us across generations.[47] *We turn to the past not because the past contains within it all of the answers to our questions, but because it is the repository of our common struggles and common commitments; it offers us invaluable*

[45] I use the term after T. G. Ash, 'Trials, Purges and History Lessons: Treating a Difficult Past in Post-communist Europe', in J. Werner Müller (ed.), *Memory and Power in Post-War Europe: Studies in the Presence of the Past* (Cambridge University Press, 2002), 265–82.

[46] T. G. Ash, *supra* note 45, 282.

[47] I draw here on the understanding of constitutional fidelity adopted by J. Balkin in 'Agreements with Hell and Other Objects of Our Faith', *Fordham Law Review* 65 (1997), 1703. As he eloquently wrote:

> Fidelity is not simply a matter of correspondence between an idea and a text, or a set of correct procedures for interpretation. It is not simply a matter of proper translation or proper synthesis or even proper political philosophy. Fidelity is not a relationship between a thing and an interpretation of that thing. Fidelity is not about texts; it is about selves. Fidelity is an orientation of a self towards something else, a relationship which is mediated through and often disguised by talk of texts, translations, correspondences and political philosophy. Fidelity is an attitude that we have towards something we attempt to understand; it is a discipline of self that is related to the discipline of a larger set of selves in a society. Fidelity is ontological and existential; it shapes us, affects us, has power over us, ennobles us, enslaves us. Fidelity is a form of power exercised over the self by the self and by the social forces that help make the self what it is. As such, fidelity is an equivocal concept, full of both good and bad, mixed inextricably together. Fidelity is the home of commitment, sacrifice, self-identification and patriotism, as well as the home of legitimation, servitude, self-deception and idolatry.

resources as we debate the most important questions of political life, which cannot fully and finally be settled.[48] Each generation should build on the best of the past and move forward with the baggage. After all, this is exactly what the Preamble to the Polish Constitution mandates. This is the kind of fidelity I am talking about, and the one that should inform our understanding of our history and the past[49] and shed critical light on the attempt to punish dissenters from the mainstream historical narrative of the day.

Given the potential breadth and severity of the Polish legislation, it stands out among legislation that criminalizes denigrating, defaming, or otherwise slandering a nation or/and people.[50] This legislation would come under scrutiny from the perspective of competing interests. Not only is the law a symbolic fig leaf devoid of any practical relevance (in most cases where such statements have been made, rectifications and official apologies were worked out through the diplomatic process and were enough to ensure that corrections were made and steps taken to prevent a repetition). The new law politicizes historical discussion and instrumentalizes law to achieve the desired reading of history and the past.[51] It crosses the line between embarrassing, yet innocuous headlines (see above) on the one hand, and dangerous resort to criminal sanctions to impose one correct vision of "what" happened and "how" on the other. Stirring up historical resentments by magnifying a glorious past as part of the "politics of memory" is one thing; threatening dissenters with criminal sanctions and jail terms for naysayers is quite another.[52] The latter takes us from the politics

[48] J. M. Balkin and R. B. Siegel, Introduction, in J. M. Balkin and R. B. Siegel (eds.), *The Constitution in 2020* (Oxford University Press, 2009), 4.

[49] *We, the Polish Nation – all citizens of the Republic . . . , Obliged to bequeath to future generations all that is valuable from our over one thousand years' heritage*

[50] For an in-depth analysis, see I. Kamiński, 'Kontrowersje prawne wokół przestępstwa polegającego na pomawianiu narodu o popełnienie zbrodni', 5–34.

[51] Instrumentalization and manipulation of the law to achieve particular objectives *contra legem* are omnipresent in the daily practice of governance a la PiS. Historical discourse aimed at abolishing the mainstream understanding of the past is only the latest victim of this more general process. See, in general, my op-ed 'Manipulacja nad Wisłą' (*Manipulation on the Vistula River*), *Gazeta Wyborcza* 30 November 2015 available at www.wyborcza.pl/1,75968,19266446,manipulacja-nad-wisla.html.

[52] As rightly put by A. Gliszczyńska-Grabias: "a dialogue about history carried out solely with the use of legal sanctions can significantly erode the space and opportunity for conflict resolution. A serious risk exists that the legal path to enforcement will exacerbate antagonisms and sometimes provoke outright hostility concerning inherently different perspectives of historical events". A. Gliszczyńska-Grabias, 'Memory Laws or Memory Loss? Europe in Search of Its Historical Identity Through National and International Law', *Polish Yearbook of International Law* XXXIV (2014), 155.

of memory to the politics of mis-memory, backed by the powerful arm of the state. Such a shift dramatically changes the basic rules of the game on the ground. In opining on the new anti-defamation law, W. Sadurski has convincingly exposed the shortcomings of the new law and its true motives. He argued that the phrase "Polish death camps" does not equal a denial of the Holocaust, as the authors of the Law claim to be the case. There is a fundamental difference between denying the Holocaust on the one hand,[53] and assigning the blame for certain facts to a state other than the one responsible for these facts. The objective of the new legislation is not really to punish anyone for "Polish death camps" (which is unattainable in both law and fact) but "rather for the government to demonstrate its patriotic zealousness and outbidding its political rivals".[54] This symbolism, though, will have real-life consequences that will be felt not by foreigners, but by people (journalists for example) on the ground in Poland who dare to question the official historic orthodoxy.

One final caveat is in order here. My analysis is not intended to belittle, nor question, the sufferings of the Polish people and the heroism of Polish Righteous among the nations of the World,[55] nor Poland's resistance in the face of the atrocities of Nazi occupation. Its unimaginable destruction of life – physical, spiritual, and cultural – would have been more than enough to wipe out entire nations less strong than the Poles. Nobody denies that. We survived because history was always a repository on which to build a new order. We relied on our accumulated constitutional fidelity and moved forward.

Rather my argument is in favour of an inclusive historical memory that is in line with that constitutional fidelity that brings together all national experiences and narratives. Fidelity is an uneasy task of reaching pacts between the past, present, and future. Such "pacting" moves away from "a historiography obsessed with minutiae and overgrown with easy

[53] On the theoretical and practical aspects of the prohibition of Holocaust denial, see the excellent analysis by L. Pech, 'The Law of Holocaust Denial in Europe. Toward a (qualified) EU-wide Criminal Prohibition', in L. Hennebel and T. Hochman (eds.), *Genocide Denials and the Law* (Oxford University Press, 2011), 185–234. See also the expert analysis, with further references, by Gliszczyńska-Grabias, *supra* note 52, 165–8, and in particular 168–71 (holocaust denial).

[54] W. Sadurski, 'Zła obrona dobrego imienia' (Misguided protection of a good name), *Gazeta Wyborcza* 5 September 2016, available at www.wyborcza.pl/1,75968,20644398,zla-obrona-dobrego-imienia.html.

[55] See T. T. Koncewicz, 'The Great YES and My Grandmother's Legacy', *Gazeta of Taube Philanthrophies* 23:2 (2016), 4–8.

assumptions about martyrology".[56] We must never forget that our history is rich and saved us in the past precisely because we remembered both the good and the bad about it. Glory aside, there is another side of our Polish story, less documented and heroic, but just as important for our collective well-being and coming to terms of who "We" are as a nation. This side is crying out for thoughtful, critical, and honest research. Facing this other part of our history is as important as glorifying our most memorable moments. J. Waldron is correct that "[o]nly the deliberate enterprise of recollection (the enterprise we call 'history'), coupled with the most determined sense that there is a difference between what happened and what we would like to think happened, can sustain the moral and cultural reality of self and community".[57] A nation that is not ready to embark on a comprehensive journey into its past is impoverished and unable to move forward with true confidence and understanding of who "We" really are. When grand gestures dominate, and less spectacular soul-searching is lacking, nations become captives of the past rather than its masters. Such nations always expect to be takers because of the injustices suffered in the past, and never givers and builders of something new and good. It is here that Polish debate over "What really happened?" must be ongoing, and is far from over. As such it must be subject to the most critical and demanding inquiry and critical exchanges.

The "politics of resentment" and exclusion of competing visions of our collective past questions Poland's overlapping consensus, which requires agreement on fundamental commitments of principle.[58] It is these essentials that I require others to respect, as the condition of my own deference to the decisions of others. Persistent differences between citizens living together in a constitutional regime create disagreements over the final shape of these constitutional essentials. At the same time, they must agree that these disagreements will be ironed out and spelt out within the discursive framework. Importantly, a European overlapping consensus never rested on a pre-agreed single doctrine of human dignity, individuality, nor even democracy. The European overlapping consensus has at its heart constitutional tolerance and agreement on fundamental commitments

[56] J. Connelly, 'Why the Poles Collaborated so Little: And Why That is No Reason for Nationalist Hubris', *Slavic Review* 64:4 (2005), 771–81 (with further references).

[57] J. Waldron, 'Superseding Historic Justice', *Ethics* 10:4 (1992), 6.

[58] I draw here on the influential work of J. Rawls, *Theory of Justice* (Harvard University Press, 1971); J. Rawls, 'The Idea of an Overlapping Consensus', *Oxford Journal of Legal Studies* 7:1 (1987); J. Rawls, *Political Liberalism* (Columbia University Press, 1993).

of principle; essentials which we require others to respect. As powerfully argued by J. H. H. Weiler in the context of European integration: *[I]t is a remarkable instance of constitutional tolerance to accept to be bound by a decision not by "my people", but by a majority among peoples which are precisely not mine – a people, if you wish, of "others". I compromise my self determination in this fashion as an expression of this kind of internal-towards myself and external-towards others tolerance.*[59] The "politics of resentment" calls into question this narrative by putting forward a competing one, that of fundamental disagreements over values[60] unless "true Poles" will be finally allowed to remedy the deficiencies of today's Poland and exclude all those who don't fall in line with the new historic orthodoxy. Overlapping consensus relies on the acknowledgment by the members of multiple societies of their persistent differences in understanding and agreeing to respect the essentials that bind them together, while at the same time honouring the influence of others on the interpretation of shared commitments. Today's Poland, engulfed by the "politics of resentment", urgently needs a discursive framework for articulating and accommodating the practical meaning of its overlapping consensus and debating its multi-dimensional past. My argument is that such a framework should be centred around basic challenges, which could be presented here as a combination of the *past*, *present*, and *the future*. The politics of resentment challenges us to revisit forgotten and/or under-researched narratives of our national history (the dimension of the PAST), rethinking our place and vocation today (the dimension of the PRESENT) and finally, opening up to, and embracing, new vistas (the dimension of the FUTURE). A resentment-driven reading of history undermines the founding narrative of "living together" and "*never again* constitutionalism" that animated Europe's Founding Fathers. As we try to move forward, the mis-memory in Poland poses the most dramatic, and once unthinkable, questions: Are "We, the Polish people" ready to continue

[59] J. H.H. Weiler, 'On the Power of the Word: Europe's Constitutional Iconography', *International Journal of Constitutional Law* 3:173 (2005), 188. For the application of overalapping consensus framework to the European pluralistic legal landscape see also interesting analysis by Ch. F. Sabel and O. Gerstenberg, Constitutionalising an Overlapping Consensus: The ECJ and the Emergence of a Coordinate Constitutional Order, *European Law Journal* 16:5 (2010).

[60] Interestingly, the crisis of the Polish overlapping consensus is reflected also on the European level, in the case law of the European Court of Justice. Recently the Court was ready to concede that member states' mutual trust in their legal systems is a rebuttable presumption, a concession that would have been unthinkable twenty years ago. See joined cases C – 411&493/10, *N.S.* (judgment of 21 December 2011, available at www.curia.europa.eu).

living together in a constitutional regime, internally divergent, and always ready to respond to the exigencies and demands of new realities? Are we ready to debate our history in a way that presupposes the confrontation of divergent points of view?[61] The challenge behind these questions has been eloquently summarized by *J. Tully's* "canoe metaphor": *Perhaps the great constitutional struggles and failures around the world today are groping towards the third way of constitutional change, symbolized by the ability of the members of the canoe to discuss and reform their constitutional arrangements in response to the demands for recognition as they paddle. A constitution can be both the foundation of democracy and, at the same time, subject to democratic discussion and change in practice.*[62] The politics of resentment and the creeping mis-memory show that overlapping consensus and tolerance is ceasing to be the dominant narrative. Instead, the "politics of resentment" and "memory capture" push Poland towards a standstill and an identity crisis. With the "politics of resentment" and the exclusion of *the Other*, and with "memory capture" elevated to the status of a new mode of governance, the challenge of *paddling together* has never been more acute. As a result of all this, in the Polish context grappling with the past remains a dream, a myth, and a forlorn hope, all at one and the same time. At least in this historical register, the winds of change have not yet started blowing in Poland. The attempts to legalize and prioritize one historical narrative contribute to the imbalance of memory: our sufferings and the crimes committed against us are internalized by Poles, while at the same time crimes committed by us against others are pushed away and a curtain of silence is brought down on this subject. With the criminalization of those who dare to put forward another narrative and/or search for answers to questions not asked, this imbalance will only grow stronger and public consciousness will be fed by a one-way vision of our history. Poles do not need the EU to tell them something is gravely wrong with today's regime and the policies it is imposing on the public: they can look into their own past and find that checks and balances, limited government, as well as the virtues of coming together and working for the common good – Poland – were all enshrined in a document ratified at Warsaw's Royal Castle on 3 May 1791,

[61] This is indeed a crucial question. As Waldron argues: "Each person establishes a sense of herself in terms of her ability to identify the subject or agency of her present thinking with that of certain acts and events that took place in the past, and in terms of her ability to hold fast to a distinction between memory so understood and wishes, fantasies, or various other ideas of things that might have happened but did not." J. Waldron, *supra* note 57, at 6.

[62] J. Tully, *Strange Multiplicity: Constitutionalism in an Age of Diversity* (Cambridge University Press, 1995), 29.

and animated the May Constitution's Founding Fathers in the true spirit of constitutional fidelity that helps build bridges that span generations, and shuns divisions.

This tradition of diversification and openness must now incline us to, using Andrzej Wajda's words, *communal action and true patriotic sentiments*, while rejecting *sterile and inert emotions and cheap feelings that serve as a smokescreen for self-satisfaction, arrogance and apathy, chauvinism and even hatred.* The last thing Poland needs today is the spreading an all-too-easy "culture of treason", (ab)using its own vision of the past and history as a tool to fight political adversaries and to divide Poles into "better" and "worse" sorts, and imposing one correct historical orthodoxy on society and enforcing it through criminal law, all as part of the wicked politics of resentment and mis-memory. Yet this politics seems to be engulfing Poland at an alarming rate. Again, as J. Błoński put it, on this Polish graveyard our obligation to carry the past must boil down to seeing this past in truth.[63] My understanding of constitutional fidelity in this context is about a generational reading of our national history. It is not about uncritical iconoclasm. It is about pragmatic recognition that our constitutional allegiances are shaped, reshaped, and re-examined as we move forward and as the world around the Constitution changes and fluctuates. There is no place for fear of failure, because failure is part of the fidelity, as no Constitution is perfect. Fidelity is about the journey and the process, rather than a boat and final destination. The past must be the key to the future, but not only. After all, Constitutions that are meant to last must be understood as documents made for people of fundamentally different views. Memory, properly understood, should challenge or subvert dominant accounts of history. It might be used to disguise and cover up, or to liberate and reveal. What matters, though, is that no one overarching master narrative exists, and that disagreement should make up for not for one, two, but many "contested pasts".[64] Unfortunately, in its most recent penal incarnation the Polish *politics of resentment* and *mis-memory* pose a danger that the Polish Past and History will become an uncontested sphere, dominated by a truth superimposed from above, and become a truly *foreign country*[65] with the keys available only to the "lucky few".

[63] J. Błoński, *supra* note 1. His essay played a fundamental role in the process of Polish renewed post-war soul-searching and grappling with the past. See M. T. Kaufman, 'Debate over Holocaust stirs passions in Poland', available at www.nytimes.com/1987/03/08/world/debate-over-holocaust-stirs-passions-in-poland.html.

[64] K. Hodgkin and S. Radstone, *Contested Pasts. The Politics of Memory* (London and New York: Routledge, 2003).

[65] L. P. Hartley, *The Go-Between* (Harmondsworth: Hamish Hamilton, 1953).

PART IV

Perspectives beyond the European Union

14

Defending Stalinism by Means of Criminal Law: Russia, 1995–2014

NIKOLAY KOPOSOV

1 Introduction

On 5 May 2014, Russia's President Vladimir Putin signed a law that introduced criminal liability for 'infringements on historical memory with regard to the events of the Second World War'. That law added the following article to the Penal Code of the Russian Federation:

> Article 354.1 Rehabilitation of Nazism
> The denial of facts established by the Judgment of the International Military Tribunal for the trial and punishment of major war criminals of European countries of the Axis, the approval of crimes established by the above-mentioned Judgment, as well as dissemination of knowingly false information on the activities of the USSR during the Second World War, committed publicly, are punishable by a fine of up to three hundred thousand roubles . . . or by deprivation of liberty for up to three years.[1]

The law also increases the punishment to up to five years of imprisonment if 'the same deeds [have been] committed with the use of one's official position or through the mass media, as well as with an artificial fabrication of prosecution evidence'.[2]

This law is commonly known as the Yarovaya Act, since Irina Yarovaya, a State Duma deputy from 'United Russia', the party in power, played the

[1] Federal'nyi zakon 'O vnesenii izmeneniy v otdel'nyie zakonodatel'nyie akty Rossiyskoy Federatsii' [Federal Law 'On the Introduction of Changes to Certain Legislative Acts of the Russian Federation'], article 1.1, *Rossiyskaya gazeta*, 7 May 2014, available at www.rg.ru/2014/05/07/reabilitacia-dok.html.

[2] *Ibid.*, article 1.2. The law also includes the following provision: 'Public distribution of information expressing manifest disrespect toward society regarding Russia's days of military glory and the commemorative dates associated with the defence of the Fatherland or public insults to the symbols of Russia's military glory are punishable by a fine of up to three hundred thousand roubles . . . or by correctional labour for up to one year' (*Ibid.*, article 1.3).

key role in its promotion.[3] Although it was adopted in the midst of the Ukrainian crisis, the law had been long in making: its first draft was presented to the Russian parliament in May 2009, while the idea of passing some kind of 'antifascist' bill dates back to the mid-1990s. Many things have changed in Russia over that period, and the history of the memory law projects illustrates those changes.

2 The Politics of History and the Cult of Second World War

The politics of history (*Geschichtspolitik*) is a hallmark of our times that is even more obvious in Russia than in most other countries. The extreme politicization of post-Soviet historical memory is partly due to the legacy of the communist regime whose legitimacy, which had been based on the Stalinist conception of history, was undermined during Mikhail Gorbachev's perestroika of the late 1980s. The unambiguous condemnation of Stalin's repressions, viewed as an inevitable consequence of the communists' coming to power, and the notion of the failure of Soviet socialism in its competition with the West were central to the new understanding of history used by President Boris Yeltsin and his team to legitimize the market reforms of the 1990s.

But after the fall of communism, history lost its appeal. It was the future rather than the past, and the economy rather than history, that interested Russians in the 1990s. The memory politics of Yeltsin's government, episodic as it was, emphasized Russia's cultural attainments, especially in the eighteenth and nineteenth centuries, which many Russians consider as comparable to, if not greater than, those of the West in the same period. Building national consensus by stimulating 'cultural patriotism' was the goal of that politics. However, the hardships of the transition period had made democratic ideology a disappointment for many Russians, and society's prime response to the unskilful attempts of an unpopular government (largely inspired by the politics of memory in the West) was an ironic distancing.[4]

3 A figure typical of the Russian political class, Yarovaya began her career as the head of a local division of the Yabloko democratic party in the Kamchatka region of the Far East. She failed twice in the legislative elections before changing her political allegiance, joining United Russia in 2007. This time she did become an MP and moved to Moscow. Shortly after that, she was appointed president of the United Russia Patriotic Club, a job that sat oddly with her former democratic identity. Since 2012, she has gained renown as the co-author of several repressive laws.

4 R.W. Davies, *Soviet History in the Gorbachev Revolution* (London: Palgrave Macmillan, 1989); K.E. Smith, *Mythmaking in the New Russia: Politics and Memory during the Yeltsin Era* (Ithaca, London: Cornell University Press, 2002); and T. Sherlock, *Historical Narratives in the Soviet Union and Post-Soviet Russia: Destroying the Settled Past, Creating an Uncertain Future* (New York: Palgrave-MacMillan, 2007).

In the 2000s, the emergence of Vladimir Putin's authoritarian regime was accompanied by a new revision of history, which has become central to 'the new Russian ideology' and was, arguably, a conscious choice on the part of Putin and his political advisors. According to Gleb Pavlovskiy, one of the architects of Putinism in the 2000s, after the collapse of the traditional ideologies (read: the great narratives), 'the politics of history will become the standard of politics as such'.[5] History politics came to be viewed as an important aspect of the latter-day propaganda state that Putin's advisors sought to create. The main goal of Putin's politics of memory was to promote a cult of the strong Russian state that would justify an immense growth of presidential power, the dominance of the bureaucracy, the destruction of the multiparty system, and a neo-imperial stance in foreign policy. However, the figure of Stalin, even after the dictator's partial rehabilitation in the official discourse, history textbooks, and movies of the early 2000s, remained too problematic to serve as the key historical symbol of Putin's Russia, which has instead selected the cult of Second World War (or the Great Patriotic War, as Russians call it) as its myth of origins.[6]

The Second World War left a powerful imprint on Soviet society. Indeed, some historians view it as the formative experience that forged the collective identity of the Soviet people. In the 1970s, the mythology of the war was cultivated by Leonid Brezhnev's administration in order to suppress another memory, that of Stalin's repressions (or the state's crimes against the people). The cult of the war lost its relevance in the period of democratic transformations under Gorbachev and Yeltsin but was restored in the 2000s.[7] An advantage of the revived cult was

[5] G. Pavlovskiy, 'Plokho s pamyatyu – plokho s politikoy' [Bad with Memory – Bad with Politics], *Russkiy zhurnal*, 9 December 2008, available at www.russ.ru/pole/Ploho-s-pamyat-yu-ploho-s-politikoj.

[6] C. Merridale, 'Redesigning History in Contemporary Russia', *Journal of Contemporary History* 38:1 (2003), 13–28; N. Adler, 'The Future of the Soviet Past Remains Unpredictable: The Resurrection of Stalinist Symbols Amidst the Exhumation of Mass Graves', *Europe-Asia Studies* 57:8 (2005), 1093–119; D. Khapaeva, 'Historical Memory in Post-Soviet Gothic Society', *Social Research* 76:1 (2009), 359–94; and N. Koposov, *Pamyat' strogogo rezhima: Istoriya i politika v Rossii [Strict-Security Memory: History and Politics in Russia]* (Moscow: Novoye literaturnoye obozreniye, 2011). On the historiographic conflict about 'Great Patriotic War' vis-à-vis 'Word War II', see chapter by Lina Klymenko in the present volume.

[7] N. Tumarkin, *The Living and the Dead: The Rise and Fall of the Cult of WWII in Russia* (New York: Basic Books, 1994); A. Weiner, *Making Sense of War: The Second World War and the Fate of the Bolshevik Revolution* (Princeton: Princeton University Press, 2001); L.A. Kirschenbaum, *The Legacy of the Siege of Leningrad, 1941–1995* (Cambridge University Press, 2006); and *Pamyat' o voine 60 let spustya: Germaniya, Rossiya, Yevropa* [Memory of War Sixty Years Later: Germany, Russia, Europe], Special Issue of *Neprikosnovennyi zapas* 2–3 (2005).

that it could leverage an enormous Soviet infrastructure of museums, associations of veterans, movies, etc. to create a widely shared ideological consensus. Not least, it has a strong mobilizing potential. It revitalizes Stalin's black-and-white formula of whoever is against communism (now Russia) is for fascism,[8] the latter being viewed as a profoundly anti-Russian force that is absolutely alien to Russia's own political tradition. This choice of a war instead of a culture as the symbol of national identity was highly significant. In particular, it reveals the roots of the Ukrainian crisis.

The myth of the war praises the USSR/Russia as the champion of peace and the world's saviour from fascism. According to sociological surveys, most Russians see 'their' victory over Hitler's Germany as the twentieth century's most important event, which gives Russia a right to universal recognition – and to those parts of Eastern Europe that Stalin occupied with the consent of his Western allies.[9] Characteristically, the Holocaust is not a part of that narrative,[10] since Russians, rather than Jews, are seen as Hitler's main victims. The USSR's ambiguous role in provoking Second World War is ignored, and the Soviet occupation of Eastern Europe is praised as its liberation. Within this framework, Eastern Europe, including Ukraine, presents as Russia's 'natural' sphere of interest. Russian memory law, furthermore, protects that narrative, which legitimizes the country's aggression against Ukraine (interpreted now as a new stage in Russia's perennial struggle against fascism).[11]

It is hard to say whether in embracing the cult of the war in the early 2000s, Vladimir Putin's government, preoccupied as it was with consolidating its domestic support, foresaw the reaction of the Eastern

[8] F. Furet, *The Passing of an Illusion: The Idea of Communism in the Twentieth Century* (Chicago, London: University of Chicago Press, 2000), 209–65.

[9] B. Dubin, *Rossiya nulevykh: Politicheskaya kul'tura, istoricheskaya pamyat', povsednevnaya zhizn' [Russia in the 2000s: Political Culture, Historical Memory, Everyday Life]* (Moscow: ROSSPEN, 2011), 47–64, 140–55.

[10] I. Altman, 'Memorializatsia Holokosta v Rossiyi: Istoriya, sovremennost', perspektivy' [Commemorating the Holocaust in Russia: History, the Current Situation, Prospects for the Future], in *Pamyat' o voine 60 let spustya*, 509–30; and K.-G. Karlsson, 'The Reception of the Holocaust in Russia: Silence, Conspiracy, and Glimpses of Light', in J.-P. Himka and J.B. Michlic (eds.), *Bringing the Dark Past to Light: The Reception of the Holocaust in Postcommunist Europe* (Lincoln: University of Nebraska Press, 2013), 487–514.

[11] T. Snyder, *Ukrainskaya istoriya, rossiyskaya politika, yevropeyskoye budushcheye [Ukrainian History, Russian Politics, European Future]* (Kiev: Dukh i litera, 2014). See also chapter by Lina Klymenko in the present volume.

European countries. That reaction was more than predictable, though. In recent years we have witnessed passionate conflicts over the interpretation of historical events between Russia and its Eastern European neighbours, Moscow claiming that Poland, Ukraine, and the Baltic countries have launched 'memory wars' against Russia. Those countries were indeed ahead of Russia in developing an infrastructure for their politics of memory (such as institutes of national memory, museums of the occupation, and de-communization laws). Often, their politics of memory were also aimed at promoting national narratives rather than democratic values. However, the question of responsibility for those memory wars is still far more complex than the Russian government would have us believe. From my point of view, Putin's neo-imperial rhetoric actually triggered them by making Russia, long before its aggression against Ukraine, appear as a danger to the Eastern European countries' newly acquired independence.[12]

3 Memory Law Projects of the 1990s

The first Russian memory law projects appeared in 1995, in the context of the Russian democrats' attempts to counter the rising far-right movement and the growing nostalgia for communism that was signally expressed in the increasing popularity of Stalin. Most of those attempts were undertaken by a group of politicians linked to the Moscow Antifascist Centre. In February 1995, Alla Gerber, an MP from the Democratic Choice of Russia, organized parliamentary hearings under the heading 'On the Prevention of Manifestations of the Fascist Danger in the Russian Federation', which introduced Russian political circles to the notion of memory law. By summer 1995, five draft antifascist laws (a term that has since become the generic name for memory laws in Russia) were presented to the State Duma; all told, no fewer than twelve such drafts were introduced into the parliament between 1995 and 1999 by the president, the government, the Moscow City Duma (the capital's legislative assembly), and various groups of deputies.[13] Four of them were submitted by the Moscow Duma on the initiative of

[12] See Koposov, *Pamyat' strogogo rezhima*, 162–8, and N. Koposov, 'Back to Yalta? Stephen Cohen and the Ukrainian Crisis', *Eurozine*, 5 September 2014, available at www.eurozine.com/articles/2014-09-05-koposov-en.html.

[13] A.M. Verkhovskiy, *Politika gosudarstva po otnosheniyu k natisonal-radikal'nym obyedineniyam, 1991–2002 [Government Policies towards Radical Nationalist Groups, 1991–2002]* (Moscow: Panorama, 2002). An abridged English translation is available at www.mhg.ru/english/1FF6AB0.

Evgeniy Proshechkin, president of the Moscow Antifascist Centre, who, as a deputy to the capital's parliament, was responsible for coordinating its anti-extremist policy in 1993–7. Three drafts were authored by Viktor Zorkaltsev, an influential Communist MP and the party's representative during the CPSU trial in 1992 (when the Constitutional Court partly invalidated Yeltsin's decrees dissolving the CPSU and allowed for the formation of a new Communist Party).

Some antifascist bills of the 1990s were purely declarative and banned fascist ideology without penalizing it, while other drafts prohibited fascist symbols and propaganda materials and introduced administrative liability for exhibiting or circulating them. Still other proposals considered the use of fascist symbols and the dissemination of fascist literature to be a criterion for recognizing as extremist any organization involved in such activities, which could result in its being shut down by a court. Finally, several bills followed the model of the 1990 French 'Gayssot Act' (the classical Western memory law, which has powerfully influenced the EU approach toward negationism and several national bills criminalizing it),[14] proposing the introduction of criminal liability for certain statements about the past, including Holocaust denial.

For Russian democrats and antifascists, promoting the memory of the Holocaust was certainly an important goal. However, they tried to expand the notion of fascism to cover 'the red-brown danger' (in other words, communist and nationalist attempts to overthrow the new democratic order), and they called for criminalizing the ideology of fascist and 'other totalitarian' regimes (above all, Stalinism). As for the communists, they did not want to cede the antifascist 'high ground' to the democrats, because the myth of the war was an important component of their own symbolic capital. In the 1990s, however, the Communist Party was becoming increasingly nationalist. The communists had to use antifascist rhetoric in such a way as to promote their myth of the war and ensure the support of the veterans' organizations without alienating their allies on the far right. That is why, in contrast to the democrats, they did not support the notion of criminalizing fascist ideology but did agree with the introduction of administrative liability for its promotion.

[14] About the Gayssot Act and French memory laws, see chapter by Ioanna Tourkochoriti in the present volume. About EU developments on historical memory, largely inspired by the punitive provisions of the Gayssot Act and the like, see chapter by Luigi Cajani in the present volume.

In May 1996, Proshechkin and his colleagues suggested an amendment to the Penal Code that provided up to four years' incarceration for:

> Public justification, approval, glorification or denial and gross diminishing of the crimes of national-socialist, fascist and other regimes that had been involved in acts of genocide, military crimes, crimes against peace and humanity, as well as public glorification and attempts to justify the leaders of such regimes that have been called criminal by the decisions of international tribunals.[15]

This would be a typical Western-style memory law. However, its language could also be extended to prohibition of the 'glorification' of Stalinism, which is usually viewed by Russian democrats as 'a regime that had been involved in acts of genocide'. Unsurprisingly, the bill was voted down by the communist-dominated parliament, not only because of its anti-Stalinist implications but also because the Holocaust-centred vision of the war challenged its Soviet/Russian myth. However, the deputies also rejected Zorkaltsev's proposals to ban 'the propaganda of fascism' and 'the distribution in public places of materials that rehabilitate the fascist leaders and clear them of the blame for genocide and other crimes against peace, humankind and humanity', on the grounds that the new Penal Code of 1996 deemed hate speech a criminal offence, while Zorkaltsev was suggesting making 'the propaganda of fascism' merely an administrative offence.[16]

The results of the legislative battles over historical memory in the 1990s were modest indeed. Article 20.3 of the new Administrative Code (2001) introduced administrative liability for 'displaying fascist attributes and symbolism for the purposes of popularization of such attributes and symbolism'.[17] A Moscow law of 1997 (adopted on Proshechkin's initiative) and a St. Petersburg law of 2000 contained similar provisions.[18] The 2002 law 'On Countering Extremist Activity' established a simplified procedure for closing public associations and mass media found guilty of such activities, including 'propaganda and public demonstration of Nazi attributes and symbols' and dissemination of 'the works of the leaders of the National-Socialist Workers Party of Germany [and] the Fascist Party of

[15] A.M. Verkhovskiy, *Politika gosudarstva po otnosheniyu k natisonal-radikal'nym obyedineniyam*, www.mhg.ru/english/1FF6905.

[16] *Ibid.*

[17] Kodeks Rossiyskoy Federatsii ob administrativnykh pravonarusheniyakh ot 20.12.2001 [Code of Administrative Offences of the Russian Federation of 20 December 2001], available at www.consultant.ru/popular/koap/. For the English translation, see www.wipo.int/edocs/lexdocs/laws/en/ru/ru073en.pdf.

[18] Verkhovskiy, *Politika gosudarstva po otnosheniyu k natisonal-radikal'nym obyedineniyam*.

Italy'.[19] Nonetheless, the law did not introduce any new criminal or administrative charges for those offences *per se*. In 2002, the main goal of the Extremist Activity law was to combat Muslim organizations and those who sympathized with the Chechen struggle for independence, rather than far-right extremism. Yet in the 2010s, the law began to be used against the democratic movement as well.

4 The 'New-Wave' Memory Bills

It was not until the end of the 2000s that Russian legislators returned to the notion of passing an 'antifascist' law in the context of the memory wars between Russia and its Eastern European neighbours. That idea reemerged during the Russian-Estonian conflict of April 2007 over the removal of a memorial to Soviet soldiers from the centre of Tallinn to a war cemetery. The Russian authorities and media had reacted violently to this as an aggressively anti-Russian act and (from their point of view) a manifestation of fascism, all the more so because pictures of parades of Estonian (and Latvian) veterans of the SS had for some time been receiving broad coverage on Russian television. In December 2008, a group of nationalist politicians led by Konstantin Zatulin, an MP from the United Russia party, began working on a bill of their own, which was published on a nationalist website in April 2009 (but has never been presented to the parliament). That was the first Russian project to use a new formula that has since become central in conceptualizing the offences that Russian partisans of memory laws wanted to forbid – 'the rehabilitation of Nazism and the heroisation of Nazi criminals and their accomplices', the latter term referring to members of various wartime and postwar anti-Soviet movements (e.g., the *Banderivtsy*, the followers of Stepan Bandera, the leader of the Organization of Ukrainian Nationalists). In fact, the bill's very name indicates that its main goal was to take a stand against the politics of memory in the 'near abroad' (the Russian term for the former Soviet republics).[20] Both key authors of the draft, Zatulin and Modest Kolerov,

[19] Federal'nyi zakon ot 25 iyulya 2002 g. 'O protivodeystvii ekstremistskoy deyatel'nosti' [Federal law of 25 July 2002 'On Countering Extremist Activity'], *Rossiyskaya gazeta*, 30 July 2002, articles 1-1, 1-2, 1-3, available at www.rg.ru/2002/07/30/extremizm-dok.html. The English translation is available at http://host.uniroma3.it/progetti/cedir/cedir/Lex-doc/Ru_Ext-2002.pdf.

[20] Proekt: Federal'nyi Zakon 'O protivodeystvii reabilitatsii v novykh nezavisimykh gosudarstvakh na territorii byvshego Soyuza SSR natsizma, natsistskikh prestupnikov i ikh posobnikov' [Project: Federal Law 'On the Struggle against the Rehabilitation of Nazism,

were deeply involved in supporting pro-Russian forces in the Baltic countries and Ukraine (especially during and after the presidential elections and the 'Orange Revolution' of 2004, when Russia began actively intervening in Ukrainian domestic politics). That formula ('the rehabilitation of Nazism and the heroisation of Nazi criminals') was prominent in the idiom of pro-Russian Ukrainian politicians such as Aleksandr Feldman and Vadim Kolesnichenko and their Russian supporters, from Zatulin and Kolerov to Boris Spiegel (whose memory law project will be discussed later in this chapter). In January 2009, when Zatulin and Kolerov were still working on their draft, Vadim Kolesnichenko, a Ukrainian MP from Viktor Yanukovych's Party of the Regions, presented to the Rada (the Ukrainian parliament) his bill 'On Banning the Rehabilitation and Heroisation of Fascist Collaborationists of 1933–1945' (which was not adopted by the parliament because of its imprecise language).[21] This was the first instance, to my knowledge, in which the new formula was used in a draft memory law.

Official Russian ideologists interpret 'the rehabilitation of Nazism' as a manifestation of 'historical revisionism', whose essence, from their point of view, consists in putting Nazi Germany and the USSR on an equal footing. Viewing the USSR as just another totalitarian regime erodes the Russian myth of the war with its black-and-white counterposition of fascism and Russia. The Foreign Policy Concept of the Russian Federation of July 2008 states that one of the government's priorities should be 'to firmly counter . . . attempts to rewrite the history . . . and revise the outcome of . . . World War Two'.[22] Here, the 'outcome of the war' refers to the Yalta System, the postwar division of the spheres of influence between the USSR and its Western allies. Calling this system (which has in fact disappeared on its own as a result of the collapse of the Soviet empire) into question is

Nazi Criminals and Their Accomplices in the New Independent States on the Territory of the Former USSR'], *Regnum*, 20 April 2009, available at www.regnum.ru/news/1153517.html.

21 Proekt Zakonu Ukrainy 3618 vid 15.01.2009 'Pro zaboronu reabilitatsii ta geroizatsii fashistskikh kollaboratsionistiv 1933–1945 rokakh' [Project of Ukrainian Law No. 3612 of 15 January 2009 'On Banning the Rehabilitation and Heroisation of Fascist Collaborationists in 1933–1945'], available at http://w1.c1.rada.gov.ua/pls/zweb2/webproc4_1?id=&pf3511=34176. See also N. Koposov, 'Ustawy memorialne w Rosji i na Ukrainie: krzyżujące się historie' [Memory Laws in Russia and Ukraine: Intersecting Stories], *Rocznik Instytutu Europy Środkowo-Wschodniej* 13:2 (2015), 198.

22 The Foreign Policy Concept of the Russian Federation, available in English at http://archive.kremlin.ru/eng/text/docs/2008/07/204750.shtml.

seen by the Kremlin as a continuation of the Cold-War-style policies of 'containing' Russia, of which the US is held to be the principal architect.[23]

In contrast to the memory law projects of the 1990s, all the memory bills of the Putin era use the term 'Nazism' rather than 'fascism'. By choosing a more historically concrete concept to refer to their country's paradigmatic enemy, Russian lawmakers were attempting to avoid the potential pitfalls of the more general 'fascism', which could also refer – and was in fact used (in the bills of the 1990s) to refer – to some aspects of Russia's own political tradition. And this, in turn, could call into question the 'us vs. them' dichotomy that is crucial to Putin's historical mythology.

Returning now to Zatulin's draft, it proposed a comprehensive series of measures to promote the Russian war myth domestically and internationally, including the creation of a Civic Tribunal whose members would be both Presidential appointees and delegates of the parliament and the Civic Chamber (an advisory body with no formal power), which (Zatulin hoped) would open it up to nationalist activists.

The Civic Tribunal's task would be to monitor manifestations of historical revisionism in the near abroad and to recommend a particular course of action with regard to a country found guilty of seeking to rehabilitate Nazism. The list of those actions ranged from economic sanctions to the outright severing of diplomatic relations. Arguably, the authors of the bill expected that a separate act would be passed to criminalize 'the rehabilitation of Nazism', but their draft did not contain any such provision.

However, United Russia did not support Zatulin's bill, most likely because the proposed 'tribunal' could potentially become a somewhat independent political actor. Zatulin was, in fact, a relatively marginal figure in his party. Instead, President Dmitry Medvedev created, in May 2009, a Presidential Commission to Counter Attempts to Falsify History to the Detriment of Russia's Interests, whose functions were suspiciously similar to those of Zatulin's tribunal but which was to consist exclusively of the President's appointees.[24] Simultaneously, United Russia proposed a bill

[23] This position was clearly formulated by Putin's foreign minister Sergei Lavrov in his 2009 article 'The Sixty-Fifth Anniversary of the Great Victory' ['65-letiye Velikoy Pobedy'], available in English at www.mid.ru/brp_4.nsf/0/019102CC71C55417C32576B80050C875.

[24] Ukaz Prezidenta Rossiyskoy Federatsii No. 549 ot 15 maya 2009 g. 'O Komissii pri Prezidente Rossiyskoy Federatsii po protivodeystviyu popytkam falsifikatsii istoriyi v ushcherb interesam Rossii' [Decree of the President of the Russian Federation No. 549 of 15 May 2009 'On the Presidential Commission to Counter Attempts to Falsify History to the Detriment of Russia's Interests'], *Rossiyskaya gazeta*, 20 May 2009, available at www.rg.ru/2009/05/20/komissia-dok.html.

making it a culpable offence to 'violate the historical memory of events which took place during the Second World War'. The bill provided:

> Distortion of the Judgment of the Nuremberg Tribunal, or of the verdicts of national courts or tribunals based on the Judgment of the Nuremberg Tribunal, with the aim of fully or partially rehabilitating Nazism and Nazi criminals; declarations that actions of countries participating in the anti-Hitler coalition were criminal, and also the public approval and denial of Nazi crimes against peace and the security of humanity shall be punishable by a fine of up to 300,000 roubles, or up to three years imprisonment.[25]

That was the first version of the Yarovaya Act, and it was co-authored by leading figures of United Russia, including the Duma President Boris Gryzlov; they obviously had pretensions of following the paradigm of the Gayssot Act (and of the European Council Framework Decision of 2008, which obliged member states to criminalize Holocaust denial).[26] The bill was formulated in such a way as to demonstrate the Kremlin's intention to protect the memory of all members of the anti-Hitler coalition and to restore an alliance with the West at the expense of the Eastern European countries, which were implicitly viewed as Nazi sympathizers. Indeed, the Russian myth of the war denies subjectivity to those countries and invites the West to do the same, as had been the case in 1945.

The parliament did not, however, adopt that bill. In the context of the rapprochement with the West that began after Barack Obama's visit to Moscow in July 2009, Russian authorities preferred to take a more moderate stand on issues of the past. In the fall of 2009, both Putin (then prime minister) and President Medvedev publicly condemned Stalin's crimes. A second (and far more moderate) version of the Yarovaya law was introduced into the parliament in April 2010 and languished there for several years.[27] It was not until a new confrontation with the West began in 2012 as a result of the radical conservative turn in Putin's politics that Yarovaya and

[25] Zakonoproekt No. 197582-5 ot 06.05.2009: Federal'nyi Zakon 'O vnesenii izmeneniya v Ugolovnyi kodeks Rossiyskoy Federatsii' [Bill No. 197582-2 of 6 May 2009: Federal Law 'On the Introduction of a Change to the Penal Code of Russian Federation'], available at http://asozd2.duma.gov.ru/main.nsf/%28SpravkaNew%29?OpenAgent&RN=197582-5&02.

[26] About the EU Council Decision, see chapter by Luigi Cajani in the present volume.

[27] The second version of the bill simply banned 'the denial or approval of Nazi crimes against the peace and security of humankind, as established by the Judgment of the Nuremberg Tribunal'. See N. Koposov, 'Does Russia Need a Memory Law?' *Open Democracy*, 16 June 2010, available at www.opendemocracy.net/od-russia/nikolai-koposov/does-russia-need-memory-law.

her colleagues returned to their draft. But in the meanwhile, another group of Russian politicians had come up with an alternative memory law project.

5 A Tale of Two Bills[28]

The alternative project was initiated by Boris Spiegel, a Russian 'oligarch', politician, and prominent Russian-Jewish activist. He was a member of the Federation Council in 2003–13 and for several years worked on its Committee on the Affairs of the Commonwealth of Independent States (CIS), of which Zatulin was deputy chair. In his capacity of president of the World Congress of Russian Jewry (a position he has held since 2007), Spiegel has worked with both the Ministry of Foreign Affairs and the Presidential Commission on the Falsification of History. In June 2010, he created 'World without Nazism', an international human rights movement, which declared the struggle against Nazi ideology and historical revisionism as its main goal. In 2012, acting as a deputy chair of the Federation Council's Committee on Constitutional Legislation, Spiegel convinced the Interparliamentary Assembly of Member Nations of the CIS to approve the model law 'On the Inadmissibility of Actions Aimed at the Rehabilitation of Nazism, and the Heroisation of Nazi Criminals and Their Accomplices'.[29] This long document, which was based on Zatulin's 2009 draft, also proposed a complex strategy for promoting the Russian war myth, but this time in combination with the memory of the Holocaust. In Spiegel's view, the CIS model law was to play a role similar to that of the European Council Framework Decision of 2008. In March 2013, Spiegel introduced two bills into the Duma, the first of which reproduced the CIS model law,[30] while the second proposed expanding the list of offences detailed in Article 282 of the Penal Code by including the rehabilitation

[28] For more details, see N. Koposov, 'Une loi pour faire la guerre: La Russie et sa mémoire', *Le Débat* 181 (2014), 103–16.

[29] Mezhparlamentskaya Assambleya gosudarstv-uchastnikov Sodruzhestva Nezavisimykh Gosudarstv. Model'nyi zakon 'O nedopustimosti deystviy po reabilitatsii natsizma, geroizatsii natsistskikh prestupnikov i ikh posobnikov', [Interparliamentary Assembly of Member Nations of the Community of Independent States. Model Law 'On the Inadmissibility of Actions Aimed at the Rehabilitation of Nazism, and the Heroisation of Nazi Criminals and Their Accomplices'], 17 May 2012, available at www.iacis.ru/upload/iblock/397/18_a_2012.pdf.

[30] Zakonoproekt No. 246071-6 ot 25.03.2013: Federal'nyi zakon 'O nedopustimosti deystviy po reabilitatsii natsizma, geroizatsii natsistskikh prestupnikov i ikh posobnikov, otritsaniyu Holokosta' [Bill No. 246071-6 of 25 March 2013: Federal Law 'On the Inadmissibility of Actions Aimed at the Rehabilitation of Nazism, and the Heroisation of Nazi Criminals and

of Nazism and Holocaust denial. The title of that Article is 'Incitement to Hatred or Hostility or the Disparagement of Human Dignity'. Had Spiegel's proposal been accepted, Article 282 would have criminalized:

> Actions aiming at exciting hatred or enmity, rehabilitating Nazism, glorifying Nazi criminals and their accomplices, denying the Holocaust, the disparagement of the human dignity of a person or a group of persons on the basis of gender, race, nationality, language, origins, religion, or belonging to a social group, committed publicly or thorough the media.[31]

Spiegel's bill was indeed similar to Western Holocaust denial laws, which consider Nazi crimes to be offences of a racist nature. According to Spiegel, the Kremlin needed to develop a politics of memory that would emphasize the involvement of some Eastern European nations in the extermination of the Jews, rather than those countries' struggle against the USSR. (He obviously thought that this narrative would have a better chance of being heard in the West than the traditional Soviet tales of Russian suffering and heroism.) Nonetheless, since Spiegel's approach eroded the 'purity' of the Russian war myth, United Russia decided to revert instead to its original bill. As for Spiegel, he had to resign from the Federation Council in March 2013, formally because of a new law that forbade combining positions in the parliament with those in international NGOs (which would include 'World without Nazism'). After Spiegel's departure from the Federation Council, his successor as deputy chair of the Committee on Constitutional Legislation Konstantin Dobrynin (a young lawyer from Saint-Petersburg reportedly close to Dmitry Medvedev) continued promoting his drafts.

The third version of the Yarovaya law was presented to the Duma in June 2013.[32] The following months witnessed a strange competition between the two houses over their projects, neither of which had the support of

Their Accomplices, and Holocaust Denial'], available at http://asozd2.duma.gov.ru/main.nsf/%28SpravkaNew%29?OpenAgent&RN=246071-6&02.

31 Zakonoproekt No. 246065-6 ot 25.03.2013: Federal'nyi zakon 'O vnesenii izmeneniy v stat'yu 282 Ugolovnogo kodeksa Rossiyskoy Federatsii' [Bill No. 246065-6 of 25 March 2013: Federal Law 'On the Introduction of Changes to Article 282 of the Criminal Code of the Russian Federation'], available at http://asozd2.duma.gov.ru/main.nsf/(Spravka)?OpenAgent&RN=246065-6.

32 Zakonoproekt No. 197582-5 ot 27.02.2104: Federal'nyi zakon 'O vnesenii izmeneniy v Ugolovnyi kodeks Rossiyskoy Federatsii i v stat'yu 151 Ugolovno-protsessual'nogo kodeksa Rossiyskoy Federatsii' [Bill No. 197582-5 of 27 February 2014: Federal Law 'On the Introduction of Changes to the Criminal Code of the Russian Federation and to Article 151 of the Code of Criminal Procedures of the Russian Federation'], available at http://asozd2.duma.gov.ru/main.nsf/%28SpravkaNew%29?OpenAgent&RN=197582-5&02.

the government, whose experts assessed the bills as underdeveloped.[33] However, the annexation of Crimea rendered those technical concerns obsolete. On 4 April 2014, the Duma approved the Yarovaya Act in its first reading by a hefty majority of 447 deputies out of 449 (the parties of the 'official opposition' also voted in favour of the bill, as they did for other repressive laws passed after Putin's return in the Kremlin in 2012).

At this point, Dobrynin and his colleagues made a last-ditch effort to stop the Yarovaya Act, by submitting new versions of their own bills.[34] Characteristically, Holocaust denial had disappeared from those drafts, which now proposed to criminalize only 'the rehabilitation of Nazism and the heroisation of Nazi criminals and their accomplices'. Yet once Holocaust denial was removed from the list of criminal offences, Dobynin's proposal ceased to be a meaningful alternative to the Yarovaya law. This last stage in the battle of the bills being primarily an expression of the institutional competition between the two houses, Dobrynin and his colleagues thought that mention of the Holocaust would undermine their bill's chances. Arguably, criminalizing Holocaust denial had for them been essentially a tactical matter.

The discussion of the Yarovaya law in the Federation Council was scheduled for 29 April. On 28 April, Dobrynin was still giving interviews predicting that the upper house would not support the bill. On the following

[33] Dmitriy Runkevich, 'Kreml' ne podderzhal zakonoproekt o zaprete reabilitatsii fashizma' [Kremlin Withholds Support from the Draft Law Banning the Rehabilitation of Fascism], *Izvestiya*, 10 February 2014, available at http://izvestia.ru/news/565382. See also Ofitsial'nyi otzyv na proekt federal'nogo zakona 'O vnesenii izmeneniy v Ugolovnyi kodeks Rossiyskoy Federatsii i v stat'yu 151 Ugolovno-protsessual'nogo kodeksa Rossiyskoy Federatsii' [Official Review of the Project of Federal Law 'On the Introduction of Changes to the Criminal Code of the Russian Federation and to Article 151 of the Code of Criminal Procedures of the Russian Federation'], available at http://asozd2.duma.gov.ru/main.nsf/%28SpravkaNew%29?OpenAgent&RN=197582-5&02.

[34] Zakonoproekt No. 504872-6 ot 22.04.2014: Federal'nyi zakon 'O protivodeystvii reabilitatsii natsizma, geroizatsii natsistskikh prestupnikov i ikh posobnikov' [Bill No. 504872-6 of 22 April 2014: Federal Law 'On Counteracting the Rehabilitation of Nazism, and the Heroisation of Nazi Criminals and Their Accomplices'], available at http://asozd2c.duma.gov.ru/addwork/scans.nsf/ID/4C9625BFB68346A943257CC2002904F0/$FILE/504872-6.PDF?OpenElement; Zakonoproekt No 504840-6 ot 22.04.2014: Federal'nyi zakon 'O vnesenii izmeneniy v stat'yu 1 Federal'nogo zakona "O protivodeystvii ekstremistskoy deyatel'nosti"' [Bill No. 504840-6 of 22 April 2014: Federal Law 'On the Introduction of Changes to Article 1 of the Federal Law "On Counteracting Extremist Activity"'], available at http://asozd2c.duma.gov.ru/addwork/scans.nsf/ID/BB1C50BC8FF7C86043257CC200371D1F/$FILE/504840-6.PDF?OpenElement.

day, however, it was almost unanimously approved, with Dobrynin being the only person to vote against it.

The final version of the Yarovaya Act is even more 'radical' than its initial draft of 2009. 'Knowingly false information' is an extremely inclusive formula that opens the way for the banning of any 'undesirable' vision of history. Significantly, this formula goes back to Article 191.1 of the Penal Code of the Russian Federation of 1960 (as amended in 1966), which prohibited 'dissemination of knowingly false information that denigrates the Soviet political and social system'.[35] That article was one of the main legal instruments used by the KGB against the dissident movement, and its reproduction in 2014 is a characteristic example of the secret services' 'institutional memory', which often manifests itself in present-day Russian politics. As for the clumsy expression 'artificial fabrication of prosecution evidence', it can be interpreted as referring to a historian's professional work on the Second World War that is not in line with the official interpretation. In fact, that phrase can hardly mean anything else.

6 Concluding Remarks

The authors of the Russian bill argued (in the explanatory note attached to it) that their proposal differed in no way from what 'countries such as Austria, Germany, Italy, Belgium, and France' had long ago done, by introducing 'criminal liability for the public denial . . . or justification of Nazi crimes . . . established by the Judgment of the Nuremberg Tribunal'.[36] This claim, however, invites several comments. First, there is a factual mistake here: Italy passed such act only in June 2016. Second, and more importantly, Western memory laws usually criminalize denial of Nazi crimes 'as defined' by the Charter of the Nuremberg Tribunal rather than as 'established' by its Judgment.[37] The difference is significant indeed, because the 1946 Judgment, which reflected a compromise between

[35] Ugolovnyi kodeks RSFSR ot 27 oktyabrya 1960 g. [Criminal Code of the RSFSR of 27 October 1960], available at www.lawrussia.ru/bigtexts/law_3558/page3.htm.

[36] See the explanatory note to the last version of the Yarovaya Act, available at http://asozd2.duma.gov.ru/main.nsf/%28SpravkaNew%29?OpenAgent&RN=197582-5&02.

[37] T. Naamat, N. Osin and D. Porat (eds.), *Legislating for Equality: A Multinational Collection of Non-Discrimination Norms, vol. I: Europe* (Leiden, Boston: Martinus Nijhoff, 2012), 156–7; and European Council Framework Decision 2008/913/JHA of 28 November 2008 on Combating Certain Forms and Expressions of Racism and Xenophobia by Means of Criminal Law, article 1, available at http://eur-lex.europa.eu/LexUriServ/LexUriServ.do?uri=OJ:L:2008:328:0055:0058:EN:PDF.

Stalin's USSR and its Western allies, can hardly be seen today as a document that is historically accurate in any single detail. Yet by claiming that the Judgment had definitively established the truth of the past, Russian lawmakers preclude any criticism of a document that in fact needs to be treated as a historical source. Characteristically, Russian authorities have themselves at times officially adopted interpretations of history that run against the Nuremberg Judgment. For example, in 1989, the Russian parliament condemned the Molotov-Ribbentrop Pact of 1939, which is presented in the Judgment as a perfectly legitimate element in Stalin's peace-seeking foreign policy. And as recently as 2010, during the 'reset' in Russian–American relationships, the State Duma adopted a declaration condemning the Katyn massacre as a Stalinist crime, although Soviet responsibility for that tragedy had by no means been 'established' by the Nuremberg Tribunal (which had been fairly ambiguous on the topic).[38] In other words, the Kremlin feels free to 'revise' parts of the Nuremberg Judgment at will, but since the Nuremberg interpretation of the war does not significantly deviate from its Stalinist conception, penalizing 'distortions' of the 1946 Judgment entails providing legal protection to that conception.

In contrast, by referring to the Nuremberg definition of Nazi crimes, the Gayssot Act and the 2008 Framework Decision only specify what kind of crimes are not to be denied, without claiming that any account of them is correct in all its details. That is, of course, not an ideal solution either, for it can imply that what is defined is what has been established, but at least it bans only attempts to deny the most basic facts about Nazism, such as the Holocaust, not interpretations of more concrete events (e.g., to what extent the USSR was responsible for the beginning of the Second World War). And I suspect that there can hardly be an ideal solution when one is seeking to judicialize the past.

To return to the claim that the Yarovaya Act is similar to its Western prototypes, I would argue, rather, that the opposite is true and that the 2014 Russian Act is almost unique among memory laws, which normally protect memories of the victims of state policy (genocide, for example, usually

[38] Zayavleniye Gosudarstvennoy Dumy 'O Katynskoy tragedii i yeyo zhertvakh' [Declaration of the State Duma 'On the Katyn Tragedy and its Victims'], *Parlamentskaya gazeta*, 3 December 2010, available at http://old.pnp.ru/newspaper/20101203/5164/print.html. In the Indictment, the Katyn massacre is listed among the crimes committed by the Nazis, but the Judgment does not mention it at all, because the USSR failed to prove its position during the trial.

being interpreted as a state crime). The Russian law protects the memory of the state – or, more specifically, the memory of Stalinism – from that of its victims, by criminalizing denial of the official Soviet/Russian narrative of the war, which includes the notion of the Yalta System and serves to justify the neo-imperialist ambitions of Putin's regime. While some of the memory law projects of the 1990s were indeed similar to their Western prototypes, the 'new-wave' bills and the 2014 Act were intended as a weapon in the memory wars rather than as a means of surmounting national narratives and promoting a shared European memory. To be sure, some Eastern European memory laws (e.g., the Polish act of 1998, the Lithuanian act of 2010, and the Ukrainian de-communization laws of 2015) also protect national narratives rather than the memory of the Holocaust, which is the opposite of what the authors of the first Western European memory laws sought to achieve. Indeed, the above-mentioned Eastern European laws prohibit the denial of both Nazi and communist crimes, which is understandable in light of those countries' historical experience; but they do it in such a way as to shift the blame for historical injustices entirely to others and whitewash national romances glorifying their respective nation-states, which entails using the past for the sake of nationalist mobilization rather than for creating a democratic culture of memory.[39] The Russian 2014 act is, I believe, an extreme case of this deplorable tendency.

[39] Thus, the 1998 Polish law prohibits the denial of 'crimes perpetrated against persons of Polish nationality and Polish citizens of other ethnicity, nationalities', which is an obvious attempt to downplay the importance of the Holocaust and present the Poles rather than the Jews as Hitler's main victims. Furthermore, political repressions 'instigated by the officers of the Polish law enforcement agencies or the judiciary' are not subsumed in the act under the notion of crimes against humanity and are seen as those functionaries' individual misdeeds rather than as crimes of the Polish state. The participation of Poles themselves in the Holocaust and ethnic cleansings is completely silenced in the law. See Law No. 155 of 18 December 1998, On the Institute of National Remembrance – Commission for the Prosecution of Crimes against the Polish Nation, available in English at https://ipn.gov.pl/en/about-the-institute/documents/institute-documents/the-act-on-the-institute-of-national-remembrance. The 2010 Lithuanian law bans the denial of 'crimes . . . committed by the USSR or Nazi Germany in the territory of the Republic of Lithuania or against the inhabitants of the Republic of Lithuania' as if Lithuanians themselves were not implicated in some of those crimes. See Law No. VIII-1968 of 26 September 2000, on the Approval and Entry into Force of the Criminal Code, consolidated version valid as of 1 April 2016, Article 170.2: http://www3.lrs.lt/pls/inter3/dokpaieska.showdoc_e?p_id=1118584&p_tr2=2. See also Koposov, 'Ustawy memorialne w Rosji i na Ukrainie', 167–216.

15

Cutting the Umbilical Cord: The Narrative of the National Past and Future in Ukrainian De-communization Policy

LINA KLYMENKO

1 Introduction

In April 2015, the Ukrainian parliament adopted four laws that included various aspects of coming to terms with the legacy of Soviet Communism (see Table 1). These laws proposed the commemoration of the seventieth anniversary of victory over Nazi Germany, defined the nature of the Soviet Communist regime, identified fighters for Ukrainian independence in the twentieth century, and regulated public access to the Soviet archives of 1917–91. Initiated by various political parties (some of which emerged in the aftermath of the 2013–14 Euromaidan revolution), these laws became a Ukrainian response to Russia's annexation of Crimea and Russia's support for the pro-Russian insurgency in the Ukrainian Donbas. The Ukrainian policy-makers included the laws in a so-called "national memory bloc," thus underlining the importance of the Ukrainian state in consolidating the Ukrainian nation through the creation of a common historical consciousness. In the preambles of two of the laws, it is explicitly stated that "[the law was adopted] with the aim of . . . removing any threats to the independence, sovereignty, territorial integrity, and national security of Ukraine."[1]

I would like to thank Christian Noack and the colleagues at the workshop "Legislating and Judging History" organized by the editors of this volume at the University of Amsterdam in June 2016 for discussing this chapter.

[1] *Verkhovna Rada Ukrainy*, 'Pro Dostup do Arkhiviv Represyvnykh Orhaniv Komunistychnoho Totalitarnoho Rezhymu 1917–91 Rokiv (On Access to the Archives of Repressive Bodies of the Communist Totalitarian Regime of 1917–91)', 9 April 2015, available at http://zakon2.rada.gov.ua/laws/show/316-19; *Verkhovna Rada Ukrainy*, 'Pro Zasudzhennia Komunistychnoho ta Natsional-Sotsialistychnoho (Natsyskoho) Totalitarnykh Rezhymiv v Ukraini ta Zaboronu Propahandy Ikhnioi Symvoliky (On the Condemnation of the Communist and National Socialism (Nazi) Regimes and Prohibition of Propaganda of their Symbols)',

Table 1 *De-communization laws adopted by the Ukrainian parliament in April 2015*

No.	Title of the law
314-VIII	On the Legal Status and Honoring the Memory of Fighters for Ukraine's Independence in the twentieth Century
315-VIII	On Perpetuation of the Victory over Nazism in World War II of 1939–1945
316-VIII	On Access to the Archives of Repressive Bodies of the Communist Totalitarian Regime of 1917–1991
317-VIII	On Condemnation of the Communist and National Socialist (Nazi) Regimes and Prohibition of Propaganda of their Symbols

The state-sponsored Ukrainian Institute of National Memory drafted the laws, and the head of the institute, Volodymyr Viatrovych, presented the drafts to the Ukrainian parliament.[2] The laws were adopted by a comfortable majority and shortly afterwards signed by the Ukrainian President Petro Poroshenko. While the degree of support for the laws varied among the various parliamentary factions (Petro Poroshenko Bloc, People's Front, Self-Reliance, Radical party, Fatherland party, Revival, People's Will, and a group of deputies non-affiliated with any faction),[3] only the Opposition Bloc completely opposed the laws.

This chapter examines the role of the Ukrainian state in the conceptualization of historical events with the aim of promoting a sense of communal belonging.[4] It explores how the Ukrainian policy-makers

Verkhovna Rada, 9 April 2015, available at http://zakon5.rada.gov.ua/laws/show/317-19. The quotes from the laws are my own translation from Ukrainian.

2 The Ukrainian Institute of National Memory is a state-sponsored institution responsible for the official interpretation of the Ukrainian history. See H. Kasianov, 'K Desiatiletiyu Ukrainskogo Instituta Natsionalnoy Pamyati (2006–2016)' (On the 10th Anniversary of the Ukrainian Institute of National Memory), *Historians.in.ua*, 14 January 2016, available at http://historians.in.ua/index.php/en/dyskusiya/1755-georgij-kas-yanov-k-desyatiletiyu-ukrainskogo-instituta-natsional-noj-pamyati-2006-2016.

3 The translated Ukrainian names for the political parties mentioned are as follows: Petro Poroshenko Bloc (*Blok Petra Poroshenka*), People's Front (*Narodnyi Front*), Self-Reliance (*Samopomich*), Radical party (*Radykalna Partiia*), Fatherland party (*Batkivshchyna*), Revival (*Vidrodzhennia*), People's Will (*Volia Narodu*), and Opposition Bloc (*Opozytsiinyi Blok*).

4 For a theoretical underpinning of the role of law in the conceptualization of historical events, see the chapter by Eric Heinze and the Introduction by Uladzislau Belavusau and Aleksandra Gliszczyńska-Grabias in the present volume.

responded to the re-configuration of the Russian–Ukrainian relations in 2013–15 through an assessment of both the experience of Ukrainians in the Soviet Union and their aspirations to join the European community. The central argument of this chapter is embedded in interpretive approaches to policy-making that emphasize the role of narratives constructed by political actors in policy-relevant situations. The chapter is based upon an analysis of policy-relevant documents, e.g. parliamentary debates, statements of political actors in the media, and also the texts of the laws themselves. This chapter demonstrates how the Ukrainian policy-makers' narrative of Ukraine's past and future reflected their intention to distinguish between the different Ukrainian and Russian forms of remembrance and to promote a commonality between Ukrainian and European values. By challenging this narrative, various policy-relevant actors (e.g. the Russian government, international organizations, scholars, and legal experts) provided their own accounts of the experience of Ukrainians in the Soviet Union and their endeavors to become part of the European community.

2 Making Sense of the World through Narratives

Originating in literary studies, narrative analysis has frequently been used in various fields of the social sciences, e.g. in nationalism studies, political science, public administration, international relations, and sociology. The notion of narrative has been thoroughly theorized in a number of scholarly works devoted to social science theory.[5] Previous studies on interpretive policy analysis have already demonstrated the role narratives perform in various policy settings.[6] Molly Patterson and Kristen R. Monroe view a narrative as a way in which one assembles disparate facts in order to make sense of the world. Individuals and collectivities

[5] J. Bruner, 'The Narrative Construction of Reality', *Critical Inquiry* 18:1 (1991), 1–21; M.R. Somers, 'The Narrative Constitution of Identity: A Relational and Network Approach', *Theory and Society* 23:5 (1994), 605–49; D. Polkinghorne, 'Narrative Configuration in Qualitative Analysis', *International Journal of Qualitative Studies in Education* 8:1 (1995), 5–23.

[6] S. Shenhav, 'We Have a Place in a Long Story. Empowered Narratives and the Construction of Communities: The Case of US Presidential Debates', *Narrative Inquiry* 19:2 (2009), 199–218; J. Subotić, 'Stories States Tell: Identity, Narrative, and Human Rights in the Balkans', *Slavic Review* 72:2 (2013), 306–26; M. van Hulst, 'Storytelling, a Model of and a Model for Planning', *Planning Theory* 11:3 (2012), 299–318; L. Klymenko, 'The Holodomor Law and National Trauma Construction in Ukraine', *Canadian Slavonic Papers* 58:4 (2016): 341–61.

(e.g. social groups or nations) create narratives in the process of understanding political reality. The constructed narrative involves human beings as characters. Their experiences are assembled in a plot, which is organized sequentially. The analysis of the narratives unpacks the cognitive maps of the narrators, i.e. the way they organize their experiences and perceive themselves and others. The narrators draw upon relevant cultural aspects, justify their decisions, explain the present, and project the future.[7]

For Patterson and Monroe, shared narratives provide individuals and collectivities with a sense of common understanding of a particular event, and therefore with a common identity. Narratives about the nation's past and future provide a sense of belonging to a particular societal group, and also a sense of a group's being, origin, and development. By interpreting history, people modify their current relationships in a community. Thus, such narratives are essential to any kind of socialization and collective functioning. This conceptualization of the notion of narrative therefore means that a narrative often becomes a site of political contestation. People's drive to change the interpretation of certain historical accounts is not only rooted in their desire to increase historical accuracy, but also to develop their understanding of who they are and how they relate to others. Ultimately, by telling the stories of the past, individuals and collectives deal with the present and imagine the future.[8]

3 Narrating a Story of Ukraine's Soviet Past . . .

The adoption of the de-communization laws was justified by the Ukrainian policy-makers through the creation of a narrative of Ukraine's Soviet past and European future. In essence, through the conceptualization of Ukraine's status in the former Soviet Union, the Ukrainian policy-makers argued for a need to distance the country from Russia's integration projects and to accelerate its rapprochement with the EU. In this sense, the de-communization laws became part of Ukraine's foreign and security policy. The Ukrainian policy-makers' intention to break with Russian ideological influence was visible in the law on the perpetuation of the victory

[7] M. Patterson and K.R. Monroe, 'Narrative in Political Science', *Annual Review of Political Science* 1:1 (1998), 315–17.

[8] *Ibid.*, 321–4.

over Nazism. By assessing the experience of Ukrainians during World War II, the policy-makers intended to promote a conceptual difference between the Ukrainian and Russian populations. According to the Head of the Ukrainian Institute of National Memory, the Russian Federation has been using the Soviet memory of the Great Patriotic War in its current struggle against Ukraine.[9] In fact, existing scholarly works have explored how in post-Soviet Russia, the discourse on World War II has been effectively reduced to a remembrance of the Great Patriotic War. Originating in the Soviet period, this narrative was used to describe only the Soviet Union's defensive war against Germany from 1941 onwards until 1945, thus omitting the Molotov–Ribbentrop Pact. After 1965, Victory Day over Nazi Germany became a day for celebrating Soviet and subsequently Russian military glory.[10]

In contrast to the Russian tradition of commemorating the Great Patriotic War of 1941–5, the Ukrainian policy-makers suggested remembering the war as World War II of 1939–45, the same as it is known in Western and European countries. Although the law retained Victory Day on 9 May as a national holiday, it called for the commemoration of both Ukrainian war heroes and war victims. Moreover, the law obliged Ukrainian citizens to respect the memory of war veterans and participants in the Ukrainian liberation movement.[11] In a Ukrainian context, the term "war veterans" usually denotes former Soviet Red Army soldiers, and the term "participants in the Ukrainian liberation movement" usually refers to the anti-Soviet wartime movement OUN (Organization of Ukrainian Nationalists) under the leadership of Stepan Bandera and its armed wing the UPA (Ukrainian Insurgent Army). The elevation of the OUN and the UPA to the level of Ukrainian national heroes contradicts the Russian discourse on the Great Patriotic War, where the above-mentioned units have a strictly negative connotation. For example, the participation of far-right organizations in the 2013–14 Ukrainian Euromaidan revolution was often presented in Russia as being representative of the whole Maidan, although

[9] Verkhovna Rada Ukrainy, 'Stenohrama Plenarnoho Zasidannia 25 (Records of the Plenary Session 25)', 9 April 2015, available at http://rada.gov.ua/meeting/stenogr/show/5842.html.

[10] R. Markwick, 'The Great Patriotic War in Soviet and Post-Soviet Collective Memory', in D. Stone (ed.), *The Oxford Handbook of Postwar European History* (Oxford University Press, 2012), 692–713.

[11] Verkhovna Rada Ukrainy, 'Pro Uvichnennia Peremohy nad Natsyzmom u Druhii Svitovii Viini 1939–1945 Rokiv (On Perpetuation of the Victory over Nazism in WWII of 1939–1945)', *Verkhovna Rada*, 9 April 2015, available at http://zakon3.rada.gov.ua/laws/show/315-19.

their role was exaggerated. By calling the Ukrainian protestors "fascists" and "followers of Stepan Bandera," the Russian government and media sought to de-legitimize the Ukrainian uprising as a whole.[12]

The difference in the perception of the Soviet past between Ukrainian and Russian policy-makers was even more visible in the law on honoring the fighters for Ukrainian statehood in the twentieth century. In the law, the policy-makers identified a number of organizations who – from their perspective – fought for Ukraine's independence between 1917 and 1991. These ranged from institutions of the Ukrainian People's Republic (UNR) to the People's Movement for Ukraine (*Rukh*), and included the OUN and the UPA.[13] During the related parliamentary debates, the Head of the Institute of National Memory conceptualized the Soviet regime as a period of Russian domination, during which Ukrainians were fighting for an independent Ukrainian state. Some deputies considered those on the Ukrainian side in the current Donbas war to be the successors to the organizations that had fought for Ukrainian independence in the twentieth century. Thus, the ongoing war was perceived by the Ukrainian policy-makers as a continuation of Ukraine's liberation struggle from Russia's domination during the Soviet era.[14]

The Ukrainian policy-makers therefore firmly categorized Soviet Ukraine, and by extension today's Ukraine, as an object of Russia's oppression. In the view of the speaker of the Ukrainian parliament Volodymyr Hroisman, "Ukraine has been leading a 100-year-old war against Russian imperialism and Russian occupation."[15] For Mykhailo Holovko, deputy from the Freedom party, the adoption of the law was therefore seen as "breaking the fetters imposed by Moscow" and demonstrating respect for Ukrainian heroes.[16] Yet, perhaps the most telling example of the policy-makers' perception of Ukrainian experiences in the Soviet Union came

[12] G. Hausmann and T. Penter, 'Der Gebrauch der Geschichte. Ukraine 2014: Ideologie vs. Historiographie', *Osteuropa* 64:9–10 (2014), 38–9. See also the chapter by Nikolay Koposov in the present volume.

[13] Verkhovna Rada Ukrainy, 'Pro Pravovyi Status ta Vshanuvannia Pamiati Bortsiv za Nezhalezhnist Ukrainy u 20 Stolitti (On the Legal Status and Honoring the Memory of Fighters for Ukraine's Independence in the 20th Century)', *Verkhovna Rada*, 9 April 2015, available at http://zakon3.rada.gov.ua/laws/show/314-19.

[14] Verkhovna Rada Ukrainy, 'Stenohrama Plenarnoho Zasidannia 25 (Records of the Plenary Session 25).'

[15] *Ibid.*

[16] *Ibid.*

from deputy Ivan Krulko of the Fatherland party. During the parliamentary debate he maintained the following:

> It is essential that we accomplish an important action, an action that will consolidate the Ukrainian state. The action that will today show that Ukraine will eventually cut the umbilical cord with the Kremlin and Moscow, which occupied Ukraine and continues its aggression against our state today.[17]

In this excerpt, Krulko expressed his support for the law through the use of the metaphor "[to] cut the umbilical cord between Ukraine and Moscow." In this way, he compared the Russian–Ukrainian relations to those of mother and child. Consequently, by saying "[to] cut the umbilical cord" he implied the birth of the Ukrainian nation by its separation from Russia.

The law on fighters for Ukraine's independence acknowledged social benefits for surviving fighters and recognized their military honors. Moreover, the Ukrainian policy-makers further acknowledged the role of the Ukrainian state in the creation of public awareness of the history of the organizations involved in the struggle for Ukrainian independence, e.g. through the construction of memorial complexes, improvement of school curricula, commemoration of their names in geographical objects, and distribution of information on the role of fighters for Ukraine's independence in Ukraine and abroad.[18] The supreme role of the state in the interpretation of Ukrainian history is also evident in the law's provision on introducing liability for the public denial of Ukrainian fighters' struggle for Ukraine's independence. The law declared that "public denial of the legitimacy of the struggle for Ukrainian independence in the twentieth century is an insult to the memory of fighters for Ukrainian independence in the twentieth century, a humiliation of the dignity of the Ukrainian people, and is unlawful."[19] According to the law, Ukrainians, foreigners, or stateless persons who publicly express disrespect towards the fighters are committing an offense.[20]

The Ukrainian policy-makers' proposition to underscore the difference between the Ukrainian and Russian societies has been further laid down in the law on the condemnation of the Communist and Nazi regimes. This law defined the Nazi regime and the Soviet Communist

[17] *Ibid.*

[18] Verkhovna Rada Ukrainy, 'Pro Pravovyi Status ta Vshanuvannia Pamiati Bortsiv za Nezhalezhnist Ukraini u 20 Stolitti (On the Legal Status and Honoring the Memory of Fighters for Ukraine's Independence in the 20th Century)'.

[19] *Ibid.*

[20] *Ibid.*

regime of 1917–91 as criminal, in that they carried out state terror expressed through the violation of human rights in various forms which are considered incompatible with fundamental human rights and civil liberties.[21] Following the definition of the Communist (and Nazi) regime as totalitarian, the law prohibited the propaganda of Communist (and Nazi) symbols used by political parties or citizens' initiatives and regulated the dismantling of symbols of the Communist regime, which were embodied in the names of streets, towns, and public places. The law introduced a criminal liability for the production, distribution, and public use of Communist (and Nazi) symbols, which may entail a five-year-term imprisonment, with or without confiscation of property.[22]

During the parliamentary debate on Holy Thursday, the speaker of the Ukrainian parliament urged the deputies to "cleanse themselves of the Communist contagion and plague."[23] The metaphor he used implied that he perceived the Communist era to be a dark age associated with disease and death. Commenting on this law, the leader of the Radical party, Oleh Liashko, stated:

> Today is really a historical day. At last, on Holy Thursday, in the 24th year of independence, the Ukrainian parliament is adopting decisions that we should have adopted 24 years ago after the collapse of the Soviet Union. That is why today our country is trembling: because we did not immediately cut that umbilical cord with totalitarianism, Communism, and Stalinism, which took away millions of lives of Ukrainian citizens.[24]

Similar to Krulko, who commented on the law on fighters for Ukrainian statehood, Liashko's use of the metaphor "[to] cut the umbilical cord of totalitarianism" implied the birth of the Ukrainian nation. Although the law did not explicitly refer to Russia, one could assume that by condemning the Soviet regime, the Ukrainian policy-makers simultaneously condemned today's Russia. As explored in previous studies, in Russia under

[21] Verkhovna Rada Ukrainy, 'Pro Zasudzhennia Komunistychnoho ta Natsional-Sotsialistychnoho (Natsyskoho) Totalitarnykh Rezhymiv v Ukraini ta Zaboronu Propahandy Ikhnioi Symvoliky (On the Condemnation of the Communist and National Socialism (Nazi) Regimes and Prohibition of Propaganda of their Symbols)'.

[22] *Ibid.*

[23] The day on which the de-communization laws were adopted happened to be Holy Thursday (the Thursday before Easter), when Orthodox Christians commemorate the Last Supper. Holy Thursday, also called Clean Thursday, is associated in Ukraine with the tradition of washing oneself and cleaning up one's home.

[24] Verkhovna Rada Ukrainy, 'Stenohrama Plenarnoho Zasidannia 25 (Records of the Plenary Session 25)'.

the leadership of Vladimir Putin, the Soviet Union has been positively perceived and often associated with great power, the gigantic construction projects of the 1930s, victory over Nazi Germany, the takeover of the Arctic, and the conquest of space. Even the figure of Stalin is perceived ambivalently in Russia – both condemned for repressions but honored for his role in the Soviet Union's victory over Nazi Germany.[25]

The Ukrainian policy-makers' intention to draw an ideological boundary between Russia and Ukraine was further elaborated in the law that regulated public access to the archives of the Soviet governmental institutions of 1917–91. Similar to the previous laws, the law defined the Communist regime as totalitarian and provided a long list of institutions that according to the policy-makers had a repressive function.[26] During the parliamentary debate, the Head of the Ukrainian Institute of National Memory argued that the main aim of opening archives was to raise public awareness about the crimes and violations of human rights in the Soviet Union.[27]

4 . . . and Its European Future

While moving away from Russia's ideological influence, the Ukrainian policy-makers have also attempted to promote ideological commonalities with European countries. This idea has been manifested in the creation of common World War II commemorative practices in the law on the perpetuation of victory over Nazism. To join the Western tradition of commemorating World War II victims, the Ukrainian policy-makers established 8 May as a new commemorative day: the Day of Remembrance and Reconciliation.[28] In this respect, the law referred to the resolutions of the UN General Assembly of 2004 and 2010 that established 8 and 9 May as a time for remembrance and reconciliation and called for paying tribute to all war victims.[29] Moreover, the law obliged Ukrainian citizens to pay respect to

[25] A. Roginskij, 'Erinnerung und Freiheit. Die Stalinismus-Diskussion in der UdSSR und Russland', *Osteuropa* 61:4 (2011), 63–4.

[26] Verkhovna Rada Ukrainy, 'Pro Dostup do Arkhiviv Represyvnykh Orhaniv Komunistychnoho Totalitarnoho Rezhymu 1917–1991 Rokiv (On Access to the Archives of Repressive Bodies of the Communist Totalitarian Regime of 1917–1991)'.

[27] Verkhovna Rada Ukrainy, 'Stenohrama Plenarnoho Zasidannia 25 (Records of the Plenary Session 25)'.

[28] Verkhovna Rada Ukrainy, 'Pro Uvichnennia Peremohy nad Natsyzmom u Druhii Svitovii Viini 1939–1945 Rokiv (On Perpetuation of the Victory over Nazism in WWII of 1939–1945)'.

[29] UN General Assembly, 'Commemoration of the Sixtieth Anniversary of the End of the Second World War', *UN*, 22 November 2004, available at www.un.org/en/events/remembranceday/.

World War II victims and explicitly named the Nazi regime of Germany and the Communist regime of the Soviet Union as being responsible for the outbreak of World War II. The law acknowledged the crimes committed by both the Nazi and Communist regimes by designating the Communist regime to be equally totalitarian as the Nazi regime.[30] Such a perception of the role of the Soviet Union under the leadership of Stalin at the outset of World War II by the Ukrainian policy-makers reflects the view expressed in some other Eastern European countries. Previous works have already explored how the condemnation of the Molotov–Ribbentrop Pact has become part of the World War II remembrance in post-Communist Poland and in the Baltic states. In Poland, the Molotov–Ribbentrop Pact stands for the beginning of what is often termed "the double occupation," whereas in the Baltic states it additionally denotes the loss of state sovereignty.[31]

The condemnation of Communism has further been seen by the Ukrainian policy-makers as a medium of Ukraine's Europeanization and democratization. The leader of the Radical party maintained that the adoption of the law on the condemnation of Nazism and Communism was a historical decision that would make Ukraine a genuinely democratic and European country.[32] The Head of the Ukrainian Institute of National Memory proposed taking Eastern European countries as a model. In his view, the condemnation of Communism may lead to Ukraine's EU and NATO membership, in the same way that it had worked for other Eastern European countries. He explained in one of his interviews:

> Today is the best time to finally complete the de-communization of the country. In contrast to other post-Communist countries of Eastern Europe, Ukraine did not do this at the beginning of the 1990s. In countries such as the Czech Republic, Poland, and the Baltic countries, similar laws were adopted in the early 1990s . . . In this way, in these countries the process of democratic revolutions was completed, and this allowed these countries to become EU and NATO members . . . I am convinced that the break with the totalitarian past is an incredibly important condition for Ukraine's development as a normal democratic state.[33]

30 Verkhovna Rada Ukrainy, 'Pro Uvichnennia Peremohy nad Natsyzmom u Druhii Svitovii Viini 1939–1945 Rokiv (On Perpetuation of the Victory over Nazism in WWII of 1939–1945)'.

31 S. Troebst, 'Der 23. August 1939. Ein europäischer Lieu de mémoire?', *Osteuropa* 59:7–8 (2009), 253–4.

32 Verkhovna Rada Ukrainy, 'Stenohrama Plenarnoho Zasidannia 25 (Records of the Plenary Session 25)'.

33 V. Viatrovych, 'Nuzhno li Zapreshchat Kommunistichenskuyu Ideologiyu v Ukraine?' (Is it Necessary to Forbid the Communist Ideology in Ukraine?), *Gordon*, 7 April 2015, available at http://gordonua.com/day_question/zapret-communisma.html.

In the spirit of Ukrainian democratization, the law claimed to ensure the protection of human rights and civil liberties and the development of an independent, democratic, and law-abiding Ukrainian state. The law emphasized the obligation of the Ukrainian state to reveal all available information about crimes of genocide, crimes against humanity, and war crimes that were committed in Ukraine by representatives of the Communist and Nazi totalitarian regimes. The law furthermore recognized the role of the state in raising public awareness about these crimes, assisting NGOs carrying out research on totalitarian regimes, providing public access to archives of former Soviet state security bodies, and developing respect for human dignity, fundamental human rights, and democracy within the Ukrainian population.[34]

The Ukrainian policy-makers' reference to the 1991 Ukrainian law on the rehabilitation of the victims of the political repressions in the Soviet Union,[35] and also to some provisions on coming to terms with the Communist and Nazi crimes in Europe in a number of resolutions by international institutions, has served to increase the credibility of the law on the condemnation of Nazism and Communism. In particular, the law referred to the 1996 Council of Europe (CoE) Parliamentary Assembly resolution on measures to dismantle the heritage of former Communist totalitarian systems;[36] the 2006 CoE Parliamentary Assembly resolution on the need for international condemnation of the crimes of the totalitarian Communist regimes;[37] the 2006 CoE Parliamentary Assembly resolution on combating the resurrection of Nazi ideology;[38] the 2009 CoE Parliamentary Assembly resolution on the attitude to memorials exposed

[34] Verkhovna Rada Ukrainy, 'Pro Zasudzhennia Komunistychnoho ta Natsional-Sotsialistychnoho (Natsyskoho) Totalitarnykh Rezhymiv v Ukraini ta Zaboronu Propahandy Ikhnioi Symvoliky (On the Condemnation of the Communist and National Socialism (Nazi) Regimes and Prohibition of Propaganda of their Symbols)'.

[35] Verkhovna Rada Ukrainy, 'Pro Reabilitatsiiu Zhertv Politychnykh Represii na Ukraini (On Rehabilitation of Victims of Political Repressions in Ukraine)', 17 April 1991, available at http://zakon3.rada.gov.ua/laws/show/962-12.

[36] Parliamentary Assembly of the Council of Europe, 'Measures to Dismantle the Heritage of Former Communist Totalitarian Systems', 1996, available at http://assembly.coe.int/nw/xml/XRef/Xref-XML2HTML-en.asp?fileid=16507&lang=en.

[37] Parliamentary Assembly of the Council of Europe, 'Resolution 1481 (2006): Need for International Condemnation of Crimes of Totalitarian Communist Regimes', 25 January 2006, available at http://assembly.coe.int/nw/xml/XRef/Xref-XML2HTML-en.asp?fileid=17403&lang=en.

[38] Parliamentary Assembly of the Council of Europe, 'Combating the Resurrection of Nazi Ideology', 12 April 2006, available at www.assembly.coe.int/nw/xml/XRef/Xref-XML2HTML-en.asp?fileid=17427&lang=en.

to different historical interpretations in CoE Member States;[39] and the 2009 OSCE Parliamentary Assembly resolution on the promotion of human rights and civil liberties in the OSCE region in the twenty-first century.[40]

In its intention to follow the European discourse on human rights by condemning Stalinist crimes, the law additionally referred to the 2008 European Parliament declaration on the proclamation of 23 August as the European Day of Remembrance for Victims of Stalinism and Nazism[41]; the 2008 European Parliament resolution on commemoration of the Holodomor[42]; the 2009 European Parliament resolution on European Conscience and Totalitarianism[43]; the 2003 UN declaration on the seventieth anniversary of the Great Famine of 1932–3 in Ukraine[44]; and the 2006 Ukrainian law on the Holodomor.[45]

Through drawing an analogy between the Nazi and Communist regimes, the Ukrainian policy-makers apparently aimed to make the nature of the Communist crimes understandable to both the Ukrainian population and the international community. There exists a fundamental Western understanding about the totalitarian nature of the Nazi regime of 1933–45 and its crimes, identified at the 1945–6 Nuremberg International Military

[39] Parliamentary Assembly of the Council of Europe, 'Resolution 1652 (2009): Attitude to Memorials Exposed to Different Historical Interpretations in Council of Europe Member States', 29 January 2009, available at http://assembly.coe.int/nw/xml/XRef/Xref-XML2HTML-EN.asp?fileid=17713&lang=en.

[40] OSCE Parliamentary Assembly, 'Vilnius Declaration of the OSCE Parliamentary Assembly and Resolutions Adopted at the 18th Annual Session', 29 July 2009, available at www.oscepa.org/documents/all-documents/annual-sessions/2009-vilnius/declaration-6/261-2009-vilnius-declaration-eng/file.

[41] European Parliament, 'Declaration of the European Parliament on the Proclamation of 23 August as European Day of Remembrance for Victims of Stalinism and Nazism', *European Parliament*, 23 September 2008, available at www.europarl.europa.eu/sides/getDoc.do?reference=P6_TA(2008)0439&language=EN.

[42] European Parliament, 'Commemoration of the Holodomor, the Artificial Famine in Ukraine (1932–1933)', 23 October 2008, available at www.europarl.europa.eu/sides/getDoc.do?type=TA&reference=P6-TA-2008-0523&language=EN.

[43] European Parliament, 'European Parliament Resolution of 2 April 2009 on European Conscience and Totalitarianism', 2 April 2009, available at www.europarl.europa.eu/sides/getDoc.do?pubRef=-//EP//TEXT+TA+P6-TA-2009-0213+0+DOC+XML+V0//EN.

[44] E.M. Williams, 'Ukraine Issues Joint Declaration at the United Nations in Connection to the 70th Anniversary of the Great Famine in Ukraine of 1932–1933', *ArtUkraine.com*, 11 November 2003, available at www.artukraine.com/famineart/ukr_un_decl.htm.

[45] Verkhovna Rada Ukrainy, 'Pro Holodomor 1932–1933 Rokiv v Ukraini (On the Holodomor of 1932–33 in Ukraine)', 28 November 2006, available at http://zakon4.rada.gov.ua/laws/show/376-16.

Tribunal. The Ukrainian policy-makers' equation of the Communist and Nazi regimes seems to follow the line taken by some Eastern European countries. As previous studies point out, by identifying similarities between Communist and Nazi crimes, many Eastern European EU member states aimed at drawing the attention of Western European countries to experiences of Eastern Europeans in the twentieth century.[46]

The intention of the Ukrainian policy-makers to adhere to European democratic values was further manifested in the Ukrainian law on archives. The law on archives declared that "the right of each citizen to obtain objective information about the history of one's country is one of the foundations of a democratic state".[47] By reference to the guidelines by the CoE Committee of Ministers on European policy on access to archives,[48] the law promoted the necessity of adopting legislation on the opening of archives. According to the Head of the Ukrainian Institute of National Memory, the Ukrainian state's dealing with its Communist archives can be modeled on the post-Communist countries of Eastern Europe. He argued that similar laws on archives have been adopted in twelve post-Communist Eastern European countries and are recommended by European institutions. In his view, the Ukrainian law on archives embodied a European approach to the people's right of access to the archives of repressive institutions. Moreover, it was supposed to lead to a discontinuation of the Ukrainian elite, some members of which originate from the Soviet time and still belong to the Ukrainian state security service and the police.[49]

5 Contesting the National Narrative

The Ukrainian policy-makers' narrative of Ukraine's past and future has, however, been challenged by several policy-relevant actors. The

46 M. Mälksoo, 'The Memory Politics of Becoming European: The East European Subalterns and the Collective Memory of Europe', *European Journal of International Relations* 15:4 (2009), 653–80. See also the chapter by Maria Mälksoo in the present volume.

47 Verkhovna Rada Ukrainy, 'Pro Dostup do Arkhiviv Represyvnykh Orhaniv Komunistychnoho Totalitarnoho Rezhymu 1917–1991 Rokiv (On Access to the Archives of Repressive Bodies of the Communist Totalitarian Regime of 1917–1991)'.

48 Council of Europe, Committee of Ministers, 'Recommendation No. R (2000) 13 of the Committee of Ministers to Member States on a European Policy on Access to Archives', 13 July 2000, available at https://search.coe.int/cm/Pages/result_details.aspx?ObjectID=09000016804cea4f.

49 Verkhovna Rada Ukrainy, 'Stenohrama Plenarnoho Zasidannia 25 (Records of the Plenary Session 25)'.

aforementioned laws have sparked an intense debate among scholars, human rights activists, and legal experts. Some international organizations and also the Russian government have contested the narrative of the Ukrainian policy-makers. The Opposition Bloc in the Ukrainian parliament issued a statement in which it challenged the definition of Soviet and European values laid out in the de-communization laws. They raised the concern that:

> By adopting the law banning propaganda of the Communist and National-Socialist (Nazi) totalitarian regimes, the war coalition has taken a new and decisive step towards strengthening confrontation in society, increasing the risk of the country's division, and eventually losing its chance to achieve national consolidation . . . The adoption of the decision to change the names of cities, streets, and squares in the form of arrant totalitarianism is a relapse to the limitation of the rights and freedoms of citizens. This does not have anything in common with democratic norms, where citizens of towns and local communities have the right to decide how to name the street on which they live. The ban on the elderly respecting the memory of their heroic deeds and on their children retaining a deserving memory of them does not have anything in common with Western values either.[50]

In this way, the Opposition Bloc questioned the adherence of Ukrainian policy-makers to Western democratic values by problematizing state-citizen relations and by raising the question of citizens' participation in the renaming of street names and cities. In this respect, it viewed the laws as being divisive for the Ukrainian society. The Opposition Bloc criticized the Ukrainian policy-makers' conceptualization of World War II and proposed to continue celebrating the heroism of former Ukrainian Red Army soldiers. In the above excerpt, it expressed its criticism towards the governing coalition by employing the word "totalitarianism" used in the de-communization laws to counter-label the governance style of the governing coalition and by characterizing it as "the war coalition."

The Russian government also rejected the Ukrainian national narrative. The Russian foreign minister Sergei Lavrov described the de-communization laws as "destructive" to the peace process in the Donbas. For him, the laws glorified the Nazis and stripped the hero status from those he called "the true heroes of the Great Patriotic War

[50] Opposition Bloc, 'Novosti Oppozitsionnogo Bloka (News of the Opposition Bloc)', 10 April 2015, available at http://opposition.org.ua/news/opozicijnij-blok-vimagae-vid-prezidenta-naklasti-veto-na-zakon-yakij-rozkolyue-suspilstvo-znevazhae-konstituciyu-i-demokratiyu-v-ukrani.html.

and World War II."[51] The Russian Ministry of Foreign Affairs issued a statement in which it challenged the Ukrainian policy-makers' view of the experience of Ukrainians in the Soviet Union. For the Ukrainian authorities, the Soviet Union embodied political repressions and Russia's domination, but for the Russian government it stood for modernization and voluntary membership. The Russian Ministry of Foreign Affairs questioned the trustworthiness of the Ukrainian view in the following manner:

> By portraying the period of 1917–1991 as a period of struggle for Ukraine's independence and declaring "the Communist totalitarian regime" as "criminal" and "as such that was executing a period of state terror," the current Ukrainian authorities are trying to erase the true history of Ukraine in the 20th century and its gradual modernization in the Soviet Union . . . It remains unclear what several generations of Ukrainians who were building the modern state were doing, those who were not sitting in the hide-outs of Banderites and were not participating in the nationalist dissident movement.[52]

Moreover, the Ukrainian policy-makers' narrative of Ukraine's past and future has been contested by some scholars. The de-communization laws sparked a short but fierce scholarly debate that unfolded mainly on the pages of the journal *Krytyka*.[53] Following the passing of the laws by the Ukrainian parliament, a group of international scholars initiated an open letter urging the Ukrainian President to abstain from signing two of the laws: the law on fighters for Ukraine's independence and the law on the condemnation of Nazism and Communism.[54] The letter

[51] UNIAN, 'Lavrov Zayavil, chto Zakony Ukrainy o Dekommunizatsii "Gubitelny" dlia Mirnogo Protsessa na Donbasse' (Lavrov Stated that the Laws on De-Communization in Ukraine are "Destructive" for the Peace Process in the Donbass), 14 April 2015, available at www.unian.net/politics/1066858-lavrov-zayavil-chto-zakonyi-ukrainyi-o-dekommunizatsii-gubitelnyi-dlya-mirnogo-protsessa-na-donbasse.html.

[52] Ministry of Foreign Affairs of the Russian Federation, 'Kommentarii Departamenta Informatsii i Pechati MID Rossii v Svyazi s Predprinimaemymi na Ukraine Shagami po Borbe s Istoriey Svoego Gosudarstva' (Comment of the Department of Information of the Ministry of Foreign Affairs of Russia Regarding the Attempt of Ukraine to Overcome its Own History), 10 April 2015, available at http://archive.mid.ru//brp_4.nsf/newsline/96F6BF69FE0EBBA543257E23005AB8B4.

[53] *Krytyka*, 'The Future of Ukraine's Past', 2015, available at http://krytyka.com/en/solutions/featured/future-ukraines-past.

[54] D.R. Marples, 'Open Letter from Scholars and Experts on Ukraine Re. the So-Called "Anti-Communist Law"' *Krytyka* 2015, available at http://krytyka.com/en/articles/open-letter-scholars-and-experts-ukraine-re-so-called-anti-communist-law.

raised the age-old question of the role of the state in the formation of historical knowledge and the democratically driven creation of a common past. The signatories of the letter opposed the Ukrainian policy-makers' narrative of the Soviet past by pointing to the crimes committed by the OUN and the UPA (e.g. the ethnic cleansing of Poles and anti-Jewish pogroms) and by citing positive examples of Ukraine's development within the Soviet Union (e.g. the promotion of the Ukrainian language in the 1920s and the emergence of Ukrainian civil society groups in the 1980s).[55]

The scholarly discussion has further focused on citizen participation in the de-communization policy and the adoption of European values in Ukraine. Several scholars have demonstrated to what extent the de-communization laws failed to incorporate a European approach to freedom of expression, and they have urged for an open debate on the Ukrainian history. In their opinion, the de-communization laws rather politicized Ukrainian history as they introduced one "correct" state-mandated narrative. Moreover, the Ukrainian policy-makers' elevation of the OUN and the UPA to the level of Ukrainian national heroes firmly contradicted the European discourse on human rights expressed through the commemoration of the Holocaust victims and condemnation of the Holocaust perpetrators.[56] Studies by historians have already revealed that these organizations collaborated with Nazi Germany and were responsible for crimes against the Jewish and Polish populations during World War II.[57] Moreover, some scholars have argued that following the adoption of the laws, it remained unclear as to how the Ukrainian state will react to the Nazi emblems of some of the far-right organizations in today's Ukraine.[58] Scholars were also suspicious of the policy-makers' intention to

[55] *Ibid.*

[56] O. Shevel, 'De-Communization Laws' Need to Be Amended to Conform to European Standards', *VoxUkraine*, 7 May 2015, available at http://voxukraine.org/2015/05/07/de-communization-laws-need-to-be-amended-to-conform-to-european-standards/; J.-P. Himka, 'Legislating Historical Truth: Ukraine's Laws of 9 April 2015', *Ab Imperio*, April 2015, available at http://net.abimperio.net/node/3442; A. Portnov, 'Andrey Portnov ob Istoricheskikh Zakonakh 9 Aprelia' (Andrey Portnov about Historical Laws on 9 April), *Ab Imperio*, 2015, available at http://net.abimperio.net/node/3437.

[57] Himka, 'Legislating Historical Truth: Ukraine's Laws of 9 April 2015'.

[58] *Ibid.*; P.A. Rudling and C. Gilley, 'Laws 2558 and 2538-1: On Critical Inquiry, the Holocaust, and Academic Freedom in Ukraine', *Political Critique*, 29 April 2015, available at http://ukraine.politicalcritique.org/2015/04/laws-2558-and-2538-1-on-critical-inquiry-the-holocaust-and-academic-freedom-in-ukraine/.

centralize all archival documents under the aegis of the state-sponsored Ukrainian Institute of National Memory. Such a procedure on the part of the Ukrainian state was feared to restrict public access to the archives.[59] Yet, scholars who were in favor of the laws argued for their necessity, despite recognizing their flaws. In their opinion, the involvement of the OUN and the UPA in war crimes and also their role in the struggle for Ukraine's independence should be acknowledged, and the crimes of the Communist era condemned.[60]

Several Ukrainian legal experts from the Kharkiv Human Rights Protection Group have criticized the laws for imposing restrictions on expressing public opinion about the Communist past.[61] The European Commission for Democracy through Law (The Venice Commission) expressed its concern regarding the law on the condemnation of the Communist and Nazi regimes. The Commission found the law's provisions on symbols, propaganda, denial of crime, sanctions, and the banning of association too vaguely defined to enable individuals to adapt their behavior to accord with the law. The Commission recommended that the Ukrainian authorities allow a multiplicity of approaches to Ukrainian history in order to promote national consolidation, solidarity, and democracy.[62] The United States Holocaust Memorial Museum likewise urged the Ukrainian government to refrain from the politicization of history, particularly that of the OUN and the UPA. It also urged Ukraine to secure scholarly research and open debate on Ukraine's national past.[63]

[59] Himka, 'Legislating Historical Truth: Ukraine's Laws of 9 April 2015'.

[60] A.J. Motyl, 'Kiev's Purge. Behind the New Legislation to Decommunize Ukraine', *Foreign Affairs*, 28 April 2015, available at www.foreignaffairs.com/articles/ukraine/2015-04-28/kievs-purge; V. Kulyk, 'On Shoddy Laws and Insensitive Critics', *Krytyka*, May 2015, available at http://krytyka.com/en/solutions/opinions/shoddy-laws-and-insensitive-critics.

[61] H. Coynash, 'President Signs Dangerously Flawed "Decommunization" Laws', *Kharkiv Human Rights Protection Group*, 16 May 2015, available at http://khpg.org/index.php?id=1431743447; V. Yavorsky, 'Analysis of the Law on Prohibiting Communist Symbols', *Human Rights in Ukraine*, 2 May 2015, available at http://khpg.org/en/index.php?id=1430564974.

[62] European Commission for Democracy through Law, 'Joint Interim Opinion', 18 December 2015, available at www.legislationline.org/download/action/download/id/6156/file/CDL-AD2015041_EN.pdf.

[63] United States Holocaust Memorial Museum, 'Statement on Ukrainian Legislation on Historical Research and Debate', 11 May 2015, available at www.ushmm.org/information/press/press-releases/statement-on-ukrainian-legislation-on-historical-research-and-debate.

6 Conclusion

This chapter has sought to explore the role of the Ukrainian state in regulating the interpretation of particular historical events in order to promote a sense of common identity. Referring to the de-communization laws adopted in Ukraine in April 2015, this chapter has demonstrated how, through the legislation of a certain interpretation of the Soviet past, Ukrainian policy-makers have set the ground for an adoption of European values and a separation from Russia's ideological influence. In the Ukrainian context, the adoption of the laws reflected the Ukrainian state's response to Russia's annexation of Crimea and Russia's support for the pro-Russian insurgency in the Donbas. The chapter has argued that the policy-makers' narrative of the Ukrainian national past and future, expressed through the de-communization laws, was aimed at counteracting Russia's aggression and demonstrated Ukraine's aspiration to join the EU. The analysis of the policy-relevant documents revealed the ways in which Ukrainian policy-makers made use of narratives to make sense of the current Russian–Ukrainian relations and to provide Ukrainians with a guideline on how to think about Russia and Europe.

Furthermore, this chapter has demonstrated how the Ukrainian policy-makers' narrative of Ukraine's national past and future has been challenged by a number of policy-relevant actors such as the opposition party, scholars, international organizations, legal experts, and the Russian government. Importantly, this narrative also found little support among the Ukrainian population. According to a survey in August 2015, 89.5 percent of Ukrainians had negative attitudes towards the de-communization policy (54.6 partly opposed and 34.9 fully opposed the laws), and only 10.5 percent of Ukrainians supported the de-communization process.[64] However, studies have pointed out that despite such low support for de-communization, there has also not been much protest. Oxana Shevel suggested several reasons for the lack of interest in de-communization policy, pointing out, for example, the public's weak support for the Soviet past, the Ukrainian government's

[64] Media Sapiens, 'Bilshist Ukraintsiv Uperedzheni do Vlady, Dekomunizatsii ta ZMI - Doslidzhennia' (The Majority of Ukrainians Have Negative Attitudes Towards the Government, De-Communization and Mass Media as Research Shows), 9 October 2015, available at http://osvita.mediasapiens.ua/mediaprosvita/research/bilshist_ukraintsiv_uperedzheni_do_vladi_dekomunizatsii_ta_zmi_doslidzhennya/; O. Shevel, 'Decommunization in Post-Euromaidan Ukraine: Law and Practice', *Ponars Eurasia*, January 2016, available at www.ponarseurasia.org/memo/decommunization-post-euromaidan-ukraine-law-and-practice.

inability to enforce the laws in the Donbas (where the majority of the places to be renamed are located), and people's concern regarding the high financial cost of de-communization.[65] However, whatever the result of the de-communization process, the media continue to report heated public debates on the issues of renaming towns, streets, and public places in Ukraine.[66]

[65] Shevel, 'Decommunization in Post-Euromaidan Ukraine: Law and Practice'.

[66] TSN, 'Trudnoshchi Dekomunizatsii: Chomu Protses Pereimenuvannia Komunistychnykh Nazv v Ukraini "Probuksovuie"' (The Difficulties of De-Communization: Why the Process of Renaming in Ukraine Is "Skidding"), 23 February 2016, available at http://tsn.ua/ukrayina/trudnoschi-dekomunizaciyi-chomu-proces-pereymenuvannya-komunistichnih-nazv-v-ukrayini-probuksovuye-596866.html.

16

Banning Genocide Denial – Should Geography Matter?

ROBERT A. KAHN

1 Introduction

Genocide denial bans are controversial – they restrict freedom of speech and are seen as establishing an official history.[1] One sees this in a recent decision of the European Court of Human Rights involving the application of Switzerland's ban on genocide denial to the Armenian genocide.[2] In explaining why bans on Armenian genocide denial violate the protection of free expression in Article 10 ECHR but Holocaust denial bans do not, the Court made reference to the "special moral responsibility" of states which have "experienced the Nazi horrors."[3] These states must "distance themselves from the mass atrocities they have perpetuated or abetted by . . . outlawing their denial."[4] Conversely, there is only a "tenuous" connection between Switzerland and the events of the Armenian genocide, the subject matter of the *Perinçek* case.[5]

Is this a good argument? Is it logical to require a nexus between the state enacting the ban and the historical act being denied? In this chapter I will explore these questions. In Section 2, I describe the type of nexus arguments one can make and present normative reasons why one might want

I would like to thank Jacqueline Baronian, Uladzislau Belavusau, Magdalena Jozwiak, Maria Mälksoo, Antoon De Baets, Gábor Halmai, Luiza Bialasiewicz, Cosmin Cercel, Salvador Herencia, Ioanna Tourkochoriti, and Eric Heinze. I dedicate this chapter to the late Neil Smith.

[1] Chapters by Luigi Cajani and Paolo Lobba in the present volume.

[2] ECtHR, *Perınçek* v. *Switzerland* (Appl. No. 27510/08), Judgment (Grand Chamber), 15 October 2015. For an extended discussion of *Perinçek*, see chapter by Paolo Lobba in the present volume.

[3] *Ibid.*, par. 243.

[4] *Ibid.*

[5] *Ibid.*, par. 244.

to support them. In Section 3, I will raise three practical objections to the nexus argument. These are: (a) *the definitional problem* (how much nexus is required?), (b) *the state reification problem* (do questions of memory, and the harms of denial, fall neatly along national lines?), and (c) *the global media problem* (given global social media (and travel), could a state ban genocide denial on its own even if it wanted to?).

Section 4 will take up normative problems posed by the nexus theory. These include the possibility that genocide denial poses universal harms, and how nexus arguments hinder discussions of other issues that should be at the heart of the legal analysis of genocide denial bans, such as whether genocide denial bans are ever justifiable and, if so, whether the denial must be accompanied by an intent to spread hate.

The harm posed by nexus arguments also extends, as Section 5 will show, into the academic study of genocide denial bans (and laws affecting memory as a whole). It does so by giving a naturalistic answer as to why a given people, or state would want to ban genocide denial: Armenians want to ban denial of the Armenian genocide because they are Armenians. This determinism drowns out other interesting explanations for the explosion of memory laws over the last twenty years.[6] I will explore some of these possibilities.

This chapter concludes by outlining how in *Perinçek*, the Court might have avoided these issues and making a few remarks about the local nature of all memory laws.

2 What Are Nexus Arguments? Why Do People Make Them?

In their most basic form, nexus arguments require a relationship between an act of genocide and a political community enacting a ban on its denial. While many different political communities might enact laws affecting memory,[7] in practice, the emphasis has been on states. Thus, the question is what business does France (or Switzerland) have in banning denial of the Armenian Genocide,[8] or to take an example from the broader category

[6] Cf. Chapter by Luigi Cajani in the present volume.

[7] Epilogue by Eric Heinze in the present volume.

[8] T. Garton Ash, 'This is the moment for Europe to dismantle taboos not erect them,' *The Guardian*, 18 October 2006, available at: www.theguardian.com/commentisfree/2006/oct/19/comment.france.

of laws affecting memory, what business does Germany have making a statement recognizing the Armenian Genocide.[9]

Nexus arguments come in two basic types – *permissive* and *restrictive*. A permissive nexus argument uses the presence of a link between the ban enactor and the genocide to support a ban that might not be otherwise justifiable. Deborah Lipstadt makes this type of argument when she says she understands why Germany, France, and Austria might want to ban genocide denial.[10] The Court in *Perinçek*, as we have seen, argued that countries that "experienced Nazi rule" had special responsibilities to the past.[11] Ironically, even opponents of memory laws, such as the historians from *Liberté pour l'Histoire*, apply this argument when they suggest it is impossible to repeal France's Holocaust denial ban.[12]

A *restrictive* nexus argument, on the other hand, uses the absence of a nexus as a limit – without necessarily approving of the genocide denial bans currently in place. For example, Timothy Garton Ash, criticizing a proposed French plan to ban denial of the Armenian genocide, wondered what was next: "[T]he Irish parliament criminalis[ing] denial of the horrors of the Spanish Inquisition," or the European Union banning denial of US crimes against Native Americans?[13] Likewise, in *Perinçek* the Court concluded that denial of the Armenian genocide was not punishable in Switzerland in part because there was "no evidence" that such denial in Switzerland "could result in serious friction between Armenians and Turks" living there.[14]

Most of this chapter will be taken up with criticism of nexus arguments. But before doing so, it is worth discussing why they are normatively appealing. The strongest argument rests on the idea that a state that commits genocide has a special responsibility to combat its denial. This argument carries weight, in part, because of the special claims that bind together

9 The German parliament made just such a statement in June 2016. See A. Kudascheff, 'Opinion: Not the right place,' *DW*, 2 June 2016, available at: www.dw.com/en/opinion-not-the-right-place/a-19298316.

10 See R. Kahn, 'Holocaust Denial and Hate Speech,' in T. Hochmann and L. Hennebel (eds.), *Genocide Denials and the Law* (Oxford: Oxford University Press, 2011), 93–4 (describing Lipstadt's views).

11 *Perinçek*, par. 243.

12 See R. Kahn, 'Does It Matter How One Opposes Hate Speech Bans? A Critical Commentary on Liberté pour l'Histoire's Opposition to French Memory Laws,' *Washington University Global Studies Law Review* 15 (2016), 55, 75–6 (noting Nora's reluctant toleration of the Gayssot Law).

13 Garton Ash, 'This is the moment.'

14 *Perinçek*, par. 244.

members of a shared community, as reflected by Avishai Margalit's distinction between morality and ethics.[15] According to Margalit, morality governs when we have thin relationships characterized by respect, while ethics governs when we have thick relationships and manifests itself through loyalty. As a consequence, morality (which encompasses "all humanity") is "long on geography and short on memory" while ethics (which arises among citizens of a state) is "short on geography and long on memory."[16] In other words, the nexus arguments (permissive and restrictive) might reflect the truth that members of a shared political community might reasonably place greater demands on each other regarding a duty to remember the past than do members of humanity as a whole.

In addition, when one leaves the narrow preserve of genocide denial bans, and takes up the broader category of what Eric Heinze calls "laws affecting memory," one encounters the dominance of local motivations for legislating about memory.[17] To take the example of the Frank Zappa statue in Lithuania Heinze raises in the Foreword, the motivation for erecting it is almost certainly local – even if Zappa fans traveling to Vilnius might be pleasantly surprised to see their hero's image.[18] If laws affecting memory are generally an expression of local biases, why should genocide denial bans be different? On this view, one would distinguish between legitimate motivations for banning genocide denial, ones based on the society's experience with the genocide in question, and illegitimate motives, one's based on pandering to lobby groups[19] or countries, such as Germany, that want to impose their issues with genocide (and genocide denial) on its neighbors.[20]

Furthermore, genocide denial bans are typically criminal laws, whose violation can lead to imprisonment. Given the nature of the penalty at stake, it might make sense to follow the maxim, *in dubio pro reo* (in doubt for the defendant) and interpret genocide denial bans, and the circumstances in which such bans are appropriate, as narrowly as possible.[21]

[15] A. Margalit, *The Ethics of Memory* (Cambridge, MA: Harvard University Press, 2002), 8.

[16] *Ibid.*

[17] Epilogue by Eric Heinze in the present volume.

[18] *Ibid.*

[19] Some of *Liberté*'s arguments about Armenian Genocide denial take this form. See R. Kahn, 'Does It Matter How One Opposes Hate Speech Bans?,' 55–92.

[20] On this view, the 2008 Framework Decision would represent a German imposition on Europe as a whole.

[21] In addition, the focus on geography is an improvement on using the Holocaust as a benchmark to evaluate the severity of genocides. See U. Belvusau, 'Memory Laws

3 Practical Objections to Nexus Arguments

While the nexus argument sounds reasonable, in practice it runs into three problems. *The definitional problem* asks how tight the nexus must be between the genocide being the denied and the state issuing the ban. The *state reification problem* concerns the tendency of the nexus argument to focus on states in a world characterized by flows of people across national borders and the emergence of regional identities such as Europe. Finally, the *global media problem* concerns whether a legal patchwork in which genocide denial is banned in one country but not another can be effective enforcement regime or a justifiable legal outcome in a global internet age.

3.1 The Definitional Problem

What does it mean to say that country X has a sufficient nexus to genocide Y, such that it can ban its denial? In some cases, such as Germany, the argument seems easy. Germany is banning the denial of a genocide committed by Germans. Some proponents of the nexus argument go further. As we have seen, Lipstadt would include Austria and France: in *Perinçek* the Court adds Belgium to this list.[22]

Fair enough. But what about other European countries? Dutch SS members helped round up Jews to go to the death camps; does this mean the Netherlands can pass a genocide denial ban?[23] Does the Hungarian role in the Final Solution explain Hungary's ban on Holocaust denial?[24] What about Argentina, a country where many Nazis fled after 1945 – including the key organizer of the trains to the death camps, Adolf Eichmann?[25] We need not stop here. Sympathetic understandings of Germany's Holocaust denial ban rely on Germany's role as a perpetrator of the Holocaust – denial sends a reassurance of "never again." But is this the only reason a state can ban genocide denial?

---

and Freedom of Speech: Governance of History in European Law,' in A. Koltay (ed.), *Comparative Perspectives on the Fundamental Freedom of Expression* (Budapest: Wolters Kluwer, 2015), 549.

22 Kahn, 'Holocaust Denial and Hate Speech'; *Perinçek*, par. 243.

23 See B. Moore, *Victims and Survivors: The Nazi Persecution of the Jews in the Netherlands, 1940–1945* (London: Arnold, 1972).

24 See R. L. Braham, *The Politics of Genocide: The Holocaust in Hungary* (Detroit: Wayne State University Press, 2000).

25 R. Weisbrot, *The Jews of Argentina from the Inquisition to Peron* (Philadelphia: Jewish Publication Society of America, 1979), 241–77 (describing an increase in anti-Semitism in Argentina in the years following the capture of Adolf Eichmann and his subsequent trial).

Perinçek is unclear. At one moment, it refers to a state having "a special moral responsibility" to distance itself from its own crimes,[26] something quite similar to the German Federal Supreme Court's 1979 ruling in the "Zionist Swindle" case, in which it held that denial was an offense to Jews living in Germany.[27] Moments later, the Court speaks of "States which have experienced the Nazi horrors," a broader category which could be read to include countries where a large number of survivors settled such as Israel.[28]

This sounds good until one looks at the debate in France over banning denial of the Armenian genocide. Just as Israel became the home to Holocaust survivors, France has a large population of Armenians, many of whom arrived in the aftermath of the Armenian genocide.[29] Yet efforts to enact genocide denial legislation have run into the argument, noted above, that the Armenian genocide did not take place on French soil. On the other hand, Ottoman historian Bernard Lewis denied the genocide on French soil, something that contributed in no small measure to the efforts of French Armenians to ban genocide denial.[30] Viewing the nexus argument in this manner may be reasonable, but in *Perinçek* the Court does not take this approach.

Another possible nexus might include countries in which the genocide physically took place. For example, the Jewish population in some eastern European countries today, such as Poland and the Czech Republic, is very small.[31] Yet Poland, which bans Holocaust denial, has a nexus with the

26 *Perinçek*, par. 243. A different nexus question arises where, as in Peru, the government passes a law banning denial of crimes committed against it – in this case by Shining Path guerillas. See chapter by Salvador Herencia Carrasco in the present volume.

27 *BGHZ (Entscheidungen des Bundesgerichthofesin Zivilsachen)* 75 (1979):160, 161 (18 September 1979); see R. Kahn, *Holocaust Denial and the Law: A Comparative Study* (Basingstoke; New York: Palgrave, 2004), 18.

28 For an overview, see T. Segev, *The Seventh Million: The Israelis and the Holocaust* (New York: Picador, 2000).

29 See Kahn, 'Does it matter . . .?,' 80. One of the parties to the *Perinçek* decision put the number of the French Armenian population at 600,000, *Perinçek*, par. 184, which is roughly equivalent to the number of Jews living in France.

30 Lewis made his comments in a *Le Monde* interview in 1994. For more, see Y. Ternon, 'Freedom and Responsibility of the Historian: The "Lewis Affair,"' in R. G. Hovannisian (ed.), *Remembrance and Denial: The Case of the Armenian Genocide* (Detroit: Wayne State University Press, 1998), 237–48.

31 For example Poland with 3,200 Jews (0.01% of the population) bans denial of Nazi crimes, as does Czech Republic where 3,900 Jews make up 0.04% of the population. U. Belavusau *Freedom of Speech: Importing European and US Constitutional Models in Transitional Democracies* (London: Routledge 2013), 191–3 (describing Polish and Czech bans of

Holocaust because the death camps were there. What is of interest here is motive: Many of the genocide denial bans enacted in Eastern Europe came after the 2008 EU Framework Decision mandating such laws.[32] If this was the motive for enacting the bans, should these countries be allowed to benefit from the nexus argument, which focuses on the impact of the Holocaust on the country in question?

In theory, the definitional problems are not insoluble. One could draw lines, even if in *Perinçek* the Court did not do this. Excluding the Armenian genocide is trickier – at least once one moves from Switzerland, which has an Armenian population of 5,000,[33] to France, where 600,000 Armenians reside. For the restrictive nexus argument to work for France, opponents of a ban on denial of the Armenian genocide need to justify defining "nexus" in a way that excludes a large survivor community. Moreover, the nexus argument faces other obstacles.

3.2 The State Reification Problem

In *Perinçek* the Court, in making its version of the nexus argument, refers to "States."[34] But why should the experience of a genocide fall neatly along state lines? Given the presence of ethnic diasporas, is it possible to speak of genocide denial as a strictly state or national issue? To paraphrase former US Speaker of the House, Tip O'Neil, all politics (and all genocide denial) is local; but in a post-modern world characterized by flows of people, the definition of "local" has become complicated. France and Germany are not simply French and German, they are also Armenian and Turkish.

On one level, the *Perinçek* Court gets this. After finding that the applicant's statements would not cause serious tension between Armenians and Turks within Switzerland, the Court also looked at the potential impact of his comments in Turkey.[35] The Court's willingness to do this undermines the strong form of the restrictive nexus argument, under which a state needs only to be concerned with its own genocides.

genocide denial); Jewish Population of the World, Virtual Jewish Library, 30 January 2016, available at: www.jewishvirtuallibrary.org/jsource/Judaism/jewpop.html.

32 Chapter by Luigi Cajani in the present volume

33 See *Perinçek*, par. 176.

34 *Ibid.*, par. 243. The Court capitalizes the word "State."

35 *Ibid.*, par. 245–8.

Here it is worth considering the recent German parliamentary vote on recognizing the Armenian genocide.[36] At first glance, it looks like a poster child for the restrictive nexus argument. The Armenian Genocide occurred on Turkish soil, not in Germany. As Heinze quotes Turkish President Recip Erdoğan, "Germany is the last country that ought to be voting about a 'so-called genocide.'"[37] In the words of Alexander Kudascheff, editor-in-chief of *Deutsche Welle*, it was "first and foremost a German matter to come to terms with our break with civilization" and while Turkey should do the same, the German parliament is "not the proper venue" for this. Kudascheff then asks if the Parliament would also condemn the crimes of "Stalinism, Maoism, the Khmer Rouge and the Vietnam war."[38]

But the more one looks at the recent vote, the more questionable the claim that there is "no nexus" between Germany and the Armenian genocide becomes. For one thing, the resolution was introduced by a Green Party member who is an ethnic Turk.[39] Meanwhile, the eleven German-Turkish members of the Bundestag who supported the Armenian genocide resolution were warned to stay out of Turkey because Germany cannot protect their safety – something the MPs recognized themselves by cancelling trips to Turkey.[40] These developments show how sometimes state boundaries that seem air tight are actually quite porous[41] and events in Germany may have implications in Turkey, and vice versa.

There is a second way in which the Bundestag resolution is relevant. While Germany was not a perpetrator of the Armenian genocide, they were military allies of the Ottoman Empire. Indeed, the resolution did not merely acknowledge the Armenian genocide, it apologized for Germany's role in it.[42] While this point goes mainly to the definitional problems of

[36] For the text of the resolution see Deustcher Bundestag 18. Wahlperiode Druchsache 18/8613, 'Erinnerung und Gedanken an den Völkermord an den Armeniern und anderen christlichen Minderheiten in den Jahren 1951 und 1916,' 31 May 2016, available at: http://dip21.bundestag.de/dip21/btd/18/086/1808613.pdf.

[37] Epilogue by Eric Heinze in the present volume (quoting Erdoğan).

[38] Kudascheff, 'Opinion: Not the Right Place.'

[39] 'Germany votes on Armenian genocide resolution amid warnings from Turkey,' *DW*, 2 June 2016, available at: www.dw.com/en/germany-votes-on-armenian-genocide-resolution-amid-warnings-from-turkey/a-19299171.

[40] 'Germany warns 11 MPs to keep out of Turkey after Armenian genocide vote – report,' *Reuters*, 11 June 2016, available at: www.rt.com/news/346215-german-lawmakers-turkey-warning/.

[41] Erdoğan seemed to recognize this when he described the MPs as "the long arm of separatist terrorists placed in Germany" and called for testing their blood for "Turkishness." *Ibid.*

[42] See 'German Bundestag Recognizes Armenian Genocide,' *The Armenian Weekly*, 2 June 2016, available at: http://armenianweekly.com/2016/06/02/bundestag-recognizes-genocide/.

the nexus concept, I mention it here because it shows how a law affecting memory that initially seems totally unrelated to the act it commemorates can actually have a fairly strong nexus to it.

This leads to a second challenge to the state-based contours of the nexus argument. What if the relevant category isn't France or Germany but Europe as a whole? Duncan Bell speaks of the potential for a "pan-European identity" that flows from "the 'Europeanization' of the memory of the Holocaust."[43] In this event, Germany's military alliance with the Ottoman Empire might, albeit in a much fainter way, tie other European countries to the Armenian genocide, much as the European Union countries are, through the Framework Decision, tied to Germany's approach to Holocaust denial. A focus on European identity might also explain some of the debates over laws affecting memory in the states of the former Soviet Union, where countries compete with differing conceptions of the Second World War, the Holocaust, and the human rights regime established in the aftermath of these events.[44]

To be sure, there are arguments against the Framework Decision, and against the idea of a shared European identity – as the recent Brexit vote shows. The creation of a "pan-European identity" is a potential that ebbs and flows. But this very uncertainty, well shown by the British vote to leave,[45] and talk of Scotland blocking Brexit (or leaving the United Kingdom),[46] should raise red flags about a theory based on the idea that state identity is stable. Should a normative theory, especially one that involves punishing speech acts with jail time, depend on this?

3.3 *The Global Media Problem*

Even if one could sketch a satisfactory geography of banning genocide denial, there is an additional obstacle based on the limited power of states to censor speech in an age characterized by open borders, easy travel,

[43] D. Bell, 'Introduction: Memory, Trauma and World Politics,' in D. Bell (ed.), *Memory, Trauma and World Politics: Reflections on the Relationship between Past and Present* (Basingstoke, New York: Palgrave, 2006), 17.

[44] See chapters by Maria Mälksoo and Lina Klymenko in the present volume.

[45] S. Castle and S. Chan, 'Boris Johnson Appeals for Calm as "Brexit" Vote Roils British Politics,' *The New York Times*, 27 June 2016, available at: www.nytimes.com/2016/06/28/world/europe/boris-johnson-brexit.html?_r=0.

[46] D. Li, 'Scotland may have power to block Brexit,' *The New York Post*, 26 June 2016, available at: http://nypost.com/2016/06/26/scotland-may-have-power-to-block-brexit/.

and global communications.[47] Assume that there is a legal regime under which Germany can ban Holocaust denial but the United Kingdom cannot because it was never occupied by Nazi Germany. Jane Doe is a German citizen. She wakes up in Hamburg where, because of Germany's historical connection to the Holocaust, she cannot express her view that the Holocaust never happened. She flies to London where, three hours later, she may say what she pleases about the Holocaust.

The Jane Doe scenario raises a practical problem for the nexus theory. If Jane is a neo-Nazi, and wants to distribute Holocaust denial flyers in Germany, it will be easy for her, when she lands in London, to draft a flyer, make copies, and return home to Hamburg in time for dinner. She can then distribute the flyer to her buddies at the beer garden later that evening. Unless the police are very diligent, Doe will get away with her crime. In a globalized world, it is harder for a nation-state to insulate itself from "foreign" ideas.

The practical problem only gets worse if one thinks about social media. Perhaps Jane does not even have to set foot in London; instead, she can visit a British website, do some cutting and pasting, and put together her own flyer without even leaving her living room. Jane may face some roadblocks; a state banning genocide denial could try to block denial Tweets and websites. But even if it enacts these measures, it will struggle. For instance, Jane may strike up contacts with private deniers who – while not questioning the Holocaust in public – are more than happy to give Jane denial material in a private email.

A supporter of the nexus argument might respond: Even if Jane can easily flout the ban, this is a problem of law enforcement. From the perspective of the moral, social, and legal order, Germany can still register its principled objection to Holocaust denial by banning it. In an increasingly global world, we expect that national boundaries will break down – especially when it comes to the exchange of ideas. Moreover, failures of enforcement do not discredit a regime of punishing genocide denial; scandals do.[48]

The possibility of scandal cuts both ways. On the one hand, to the extent internet enforcement is low key, scandals should be rare. On the

[47] To its credit, the *Perinçek* majority recognized the possibility that "electronic communications" would help the applicant's message reach beyond the borders of Switzerland, although it largely limited its analysis to Turkey. See *Perinçek*, par. 245–6.

[48] See Kahn, *Holocaust Denial and the Law*. Moreover over time societies may even learn to tolerate scandals. See *Ibid.*, 82, 160.

other hand, the very nature behind the nexus argument – under which Holocaust denial material is offensive (and embarrassing) in Germany but not in Britain – might lend itself to scandal if the wrong material winds up in the wrong country.

Now let's reverse the example and focus on Sally, the neo-Nazi in London who is supplying Jane with her material. Thanks to the valor of Royal Air Force pilots in the summer of 1940, Nazi troops never crossed the English Channel. As a result, Sally may deny the Holocaust so long as she does not engage in explicit hate speech against a religious or racial group – for example, by calling the Holocaust a "Jewish lie." Sally can do this because British Jews did not go to the gas chambers and while survivors live in Britain, the number is relatively small. So Sally is off the hook.

Or is she? As the example with Jane demonstrates, many people come to Britain. Some come in person; others travel virtually. Some of these people will come from countries – like Germany – with sensitive pasts. If enough people from Germany, or Armenia, or Rwanda come and visit, the insulation between the event being denied (the Holocaust in Germany) and the place considering banning denial (the United Kingdom) starts to break down.

Not only that, as globalized social media grows, the connection between Germany's concern with Holocaust denial and suppliers of denial in the United Kingdom will grow as well. Unlike the first example where Germany's effort to protect itself from global Holocaust denial recalls King Canute trying to hold back the waves, the call for the United Kingdom to take responsibility for people in other countries who will read Sally's denial leaflets in their home countries has a postmodern feel. The communications revolution has made censorship a worldwide affair. Yale University Press prevented Jytte Klausen from including reproductions of the "Danish cartoons" in her book *Twelve Cartoons that Shook the World* (2009) because of fears their inclusion would cause violence in Western Africa.[49] If the harm posed by Holocaust denial (or denial of the Rwandan genocide) were great enough, it might be reasonable to ask Sally to stop making genocide denial material available on her website.

Finally, the state is not the only morally relevant party in this scenario. The nexus argument creates a universe in which the professional historian has to be careful about what can be said about a given genocide in a

[49] P. Cohen, 'Yale bans images of Muhammad in New Book by Jytte Klausen,' *The New York Times*, 12 August 2009, available at: www.nytimes.com/2009/08/13/books/13book.html?_r=0.

given country.[50] This is yet another way the nexus argument advanced in *Perinçek* does not yield stable results. Indeed, the more the nexus argument moves in a nuanced fashion away from the narrow formulation that a perpetrator state can deny its own crimes, the more uncertain things become for the historian. This is the ultimate dilemma of the nexus approach. Either it is too blunt an instrument to be used credibly, or in making fine distinctions, it fails to yield reliable results.

4 Normative Objections to Nexus Arguments

But the nexus argument raised in *Perinçek* also has a second, normative set of problems. First, ironically for a theory based on geography, the nexus argument ignores one of the discipline's key teachings – that human beings share certain similarities, despite place. Second, the attention on geography draws attention away from other normative concerns raised by genocide denial bans.

4.1 Rejection of Universalism

The commonality of the human species is not simply a reflection of the globalized world, it also reflects a shared understanding that denial of past crimes against humanity offends the victims and their descendants, regardless of where they live. This is because, as Margalit puts it, genocide is "an attack on the very notion of shared humanity."[51] Genocide is not simply a concern of perpetrators and victims, it is a concern for all of us.

Likewise, genocide denial prevents perpetrators and bystanders from working through the past, again regardless of where they live. What is more, there is a growing understanding that genocide denial itself is a global problem – as opposed to the denial of specific genocides.[52] To the

[50] For an example of the problems historians might encounter with memory laws in general, see J. Mchangama, 'First They Came for the Holocaust Deniers, and I Did Not Speak Out,' *Foreign Policy*, 2 October 2016. Mchangama describes how Russian blogger Vladimir Luzgin was punished under a law banning Nazi rehabilitation for stating: "The Communists and Germany invaded Poland, sparking off World War II." *Ibid.* (quoting Luzgin). The nexus theory should, in theory at least, have no difficulty with the Luzgin prosecution since it involves a Russian blogger being tried under a Russian law. But from a free speech perspective, it is hard to find imagine a less justifiable application of a memory law.

[51] Margalit, *The Ethics of Memory*, at 9.

[52] This was a major theme of the Denialism and Human Rights Conference at Maastricht University, which brought together experts on genocide denial and other forms of denial

extent this is true, the logic of geographic limitations on denial bans starts to break down. If denial itself is a global problem, then why should Denmark tolerate denial of the Rwandan genocide even if very few Rwandans live there?[53] The joint dissenting opinion in *Perinçek* highlighted this point nicely. Accusing the majority of "[m]inimizing the significance of the applicant's statements by seeking to limit their global reach," the dissenters conclude that the majority has "water[ed] down the universal, *erga omnes* scope of human rights."[54]

Let me be clear, I am not calling for a globalization of genocide denial bans. As noted below, there are good reasons to be skeptical of such laws – starting with concerns about freedom of speech. But when opponents of genocide denial bans rely on the nexus argument, they run the risk of downplaying the shared humanity that stands at the heart of efforts to comfort genocide victims and prevent the recurrence of genocide in the future.

4.2 *Distraction from Other, More Substantial Normative Arguments for and against Genocide Denial Bans*

As noted above, genocide denial bans are controversial, and the positions lawyers, academic and citizens take about such laws are quite varied. There are some who reject genocide denial bans because they reject hate speech laws,[55] others who support hate speech laws but not genocide denial bans,[56] and still others who support genocide denial bans outright.[57] Assuming such laws are to exist, there are debates about the form a genocide denial ban should take: Must it include a requirement that speech acts denying

including global warming denial, denial of the AIDS epidemic, and denial of child abuse. S. Cohen, *States of Denial: Knowing about Atrocities and Suffering* (Cambridge: Polity Press, 2001).

53 This is especially true when one focuses on the type of denial that appears to pave the way for future acts of genocide.

54 *Perinçek*. Dissenting opinion of Judges Spielmann, Casadevall, Berro, De Gaetano, Sicilianos, Silvis, and Kūris, par. 6 (hereinafter "Joint Dissent"). There was also a dissent signed by Judges Casadevall, Berro, and Kūris.

55 See R. Dworkin, 'The Unbearable Cost of Liberty,' *Index on Censorship* 24:3 (1994). Heinze would take this position for prosperous, long-standing, stable democracies. See E. Heinze, *Hate Speech and Democratic Citizenship* (Oxford: Oxford University Press, 2016).

56 Belavusau, *Freedom of Speech* takes this position.

57 This is the perspective of Sévane Garibian. See S. Garibian 'Taking Denial Seriously: Genocide Denial and Freedom of Speech in the French Law,' *Cardozo Journal of Conflict Resolution* 9 (2009), 479–89.

genocide also denigrate the human dignity of the victim group? Is genocide denial best seen as a separate crime, or as an aggravating circumstance, as Italy now deals with genocide denial?[58]

Furthermore, the *Perinçek* case raised a number of factual issues. For example, was Perinçek's statement that the Armenian genocide was an "international lie" a form of hate speech directed at Armenians?[59] Or was it merely refusal to categorize the facts of the Armenian genocide as a genocide, without denying the facts themselves.[60] What should one make of the *Perinçek* majority's refusal to state for the record that the Armenian genocide was a historical fact? Is this an appropriate refusal of the Court to adjudicate a question of history?[61] Or was the joint dissent correct when they stated at the start of their opinion that the Armenian genocide was "a clearly established historical fact."[62]

The nexus argument, especially when applied in a restrictive fashion, prevents a fulsome discussion of these questions. While the expansion of genocide denial bans (and speech restrictive memory laws) is a serious concern, especially in France, the critics go too far. Too often, the nexus argument is a debating point, one that raises the specter of a Pandora's Box of censorship. But just as in the myth the critics close the box before hope can escape. Instead of engaging in the ongoing controversies concerning the scope, application, and justifiability of genocide denial bans, supporters of the restrictive nexus argument reduce everything to geography. In the process, much is lost.

58 See chapter by Luigi Cajani in the present volume.

59 The Joint Dissent of seven judges reached this conclusion. *Perinçek*, Joint dissent, par. 4.

60 The lawyers for the applicant and Turkey made this argument. See *Perinçek*, par. 159, 174. The majority seemed to agree up to a point. *Ibid.*, par. 240 (writing that "genocide justification does not consist in assertions that a particular event did not constitute a genocide," language suggesting that it agreed with the applicant).

61 See chapter by Paolo Lobba in the present volume. Judge Hugh Locke, in the 1985 trial of Holocaust denier Ernst Zundel for spreading false news in Canada took a similar position, but for slightly different reasons. Operating in an adversarial, common law system, Judge Locke refused to rule for the prosecution on a question he found essential to the finding of the innocence or guilt of the defendant, something Canada's legal system reserves for a jury. Kahn, *Holocaust Denial and the Law*, 40–1.

62 *Perinçek*, Joint Dissent, par. 2. The dissenters sharply criticized the majority for taking "a decidedly timid approach." *Ibid.* Interestingly, the judge in Ernst Zundel's 1988 trial for spreading false news (the 1985 trial, which resulted in a conviction, was reversed on appeal) had little trouble taking judicial notice of the Holocaust. Kahn, *Holocaust Denial and the Law*, 43.

5 The Nexus Argument and the Academic Study of Genocide Denial and Genocide Denial Bans

As we have seen, the nexus argument advanced in *Perinçek* is hard to use in practice, and fails to address important normative concerns raised by genocide denial bans. However, its greatest damage may arise from the way in which it stunts the study of genocide denial bans, genocide denial, and memory laws more generally. A society with a sensitive past – one in which a genocide or crime against humanity occurred – is assumed to naturally want to ban speech that questions that past. Thus Germans, Jews, and Holocaust survivors demand bans on Holocaust denial; Armenians seek bans of the Armenian Genocide denial; and Rwandans seek to punish those who deny the Rwandan Genocide. What could be simpler than that?

In essence, the nexus argument is a retreat to determinism: Germans support Holocaust denial bans because they are German – this is what they are called upon to do.[63] On this view, victim groups and perpetrators always play the same role. There is no space for Germans who oppose Holocaust denial bans; nor is there a place for residents of any number of countries who, despite lacking a nexus, view themselves as global citizens, ready to fight injustice everywhere. Taken to its extremes, the nexus argument is a form of "geographic determinism" which assumes "iron links between environmental conditioning and social response."[64]

As such, it makes it hard to answer another important question: Why the recent upsurge of genocide denial bans? Until 1970, prosecutions based on denial of historical facts were almost unheard of; since then, Holocaust deniers have been prosecuted in Canada and across Europe.[65] More recently, the impetus to ban denial has spread to other genocides and historical acts.[66] What accounts for this change?

There are some interesting answers to these questions. One possibility is that, after the passage of the French Gayssot Law (which bans Holocaust denial), other countries – and victims of other genocides – sought to copy it. Another possibility, raised by historian Jay Winter, is that the rise of affluence in the postwar era led to a demand for memory

[63] For a critique of determinism in hate speech laws more generally, see Heinze, *Hate Speech*, 181–94.

[64] M. W. Lewis and K. E. Wigen, *The Myth of the Continents: A Critique of Metageography* (Berkeley: University of California Press, 1997), 194–5.

[65] For an account of some of the early trials, see Kahn, *Holocaust Denial and the Law*.

[66] See chapter by Ioanna Tourkochoriti in the present volume.

products by college educated elites[67]; genocide denial bans could be one such product.

A final possibility relates to the emergence of denial itself. After 1945 there were German citizens (and others) who refused to believe the accounts of gas chambers and mass murder. But in 1950s and 1960s this was not how one expressed anti-Semitism. Rather, one would engage in name calling ("Jews are evil, rich, rule the world") or glorify the violence of the Nazi regime. ("Hitler was right: You should have been gassed.") After a global move toward punishing hate speech and racial incitement – through criminal sanctions and/or employment discrimination laws – traditional expressions of hate became much harder to justify, even in countries like the United States that have traditionally protected hate speech.[68]

On this view, denial is a rhetorical strategy used by people who formerly engaged in hate speech. Sometimes the connection is easy to spot, as when the Holocaust is called a "Zionist lie"; at other times, the connection is a bit more tenuous. Indeed, Deborah Lipstadt devoted *Denying the Holocaust* (1993) to exposing the racist and anti-Semitic agenda of Holocaust deniers who sometimes appeared to speak in neutral, measured language.[69] The same strategies are present in Armenian Genocide denial. Even in *Perinçek* the majority conceded that genocide denial could stoke the flames of anti-Armenian sentiment in Turkey; they merely questioned whether the applicant's comments had that effect.[70]

Here let me draw an example from India. Adolf Hitler's *Mein Kampf* has enjoyed a surprising run of success in India.[71] According to one commentator, Indians are not reading the parts focusing on the Jews; instead, they rely on Hitler's account of the creation of the Nazi party as a source

[67] J. Winter, 'Notes on the Memory Boom: War, Remembrance and the Uses of the Past,' in D. Bell, *Memory, Trauma and World Politics: Reflections on the Relationship between Past and Present* (Basingstoke, New York: Palgrave, 2006), 67–9. Winter also attributes what he calls the "memory boom" to the emergence of "new forms of information technology." *Ibid.*, 72.

[68] See A. Jacobson and B. Schlink, 'Hate Speech and Self-Restraint,' in M. Herz and P. Molnar, *The Content and Context of Hate Speech* (New York: Cambridge University Press, 2012), 217–41 (comparing US and European speech restrictions in education, employment, and broadcast regulation settings).

[69] See also A. Gliszczynska-Grabias, 'Memory Laws or Memory Loss? Europe in Search of its Historical Identity through National and International Law,' *Polish Yearbook of International Law* 14 (2014), 164.

[70] *Perinçek*, par. 247. For more, see chapter by Paolo Lobba in the present volume (arguing that the ruling may weaken the tendency to treat the Holocaust differently from the denial of other crimes).

[71] D. Shaftel, 'Hitler has a following in India,' *Business Week*, 6 December 2012, available at: www.bloomberg.com/news/articles/2012-12-06/hitler-has-a-following-in-india.

of "business advice."[72] On one level, this sounds innocent enough – if a bit odd.[73] This interpretation flows logically from the nexus argument. Given the distance between Mumbai and Calcutta and the killing fields of east Europe, Hitler's popularity in India must be harmless.[74]

However, there are other, more sinister interpretations. When asked about Hitler's references to Jews in *Mein Kampf*, and the book's relationship to the Holocaust, one common response in India was to dismiss those who Hitler killed as "traitors."[75] Meanwhile, Hindu right-wing nationalist Bal Thackeray said of Hitler's manifesto: "If you take *Mein Kampf* and if you remove the word Jew and put in the word Muslim, that is what I believe in."[76] In a world taught to "never forget" the horrors of genocide, certain books, ideas and people have been declared taboo; denial represents an attempt to circumvent those taboos. If so, then genocide denial bans might be seen as attempts to make this act of circumvention more difficult. They come out of a fear that the normalization of past acts of genocide is the first step toward their repetition.

Maybe this is a convincing explanation for the success of *Mein Kampf* in India, and more generally, for the emergence of genocide denial bans. Or maybe other arguments better explain these bans, such as copying the model of the Gayssot law, or the impact of affluence and information technology. One thing is certain: The nexus argument cannot explain the origins of the current landscape, except in the most essentialist, naturalizing way.

6 Conclusion: Toward a More Nuanced Understanding of Nexus

The nexus argument is something of a puzzle. The normative foundations behind the argument are solid. None of the points raised in this chapter challenge Margalit's suggestion about the connection between community, loyalty and an ethical duty – although he does say that "gross crimes

[72] *Ibid.*

[73] The easy availability of *Mein Kampf* in India may, however, say something about the limits of Germany's ban on the book, a ban that ended in 2016 when Bavaria's copyright on the book expired. See M. Doerry and K. Wiegrefe, 'Book of Hate: The Bold Attempt to Demystify *Mein Kampf*,' *Spiegel Online*, 15 January 2016, available at: www.spiegel.de/international/germany/new-annotated-mein-kampf-offers-insight-into-hitler-a-1072032.html.

[74] From a broader perspective, one might argue that given Britain's participation in the Second World War and the impact of the war years on India's move toward independence, there may some nexus here after all – something that demonstrates the contingent, fluid nature of the nexus concept.

[75] D'Souza, 'Hitler's Strange Afterlife in India,' *The Daily Beast*, 30 November 2012, available at: www.thedailybeast.com/articles/2012/11/30/hitler-s-strange-afterlife-in-india.html.

[76] *Ibid.* (quoting Thackeray).

against humanity," such as the Holocaust, are "glaring examples of what humanity requires us to remember."[77] Still, Margalit does not discuss genocide denial or attempts to ban it. The focus on the broader universe of laws affecting memory, as described by Heinze, reminds us of the great many memory laws that are local in inspiration and impact. Furthermore, while the identity and community are contingent, enacting a law – especially a genocide denial ban – requires a legislature that is necessarily anchored in time and place. So the nexus argument, in both in its permissive and restrictive form, is logically coherent. In many situations, one can identify what is local, and what is not. Finally, the restrictive form of the nexus argument will protect some speech – to be sure, not as much as an outright rejection of genocide denial bans – but enough to be seen by opponents of genocide denial bans as a step in the right direction.

That said, there is something unsettling about the argument, particularly how it is used in *Perinçek*. This goes beyond the problems with defining the limited geography of nexus argument, the way it distracts from other normative issues raised by genocide denial bans and how its determinism dampens scholarly research into the motivations behind genocide denial and genocide denial bans. The problem is one of exclusion. Paragraphs 243–4 of the majority opinion, in which the Court states that Holocaust denial "invariably" connotes "an anti-democratic ideology and anti-Semitism"[78] yet views the connection between Switzerland and the Armenian genocide as "tenuous,"[79] can be read to suggest that Armenians, and the Armenian Genocide, have no place in Europe, or its memory. The majority reached this conclusion even though the genocide took place during (and may have been enabled by)[80] the First World War, a quintessentially European event. Coupled with the Court's refusal to describe the Armenian Genocide as "an established historical fact," the opinion says to European Armenians: "You're not part of us." To put it another way, the Court not only mistakenly relied on the concept of nexus – it arguably misapplied it.

This is not to say that the legal conclusion of *Perinçek* was necessarily wrong. [81] As an American, I find it hard to come to terms with genocide

[77] Margalit, *The Ethics of Memory*, at 9.

[78] Perinçek, par. 243.

[79] *Ibid.*, par. 244.

[80] See R. Melson, *Revolution and Genocide: On the Origins of the Armenian Genocide and the Holocaust.* (Chicago: University of Chicago Press, 1992) (arguing that war enabled the Armenian Genocide and Holocaust).

[81] For instance, the Spanish Constitutional Court concluded that bare denial of the Holocaust violates freedom of expression without deploying a full-fledged nexus argument.

denial bans. While I personally believe that the applicant did more than simply refuse to apply the genocide label to a set of underlying facts – the statement "It was a battle between peoples and we suffered many casualties" strikes me as factual[82] – the Court could have based its decision on the conclusion that the statements, while hateful, did not rise to the level necessary to justify a criminal prosecution, without bringing nexus into play. Instead, *Perinçek* establishes a double standard – for the Holocaust there is a "special moral responsibility"[83] – while in the Armenian context the Court requires a showing of "serious friction."[84] Given the extent to which Holocaust denial is associated with anti-Semitism, I am not sure the Court needed to make such a distinction to justify its result.

Turning to the broader context of laws affecting memory, the nexus argument strikes me as an artificial restriction on the scope of memory laws. To the extent, as Heinze puts it, "law inherently reflects official positions taken on past events,"[85] efforts to limit officials to taking positions on "local" memory issues will likely be futile, precisely because from the enactor's perspective all politics is ultimately local. Instead of struggling to define what is, or is not, appropriately "local," the focus should be on motives (why is a given genocide, war, or other historical event being commemorated?) and outcomes (is the commemoration a good thing?). In answering these questions, unraveling connections – be they regional, national, ethnic, religious, or personal – might well be helpful. But this is only true if the enterprise is approached with an understanding of the contingent, unexpected connections between commemoration and the past that can arise. Otherwise, we risk becoming like an ill-informed traveler who, seeing the Frank Zappa statue in Vilnius, assumes that he was born there.

See Tribunal Constitutional (Constitutional Court of Spain), judgment No. 2352007 (7 November 2007), par. 8 (referring to bare genocide denial as "pointless" and questioning whether such denial necessarily "creates a climate of social hostility against victims"). Indeed, for some dissenting justices this lack attention to nexus was the precisely the problem. P. S. Codrech and R. P. Puig, 'Genocide Denial and Freedom of Speech: Comments on the Spanish Constitutional Court's Judgment 235/2007, November 7th.' *InDret, Revista para el Análysis del Derecho*, 4/2008, available at www.indret.com (noting that some of the dissenters warned that allowing denial to go unharmed ignored Spain's history and risked its position in Europe).

82 *Perinçek*, par. 3 (quoting applicant).

83 *Ibid.*, par. 243.

84 *Ibid.*, par. 244.

85 Epilogue by Eric Heinze in the present volume.

17

"From Banning Nakba to Bridging Narratives": The Collective Memory of 1948 and Transitional Justice for Israelis and Palestinians

JEREMIE M. BRACKA

1 Introduction

Notwithstanding the significance of 1948 for Israelis and Palestinians, or perhaps precisely because of it, there have been few attempts to address the historical legacy of the conflict's genesis in international law or the political arena. This chapter is devoted to unstitching the collective memory woven by this event, and the role it has played in shaping national identity, legal discourse, political narrative, and the escalation of the conflict. Given its centrality to both sides, this chapter will also examine the power of re-shaping collective memory through the creation of a "bridging narrative" based on the applicability of transitional justice mechanisms, like an Israeli–Palestinian Truth Commission (IPTC).

Sections 2 and 3 of this chapter will outline the significance of the historic dimensions of 1948 and the conflicting meta-narratives of victimhood and nationalism. It is worth pointing out that propagating a simplified and varnished version of the 1948 war has created the moral prism through which both sides view all aspects of the dispute and its escalation. Section 4 will examine legal attempts to institutionalize collective denial and suppression of 1948 in Israeli Jewish society. Finally, Section 5 will propose a pivotal role for transitional justice and civil society to challenge the political landscape and widen debate. Indeed, it is contended that, rather than obstructing resolution, a meaningful and nuanced accounting of the past may in fact be the discursive and cognitive bridge required to reconcile both nations.

2 Historical Resonance of 1948

2.1 *The Palestinian Displacement: Origins of the Conflict*

Outlining the historical genesis of the Israeli–Palestinian conflict is an undertaking fraught with perils, both political and analytical. The essentially contentious character of the struggle flows from the fact that the original cause of the refugee problem, rooted in the 1948–9 Arab Israeli war, remains largely unresolved. More often than not, it is a question considered through the prisms of irreconcilable political and ideological narratives. Nevertheless, what is incontrovertible is that the 1948 hostilities, which began in the wake of the United Nations (UN) partition of Palestine in November 1947[1] and erupted into full-scale war between Israel and several Arab States after the Declaration of Israeli Independence in May 1948,[2] resulted in the exile of much of Arab Palestine. Between December 1947 and September 1949, some 600,000–760,000 Palestinians departed, fled, or were expelled from those regions in Palestine which are now territories within the State of Israel.[3]

The massive dislocation of roughly half of the territory's population profoundly altered the demographics of Jews and Arabs within the new borders.[4] "Only 150,000 of the Arab population of pre-1948 Palestine remained behind and they became Israeli citizens, an Arab minority in the Jewish State."[5] By the war's end with the armistices of 1949, the vast majority of Palestinians were plunged into makeshift refugee camps under Egyptian or Jordanian control, and the United Nations Relief and Works Agency for Palestine Refugees in the Near East [UNRWA] was subsequently created to

[1] G.A. Res. 181(II), U.N. Doc. A/519, at 131 adopted a plan to partition Palestine into separate States, one Jewish and the other Arab.

[2] On 14 May 1948, the Jewish leaders declared the establishment of the State of Israel on the heels of the final withdrawal of British troops from Palestine. On the following day, the armies of Transjordan, Syria, Lebanon, Egypt, and Iraq invaded the newly declared State. After several successful Israeli military campaigns, Israel assured its existence.

[3] Y. Tadmor, 'The Palestinian Refugees of 1948: The Right to Compensation and Return', *Temple International and Comparative Law Journal* 8 (1994), 403; See also K. R. Radley, 'The Palestinian Refugees: The Right to Return in International Law', *American Journal of International Law* 72 (1978), 587, 595; D. E. Artzt and K. Zughaib, 'Return to Negotiated Lands: The Likelihood and Legality of a Population Transfer Between Israel and a Future Palestinian State', *New York University Journal of International Law and Politics* 24 (1991–2), 1420–2.

[4] E. Benvenisti and E. Zamir, 'Private Claims to Property Rights in the Future Israeli–Palestinian Settlement', *American Journal of International Law* 89 (1995), 295, 297.

[5] L. Takkenberg, *The Status of Palestinian Refugees in International Law* (Oxford: Clarendon Press, 1998), 14.

take care of needy Palestinians.[6] Many of these refugees, whose numbers have increased considerably over the decades due to natural growth, continue to live in squalid camps where they first relocated and are dependent on help from the UNRWA.[7] Thus, the creation and continuing unresolved status of the Palestinian refugees from 1948 is pivotal to the conflict.

2.2 *The "1948" Blame-Game*

As with any intractable ethno-national conflict, there is no authoritative and legitimated determination of the immediate causes or motivations for the Palestinian exodus. Rather, both sides, Israeli and Arab, traditionally ascribe responsibility for the mass displacement entirely to the other and maintain conflicting factual assessments in what might best be termed "official history."[8] It is worth pointing out that propagating a reductive version of the 1948 war has been integral in pursuing political and moral leverage. In Israel, nationalist historians, conventionally claim that the Palestinians either voluntarily fled free from Jewish compulsion, due to a "general sense of fear and confusion,"[9] or that they were prompted or ordered to evacuate by leaders of the Arab States bent on Israel's destruction.[10] Israeli government sources also stress that hundreds of thousands of Jewish refugees simultaneously fled their homes in Arab countries to Israel as a direct consequence of the 1948 hostilities.[11] Accordingly, Israel contends that it was the Arabs who caused the Palestinian refugee problem, by rejecting the creation of the State of Israel

[6] *Ibid.*, 6.

[7] R. Lapidoth, 'Legal Aspects of the Palestinian Refugee Question', *Jerusalem Viewpoints, Jerusalem Centre for Public Affairs* 485 (2002), available at: www.jcpa.org/jl/vp485.htm (date accessed: 6 July 2015) 2.

[8] E. Rogan and A. Shlaim (eds.), *The War for Palestine, The War for Palestine: Rewriting the History of 1948* (Cambridge: Cambridge University Press, 2007), 79–103.

[9] L. J. Silberstein, *The Post Zionism Debates: Knowledge and Power in Israeli Culture* (New York and London: Routledge, 1999), 88.

[10] See generally L. J. Silberstein, *The Postzionism Debates: Knowledge and Power in Israeli Culture* (New York and London: Routledge, 1999), 97–8; Israel Office of Information, The Arab Refugees (1953) 11, as cited in T. Kramer, 'The Controversy of a Palestinian "Right of Return" to Israel', *Arizona Journal of International and Comparative Law* 18 (2001), 997, 998. See also R. Khalidi, 'The Palestinians and 1948: The Underlying Causes of Failure', in E. Rogan and A. Shlaim (eds.), *The War for Palestine* (Cambridge: Cambridge University Press, 2007), 12, 14; C. Sykes, *Crossroads to Israel* (Bloomington, London: Indiana University Press, 1965), 353–4.

[11] State of Israel, 'The Refugee Issue: A Background Paper, Government Press office' (October 1994) 3, cited in Takkenberg, *The Status of Palestinian Refugees*, 14.

and declaring war upon it – "a war, which, like most wars created refugee problems, including a Jewish one."[12]

Conversely, Palestinian and Arab accounts insist that the Israelis forcibly expelled the Palestinians as a part of a premeditated and prearranged "grand political-military design."[13] Palestinian historians[14] highlight Deir Yassin[15] and other massacres[16] as indicative of a Jewish conspiracy to rid Palestine of its Arab inhabitants. Upon this historical construction, the Palestinians insist on the right of the refugees to return to their homes and demand that Israel unilaterally acknowledge complete moral responsibility for the injustice of their expulsion and present refugee status.[17] Both evaluations of 1948 thus subscribe to an uncritically nationalist account of the Palestinian displacement, and accordingly "the pretense of objectivity is particularly misplaced, if not totally unfounded."[18]

2.3 The "New Historians" – Critiquing "1948"

Nevertheless, in recent decades, new scholarship has subverted the foundational premises of these dominant narratives. The most significant reappraisals have emerged from mostly Israeli historians relying on newly discovered archival evidence.[19] Dubbed the "New Historians,"[20]

[12] Y. Alpher and K. Shikaki, 'Concept Paper: The Palestinian Refugee Problem and the Right of Return', *Middle East Policy* 6:3 (1999), 172.

[13] Tadmor, 'The Palestinian Refugees of 1948', 403; See also W. E. Said, 'Palestinian Refugees: Host Countries', 89, citing N. Masalha, *A Land without a People: Israel, Transfer and the Palestinians 1949–96* (London: Faber and Faber, 1997).

[14] On the early Palestinian historiography, see B. B. Doumani, 'Rediscovering Ottoman Palestine: Writing Palestinians into History', *Journal of Palestine Studies* 21:2 (1992), 13–17.

[15] On 9 April 1948, Jewish members of the Irgun and Stern militias (Jewish fringe militant factions) attacked Deir Yassin, an Arab village located next to a major thoroughfare connecting Jerusalem to the coast.

[16] Palestinian historian Saleh Abdel Jawad lists around twenty villages where indiscriminate killings of Palestinian civilians occurred. S. Abdel Jawad, 'Zionist Massacres: The Creation of the Palestinian Refugee Problem in the 1948 War', in E. Benvenisti, C. Gans and S. Hanafi (eds.), *Israel and the Palestinian Refugees* (Berlin: Springer, 2007), 59–127.

[17] Alpher and Shikaki, 'Concept Paper: The Palestinian Refugee Problem', 171.

[18] I. Pappe, 'Humanising the Text: Israeli "New History" and the Trajectory of 1948 Historiography', *Radical History Review* 86 (2003), 102, 103.

[19] As a result of Israel's 5715–1955 *Archives Law* and its attending regulations, hundreds of thousands of previously closed State papers became available to researchers in the early 1980s. For an exhaustive review of the drafting, legislation and amendment history of the Archives Law, see P. A. Alsberg, 'The Israel Archives Law, History and Implementation', *Arkhyon: Reader in Archives Studies and Documentation* 1 (1987), 7–29 (Hebrew).

[20] A. Shlaim, *Collusion across the Jordan: King Abdullah, the Zionist Movement and the Partition of Palestine* (New York: Columbia University Press, 1988). See also S. Flapan,

they depict the 1948 war as something other than "a miraculous victory of beleaguered underdogs."[21] Indeed, Benny Morris[22] was the first Israeli historian to admit that mass expulsions of Palestinians occurred in 1948, and decisively refute the claim that Arab leaders ordered the Palestinians to flee and clear the way for impending armies.[23] Most shocking was the disclosure that Zionist leaders had actively driven out the Arab inhabitants of Palestine.[24] Morris determined, however, that neither the expulsions nor the subsequent refugee problem were the result of a Jewish blueprint or "master plan," but rather the consequence of war and associated circumstances.[25]

More generally, revisionist scholarship challenged mobilizing myths of official history with a "post-Zionist" conflict narrative.[26] Some historians, like Baruch Kimmerling, examined Zionism through a colonial prism.[27] During the 1990s, the Oslo peace process fanned debates about 1948.[28] Ultimately, they raised a wide-ranging debate that spilled over from scholarly journals and academic conferences into the public domain. In the words of Uri Ram: "One way or another, the new historians have radically

---

The Birth of Israel, Myths and Realities (New York: Pantheon Books, 1987); I. Pappe, *Britain and the Arab–Israeli conflict, 1948–51* (London: Macmillan Press, 1988).

21 L. Takkenberg, *The Status of Palestinian Refugees*, 15 citing N. Caplan, 'The New Historians', *Journal of Palestine Studies* 24:4 (1994/5), 96.

22 B. Morris, *The Birth of the Palestinian Refugee Problem 1947–1949* (New York: Cambridge University Press, 1987). Morris has written critically for example about the expulsion of 60,000 Arab residents from the towns of Lydda and Ramle.

23 Flapan, *The Birth of Israel*, 85, also dismisses this contention as illogical, cited in Artzt and Zughaib, *Return to Negotiated Lands*, 1421.

24 See both Morris, *The Birth of the Palestinian Refugee Problem*, and Pappe, *The Ethnic Cleansing of Palestine* (London and New York: Oneworld Publications, 2006) for clashing interpretations of how this flight unfolded.

25 Morris, *The Birth of the Palestinian Refugee Problem*, 286.

26 Generally, the post-Zionist narrative criticizes the Zionist narrative. Some of the Post-Zionists associate themselves with post-modernism. See U. Ram, 'Post Nationalist Pasts – The Case of Israel', *Social Science History* 24:4 (1998), 515–23. See also D. Ohana and R. Wistrich, *Myth and Memory: Genealogy of the Israeli Consciousness* (Jerusalem: Ha Kibbutz Hamehoohad and Van-Leer Institute, 1996), 21–32.

27 From this standpoint, Palestine was no empty land and Zionism was just another Western colonial exploitative force. See B. Kimmerling, *Zionism and Territory: The Socio-Territorial Dimensions of Zionist Politics* (Berkeley: University of California Press, 1983) and G. Shafir, *Land, Labor and the Origins of the Israeli–Palestinian Conflict, 1882–1914* (Cambridge: Cambridge University Press, 1989).

28 "The current peace process and the concomitant changes in perceiving reality have made Israeli society more willing than ever before to reassess the historical events that gave birth to the state." A. Shapira and O. Wiskind-Elper, 'Politics and Collective Memory: The Debate over the "New Historians" in Israel', *History and Memory* 7 (1995), 9–55.

transformed the historical consciousness . . . in Israel."[29] Consequently, there is at present an increasing academic recognition of Israel's shared accountability for 1948.[30]

3 Meta-Narratives of Memory: The 1948 "Dialogue of the Deaf"

3.1 *Collective Memory, Identity, and Conflict*

> In Israel and Palestine, remembering and forgetting thus continues to serve as weapons in the national battlefield.[31]

Historical inquiry aside, the ostensible intractability of 1948 cannot be understood without outlining its ideological roots. According to Shapira "the debate is less about historiography than it is about collective memory."[32] Indeed, this event is deeply embedded in each side's nationalism and meta-narratives of entitlement, villain, victimhood, and utopia. From this standpoint, every historical event since 1948, from Oslo to the Gaza disengagement, continues to be viewed through the same nationalistic prism. For Palestinians since 1967, the Israeli military occupation[33] of the West Bank (and formerly of the Gaza Strip), which controls the daily lives and rights of Palestinians, coupled with the expansion of Jewish settlements is a perennial reminder of the humiliation and dispossession of 1948.[34] For Israelis, the sense of Jewish victimhood and isolation was only exacerbated by the subsequent Arab-Israeli wars, the regional rejection of Israel's right to exist, and by Palestinian terrorist attacks against Israelis and Jews worldwide.

[29] U. Ram, *Israeli Nationalism: Social Conflicts and the Politics of Knowledge* (New York: Routledge, 2010), 34.

[30] See Takkenberg, *The Status of Palestinian Refugees*, 6; See also Shapira and Wiskind-Elper, 'Politics and Collective Memory', 9, 14. "The details published about Jews slaughtering Arabs increased Israeli sensitivity to the fact that the 1948 war had not been a war of the righteous against the wicked, a question of black and white, and paved the way for a more balanced view of the events."

[31] U. Ram, *Israeli Nationalism: Social Conflicts and the Politics of Knowledge* (New York: Routledge, 2010), 110.

[32] Shapira and Wiskind-Elper, 'Politics and Collective Memory', 9–12.

[33] The ongoing humanitarian crisis, coupled with the repression of the Israeli occupation (house demolitions, restriction of movement, humiliating checkpoints, and extra-judicial killings) only reinforces notions of Palestinian injustice.

[34] A. Meyerstein, 'Transitional Justice and Post-conflict Israel/Palestine: Assessing the Applicability of the Truth Commission Paradigm', *Case Western Reserve Journal of International Law* 38 (2006–7), 281, 299.

Both Israelis and Palestinians have thus drawn on 1948 to cope with the conflict and enable its members to contribute to the ongoing struggle.[35] The meanings and implications, derived from 1948, strike at the very heart of both parties' legitimacy, obstructing even partial acceptance, of either side's discourse. These incongruent paradigms both rigidly "construct and delimit each people's own reality as well as their interpretation of the other's."[36] What for Palestinians is a historic right to return, is for Israeli Jews an attack on the Jewish State's legitimacy and survival. Thus, each group conceives rights as unquestionable and irrevocable with regard to itself, while illegitimate with regard to the other. In short, the conflict over 1948 is as much about a clash of constructed discourses, as it is a factual debate over entitlement to land.

3.2 Mutually Exclusive Notions of Victimhood ("Nakba" vs. "Holocaust")

Within this 1948 dialectic, each side perceives itself as the sole victim of the conflict. Whilst the Palestinians recount a story of dispossession and catastrophe based on the Nakba, the Israelis recall the War of Independence and its symbolic compensation for the Holocaust. Both nations have their own cosmic catastrophes, and both draw on a strong memory of victimhood in what is perceived as an existential struggle.

> We Israelis often look at Arabs not as fellow victims, but as an incarnation of our past oppressors . . . Nazis who have grown moustaches and wrapped themselves in Kaffiyehs.[37]
>
> Amos Oz, Israeli author

For Israelis, the trauma of Nazi genocide makes Arab threats of destruction credible "casting the conflict as one of basic survival, aimed at preventing a second Holocaust."[38] It has assumed "meta-physical

[35] R. Nets-Zehngut, 'The Israeli National Information Center and Collective Memory of the Israeli–Arab Conflict', *Middle East Journal* 62:4 (Autumn 2008), 653, 669.

[36] A. Friedman, 'Unraveling the Right of Return', *Refuge* 21:2 (2003), 62.

[37] Amos Oz as quoted in N. Caplan, 'Victimhood and Identity: Psychological Obstacles to Israeli Reconciliation with the Palestinians', in K. Abdel-Malek and D. C. Jacobson (eds.), *Israeli and Palestinian Identities in History and Literature* (New York: St. Martin's Press, 1999), 64.

[38] D. Waxman, *The Pursuit of Peace and the Crisis of Israeli Identity* (New York: Palgrave Macmillan, 2006), 49.

proportions" in the Jewish Israeli psyche.[39] As the current debate over Iran's nuclear ambitions demonstrates, Israeli fears of decimation are more prevalent than ever before, increasingly fueled by their anxious leaders.[40]

Moreover, the memory of 1948, and above all the Holocaust, is appropriated politically and militarily. To varying degrees, this legacy has served to justify the primacy of national security in Israeli foreign policy.[41] Since 1948, Israel maintains an endless state of emergency whereby legal norms are suspended. Thus, "It is not a formidable army that penetrates Lebanon . . . but a handful of survivors that go out to avenge Auschwitz."[42] This motif is woven into the conflict with the Palestinians, by drawing comparisons between Arafat and Hitler, the PLO and the Nazi party. On the global stage, Israeli PM Benjamin Netanyahu frequently refers to the Nazi genocide of Jews in his speeches at the UN General Assembly.[43] Thus, the palpable memory of Jewish persecution plays a seminal role in Israeli identity and politics.

> Thus, we [Palestinians] are the victims of the victims, the refugees of the refugees.[44]
>
> Edward Said, 1999

[39] "The Holocaust increasingly took on meta-physical proportions, perceived not only as a German atrocity committed against the Jews, but as the culmination of centuries-long gentile persecution of Jews." See D. Waxman, *The Pursuit of Peace and the Crisis of Israeli Identity* (New York: Palgrave Macmillan, 2006), 49.

[40] Speaking at the Yad Vashem Holocaust Memorial in Jerusalem in April 2014, PM Netanyahu told the crowd, "we must identify an existential threat in time and act against it this time . . . Iran calls for our destruction." See also B. Morris, 'This Holocaust will be different', *The Jerusalem Post* (Jerusalem), 18 January 2007.

[41] See D. Waxman, *The Pursuit of Peace and the Crisis of Israeli Identity* (New York: Palgrave Macmillan, 2006), 188. See generally I. Zertal, *Israel's Holocaust and the Politics of Nationhood* (Cambridge: Cambridge University Press, 2010) demonstrating the use of the Holocaust discourse to rationalize the building of Israel's military power.

[42] I. Zertal, 'Du bon usage du souvenir: Les Israéliens et le Shoa', *Le Debat* 11:58 (1990), 92, 101 as cited in S. Atran, 'Stones Against the Iron Fist, Terror within the Nation: Alternating Structures of Violence and Cultural Identity in the Israeli–Palestinian Conflict', *Politics and Society* 18:4 (1990), 484, 498.

[43] On 24 September 2009, Israeli PM Benjamin Netanyahu displayed original construction plans for the Auschwitz-Birkenau concentration camp during his speech to the UN General Assembly.

[44] E. Said, 'The One State Solution', *The New York Times* (New York), 10 January 1999. Many Palestinians claim that the Nakba has brought about an exchange of historical roles, and the Palestinians have been transformed into the "victims of the victims." See M. Milshtein, 'The Memory that Never Dies: The Nakba Memory and the Palestinian National Movement', in M. Litvak (ed.), *Palestinian Collective Memory and National Identity* (New York: Palgrave Macmillan, 2009), 50. See also generally R. Khalidi, *Palestinian Identity: The Construction of Modern National Consciousness* (New York: Columbia University Press, 1997).

For Palestinians, the Nakba has become a hallowed symbol of identity, "a unique and unprecedented historical experience."[45] Mirroring Holocaust discourse, Palestinians regard themselves as casualties of a colossal tragedy.[46] "We are the only people left in the world who still live under occupation."[47] In the eyes of the refugees "the Palestinian tragedy was graded higher than Jewish suffering."[48] Striking similarities exist therefore in how both communities cultivate an ethos of victimhood through tradition,[49] historiography,[50] and commemoration.

For example, Deir Yassin evolved into a symbol of memorialization[51] like Auschwitz. Established in 1999, the Palestinian state Nakba museum Dar al Dahkira[52] resembles Israel's Yad Vashem, and akin to Holocaust Memorial day, Palestinians officially mark "Nakba" day through national ceremony and siren sounding.[53] Each year on May 15 (the day after Israel declared its independence), Palestinian communities both inside Israel[54]

[45] Al Quds, 15 May 1998 cited in Webman, 'The Evolution of a Founding Myth', 35. See R. Khalidi, 'Attainable Justice: Elements of a Solution to the Palestinian Refugee Issue', *International Journal* 33:2 (Spring 1998), 233, 245.

[46] Webman, 'The Evolution of a Founding Myth', 35–6. While these two events cannot be factually compared, it is notable that Palestinians argue that the Nakba "is no less catastrophic to destroy a whole society with its material, social, and cultural presence on a certain land and to drive its people out their homeland into exile." See A. Qaymari, 'The Holocaust in the Palestinian Perspective', in B. Pogrund, W. Salem, and P. Scham (eds.), *Shared Histories: A Palestinian–Israeli Dialogue* (Walnut Creek: Left Coast Press, 2005), 151.

[47] *Ibid.*

[48] "The analogy between what befell the Jews and the Palestinian Arabs was a major motif in the Palestinian and Arab discourse on the Holocaust. Whereas the wrongdoings toward the Jews were minimized, the injustice toward the Palestinians was magnified." Webman, 'The Evolution of a Founding Myth', 35.

[49] Notably, Palestinians preserve keys of the refugee's original houses, and Palestinian refugees commonly refer to themselves by the original names of their villages and not the refugee camps they live in. See Qaymari, 'The Holocaust in the Palestinian Perspective', 151.

[50] Collecting oral testimony from 1948 is a popular historiographical approach among Palestinian researchers and historians. See *Ibid.*

[51] Deir Yassin has become a key element in the Palestinian transformation of the events of 1947–9 into a 'cosmic injustice'. See generally W. Khalidi, 'Deir Yassine: Autopsie d'un Massacre', *Revue d'etudes Palestiniennes* 17:69 (1998), 20–58.

[52] The site, located at Kafr Ayn Siniya near Ramallah, exhibits numerous data based on the Nakba in general and destroyed villages in particular. See Milshtein, 'The Memory that Never Dies', 55.

[53] In 1998, the PNA set up May 15 as the official Nakba day, marking the date on which the State of Israel was established.

[54] By the early 1990s, annual commemorations of the day by Palestinian Arab citizens of Israel held a prominent place in the community's public discourse. In 2006, for example, Azmi Bishara, an Arab member of the Knesset told the Israeli newspaper Maariv: "Independence Day is your holiday, not ours. We mark this as the day of our Nakba, the tragedy that

and across the globe commemorate this day through protests,[55] marches, lectures, and public events. As a day of mourning, it has become a significant milestone with deep resonance in Palestinian society and identity.

Moreover, 1948 serves as a powerful political tool for mobilizing Palestinians in their national struggle. The Palestinian National Authority (PNA) has consciously cultivated the Nakba memory in schools[56] and demonstrations.[57] Symbols and rituals of suffering have become what Pierre Nora calls: 'sites of memory' or '*lieux de memoire*' creating a continuum between the past and present.[58] Like the Holocaust, the Nakba is not merely a passing historical event, but an ongoing process of victimization that heightens threat perceptions and bolsters political and legal claims. It is also contended that an ethos of victimhood cultivated on both sides contributes to the sustenance of the conditions and experiences of intractable conflict.[59]

Thus, the Israeli–Palestinian conflict is not only a conventional one for power and territory, but also an existential one drawn from the collective memories of catastrophic events. Tragically, there is an ironic symmetry to each nation's exclusive claim to victimhood and refusals to acknowledge the national trauma of the other. "For many Palestinians, the Holocaust seems an excuse and a camouflage for the atrocities . . . which Israel thrusts upon them."[60] In Israel, the incomparable trauma of the Holocaust appears

befell the Palestinian nation in 1948" (Maariv article, in Hebrew). See also N. Masalha, *Catastrophe Remembered: Palestine, Israel and the Internal Refugees: Essays in Memory of Edward W. Said (1935–2003)* (New York: Zed Books, 2005), 221.

55 At times protests develop into clashes between Palestinians and the IDF in the West Bank and Gaza Strip.

56 For example, in textbooks and teacher's guides published by the Palestinian Ministry of Education, the Nakba and its aftermath, receive comprehensive treatment, while the existence of Israel is patently ignored. See Milshtein, 'The Memory that Never Dies', 55.

57 Yasser Arafat's address to the "march of millions" on 14 May 1998 connected the Nakba with the creation of a Palestinian State and the right of return. "We ask only that the page of the *Nakba* be turned over forever, that the emigrant return to his homeland, and that we build our Palestinian state on our land" quoting Yasser Arafat in Webman, 'The Evolution of a Founding Myth', 34.

58 See P. Nora, 'Between Memory and History: Les lieux de memoire', *Representations* 26 (1989), 19 as quoted in M. Bar-On, 'Conflicting Narratives or Narratives of a Conflict: Can the Zionist and Palestinian Narratives of the 1948 War Be Bridged?', in Robert Rotberg (ed.), *Israeli–Palestinian Narratives of Conflict: History's Double Helix* (Bloomington: Indiana University Press, 2006), 164.

59 See D. Bar-Tal, 'Socio-psychological Foundations of Intractable Conflicts', *American Behavioural Scientist* 50 (2007), 1430, 1443. See also B. Tint, 'History, Memory and Intractable Conflict', *Conflict Resolution Quarterly* 27:3 (Spring 2010), 239, 242.

60 Qaymari, 'The Holocaust in the Palestinian Perspective', 150.

to blind Israelis to the plight of Palestinians,[61] whilst the notion of the Palestinian right of return is a euphemism for calls to destroy the Jewish nation.

4 Legal Footprints of Collective Memory

4.1 Palestinian Return

The bitter struggle over 1948 is also reflected in Israel's legal and official memory. Israeli laws and legal institutions reproduce denial of the Palestinian past, refraining from addressing the rights of Palestinian refugees, particularly the right of return, and thus reifying the silencing of this issue in the public space. Thus, a corollary of Jewish return (which guarantees all Jews a virtually automatic right to Israeli citizenship) embodied in the Israeli Declaration of Independence, the Law of Return[62] and the Nationality Law (1952),[63] is the staunch resistance to the notion of a Palestinian right of return. Indeed, the *Nationality Law* was arguably expressly drafted to render the Palestinians displaced in 1948 ineligible for citizenship.[64] By confining the granting of nationality to those Palestinians physically present within Israel's borders upon the termination of the 1948 war, Israel could effectively prevent hundreds of thousands of Palestinian refugees from acquiring nationality.[65] In Israeli eyes, the basis for the legal obstruction through exclusionary statutory categories is deeply rooted in the Zionist narrative of 1948, in which, the Palestinian refugee issue is perceived first and foremost as an existential security one.

[61] "Tragically, most Israelis . . . are mesmerized by their own profound fears . . . Those fears are rooted . . . in the Holocaust. Such fears seem to blind those in their grip to the fact that the Palestinians are tormented by their own profound existential crisis as a people." See Khalidi, *Palestinian Identity*, 26.

[62] Law of Return 4 Laws of the State of Israel, 114 (1950).

[63] Nationality Law, 6 Laws of the State of Israel, 50 (1952).

[64] Section 3 of the *Nationality Law* (1952) provides that "[a] person who resided in Palestine immediately prior to the establishment of the state is only automatically regarded as a resident if they were registered as a resident prior to the enactment" of the *Nationality Law*. See T. Kramer, 'The Controversy of a Palestinian "Right of Return" to Israel', *Arizona Journal of International and Comparative Law* 18 (2001), 979, 998. See also S. A. Sitta, 'The Israeli Law of Return, Dual Loyalty and the Status of Jewish Communities Outside Israel', in D. Abdullah (ed.), *The Israeli Law of Return & Its Impact on the Struggle in Palestine* (London: Palestinian Return Centre, 2004), 120–2.

[65] A. Shachar, 'Whose Republic: Citizenship and Membership in the Israeli Polity', *Georgetown Immigration Law Journal* 13 (1999), 107; S. Jiryes, 'Domination by the Law', *Journal of Palestine Studies* 11:1, 10th Anniversary Issue: Palestinians under Occupation (1981), 80.

Israel's staunch legal resistance to Palestinian return applies not only to those living across the border, but also to those Palestinians internally displaced within Israel (often referred to as Israeli-Arabs). Official policy continues to block 1948 refugees from returning to their original places of residence, even nationals of Israel, and even when return is sought to areas unused by the State.[66] In this regard, the case of the Galilee villages of *Ikrit* and *Biram* is illustrative. For over five decades, its former residents ordered to evacuate during the 1948 war, petitioned Israeli courts to return to their original homes,[67] or at least to unused areas nearby.[68]

On 26 June 2003, Israel's High Court of Justice (HCJ) rejected yet another appeal against the Israeli government. The Court accepted the State's claim that "political" interests do not justify allowing the former residents to return because of security reasons, and the Palestinian demand for a general right of return.[69] Among the documents submitted by the State was an affidavit by Prime Minister Ariel Sharon from 2001 that the right of return issue was significant at Camp David, and that the subsequent wave of hostility casts a shadow over the case. The government claimed that the PA would take advantage of any precedent concerning the return of displaced residents for political and propaganda purposes.[70] The petitioners rejected any link between their right to return to their homes as

[66] Y. Peled and N. N. Rouhana, 'Transitional Justice and the Right to Return of the Palestinian Refugees,' *Theoretical Inquiries in Law* 5 (2004), 317, 325.

[67] The HCJ originally ruled in July 1951 that the residents were entitled to return to their village because the legal basis for temporary evacuation no longer existed after the war (HCJ 64/51 *Dawwod vs. Defence Minister* 1951, P.D. 5(2): 1118). However, on Christmas Day 1951 the military defied the order, issued the inhabitants with expulsion orders, and destroyed both villages.

[68] In the 2003 petition (this was the fourth plea made by the former residents of Ikrit), the displaced residents referred to the statement in the Libai Committee's report (headed by former Justice Minister David Libai) that indicated defined areas near the village on which community settlements could be built without causing harm to the neighbors. The petitioners claimed that these areas are still not used, and therefore are not needed any more for the public interest for which they were confiscated.

[69] According to the HCJ ruling, since the issue is mainly "political," the State enjoys broad discretion, and the government's position in this case was "reasonable." HCJ 840/97 paragraph 6.

[70] The government also claimed that accepting the petition would have far-reaching and strategic implications, because 200,000 other displaced citizens have also demanded they be allowed to return to their former villages. See Hussein Abu Hussein, 'Refugee Protection: Right of Return – The Ever-Present Fear, The Iqrit Model Israeli Supreme Court Denies IDPs Latest Attempt to Return Home' (2003) 19 *BADIL Resource Center for Palestinian Residency and Refugee Rights: Back to Basics.*

Israeli nationals, and the political issue of 1948 generally.[71] Nevertheless, as Gad Barzilai concludes, the case was ultimately decided based on "the judicial fear that such legal precedent would restore the right of return and hence threaten the foundations of the Jewish state."[72] The *Ikrit* decision thus reveals the extent to which Israeli courts are equally subverted by the Zionist collective memory of 1948, and in particular official resistance to any aspect of the Palestinian narrative of return.

4.2 Critical Representation of 1948

Regarding cultural expressions of 1948, Israeli legal institutions are also compelled to negotiate the fraught intersection between the contested past, democratic notions of free speech, and official memory. One of the earliest High Court cases to squarely address critical representation of 1948 was the *Ein Gal* decision from the late 1970s. In this case, the Censorship Board banned the screening of a documentary film entitled *The Struggle over the Land*, which depicted Zionism as a colonialist movement, and claimed that the Arabs of Israel were expelled from their land by the Jews in 1948.[73] A large part of the judgment was devoted to history in the film that could threaten the legitimacy of the State and incite violence. Justice Landau indicated that, "in describing the events of 1948, the film producers avoided mentioning that they occurred at the height of a war of self-defense in which the Jewish community was fighting for its survival"[74] and that the filmmakers ignored that the lands of Petah Tikvah and Tel-Aviv had been purchased for full consideration. Ultimately, guided by popular memory of 1948 at the time, Justice Landau approved the banning of the film based on its potential for incitement, primarily of the Arab public.[75]

71 The petitioners based their demand to return to their village on three grounds: the lack of a security reason for the issue of the closure order; the promise of the State; and the new precedent given by the Supreme Court in the 1990s regarding the ability of the government to cancel a confiscation.

72 G. Barzilai, *Communities and Law: Politics and Cultures of Legal Identities* (Ann Arbor: University of Michigan Press, 2003), 92.

73 HCJ 807/78 Ein Gal, IsrSC 33(1) 274 at 275. See Daphne Barak-Erez, 'The Law of Historical Films: In the Aftermath of *Jenin Jenin*', *Southern California Interdisciplinary Law Journal* 16 (2007), 495. Notably, another film *Hirbet Hiz'eh* was broadcast on television in the same year (1978) after a protracted public controversy. The film was based on a book, which portrays the expulsion of an Arab village by the IDF at the end of the war.

74 HCJ 807/78 Ein Gal, IsrSC 33(1) 274 at 275–6.

75 *Ibid.*, 278. "Were this film to be shown in Israel, there is an imminent danger that . . . it could become an effective tool of incitement among Arabs living here and encourage them to engage in criminal activities."

It is worth noting that Israeli case law has repeatedly ruled that distortions of history are not adequate grounds for censorship of films.[76] From this perspective, the *Ein Gal* decision is a somewhat isolated case. It can perhaps be explained by the fact that during the 1970s, critical engagement with 1948 was still anathema to Israeli society.[77] Indeed, mirroring shifts in Israeli popular memory,[78] this decision was reversed some two and half decades later in *Bakri v. Film Censorship Board*[79] (2003) ("Bakri"). In that case, the Censorship Board banned the screening of a documentary film that sought to present the Palestinian narrative of the battle in the Jenin refugee camp in April 2002. In her decision, Justice Dalia Dorner refers to the *Ein Gal* ruling and concludes that: "since this ruling was issued in 1979, times have changed and so has the law. Given the case law since then, the precedent set there can no longer stand. In any event, I hold that Israeli society is currently able to deal with such expressions."[80] Thus, at least as it concerns freedom of expression, there is hope that judicial narrative on 1948 is capable of adapting to shifts in popular memory.

4.3 *Holocaust Denial*

From a different standpoint, section 2 of the Denial of Holocaust (Prohibition) law (1986)[81] ("Holocaust Denial Law") is a striking example of Israeli attempts to regulate and preserve Jewish historical memory. The Israeli law criminalizes publication of any statement (written or verbal), that denies or diminishes the extent of the "crimes against the Jewish people

[76] See HCJ 1/81 *Shiran v. Broadcasting Authority* [1981] IsrSC 35(3) 365. The petition was dismissed in view of the Court's fundamental approach that an unfair and even biased presentation of content does not justify the infringement of the right to freedom of expression. See also HCJ 2137/98 *Elias v. Chairman of Managerial Committee of Broadcasting Authority* (unpublished). Another judgment marking the freedom to distort historical truth was delivered in HCJ 6126/94 *Senesh v. Broadcasting Authority* [1999] IsrSC 53(3) 817. See Barak-Erez, 'The Law of Historical Films', 507.

[77] *Ibid.*, 506.

[78] As discussed, a series of momentous events since the 1970s from the "New Historians" to the *Oslo Accords* reconfigured Israeli collective memory of 1948. Uri Ram, 'Ways of Forgetting: Israel and the obliterated Memory of the Palestinian Nakba', *Journal of Historical Sociology* 22:3 (2009), 366, 384–5.

[79] See generally HCJ 316/03 *Bakri* [2003] IsrSC 58(1) 249.

[80] See generally HCJ 316/03 *Bakri* [2003] IsrSC 58(1) 249 at 270.

[81] The Knesset passed Israel's Denial of Holocaust (Prohibition) Law 5746 on 8 July 1986 (published in Sefer Ha-Chukkim No. 1187, 16 July 1986), 196. Available at www.mfa.gov.il/MFA/Anti-Semitism+and+the+Holocaust/Documents+and+communiques/Denial+of+Holo caust+-Prohibition-+Law-+5746-1986-.htm (Isr.).

or crimes against humanity" committed during the Nazi regime, if made "with intent to defend the perpetrators of those acts or to express sympathy or identification with them." An offender is "liable to imprisonment for a term of five years."[82]

Notably, the law was passed during the same period as the Israeli Knesset adopted legal measures to ban racial incitement against Israeli-Arabs, in response to the racist politics of Rabbi Meir Kahane.[83] New legislation outlawed racist parties from the Knesset,[84] and criminalized certain modes of racist behavior.[85] As if to create a common discourse against racism, the Holocaust Denial Law seemed intended to equally limit incitement against Jews. Yet it seems somewhat redundant in a Jewish State where Holocaust denial is almost uniformly rejected, whereas racism against Arabs finds receptive audiences.[86] Indeed, a review of Israeli case law failed to uncover a single instance in which charges were brought under the statute.[87] In this light, the law is merely symbolic and politically instrumental.[88] It is particularly noteworthy compared with Israel's regulation of 1948. Arguably, the legislation reflects a double mnemonic standard, under which Jewish

[82] *Ibid.*

[83] Rabbi Meir Kahane established a political–racial movement, Kach, whose platform advocated the expulsion of Arabs from Israel and the establishment of a Jewish theocracy. After his election to the Knesset in 1974, Kahane intensified his provocative public statements, calling for the persecution of the Arab residents of Israel.

[84] See Basic Law: The Knesset section 7(a) amended in Basic Law: The Knesset Amendment. No. 9 1155 Sefer Hahukim (SH) 196 (1985).

[85] In 1986, the Knesset amended the Penal Law to create two related offenses: a prohibition against publishing material with the purpose of inciting racism (section 144B), and a prohibition against possession of any racist publication with intent to distribute it so as to bring about racism (section 144D). Penal Law Amend. No. 20, 1191 S.H. 219 (1986). Both criminal offenses are punishable by three to five years' imprisonment.

[86] The historical and cultural context in Israel is obviously of great significance. Propagating Holocaust denial here is quite different from propagating this idea in Europe. Most Israeli Jews will hardly be persuaded by such propaganda.

[87] Notably, the 1986 amendment to Israel's Penal law (banning racist rhetoric) has led to only one conviction that of an Israeli Arab for pursuing anti-government propaganda. See J. Schoffman, 'Legislation Against Racist Incitement in Israel: A 1992 Appraisal', 194, in S. Colliver (ed.), *Striking a Balance: Hate Speech, Freedom of Expression and Non-Discrimination* (London: Article 19, London and Human Rights Centre, University of Essex, 1992).

[88] According to Lederman and Tabory, the ostensible purpose of this type of legislation was to make a political statement, one that "reinforced anti-racist ideology and influenced modes of behavior through its normative proscription against racism." E. Lederman and M. Tabory, 'Criminalisation of Racial Incitement in Israel', *Stanford Journal of International Law* 24 (1987), 55–84.

Holocaust memory remains sacred, whilst the mere invocation of the Palestinian "Nakba" is sacrilege.

4.4 "The Nakba Law"

Thus, the Nakba taboo is firmly embedded into Israeli discourse. Indeed, in recent years (particularly under the "right-wing" Netanyahu coalition government), strident attempts are being made to revive traditional Zionist narratives of 1948. In 2009, the Israeli Ministry of Education ordered the removal of any reference to the Nakba from Israeli-Arab high-school textbooks.[89] In Jewish-Israeli political circles, there is also a growing trend of denying the Nakba "as a sort of conservative counter-attack to the post-Zionism of the 1990s."[90] For example, *Im Tirzu*, an Israeli right-wing group published and distributed a booklet called "Nakba-Bullshit" (it rhymes in Hebrew) at University gates, and stages counter-protests against memorial ceremonies.[91]

Against this backdrop, the Knesset (Israeli parliament), passed an amendment in March 2011 empowering the Minister of Finance to reduce monetary support for bodies or institutions (for example schools, universities or local authorities) that fund events or actions marking the date of Israel's establishment as a day of mourning (or undermining the existence of Israel as a Jewish and democratic State).[92] This amendment, known as "the Nakba Law," mirrors the current political trajectory against critical engagement with 1948.[93] The original Bill intended to criminalize Nakba

[89] Since 2009, Palestinian Arab–Israeli schools have been effectively prevented from discussing or even using the term Nakba as part of their curriculum. Originally, the term "Nakba" was introduced in books for use in Arab schools in 2007 when the Education Ministry was run by Yuli Tamir of the Labour party.

[90] See N. Sheizaf, 'Despite efforts to erase it, the Nakba's memory is more present than ever in Israel', *+972*, 14 May 2013.

[91] The Booklet repeats many of the traditional Zionist views on the 1948 refugees: from "there is no such thing as a Palestinian people" to "they fled of their own free will." Activists from *Im Tirzu* also urged students to avoid classes that mention the Nakba, distributed the booklet at university gates, and staged counter-protests against memorial ceremonies on Nakba Day. See *Ibid.*

[92] Budget Principles Law (Amendment #40), 5771-2011, SH No. 2286, 686–7.

[93] This and other Knesset measures, from a Bill attempting to cancel Arabic's status as an official language in Israel to proposals for a mandatory loyalty oath, have sharpened feelings of alienation among many Arab citizens of Israel that their presence and history in the land is under attack. See D. Kraft, 'Arab Alienation abound on Israel's 63rd birthday', *Washington Jewish Week*, 12 May 2011.

commemoration by proposing a three-year prison sentence for any person organizing such acts of remembrance. Ultimately, the Knesset passed a more diluted version of the Bill, which basically threatens any institution – even an Arab-Israeli one – with loss of state funding if it sponsors a Nakba-related event. Given that one in every five Israelis is Arab-Israeli, the law effectively denies a sizeable minority from freely expressing its own collective memory and historical narrative of 1948.[94]

According to Orr and Golan: "The Nakba Law denotes the institutionalisation of silencing of public discourse on the Nakba."[95] Some even suggest it amounts to official rewriting of history and censorship of Palestinian culture and history.[96] Arab-Israeli Knesset Member Hanin Zoabi protests: "The Nakba is a historic truth, not a position or freedom of expression . . . those memories and that history are more resonant than ever."[97] Others defend the law, claiming that: "as a Jewish state, Israel cannot be expected to use taxpayers' money to perpetuate a Palestinian narrative of victimization that intentionally distorts reality in order to delegitimize Zionism."[98] Either way, since 2011, Israeli legislation has made publicly marking the Nakba more difficult for Palestinians and activists in Israel.[99] By targeting commemoration, this law limits the space for open discussion of 1948, and invalidates Palestinian political and moral claims to justice and the right of return.

[94] This law has the potential to limit the ability of Arab educational, cultural, and political organizations to teach, explore, express, and preserve their collective memory of 1948.

[95] "This was partially in response to a nascent crack in hegemonic denial of the event, the blurring and erasure of the Palestinian past in Israeli discourse since 1948 having failed to preclude discussion of the Nakba in Israel," Z. Orr and D. Golan, 'Human Rights NGOs in Israel: Collective Memory and Denial', *The International Journal of Human Rights* 18:1 (2014), 68.

[96] Ali Abumnima (Palestinian American journalist) writes that the Nakba law amounts to "outlawing history" quoted in Yosefa Loshitzky, 'Reviews: Ella Shohat Israeli Cinema', *Third Text* 26:5 (2012), 615, 618.

[97] See Middle East Policy Council, 'Commentary: Knesset Passes Nakba Law Targeted at Its Arab Citizens: Middle East in Focus', April 2011.

[98] The Jerusalem Post Editorial 'Nakba and Freedom', 14 May 2012. See also Yoaz Hendel writing on Ynet: "A sovereign state seeks to cut the budgets of institutions and bodies that reject its basic values, yet some people around here characterize this as an undemocratic step. The debate over the Nakba Law . . . is not fundamental at all." Yoaz Hendel, 'In Praise of Nakba Law', 28 March 2011, Y-net.

[99] "The bottom line is that the law makes commemorating the Nakba illegitimate and unacceptable, an activity that requires regulation in the form of penalisation." Fady Khoury, 'High Court Ruling on Nakba Law Reveals Its Waning Power', *+972*, published 7 January 2012.

From a legal standpoint, the Nakba Law is rather vague in both language and scope. The ambiguous wording raises concerns about which state-funded institutions are at risk,[100] what activity warrants reduction of public funding (Does it include critical plays and films on 1948?), at what point (Is it only on Israel's Independence Day or throughout the year?), and which criteria exist to define rejection of Israel as a Jewish and democratic State.[101] In the petition filed against the Nakba Law on 4 May 2011 to the HCJ, Adalah[102] and the Association for Civil Rights in Israel (ACRI) challenged the law as anti-democratic, and as severely injuring basic civil and constitutional rights of Arab-Israelis, including freedom of expression, artistic and political freedom, the right to equality, the right to dignity, the right to education, and academic freedom and freedom of occupation.[103]

The HCJ dismissed the petition in 2012, ruling that since the law had not yet been technically implemented, constitutional inquiry was premature.[104] The Court's decision did not deal with the issues substantively, despite noting that they "raise complex questions of public importance, which go to the root of problems that divide Israeli society."[105] In her

[100] The law threatens a broad swath of government-funded institutions. Organizations at risk include research institutions found to be challenging the definition of the Israeli State as Jewish and democratic; educational institutions, such as bilingual schools, which hold events acknowledging the shared history of Jews and Arabs; and state-funded community organizations, such as theaters showing plays about the Nakba.

[101] According to ACRI's letter to the Knesset, 9 March 2011, "the law is exceedingly vague and might lead to selective and discriminatory enforcement, subject to the changing political whim of the hour. It would require civil servants, politicians and public bodies to become involved in administrative proceedings, which would then have to determine whether the law was broken based on ideological or political interpretation." See Adalah and ACRI: 'Israeli High Court Ignored the Chilling Effect Already Caused by the Nakba Law', 5 January 2012 available at www.adalah.org/en/content/view/7188 (accessed on 10 January 2016).

[102] Adalah is the legal center for Arab minority rights in Israel.

[103] The petition was submitted by both organizations on behalf of the Alumni Association of the Arab-Orthodox High School in Haifa, which holds various public education events about the Nakba and the nature of the "Jewish and democratic" State in the school; parents of students at the Arab–Jewish school "Galilee" in Misgav, in which educational activities are held commemorating Independence Day alongside events commemorating the Nakba; and geographer Professor Oren Yiftachel of Ben Gurion University whose research and academic work criticizes the definition of the State as "Jewish and democratic."

[104] The ruling is grounded in the ripeness doctrine from US Constitutional law, which essentially prevents Courts from entangling themselves in abstract disagreements or premature adjudication. HCJ 3429/11; delivered 5 January 2012.

[105] HCJ 3429/11 President Benisch judgment.

leading judgment, Justice Naor wrote that "The petitioners request the repeal of sections of the law that have not yet been used by the Finance Minister, and there is no way of knowing whether, when, and under what circumstances he will use that authority."[106]

Nevertheless, human rights groups retorted that the law has a chilling effect,[107] which regardless of use by the Minister, serves to intimidate state-supported entities. It appears that the Court erroneously ignored the insidious impact of the Nakba law on free speech. Indeed, four months after the HCJ's decision, the Nakba Law was used to prevent Tel Aviv University groups from holding Nakba Day events on campus, and requiring students to pay for their own security.[108] In similar circumstances, the Mayor of Haifa withdrew municipal funding for a film festival about the Nakba in February 2015, resulting in the event's cancellation.[109] The HCJ thus discounted the infringement on constitutional rights arising from the mere existence of the law on the statute books. In this way, the Nakba Law is an excellent example of official Israeli attempts to regulate collective memory. The continued sensitivity around 1948 is also partially reflected in the Court's reluctance to intervene.[110]

106 HCJ 3429/11; paragraph 28.

107 Attorney Dan Yakir, Legal Advisor of ACRI states: "The court completely ignored the claims regarding the chilling effect of this law, which forces state-supported entities to risk a significant reduction in their budgets before the law will be considered for judicial review. In this, it limits free speech." See Adalah and ACRI: 'Israeli High Court Ignored the Chilling Effect'.

108 In 2012, a group of students at Tel Aviv University sought to hold a ceremony marking Nakba Day in which they would offer an alternative memorial, including a moment of silence. The dean of students approved the event, but the university's security department announced that organizers would have to hire at least six ushers to maintain order. This was the first time that the university requested organizers of events on campus to fund security out of their own pockets, and it cited the Nakba Law as a reason. Available at www.haaretz.com/opinion/chilling-effect-of-the-nakba-law-on-israel-s-human-rights-1.430942 (accessed 2 January 2016). See also P. Strickland, 'Israel Continues to Criminalise Marking Nakba Day', *Al Jazeera English*, 14 May 2015.

109 The cancellation of the film festival on 23 April 2015 in Haifa followed a political uproar that surrounded a similar film festival that did take place in Tel Aviv's public cinema in November 2014.

110 According to Fady Khouri: "The decision by Israel's Supreme Court to keep the Nakba Bill intact demonstrates its capitulation to right-wing pressure and increasing struggle to survive as an independent body." F. Khoury, 'High Court Ruling on Nakba Law Reveals Its Waning Power', *+972*, 7 January 2012.

5 Challenges and Opportunities for Transitional Justice

5.1 Challenging Avoidance of 1948

Notwithstanding the Nakba Law, the memory of 1948 remains enduring. Paradoxically, "The more legislative attempts to limit the space for discussion [about the Nakba], the greater the public interest becomes."[111] As discussed, many of the anxieties and fears permeating Israeli and Palestinian society are traceable to the conflict's genesis. Thus, it is crucially important to find ways to engage the psychological repertoires of 1948 so as to assist in the reduction, de-escalation, and potential resolution of the conflict.

Engaging 1948 is no small feat, as there have been few attempts to comprehensively address this event in peace building efforts. Notably, both *Oslo 1* (DOP) and *Oslo II* (Interim Agreement 1995) expressly deferred the question of the Palestinian refugees until final negotiations "postponing any 'policing of the past' to a future unspecified stage."[112] The brokered settlements failed to mention any efforts to compensate or acknowledge Palestinian refugees, or consider symbolic measures to address the return issue. While some peace plans exhibited attempts to deal with 1948,[113] none of them sought to fully grapple with the psychological and historical barriers impeding the parties. Rather, Israeli negotiators flatly dismissed Palestinian demands for transitional and compensatory "justice" in relation to 1948.[114] In some ways, *Oslo* attempted to re-frame the conflict's narrative: "History now began in 1967 . . . Fundamental questions

[111] See P. Strickland, 'Israel Continues to Criminalise': "A strange thing regarding the debate on Nakba: the responses it generates in Israeli society are becoming more and more hostile, while at the same time the *Nakba* is mentioned more and more often." See Sheizaf, 'Despite efforts to erase it'; See also N. Sheizaf, 'Between Anger and Denial: Israeli Collective Memory and the Nakba', *+972*, 16 October 2012.

[112] L. King-Irani, 'To Reconcile or be Reconciled?: Agency, Accountability and Law in Middle-Eastern Conflicts', *Hastings and International and Comparative Law Review* 28 (2004–5), 369, 375; See also K. A. Cavanaugh, 'Selective Justice: The Case of Israel and the Occupied Territories', *Fordham International Law Journal* 26 (2002–3), 934, 940–1.

[113] At Camp David (2000) former Israeli Prime Minister Ehud Barak offered "symbolic return" of the 1,948 refugees involving up to 70,000 refugees over ten years. The Geneva Initiative (2003) was the most far-reaching on this issue. Nevertheless, it too did not engage the Palestinian demand that Israel acknowledge its responsibility for 1948 and associated the right of return solely within the territory of the Palestinian State.

[114] Y. Bar-Siman-Tov, 'Chapter 5: Justice and Fairness as Barriers to the Resolution of the Israeli–Palestinian Conflict', in Y. Bar -Siman-Tov (ed.), *Barriers to Peace in the Israeli–Palestinian Conflict* (Jerusalem: Jerusalem Institute for Israel Studies, 2011), 178–226, 201.

of justice, such as the 1948 refugees were placed on the political back burner."[115]

More broadly, "the terms transitional justice and dealing with the past have not yet been popularized in the Israeli–Palestinian setting."[116] Indeed, Israeli human rights NGOs have tended to refrain from addressing the rights of 1948 refugees, particularly the right of return.[117] Thus, the deepest desires of both parties for mutual validation of their collective memories from 1948, namely Palestinian acceptance of a Jewish State, and Israeli recognition of the Nakba have been somewhat sidelined.[118] It is therefore no coincidence that Oslo's demise is commonly attributed to the political intractability over 1948 and the right of return.[119] Accordingly, it appears worthwhile convincing the parties that squarely addressing this event is not an obstruction to peace, but could be part of the conflict's resolution.

5.2 *Desirability of Transitional Justice and Civil Society*

In this light, transitional justice may serve as a relevant tool to foster truth-telling, justice, and reconciliation efforts around 1948. Engaging the historical record could help challenge the competing meta-narratives of victimhood to which both sides are wedded. Broadly speaking, transitional justice may be defined as a "process" that "seeks recognition for victims and to promote possibilities for peace, reconciliation, and democracy."[120] While

[115] A. Ghazi-Bouillon, *Understanding the Middle East Peace Process: Israeli Academia and the Struggle for Identity* (New York: Routledge, 2009), 78.

[116] These terms have not fully entered the language of human rights organizations or the public and do not serve as established signifiers of this line of work. R. Shaw, L. Waldorf with P. Hazan (eds.), *Localizing Transitional Justice: Interventions and Priorities after Mass Violence* (Stanford: Stanford University Press, 2010), 237.

[117] According to Golan and Orr, 1948 does not constitute a significant element of the human rights discourse in Israel as Israeli NGOs tend to focus on 1967 and documenting human rights violations in the occupied territories. Z. Orr and D. Golan, 'Human Rights NGOs in Israel: Collective Memory and Denial', *The International Journal of Human Rights* 18:1 (2014), 68–72.

[118] Shamir and Shikaki confirm that "The identity of Israel as a Jewish State and the Palestinian demand for their right to return have become among the most difficult obstacles for reaching a comprehensive peace agreement." J. Shamir and K. Shikaki, 'Public Opinion in the Israeli–Palestinian Two Level Game', *Journal of Peace Research* 42 (2005), 311, 315.

[119] Friedman, 'Unraveling the Right', 64.

[120] International Centre for Transitional Justice, 'What is Transitional Justice Fact Sheet', 2009.

some adhere to a narrower legalistic concept of transitional justice,[121] others argue for a thicker understanding, in which "dealing with the past" extends beyond fixed transitional periods or juridical mechanisms.[122] In the Israeli/Palestinian scenario, Ron Dudai proposes "an incremental process . . . through a long process of transition, rather than one high-profile and all-encompassing mechanism in the post-conflict stage."[123]

Given the ongoing violence and official resistance to transitional justice, this seems to be a sensible approach. Indeed, projects like memorials, textbook reform, and truth committees, could be presently contemplated by civil society as transitional justice measures, to sow the seeds of reconciling 1948 before a political settlement.[124] Arguably, such measures have the potential to herald earlier support, healing, and trust between the parties and to promote termination of the conflict by extending the boundaries of discussion.[125]

In this regard, it is worth noting the work of Israeli NGO *Zochrot*[126] (remembering in Hebrew), which conducts truth-telling activities on 1948 to promote *Nakba* awareness and to recast public debate in Israel. The movement was established in the belief that Israeli Jewish denial of the Nakba obstructs reconciliation between the two nations.[127] In practical terms, *Zochrot* distributes informational resources, organizes memorial events and historical tours.[128] One of its signature activities is signposting

121 See C. Campbell, F. Ni Aolain and C. Harvey, 'The Frontiers of Legal Analysis: Reframing the Transition in Northern Ireland', *Modern Law Review* 66:3 (2003), 17–45. See also C. Bell, 'Transitional Justice, Interdisciplinarity and the State of the "Field" or "NonField"', *International Journal of Transitional Justice* 3:1 (2009), 5–27.

122 See McEvoy and Kieran, 'Beyond Legalism: Towards a Thicker Understanding of Transitional Justice', *Journal of Law and Society* 34:4 (2007), 411–40. See also R. Dudai, 'A Model for Dealing with the Past in the Israeli–Palestinian Context', *International Journal of Transitional Justice* 1 (2007), 249; R. Nets-Zehngut, 'Transitional Justice and Addressing the History of Active Conflicts: The Case of the Israeli–Palestinian Conflict' (2011) 1–27.

123 R. Dudai, 'A Model for Dealing with the Past in the Israeli–Palestinian Context', *International Journal of Transitional Justice* 1 (2007), 249, 250.

124 R. Nets-Zehngut, 'Transitional Justice and Addressing the History of Active Conflicts: The Case of the Israeli Palestinian Conflict' (2012) The Leonard Davis Institute for International Relations, The Hebrew University of Jerusalem (Under Review), 2–3.

125 *Ibid.*, 20.

126 *Zochrot* (remembering in Hebrew) is an Israeli group, which seeks to stimulate debate and promote awareness within Israeli–Jewish society about the Palestinian Nakba. See the Organization's website: http://zochrot.org/en.

127 One of the self-defined purposes of Zochrot is to for Israeli Jews to acknowledge practical and moral responsibility for the part they played in the Palestinian Nakba.

128 U. Ram, 'Ways of Forgetting: Israel and the Obliterated Memory of the Palestinian Nakba', *Journal of Historical Sociology* 22:3 (2009), 366, 389.

around Israel to mark destroyed Palestinian villages from 1948.[129] In the Director's words: "Physically marking these villages . . . is intended to set in motion a process of catharsis."[130]

Zochrot is also engaged in legal advocacy. In March 2006, after petitioning the HCJ, Israeli authorities conceded to post new signs at Canada Park that commemorate the prior existence of Palestinian villages on this site.[131] *Zochrot* claimed the signs originally posted by the Jewish National Fund (JNF) were "selective exclusions of segments of local history."[132] Notably after the case, one of the new signs posted in Canada Park disappeared, and the other was vandalized. Despite these setbacks, one must not underestimate *Zochrot*'s discursive contribution to the present political landscape, as a "movement of alternative memory."[133] Such activities and other civil society groups serve as a counter-weight to current trends of forgetting and regulation of memory.[134]

5.3 *Bridging Narrative: From Mutual Denial to Joint Acknowledgment*

Beyond unilateral initiatives directed at the Israeli–Jewish public, it is also important to contemplate collaborative mechanisms that address

[129] Posting signs at destroyed Palestinian villages is part of a larger campaign to bring Nakba awareness to the country. In this context Zochrot has invited Jewish people to join guided visits.

[130] He continues: "As long as razed Palestinian villages remain un-commemorated on the Israeli landscape, their existence in the past and their destruction is repressed." E. Bronstein, 'The Nakba – Something That did not Occur (Although It has to Occur)', in T. Rempel (ed.), *Rights in Principle – Rights in Practice: Revisiting the Role of International Law in Crafting Durable Solutions for Palestinian Refugees* (Bethlehem: BADIL Resource Centre, 2011), 321.

[131] See HCJ 5580/05 *Zochrot v. The Military Commander for Judea and Samara* (5 June 2006) (unpublished). In sum, the petition sought to include a historic account of the prior existence of Palestinian villages *Yalu* and *Imwas* that were destroyed following the Six-Day War in 1967.

[132] See, the High Court of Justice Petition No. 5580/05 Id. See also, A. Barakat, 'The JNF will Post Signs Commemorating the Palestinian Villages that were Destroyed', *Ha'aretz*, 26 July 2005.

[133] Uri Ram observes: "What is remarkable about Zochrot is not its size or impact, but rather the fact that it openly offers an explicit and direct antithesis to the Israeli regime of forgetting." Ram, 'Ways of Forgetting', 389.

[134] For the past eleven years, Israeli group "Combatants for Peace" hold an alternative joint Israeli–Palestinian Memorial Day to commemorate 1948. Also, the Israeli–Palestinian Narrative Project (initiated by the Parents Circle-Families Forum) promotes reconciliation through historic, national, and personal narrative sharing.

both sides' demands to have their historical rights and injustices acknowledged. Accountability for the Nakba remains central to the self-view of the Palestinian people. [135] Similarly, Israel continues to demand Palestinian recognition of its legitimacy as a Jewish State.[136] Beyond polarized rhetoric or technical debate, any meaningful conversation on 1948 will need to include questions of responsibility, and account for the existential aspects of the past. Despite the asymmetry of power between Israelis and Palestinians, it is contended that, psychologically both nations are traumatized by "a victim ideology affecting their deepest levels of existence."[137]

In this light, a mechanism could be conceived that transcends the narrow legal and political framing of 1948, and which can "encompass the requirements of narrative, history, reparations, and repair."[138] For Palestinians, this means trading utopian conceptions of return[139] and absolute justice with compensation, resettlement, and attainable justice for the refugees. Despite inroads made by the "New Historians," Israelis still need to forgo self-righteous mythologizing of 1948 in order to assume ownership of their role in the Palestinian displacement. Thus, creative and innovative approaches should be trialed that produce a common narrative on the origins of the refugee problem.

5.4 Contemplating an Israeli–Palestinian Truth Commission

In this light, one could envisage a collaborative project between Israeli and Palestinian academics and NGOs, in which an IPTC model is jointly formulated to inform negotiations and provoke wider public debate.

[135] R. Khalidi, 'Observations on the Right of Return', *Journal of Palestine Studies* 82 (1992), 29–30.

[136] In May 2014, Prime Minister Benjamin Netanyahu ruled out any deal with the Palestinians unless they recognize Israel as the Jewish State and give up their refugees' right of return.

[137] "While a suicide bomber may kill only a handful of civilians and perhaps injure dozens more, the real violence done is psychological." See Meyerstein, 'Transitional Justice and Post-Conflict', 301 and 313.

[138] Z. Miller, 'Settling with History: A Hybrid Commission of Inquiry for Israel/Palestine', *Harvard Human Rights Journal* 20 (2007), 293, 306.

[139] "Palestinian discourse on return remains utopian, abstract and nostalgic . . . justified as it may be, however nostalgia cannot substitute a plan of action or forever postpone it." See D. Rabinowitz, 'Israel and the Palestinian Refugees: Postpragmatic Reflections on Historical Narratives, Closure, Transitional Justice, and Palestinian Refugees' Right to Refuse', in B. R. Johnston and S. Slyomovics (eds.), *Waging War, Making Peace: Reparations and Human Rights* (Walnut Creek: Left Coast Press, 2009), 225–39, 230.

Just as critical scholarship of 1948 sensitized Israeli public opinion,[140] an academic initiative of this kind could break taboos, propose counter-narratives, and envisage a post-conflict reality before a political accord is concluded. Indeed, Michal Ben-Josef Hirsch persuasively demonstrates how the Israeli "New Historians" reconfigured social attitudes and representations of the conflict.[141]

In a similar vein, a bi-national IPTC committee could attract media attention and extend the boundaries of discussion. The collection of personal stories and scholarship might begin the process of challenging exclusive notions of victimhood.[142] Moreover, a model IPTC could provide creative strategies for diplomatic resolution of 1948 and influence political elites.[143] Opening new channels of dialogue could undermine the entrenched view that "there is nobody to talk with"[144] in the diplomatic arena. According to Nets-Zehngut[145] and Ben-Josef Hirsch,[146] critical scholarship of 1948 enabled negotiators to revisit the issue of Palestinian refugees with new political trade-offs.[147] It is submitted that a model IPTC

[140] A 2008 public opinion reflected a major shift in Israeli–Jewish popular memory of the conflict, which used to be more Zionist-orientated. See Nets-Zehngut, 'Transitional Justice', 15.

[141] See M. Ben-Josef Hirsch, 'From Taboo to the Negotiable: The Israeli New Historians and Changing Representations of Palestinian Refugees', *Perspectives on Politics* 5:2 (2007), 241, 242.

[142] "The rival then can be viewed in a more legitimized, humanized, personalized and differentiated manner." Y. Auerbach, 'National Narratives in a Conflict of Identity', in J. Bar-Simon-Tov (ed.), *Barriers to Peace in the Israeli–Palestinian Conflict* (Jerusalem: The Jerusalem Institute for Israel Studies, 2010), 99–133.

[143] According to Daniel Levy, a member of the Israeli Delegation to Taba, "the historical work or the New Historians was part of the material they read in preparation for the negotiation." Cited *Ibid.*, 251.

[144] Ben-Josef Hirsch, 'From Taboo to the Negotiable', 244.

[145] At Camp David (2000) "the Critical narrative regarding the exodus was so prevalent in Israel that it was hard for Israeli negotiators to ignore it." See Nets-Zehngut. 'Transitional Justice', 14.

[146] "At the Taba Conference (January 2001), Israeli negotiators went where no Israeli officials went before: they considered the right of return, and a quasi-statement that acknowledges the Palestinian tragedy and Israel's share of the responsibility." Ben-Josef Hirsch, 'From Taboo to the Negotiable', 241.

[147] For example, an Israeli public apology, compensation to refugees, and an official report whose findings or recommendations would address past abuses, may all be contemplated as political concessions. As was the case in Sierra Leone and El Salvador, negotiators can agree upon a truth and reconciliation mechanism "in principle" to be implemented once an agreement is achieved. See Dudai, 'A Model for Dealing with the Past', 264.

be broader than 1948,[148] and akin to the South African model address human rights abuses of both parties.

6 Conclusion

Ultimately, the Israeli case is a striking example of the legal proscription of history and the politics of memory. Judicial engagement with 1948, and the legislative ban on Nakba commemoration, have been instrumental to enforcing a nationalist past, and an exclusive claim to victimhood. Pitted against the Holocaust Denial Law, Israeli society is at once commanded to sanctify the Holocaust, and to silence the Palestinian Nakba. For this reason, this author is wary of memory laws that serve partisan political ends and censorship in democracies like Israel's.

Notwithstanding current trends, the legacy of the New Historians, and the *Ein Gal* ruling demonstrate the capacity of Israeli society to adapt to shifts in popular memory. A broader view of transitional justice involving civil society might herald a more conciliatory and bridging approach to 1948. No doubt, this is no small task, given the present Israeli landscape of "regulatory" and "punitive" approaches to historical memory.[149] Still, it is arguably part of a necessary process of transforming cultures of denial and victimhood into "a morally more responsible and historically constructive cycle of acknowledgement of the past."[150]

[148] Ideally the IPTC should address two historical periods, one of 1947–50 and the second of 2000–present, to treat abuses under the Israeli occupation and Palestinian suicide bombing and attacks on Israeli civilians.

[149] For a theoretical overview of the distinction between "regulatory" and "non-regulatory" memory laws and "punitive" and "non-punitive" laws, see Epilogue by Eric Heinze in the present volume.

[150] Rami Khouri (Jordanian commentator and writer) as quoted by Webman, 'The Evolution of a Founding Myth', 40.

18

Historical Revisionism and the Settler State: The Canadian Experience

MICHAEL MORDEN

1 Introduction

There are several approaches that states may adopt to engineer the diffusion of specific historical narratives, and the suppression of others. Memory laws are one. Truth commissions are another, and one of the most common instruments deployed by states to engineer historical revision on a societal scale. Rather than using coercion, as in forbidding the transmission of particular versions of history, their method is persuasion, inviting broad public participation in the interest of promoting an ostensibly more accurate and consensual understanding of recent history. In the words of Michael Ignatieff: 'The past is an argument, and the function of truth commissions, like the function of honest historians, is simply to purify the argument, to narrow the range of permissible lies'.[1] But truth commissions are not exercises in inductive history. They are built to tell a preferred story about the past, and they invite testimony to bolster and support this argument, as well as foster a critical mass of adherents. As policy instruments intended to produce public historical narrative, which often yield important legal outcomes, truth commissions merit attention in discussions about law and public memory.

Truth commissions have provoked proportionate scholarly interest in recent decades,[2] but have also proven difficult creatures to study. They

[1] M. Ignatieff, 'Overview: Articles of Faith,' *Index on Censorship* 25 (1996), 113.

[2] See for example, K. Avruch, 'Truth and Reconciliation Commissions: Problems in Transitional Justice and the Reconstruction of Identity,' *Transcultural Psychiatry* 47 (2010), 33–49, K. Brounéus, 'Truth-Telling as Talking Cure? Insecurity and Retraumatization in the Rwandan Gacaca Courts,' *Security Dialogue* 39 (2008), 55–76, P. B. Hayner, *Unspeakable Truths: Transitional Justice and the Challenge of Truth Commissions* (New York: Routledge, 2010), M. Hirsch, M. MacKenzie, and M. Sesay, 'Measuring the Impacts of Truth and Reconciliation Commissions: Placing the Global "Success" of TRCs in Local Perspective,'

mostly occur in deeply unsettled contexts, immediately in the aftermath of conflict or regime collapse, which makes it very difficult to establish casual relationships between them and (for instance) legal outcomes, or relapses into conflict, improved social peace, justice, and intergroup relationships. Much literature on this topic has presumed rather than proved the value of truth commissions.[3] They also, by definition, entail deep historical contexts, which differ widely from case to case, sometimes limiting cross-national comparison to strictly legalistic or policy-based analysis.

Canada, in its efforts to address historical injustices visited on Indigenous people in its territory, offers a useful case study, which evades both of these problems. The Canadian state has not, through memory law, legislated limits on historical remembrance regarding Indigenous people. But the country has recently concluded a major and relatively high-profile truth and reconciliation commission focused on Indian residential schools – boarding schools that operated for roughly one hundred years from the late nineteenth to the late twentieth century, which thousands of Indigenous students were compelled to attend. Living conditions were poor, students suffered physical and sexual abuse, and the schools were specifically dedicated to assimilation, including the elimination of Indigenous languages and certain cultural practices. In 2008, the prime minister apologized to Indigenous people for the residential schools system, and in 2009 the Indian Residential Schools Truth and Reconciliation Commission (IRSTRC) commenced its work. It is itself a unique exercise in reconciliation policy – the first major truth commission to occur in a stable liberal democracy, and entirely apart from any transition or regime change.[4] Its goal was to establish a new, widely disseminated and definitive history of this particular episode in Canada's settler colonial history.

Cooperation and Conflict 47 (2012), 386–403 (hereinafter Hirsch et al., 'Measuring the Impacts of Truth and Reconciliation Commissions'), D. Mendeloff, 'Truth-Seeking, Truth-Telling, and Postconflict Peacebuilding: Curb the Enthusiasm?,' *International Studies Review* 6 (2004), 355–80 (hereinafter Mendeloff, 'Truth-Seeking, Truth-Telling, and Postconflict Peacebuilding'), D. J. Stein, S. Seedat, D. Kaminer et al., 'The Impact of the Truth and Reconciliation Commission on Psychological Distress and Forgiveness in South Africa,' *Social Psychiatry and Psychiatric Epidemiology* 43 (2008), 462–8.

[3] Hirsch et al., 'Measuring the Impacts of Truth and Reconciliation Commissions,' Mendeloff, 'Truth-Seeking, Truth-Telling, and Postconflict Peacebuilding.'

[4] C. Jung, 'Transitional Justice for Indigenous People in a Non-Transitional Society,' *International Centre for Transitional Justice* (2009), available at ictj.org/sites/default/files/ICTJ-Identities-NonTransitionalSocieties-ResearchBrief-2009-English.pdf (8 October 2013), R. Niezen, *Truth and Indignation: Canada's Truth and Reconciliation Commission on*

But while the IRSTRC is the first explicit truth commission, it is not the first formal state-led effort to address the settler state's historical relationship to Indigenous people. There have been several attempts in the past twenty years, albeit with divergent scopes, on different scales, and using distinct formats. I contend that there are two other meaningful truth commissions (adopting a broad understanding of the term), which should be studied alongside the IRSTRC, and which make for rich comparison within the single political and historical context. The first was the Royal Commission on Aboriginal Peoples (RCAP), a massive commission called to inquire into the place of Indigenous peoples in Canada after a violent conflict took place between Kanien'kehá:ka (Mohawks) and the Canadian army in 1990. RCAP produced a 4,000-page report, published in 1996, which called for dramatic changes to laws, institutions, and existing settler narratives of Canadian history.[5] The second was the Ipperwash Inquiry, a public inquiry commissioned in 2003 to investigate the shooting death of an unarmed Anishinabek (Ojibway) protester. The Ipperwash Inquiry reported in 2007, and its research and recommendations extended well beyond the specific violent act into wide-ranging legal reforms and a broader accounting of history.

RCAP, the Ipperwash Inquiry, and the IRSTRC therefore represent three separate policy interventions that share the basic goal of performing an historical accounting of past injustices, in the interest of publicizing a new historical narrative, and generating legal and political improvements in the relationship between Indigenous and non-Indigenous peoples. In other words, they are exercises in public memory that are non-coercive, but are similar in objectives to some memory laws. They also are intended to engender changes in law to reflect the promoted historical understanding. In most other respects they are widely different. They each operate at different narrative levels. RCAP was conceived most broadly, as an inclusive examination of the history of Indigenous-non-Indigenous relations (as well as an inquiry into legal and policy failures, and more). The IRSTRC adopts a more limited focus on the sole issue of residential schools, a vastly significant programme, but only one policy amongst the suite of laws and policies employed by the federal government to dispossess Indigenous

Indian Residential Schools (Toronto: University of Toronto Press, 2013) (hereinafter Niezin, *Truth and Indignation*).

[5] Royal Commission on Aboriginal Peoples. *Report of the Royal Commission on Aboriginal Peoples. Volume 1: Looking Forward, Looking Back* (Ottawa: Ministry of Supply and Services, 1996b) (hereafter Royal Commission on Aboriginal Peoples).

peoples of their lands, resources, and cultural identities. The Ipperwash Inquiry was narrower still, initiated to investigate a single land dispute and the recent violence it produced (although we shall see that in practice, the inquiry stretched and likely exceeded its original mandate). All three truth commissions followed different formats, and their sponsor governments made different decisions about what powers the commissions should wield, who should be granted standing, how ostensible perpetrators of the discussed injustices should be treated, and what specific legal outputs were sought. This chapter will examine the three initiatives with an eye to what planning decisions were taken, what sorts of narratives were promoted, and finally, what effect in law each truth commission has had (so far).

I will argue that scope and scale should be regarded as key determinants of the effectiveness of truth commissions, and key considerations generally in the study of truth commissions. Historical narratives themselves exist at multiple levels of analysis: as definitive metanarratives of nationhood, as well as limited stories about particular people, places, and things.[6] Not all historical narratives are equally amenable to state-led change, and this is reflected in the differential impacts of the three commissions. The Ipperwash Inquiry adopted the most constrained scope, and arguably has had the most significant impact in the areas of historical narrative and legal output in which it deals. The IRSTRC has only recently concluded, and therefore beyond any certain verdict, but it already appears that it has failed some of the grander expectations it carried, but succeeded in making 'unsayable'[7] certain older narratives about the residential schools themselves. RCAP adopted the most ambitious agenda by far, and has perhaps had the most insubstantial impact; its volumes have collected dust in government libraries, and it lives on primarily as an academic curiosity and still-radical aspiration. Herein lie lessons for the comparative study of memory law and policy, and the importance of scope and scale.

2 Royal Commission on Aboriginal Peoples

The first major truth commission on the subject of Indigenous peoples and colonialism in Canada was commissioned in the aftermath of some of the worst violence between First Nations and the Canadian state in the

[6] Y. Auerbach, 'The Reconciliation Pyramid – A Narrative-Based Framework for Analyzing Identity Conflicts,' *Political Psychology* 20 (2009), 291–318 (hereinafter Auerbach, 'The Reconciliation Pyramid').

[7] Niezen, *Truth and Indignation*, 58.

modern era. The precipitant was a decision taken by the municipality of Oka, Québec to expand a golf course onto disputed territory, which the neighbouring Kanien'kehá:ka (or Mohawk) community claimed had been reserved for their use and later appropriated. Some Kanien'kehá:ka protesters established a road barricade in the spring of 1990, to prevent construction of the golf course. In July, the provincial police force mobilized against the protesters, and in a firefight one officer was killed. Sympathy demonstrations occurred across the country, in what became known as the 'Indian Summer', and Mohawks from another reserve established supportive road blockades disrupting major traffic corridors in Quebec. The Royal Canadian Mounted Police were also unable to establish control of the situation, and in August, the Canadian army was deployed. The Mohawk resistance ended in late September. Over the course of the crisis, images of Canadian soldiers facing off with armed Indigenous warriors shocked the country, and garnered significant international attention. The episode attracted an unprecedented degree of public concern for the state of the Indigenous-non-Indigenous relationship.[8]

Prime Minister Brian Mulroney responded to this unrest in 1991 by calling for a Royal Commission on Aboriginal Peoples (RCAP). Its mandate was sweeping, intended to take in 'the economic, social and cultural situation of the aboriginal peoples of this country'.[9] The commission was expected to produce myriad policy insights, and possibly guide future legal change – including changes to the constitution itself. But settling the past was clearly also an intended function: 'The primary objective is to deal with literally centuries of injustice' explained the Prime Minister.[10] The historical dimension of the commission's work is described throughout its published output. In a sub-chapter titled 'The Ghosts of History', for example, the report explains why historical analysis is central to RCAP: 'Studying the past tells us who we are and where we came from. It often reveals a cache of secrets that some people are striving to keep hidden and others are striving to tell. In this case, it helps explain how the tensions

[8] See K. L. Ladner and L. Simpson (eds.), *This is an Honour Song: Twenty Years Since the Blockades: An Anthology of Writing on the 'Oka Crisis'* (Winnipeg: Arbeiter Ring Pub., 2010); H. Swain, *Oka: A Political Crisis and Its Legacy* (Toronto: Douglas & McIntyre, 2010); G. York and L. Pindera, *People of the Pines: The Warriors and the Legacy of Oka* (Boston and Toronto: Little, Brown, 1991).

[9] Globe and Mail, 'Striking a Commission on Aboriginal Issues,' *The Globe and Mail*, 24 April 1991.

[10] G. Fraser, 'Erasmus Appointed to Commission Quebec Judge to Co-chair Inquiry on Native Issues,' *The Globe and Mail*, 28 August 1991, A1.

between Aboriginal and non-Aboriginal people came to be, and why they are so hard to resolve'.[11]

Indeed, the first purpose identified in RCAP's terms of reference was to make recommendations concerning 'the history of relations between aboriginal peoples, the Canadian government and Canadian society as a whole', and to martial this historical analysis in 'recommendations promoting reconciliation between aboriginal peoples and Canadian society as a whole', including finding ways that Indigenous historical narratives can be 'better integrated into the public and ceremonial life of the country'.[12] In the address for the launch of RCAP's report, Commissioner Georges Erasmus declared 'the roots of injustice lie in history and it is there where the key to the regeneration of Aboriginal society and a new and better relationship with the rest of Canada can be found'.[13] While not solely dedicated to historical analysis, this function was at the core of RCAP's process and output, and in this way, it operated as a *de facto* truth commission.

Seven commissioners were appointed to lead RCAP, of which four were Indigenous. Three of the four Indigenous commissioners had previously held leadership roles in Indigenous political organizations. In practice, RCAP largely followed the template of other royal commissions in Canada, which have been created on an *ad hoc* basis since the nineteenth century to investigate various issues of public concern, ranging from political scandal to immigration, economic change, transportation, the status of women, and various policy areas beyond.[14] Its primary function was research, and to lead this effort, an Aboriginal and a non-Aboriginal co-director of research were appointed. The commission originally intended to author a comprehensive 'new history of Aboriginal peoples in Canada', but because of time and resource constraints, instead simply built historical analysis into each of the four main themes of enquiry: governance, land and the

[11] Royal Commission on Aboriginal Peoples, *People to People, Nation to Nation: Highlights from the Report of the Royal Commission on Aboriginal Peoples* (Ottawa: Ministry of Supply and Services, 1996), at 4 (hereinafter Royal Commission on Aboriginal Peoples, *People to People, Nation to Nation*).

[12] Royal Commission on Aboriginal Peoples, *Appendix A: Commissioner's Terms of Reference* (Ottawa: Government of Canada, 1991).

[13] G. Erasmus and R. Dussault, *Address for the Launch of the Royal Commission on Aboriginal Peoples* (Ottawa: Government of Canada, 1991). Available at: www.aadnc-aandc.gc.ca/eng/1100100014639/1100100014640 (31 January 2016).

[14] J. Courtney, 'In Defence of Royal Commissions,' *Canadian Public Administration* 12 (1969), 198–212.

economy, social/cultural, and the north.[15] In total, hundreds of researchers were engaged for more than 350 commissioned studies.[16] There was also a public face to the commission. Hearings were held in communities across the country, presided over by either some or all of the commissioners.[17] They received submissions from both individuals and organizations – a total of 2,200 submissions.[18] Despite extensive hearings, media coverage of the public activity of RCAP was spotty, and tended to focus on the rising costs of the commission, as well as of organizational challenges it faced.[19]

In 1996, RCAP delivered its report in five volumes, amidst pomp and ceremony. The report suggested that non-Indigenous Canadians were ignorant of the historical trauma suffered by Indigenous peoples, and argued this was a primary driver of conflict. Drawing on contemporary historical scholarship, the report derived a periodization of Indigenous-non-Indigenous relations, from an early condition of 'separate worlds', to a period of 'contact and cooperation', to 'displacement and assimilation', and finally the present period, which is anointed an era of 'negotiation and renewal'. The report castigates the 'ethnocentric triumphalism' of the Canadian makers of laws governing Indigenous communities, and their racist, authoritarian, and openly assimilationist interventions into Indigenous lives. Its recommendations comprised a suite of legal changes, including to foundational legislation governing Indigenous communities, and prospective constitutional change entrenching Indigenous self-government within the Canadian federation.

The federal government's response to RCAP was muted. In 1998, the Minister of Indian Affairs and Northern Development offered a 'statement of reconciliation'. Aboriginal politicians noted at the time that while the statement expressed 'profound regret for past actions of the federal government which have contributed to these difficult pages in the history of our relationship together',[20] it avoided a full formal apology for the historical

[15] J. Wherrett, 'The Research Agenda of the Royal Commission on Aboriginal Peoples,' *Canadian Public Administration* 38 (1995), 272–82 (hereinafter Wherrett, 'The Research Agenda of the Royal Commission on Aboriginal Peoples').

[16] Ibid., 278.

[17] J. Frideres, 'The Royal Commission on Aboriginal Peoples: the Route to Self-Government?,' *Canadian Journal of Native Studies* 16 (1996), 247–66 (hereinafter Frideres, 'The Royal Commission on Aboriginal Peoples').

[18] Ibid., 256.

[19] Ibid., 255.

[20] J. Stewart, 'Address by the Honourable Jane Stewart Minister of Indian Affairs and Northern Development on the Occasion of the Unveiling of Gathering Strength – Canada's

injustices detailed in the report. The fact that it was not delivered by the prime minister personally further diminished its symbolic effect. On the same occasion, the federal government announced a vision document titled *Gathering Strength* – its commitment to fulfil some of the legal and policy recommendations of RCAP. Some from this already incomplete suite of policies made it into law, but the document is widely regarded as unrealized and aspirational – commonly re-named by Indigenous peoples as 'Gathering Dust'.[21]

3 The Ipperwash Inquiry

The second truth commission to reflect on historical injustices experienced by Indigenous peoples at the hands of the Canadian state emerged from similar circumstances, but adopted a radically different focus, scope, and scale. The Oka Crisis had signalled a qualitative change in Indigenous direct action in Canada, and in its aftermath, more militant repertoires of action – such as road blockades and sustained occupations of disputed territory – became more common. This was true in the Anishinabek (or Ojibway) community around Ipperwash, in southwestern Ontario. The community had lost one of its two reserves during the Second World War, when it was appropriated by the Canadian government in order to construct an army base. The land was not returned after the conclusion of the war, and in the early 1990s, Anishinabek protesters engaged in escalating direct action. In 1993 protesters began an occupation of the Ipperwash army base. In 1995, they expanded their occupation to take in a neighbouring park. This provoked conflict with the police, who deployed in force and opened fire, killing an unarmed Anishinabek protester. The provincial government was widely alleged to have applied pressure on the police to act quickly and with force.

After a change in government in 2003, the new provincial government announced that it would convene a non-judicial inquiry into the police action. The order-in-council that created the commission of inquiry suggested a very limited mandate: 'a) inquire into and report on events surrounding the death of Dudley George; and b) make recommendations

---

Aboriginal Action Plan,' *Indian Affairs and Northern Development Canada* (1998), available at www.aadnc-aandc.gc.ca/eng/1100100015725/1100100015726 (11 May 2016).

21 M. Switzer, 'Reserve Judgement,' *The Globe and Mail*, 12 November 2005, available at www.theglobeandmail.com/arts/reserve-judgment/article740059/ (31 January 2016).

directed to the avoidance of violence in similar circumstances'.[22] It was to be presided over by a single judge commissioner. The inquiry primarily consisted of public hearings held near Ipperwash, with invited testimony from participants in the conflict, who were examined and cross-examined by counsellors. In addition to testimony, the inquiry commissioned historical and policy research, and convened thematically focussed roundtable meetings. Despite the largely judicial format, the inquiry was not able to assess criminal wrongdoing or civil liability, which had been dealt with to a limited extent in trials that predated the inquiry.[23]

Little in the above suggests a truth commission. However, it early became clear that those involved in the inquiry imagined a somewhat broader focus. A 2004 press release from the inquiry argued that 'One of the purposes of a public inquiry is to educate the public on the matters in issue. An understanding by Ontarians of the Aboriginal history of the region and the historical context of the incident is fundamental to the Inquiry and our educational mandate'.[24] In an early address, the commissioner suggested there was 'an element of public education as part of [the inquiry's] mandate . . . because in my view, it is also important to establish the context of events, that is, cultural, historical or otherwise, [so] I believe it is appropriate to allow some latitude'.[25] In 2005, justifying the expanding scope of the inquiry, he spoke of 'an obligation to acknowledge that systemic or historic circumstances may have contributed to the actions taken and decisions made. While many of these circumstances pre-date the events that gave rise to this Inquiry or appear to fall outside its jurisdiction or mandate, in my view they shed light on why the events occurred'.[26]

22 Ontario, *Order in Council 1662/2003* (Toronto: Executive Council of Ontario 2003).

23 Most notably, in 1997 Kenneth Deane, the police officer responsible for shooting Dudley George, had been convicted individually of criminal negligence causing death, but was not incarcerated or initially fired from the provincial police force. The family of the victim also launched a wrongful death suit against the government and provincial police force, settling the suit in 2003.

24 Ontario, *Experts on Aboriginal Culture and History to Testify at Start of Ipperwash Inquiry Next Week* [press release], 7 July 2004, available at: www.attorneygeneral.jus.gov.on.ca/inquiries/ipperwash/m_releases/pdf/July_7_2004.pdf (31 January 2016).

25 S. Linden, *Commissioner's Statement: Observations Regarding Progress on the Inquiry*, 2004, available at: www.attorneygeneral.jus.gov.on.ca/inquiries/ipperwash/li/pdf/Commissioner_Remarks_Nov1_04.pdf (31 January 2016).

26 S. Linden, *Commissioner Linden's Opening Remarks Ipperwash Inquiry Hearings*, 2005, available at: www.attorneygeneral.jus.gov.on.ca/inquiries/ipperwash/li/pdf/Commissioner OpeningRemarks_March30_05.pdf (31 January 2016).

The final report, released in 2007, gave considerable space over to exploration of the underlying contention between Indigenous people and the Canadian state, particularly over the historical loss of land and associated abuses. The commissioner wrote:

> The events . . . arose from a long-standing dispute about treaty and Aboriginal rights. Building a better relationship with Aboriginal peoples requires that governments and citizens recognize that treaties with Aboriginal peoples are the foundation that allowed non-Aboriginal people to settle in Ontario and enjoy its bounty. Nearly all of the lands and inland waters in Ontario are subject to treaties between First Nations and the British and Canadian governments. These treaties are not, as some people believe, relics of the distant past. They are living agreements, and the understandings on which they are based continue to have the full force of law in Canada today.[27]

It went on to describe the settler state's betrayal of treaty promises. Deep historical context was provided for the specific land dispute that produced the Ipperwash conflict, and the occupation of the army base and provincial park were simply the expression of 'the frustration and anger that can result from the failure of the federal and provincial governments to take treaty obligations seriously'.[28]

The Ontario provincial government responded to the report with enthusiasm, and implemented several of its key legal and policy recommendations shortly. This included creating a stand-along Ministry of Aboriginal Affairs, which had not existed at the provincial level previously. The government also announced, at the end of 2007, that it would transfer ownership of the occupied park back to the Anishinabek – an act which was in some ways outside of the existing legal processes for settling Indigenous land claims. This was a surprising and fairly dramatic outcome, which actually exceeded the recommendations of the report. It was well received by the Ontarian public. In general, media content analysis has suggested that the public activity and report of the Ipperwash Inquiry affected strong change in public perceptions of the conflict – its historical context, the veracity of the Indigenous claim to territory, and the necessity of some forms of restitution and legal reform.[29]

[27] S. Linden, *Report of the Ipperwash Inquiry* (Toronto: Ministry of the Attorney General, Queen's Printer for Ontario, 2007) (hereinafter Linden, *Report of the Ipperwash Inquiry*).

[28] Ibid., 81.

[29] M. Morden, 'Telling Stories about Conflict: The Symbolic Politics of the Ipperwash Land Transfer,' *Canadian Journal of Political Science* 46 (2013), 505–24 (hereinafter Morden, 'Telling Stories about Conflict').

4 Indian Residential Schools Truth and Reconciliation Commission

Indian residential schools were created in the late nineteenth century as boarding schools for Indigenous children. They were openly assimilationist in their intent – adopting a policy of 'aggressive civilization', which saw expressions of Indigenous culture, and the speaking of Indigenous languages punished by the priests, ministers, and nuns who were empowered by the state to operate the schools. At points in history, attendance in residential schools was compelled. The schools often became squalid, and over 6,000 children died in attendance – in fires, of tuberculosis and other diseases, during attempted escapes, and by suicide. Moreover, sexual and physical abuse was endemic to the schools. Residential schools have been described as constituting 'the worst crime in private life, the sexual abuse of children, applied in the context of one of the worst wrongs in public life, the purposeful, policy-driven elimination of a people'.[30] The residential schools system was wound down beginning in the 1970s.

Momentum towards some form of official recognition of the historical wrong originated in the mid-1980s, when some high-profile Indigenous political leaders went public with their experiences of abuse at residential schools. Initially they sought restitution from the religious orders that had operated the schools. Several of those churches did enter into reconciliatory dialogue with Indigenous people. The United Church of Canada, Anglican Church, Presbyterian Church, and some authorities within the Catholic Church issued apologies or acknowledgements at various points throughout the 1980s and 1990s. The report and proceedings of RCAP, which placed special emphasis on residential schools and even called for further public inquiry on the issue, created further momentum – but no inquiry was called.[31] After a rash of litigation, peak Indigenous advocacy organizations entered into negotiations with the federal government and churches to reach a settlement. The settlement agreement, which came into effect in 2007, represented the largest class action settlement in Canadian history.[32] It includes a common lump sum payout to all residential schools 'survivors', as former students came to be known, as well as additional funds for survivors with specific experiences of abuse, money for various

[30] Niezen, *Truth and Indignation*, 150.

[31] K. Stanton, 'Canada's Truth and Reconciliation Commission: Settling the Past?,' *International Indigenous Policy Journal* 2 (2011), 1–18 (hereinafter Stanton, 'Canada's Truth and Reconciliation Commission').

[32] Ibid., 4.

healing projects, an official apology, and a truth and reconciliation commission. A change in government put the official apology in question, but after lobbying from both Indigenous people and the churches, it was delivered by the prime minister on the floor of the House of Commons in 2008. The TRC began its work in 2009 with a five-year framework, but later had its mandate extended to June 2015.

The mandate of the commission speaks strongly of an orientation towards historical accounting: 'There is an emerging and compelling desire to put the events of the past behind us so that we can work towards a stronger and healthier future. The [TRC] . . . is a sincere indication and acknowledgement of the injustices and harms experienced by Aboriginal people and the need for continued healing.'[33] Stated goals of the commission include to 'acknowledge Residential Schools experiences, impacts, and consequences', 'promote awareness and public education', and 'create as complete an historical record as possible'.[34]

It drew inspiration from other international truth commissions, and especially the South African Truth and Reconciliation Commission. But it was unique for several reasons. Ronald Niezen identifies four: (a) it emerged from civil litigation, rather than transition from war or authoritarianism; (b) as the product of a settlement, it was a deeply 'a-judicial' body, lacking the powers and responsibilities of judicial inquiry; (c) it focussed only on the victimization of children; and (d) it placed an unusually large emphasis on mental health and the healing of trauma – though this function is certainly also served by other truth commissions.[35] The first two factors in particular played a major role in shaping the format of the commission.

If truth commissions are placed on a spectrum between the goals of judicial prosecution at one pole, and pure information-gathering at the other, the Canadian TRC is likely furthest to the latter pole. Its mandate expressly forbade formal hearings or legal processes. It lacked subpoena power, and could not compel participation or attendance. It could not recommend civil or criminal liability of any individual or organization, or find in an informal way against any individual. There was no naming of names, in public proceedings or the written output of the commission. The

[33] Indian and Northern Affairs Canada, *Indian Residential Schools Settlement Agreement* (Ottawa, 2006), available at www.residentialschoolsettlement.ca/ (29 January 2016), at Schedule N (hereinafter Indian and Northern Affairs Canada, *Indian Residential Schools Settlement Agreement*).

[34] Indian and Northern Affairs Canada, *Indian Residential Schools Settlement Agreement*, at Schedule N.

[35] Niezen, *Truth and Indignation*, 3–5.

result was a 'victim-centred' approach that left perpetrators largely absent from the proceedings.[36]

The commission undertook three major activities: national and regional events in cities, meant to engage the broader Canadian public and feature prominent state and church leaders; community events in Indigenous communities throughout the country, featuring survivor testimony at smaller and more intimate gatherings; and individual statement-gathering, which invited survivors to share their stories privately, electronically or in person. Some statements were also given publicly in Sharing Panels and Sharing Circles. It also conducted ongoing research, and had to fight the federal government in courts for the release of archival documents pertaining to the residential schools. The hearings themselves were deeply emotional, and were staffed by 'health supports' – mental health workers who attend to distressed audience-members. The in-house audience to hearings largely consists of survivors themselves, along with researchers, health care workers, some church officials, and other interested parties. There was limited attendance from the Canadian public at large.[37]

The commission concluded ceremoniously and released its interim findings in June 2015, following with the complete report later in the year. Any evaluations of the impact of the IRSTRC are necessarily preliminary, even premature – but concerns have been expressed about the possible inattentiveness of the Canadian public, as well as the degree to which it has embraced the commission-promoted narrative.[38] During the tenure of the commission, the country has also witnessed an upsurge in Indigenous direct action, and mainstream Indigenous political actors faced increased pressure to adopt a more confrontational posture vis-à-vis the Canadian state. This has raised questions about the efficacy of the TRC in facilitating reconciliation. But the governing Liberal party has pledged to enact all of the legal and policy recommendations of the commission, and while time will reveal the seriousness of this promise, it must be viewed as a measure of success with respect to legal outcomes.

5 Discussion – Creating Public Historical Truth with Truth Commissions

How to evaluate the relative successes of the truth and reconciliation commissions described above? This is a question that merits a broad discussion,

[36] Ibid.
[37] Ibid., 85.
[38] Ibid., 146.

but for our purposes I will suggest that there are at least two general bases for measuring the causal impact of truth commissions. The first involves weighing commissions' impact on law, public policy, and sustained change in the behaviour of political elites. Unlike memory law approaches, in the case of commissions, legal change undergirding historical revisionism is an output rather than an input. The second focuses on the ideational, discursive, and public opinion change that truth commissions affect in society more broadly – in particular, alterations to national public memory about historical events. Though distinct, these two expressions of impact are likely to track each other fairly closely. Truth commissions are novel from other forms of governmental inquiry in that they seek large lay audiences. Therefore, where they have failed to produce change in the hearts and minds of publics, they are unlikely to yield major legal outputs.

Admitting some crudity in the following analysis, I will suggest that of the three truth commissions, the Ipperwash Inquiry has proven to be the most effective against these measures. As outlined above, there are indications that the public understanding of the Ipperwash conflict was substantially revised as a result of the commission's work.[39] In the immediate aftermath of the conflict itself, opinion leaders in the majority public expressed sympathy for the government, and a belief that it acted in good faith – while portraying Indigenous activists as irresponsible, impatient, violent 'joker[s] in battle fatigues' who could reasonably be ignored.[40] By the time the Inquiry had completed its hearing and delivered its findings, a very different narrative had taken root, which portrayed the same activists as patient and reasonable, and placed blame for the violence at the feet of the state for a history of inequitable treatment: 'Militancy will find less fertile soil if Canada acts honourably. But the reason for settling native grievances in a fair and dispassionate way, as Ontario has done at Ipperwash, is that it is the right thing to do.'[41] With the limited indicators available to us, it appears that the commission achieved a genuine narrative shift. Moreover, it was followed closely with a range of concrete legal and policy measures that reflected its recommendations, including an across-government commitment to reform the legal processes related to settling land-based historical grievances. The strongest indicator of the change that the Inquiry engendered, at both narrative and legal levels, is

[39] Morden, 'Telling Stories about Conflict.'

[40] Globe and Mail, 'Move Cautiously on Land Claims,' *The Globe and Mail*, 19 September 1995.

[41] Globe and Mail. 'Overdue Justice at Ipperwash,' *The Globe and Mail*, 21 December 2007, A22.

the provincial government's decision to return the disputed land to the Indigenous community in question – a decision that even exceeded the recommendations of the inquiry itself.

As I have already outlined above, RCAP, by most evaluations, failed to engender major change on either dimension. Its concrete recommendations are the most far-reaching of the three. Even twenty years after the report of RCAP was published, many of the proposed legal reforms appear radical relative to the current state of public and elite opinion. These recommendations – calling, for example, for major reform of central political institutions to guarantee representation of Indigenous peoples – have entirely fallen out of the political discourse, and have never really commanded serious attention by either the Canadian public or policy- and law-makers. There is little evidence of discursive or narrative change contemporary with and reflecting the work of the commission, and indeed, at least some evidence of generally declining sympathy in the Canadian public for Indigenous peoples at the time of the commission's final report.[42] Ten years after the release of the report, the Assembly of First Nations, a peak advocacy organization representing some Indigenous peoples, produced a detailed assessment of government responses to RCAP, and concluded there has been 'no structural change in the relationship between First Nations and the Canadian government', an extremely limited government response to the truth commission, and no political will to make concrete its legal recommendations.[43]

The IRSTRC is hardest to assess, because there has simply not been time to reflect the changes it has engendered. But an early read suggests that its effectiveness falls somewhere in between the poles represented by Ipperwash and RCAP. The governing Liberal Party committed to and campaigned on a promise to implement all recommendations made in the report – a striking result, but, it must be acknowledged, one which can only be evaluated after concrete action has been taken. With respective to narrative change, a near-complete public consensus historical narrative about the residential schools has been achieved. This was on display, for example, when two academics wrote an op-ed accusing the IRSTRC of exaggerating claims made against the residential schools, and were subsequently widely

[42] J. Aubry, 'Natives to Blame for Their Problems – Poll,' *Edmonton Journal*, 8 July 1996, A3.

[43] Assembly of First Nations, *Royal Commission on Aboriginal Peoples at Ten Years: A Report Card* (Assembly of First Nations, 2006), available at: www.turtleisland.org/resources/afnrcap2006.pdf (11 April 2016).

condemned in public, and rebuked by their colleagues.[44] However, to the extent that residential schools were known to a broader Canadian public, they were already generally regarded as a national embarrassment even before the commission undertook its work. In other words, the narrative produced from the commission was largely resonant with the received understanding of the schools already. And observers of the IRSTRC have expressed concern that the commission was largely attended by survivors of residential schools themselves or other concerned parties, but was largely absent from the attention of a broader Canadian public. Media coverage of the hearings was minor and inconsistent, and there were at least some indicators – for example, one observer cites internet comment threads[45] – which suggest apathy at best, and scepticism or even hostility at worst on the part of the Canadian public. But it must once again be conceded that a proper assessment of the IRSTRC against either measure of impact requires more time.

How, then, do we explain the differing outcomes of truth commissions, holding constant the state and societal context? The cases presented above allow us, at least, to formulate some hypotheses to be tested in future work. In particular, I wish to draw attention to decisions about scope and scale of truth commissions, and how they are integral to the effectiveness of truth commissions in engendering legal and narrative change. This requires some more precise conceptualization of historical narrative in political life.

There is a longstanding tradition in the study of nations and nationalism to identify the causal importance of national narratives, which 'form integral parts of the fabric of popular visions, and of the social structures and processes in which the designated populations are embedded and through which their elites must forge their strategies'.[46] National myths are intrinsic to individual and collective identity, and to national bodies of law, which are constructed against a normative backdrop. These stories provide us with a stylized version of our national pasts, our group boundaries, our place in the world, our relationship to various out-groups, and appropriate legal rendering of all of this content. Arguably, national myths are what are targeted in the politics of truth and reconciliation. Where multiple groups within society foster separate and dissonant national myths, or where

[44] CBC News, 'University of Manitoba profs rebuke anti-TRC editorial by colleagues,' *CBC News*, 5 June 2015, available at: www.cbc.ca/news/canada/manitoba/university-of-manitoba-profs-rebuke-anti-trc-editorial-by-colleagues-1.3101710 (31 January 2016).

[45] Niezen, *Truth and Indignation*, at 146.

[46] A. Smith, *Myths and Memories of the Nation* (Oxford: Oxford University Press, 1999), 9.

one body of national mythology excludes vital historical content that is required for a re-contextualized present, the truth commission seeks to engineer and embed a revision.

But some have argued that to properly understand the relationship of truth and reconciliation to national mythology, we must disaggregate the mythological body, and recognize that myths exist at several levels of analysis.[47] For example, Auerbach distinguishes between two basic levels of myth. A 'Meta-narrative', in Auerbach's rendering, is the big broad, existential national narrative – a 'stor[y] about stories . . . [that] locate[s] national stories within a wider, holistic scheme'.[48] In the case of non-Indigenous Canada, the meta-narrative describes the achievement of a peaceful, multicultural and egalitarian society, founded on legal principles of liberalism and individual rights. The other level, which I have termed 'micro-narratives', refer to the narrower, more specific, and more concrete stories embedded within a meta-narrative, that tell about events, experiences, key actors in a nation's past. Generally, they perform one or several of the following functions: presenting a glorified image of the in-group, ascribing negative or irrational characteristics to members of an out-group, reflecting on historical triumphs, mourning tragedies that have befallen the nation, and – especially in the context of societal or narrative conflict – externalizing causality for conflict or misfortune.[49] One can identify numerous key micro-narratives that buttress the Canadian meta-narrative. For example, a conventional telling of Canadian history identifies ways in which Indigenous peoples in Canada were dealt with peacefully and honourably historically, in contrast to the more conflictual and brutal experience of the American West. The peacekeeper is a key figure that appears in countless micro-narratives within Canadian national mythology – in domestic stories about the treatment of Indigenous peoples and ethnic minorities, and in international stories about the invention of United Nations peacekeeping missions (for example). In this way, micro-narratives support the meta-narrative and are also imbued with meaning because of it.

All levels of narrative are not equally pliable under the politics of truth and historical revision. I would argue that meta-narratives are basically structures. They are powerfully intrinsic to identity, live inside of

[47] Morden, 'Telling Stories about Conflict.'

[48] Auerbach, 'The Reconciliation Pyramid,' 295.

[49] See D. Bar-Tal, N. Oren, and R. Nets-Zehngut, 'Sociopsychological Analysis of Conflict-Supporting Narratives: A General Framework,' *Journal of Peace Research* 51 (2014), 662–75.

institutions and social norms, and (irrespective of their actual origins) are experienced by members of a national community as ancient and profound. It is immensely costly to the individual to critically interrogate one's meta-narrative. They are moral narratives; as the social psychologist Jonathan Haidt suggests, 'Once [people] accept a particular [moral] narrative, they become blind to alternative moral worlds'.[50] As a result, it is difficult to imagine a truth commission substantially altering the broad outline of a meta-narrative, unless structural change in the national mythology was already and independently underway. The meta-narrative is too robust, too concrete for policy and elite agency to topple. From a legal standpoint, meta-narratives live inside of constitutions; they are the basic stories against which basic laws are written. The likely result of a truth commission that targets meta-narrative, then, is relative failure.

Micro-narratives, on the other hand, are much more plastic. No single micro-narrative carries the same existential weight and importance to members of a national community as a meta-narrative does. Moreover, and importantly, a meta-narrative can accommodate new micro-narratives, even micro-narratives that are not immediately resonant with its general theme. Negative micro-narratives, micro-narratives that reflect poorly on the nation, can become stylized as outliers, exceptions to prove the rule. As a consequence, I hypothesize that truth commissions which seek to alter historical micro-narratives, or contribute new micro-narratives are far more likely to be successful. They do their work inside of the structural framework imposed by the national meta-narrative, and are therefore able to affect narrative change without transforming national identities. They are also more likely to affect legal change, albeit of a limited nature. Remedying specific instances of wrongdoing does not require the kind of profound legal and constitutional change that is often demanded in revisions to meta-narrative.

The cases I have detailed above provide at least some support for this hypothesis – and here we encounter the importance of decisions governing scope and scale. RCAP, in adopting an enormous scope and scale – encompassing the entire history of Indigenous-non-Indigenous relations in Canada, seeking to engender a radically new understanding (from the non-Indigenous perspective) of that history, and to produce fundamental legal and political transformation to reflect this new understanding – clearly sought change to the Canadian meta-narrative. This could play a

[50] J. Haidt, *The Righteous Mind: Why Good People are Divided by Politics and Religion* (New York: Random House, 2012), 23.

significant role in why RCAP was unable to substantially alter attitudes held by the Canadian public, or compel elites to see through its recommended legal reforms. By bringing to light 400 years of what it characterized as unjust and dishonourable dealings with Indigenous peoples, it sought – in a sense – a too-deep narrative concession from Canadians, who continued to adhere to the meta-narrative which spoke of a fair and equal political community, embodied in a liberal individualist constitution (albeit with some recognition of group rights). It would have been difficult or impossible to accommodate the RCAP historical narrative to existing national mythology. As a result, the message of RCAP went unheeded and became badly marginalized, and its legal outcomes were profoundly limited.

The Ipperwash Report represents scope and scale decisions taken in the other extreme. It nominally focused on a single unlawful incident, the shooting death of the Anishinabek protester. Though in practice the commission participated in a broader historical accounting, its promoted narrative and recommendations were nevertheless bounded by its foundational mandate and impetus. What it produced, then, was a micro-narrative – a specific story about a specific Indigenous community and the injustice and indignation it suffered. This was a narrative the Canadian public was much more capable of embracing, and even assimilating to the meta-narrative. The Ipperwash experience was treated as exceptional, and this permitted not only a change in narrative, but also legal, material and political accommodation of the Indigenous community in question.[51]

The IRSTRC, again, falls somewhere in the middle. In tackling the malignant effects of a century of education policy, it shone a profoundly critical light on the conduct of the Canadian state over multiple generations. Moreover, in emphasizing the lingering social pathologies produced from residential schools, it demanded that a majority public recognize the state's enduring responsibility for social problems – poverty, crime – affecting the Indigenous out-group. So the micro-narrative it produced was difficult, certainly, to accommodate to the broader national mythology. Nevertheless, it required less than a fundamental re-evaluation of the character and past practice of the nation. Residential schools can be set apart as a specific, lamentable failing of the state and churches, rather than just a symptom of the broader problem of colonialism. Elements within the promoted narrative – such as the abuses of exploitative priests – were

[51] Morden, 'Telling Stories about Conflict.'

even already familiar narrative clichés. In other words, inside the micro-narrative the residential schools could be treated as a series of private transgressions against a backdrop of governmental failure. Its legal recommendations are wide-reaching, and some will be easier to adopt than others – but at their core seek social investments to atone for the particular sin of residential schools. That scale and scope of narrative revision likely falls inside the range in which the politics of truth and historical revision can succeed.

6 Conclusions

I have suggested that Canada offers an overlooked and potentially useful case for assessing the project of historical revision, not through memory law but through truth commissions. Despite not being a society in transition, either from war or autocracy, Canada has experimented in recent decades with variations on the truth commission instrument. These exercises have been focused on rendering a more just and consensual historical understanding about the relationship of the settler state to Indigenous peoples within, and in doing so, to develop public support for concrete legal and policy efforts at restitution, recognition, and reconciliation. The success of these initiatives has been distinctly mixed, as the three cases presented above illustrate.

Comparing these three cases presents an hypothesis about why some truth commissions successfully engender new historical understandings on the part of publics, and legal reform to underpin those new understandings, while others do not. I have argued that at least one key variable determining this outcome is the scope and scale of revision that is attempted. Endeavouring to re-write essential, existential stories about a nation's past – that is, trying to alter elements of the nation's meta-narrative – is likely to overestimate the efficacy of truth politics. By limiting scope and scale, and focusing only on micro-narratives that represent single figures within the broader national mythology, policy-makers are more likely to achieve the kinds of changes in public history that they seek. This is, I would reiterate, only an hypothesis – but one that should be incorporated into future research on the processes and impacts of truth commissions.

Of course, there are normative objections to the implicit prescription of the paper. These are precisely the sort of objections that Indigenous scholars and activists have made against the Canadian politics of truth and reconciliation. They have criticized instruments such as the IRSTRC as arbitrarily isolating a single element in the broad suite of colonial policies wielded against Indigenous communities. They have argued that permitting the settler public to feel as though it has atoned for some limited, finite sin makes more difficult the work of accounting for the totality of colonialist history. And some have counselled against participation in these exercises while the Canadian state, in other respects, continues to act dishonourably to Indigenous peoples.[52] This is a persuasive objection, and there is no simple response. It may be that in seeking historical revision on a societal scale through policy, we are compelled to balance moral and historical gratification against the limitations inherent in such an exercise. Knowing more about the dynamics of truth policy, and national mythology, will allow us to strike a more precise and progressive balance.

[52] L. Simpson, *Dancing on Our Turtle's Back: Stories of Nishnaabeg Re-Creation, Resurgence, and a New Emergence* (Winnipeg: Arbeiter Ring Publishing, 2011), 21.

19

Defense of Democracy and the Preservation of Collective Memory through Criminal Legislation: The Challenges of Reconciliation in Peru

SALVADOR HERENCIA CARRASCO

1 Introduction

"What type of memory could we use to lead to a reconciliation with the past without its becoming a simple evocation of conformity with the violence?"[1] This question, posited by the former President of the Peruvian Truth and Reconciliation (hereinafter "TRC")[2] still remains valid in a country that has been unable to come to terms with its violent past. Sixteen years after the return to democracy, Peruvian society still can't agree on a term to describe the most violent period of its republican history, which took place between May 1980 and November 2000.[3]

The terms "internal armed conflict" or "fight against terrorism" are often used to describe this period of violence in Peru. These expressions are in no way interchangeable nor synonymous, as they have different political and legal implications. "Internal armed conflict,"[4] a term defined by the common Art. 3 to the Geneva Conventions and its 1977 Additional Protocol II, is usually used by a liberal sector of society and academics with the aim of acknowledging that all parties in the Peruvian conflict breached international human rights and/or international humanitarian law. On the other

[1] S. Lerner Fabres, 'Memory and the Search for a Democratic Society', in M.S. Grindle and E.E. Goodman (eds.), *Reflections on Memory and Democracy* (Cambridge: The David Rockefeller Center Series on Latin American Studies, Harvard University Press, 2016), 86.

[2] The Peruvian Truth and Reconciliation Commission was created by the Peruvian Government via Supreme Decree No. 065-2001-PCM.

[3] See: Report of the Commission on Truth and Reconciliation, Peru, General Conclusions, 28 August 2003. Available at: www.cverdad.org.pe/ingles/ifinal/conclusiones.php (last accessed 21 October 2016).

[4] See: M. Sassòli, A.A. Bouvier and A. Quintin, *How Does Law Protect in War?* (Geneva: International Committee of the Red Cross, 2011).

hand, conservative sectors of society describe this same period as a "fight against terrorism," declaring that everything that the state did (particularly its Armed Forces and National Police) was to preserve the integrity of the nation and to avoid illegal armed groups from taking over the country.

The words used to describe this period are important, as they contribute to shaping the historical or collective memory, as well as public policy and legal reforms toward democratic governance and respect for human rights.[5] In order to avoid the polarization and the politicization of legal reforms addressing the Peruvian conflict, the legislation adopted to implement the recommendations of the TRC, as well as to pay compensation to victims, uses the neutral term "period of violence."[6]

The inability to come to terms with the past also poses a challenge that affects state programs addressing the rights of victims, fostering an open debate regarding the preservation of memory and over the impact of the transitional efforts in the country. If the final report of the TRC and the inconsistent implementation of its Final Recommendations have been unable to achieve reconciliation, the question arises whether a memory law could fill this gap? Depending on the content of the law it could, as long as it is "true to the facts and respectful of the experiences to which those facts pertain."[7]

The challenge in adopting memory laws is the choice that lawmakers make in selecting what is worthy to of remembrance and what should be, or is attempted to be, negated, discarded, or forgotten. Another element is how and if the state plans to oversee the fulfillment of this provision (prescriptive v. ban/proscriptive).[8] In this context, we build on the distinction made by Eric Heinze[9] in Epilogue to this volume, where he calls our attention to the distinction between memory laws and laws affecting public memory. In his view, with which I agree, the latter category has always existed and is part of the *auctoritas* of Constitutional institutions, while memory laws are more associated with post-World War II legislation and the Holocaust. In the Peruvian context, particularly in the draft bill that will be examined in this chapter, we are faced with an example of a draft memory law that has both a regulatory and a punitive element to it.[10]

[5] See: E. Jenin, 'Memory and Democracy: An Uncertain Relationship', *Revista Mexicana de Ciencias Políticas y Sociales* 59:221 (2014), 207–20.

[6] Law No. 28592, *Law that Creates the Integral Reparation Plans*. Lima, 28 July 2005.

[7] S. Lerner Fabres, 'Memory and the Search for a Democratic Society', 86.

[8] See chapter by Antoon De Baets in the present volume.

[9] See Epilogue by Eric Heinze in the present volume.

[10] *Ibid.*

The Peruvian transition toward democracy has been the object of several studies, being one of the most prominent cases and experiences in Latin America.[11] This literature has focused on the work and impact of the TRC[12] and the criminal prosecutions – mainly of state agents – for their human right breaches during the violent years.[13] The reparation programs adopted by the state have also been analyzed by the specialized literature, albeit to a lesser degree.[14] While acknowledging these academic works, the purpose of this paper is to analyze whether this framework has contributed to reconciliation, or at least "to [coming] to terms with the past."

The novel element analyzed in this chapter is the draft bill proposed by the Peruvian government to criminalize those that deny that the acts perpetrated by Shining Path and the *Movimimiento Recolucionario Túpac Amaru* (MRTA) were acts of terrorism. The proposed bill bases its justification on the comparative experience of laws criminalizing Holocaust denials, except that its purpose is exclusively focused on those denying the acts perpetrated by Shining Path and MRTA.

One of the issues presented by the editors of this book is to determine the "place and scope of memory laws in social reality." If we understand and build on the jurisprudence of national and international courts on issues related to memory and apply it to the draft bill described above,

[11] See, among others: K. Ambos, G. Elsner and E. Malarino (eds.), *Justicia de Transición con Informes de América Latina, Alemania, Italia y España* (Montevideo: Fundación Konrad Adenauer and Georg-August-Universität-Göttingen, 2009); R.K. Root, *Transitional Justice in Peru* (New York: Palgrave Macmillan, 2012); E. Allier-Montaño and E. Crenzel (eds.), *The Struggle for Memory in Latin America: Recent History and Political Violence* (New York: Palgrave Macmillan, 2015).

[12] See, among others: S. Macher, *¿Hemos Avanzado? A 10 años de las Recomendaciones de la Comisión de la Verdad y Reconciliación* (Lima: Instituto de Estudios Peruanos, 2014); L.J. Laplante and K. Theidon, 'Truth with Consequences: Justice and Reparations in Post-Truth Commission Peru', *Human Rights Quarterly* 29:1 (2007), 228–50.

[13] See, among others: J.M. Burt, 'Guilty as Charged: The Trial of Former Peruvian President Alberto Fujimori for Human Rights Violations', *International Journal of Transitional Justice* 3:3 (2009), 384–405; E. González-Cueva, 'The Contribution of the Peruvian Truth and Reconciliation Commission to Prosecutions', *Criminal Law Forum*, 15:1 (2004), 55–66.

[14] See, among others: J. Garcia-Godos, 'Victim Reparations in the Peruvian Truth Commission and the Challenge of Historical Interpretation', *International Journal of Transitional Justice* 2:1 (2008), 63–82; M. de Waardt, 'Are Peruvian Victims Being Mocked?: Politicization of Victimhood and Victims' Motivations for Reparations', *Human Rights Quarterly* 35:4 (2013), 830–49. On this note, it is worth mentioning that the legislative authorization for the registration of victims to receive compensation from the state closed on 31 December 2011. This was much criticized by human rights organizations, and in September 2016 this registry was re-opened by the Peruvian Ministry of Justice and Human Rights (*Decreto Supremo No. 12-2016-JUS*).

a number of questions arise: What are the benefits of a criminal law of such nature? Does it contribute to reconciliation? What are the institutional deficiencies that have enabled the proposal of such legislation? Is reconciliation an aim of this particular memory law?

Section 2 of this chapter focuses on how the pursuit and preservation of memory has been developed by the Inter-American Court of Human Rights (hereinafter, "IACtHR") as part of the right to truth. Section 3 assesses what has been done in Peru to address the transition toward democracy, and its impact on historical memory. Section 4 analyzes the bill criminalizing the denial of a specific form of terrorism and examines how, if adopted, it might affect the "coming to terms with the past."

2 The Inter-American Court of Human Rights and the Pursuit of Memory

Latin America's recent past, and its efforts to address human rights violations perpetrated by both states and illegal armed groups, provide a rich field of study.[15] Despite significant efforts to implement transitional justice, the "[d]ivision about how past crimes are to be understood and judged, how those accused of the abuse of human rights are to be held responsible for their actions, and how victims are to be compensated continue to generate debate and dissonance in many Latin American polities."[16]

The IACtHR is a regional human rights tribunal created by the American Convention on Human Rights,[17] which entered into force in July 1978. The decisions of the Court are binding and final upon the State Parties that have accepted its jurisdiction.[18] Owing to the fact that most of the cases decided by the IACtHR, particularly in its initial phase, have addressed

[15] See, among others: K. Sikkink, *The Justice Cascade: How Human Rights Prosecutions are Changing World Politics* (New York: W. W. Norton & Co., 2011), 129–61; A.J. Carrillo, 'The Relevance of Inter-American Human Rights Law and Practice to Repairing the Past', in P. de Greiff (ed.), *The Handbook of Reparations* (New York: Oxford University Press, 2006), 504–38.

[16] M.S. Grindle, 'Democracies in the Shadow of Memories', in M.S. Grindle and E.E. Goodman (eds.), *Reflections on Memory and Democracy* (Cambridge: The David Rockefeller Center Series on Latin American Studies, Harvard University Press, 2016), 3.

[17] *American Convention on Human Rights*, 22 November 1969, 1144 UNTS 123, 9 ILM. 99 (entered into force 7 July 1978).

[18] *American Convention on Human Rights*, Art. 67.

cases of systematic practices[19] of torture and forced disappearances,[20] the issue of memory (although victim-centered) and the adoption of reparations to avoid the recurrence of these types of crimes have been at the core of its jurisprudence.[21]

The decisions of the IACtHR have triggered prosecutions of grave human rights violations[22] perpetrated during the rule of military and authoritarian regimes in Latin America.[23] The IACtHR has interpreted the scope of human rights obligations of states based on institutions of International Criminal Law, International Humanitarian Law[24] and other international Human Rights Treaties in order to determine the obligation of State Parties vis-à-vis the American Convention on Human Rights. This practice has enabled the Court to analyze human rights violations in the light of other branches of Public International Law, ordering remedies that go beyond individual compensation[25] to victims.[26]

In this regard, the IACtHR has (i) declared the inadmissibility of amnesty laws to avoid national investigations[27]; (ii) established an unenumerated right to truth[28]; (iii) determined the scope of the obligation to respect and fulfill the object and purpose of treaties, even those that

[19] See: J. Davis, *Seeking Human Rights Justice in Latin America – Truth, Extra-Territorial Courts, and the Process of Justice* (Cambridge: Cambridge University Press, 2014).

[20] R. Sieder, 'War, Peace, and Memory Politics in Central America', in A.B. de Brito, C. González-Enríquez and P. Aguilar (eds.), *The Politics of Memory – Transitional Justice in Democratizing Societies* (Oxford: Oxford University Press, 2001), 161–89.

[21] A.B. de Brito, 'Truth, Justice, Memory, and Democratization in the Southern Cone', in A.B. de Brito, C. González-Enríquez and P. Aguilar (eds.), *The Politics of Memory – Transitional Justice in Democratizing Societies* (Oxford: Oxford University Press, 2001), 119–60.

[22] See: B.D. Tittemore, 'Ending Impunity in the Americas: The Role of the Inter-American Human Rights System in Advancing Accountability for Serious Crimes Under International Law', *Southwestern Journal of Law and Trade in the Americas* 12:2 (2006), 429–75.

[23] See: Ambos et al. *Justicia de Transición con Informes de América Latina, Alemania, Italia y España.*

[24] See: S. Herencia Carrasco, 'Implementation of War Crimes in Latin America: An Assessment of the Impact of the Rome Statute of the International Criminal Court', *International Criminal Law Review* 10:4 (2010), 461–73.

[25] *American Convention on Human Rights*, Art. 63.

[26] S. Herencia Carrasco, 'Las Reparaciones en la Jurisprudencia de la Corte Interamericana de Derechos Humanos' in K. Ambos, E. Malarino and G. Elsner (eds.), *El Sistema Interamericano de Protección de los Derechos Humanos y el Derecho penal Internacional* (Montevideo: Fundación Konrad Adenauer and Georg-August-Universität-Göttingen, 2011), 381–402.

[27] IACtHR, *Case of Barrios Altos (Chumbipuma Aguirre v. Peru)* (Merits), 14 March 2001, No. 75, par. 41.

[28] IACtHR, *Case of Castillo Paez (Peru)* (Merits), 3 November 1997, No. 34.

have not been ratified by states[29] but share the same principles stated in the American Convention on Human Rights; and (iv) ordered a state to implement legislation regarding crimes against humanity according to the guidelines set by, *inter alia*, specific international treaties.[30]

Despite the controversies that have accompanied some of its decisions,[31] the advancement of human rights and the prosecution of gross human rights violations in Latin America[32] would not have been possible without the rulings of the IACtHR. The decisions adopted by the Court have prompted legal and institutional reforms, consolidating the rule of law and democratization processes in transitional Latin American societies.[33]

This has been particularly true in Peru, where most of the cases that have been decided by the Court against Peru address the issues of memory, truth and justice in the internal conflict involving Shining Path and the MRTA. Some of these cases, due to the sensitivity of Peruvian society vis-à-vis the years of violence it suffered through, have triggered a debate in the country about the meaning of human rights and the limitations that International Human Rights Law should have in "the fight against terrorism." For example, the *Case of Loayza Tamayo*[34] brought into the international sphere the issue of the limits that Peruvian authorities had put on the right to due process, including the creation of faceless tribunals. In a more recent decision, the *Case of Cruz Sánchez* addressed the alleged violations of the right to life and access to justice in the "Chavín de Huantar" military operation, which rescued civilians kidnapped by the MRTA in the Japanese Embassy in Peru.[35]

At the same time, the preservation of memory in the jurisprudence of the IACtHR has focused on highlighting the role of Truth and Reconciliation Commissions, as well as the ordering of reparation measures on behalf of

[29] See: IACtHR, *Case of Almonacid Arellano et. al. (Chile)* (Preliminary Objections, Merits, Reparations and Costs), 26 September 2006, No. 154.

[30] See: IACtHR, *Case of Goiburu et. al. (Paraguay)* (Merits, Reparations and Costs), 22 September 2006, No. 153.

[31] The most common criticisms to these rulings relate to the amount of pecuniary compensation awarded to victims and the fact that some of the reparations go beyond the merits of the case, especially the non-repetition guarantees.

[32] See: J.E. Méndez and C. Cone, 'Human Rights Make a Difference: Lessons from Latin America', in D. Shelton (ed.), *The Oxford Handbook of International Human Rights Law* (Oxford: Oxford University Press, 2013), 955–80.

[33] See: R. Gargarella, *Latin American Constitutionalism 1810–2010: The Engine Room of the Constitution* (Oxford: Oxford University Press, 2013).

[34] IACtHR, *Case of Loayza Tamayo (Peru)* (Merits), 17 September 1997, No. 33.

[35] IACtHR, *Case of Cruz Sánchez et al. (Peru)* (Preliminary Objections, Merits, Reparations and Costs), 17 April 2015, No. 292.

victims. These include the renaming of streets, the inclusion of victims' names in public spaces, and the adoption of commemorative plaques, all of which are examples of non-regulatory memory laws.[36] To date no regulatory and/or punitive memory law has been analyzed by the IACtHR. However, the emphasis that the Court has put on the declassification of secret documents as part of the right to information has contributed to granting the public access to the full scope of human rights violations perpetrated in the past.[37] In this context, the Inter-American Commission on Human Rights has reported that this right of access to information allows society:

> 108. . . . (i) to learn the conduct of those who have been involved in committing serious violations of human rights or international humanitarian law, especially in the case of mass or systematic violations; (ii) to understand the objective and subjective elements that helped create the conditions and circumstances in which atrocious conduct was perpetrated, and to identify the legal and factual factors that gave rise to the appearance and persistence of impunity; (iii) to have a basis for determining whether state mechanisms served as a context for punishable conduct; (iv) to identify the victims and the groups they belong to, as well as those who have participated in acts victimizing others; and (v) to understand the impact of impunity.[38]

As stated earlier, so far no case specifically addressing the issue of memory laws has been presented before the IACtHR, but in the likely eventuality that such a case be addressed by this forum, issues such as the right to truth, justice, and reparation by victims would be among the elements under consideration. In the case of the Peruvian draft bill of a memory law, freedom of expression would also play a significant role in its analysis.

3 The Peruvian Transitional Experience and the Role of the Inter-American Human Rights System

The period of violence in Peru began in May 1980, when the illegal armed group *Sendero Luminoso* (Shining Path) entered the small community of Chuschi, Ayacucho (in central Peru) and burned the ballot boxes as a form of protest against the presidential elections. This period of violence ended in November 2000 with the resignation of former President Alberto Fujimori who, facing corruption charges, fled the country. It is estimated

[36] E. Heinze, *supra* note 9.

[37] See: IACtHR, *Case of Gomes Lund et al. ("Guerrilha do Araguaia" v. Brazil)* (Preliminary Objections, Merits, Reparations and Costs), 24 November 2010, No. 219.

[38] Inter-American Commission on Human Rights, *The Right to Truth in the Americas* (Washington: Inter-American Commission on Human Rights, 2014), 52.

that more than 69,000 people died[39] in the conflict between the state and the Maoist illegal armed group of Shining Path and the MRTA. According to the TRC, Shining Path was responsible for 54 percent of the deaths,[40] mostly low-income peasants.[41] The Andean region of Ayacucho in central Peru was the most affected by the violence.[42]

Together with the return to democracy, the Peruvian government has adopted legal and institutional measures to address and shed light on the underlying causes of this conflict. These include: (i) the establishment of an official Truth and Reconciliation Commission (*Comisión de la Verdad y Reconciliación*)[43]; (ii) the outlawing of amnesty and broad antiterrorist legislation by the Constitutional Court; (iii) the prosecution of the main perpetrators of crimes against humanity, including former President Alberto Fujimori[44]; (iv) specific legislation encompassing reparation programs for the victims of violence perpetrated between 1980 and 2000[45]; and (v) the recent opening of a Museum of Memory, now called the Place of Memory, Tolerance and Social Inclusion (*Lugar de la Memoria, la Tolerancia y la Inclusión Social*).

As of December 2015, the Peruvian state has financially compensated 78,123 victims in a total amount of approximately USD 77 million. Those who have received compensation constitute 95 percent of the "accredited" victims entitled to individual financial reparations.[46] The state has also paid USD 66 million in the form of collective reparations to affected communities. In addition, the state has financed reparations in health, education, and restitution of memory in a total sum of approximately USD 146 million, benefiting 220,000 families.[47] With respect to the restitution

[39] Report of the Commission on Truth and Reconciliation, Peru, General Conclusions, 28 August 2003, par. 2.

[40] *Ibid.*, par. 13.

[41] *Ibid.*, par. 5.

[42] *Ibid.*, par. 8.

[43] Peruvian Truth and Reconciliation Commission, *supra* note 2.

[44] See: C.T. Prusak, 'The Trial of Alberto Fujimori: Navigating the Show Trial Dilemma in Pursuit of Transitional Justice', *New York University Law Review*, 85:3 (2010), 867–904; D.C. Caro Coria, 'Sobre la punición del ex presidente Alberto Fujimori Fujimori como autor mediato de una organización criminal estatal', *Zeitschrift für Internationale Strafrechtsdogmatik*, 11:4 (2009) 581–95.

[45] Law No. 28592, *Law that Creates the Integral Reparation Plans*. Lima, 28 July 2005, and subsequent amendments.

[46] The Peruvian state presented an oral report to the Inter-American Commission on Human Rights regarding its efforts to compensate victims, in a hearing which took place on 8 April 2016 in Washington, D.C. during the Commission's 157th period of sessions. Available at: www.youtube.com/watch?v=MukmvZ0Ale0 (last accessed 21 October 2016).

[47] *Ibid.*

of memory, the main challenges are the construction of sanctuaries in places where mass graves have been found, the implementation of a forensic national strategy for the restitution of the remains of victims to their families, and the operation of the National Museum of Memory as an effort to preserve collective and historic memory.

Despite these efforts, the measures undertaken have not been sufficient to foster reconciliation among Peruvians. As an example of the extent to which polarization persists, the political discourse offered by state officials refers this period as the "age of terrorism," while Shining Path's political arm, MOVADEF, refers to their former leaders as political prisoners, often calling for an amnesty as a means toward national reconciliation. Since the adoption of the TRC Final Report in August 2003, the division in Peruvian society has continued and public opinion polls indicate that there is both a lack of knowledge and mistrust toward the work of the TRC.

In an urban opinion poll in October 2015,[48] 76 percent of the population did not know about the TRC. Of the 22 percent that affirmed that they knew or had heard about the TRC, 55 percent approved of its work and 33 percent disapproved it. In a follow-up question, 57 percent considered that the final report of the TRC was too soft with respect to Shining Path and too harsh on the Armed Forces. This suggests that some respondents approved of the report while at the same time registering reservations. This latter view represents a direct contradiction with one of the main conclusions from the TRC's Final Report, which stated that[49]:

> 12. The TRC believes that the immediate and fundamental cause of the unleashing of the internal armed conflict was the PCP-SL's decision to start the armed struggle against the Peruvian State, in opposition to the will of the overwhelming majority of Peruvians, men and women, and at a time in which democracy was being restored through free elections.
>
> 13. In the TRC's view, based on the number of persons killed and disappeared, the PCP-SL was the principal perpetrator of crimes and violations of human rights. It was responsible for 54 percent of victim deaths reported to the TRC. This high degree of responsibility on the part of the PCP-SL is an exceptional case among subversive groups in Latin America, and one of the most notable and unique features of the process that the TRC has had to analyze.

[48] Ipsos Opinión Data, 'Opinión Data', *Resumen de Encuestas a la Opinión Pública*, Año 15, No. 196 (19 October 2015), 5.

[49] Report of the Commission on Truth and Reconciliation, Peru, General Conclusions, PART II.A. Available at: www.cverdad.org.pe/ingles/ifinal/conclusiones.php (last accessed 21 October 2016).

This dissociation between the official institutions and civil society, as well as the enforcement of the rulings of the IACtHR, public sentiment, and (lack of) memory, has led the Peruvian state to propose criminal legislation prosecuting those that deny the existence of terrorism and its moral and legal responsibility. Building on the allegedly comparable experience of European legislation criminalizing Holocaust denials, a draft bill has been proposed that would allow the public prosecutor (*Ministerio Público*) to commence a legal action against the "terrorism deniers."

4 Criminalization of Terrorism-Denial in Peru: A Failed Attempt Toward the Adoption of a Memory Law

On 28 August 2012,[50] the Peruvian Government submitted to Congress a bill to amend the Penal Code, which would have criminalized the public approval, justification, denial, or minimization of crimes perpetrated by members of illegal organizations that have been convicted by the judiciary under the Peruvian Anti-terrorism legislation.[51] On 13 December 2012, this proposal was approved, with modifications,[52] by Parliament's Commission of Constitution and Procedures, as well as the Commission on Justice and Human Rights.[53] As of this date, the draft bill has to be

[50] Poder Ejecutivo del Perú, Proyecto de Ley No. 1464/2012-PE mediante el cual se Incorpora el Art. 316-A al Código Penal. 28 August 2012.

[51] The original bill submitted by the Executive Branch reads as follows:

> *Será reprimido con pena privativa de libertad no menor de cuatro ni mayor de ocho años el que públicamente apruebe, justifique, niegue o minimice los delitos cometidos por integrantes de organizaciones terroristas, previstos en el artículo 2° del Decreto Ley N° 25475 y establecidos en una sentencia judicial firme, de modo tal que el contenido de esas expresiones resulte idóneo y suficiente para cualquiera de los siguientes fines:*
>
> (a) Menospreciar, hostilizar u ofender gravemente a un colectivo social.
> (b) Enaltecer a los responsables de dichos delitos.
> (c) Propiciar o estimular la violencia terrorista.
> (d) Sirva como medio para adoctrinar con fines terroristas.

[52] Comisión de Justicia y Derechos Humanos, Comisión de Constitución y Reglamento, Dictamen Conjunto recaído en el Proyecto de Ley 1464/2012-PE que propone incorporar el artículo 316-A al Código Penal, referido al negacionismo de los delitos de terrorismo. 13 December 2012.

[53] The bill, as modified and approved by the Congressional Commissions, reads as follows:

> *Será reprimido con pena privativa de libertad no menor de seis ni mayor de doce años, el que públicamente niegue cualquiera de los delitos de terrorismo previstos en el Decreto Legislativo 046, el Código Penal de 1924 modificado por las Leyes 24651 y 24953, y el Decreto Ley 15475, o la calidad de autor o partícipe de una*

submitted to the plenary of Parliament for final discussion and vote. Although a new government was sworn in on 28 July 2016, this bill could still be passed by Congress, particularly now that *Fuerza Popular*, the political party of former President Alberto Fujimori, has the overwhelming majority of Parliamentary seats. If approved by Congress and signed by the Executive, those convicted under the new law would face six to twelve years in prison for violation of the law.

Regardless of the final outcome of this bill, the adoption of criminal laws focusing on the criminalization of particular views expressed by a specific group of people reveals, at the very least, a selective view of the collective truth that the norm is trying to preserve. As stated before, opinion polls show a direct rejection of the actions perpetrated by Shining Path and the MRTA. Organizations and other grassroots movements attempting to justify the actions perpetrated by these terrorist groups have never achieved significant political representation nor access to the public sphere. Thus there is no clear indication of a significant revisionist or denial movement which could justify such a drastic measure, one that would trump the fundamental freedoms[54] protected by the 1993 Political Constitution and/or the American Convention on Human Rights.[55]

4.1 *The Criminal Code and the Over-Criminalization of Social Conduct*

At the outset it is important to highlight that the over-criminalization of social conduct has been a common phenomenon in Peru. This practice is correlated with the "tough on crime" narrative and offered as a solution to complex socioeconomic problems in society, including sensitive issues related to the preservation of memory. This situation is faced by many Latin American countries, but in the Peruvian context a number of

---

persona respecto de esos delitos, establecidos en sentencia judicial firme, con la finalidad de promover la comisión de los delitos de terrorismo o apología de terrorismo o sirva como medo para adoctrinar para fines terroristas.

Si la negación se realiza a través de medios de comunicación social o mediante el uso de tecnologías de la información y comunicaciones, la pena será no menor de ocho ni mayor de quince años, imponiéndose trescientos sesenta y cinco días de multa e inhabilitación conforme a los incisos 2, 4 y 8 del artículo 36 del Código Penal.

[54] See: B.G. Cano Suárez, 'El delito de negacionismo. Su problemática en el Perú', *Anuario de Derecho Penal y Ciencias Penales* 45:1 (2012), 305–24.

[55] See: J.R. Vanossi, 'La criminalización del «negacionismo» frente a la libertad de expresión: un tremedal del derecho', *Revista Pensamiento Constitucional* 19:19 (2014), 123–62.

reforms to the current Criminal Code provide a better understanding of the rationale behind this proposed Memory Law bill.

The current Penal Code was adopted in 1993 and up until January 2013 there were 408 modifications to the Statute. Of these reforms, 73.5 percent increased the criminal penalties and 22 percent defined new crimes, while the remaining 4.5 percent struck down statutory provisions. This phenomenon is equally applicable to the Penitentiary Code. Since the adoption of this Code in 1991 and up until December 2012, twenty-eight reforms to this piece of legislation were adopted; of which 72 percent restricted access to penitentiary benefits, 14 percent increased the number of requirements to access such benefits, and the remaining 14 percent struck down provisions.[56] This over-criminalization has contributed to the over-crowding of prisons,[57] corrupt practices, and a judicial system that is unable to address its burgeoning caseload, affecting fundamental rights and the guarantees of due process and access to justice.[58]

4.2 The Criminalization of Terrorism-Denials and European Memory Laws on the Holocaust: Are They Equivalent?

The purpose of the proposed new amendment is to imprison those who deny the acts of terrorism perpetrated by Shining Path and the MRTA. It is worth mentioning that up until now, Shining Path and its political movement, MOVADEF, have not accepted responsibility for the human rights violations that they perpetrated against civilians.

To justify this amendment to the Criminal Code, the Government used some of the conclusions presented by the TRC with respect to the responsibility of Shining Path for systematic violations of human rights.[59] However, the TRC also documented grave violations of human rights perpetrated by Armed Forces. These led to the prosecution and conviction of former military and paramilitary groups on charges of homicide,

[56] Ministerio de Justicia y Derechos Humanos, *La Delincuencia en el Perú: Propuesta de Intervención Articulada* (Lima: Consejo Nacional de Política Criminal- Documento de Trabajo No. 01, 2013), 29–30.

[57] See: Inter-American Commission on Human Rights, *Report on the Human Rights of Persons Deprived of Liberty in the Americas* (Washington: Inter-American Commission on Human Rights, 2011).

[58] See: Inter-American Commission on Human Rights, *Report on the Use of Pretrial Detention in the Americas* (Washington: Inter-American Commission on Human Rights, 2013).

[59] Poder Ejecutivo del Perú, Proyecto de Ley No. 1464/2012-PE mediante el cual se Incorpora el Art. 316-A al Código Penal. 28 August 2012, p. 9.

torture and forced disappearances.[60] However, those who deny these serious breaches to human rights perpetrated by state actors (like the *Barrios Altos*[61] or *La Cantuta*[62] killings), which include political parties and presidential candidates that ran in the 2016 general elections, would not be covered by this bill.

While major criticisms of the proposed bill have presented it as an unconstitutional limitation on freedom of expression, the Congressional Joint Commission report approving the bill based its decision on the principle that human rights are not absolute[63] and that International Law, including the American Convention on Human Rights,[64] allows the imposition of certain restrictions to these rights[65] in order to preserve democracy. Additionally, the justification of the bill draws a parallel between the bill and Holocaust denial legislation in Europe, arguing that the proposed bill adapts the Holocaust denial framework to terrorist deniers in Peru.[66] In one of its paragraphs to justify the bill, the joint Congressional Commission report states that:

> 40. Therefore, to deny the existence of the crime of terrorism is assimilable to one of the goals of the legislation against those that deny the Holocaust: to punish those who offend the memory of victims and their families in

[60] D.C. Caro Coria, 'Prosecuting International Crimes in Peru', *International Criminal Law Review*, 10:4 (2010), 583–600.

[61] See: *Case of Barrios Altos (Chumbipuma Aguirre v. Peru)*, Inter-Am. Ct. H.R. (ser. C) No. 75 (2001).

[62] *Case of La Cantuta (Peru)* Inter-Am. Ct. H.R. (ser. C) No. 162 (2006).

[63] Comisión de Justicia y Derechos Humanos, Comisión de Constitución y Reglamento, Dictamen Conjunto recaído en el Proyecto de Ley 1464/2012-PE que propone incorporar el artículo 316-A al Código Penal, referido al negacionismo de los delitos de terrorismo. 13 December 2012, 6–12.

[64] For example, Art. 13.5 of the American Convention on Human Rights states:

> *Article 13. Freedom of Thought and Expression 5. Any propaganda for war and any advocacy of national, racial, or religious hatred that constitute incitements to lawless violence or to any other similar action against any person or group of persons on any grounds including those of race, color, religion, language, or national origin shall be considered as offenses punishable by law.*

[65] On the limits of freedom of expression vis-à-vis the legislation criminalizing Holocaust denials, see: K. Lasson, 'Defending Truth: Holocaust Denial in the Twenty-First Century', in L. Hennebel and T. Hochmann (eds.), *Genocide Denials and the Law* (Oxford: Oxford University Press, 2011), 109–82.

[66] Comisión de Justicia y Derechos Humanos, Comisión de Constitución y Reglamento, Dictamen Conjunto recaído en el Proyecto de Ley 1464/2012-PE que propone incorporar el artículo 316-A al Código Penal, referido al negacionismo de los delitos de terrorismo. 13 December 2012, 12–19.

> relation to these facts, and in this way to prevent the chronic repetition of these execrable acts.[67]

Memory laws criminalizing Holocaust denials have been widely analyzed with the aim of determining whether they constitute a valid or impermissible limitation to freedom of expression.[68] The supporters of the Peruvian bill are correct when stating that no human right is absolute, particularly when freedom of expression is invoked to protect incitement to violence, hate speech, or the perpetration of crimes. However, where the Commission's reasoning behind the bill is not convincing is in its assertion that the human rights situation in Peru between 1980 and 2000 was sufficiently equivalent to what happened during World War II that both deserve the same criminal law approach.

Inasmuch as the draft bill attempts to mirror, and justify its provisions, based on the adoption of laws criminalizing Holocaust denials within the European context, it should be underlined that there are significant differences between them. One could focus on the historical impact of these events, different existing international obligations at the time they occurred, the magnitude of the victims, or even the acceptance of responsibility by the perpetrators of the Holocaust, while in the case of the Peruvian armed conflicts, this "acceptance of responsibility" has been mainly manifested by criminal convictions of the main perpetrators.

However, the major difference is that these two examples are not factually comparable. Holocaust denial legislation in Europe, which is examined in this volume, criminalizes those that deny that the killing and extermination of the Jewish population during World War II took place. In the Peruvian case, neither the members nor supporters of illegal armed groups deny the existence of the period of violence, referring to is as, among other terms, the period of *lucha armada* (armed struggle) or the *lucha del pueblo* (the people's fight). What they deny is that their acts were criminal offenses or human rights violations. Therefore, they are not challenging the factual

[67] *Ibid.*, par. 40. The original text reads as follows:

> 40. Por tanto, negar la existencia del delito de terrorismo es asimilable a una de las finalidades de los tipos penales de negacionismo del Holocausto: reprimir la ofensa a la memoria de las víctimas y sus familiares en relación con estos hechos y, de esta manera, prevenir la repetición crónica de tan execrables hechos.

[68] See, for example: Human Rights Committee, *Robert Faurisson v. France*, Communication No. 550/1993, U.N. Doc. CCPR/C/58/D/550/1993 (1996); ECtHR, *Janowiec and others v. Russia* (Appl. No. 55508/07 and 29520/09), Judgment (Grand Chamber), 21 October 2013.

elements, but rather calling into question their legal characterization and criminal prosecution.

Another problem with the proposed bill is its selectivity. In the case of the Peruvian legislation, the draft bill seeks to criminalize deniers of the actions of Shining Path or MRTA, but remains silent about those who deny or minimize the actions of the state. This is problematic because it attempts to direct or condition, with the use of criminal law instruments, a selective memory law that is in contradiction with the other attempts on the part of the state to address the human right crisis that took place. The work of the TRC, the reparation programs, the creation of a Museum of Memory, and other particular and institutional efforts to recover and preserve memory are thus affected by a biased and unnecessary view of what the memory law should preserve.

Another equally problematic aspect concerns the issue of how memory can be manipulated when a particular narrative is conveyed. In this case, the purpose is not to remember a specific and problematic period of Peruvian history that took the lives of more than 69,000 people, but to establish a good-bad dichotomy that excludes the inevitable shades of grey that accompany internal armed conflicts. In addition, this type of legislation would not contribute to "coming to terms with the past," but it could potentially undermine other efforts made to preserve historical memory, like the opening of a Museum of Memory, the public pardon for victims of human rights violations ordered by the IACtHR, or the restitution programs for victims.

Another issue of concern is that this bill would place criminal judges in the role of being the guardians of collective memory. This would lead to the assumption that "what is recorded within the court room or inquiry hall can constitute the irrefutable history of the past. This is both intellectually circumspect and historically dangerous."[69] In addition, it means that the state relinquishes the alternative of incorporating this group into society, prioritizing *ultima ratio* measures like the application of criminal law.

Regardless of the final outcome, this bill sends the wrong message about how memory should be portrayed in a transitional country like Peru. In my view, Shining Path and the MRTA are indeed organizations that killed and caused the disappearance of innocent people, and charges and convictions of terrorism alone do not do justice to their victims. The acts perpetrated by these organizations were crimes against humanity. However, the

[69] T. Hunt, 'Whose Truth? Objective Truth and a Challenge for History', *Criminal Law Forum* 15:1 (2004), 193–8.

attempt of the Peruvian government to exclusively criminalize the denial of the acts perpetrated by these organizations could have the unintended consequence of creating doubts in future generations about the real social, political, and economic implications of their acts. This draft memory law, which wrongly builds on Holocaust denial laws, affects the thorough and critical understanding needed of this period in Peruvian history.

5 Conclusions

The transitional experience in Peru has been inconsistent, and exclusively dependent on the political will of the Executive branch. Despite the significant amount of resources that have been allocated to reparation programs, successive governments have not yet lent their unequivocal support to the implementation of the Truth and Reconciliation Commission's recommendations with respect to collective memory efforts.

Memory laws may have a significant impact on the reconstruction of a fractured society.[70] They may provide a legal and institutional framework in order to prevent atrocities from happening again.[71] This includes the adoption of educational programs, access to information, reparation initiatives, and even the adoption of criminal laws protecting victims and criminalizing the desecration of historic sites and historical accounts. But if memory laws are limited to just one aspect, instead of fostering reconciliation and remembrance they can instead halt reconciliation processes.

With respect to memory laws, I agree with the premise of the editors of this book concerning the role that law can play in the shaping of collective memory. However, the attempt of the Peruvian government to adopt a specific bill only targeting those that deny the acts of terrorism by Shining Path and the MRTA, while remaining silent about those that deny the

[70] For more on the Peruvian context see, among others: M. Saona, *Memory Matters in Transitional Peru* (New York: Palgrave Macmillan, 2014); M. Hamann, S.L. Maguiña, G. Portocarrero and V. Vich (eds.), *Batallas por la Memoria: Antagonismos de la Promesa Peruana* (Lima: Pontificia Universidad Católica del Peru, Universidad del Pacífico and Instituto de Estudios Peruanos, 2003); P. del Pino and C. Yezer (eds.), *Las Formas del Recuerdo: Etnografías de la Violencia Política en el Perú* (Lima: Instituto de Estudios Peruanos and Instituto Francés de Estudios Andinos, 2013); C.I. Degregori, T. Portugal, G. Salazar and R. Aroni (eds.), *No hay Mañana sin Ayer: Batallas por la Memoria y Consolidación Democrática en el Perú* (Lima: Instituto de Estudios Peruanos, 2015).

[71] See: S. Loytomaki, *Law and the Politics of Memory – Confronting the Past* (New York: Routledge, 2014).

human right violations perpetrated and ordered by the Peruvian state, is blatantly one-sided and does nothing to promote a thorough understanding of the conditions that triggered this period of violence.

If adopted, the memory law discussed herein would mandate a particular view of events, but do nothing to promote an open discussion or reconciliation among Peruvians. In analyzing the proposed law, it is important to include the warning that a manipulative use of Holocaust denial legislation can subvert the preservation of collective memory, the rights of victims, and the guarantees of non-repetition.

As has been noted this bill has not yet been finally approved by Congress, but regardless of its final outcome it is a matter of serious concern that a populist "tough on crime" narrative can trump other efforts made by the state in its never-ending transition to democracy. While it remains uncertain that this bill, if passed, will actually be put into practice by prosecutors, the problem is that its very passage could trigger similar "memory laws" in other Latin American countries.

At present there are no comparable experiences in Latin America of similar legislation aimed at preventing and prosecuting those who oppose a particular view of a particular period of time. However, recent events regarding the killing of forty-three students in Ayotzinapa, Mexico,[72] together with the expressed will of the government to establish an official truth[73] despite the fact that nobody has been prosecuted or the remains of the bodies of the victims have been found, demonstrate that in the context of gross human rights violations there could be a tendency to block investigations or to establish an "official truth" by force. Colombia is another situation that should be observed closely, with its adoption of a Final Peace Agreement with the illegal armed group FARC, aimed at bringing to an end a fifty-year internal conflict. The polarization that this agreement has given rise to in Colombian society, along with the uncertainties regarding its implementation, could give rise to memory laws that, despite their name, would have the purpose of blocking, selecting, or arbitrarily determining what is the truth with respect to particular sets of events.

[72] See: Interdisciplinary Group of Independent Experts, *Ayotzinapa Report Summary – Research and Initial Conclusions of the Disappearances and Homicides of the Normalistas from Ayotzinapa* (GIEI: Creative Commons, 2015).

[73] See: Grupo Interdisciplinario de Expertos Independientes, *Informe Ayotzinapa II – Avances y nuevas conclusiones sobre la investigación, búsqueda y atención a las víctimas* (GIEI: Creative Commons, 2016).

EPILOGUE: BEYOND 'MEMORY LAWS': TOWARDS A GENERAL THEORY OF LAW AND HISTORICAL DISCOURSE

Eric Heinze

> Germany is the last country that ought to be voting about a so-called genocide.[1]
>
> Memory should never be watered-down or forgotten. Memory is the source of peace and the future.[2]

1 Introduction

Law constantly moulds collective understandings of the past, in ways falling along a spectrum from the benign to the brutal. At the mild end, we find a 1992 Vilnius town ordinance authorising a public monument to honour rock legend Frank Zappa. 'We were desperate', quips a Lithuanian civil servant who had favoured the move, 'to find a symbol that would mark the end of communism'.[3] That symbol had to remind people that history 'wasn't always doom and gloom'.[4] At the opposite end we find systemic executions and labour-camp imprisonment of whole families for a North

Some material in this chapter is adapted from E. Heinze, 'Law can enshrine a country's history, but it is a citizen's right to question it'. Retrieved 1 July 2017, from *The Conversation*: available at: https://theconversation.com/law-can-enshrine-a-countrys-history-but-it-is-a-citizens-right-to-question-it-59561 (19 May 2016). I would like to thank Uladzislau Belavusau, Aleksandra Gliszczyńska-Grabias, and Antoon De Baets for their comments, as well as Matthijs Lok for acting as respondent. Ideas in this essay were also presented at the conference 'Denialism and Human Rights', Faculty of Law, Maastricht University, 22–3 January 2015.

[1] Turkish President Recep Tayyip Erdoğan cited in *Mordaufrufe gegen Bundestagsabgeordnete*, Retrieved 1 July 2017, from *Die Zeit*, available at: www.zeit.de/politik/ausland/2016-06/tuerkei-recep-tayyip-erdogan-armenien-resolution-morddrohungen (6 June 2016).

[2] Pope Francis during June 2016 visit to Armenia, cited in '*Mentality of the Crusades*': *Turkey slams Pope Francis Armenian genocide comment*. Retrieved 1 July 2017, from *The Guardian*, avaliable at: www.theguardian.com/world/2016/jun/26/mentality-of-the-crusades-turkey-slams-pope-francis-armenian-genocide-comment (26 June 2016).

[3] K. Connolly, *They tore down Lenin's statue – and raised one to Frank Zappa*. Retrieved 1 July 2017, from *The Guardian*, available at: www.theguardian.com/travel/2000/jan/29/lithuania (29 January 2000). Cf. in the present volume the chapters by Cosmin Sebastian Cercel, Lina Klymenko, Nikolay Koposov, Maria Mälksoo, Ieva Miluna, and Jiří Přibáň.

[4] *Ibid.*

Korean who challenges official history.[5] Between those two poles, states devise countless ways to inscribe their preferred versions of history into law.[6] Can approaches diverging throughout a vast range of nations and historical settings share any meaningful characteristics? Can we write a general theory of law as a tool for ordering public knowledge of the past?

Most professional historians find it laborious enough, after all, to write about love in ancient Phoenicia, or markets in seventeenth-century China, or navigation in medieval Scandinavia, without also having to answer the ultimate question, 'What is history?' Some would insist that history is nothing but a plethora of histories,[7] concealing no transcendent essence such as 'History is the progressive achievement of democracy' or 'of reason' or 'of proletarian revolution' beneath its variegated surface.[8] Any universalist claim seems either ideologically laden or plausible only as to obvious and trivial elements ('History concerns past events'). Laws affecting historical memory, too, remain deeply embedded within cultural contexts. Age-old debates still rage about whether law itself – irrespective of any given system's distinct norms, institutions, and practices – 'is' the same type of thing from one culture to the next.[9] Can it be meaningful to ask about law's effect on historical memory in general terms?

[5] See, e.g., UN Human Rights Council, *Report of the detailed findings of the commission of inquiry on human rights in the Democratic People's Republic of Korea*. United Nations, 2014, 45–8; 323–30. Information drawn also from A. De Baets, *Censorship of Historical Thought: A World Guide 1945–2000* (Westport: Greenwood Press, 2002), 328 (version of 24 June 2016 updated by De Baets, on file with author).

[6] See generally, e.g., U. Belavusau, 'Memory Laws and Freedom of Speech: Governance of History in European Law', in A. Koltay (ed.), *Comparative Perspectives on Fundamentals of Freedom of Speech* (Budapest: Wolters Kluwer), 537–58; L. Cajani, 'L'histoire, les lois, les mémoires. Sur quelques conflits récents en Europe', *Revue française de Pédagogie* 165 (2008), 65–76; E. Fronza, *Il negazionismo come reato* (Milano: Giuffré, 2012); S. Garibian, 'Pour une lecture juridique des quatre lois «mémorielles»', *Esprit* (2006, February), 158–73; A. Gliszczynska-Grabias, 'Coping with the Past in a Multicultural Europe: The European Court of Human Rights on Memory and Law', D. Gozdecka and M. Kmak (eds.), *Europe at the Edge of Pluralism* (Cambridge – Antwerp – Portland: Intersentia, 2015); M.J. Osiel, *Mass Atrocity, Collective Memory, and the Law* (New Brunswick: Transaction, 1997). For annual global surveys of law and policies affecting historical memory or research, see, e.g., *Liberté pour l'Histoire*. Retrieved 1 July 2017 from www.lph-asso.fr/, *Network of Concerned Historians*, available at: www.concernedhistorians.org/content/home.html (1 July 2017).

[7] Cf. famously L. Tolstoy, Second Epilogue. In *War and Peace* (L. Maude and A. Maude, Trans., 929–64) (Wordsworth, [1869] 1993).

[8] The references being, respectively, to de Tocqueville, Hegel, and Marx. Cf. critically, e.g., K. Popper, *The Poverty of Historicism* (London: Routledge, [1957] 2002a) and K. Popper, *The Open Society and Its Enemies*, Vols. 1–2 (London: Routledge, [1945] 2002b) (challenging determinist theories of history).

[9] Cf., e.g., J. Vanderlinden, *Anthropologie juridique* (Paris: Dalloz, 1996).

Law's distinct feature as a vehicle of memory, I shall argue, is its aim or effect of increasing the *expressive weight* of some version of history, irrespective of that version's *substantive weight*. In order to proceed towards that observation, I begin in Section 2 by examining the notion of a *memory law*. It is a new phrase, but derives from something as old as law itself. The phrase admittedly helps us to understand certain debates within law emerging from a post-World War II and post-colonial world, but accounts for only certain types of specially consecrated norms. I shall propose that we instead adopt a phrase like *law affecting historical memory* (or some cognate) if we wish to grasp the broader processes through which law guides the public's understanding of the past.

In Section 3, I examine public discourse as the matrix within which facts and norms relevant to the past are expressed. Claims about the past gain *substantive* weight through factual and normative claims as perceived within respective epistemic communities. We must distinguish substantive weight, however, from a claim's *expressive* weight, the claim's opportunity to be heard and discussed. In Section 4, I argue that law serves to add expressive weight to some preferred version of history and to subtract expressive weight from rival versions, irrespective of those respective versions' substantive merits. I draw a further distinction in Section 5 between legal-formalist and legal-realist approaches in order to propose, in conclusion, a general description of law as a vehicle for shaping public understandings of the past.

2 From 'Memory Laws' to Laws Affecting Memory

For as long as human society has existed, law has shaped historical memory. I make that claim not with any privileged insight into all societies, but because law can scarcely do otherwise. 'The life of the law has not been logic', in Oliver Wendell Holmes's time-honoured words, 'it has been experience . . . The law embodies the story of a nation's development through many centuries'.[10] Well before establishing their democracy, the ancient Athenians had 'committed the whole constitution (πολιτείαν)' into the 'hands' of the statesman Solon.[11] Solon's steps towards citizen enfranchisement followed from more than moral abstractions. '[T]he hardest and bitterest part' of their earlier constitution, Aristotle would later write, had been

10 O.W. Holmes, Jr., *The Common Law* (Cambridge: Belknap, [1881] 2009), 3.

11 Constitution of Athens, ch. 5, in Aristotle, J. Barnes (ed.), *The Complete Works of Aristotle: The Revised Oxford Translations* (Princeton, NJ: Princeton University Press, 1984 [fourth-century BCE]), vol. 2, 2243.

'their state of serfdom (δουλεύειν)'.[12] Among the democratising features of Solon's new regime were: prohibitions on loans secured by 'the debtor's person'; the right of each citizen 'to claim redress on behalf of any one to whom wrong was being done'; and the 'institution of the appeal of the jury-courts'.[13] Those are no humdrum, blackletter norms. They are the codified memories of an overthrown past.

Modern constitutions stand largely as responses to the arrival or overthrow of some monarchical, dictatorial, oligarchic, colonial, or imperial power. The preamble to the 1996 South African Constitution, for example, enshrines core legal principles through the recollection of a chilling history:

> We, the people of South Africa, Recognise the injustices of our past; Honour those who suffered for justice and freedom in our land . . . We therefore, through our freely elected representatives, adopt this Constitution as the supreme law of the Republic so as to – Heal the divisions of the past and establish a society based on democratic values, social justice and fundamental human rights.[14]

We need not, moreover, assume the concept of a legal system to overlap entirely with that of a *national* legal system. Law at supra-state, sub-state, and indeed non-state levels is equally framed in response to dramatic histories. The 1948 Universal Declaration of Human Rights (UDHR) cloaks its otherwise conventionally humanist goals as the remembrance of a grievous past:

> Whereas disregard and contempt for human rights have resulted in barbarous acts which have outraged the conscience of mankind ... ,
>
> Whereas it is essential, if man is not to be compelled to have recourse, as a last resort, to rebellion against tyranny and oppression, that human rights should be protected by the rule of law ... .[15]

Curiously, however, the phrase 'memory laws' is remarkably new, sometimes mentioned as a legal aberration. But we can easily close the gap between law's age-old incorporation of memory and the recent emergence

[12] Constitution of Athens, ch. 2, *in* Aristotle, [fourth century BCE] 1984, vol. 2, p. 2241. The reference is principally to Draco's regime.

[13] Constitution of Athens, ch. 9, *in* Aristotle, [fourth century BCE] 1984, vol. 2, p. 2245.

[14] Constitution of the Republic of South Africa, preamble (1996).

[15] G.A. res. 217A (III), U.N. Doc A/810 at 71, art. 19 (1948), preambular par. 1–2. The European Convention on Human Rights, albeit not expressly reciting that history, remains unmistakably embedded in it. Its drafting followed closely in the footsteps of the UDHR. On relevant comments of the UN Human Rights Committee, see chapter by Antoon De Baets in the present volume.

of a specialist discourse. We can distinguish between, on the one hand, a narrow category of specifically dedicated *memory laws* and, on the other hand, the inherent and far broader phenomenon of *laws affecting public memory*. As a recent term of art, *memory laws* translates, not altogether accurately, the phrase *lois mémorielles*, which emerged in post-World War II French political discourse. It designates actual and proposed laws[16] formulated to proclaim authoritative versions of some invariably sensitive history. Such laws might well 'prove repressive by penalising alternative opinions'.[17] But they can also be purely 'declaratory',[18] adopted solely to confer solemnity upon a brutal past without penalising the expression of contrary views.

That distinction between declaratory and punitive norms does not, however, wholly capture even this recent and narrower concept of 'memory laws'. Some laws are non-punitive yet more than just declaratory. They authorise specific government action, albeit without imposing penalties for breach. These include laws designating a commemorative garden, a souvenir postage stamp, or a national holiday. The Vilnius ordinance may seem harmless enough, yet those more-than-just-declaratory and yet non-punitive norms often spark as much controversy as punitive norms. The 2014 Hungarian law purporting to create a World War II memorial was widely condemned as a ploy to whitewash the Horthy regime's complicity in Nazi atrocities.[19] Even something as seemingly benign as the Hyde Park Diana Princess of Wales Memorial Fountain ends up scorned as royalist propaganda.[20]

[16] See, e.g., *Les termes du débat sur les "lois mémorielles"*. Retrieved 1 July 2017 from *La Documentation française*, available at: www.ladocumentationfrancaise.fr/dossiers/d000078-loi-et-memoire/les-termes-du-debat-sur-les-lois-memorielles (23 October 2006). See also, in the present volume, the chapters by Luigi Cajani, Antoon De Baets, Robert A. Kahn, Ieva Miluna, and Ioanna Tourkochoriti.

[17] *Les lois mémorielles doivent être abrogées*. Retrieved 10 June 2016 from *Le Nouvel Observateur*, available at: http://danielclairvaux.blogs.nouvelobs.com/archive/2012/01/02/les-lois-memorielles-doivent-etre-abrogees.html (7 January 2012). Punitive laws commonly rely upon both consequentialist and deontological rationales. Elsewhere, however, I argue that neither rationale can command legitimacy within a sufficiently longstanding, stable and prosperous democracy. E. Heinze, *Hate Speech and Democratic Citizenship* (Oxford: Oxford University Press, 2016), 32–5, 125–62.

[18] *Ibid.* For a critical assessment of declaratory norms, see, e.g., chapter by Miklós Könczöl in the present volume.

[19] See, e.g., M. Feher, *Hungarian Sculptor Defends Monument to Victims of Nazis*. Retrieved 1 July 2017, from *The Wall Street Journal*, available at: www.wsj.com/articles/hungarian-sculptor-defends-monument-to-nazi-occupation-1406910612 (1 August 2014).

[20] See, e.g., R. English and D. Sherwood, *Controversial Diana Memorial Fund to Close after 14 years*. Retrieved 1 July 2017, from *Daily Mail*, available at: www.dailymail.co.uk/news/article-2016638/Diana-memorial-fund-close-14-years.html (20 July 2011).

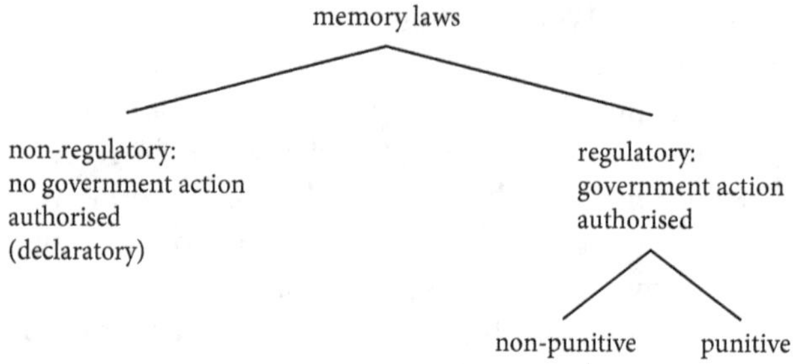

Figure 1 Types of memory laws

As illustrated in Figure 1, we can distinguish between, on the one hand, declaratory, hence *non-regulatory* measures, and, on the other hand, measures that are *regulatory* in the sense of authorising action in ways that may be either punitive, entailing limits on freedom, or non-punitive yet entailing some state action. A strictly declaratory norm is not only non-punitive, but more generally non-regulatory.

Antoon De Baets, for example, defines a memory law as serving to 'prescribe or proscribe certain views of historical figures, dates, symbols or events'.[21] The word 'proscribe', on his view, entails punitive norms, whereas 'prescribe' includes both non-punitive and declaratory norms. The distinction between regulatory and non-regulatory norms arises largely at the level of prospective, legislative norm creation. Yet it echoes a parallel distinction at the level of retrospective dispute settlement. We find, on the one hand, traditionally judicial procedures of full-fledged prosecutions containing a punitive element, as with war crimes tribunals. On the other hand, we find conciliatory 'truth commissions' or 'bridging' approaches[22] of a non-judicial or only quasi-judicial type, aiming more to establish a declaratory record than to punish.

As suggested in this chapter's epigraph, it is not only regulatory laws that spark controversy. The German Parliament's 2016 resolution recognising

[21] See chapter by Antoon De Baets in the present volume.

[22] For critical analyses see, e.g., chapters by Jeremie Bracka and Salvador Herencia Carrasco in the present volume. The distinction between non-regulatory and regulatory approaches cannot, however, be pushed too far. For a state even to 'declare' some activity to be criminal, for example, can in some instances constitute an affirmative step towards subsequent coercive or punitive measures. In the case of genocide, for example, declaratory recognition may subsequently be invoked to justify use of force to prevent further killing or criminal procedures to punish it.

the mass Ottoman killings of Armenians as genocide sparked a hefty Turkish backlash.[23] Many have argued that even a good-faith declaratory law, e.g., acknowledging complicity in the Holocaust or the trans-Atlantic slave trade, wrongly distorts historical enquiry by throwing too much weight behind governments entering an arena where they command insufficient scholarly competence. States or supra-national bodies such as the United Nations or Council of Europe, on that view, cannot match the political authority they wield to any correlative epistemic authority. The temptation, moreover, for non-democratic or only quasi-democratic regimes to declare their own readings of history only further frustrates serious historical enquiry and education.

Within the contexts of strong democracies, however, I have elsewhere supported declaratory (and indeed other non-punitive) laws. I do so by challenging any background assumption that the state can retreat to neutrality on controversial ethical disputes,[24] including those involving historical interpretation. States perforce take positions on history, and can scarcely do otherwise. Every authorised grade-school history curriculum stamps an official imprimatur upon particular readings of history. Few modern democracies are prepared to abandon historical education on the grounds that it cannot be done with perfect ethical or political neutrality.

More importantly, that particular and recent concept of *memory law*, in both its regulatory and non-regulatory forms, only partly accounts for the broader and older panoplies of ways in which law directs public memory. Even in today's France or Germany, where such laws have attracted attention, they become dwarfed by the far broader means through which law shapes popular understandings of history in schools or through the media. Particularly in contemporary democracies, law's power simply to *promote* certain views of history and to *sideline* other views far exceeds its power to 'prescribe' and to 'proscribe' this or that particular view through formal sanctions.

The Vilnius ordinance *promotes* a particular understanding of history. Through its conspicuously idiosyncratic irony and nuance, however, it neither 'prescribes' any officially endorsed history nor 'proscribes' any

[23] See, e.g., A. Smale and M. Eddy, *German Parliament recognizes Armenian genocide, angering Turkey*. Retrieved 1 July 2017, from *The New York Times*, available at: www.nytimes.com/2016/06/03/world/europe/armenian-genocide-germany-turkey.html (2 June 2016).

[24] E. Heinze, *Hate Speech and Democratic Citizenship*, 6, 22, 186, 111–16, 211.

contrary one.[25] The Zappa monument lampoons the whole notion of states prescribing or proscribing particular accounts of history. There is no obvious way to 'violate' the Vilnius ordinance. (One might well incur penalties for defacing such a structure, but that prospect holds under laws protecting public property generally. It is not unique to memory laws as such, although some laws might impose penalties disproportionate to those authorised for defiling other public property.) The Zappa bust satirises the po-faced, taboo-laden colossuses of state-approved heroes imposed throughout the Soviet imperial space, which could once be ridiculed only through precarious whispers. It is anti-iconographic iconography.

To be sure, that monument is highly idiosyncratic. I invoke it not as typical, but as a test case to ensure that general principles can apply even to an unusual specimen. More typical forms of non-punitive commemoration, like postage stamps or the Princess Diana fountain, serve more to promote than to prescribe a particular view of persons or events from the past. Law, after all, always acts beyond sheer prescription and proscription.[26] We would err if, failing to see prescription and proscription, we saw no law at all. Not to legislate is also to legislate. Legal power acts through law's proceedings but also though law's abstentions. Alfons Aragoneses reminds us, for example, that by remaining ostensibly neutral, ostensibly silent about its fascist past,[27] Spanish law ends up pervasively and systemically bolstering a politically expedient, albeit ethically questionable *status quo* of unreflective forgetfulness. The power of law in a Spain which withholds even a declaratory legislative resolution on Francoist crimes is a power indeed. It is a power for schools and public institutions to avoid taking an essential ethical stance. It is a power to sideline public instruction and debate.

We must forever anew shake off the popular view of law as operating on the criminal paradigm, namely, that law consists essentially of 'orders

[25] This is not to say that all Lithuanian law and practice are equally liberal. See, e.g., Prosecution and persecution, 2008 (noting prosecutions brought against elderly Holocaust survivors on dubious charges of collaboration).

[26] That is of course an ancient insight, albeit revived in modern theory, e.g., in H. Hart, *The Concept of Law* (2nd ed.), P.A. Bulloch and J. Raz (eds.) (New York: Oxford University Press, 1994), 7, 20–5.

[27] See chapter by Alfons Aragoneses in the present volume. Cf. also chapters by Salvador Herencia Carrasco and Miklós Könczöl in the present volume and M.M. Lok, '"Un oubli total du passé"?: The Political and Social Construction of Silence', *History & Memory* 26:2 (2014), 40–75.

backed by threats'[28] which 'get you into trouble' when you break them. When Germany adopts a law punishing Holocaust denial, it admittedly creates a rule in the recent sense of a *loi mémorielle*. By contrast, Britain's omission to punish Holocaust denial does not rob it of relevant law, indeed of *equal force*. For Germany, such a law powerfully restricts individual freedom. For Britain, law serves just as powerfully to protect individual speakers as to the utterances in question. Britain does not lack relevant law and retains no sphere of 'no law' on Holocaust denial. For many a German mindful of the past, it is the power of the British law that is the more ominous, the more dangerous for preserving historical memory (however passionately we free speech advocates may disagree).[29] In both states, irrespective of having or not having some memory law, there is plenary law affecting historical memory. The *memory law* is but a recent subset of the far broader, age-old category of *law affecting historical memory*. Our question, then, is not *whether* law shapes memory, as if it could do anything else, but rather *how* it performs that task.

3 Discursive Contexts: Substantive versus Expressive Weight

Any claim about history, certainly within a contemporary state, is arguably relevant to memory laws, insofar as it seeks to influence someone's understanding of the past. Some such views end up reflected within law and policy. Historical memory arises largely through *public discourse*. Public discourse does not necessarily entail candid *public conversation*, even if the greatest possible overlap between the two remains central to democracy.[30] In repressive states, public discourse often amounts to little more than endless reiteration of state-approved messages.

Consider the following Context C_1. A township committee plans to facilitate a public discussion about some controversial history. The organisers expect in advance that not all views will carry equal *substantive* weight as to their intellectual or moral content. Some views, they predict, will entail glaring factual inaccuracies or repugnant normative assumptions. The organisers decide that each view must nonetheless be accorded

[28] Hart (1994, 7).

[29] See generally, e.g., M. Thiel (ed.), *Wehrhafte Demokratie: Beiträge über die Regelungen zum Schutze der freiheitlichen demokratischen Grundordnung* (Tübingen: Mohr Siebeck, 2003). Cf. critically, E. Heinze, *Hate Speech and Democratic Citizenship*, 129–37.

[30] See generally, e.g., J. Habermas, *Moralbewußtsein und kommunikatives Handeln* (Frankfurt a.M.: Suhrkamp, 1983). On the concept of 'public discourse', see also E. Heinze, *Hate Speech and Democratic Citizenship*, 26–30.

the same *expressive* weight through an equal opportunity for all views to be recited and discussed.

That difference between substantive and expressive weight is crucial.[31] A history of the Holocaust may carry overwhelming substantive weight through voluminous and intricate factual evidence about its organisation and execution, and may carry expressive weight within a small, specialist community. For the broad public, however, it may carry expressive weight only once it translates into accessible terms. Run-of-the-mill populists, by contrast, may carry strong expressive weight through sheer charisma. But they often bear little substantive weight in view of their implausible factual or normative assumptions. The founder of the French *Front National* Jean-Marie Le Pen entertained Holocaust denial of both the factual type, casting doubt on the existence or extent of Nazi gas chambers, and of a normative type, sidestepping such factual questions on the view that any Jewish genocide under the Nazis amounted, in any event, to little more than a 'detail' of history.[32]

Sheer repetition or amplification of an idea cannot increase its substantive weight – its materially factual record or its presupposed ethical principles – but does aim to enhance its expressive weight. From the late 1930s through to 1945, Germans under Nazi rule became exposed to incessant messages in school and the media about Jews as dangerous and perfidious vermin (*Die Juden sind unser Unglück*) to the exclusion of any counter-narrative. That communicative monopoly lent to antisemitism colossal expressive weight, persuading much of the population of its factual accuracy and ethical force. It in no way, however, endowed

[31] Cf. E. Heinze, *Hate Speech and Democratic Citizenship*, 104 (distinguishing between epistemic equality and democratic equality).

[32] See, e.g., N. Gauthier, *Le «détail» de Le Pen sera jugé en Allemagne*. Retrieved 1 July 2017, from *Libération*, available at: www.liberation.fr/france/1998/10/07/le-detail-de-le-pen-sera-juge-en-allemagne-le-parlement-europeen-a-leve-hier-son-immunite-parlementa_250214 (7 October 1998). My observations here are relative, not absolute. I seek neither to attribute uncontested authority to academic histories nor to dismiss all ideas spoken within popular contexts. Well into the twentieth century, Western histories issuing from the most prestigious scholars remained strongly patriarchal and Eurocentric. Only recently, and still uneasily, have alternative histories gained a stronger voice. Nor ought popular history to be confused with populism in the derisive, Le Penist sense. The 'storytelling' or 'microhistory' movement gained recognition in the twentieth century largely as a counter-current to the traditionalist historical narratives within the academy and the media. See, e.g., R. Delgado, 'Storytelling for Oppositionists and Others: A Plea for Narrative', *Michigan Law Review* 87 (1989) 2411. See also, e.g., D. Van Reybrouck, *Pleidooi voor populisme* (Amsterdam: Querido, 2008) (distinguishing different meanings of 'populism').

antisemitism with greater substantive weight through a materially superior factual record or rigour of ethical reason (except perhaps under an extreme social constructionist view, which would collapse substantive weight altogether into expressive weight).[33] The Nuremburg rally will forever stand as the epitome of crushing expressive weight coupled with substantive vacuity. Conversely, no addition of substantive weight through factual clarification or ethical reason inherently increases an idea's expressive weight. To the contrary, the more fastidious and comprehensive a history of the Holocaust, the fewer its readers.

The organisers in Context C_1 strive for an 'ideal speech situation'.[34] They aim to avoid, as far as possible, unfair weighting of the discussion in favour of any one reading of the historical event in question, even if they recognise that such a situation can never be perfectly achieved. As has been noted by critics of classical liberalism, power dynamics long embedded within culture impair equal opportunities for all views to receive the fair and equal hearing that the liberal paradigm purports to vindicate. Exponents of a mainstream opinion enter the conversation with attitudes already strongly weighted in their favour; with, so to speak, countless hours 'awarded' to their opinion even before this particular event begins. No discussion about something as value-laden as a controversial historical event can start with a clean slate.[35]

Nor could adjustments in the conversation's rules ever erase those predispositions. A gap separates, on the one hand, the conversation as a particular event in space and time ('next Thursday evening at the Town Hall') from, on the other hand, its inscription within a matrix of opinion

[33] Modern controversies surrounding the ethical implications of social constructionism echo an inveterate concern about the discrepancy between the substantive and the purely expressive force of arguments. That anxiety became, in Athens, pivotal for assessing political legitimacy. For Plato, the disjunction between substantive essence and rhetorical appearance engenders endless injustice. See, e.g., *Gorgias*, in Plato, *Plato: Complete Works*, J.M. Cooper (ed.) (Indianapolis, IN: Hackett 1997 [fourth-century BCE]), 791–869; *Rhetoric*, in Aristotle [fourth-century BCE], 1984:2, 2152–269.

[34] See, e.g., Habermas, 1983, 53–125. Unlike the English translation, which creates ambiguity between the two nouns 'speech' and 'situation', the adjective 'ideal' in the original *ideale Sprechsituation* unambiguously modifies 'situation' and not 'speech'. We might instead translate the phase as 'ideal *speaking* situation' to emphasise not the product but rather the process of expression, even if we admittedly refine the process in the hope of refining the product.

[35] See, e.g., H.-G. Gadamer, *Wahrheit und Methode: Grundzüge einer phiosophischen Hermeneutik*, 4th ed. (Tübingen: J.C.B. Mohr (Paul Siebeck), 1986). Cf., e.g., D. Cornell, M. Rosenfeld, and D.G. Carlson (eds.), *Deconstruction and the Possibility of Justice* (London: Routledge, 1992).

Discursive contexts for historical interpretation		
	Strong substantive weight	**Weak substantive weight**
Strong expressive weight	[1] **Aspiration in principle:** Satisfactory positions *prevailing* through satisfactory discursive processes	[2] **Defect in practice:** Unsatisfactory positions *prevailing* through unsatisfactory discursive processes
Weak expressive weight	[3] **Defect in practice:** Satisfactory positions *dissipated* through unsatisfactory discursive processes	[4] **Aspiration in principle:** Unsatisfactory positions *dissipated* through satisfactory discursive processes

Figure 2 Discursive contexts for historical interpretation

weighted in favour of the *status quo*. The organisers might, for example, adopt a rule granting additional time to representatives claiming to present historically repressed minority perspectives. For some participants, however, that attempt to redress an historical imbalance risks inserting an opposite yet equally unsatisfactory imbalance into the conversation scheduled for that particular date and place. Many blacks within a white majority situation might well shun a rule of 'Twenty minutes more for black people', which would seem merely to patronise them. They might well prefer to rely on their arguments' inherent substantive weight even despite an expressive weight historically skewed against them. There is no infallible remedy to that dilemma of democratic public discourse. We would immobilise ourselves, however, if we were to swing from one naïve extreme, assuming perfect expressive fairness, to the opposite yet equally untenable extreme of assuming the impossibility of expressive weight for historically marginalised viewpoints.

Figure 2 proposes various correlations between substantive and expressive weight, representing four basic contexts within which public discourse about history can proceed. As an ideal we might hope that the views carrying strong substantive weight, through strong factual and normative bases, will emerge through strong expressive weight (quadrant 1), in effect marrying 'essence' and 'appearance'. The best arguments in substance – proclaiming the injustices of genocides, of the transatlantic slave trade, of women's subordination – would then acquire expressive weight *through* their substantive weight. That ideal speech situation would conversely entail weak expressive weight for views carrying weak substantive weight (quadrant 4). Ideally, in that situation, attempts at factual and ethical denial or trivialisation of genocides, slavery, or patriarchy would, precisely *through* their substantive weakness, progressively dissipate, enjoying only weak expressive force.

Together, then, quadrants 1 and 4 present an aspirational context for historical debate. Quadrants 2 and 3, by contrast, counter that ideal with the flaws of everyday, fallible discursive reality. One such realistic, hence commonly defective type of discourse would be a position enjoying strong substantive weight through rigorous factual and normative bases, yet dissipated through weak expressive weight (quadrant 3), as we witness among dissidents within highly oppressive regimes, or with the aforementioned example of a Holocaust history too meticulous to be widely accessible. The final situation, conversely, involves strong expressive weight enjoyed by a view carrying only weak substantive weight (quadrant 2), as with Jean-Marie Le Pen's type of populism.

Those four categories are admittedly limited. For any discussion about a controversial history, substantive and expressive strength will always be context- and viewpoint-dependent, often subject to the assessments of epistemic communities themselves either defective in their own factual or ethical foundations, or simply lacking consensus. (While the concept of 'epistemic community' often refers to expert groups, I construe it here more broadly to mean any locus of identifiably shared understandings, not limited to scholars or professionals.) For simplicity's sake, moreover, I have merged factual and normative elements, as they do not readily disaggregate. A dispute, for example, as to whether it was justified for allied forces to bomb Dresden in 1945 deeply embeds factual claims within ethical assumptions, yet those same ethical assumptions within further factual claims (*A* was ethically legitimate if *B* was factually the case, but *B* was factually the case only if ethically necessitated by *C*, and so forth).[36] Even if we assume agreement on a set of factual claims, divergent normative positions

[36] See, e.g., D. Selwood, *Dresden was a civilian town with no military significance. Why did we burn its people?* Retrieved 1 July 2017, from *The Telegraph*, available at: www.telegraph.co.uk/history/world-war-two/11410633/Dresden-was-a-civilian-town-with-no-military-significance.-Why-did-we-burn-its-people.html (13 February 2015).

will accord different importance to some facts over others. A speaker may take a substantively compelling normative position but may lack depth of factual support, or may, conversely, turn factually sound evidence towards an ethically questionable aim. The seductive way to perpetrate Holocaust denial is not by reciting wholly false facts, but by blending the false with the true.[37]

The axis of real-world, hence often or even inherently defective discourse running between quadrants 2 and 3 raises a problem central to law's role in shaping memory. Situations represented by quadrant 3, where expressive weakness inhibits substantive strength, might seem to suggest that state interventions become most likely through measures aimed at adding expressive strength. In repressive states, we would expect any use of law to maintain that dynamic. North Korea embodies an arch-typical 'Quadrant 3 regime', relentlessly directed towards suppressing substantive evidence of both past and current affairs through a state monopoly on expressive strength for its viewpoint. In stable and prosperous democracies, by contrast, we witness many debates about (a) whether the state ought to add expressive weight to histories threatened by neglect or counter-narratives; and, if so, (b) whether that should be done in punitive ways, as with punitive anti-negationist laws, or only in non-punitive or declaratory ways. That prospect raises concerns for those who distrust government as a protagonist within historical discourse. The question, again, is not whether law enters historical discourse, but *how* it enters. Quadrant 3 by no means compels, say, a ban on Holocaust denial. It might well, however, be cited to demand more effective primary education, better coverage within state-operated media, or more effective state commemorative and cultural events.

The concept of substantive weight presupposes no *telos*, no inevitable end-point, no final or objectively verifiable completion of historical knowledge. History remains a hermeneutic enterprise, rarely enjoying any Archimedian point hovering above sensitive and complex histories. Ioanna Tourkochoriti rightly invokes Durkheim, Castoriades, Foucault, and Ricoeur to recall the impossibility of fixed or canonical histories.[38]

[37] See generally, e.g., M. Tiedemann, '*In Auschwitz wurde niemand vergast.*' – *60 rechtsradikale Lügen und wie man sie widerlegt* (Munich: Goldmann, 1996). See also, e.g., A. De Baets, *Responsible History* (New York/Oxford: Berghahn, 2008).

[38] See chapter by Ioanna Tourkochoriti in the present volume. See also chapter by Cosmin Sebastian Cercel (developing an anti-essentialist approach), and the notion of 'ontological security' developed in the chapter by Maria Mälksoo.

Greater and lesser substantive weight will always depend upon the epistemic communities within which claims are adduced.[39] We may aim to avoid the relativism that would equate, for example, affirmation and denial of the Holocaust as positions of equal validity; yet those writers, along with such historians as Maurice Halbwachs and François Hartog, remind us of history's polysemic character. The distinction between substantive and expressive weight does not correspond to any distinction between, respectively, objectivist and subjectivist assumptions about history. To the contrary, the distinction emerges from post-Wittgensteinian and post-Heideggerian understandings, particularly prominent in the work of Habermas, that substantive knowledge and debate about history cannot proceed independently of the socio-linguistically expressive contexts within which they find their articulation and thereby, for present purposes, their expressive weight.

4 State Intervention as 'Expressive Weighting'

Now consider Context C_2, in which the committee members further adopt a portentous exception to their seeming quest for expressive parity among speakers and viewpoints. They agree to exclude speakers whose statements 'undermine or insult any of our deceased Heads of State'.[40] That restriction aims to subtract expressive weight from views critical of, and to add expressive weight either to overt praise for, or to the silence which sidelines scrutiny of, those former Heads of State. Law, from that perspective, affects historical memory *through the aim or effect of adding expressive weight within public discourse to some preferred version of a given history, commensurately subtracting from the expressive weight of rival versions.* That 'subtraction' clause may seem tautological or redundant, but emphasises a salient factor. Expression within public discourse may be open-ended in principle, since there is no limit *a priori* to how many or how much people *might* speak; but its effectiveness is zero-sum in practice, since none of us can absorb all views without end. In practice, greater

[39] Whether a claim within natural science envisages truth irrespective of any epistemic community, indeed in a way fundamentally distinct from truth claims within social science, remains an ongoing dispute central to the philosophy of science. The notion of absolute objectivism as necessarily presupposed by natural science still presupposes epistemic communities setting criteria of experimental and pragmatic veracity.

[40] Cf., e.g., Turkish Criminal Code, Law no. 5273 of 26 September 2004 (Official Gazette No. 25611 of 12 December 2004), sec. 13, arts. 297–9.

exposure, hence greater expressive weight for one view does indeed subtract to some extent, even if only minimally, from competing views

North Korea again dramatises such a point at the extreme end. Upon the death of Kim Jong-il in 2011, state media carried the claim that magpies had mourned the leader's death.[41] Within the modernist, scientific context to which that state strenuously proclaims its adherence,[42] and yet which yields no empirical evidence that birds emote over conventionally political events, such claims enjoy scant substantive weight yet overwhelming expressive weight through public discourse barring dissent. (What distinguishes our extreme poles running from Zappa to magpies is not humour versus seriousness, but rather deliberate versus unintended humour.) Yet even the mild state action of a Vilnius ordinance deliberately satirical of official statuary nevertheless enhances the expressive weight of a twentieth-century Americanist myth of individual freedom. The sculpture thereby subtracts, albeit to an equally mild degree, from rival views about individualism. Persons viewing even an intentionally funny monument may still be impacted so as more strongly to favour its message over rival views. After all, if public art lacked all impact, nations would scarcely bother with it.

The emphasis on 'aim' as well as effect in that provisional account is crucial, as actual effects are unpredictable. In some contexts, a law could boomerang, provoking a backlash which would undermine the additional expressive weight envisaged for the official version.[43] A categorical statement can be made, then, only about the expected effects of laws influencing historical memory, and not about their actual effects. All such laws aim to enhance the expressive weight of the state's view[44] vis-à-vis rival views,

[41] *Magpies 'mourn' Kim Jong-il in North Korea*. Retrieved 1 July 2017, from *The Telegraph*, available at: www.telegraph.co.uk/news/worldnews/asia/northkorea/8977961/Magpies-mourn-Kim-Jong-il-in-North-Korea.html (26 December 2011).

[42] See, e.g., *Foundation of socialism*. Retrieved 1 July 2017, from Official webpage of the DPR of Korea, available at: www.korea-dpr.com/foundation_socialism.html (2011). That qualification is crucial, particularly in the repressive context within which the North Korean state operates. I by no means deny the ascription of symbolically rich animal interaction with humans recognised within cultures throughout history, as reported, for example, by Herodotus.

[43] See, e.g., E. Heinze, *Hate Speech and Democratic Citizenship*, 145–53 (arguing that bans within full-fledged democracies on Holocaust denial or other forms of provocative speech, while aiming to promote a preferred reading of history, may serve more to strengthen than to dissipate those provocative readings).

[44] Cf., e.g., C. Brettschneider, *When the State Speaks, What Should It Say?: How Democracies Can Protect Expression and Promote Equality* (Princeton: Princeton University Press, 2012)

be it dramatically through Draconian laws or minimally through mild ones. For Draconian regimes, such readjustments are made through harsh penalties. For the mild ones, the readjustments can be deemed *de minimis* both in expressive weight and in legal enforcement.

When law is used to add expressive weight to views already carrying strong substantive weight (Figure 2, quadrant 1), it is with an anxiety about the better view languishing. We witness that aspiration through laws prohibiting Holocaust denial,[45] even if it can be challenged through rival aspirations, such as free speech principles.[46] Commensurately weaker expressive weight is then accorded to substantively weaker rival views (quadrant 4), such as Holocaust denial, with the aspiration of dissipating them. Strong expressive weight added to views carrying only weak substantive weight (quadrant 2), by contrast, typifies a bad-faith, propagandising effort. An unsatisfactory stance is offered a better opportunity to prevail through a discursive process commensurately subtracting expressive weight from alternative views which carry a stronger substantive weight. Commensurately weaker expressive weight is then accorded to stronger substantive views with the aim of diluting them (quadrant 3), which is the classic predicament of dissidents within dictatorial or censorious regimes.

Through the Zappa monument's self-parody, a Lithuanian public authority adds only a *de minimis* expressive weight to the view that the entertainer once represented a freedom of anti-establishment expression denied under Soviet rule. The almost imperceptibly slight expressive weighting of the public conversation through that intervention emerges through Lithuanians' freedom to detest Zappa, or anything he represents, as loudly as they wish. The Vilnius ordinance certainly exemplifies a local government intervening to tilt public discourse in favour of a certain reading of history, but does so with an adjustment of expressive weight no

(examining the aims and effects of the state as a distinctly powerful speaker within public discourse).

45 See, e.g., M. Imbleau, *La négation du génocide nazi, liberté d'expression ou crime raciste?: Le négationnisme de la Shoah en droit international et comparé* (Paris: L'Harmattan, 2003).

46 See, e.g., E. Heinze, *Hate Speech and Democratic Citizenship*, 22, 23, 102, 103, 113, 144, 150, 151, 154, 155. De Baets recommends that we 'distinguish three possible effects of laws: their *symbolic* effects (emphasizing social values), their *repressive* effects (punishing offenders) and their *pragmatic* effects (steering conduct in a certain direction). Genocide denial laws can have powerful symbolic effects, but usually have poor repressive and pragmatic effects. The same goes for hate speech laws' (personal communication of 22 June 2016, on file with author).

heavier than that of a feather. The North Korean state, in polar opposition, crushes with the weight of an avalanche even featherweight departures from its approved history. There is no obvious way to violate the Vilnius ordinance, and no obvious way, beyond ritual obedience, *not* to violate *any* North Korean law affecting historical memory.

Re-adjustment of expressive weight need not proceed wholly against popular will. On a socially divisive historical event, a memory law will often add expressive weight to the view of one constitutive social group, subtracting it from the view of another. Many members of ethnic minorities, for example, decry a media which they claim to be dominated by, thereby according unfairly strong expressive weight to, the views of an ethnic elite. Many conservatives condemn mainstream media for being rigged by, hence according undue expressive weight to, a leftist elite. Many progressives reject the media for being controlled by, according undue expressive weight to, a corporate elite. The readjustment may, moreover, entail both local and global levels of influence. Russian or Chinese nationalists warn of media manipulated by, according undue expressive weight to, a Washington-based elite. The far-right and far-left blast the media worldwide as puppeted by, according undue expressive weight to, a Jewish elite; and so forth.

5 Formalist versus Realist Aspects

Memory laws must be viewed from both legal-formalist and legal-realist perspectives. As a matter of sheer formalism, a state may, for example, keep a law on the books that penalises speakers who 'undermine or insult the nation's President', but which has long ceased to be enforced, falling into desuetude. From a legal-realist perspective, that law's expressive weight within general historical discussion may turn out to be null. To be sure, as long as the law remains on the books, it might suddenly be invoked at any time, which is why people sometimes agitate for repeal even of neglected laws. People may also push for the law's removal on the symbolic grounds that its ongoing enshrinement lends it an inadmissible legitimacy.[47]

Conversely, from a legal-realist perspective, a state may clandestinely engage thugs or hitmen to attack individuals, groups, or organisations dissenting from a state-approved history, even if no formal, blackletter law

[47] For De Baets, 'a comparable (partly overlapping, partly more important) case is the case of survivals: flawed laws promulgated under dictatorship, or their remnants, sometimes survive in democracies' (personal communication of 22 June 2016, on file with author).

forbids the airing of such opinions – indeed even if officials laud their nation as a paradise of free speech. In 2016, the Russian Prime Minister Dmitry Medvedev maintained that 'no one bans' access by the political opposition to Russia's central mass media. 'It is absolutely impossible to impose any restrictions on the freedom of speech in the era of Internet'.[48] Legal-realist theory emphasises that state power may operate through material albeit formally unacknowledged effects.[49] That point expands the aforementioned observation that law never retreats from its role of shaping memory, even, or especially, when it appears silent.

Refining the prior account, then, it can be said that law affects historical knowledge through formal norms as well as informal, institutionally supported practices, with the primary aim or effect of adding expressive weight within public discourse to some preferred version of a given history, thereby commensurately subtracting from the expressive weight of rival versions. That description aims to avoid a scope so broad as to attribute commemorative aims to virtually any law, but also to avoid a scope so narrow as to include only 'memory laws', *lois mémorielles*, tailored expressly for a commemorative purpose.

The German Justice Minister announced in 2016 proposed legislation to compensate individuals who had been convicted under the now-repealed § 175 of the Criminal Code (*Strafgesetzbuch*), which had penalised homosexual acts between consulting adults.[50] Ordinarily legal systems recognise no presumption of compensation to persons previously disadvantaged under later-repealed laws. For example, a 95 per cent marginal tax rate for highest earners may be repealed in favour of a 50 per cent rate without any assumption of repayment to those who had once paid the higher rate. The German proposal recognises not merely that the earlier law is no longer necessary as a practical matter. Rather it stakes out an ethical position on German history, namely, that the conception or implementation

[48] *Russian PM: no restrictions on freedom of speech possible in internet era*. Retrieved 1 July 2017, from *TASS Russian News Agency*, available at: http:/tass.ru/en/society/856689 (14 February 2016). But see UN Human Rights Committee, 2015 (citing systemic abuse of rights of free expression, association, and media in Russia).

[49] See, e.g., R. Cotterrell, *The Politics of Jurisprudence* (2nd ed.) (London: Butterworths, 2003), 175–207; E. Heinze, 'Truth and Myth in Critical Race Theory and LatCrit: Human Rights and the Ethnocentrism of Anti-Ethnocentrism', *National Black Law Journal* 20 (2008), 107–62, at 121–33.

[50] See, e.g., J. Leithäuser, *Homosexuelle werden rehabilitiert*. Retrieved 1 July 2017, from *Frankfurter Allgemeine*, available at: www.faz.net/aktuell/politik/inland/heiko-maas-will-nach-175-stgb-verurteilte-homosexuelle-entschaedigen-14227386.html (11 May 2016).

of § 175 StGB had visited a fundamentally unjust form of persecution upon those convicted. As the law's overtly stated purpose is to compensate former convicts, it does not impose penalties to enforce its view of the past in any prescriptive or proscriptive way. It might admittedly be identified under Figure 1 as regulatory but non-punitive; yet it cannot altogether, or at least not primarily, be recognised as a *loi mémorielle*, as it is not obviously adopted for a specifically commemorative purpose. We can recognise memory laws as only sample, particularly obvious manifestations of the broader phenomenon of laws affecting historical memory, by also acknowledging such borderline cases in which a norm's or practice's specifically commemorative purpose may not be wholly clear.

More generally, a law may delegate decisions about primary educational curricula, including the teaching of history, to expert educational bodies or to school oversight committees. Insofar as primary education is compulsory, such a law adds formal state power to the choices made by such bodies even if the law itself makes no such choices. The phrase 'institutionally supported' in that definition again reminds us, moreover, that the concept of a 'legal system' is not fully coextensive with the concept of a national system. Within national legal systems, 'institutionally supported' will indeed largely mean 'state-supported', but law at supra-state, sub-state, and indeed non-state levels is equally framed within historical contexts and in response to decisive histories.

Lines between punitive and non-punitive laws can blur once we take the synthesis of formalist and realist elements into account. A law may, for example, mandate a schoolroom curriculum, which includes state-approved instruction of important past events. On its face, the blackletter text prescribing that educational programme, albeit regulatory, need not set forth penalties for particular departures from it. State measures could nevertheless be taken against teachers who express contrary views, or who allow open student discussion of such views, perhaps under a different law, such as one setting forth general conditions governing professional insubordination. In such a case, the law may indeed be non-punitive in its literal formulation, yet becomes *de facto* punitive in its application.

The distinction between punitive and non-punitive laws should not be confused with the distinction between mild and harsh laws. Here too we must consider both formalist and realist elements. A law imposing only negligible penalties, such as token fines that even the poor can easily pay, may fall on the milder end of the spectrum, and may even be deemed to be effectively non-punitive as a practical matter, but is still punitive in its literal formulation. Or a law may formally provide for harsh penalties, but if only small penalties are in fact applied, then it too remains punitive in form but mild in practice. Conversely, as already mentioned, a law may formally include no penalty at all, but prompt either mild or harsh punishments in practice. De Baets observes, 'the mere fact of a conviction is punitive, the mere fact of an acquittal is reparatory. Therefore international human rights courts, when ruling that states have committed human rights violations, often stress the reparatory nature of their judgments for the victims of these violations'.[51]

Law affecting memory commonly arises in contexts of dramatic histories, such as genocides, brutal dictatorships, or other incidents of gross and systemic human rights violations, well within the context of 'history' as conventionally understood. In view of the foregoing definition, however, any norm, policy or practice can count as a state intervention into public memory as long as it is imposed through some constitutional power, with the primary aim or effect of adding expressive weight within public discourse to some preferred version of a given history.[52] 'Memory laws', *lois mémorielles*, in the current and familiar sense have certainly focussed recent scholarly and media attention on the ways in which states act to influence public understandings of history. Those seemingly recent developments must not, however, divert our attention from something far older and far deeper within law. We must examine all the more closely the links between law and historical memory. For as long as human societies have existed, law inherently reflects official positions taken on past events.

[51] Personal communication of 22 June 2016 (on file with author).

[52] Cf. Heinze, 2017 (identifying both minor, isolated abuses and mass atrocities as equally vulnerable to suspect state denials).

INDEX

abuse clause, 113–15, 117
academic freedom, 15, 162, 173, 270, 271
access to justice, 77, 400, 406
access to the past, 212
accountability, 72, 76, 104, 353, 371
  United Nations, lack of, 87
actio popularis (complaint in the public interest), 32
ad hoc tribunals, 48, 64, 68
Afghanistan, 76
Ahmadinejad, Mahmoud, 8
aider and abettor, 65
Akayesu, 50, 63, 69
Al Nashiri v. *Poland*, 54
Algeria, 43, 158
Allied forces, 59, 61, 106, 144, 425
Allied soldiers, 21, 107
Al-Qaida, 76
American Convention on Human Rights (ACHR), 75, 79, 83, 398, 399, 400, 405, 407
American Historical Association, 142
amicus curiae briefs, 73
amnesty, 41, 43, 47, 74, 73–4, 79, 85, 181
  Germany, 54
  IACtHR, 399
  Peru, 402, 403
  South Africa, 74
anti-European sentiments, 265
anti-Semitism, 45
  activities, 113, 131, 170, 344
  Article 17 of the Human Rights Act, 115
  Holocaust denial, 128, 130, 346, 347
  ideology, 118, 126, 131, 191
  memory laws, vehicle for, 19, 45, 125, 156
Antonescu, Marshal of Romania, 233, 235, 237, 242
apology, 86, 380, 385
archives, public access to, 42, 75, 84, 310
  Ukraine, 318, 322
Argentina, 43, 73, 185, 190, 333
Aristotle, 415
Armenian genocide, 12, 116, 130, 142, 146, 157
  denial, 157, 329, 343, 344
  differences with Holocaust, 173
  France, 154, 331, 334
  Germany, 336, 419
  Switzerland, 329, 330, 346
  Turkey, 172
Armenians, 119, 122
  deportations, 110
  dignity, 118, 172
  living in Turkey, 119
Armistice agreement, 238, 239, 349
Article 3 of the Human Rights Act, 54
Article 8 of the Human Rights Act, 275
Article 10 of the Human Rights Act, 16, 76, 113, 274, 275, 329
  access to information, 83
  admissability, 170
  applicant's statements, 118
  freedom of expression, 75, 153, 162
  freedom of speech, 109
  Hungary, 251

Article 10 of the Human Rights Act (*cont.*)
importance for truth activists, 77
interaction with Article 17, 112, 115, 125, 127
limits that states may impose, 275
refusal to consider right to truth, 83
violations of, 120
Assembly of First Nations, 388
Association '21 December 1989' v. *Romania*, 81
atomic bombings, 8
Audiencia Provincial de Madrid, 184, 185
Auschwitz, 53, 171, 355, 356
Austria, 9, 172, 331, 333
Holocaust denial, 132
memory law, 307
right wing parties, 265

Bakri v. *Film Censorship Board*, 361
Baltic states, 14, 22, 25, 96, 106, 138, 216
criminal laws, 217, 223
deportation, 217
entry to USSR, 97
memory wars against Russia, 297
Molotov-Ribbentrop Pact, 319
occupation damages, 108
Barbie, Klaus, 7
Belarus, 37
Belgium, 307, 333
biographical narratives, 93, 95, 103, 105, 108
Bosnia, 64, 67
Bosnia-Herzegovina, 86
Brazil, 75, 79, 85
Brezhnev, Leonid, 295
Bulgaria, 137, 233
burial grounds, 34
burial places, 36, 80
Burundi, 56
Bush, George W., 76

Cambodia, 4
Canada, 7, 18, 20, 21, 24, 374–94
Anishinabek, 376, 381, 383, 392
Assembly of First Nations, 388
class action settlement, 384
evaluating truth and reconciliation commissions, 386–93
Holocaust denial, 343
Indian Residential Schools Truth and Reconciliation Commission (IRSTRC), 375, 386, 388, 392
inspration from South African truth and reconciliation commission, 385
Ipperwash Inquiry, 376, 381–4, 387, 392
Mohawks, 378
Mulroney, Brian, 378
Ontario, 381, 387
Quebec, 378
residential schools, 384–6
restitution, 383
Royal Commission on Aboriginal Peoples (RCAP), 376, 377–81, 384, 388, 391, 392
statement of reconciliation, 380
truth and reconciliation commissions, 377
Carol II, king of Romania, 233
censorship, 6, 15, 268, 339, 342
Israel, 360
Charter of the International Military Tribunal, 131, 132, 133, 153
Chile, 43, 74, 185, 190
Chirac, Jacques, 152, 155
Churchill, Winston, 213
CIA, 54, 76
Cifuentes v. *Chile*, 36
civil liability, 281, 382
closure, 72
coercion, 38, 40, 47, 374
Cold War, 302
collective consciousness, 164, 165, 169, 173
collective identity, 19–20, 53, 177, 295, 389

Colombia, 85, 87, 411
colonialism, 6, 12, 154, 167, 377, 392
communicative monopoly, 422
Conducător (Leader), 236, 242, 243
confiscation of property, 35, 42, 317
continuing violations, 33, 46, 47
Convention on the Prevention and Punishment of the Crime of Genocide, 140
Council of Europe (CoE), 320, 322, 419
coup d'état, 176, 178, 234, 238
Covenant (International Covenant on Civil and Political Rights), 29, 32
crimes against humanity, 33, 50, 60, 61, 131, 151, 153
  Allied forces, 144
crimes against peace, 59, 60, 131, 133, 209, 221
culture of remembrance, 192, 193
Czech Republic, 16, 22, 140, 195–215
  Act of Judicial Rehabilitation, 202
  ANO movement, 196
  communist past, 199
  history, 195–8
  Institute for the Study of Totalitarian Regimes, 197, 199, 201, 202, 207–10, 210–12, 212, 213
  Jewish population, 334
  Kundera case, 197, 198–201, 206, 214
  lustration law, 197, 203–5
  Nation's Memory Institute of Slovakia, 207–10
  rehabilitative and restitutive justice, 201–3
  secret police information, 206–7
  Velvet Revolution, 204

Daesh, 69
Darfur, 143
Declaration of Independence, 5
defamation, 45, 158, 171, 269, 271, 272
degree of consensus, 125
Deir Yassin, 351, 356
Demjanjuk, Ivan, 6
Denmark, 136, 341
disappearance of persons, 41, 77, 80
Dobrynin, Konstantin, 305, 306
documentary films, 179, 360, 361
domestic penal law, 52
double occupation, 99, 226, 319
dual presumption, 128
due process, 406
Durkheim, Emile, 57, 164, 165, 426
duty to cooperate, 83
duty to remember, 6, 11, 13, 38, 70, 71, 332

Eichmann, Adolf, 6, 53, 333
Ein Gal case, 360, 361
El Salvador, 74
El-Masri v. *Macedonia*, 76, 81, 83
epistemic communities, 49, 415, 425, 427
Erdemović case, 54, 56
Estonia, 96, 216, 220, 225
  criminal code, 225, 226
  deportation, 217
  war memorial, 300
ethnic cleansing, 212, 232, 325
EU Framework Decision 2008, 11, 133, 134, 135, 174, 308
  collective consciousness, 173
  communist regimes, 138–40
  crimes, 129–30
  criticism by historians, 142
  genocide denial bans, 335
  Greek implementation, 163
  Holocaust denial, 303
  implementation, 138
  opposition to, 337
  overview, 151
  pitfalls, 142–7
  purpose, 153
  Spain implementation, 192
Europe for Citizens Program, 10
European Commission for Democracy through Law (The Venice Commission), 326

European Court of Human Rights, 54, 81–84, 92, 152, 170, 216, 251, 329
European Day of Remembrance for Victims of Stalinism and Nazism, 140, 321
European Union, 97, 129, 133, 134, 138, 139, 142, 151, 153, 174, 175, 215, 331, 337
exhaustion of local remedies, 221
European Court of Human Rights
exhumation of bodies, 84, 185, 186, 188, 189
  funding, 189, 191

Farbtuhs case, 219, 223
Faurisson v. *France*, 38, 169
film festival, 366
Final Solution, 333
Finland, 44, 136
forensic science, 34, 84, 85, 403
France
  Armenian genocide, 152, 154
  Armenian population, 334
  collective consciousness, 169
  Constitutional Council, 156
  Court of Cassation, 156
  French Revolution, 4, 26, 158
  Gayssot, 19, 38, 130, 131, 141, 146, 154, 156, 303, 343
  Holocaust denial, 20, 422
  Mekachera, 154, 165
  memory laws, 152, 154–9, 307
  right wing parties, 265
  Taubira, 154, 157, 158
  War in Algeria, 158
Franco, Francisco, 178, 179, 180, 188, 193, 194
freedom of association, 136, 152, 153, 160, 161, 164, 173
freedom of expression, 15, 120, 127, 146, 162, 163, 173, 272
  balancing of interests, 274
  Belarus, 37
  consideration of, 280
  Holocaust denial, 46, 170
  Hungary, 246
  Israeli-Palestinian conflict, 361
  limits, 164
  matters of public interest, 276
  Peru, 401, 407
  Poland, 273
  preserving democracy, 9
  United Nations, 40, 45
freedom of research, 130, 144, 146, 147
Fujimori, Alberto, 401, 402, 405
fundamental rights, 9, 26, 81, 406

Gacaca, 68
Garaudy v. *France*, 115, 169–71
Garzón case, 189, 190
General Assembly of the International Committee of Historical Sciences (ICHS), 142
Geneva Conventions, 395
genocide, 7, 14, 19, 33, 45, 50, 56, 116
  colonial, 143
  crimes, 153
  definition of, 62, 69, 143, 219, 221, 223
  emergence as a legal category, 60
  jurisdiction, 69
  shared concern, 340
  specific intent, 65, 66
  targeting of groups, 223
  Ukraine, 320
Genocide Convention, 63, 218–21, 223
Genocide in the Vendée of 1793–1794, 155
George III, king of England, 5
Germany
  Armenian genocide, 336, 418
  battle of Crete, 162
  crimes against humanity, 137
  global media, 338
  Holocaust denial ban, 343, 421
  homosexuals, 431
  Hungary, relations with, 257
  loss to Russia in World War II, 296, 314, 318
  memory law, 8, 132, 307

nexus arguments, 331, 332, 333
Nuremberg Tribunal, 48
right wing parties, 265
Gomes Lund v. *Brazil*, 79
Gorbachev, Mikhail, 294, 295
Great Patriotic War, mnemonic narrative, 93, 97, 103, 105, 106, 295, 314
Greece, 21, 137, 138, 152, 153, 164, 165
Guatemala, 74
guillotine effect, 112, 113, 114, 123, 127
Gypsy Genocide, 155

Haïti, 74
Hartikainen v. *Finland*, 44, 45
hate speech, 45, 122, 126, 128
criminalization of, 7, 344
genocide denial ban, 341, 342
Peru, 408
Poland, 280, 281
Russia, 299
spread of, 265
heirs, 32, 46, 284
historians, 44, 47, 201
analysis of historical facts, 167, 168
Armenian genocide, 334
challenges of, 414
critcism of institute of national memory, 214
expert testimony, 171
Framework Decision criticism, 141–2
France, 141, 155, 331
Israeli New Historians, 351, 352
Kundera case (Czech Republic), 199
matters of public concern, 275
Palestinian, 351
Poland, treatment of, 271
prosecution of, 157, 161
Russia's Yaravaya Act, 307
standards expected of, 279
Ukraine, 325
World War II impact on Soviet people, 295
historical narratives, 55, 96
Canada, 376, 377, 379, 388
Hungary, 246, 248, 261
Israeli-Palestinian conflict, 364
manipulation, 409
meta-narratives, 392
micro-narratives, 390–1, 392
Poland, 279, 285, 289
Rwanda, 49
truth commissions, 389
use in prosecutions, 50
Hitler, Adolf, 193, 344
Hobbes, Thomas, 3
holidays, 179, 256
Home of Macedonian Civilisation, 159
homosexual acts, 431
Hopu and Bessert v. *France*, 34
human dignity, 39, 209, 251, 288, 305, 342
Human Rights Committee, 46, 47
view of memory as a right, 35–40
view of time, 31–5
Hungary, 13, 22–23, 25, 137, 138, 140, 191, 195, 233, 246–62
1949 constitution, 257
1989 constitution, 259, 260
Act 1 of 2000, 249, 254, 255
Act 20 of 1949, 259
Act 23 of 1994, 248
Act 90 of 1993, 249
communist takeover, 257
democratic transition, 258
disabling of checks and balances, 265
free elections in 1990, 257
freedom of expression, 250–2
Fundamental Law, 246
Fundamental Law, Christianity, 254–5
Fundamental Law, Holy Crown, 255–7
Fundamental Law, making of, 252
Fundamental Law, National Avowal, 252, 254, 258
Fundamental Law, post-war periods, 257–60, 262
German occupation, 257

Hungary (*cont.*)
  historical continuity, 249–50
  Holocaust denial ban, 333
  regime change in 2011, 195
  responsibility under community regime, 247–9
  Romania, relations with, 242
  secret service, 248

India, 24, 344, 345
inhuman treatment, 36, 41, 42, 81
institutes of national memory, 208, 211, 214, 311, 318, 326
internal armed conflict, 73, 395, 403, 409
International Court of Justice (ICJ), 66, 67
International Covenant on Civil and Political Rights, 29, 30
  Optional Protocol, 29, 31
International Criminal Court (ICC), 51, 52, 56, 62, 140
international criminal justice, 69
  legitimacy, 59
  purpose, 52, 54
  symbolic function, 57
International Day for the Right to the Truth, 84
International Military Tribunal (IMT), 59, 60, 61, 101, 145, 293
Iran, 8, 355
Ireland, 136
Islam, 8
Israel
  Holocaust denial law, 130
  home to Holocaust survivors, 334
Israeli-Palestinian conflict, 14, 18, 24, 26, 348–73
  1948–49 Arab Israeli war, 349
  challenging avoidance of 1948, 367–8
  collective memory legal footprints, 358–61
  Holocaust denial, 361–3
  ideological roots, 353–4
  Israeli-Palestinian Truth Commission (IPTC), 371–3
  joint acknowledgement, 370–1
  mutual notions of victimhood, 353–8
  Nakba law, 363–7
  Nationality Law, 358
  New Historians, 351–3, 371
  origins, 348–51
  Oslo accords, 352, 367
  Palestinian National Authority (PNA), 357
  transitional justice, 368–70
Italy, 138, 141, 307

Janowiec v. *Russia*, 76, 82
Japan, 6, 9, 144
Japanese Embassy, 400
Jewish National Fund (JNF), 370
Joint Action to Combat Racism and Xenophobia, 133
journalists, 199, 286
Juan Carlos I, king of Spain, 181
Judt, T., 282, 283

Kayishema, 63
Keegstra. James, 7
Khmer Rouge, 14
Kim II-Sung, 4
Kim Jong-il, 428
Knonov v. *Latvia*
  reaction, 100–2
Kolk and Kislyiy v. *Estonia*, 225
Kononov v. *Latvia*, 17, 21, 97, 226
  decision, 96–100
  implications, 106–8
  introduction, 91–6
  ontological security, 102–6
Kononov, Vasily Makarovich, 98
Kosovo, 87
Kovalenko v. *Belarus*, 37
Krstić, 50, 64–6
Kühnen v. *Germany*, 113, 114
Kundera, Milan, 198

Laptsevich v. *Belarus*, 37
Laptsevich and Tess v. *Latvia*, 220, 221, 223, 224
Latin America, 13, 18, 70, 73, 398, 405, 411
Latvia, 21, 22, 96, 97, 137, 138, 216–27
  Constitutional Court, 221
  Criminal Code, 217, 218, 220, 221, 222
  deportation cases, 216, 217–23, 227
  double occupation, 226
  European Court of Human Rights (ECtHR), 220–3, 227
  genocide, definition of, 218
  Russian mnemonical disagreement, 95
leaflets, 37
legitimacy, 56, 195
  attempts to de-legitimize, 315
  Israeli-Palestinian conflict, 354, 371
  memory laws, 430
  Poland, 268
  Romania, 240, 241
  Russia, 294
  Spain, 191
Lehideux and Isorni v. *France*, 114
LePen, Jean-Marie, 422, 425
Lewis, Bernard, 157, 334
libel, 7
Liberté pour l'histoire, 141
Lipstad, Deborah, 7
Lithuania, 96, 137, 138, 140, 216, 332
  memory law, 309
  Vilnius ordinance, 413, 417, 419, 428, 429
loi Taubira, 146
Lowes v. *United Kingdom*, 113
Lund v. *Brazil*, 75
Luxembourg, 132

Maastricht Treaty, 9
Malta, 137, 138
Marxist theory, 166
mass graves, 84, 188, 189
  appropriations, 191
media
  criticism by progressives, 430
  duty to report, 275
  lack of coverage, 380
  law shaping understanding of history, 419
  state operated, 426, 428
  stirring up a new controversy, 282
Medvedev, Dmitry, 302, 303, 305, 431
Mein Kampf, 344, 345
memorial complexes, 316
memorials, 80, 320, 369
  Diana, Princess of Wales, 417
  Hungary, 417
  Soviet soldiers, 300
memory capture, 265, 266
  politics of, 289
  rationale, 267
memory laws
  commemorative purpose, 431
  contexts and state action, 433
  cultural context, 414
  declaratory-punitive distinction, 417, 418, 432
  distinction with laws affecting public memory, 396
  expansion, 342
  Israel, 358
  laws affecting historical memory, 415, 421
  laws affecting public memory, 417
  penalties, 432
  prescription and proscription, 419, 420
  promoting understanding of history, 419
  truth and reconciliation commissions, contrast with, 387
memory wars, 93, 145, 297
  Kononov v. *Latvia*, 106
  Russia, 297, 300, 309
mens rea, 221
Mexico, 411

Michael, king of Romania, 234
Middle Ages, 241, 242
militant democracy (*streitbare* or *wehrhafte*), 9
Mill, John Stuart, 44
mismemory
  definition of, 266
  manifestations, 267
  Poland, 282, 288
  politics of, 267, 269, 289
mnemonic narratives, 92, 93, 94, 103, 105
Molotov-Ribbentrop Pact, 96, 140, 226, 308, 314, 319
Monnat v. *Switzerland*, 275
monuments, 178, 180, 188, 193, 413, 420
  impact on public, 428
moral narratives, 391
moral relativism, 158, 169
moral retribution, 205
Morocco, 85
mourn, right to, 35–7, 46
museums
  funding, 10
  Hungary, 249
  Israeli-Palestinian conflict, 356
  memory laws, 19
  Peru, 402, 409
  purpose, 5
  reforms, 4
Muslim organizations, 300
Myjer, Egbert, 98, 99, 102

name calling, 344
national identity, 153, 159, 166
  definition, 165
  Spain, 177
national security, 40, 73, 76, 160, 310
  Israeli-Palestinian conflict, 355
NATO, 319
Nazi emblems, 325
neo-Nazi propaganda, 113
Netanyahu, Benjamin, 355
Netherlands, 98, 136, 333
neurotic collective memory, 197, 215
neutrality, 420
nexus of arguments, 23, 329–47
  academic study, 343–5
  definitional problem, 333–5
  geographic determinism, 343
  global media problem, 337–40
  normative objections, 340–3
  nuanced understanding, 345–7
  practical objections, 333
  purposes, 330–3
  state reification problem, 335–7
NGOs
  international human rights, 87
  Israeli-Palestinian conflict, 368, 371
  Zochrot (Israeli), 369
Nicaragua v. *United States of America*, 67
Nietzsche, 166
North Korea, 413, 414, 426, 428, 430
Noviks case, 218, 223
Nuremberg Charter, 219, 220
  crime of genocide, 61
  crimes against humanity standard, 225
  deportations, 226
  jurisdiction, 60
  predecessor of international criminal courts, 52
  standard for denial of Nazi crimes, 307
Nuremberg Tribunal, 48, 59, 60, 134, 307, 308
  basis for memory laws, 307
  conspiracy charge, failure of, 66
  genocide not prosecuted, 61
  Russia, 101
  standard for crimes against humanity, 97, 100, 170

Obama, Barack, 303
oblivion, act of, 213
oblivion model, 3, 4

ontological security, 92, 93, 95
Baltic states, 93
definition, 91
ECtHR, 92
Russia, 105, 106
Open Society Justice Initiative (OSJI), 75, 76, 77, 78, 79
Ottoman Empire, 111, 118, 130, 142, 337

pardons, 3, 8, 409
Pătrăşcanu, Lucreţiu, 240
peaceful assembly, 37
peacekeepers, 390
Penart v. *Estonia*, 224
Perinçek v. *Switzerland*, 172, 277, 279, 281, 329, 333, 334, 335, 340, 343
anti-Armenian sentiment in Turkey, 344
application of decision, 120–5
criticism of decision, 346, 347
decision, 116–18
distinguished from other cases, 125–8
factual issues, 342
Grand Chamber decision, 119–20
introduction, 109–11
no evidence of serious friction, 331
reference to "States", 335
statements at issue, 118–19
uncertainty, 334
Perinçek, Doğu, 115
Peru, 24, 395–412
comparison to Holocaust denial laws, 408
Criminal Code, 406
criminalization of terrorism-denial, 404–10
Inter-American Court of Human Rights (IACtHR), 398–401
memory museum, 402
MOVADEF, 403, 406
Movimimiento Recolucionario Túpac Amaru (MRTA), 397, 400, 402, 406, 409, 410
National Museum of Memory, 403, 409
Peruvian Truth and Reconciliation (TRC), 402, 403, 406
public opinion polls, 403
public pardons, 409
reparations, 409
Shining Path, 397, 400, 401, 402, 403, 406, 409, 410
transitional experience, 401–4
Pétré-Grenouilleau, Olivier, 157, 169
Pezoldova v. *Czech Republic*, 42
Pol Pot, 4
Poland, 25, 77, 96, 138, 195, 263–90
anticipated litigation, 272–81
Art. 55a, 270
Article 10 of the Human Rights Act, 274
Article 8 of the Human Rights Act, 275
Constitution Preamble, 285
Criminal Code, 270, 271, 273
criminalizing historical debate, 268–72
culture of treason, 290
defamation, 272
disabling of checks and balances, 265
foreigners, liability of, 269
freedom of expression, 271, 273
institute of national memory, 208, 211
Jewish population, 334
Law and Justice party (PiS), 267
memories contrasted with Western Europe, 283
memory law, 309
memory wars against Russia, 297
mismemory and memory capture, 265–8, 290
Molotov-Ribbentrop Pact, 319
new memory law shortcomings, 285–6
nexus with Holocaust, 335
"Polish death camps" expression, 269, 272, 279, 280, 281, 286

Poland (*cont.*)
  Polish Institute of National Remembrance (IPN), 267
  politics of resentment, 263–5, 287, 288, 290
  revisionist rationale, 271
  Third Republic, 268
  unconditional protective principle, 269
political speech, 118, 172
political will, lack of, 85
Polynesia, 34
populism, 195, 263, 425
Portugal, 6
postage stamps, 420
post-communist liberal democratic politics, 195
post-totalitarian transformations, 202
pragmatic meaning, 203
pre-existing law, 33
preservation of memories, 209
propaganda, 180, 210, 298, 299, 429
  Nazi symbols, 299
  of fascism, 299
proportionality, 53, 123, 124, 281
Prussian empire, 6
public access to information, 401
public apologies, 80
public discourse, 282, 421
public health, 40
public morals, 40
public opinion polls, 403, 405
public order, 40
punishment rationales, 53
Putin, Vladimir, 16
  authoritarian regime, 295
  criticism of, 139
  as prime minister, 303
  Yarovaya Act, 293

Quinteros v. *Uruguay*, 41

racial discrimination, 116
racist crimes, 129
racist motive, 118
ratione temporis, 31, 32, 46
reconciliation, 56, 397
red judicata, 144
REDRESS, 77, 78, 81
refugees, 367, 372
  Palestinians, 359
regime of truth, 94
rehabilitation, 202
relatives as victims, 41
religious beliefs, 80
religious freedom, 255
religious rituals, 57, 58
Remembrance Days, 19
reparations, 73, 77–8, 82, 184, 185, 202, 397
  Germany, homosexuals, 431
  Peru, 396, 400, 402, 409
Report to the European Parliament and to the Council, 19
republican citizenship, 5
researchers, 380
Respekt magazine, 200, 201
restitution, 203, 204, 248, 403
  Canada, 383
  United States, 67
retroactive application of criminal law, 99, 220
Richter, Heinz, 146, 161, 162, 163, 165, 167, 168
right to fair trial, 221
right to history, 47
right to obtain information, 71
right to silence, 214
right to truth, 20, 41, 55, 70, 71, 72
  alternatives, 74
  historians, 42
  limiting state secrecy, 75–7
  punitive justice, 79
  substnatial violation, 83
right wing parties, 265, 267
Rizvanović v. *Bosnia and Herzegovina*, 42
Rodrigues, Almiro, 65

Romania, 22, 81, 133, 228–45
  Antonescu trial, 242, 243–5
  Constitution of 1923, 233, 234, 238
  Constitution of 1938, 233, 234
  dictatorship and fascism, 233–8
  Holocaust, participation in, 237
  paradox of the exception, 231
  postwar trials, 242
  return to democracy, 238–44
  royal dictatorship, 233
  royal-dictatorship, 235, 236
  state of exception, 229, 230–3
Ross v. *Canada*, 44, 45
Russia, 23, 25, 293–309
  administrative liabilty for fascist ideology, 298
  Chechen struggle for independence, 300
  Civil Tribunal, 302
  Criminal Code, 103
  cult of the war, 295
  Duma, 101
  Federation Council, 304, 305, 306
  Framework Decision, 139
  Holocaust denial, 298
  Katyn massacres, 77, 82
  memory laws of 1990s, 297–300
  memory wars with former Soviet states, 93
  Penal Code, 145
  Penal Code of 1996, 299
  politics of history and cult of the war, 294–7
  Putin regime, 103, 302, 309, 318
  Yarovaya Act, adoption of, 304–7
  Yarovaya Act, contrast with other memory laws, 307–9
  Yarovaya Act, introduction to, 293–4
  Yarovaya Act, prior versions, 300–4
Russian
  Putin regime, 104, 295, 296, 306
  Yeltsin government, 294
Russian Ministry of Foreign Affairs, 100
Russian–Ukrainian relations, 296, 297, 312, 316
  criticism of Ukraine memory law, 324
  memory use of World War II, 314
Rutuganda, 64
Rwanda, 14, 24, 339
  genocide, 343
  Hutu, 56
  International Criminal Tribunal for Rwanda (ICTR), 49, 50, 54, 56, 58, 63, 64, 68
  Tutsi, 63

satire and ridicule, 420, 428
Savenko case, 219, 223
Schedko v. *Belarus*, 36
scholarly research, 346
schools, 420, 426
  Canada, 384–6
  delegated powers under memory laws, 432
secret police, 205, 206
  KGB, 307
  Poland, 267
secret service, 236
  Hungary, 248
separation of church and state, 250
Serbian, 65
shared narratives, 313
Sharon, Ariel, 359
Siberia, 217, 218, 219
Sidiropoulos and others v. *Greece*, 160, 161
slave trade, 154, 157, 419
slavery, 5, 33, 425
Slovakia, 137, 138
  institute of national memory, 208, 209, 211
Slovenia, 138, 139
social media, 338, 339
social performances, 58
social space, 165

South Africa, 74, 207
Constitution Preamble, 416
Truth and Reconciliation Commission, 211, 385
Spain, 13, 26, 132, 175–94
Amnesty Act, 181, 182, 184, 190
Balearic Parliament, 189
Catalan Parliament, 189
Civil War, 179, 183
condemnation of Francoism, 187
Constitutional Court, 183
cultural references to World War II, 193
Francoism, 178–80
Historical Memory Act, 176, 185–91, 193
Holocaust denial law, 176
lack of financial support, 191
Mass Graves Act, 189
Ministry of Justice, 187
pact of silence, 182, 184
rebellion of the grandchildren, 185, 186
Sephardic Jews, 192
silence on fascist past, 420
Spanish Inquisition, 331
special tribunals, 187
Valley of the Fallen, 188
war memories, 175–8
speech
academic, 153
chilling effect, 16, 123, 154, 271, 366
dangers of limiting, 270
freedom of, 12, 109, 110, 250, 329, 341, 360, 429, 431
incitement to violence, 153, 276, 360
justification for interference, 277
restrictions, 127
rights of third persons, 277, 278
vagueness, 249
Spiegel, Boris, 304, 305
Srebrenica, 49, 64, 65, 86, 143
Stalinism, 176, 229, 233, 298, 299, 309, 317
state secrets, 81
state secrets privilege, 76
statues and plaques, 188, 332, 347, 401
status quo, 424
statute of limitations, 249
Stephen I, king of Hungary, 249
Strasbourg jurisprudence, 109
street names, 178, 188, 316, 328
Peru, 401
subjectivity of reflection, 167
substantive and expressive weight distinction, 422, 423, 424, 425, 426, 428, 429
summary executions, 59
Sweden, 136
Swiss Federal Tribunal, 116
Switzerland, 132
Armenian genocide, 346
Armenian population, 335
ban on genocide denial, 329
symbolic laws, 362, 430
symbolic meaning, 203, 204, 205
symbols, 251, 256
Communist era, 251
Deir Yassin, 356
end of communism, 413
fascism, 298, 299
Nabka, 357
Palestinians, 356
removal of, 188
system criminality, 66

Tadić, 67
Tahiti, 34
Tel Aviv University, 366
Tess case, 219, 220
textbook reform, 369
Tokyo Charter, 52
torture, 33, 54, 71, 76, 77
totalitarianism, 175, 234, 298, 317, 323
transitional justice, 202, 368
transnational resonance, 94
treason, 267, 290
Treaty of Versailles, 6

Treaty of Westphalia, 3
truth and reconciliation commissions
  Canada, 376
  Peru, 400
  proliferation of, 74
  right to truth, 84
  role of, 79, 369, 385
  South Africa, 385
Turkey, 6, 77, 116, 119, 152, 336, 344
  Armenian genocide, 171, 336

Ukraine, 25, 310–28
  access to archives, 318, 322
  condemnation of Nazism and Communism, 320
  contesting the national narrative, 322–7, 327
  Day of Remembrance and Reconciliation, 318
  de-communization laws, 327, 328
  EU and NATO membership, 319
  European Day of Rememberance for Victims of Stalinism and Nazism, 321
  famine, 142, 145, 155, 321
  Holodomor, 145, 321
  honoring fighters for statehood, 315–16
  joining European countries, 318–22
  memory law, 309
  memory law draft, 301
  memory wars against Russia, 297
  Molotov-Ribbentrop Pact, 319
  narrative history theories, 310–13
  narrative of Soviet past, 313–18
  national memory bloc, 310
  Opposition Bloc, 311, 323
  OUN (Organization of Ukrainian Nationalists), 314, 315, 325
  Ukrainian Institute of National Memory, 318
  Ukrainian language, 325
  Ukrainian People's Republic (UNR), 315
  UPA (Ukrainian Insurgent Army), 314, 325
  war veterans, definition of, 314
United Kingdom, 337, 338, 339
  Brexit, 265, 337
  Diana, Princess of Wales, 417
  distinction with Germany, 421
  Framework Decision, 136, 139
  House of Lords, 136
  omission of Holocaust denial law, 421
United Nations
  Convention on the Prevention and Punishment of the Crime of Genocide, 7
  General Assembly, 62, 355
  Human Rights Committee, 29, 169
  Human Rights Council, 85
  Independent Expert on the Promotion of a Democratic and Equitable International Order, 39
  memory laws, 419
  Office of the High Commissioner for Human Rights, 84
  peacekeeping missions, 390
  Relief and Works Agency for Palestine Refugees in the Near East (UNRWA), 349
  Security Council, 104
  Special Rapporteur on Free Expression, 39
  Srebrenica massacres, 86
  Ukraine famine, 321
  War Crimes Commission, 59, 60
United States, 76
  crimes against Native Americans, 331
  hate speech, 344
  Holocaust Memorial Museum, 326
  Russia, relations with, 302
Universal Declaration of Human Rights (UDHR), 221, 416
Uruguay, 43, 85

USSR
  Criminal Code, application to
    Estonia, 225
  deportation to Siberia, 217
  Member of the United Nations, 225
  Party to the London Agreement of
    1945, 225, 226
  Poland, relations with, 283
  Romania, relations with, 233, 239,
    240
  Romanian war, 234
  UN Human Rights Committee, 32
utopias, 71, 72, 84, 85, 86
  Israeli-Palestinian conflict, 353, 371

Valley of the Fallen, 180, 193
Varnava and others v. *Turkey*, 77, 81
Vasiliauskas v. *Lithuania*, 227
victimhood, 25, 46, 348
  dangers, 279
  Israeli-Palestinian conflict, 353, 354,
    357, 372
Victory Day, 314

war coalition, 323
war crimes, 19, 22, 33, 50, 60, 97, 105,
    131, 153
  by Allied soldiers, 107
  conviction, 226
  Ukraine, 320
War Guilt Clause, 6
Weber, Max, 46
Weil, Simone, 171
witness protection, 84
Witzsch v. *Germany*, 115

xenophobia, 21, 129, 130, 131,
    136, 276

Yalta System, 301, 309
Yarovaya, Irina, 293
Yazidi community, 69
Yeltsin, Boris, 294, 295
Yugoslavia, 14, 32
  International Criminal Tribunal for
    the Former Yugoslavia (ICTY),
    49, 55, 56, 58, 65, 67

Zappa, Frank, 332, 347, 413
Zatulin, Konstantin, 300, 301,
    302, 304
Zionist Swindle case, 334
Zündel, Ernst, 7
Zypries, 141